FUGITIVE FROM THE CUBICLE POLICE

FUGITIVE FROM THE CUBICLE POLICE

A DILBERT™ BOOK BY SCOTT ADAMS

B※XTREE

First published 1996 by Andrews & McMeel Publishing, Kansas City

This edition published 1998 by Boxtree
an imprint of Macmillan Publishers Ltd
25 Eccleston Place London SW1W 9NF
and Basingstoke

Associated companies throughout the world

ISBN 0 7522 2431 X

www.dilbert.com

3 5 7 9 8 6 4 2

A CIP catalogue record for this book is available from
the British Library.

Printed and bound in Great Britain by
Butler & Tanner Ltd, Frome and London

For Pam and the Cats.

Introduction

I was doing some thinking today. But I didn't enjoy it very much, so I decided to write this introduction instead.

It seems as though every time I turn around, well, I get dizzy. So I stopped doing that. Now I only walk straight forward and backward and it has made my life much simpler. Granted, sometimes I have to tunnel through sheetrock, which is hard on my teeth. And my annoying neighbors are starting to whine about the holes in their houses. And it can take a VERY long time to get where I'm going, given the circumference of the earth and the hassle with immigration.

But when it starts to get me down I remember the story about the tortoise and his hair. If I recall, the tortoise had hair that grew very quickly. For some reason this was a problem. The tortoise eventually triumphed by beating his hair with his flipper.

Now you might say that tortoises (torti to be proper) do not have flippers. But if that's true, how could they fly? Or you might say that torti do indeed have flippers—I'm not really doing a whole lot of research for this part of the book—in which case, shut up.

And this brings me to my main point: I've been spending far too much time alone in my house since I became a cartoonist. My friends told me that the isolation, combined with my newfound prosperity, would have a negative impact on my mental state. So I paid a guy to kill them.

I'm kidding. I don't have friends. At least not good ones.

But if you'd like to be my friend—and Lord knows that's a hot ticket—you can do that by joining Dogbert's New Ruling Class.

As you might already know, when Dogbert conquers the planet and becomes supreme ruler, everyone who subscribes to the free Dilbert Newsletter will form the New Ruling Class and have complete dominion over everyone else. The others (we call them induhviduals) will be our domestic servants. Don't let that happen to you.

The Dilbert newsletter is free and it's published approximately "whenever I feel like it," which is about four times a year. There's an e-mail version and a snail mail version. The e-mail version is better.

E-mail subscription (preferred): write to scottadams@aol.com

Snail mail:

Dilbert Mailing List
c/o United Media
200 Madison Avenue
New York, NY 10016

S. Adams

http://www.unitedmedia.com/comics/dilbert

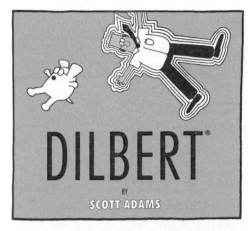

DILBERT®
BY
SCOTT ADAMS
I JUST ARRANGED TO HAVE MY BODY CRYO-GENICALLY FROZEN BEFORE MY DEATH.
S. Adams
IN A HUNDRED YEARS I'LL BE REVIVED AND CURED. THAT WAY, FUTURE GENERATIONS WILL GET THE BENEFITS OF KNOWING ME.
I HOPE YOU HAVE A GOOD WARM COAT.
COAT? NOBODY SAID ANYTHING ABOUT NEEDING A COAT.
OBVIOUSLY YOU NEED A COAT. IT'S FREEZING IN THAT CRYOGENIC CHAMBER. YOU'D BETTER WEAR LONG UNDERWEAR TOO.
9-19
© 1993 United Feature Syndicate, Inc.
DON'T LET THEM TELL YOU OTHERWISE. REMEMBER, THE CUSTOMER IS ALWAYS RIGHT!
I WANT A SPACE HEATER IN THERE TOO!
THAT WASN'T NICE.
I DID IT FOR FUTURE GENERATIONS.

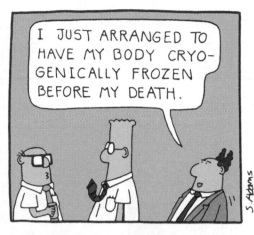

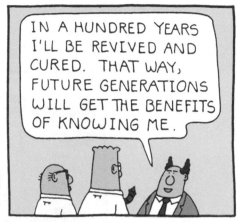

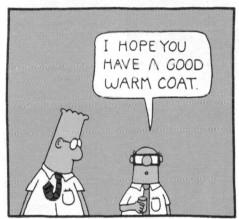

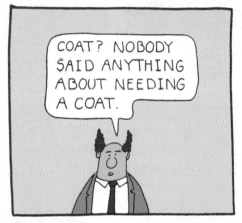

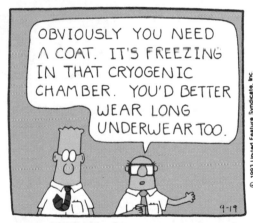

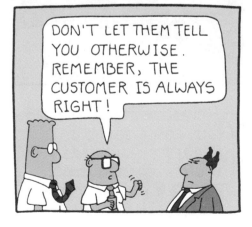

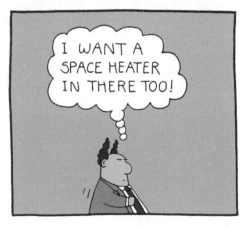

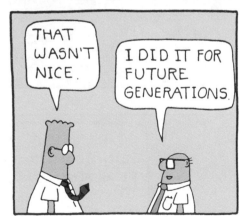

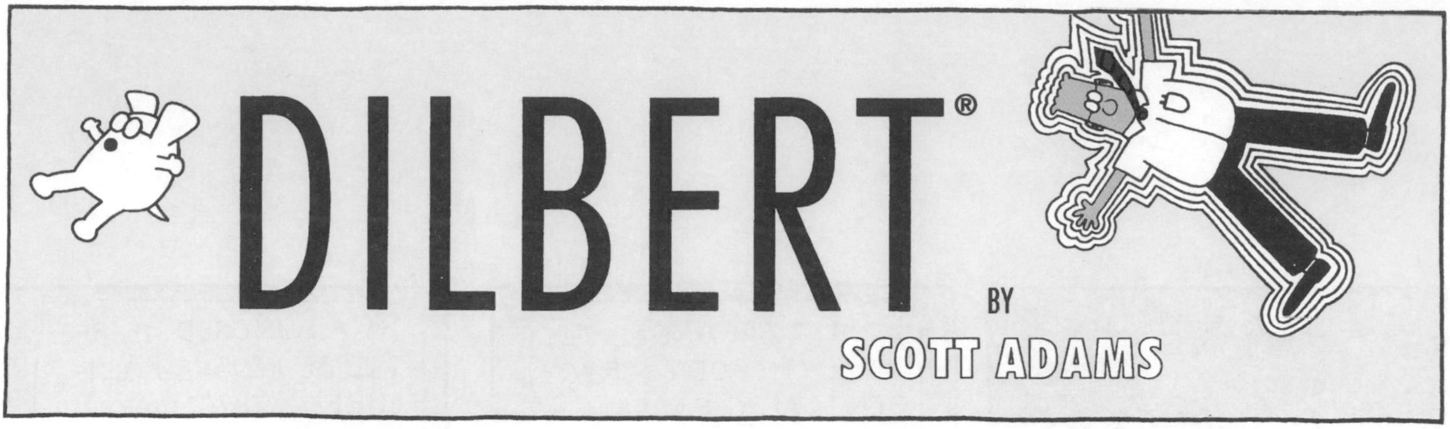
DILBERT®
BY
SCOTT ADAMS

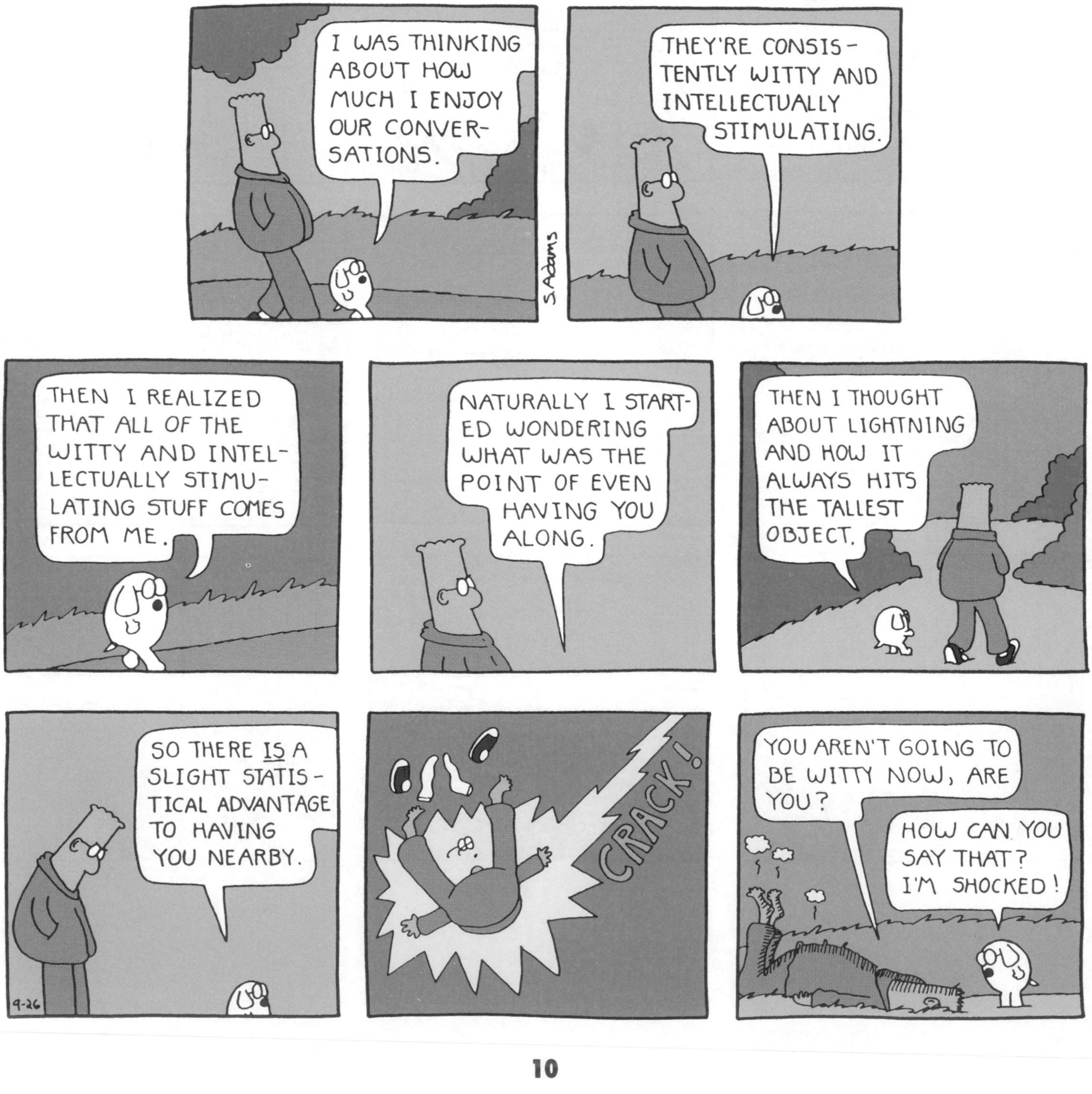
I WAS THINKING ABOUT HOW MUCH I ENJOY OUR CONVERSATIONS.
S. Adams
THEY'RE CONSISTENTLY WITTY AND INTELLECTUALLY STIMULATING.
THEN I REALIZED THAT ALL OF THE WITTY AND INTELLECTUALLY STIMULATING STUFF COMES FROM ME.
NATURALLY I STARTED WONDERING WHAT WAS THE POINT OF EVEN HAVING YOU ALONG.
THEN I THOUGHT ABOUT LIGHTNING AND HOW IT ALWAYS HITS THE TALLEST OBJECT.
SO THERE IS A SLIGHT STATISTICAL ADVANTAGE TO HAVING YOU NEARBY.
9-26
CRACK!
YOU AREN'T GOING TO BE WITTY NOW, ARE YOU?
HOW CAN YOU SAY THAT? I'M SHOCKED!

HAVE I TOLD YOU RECENTLY THAT I HAVE A LUCRATIVE JOB OFFER FROM OUR COMPETITOR?

YES

THE PAY IS OBSCENE, THEY WEAR CASUAL CLOTHES AT WORK, AND WEDNESDAY THROUGH FRIDAY IS FREE BEER AND PIZZA.

AS THE NEW GUY I GET TO DATE THE MASSEUSE UNTIL THE COMPANY MATCHES ME WITH AN ATTRACTIVE CO-WORKER.

SOB°°

© 1993 United Feature Syndicate, Inc.

NEXT WEEK I'LL BE AT MY NEW JOB, REAPING HUGE REWARDS.

WE'RE SO HAPPY FOR YOU.

BUT I'LL STILL HAVE A LITTLE CUBICLE LIKE YOURS.

THE ONLY DIFFERENCE BEING THAT I'LL KEEP A PONY THERE. THAT WAY IT'S CLOSE TO MY OFFICE.

© 1993 United Feature Syndicate, Inc.

9-28

9-29

S. Adams

S. Adams

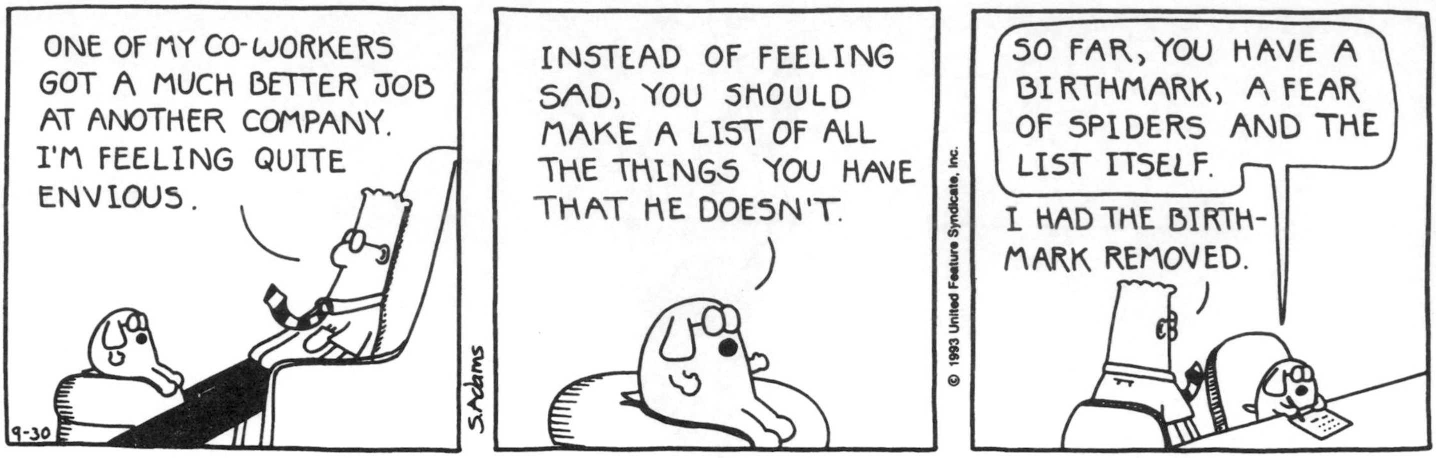
ONE OF MY CO-WORKERS GOT A MUCH BETTER JOB AT ANOTHER COMPANY. I'M FEELING QUITE ENVIOUS.
9-30
S. Adams
INSTEAD OF FEELING SAD, YOU SHOULD MAKE A LIST OF ALL THE THINGS YOU HAVE THAT HE DOESN'T.
© 1993 United Feature Syndicate, Inc.
SO FAR, YOU HAVE A BIRTHMARK, A FEAR OF SPIDERS AND THE LIST ITSELF.
I HAD THE BIRTH-MARK REMOVED.

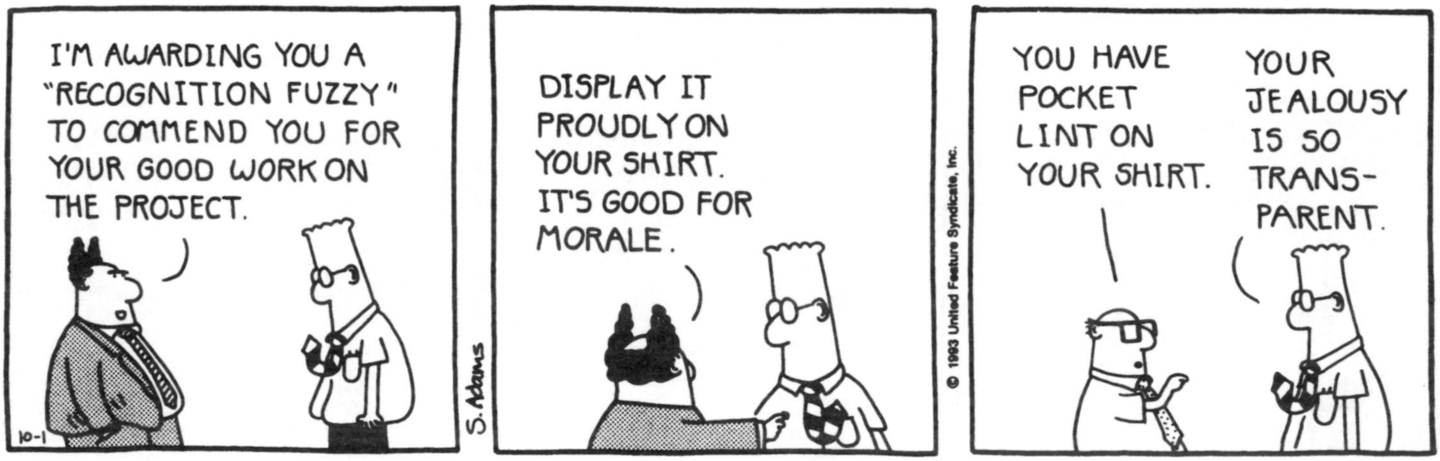
I'M AWARDING YOU A "RECOGNITION FUZZY" TO COMMEND YOU FOR YOUR GOOD WORK ON THE PROJECT.
10-1
S. Adams
DISPLAY IT PROUDLY ON YOUR SHIRT. IT'S GOOD FOR MORALE.
© 1993 United Feature Syndicate, Inc.
YOU HAVE POCKET LINT ON YOUR SHIRT.
YOUR JEALOUSY IS SO TRANS-PARENT.

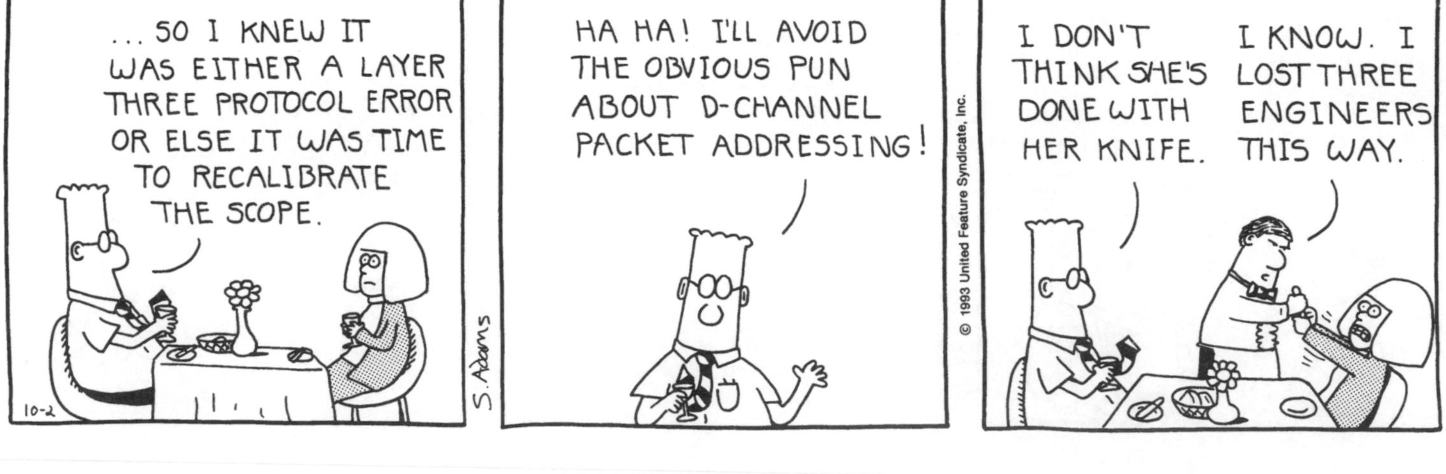
... SO I KNEW IT WAS EITHER A LAYER THREE PROTOCOL ERROR OR ELSE IT WAS TIME TO RECALIBRATE THE SCOPE.
10-2
S. Adams
HA HA! I'LL AVOID THE OBVIOUS PUN ABOUT D-CHANNEL PACKET ADDRESSING!
© 1993 United Feature Syndicate, Inc.
I DON'T THINK SHE'S DONE WITH HER KNIFE.
I KNOW. I LOST THREE ENGINEERS THIS WAY.

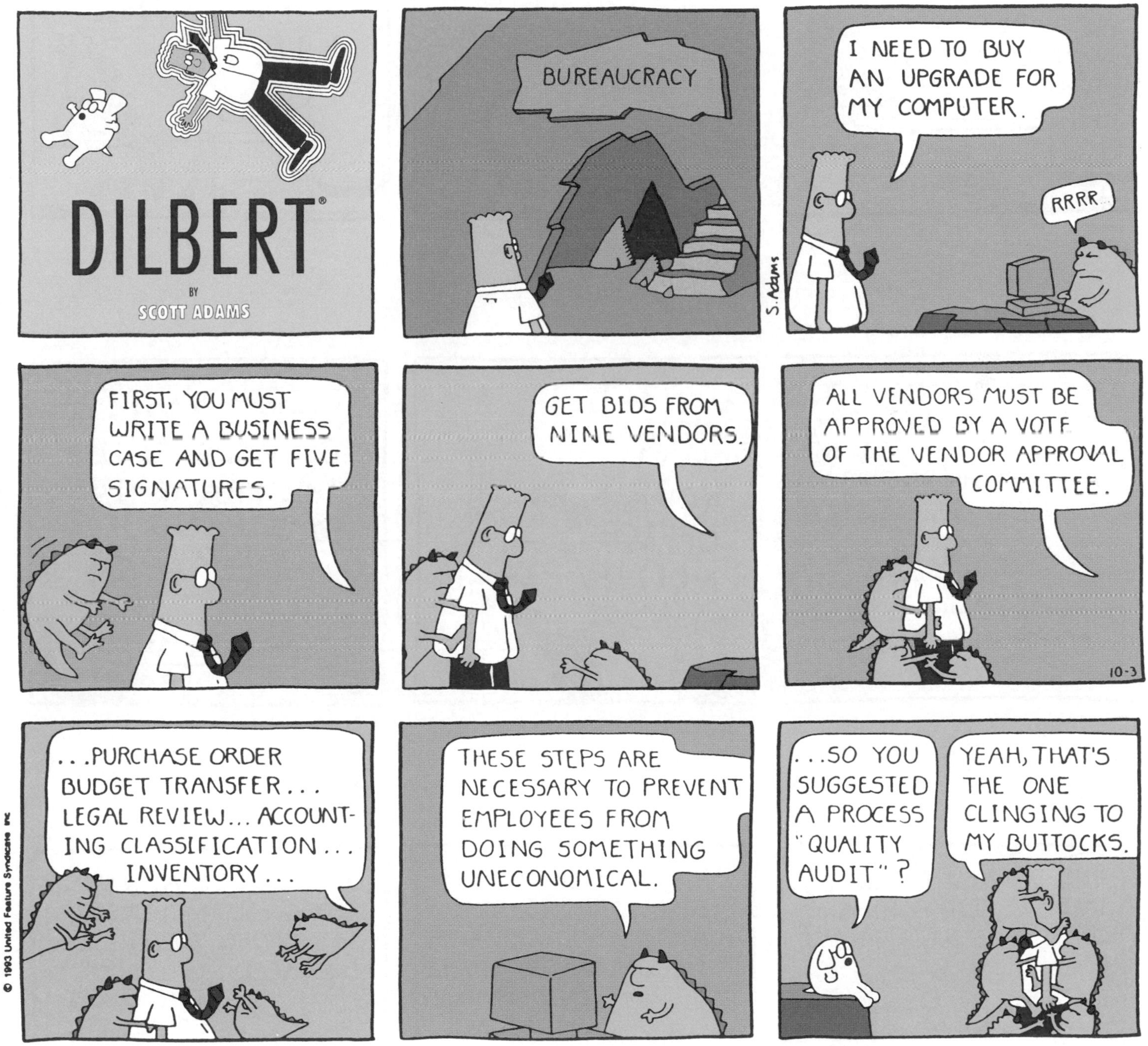
DILBERT®
BY
SCOTT ADAMS
BUREAUCRACY
I NEED TO BUY AN UPGRADE FOR MY COMPUTER.
RRRR...
S. Adams
FIRST, YOU MUST WRITE A BUSINESS CASE AND GET FIVE SIGNATURES.
GET BIDS FROM NINE VENDORS.
ALL VENDORS MUST BE APPROVED BY A VOTE OF THE VENDOR APPROVAL COMMITTEE.
10-3
...PURCHASE ORDER BUDGET TRANSFER... LEGAL REVIEW... ACCOUNTING CLASSIFICATION... INVENTORY...
THESE STEPS ARE NECESSARY TO PREVENT EMPLOYEES FROM DOING SOMETHING UNECONOMICAL.
...SO YOU SUGGESTED A PROCESS "QUALITY AUDIT"?
YEAH, THAT'S THE ONE CLINGING TO MY BUTTOCKS.
© 1993 United Feature Syndicate Inc

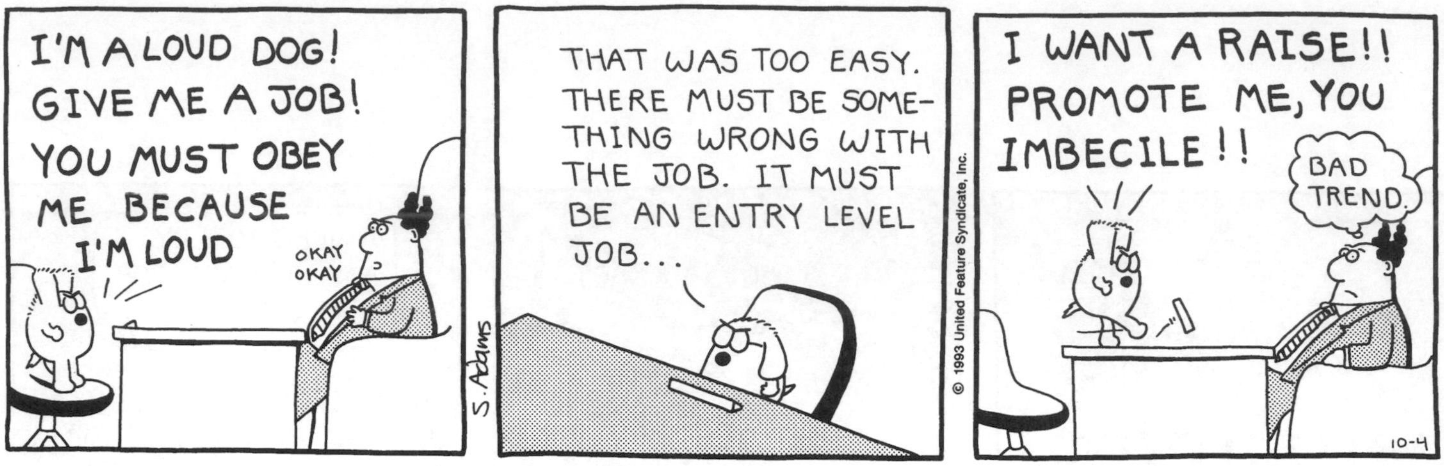
I'M A LOUD DOG! GIVE ME A JOB! YOU MUST OBEY ME BECAUSE I'M LOUD
OKAY OKAY
THAT WAS TOO EASY. THERE MUST BE SOMETHING WRONG WITH THE JOB. IT MUST BE AN ENTRY LEVEL JOB...
S. Adams
© 1993 United Feature Syndicate, Inc.
I WANT A RAISE!! PROMOTE ME, YOU IMBECILE!!
BAD TREND.
10-4

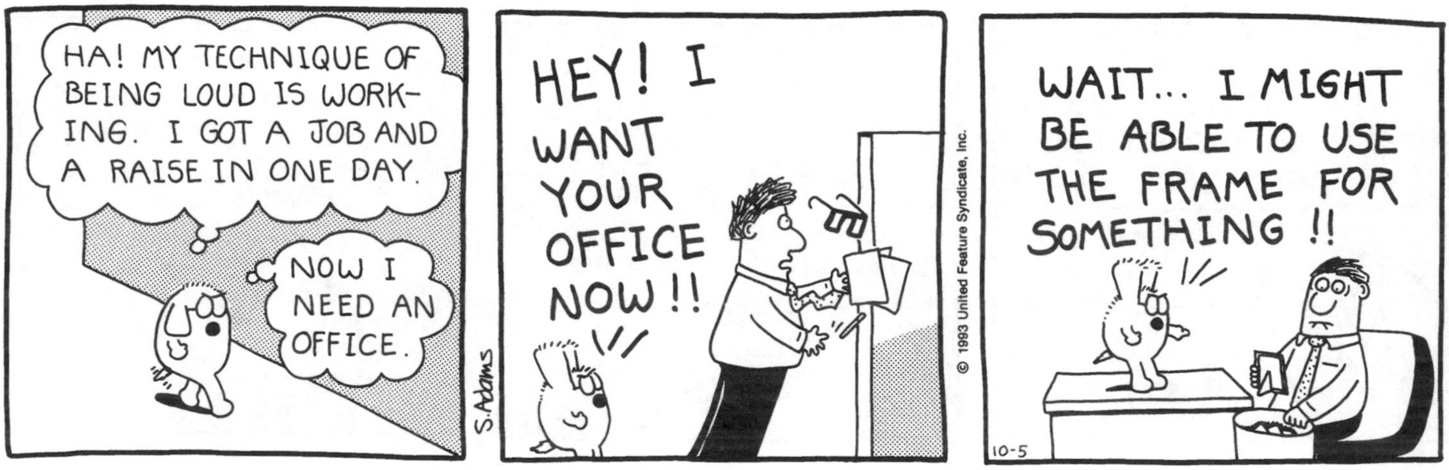
HA! MY TECHNIQUE OF BEING LOUD IS WORKING. I GOT A JOB AND A RAISE IN ONE DAY.
NOW I NEED AN OFFICE.
S. Adams
HEY! I WANT YOUR OFFICE NOW!!
© 1993 United Feature Syndicate, Inc.
WAIT... I MIGHT BE ABLE TO USE THE FRAME FOR SOMETHING !!
10-5

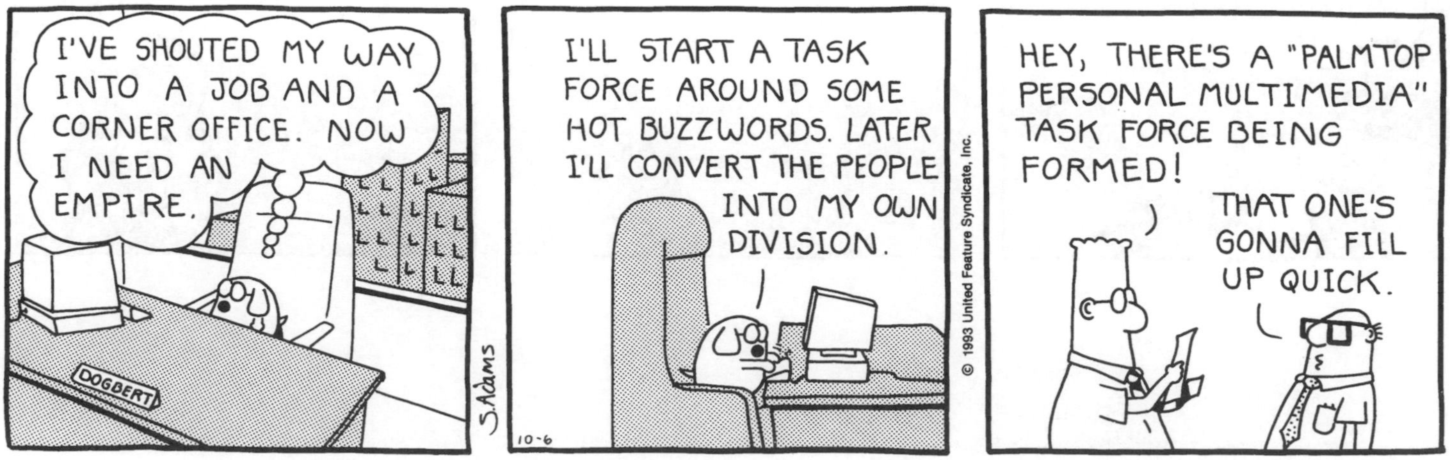
I'VE SHOUTED MY WAY INTO A JOB AND A CORNER OFFICE. NOW I NEED AN EMPIRE.
DOGBERT
S. Adams
10-6
I'LL START A TASK FORCE AROUND SOME HOT BUZZWORDS. LATER I'LL CONVERT THE PEOPLE INTO MY OWN DIVISION.
© 1993 United Feature Syndicate, Inc.
HEY, THERE'S A "PALMTOP PERSONAL MULTIMEDIA" TASK FORCE BEING FORMED!
THAT ONE'S GONNA FILL UP QUICK.

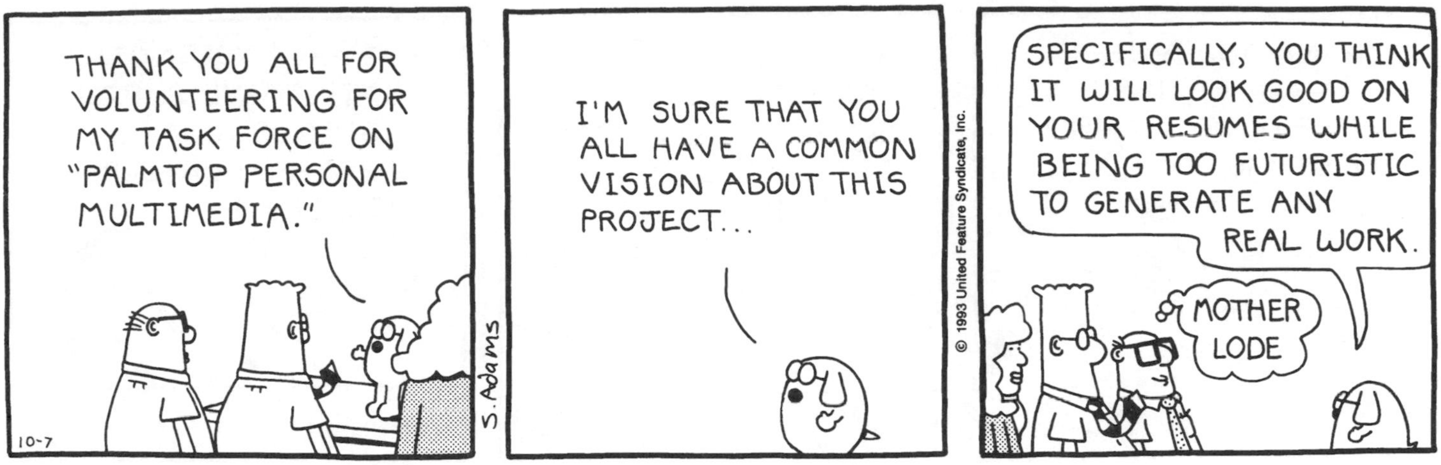
THANK YOU ALL FOR VOLUNTEERING FOR MY TASK FORCE ON "PALMTOP PERSONAL MULTIMEDIA."
10-7
S. Adams
I'M SURE THAT YOU ALL HAVE A COMMON VISION ABOUT THIS PROJECT...
© 1993 United Feature Syndicate, Inc.
SPECIFICALLY, YOU THINK IT WILL LOOK GOOD ON YOUR RESUMES WHILE BEING TOO FUTURISTIC TO GENERATE ANY REAL WORK.
MOTHER LODE

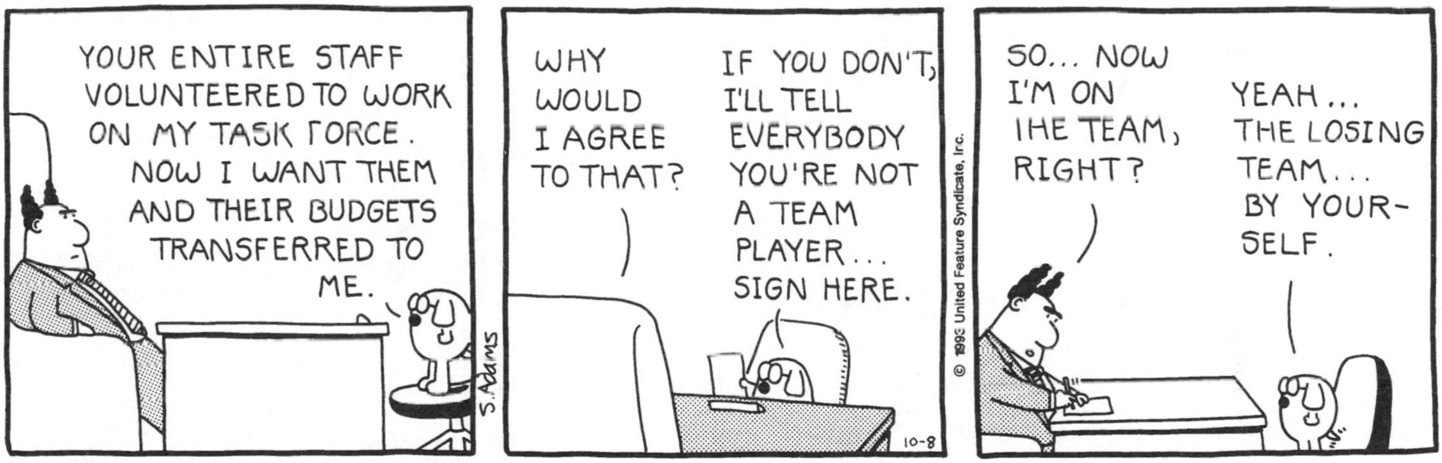
YOUR ENTIRE STAFF VOLUNTEERED TO WORK ON MY TASK FORCE. NOW I WANT THEM AND THEIR BUDGETS TRANSFERRED TO ME.
S. Adams
WHY WOULD I AGREE TO THAT?
IF YOU DON'T, I'LL TELL EVERYBODY YOU'RE NOT A TEAM PLAYER... SIGN HERE.
10-8
© 1993 United Feature Syndicate, Inc.
SO... NOW I'M ON THE TEAM, RIGHT?
YEAH... THE LOSING TEAM... BY YOURSELF.

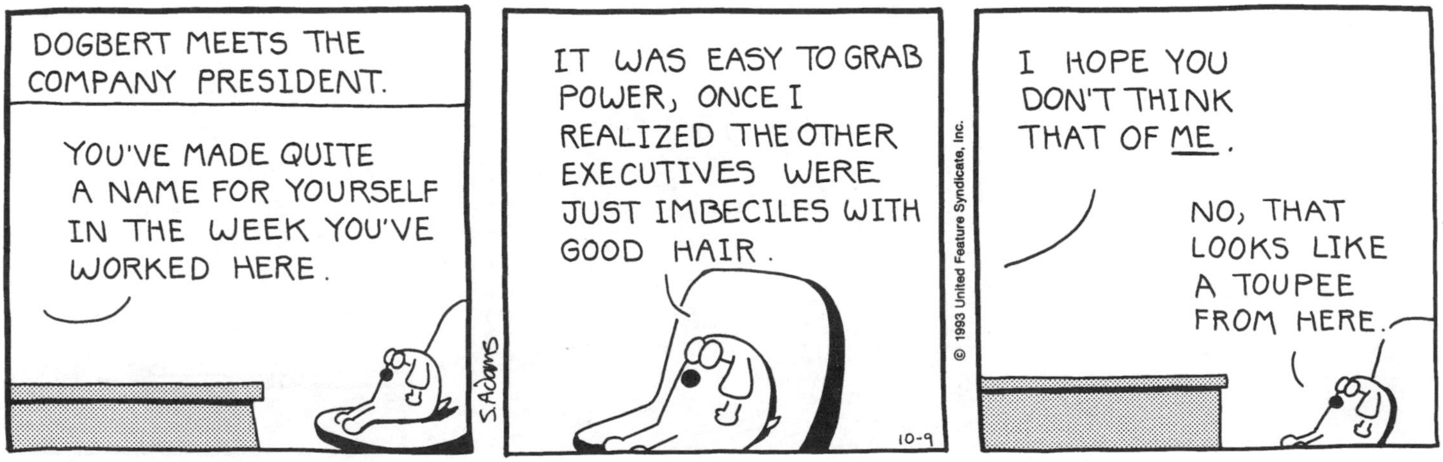
DOGBERT MEETS THE COMPANY PRESIDENT.
YOU'VE MADE QUITE A NAME FOR YOURSELF IN THE WEEK YOU'VE WORKED HERE.
S. Adams
IT WAS EASY TO GRAB POWER, ONCE I REALIZED THE OTHER EXECUTIVES WERE JUST IMBECILES WITH GOOD HAIR.
10-9
© 1993 United Feature Syndicate, Inc.
I HOPE YOU DON'T THINK THAT OF ME.
NO, THAT LOOKS LIKE A TOUPEE FROM HERE.

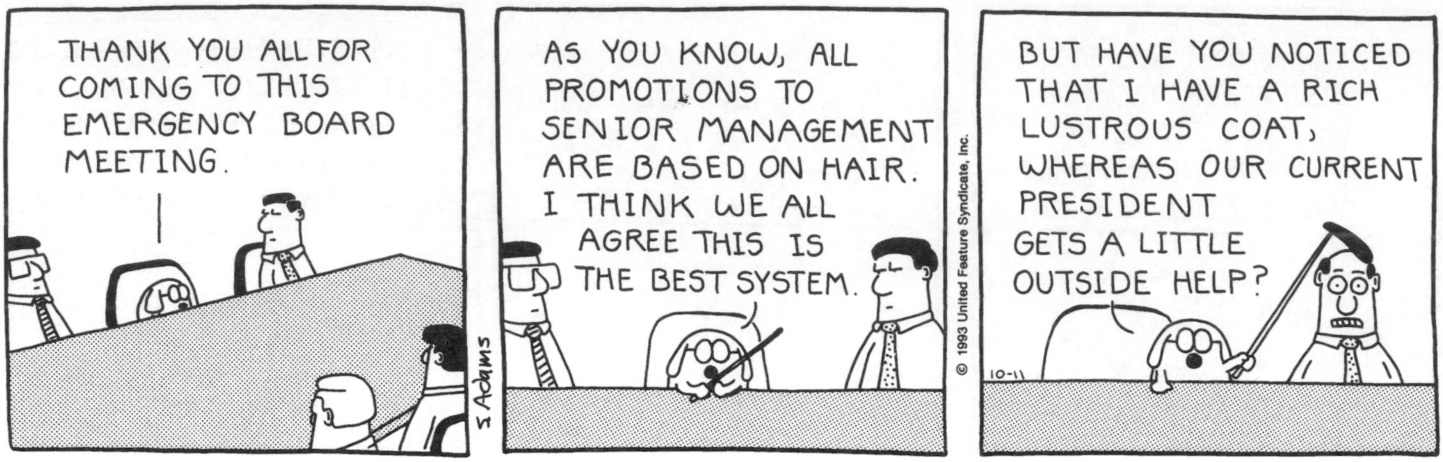
THANK YOU ALL FOR COMING TO THIS EMERGENCY BOARD MEETING.
S. Adams
AS YOU KNOW, ALL PROMOTIONS TO SENIOR MANAGEMENT ARE BASED ON HAIR. I THINK WE ALL AGREE THIS IS THE BEST SYSTEM.
© 1993 United Feature Syndicate, Inc.
BUT HAVE YOU NOTICED THAT I HAVE A RICH LUSTROUS COAT, WHEREAS OUR CURRENT PRESIDENT GETS A LITTLE OUTSIDE HELP?
10-11

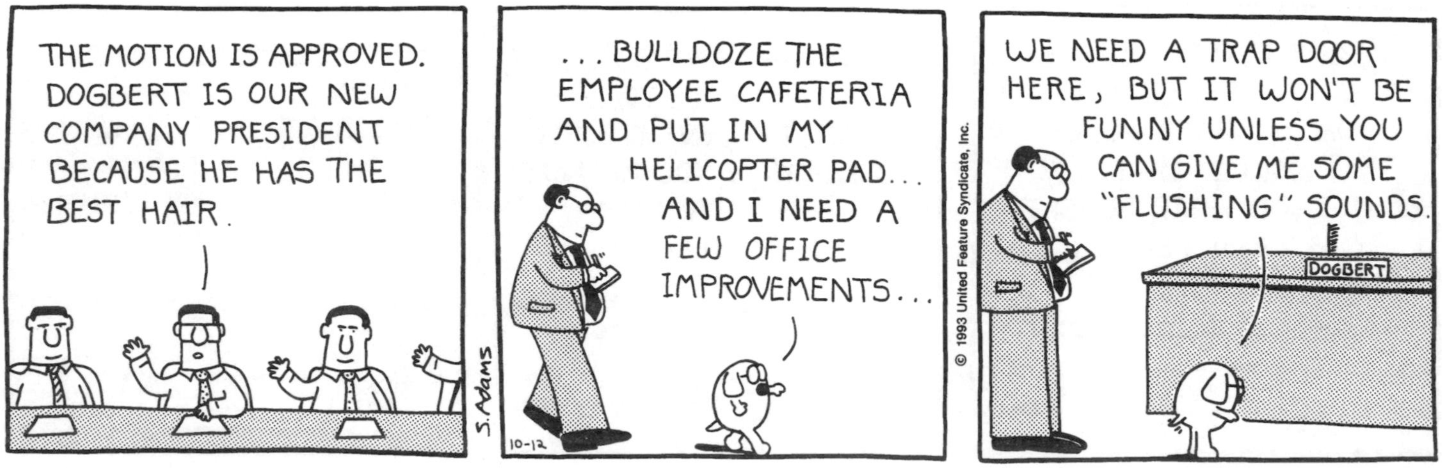
THE MOTION IS APPROVED. DOGBERT IS OUR NEW COMPANY PRESIDENT BECAUSE HE HAS THE BEST HAIR.
S. Adams
10-12
. . . BULLDOZE THE EMPLOYEE CAFETERIA AND PUT IN MY HELICOPTER PAD. . . AND I NEED A FEW OFFICE IMPROVEMENTS. . .
© 1993 United Feature Syndicate, Inc.
WE NEED A TRAP DOOR HERE, BUT IT WON'T BE FUNNY UNLESS YOU CAN GIVE ME SOME "FLUSHING" SOUNDS.
DOGBERT

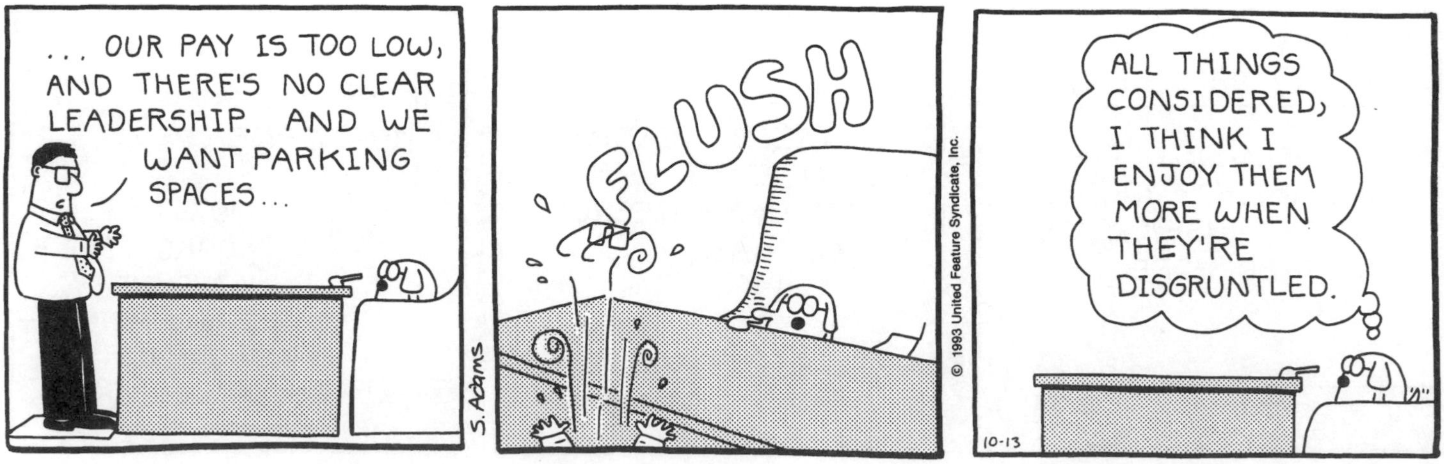
. . . OUR PAY IS TOO LOW, AND THERE'S NO CLEAR LEADERSHIP. AND WE WANT PARKING SPACES. . .
S. Adams
FLUSH
© 1993 United Feature Syndicate, Inc.
ALL THINGS CONSIDERED, I THINK I ENJOY THEM MORE WHEN THEY'RE DISGRUNTLED.
10-13

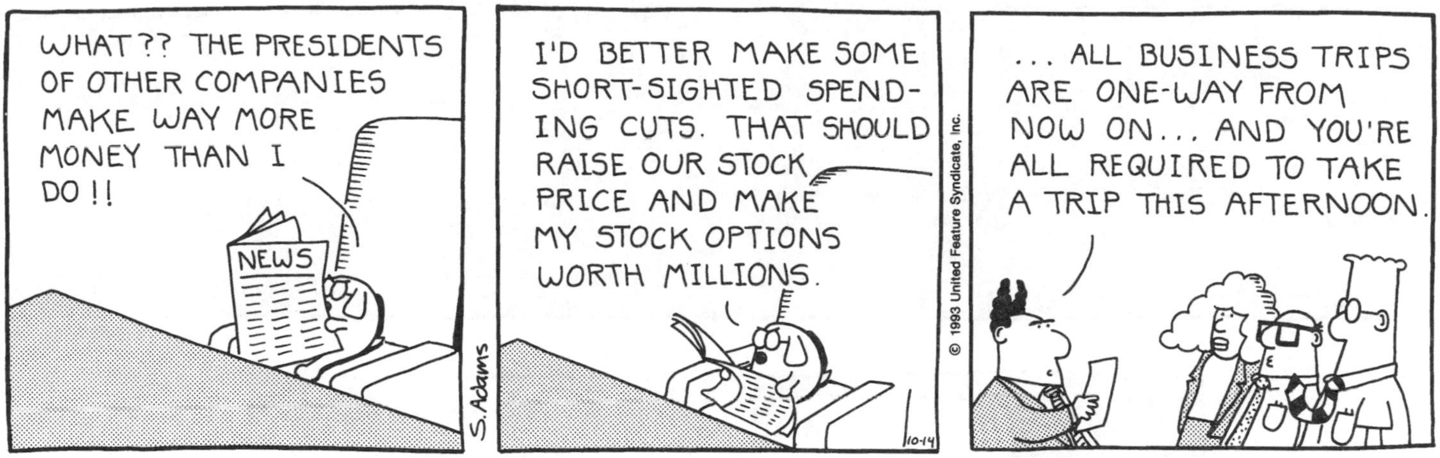
WHAT?? THE PRESIDENTS OF OTHER COMPANIES MAKE WAY MORE MONEY THAN I DO!!
NEWS
S. Adams
I'D BETTER MAKE SOME SHORT-SIGHTED SPENDING CUTS. THAT SHOULD RAISE OUR STOCK PRICE AND MAKE MY STOCK OPTIONS WORTH MILLIONS.
10-14
© 1993 United Feature Syndicate, Inc.
... ALL BUSINESS TRIPS ARE ONE-WAY FROM NOW ON... AND YOU'RE ALL REQUIRED TO TAKE A TRIP THIS AFTERNOON.

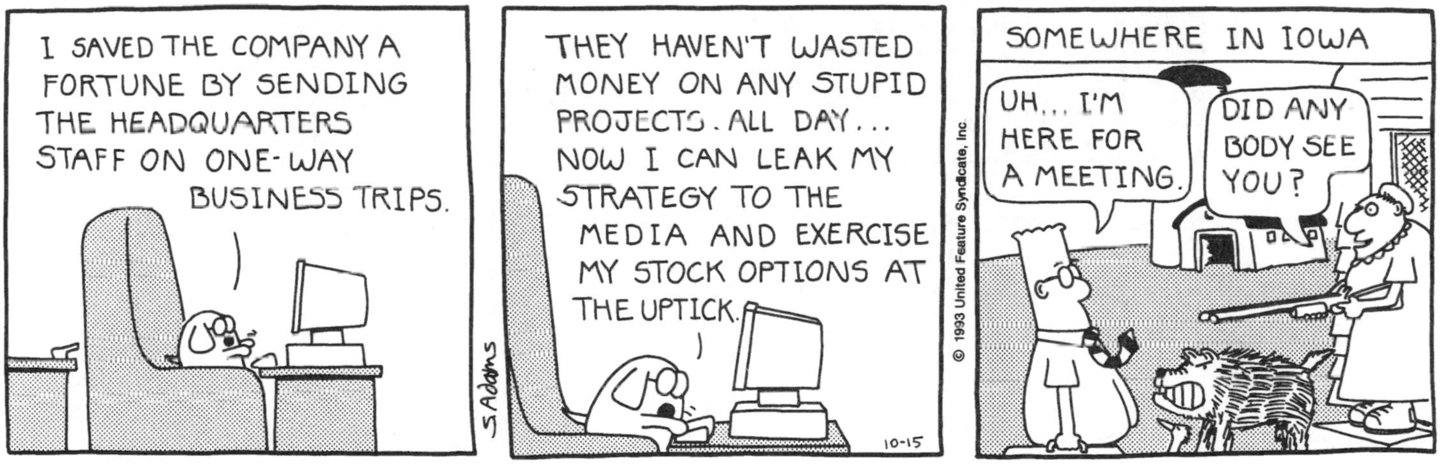
I SAVED THE COMPANY A FORTUNE BY SENDING THE HEADQUARTERS STAFF ON ONE-WAY BUSINESS TRIPS.
S. Adams
THEY HAVEN'T WASTED MONEY ON ANY STUPID PROJECTS ALL DAY... NOW I CAN LEAK MY STRATEGY TO THE MEDIA AND EXERCISE MY STOCK OPTIONS AT THE UPTICK.
10-15
© 1993 United Feature Syndicate, Inc.
SOMEWHERE IN IOWA
UH... I'M HERE FOR A MEETING.
DID ANY BODY SEE YOU?

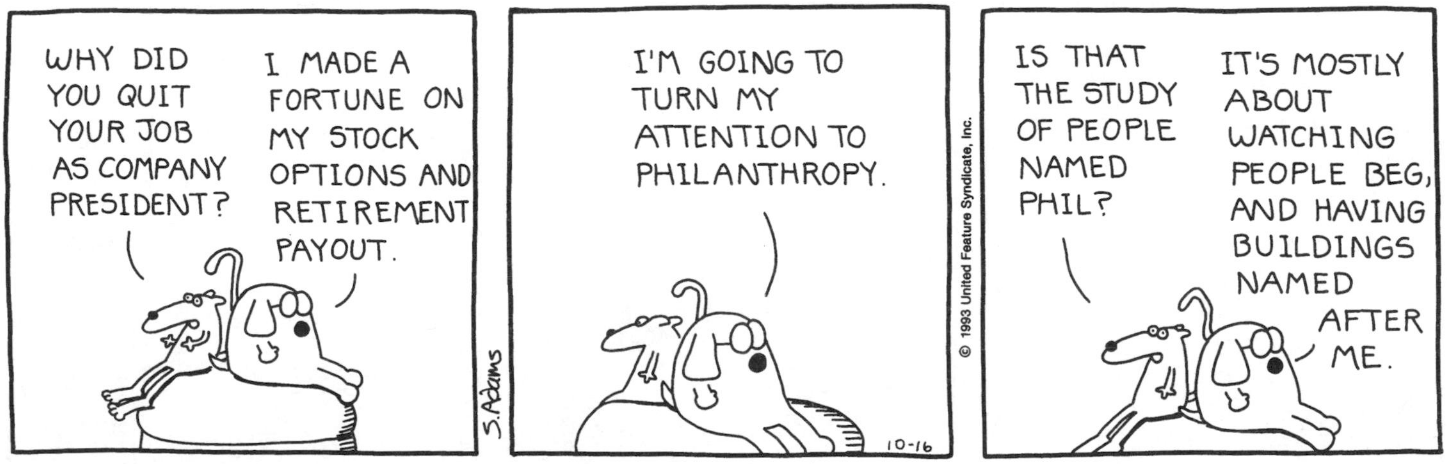
WHY DID YOU QUIT YOUR JOB AS COMPANY PRESIDENT?
I MADE A FORTUNE ON MY STOCK OPTIONS AND RETIREMENT PAYOUT.
S. Adams
I'M GOING TO TURN MY ATTENTION TO PHILANTHROPY.
10-16
© 1993 United Feature Syndicate, Inc.
IS THAT THE STUDY OF PEOPLE NAMED PHIL?
IT'S MOSTLY ABOUT WATCHING PEOPLE BEG, AND HAVING BUILDINGS NAMED AFTER ME.

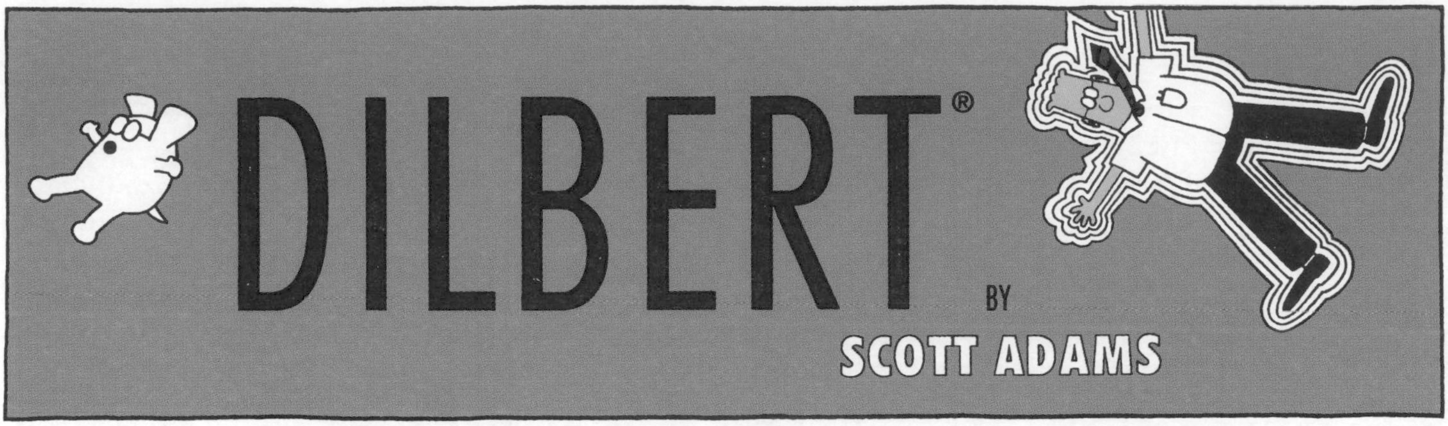
DILBERT®
BY
SCOTT ADAMS

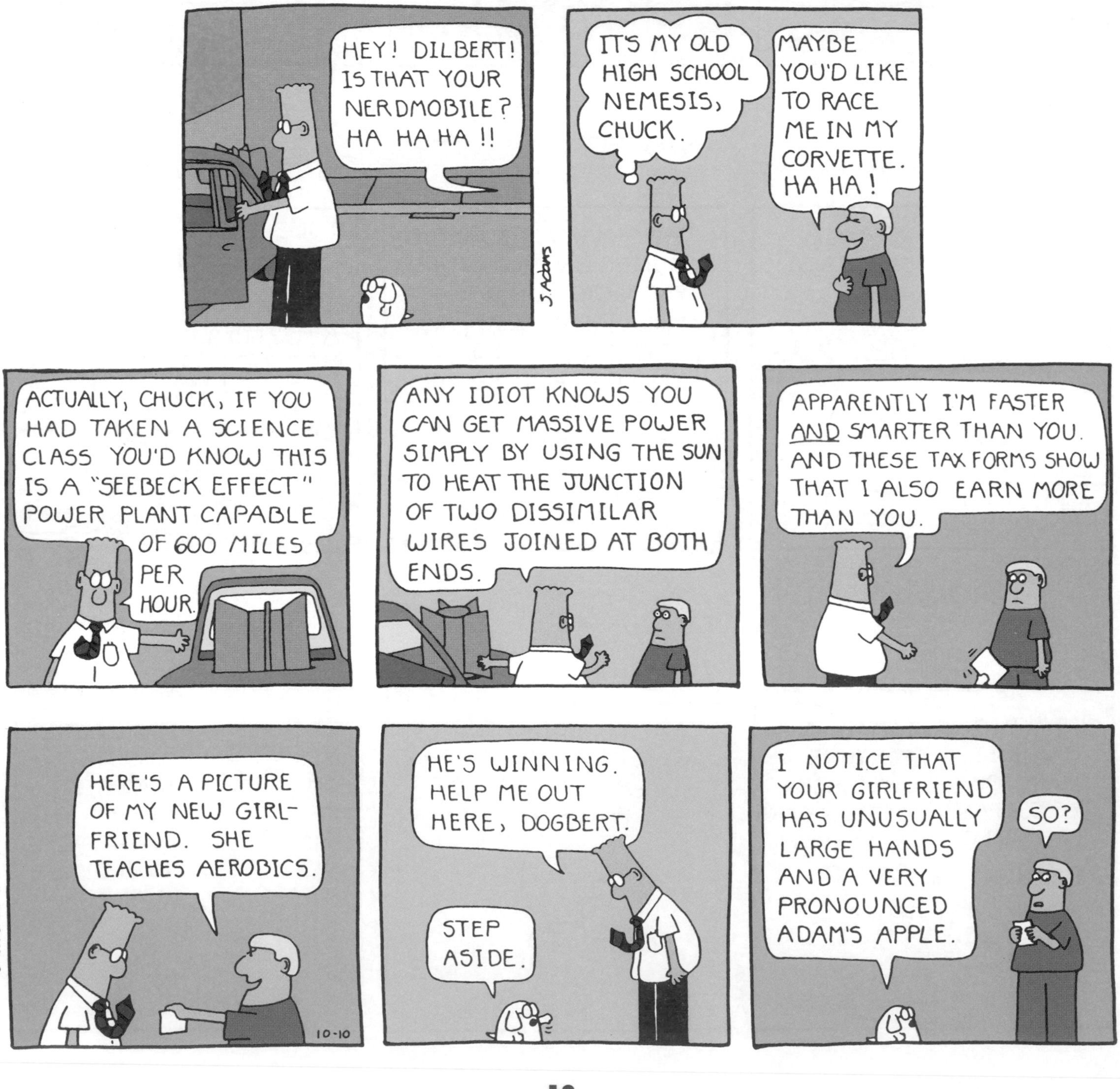
HEY! DILBERT! IS THAT YOUR NERDMOBILE? HA HA HA!!
S. Adams
IT'S MY OLD HIGH SCHOOL NEMESIS, CHUCK.
MAYBE YOU'D LIKE TO RACE ME IN MY CORVETTE. HA HA!
ACTUALLY, CHUCK, IF YOU HAD TAKEN A SCIENCE CLASS YOU'D KNOW THIS IS A "SEEBECK EFFECT" POWER PLANT CAPABLE OF 600 MILES PER HOUR.
ANY IDIOT KNOWS YOU CAN GET MASSIVE POWER SIMPLY BY USING THE SUN TO HEAT THE JUNCTION OF TWO DISSIMILAR WIRES JOINED AT BOTH ENDS.
APPARENTLY I'M FASTER AND SMARTER THAN YOU. AND THESE TAX FORMS SHOW THAT I ALSO EARN MORE THAN YOU.
© 1993 United Feature Syndicate, Inc
HERE'S A PICTURE OF MY NEW GIRLFRIEND. SHE TEACHES AEROBICS.
10-10
HE'S WINNING. HELP ME OUT HERE, DOGBERT.
STEP ASIDE.
I NOTICE THAT YOUR GIRLFRIEND HAS UNUSUALLY LARGE HANDS AND A VERY PRONOUNCED ADAM'S APPLE.
SO?

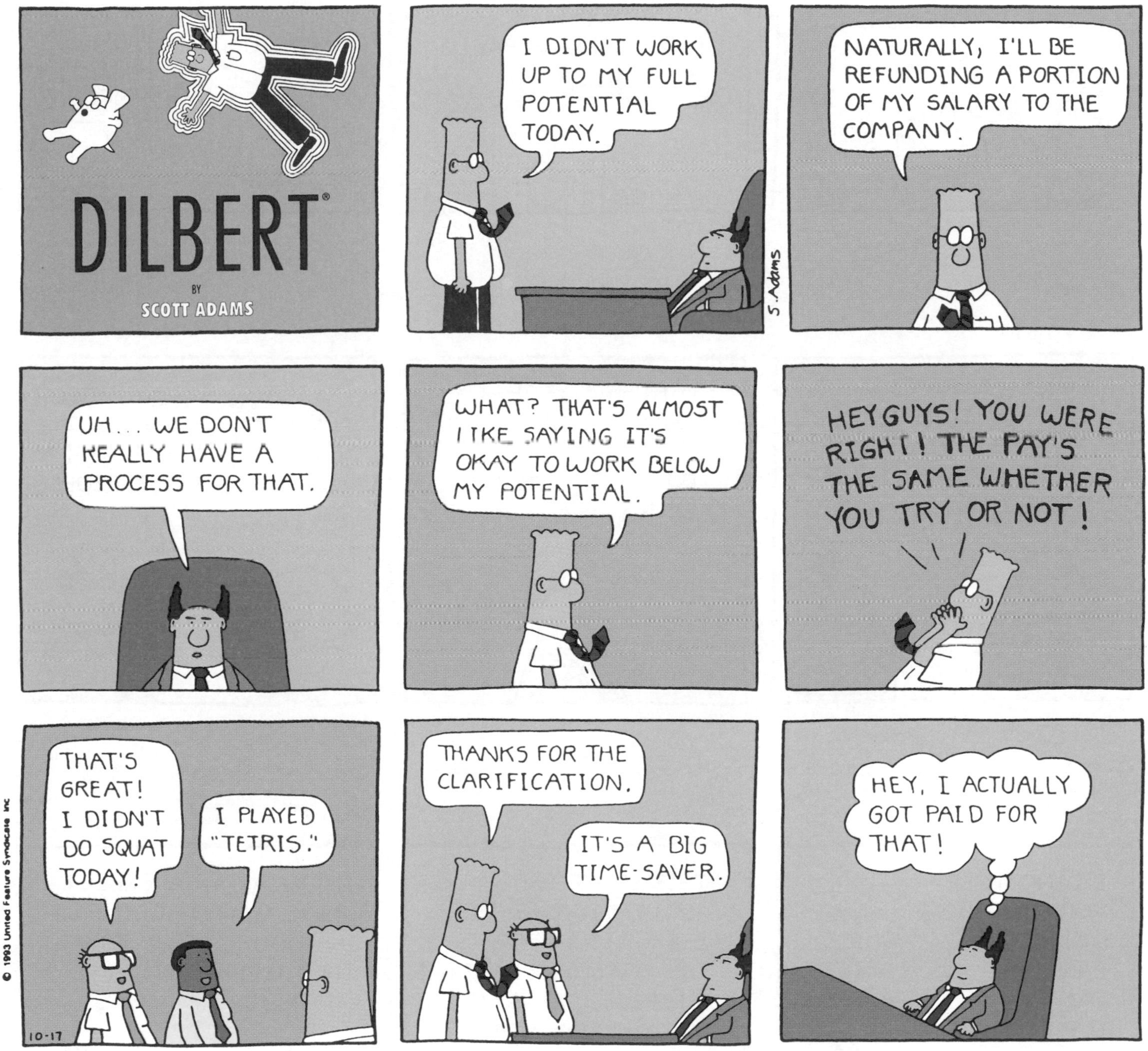
DILBERT®
BY
SCOTT ADAMS
I DIDN'T WORK UP TO MY FULL POTENTIAL TODAY.
S. Adams
NATURALLY, I'LL BE REFUNDING A PORTION OF MY SALARY TO THE COMPANY.
UH... WE DON'T REALLY HAVE A PROCESS FOR THAT.
WHAT? THAT'S ALMOST LIKE SAYING IT'S OKAY TO WORK BELOW MY POTENTIAL.
HEY GUYS! YOU WERE RIGHT! THE PAY'S THE SAME WHETHER YOU TRY OR NOT!
THAT'S GREAT! I DIDN'T DO SQUAT TODAY!
I PLAYED "TETRIS."
10-17
© 1993 United Feature Syndicate Inc
THANKS FOR THE CLARIFICATION.
IT'S A BIG TIME-SAVER.
HEY, I ACTUALLY GOT PAID FOR THAT!

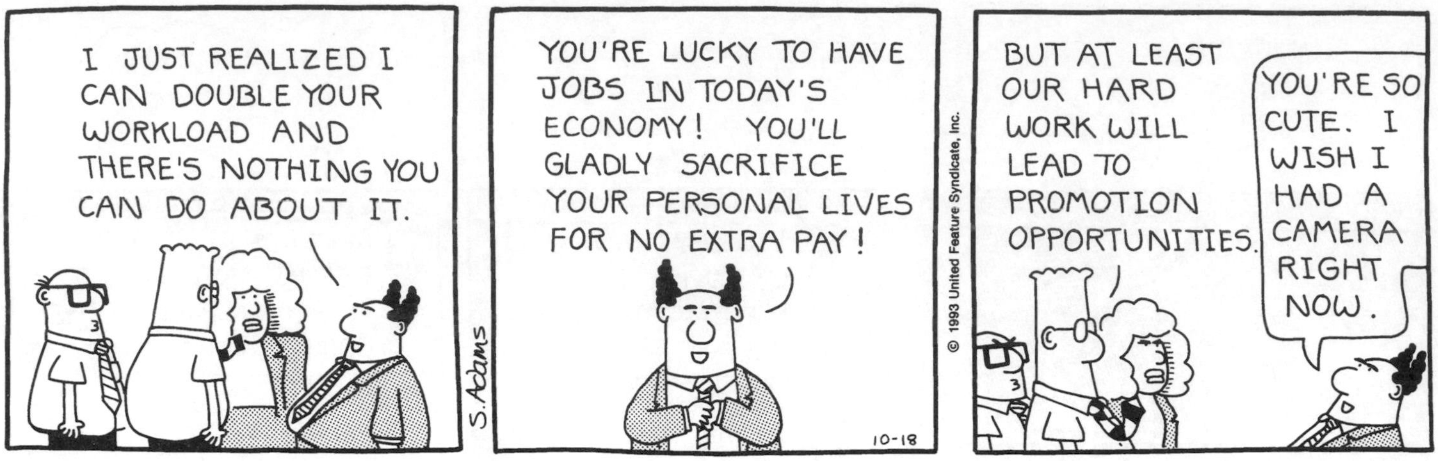
I JUST REALIZED I CAN DOUBLE YOUR WORKLOAD AND THERE'S NOTHING YOU CAN DO ABOUT IT.
S. Adams
YOU'RE LUCKY TO HAVE JOBS IN TODAY'S ECONOMY! YOU'LL GLADLY SACRIFICE YOUR PERSONAL LIVES FOR NO EXTRA PAY!
10-18
© 1993 United Feature Syndicate, Inc.
BUT AT LEAST OUR HARD WORK WILL LEAD TO PROMOTION OPPORTUNITIES.
YOU'RE SO CUTE. I WISH I HAD A CAMERA RIGHT NOW.

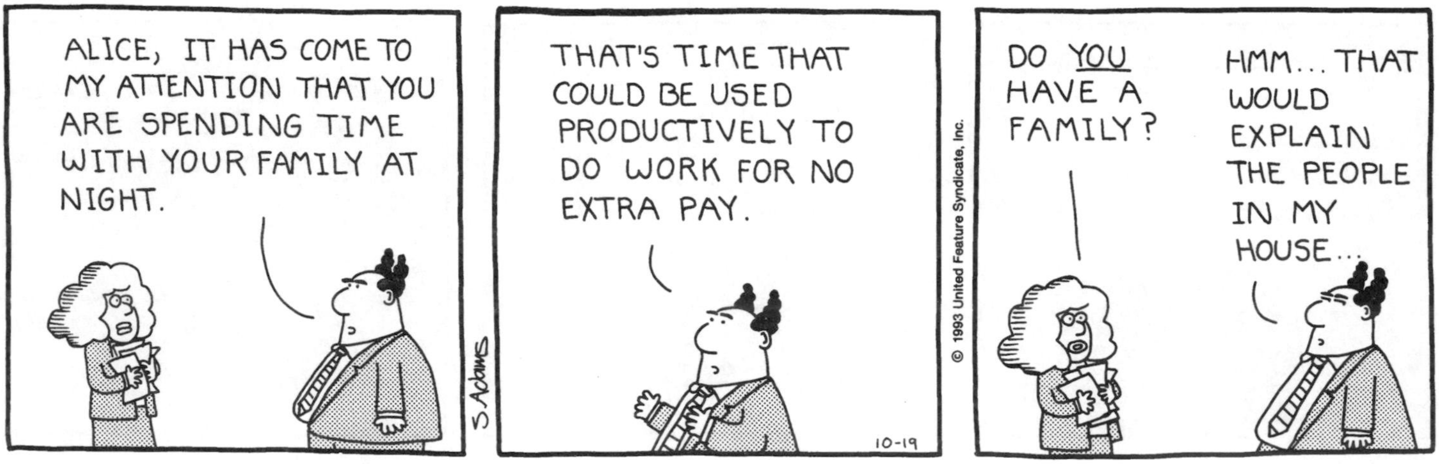
ALICE, IT HAS COME TO MY ATTENTION THAT YOU ARE SPENDING TIME WITH YOUR FAMILY AT NIGHT.
S. Adams
THAT'S TIME THAT COULD BE USED PRODUCTIVELY TO DO WORK FOR NO EXTRA PAY.
10-19
© 1993 United Feature Syndicate, Inc.
DO YOU HAVE A FAMILY?
HMM... THAT WOULD EXPLAIN THE PEOPLE IN MY HOUSE...

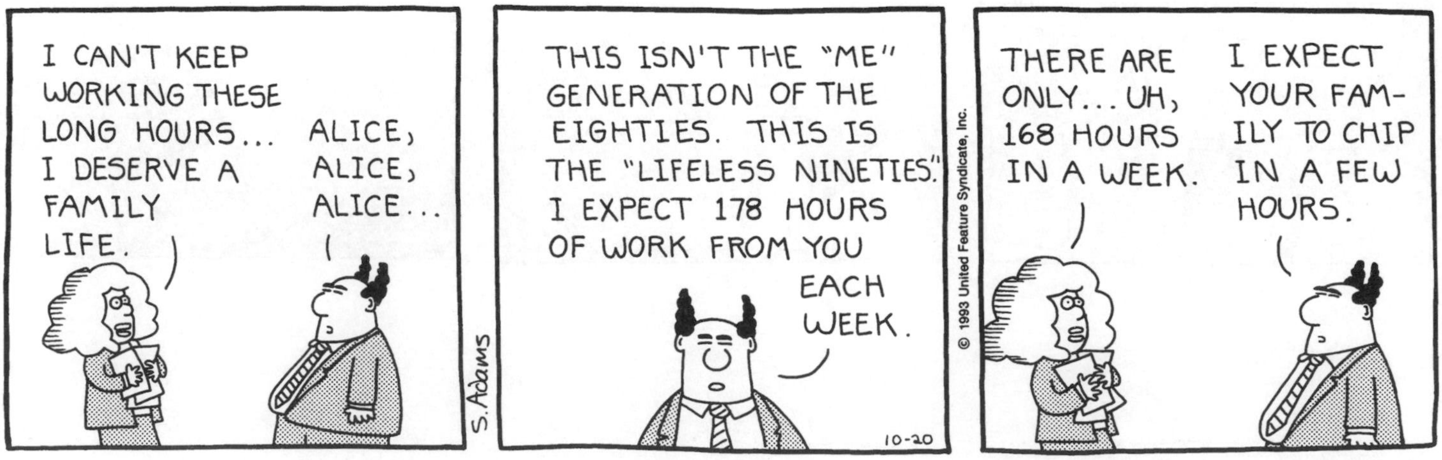
I CAN'T KEEP WORKING THESE LONG HOURS... I DESERVE A FAMILY LIFE.
ALICE, ALICE, ALICE...
S. Adams
THIS ISN'T THE "ME" GENERATION OF THE EIGHTIES. THIS IS THE "LIFELESS NINETIES." I EXPECT 178 HOURS OF WORK FROM YOU EACH WEEK.
10-20
© 1993 United Feature Syndicate, Inc.
THERE ARE ONLY... UH, 168 HOURS IN A WEEK.
I EXPECT YOUR FAMILY TO CHIP IN A FEW HOURS.

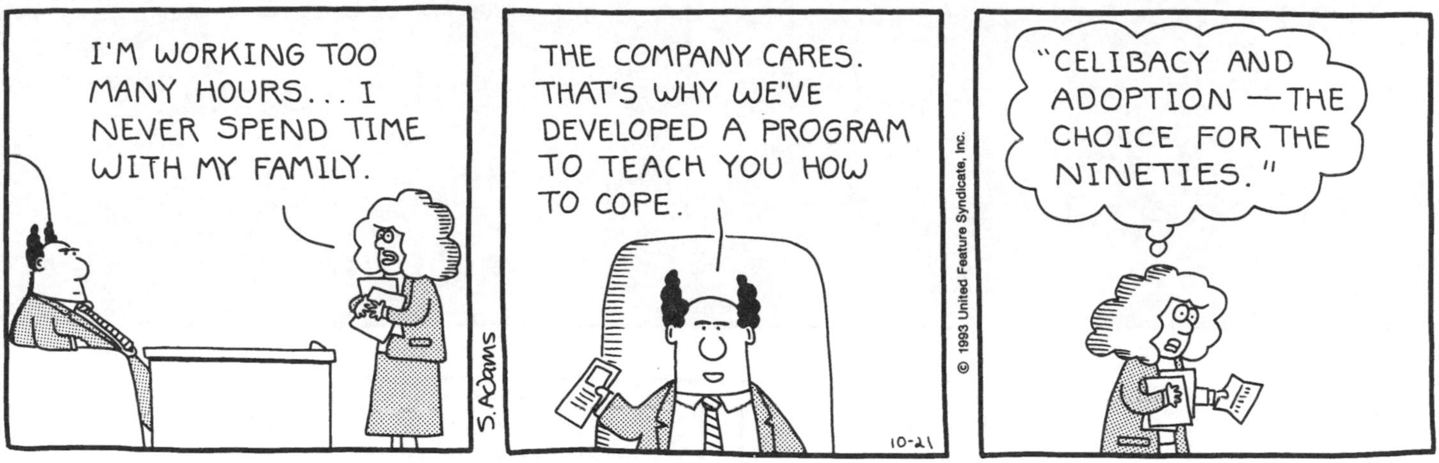
I'M WORKING TOO MANY HOURS... I NEVER SPEND TIME WITH MY FAMILY.
S. Adams
THE COMPANY CARES. THAT'S WHY WE'VE DEVELOPED A PROGRAM TO TEACH YOU HOW TO COPE.
10-21
© 1993 United Feature Syndicate, Inc.
"CELIBACY AND ADOPTION — THE CHOICE FOR THE NINETIES."

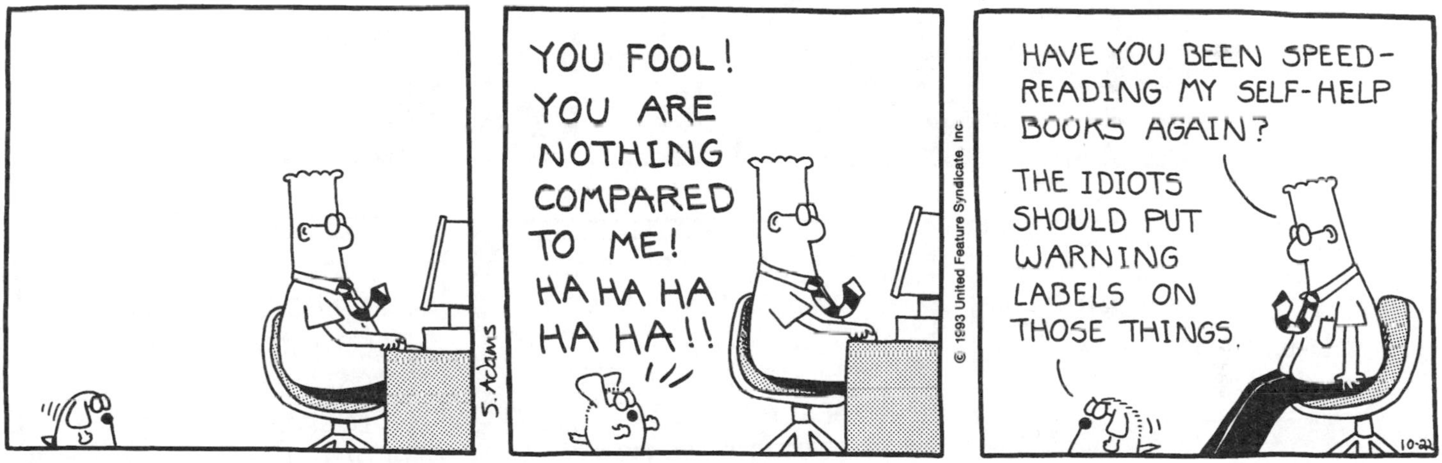
S. Adams
YOU FOOL! YOU ARE NOTHING COMPARED TO ME! HA HA HA HA HA!!
© 1993 United Feature Syndicate Inc
HAVE YOU BEEN SPEED-READING MY SELF-HELP BOOKS AGAIN?
THE IDIOTS SHOULD PUT WARNING LABELS ON THOSE THINGS.
10-22

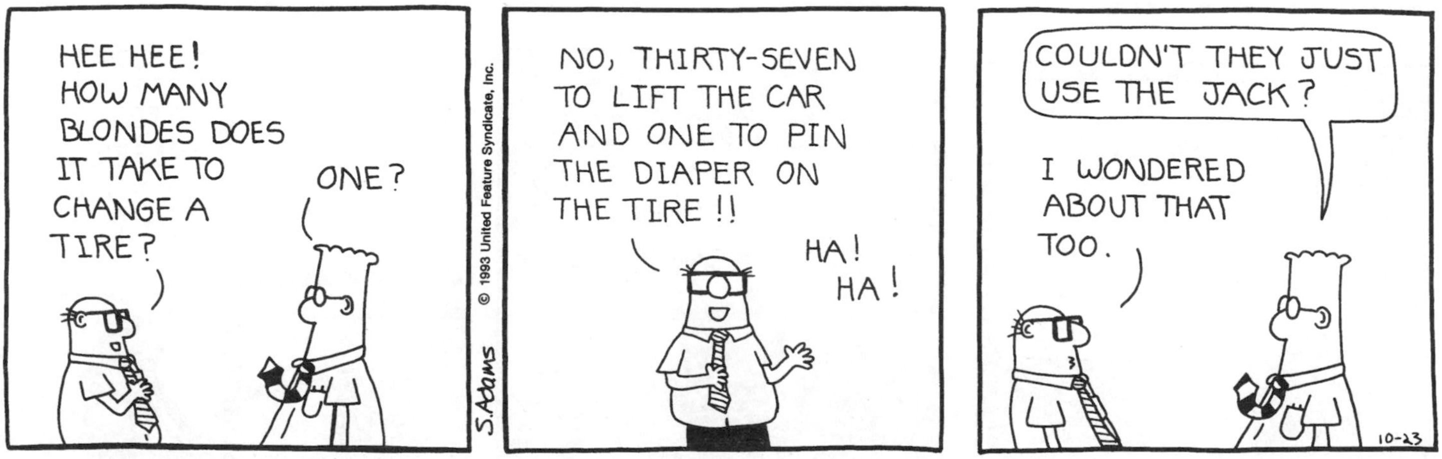
HEE HEE! HOW MANY BLONDES DOES IT TAKE TO CHANGE A TIRE?
ONE?
S. Adams
© 1993 United Feature Syndicate, Inc.
NO, THIRTY-SEVEN TO LIFT THE CAR AND ONE TO PIN THE DIAPER ON THE TIRE!!
HA! HA!
COULDN'T THEY JUST USE THE JACK?
I WONDERED ABOUT THAT TOO.
10-23

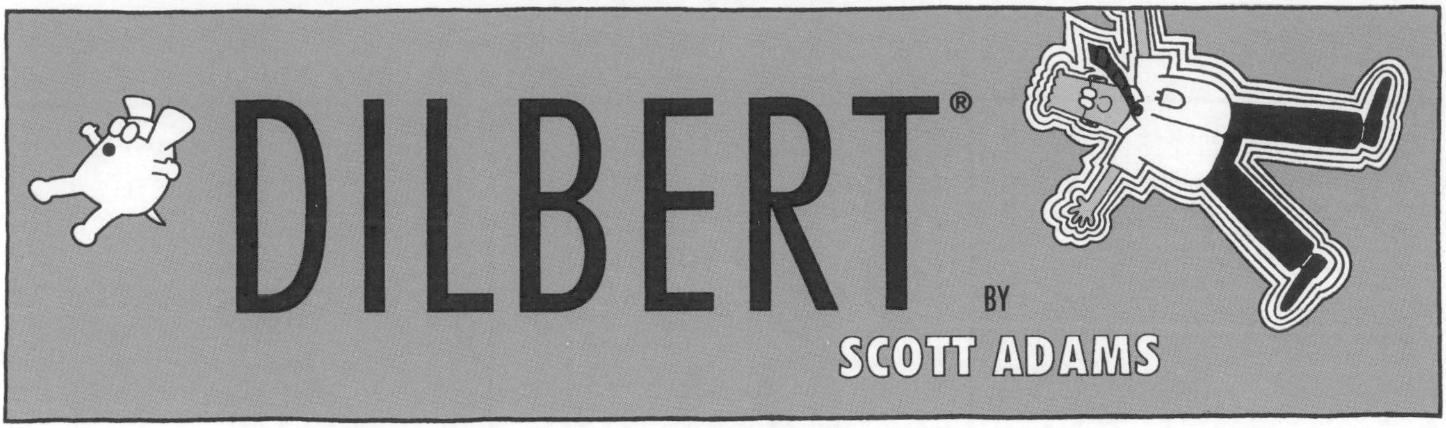
DILBERT®
BY
SCOTT ADAMS

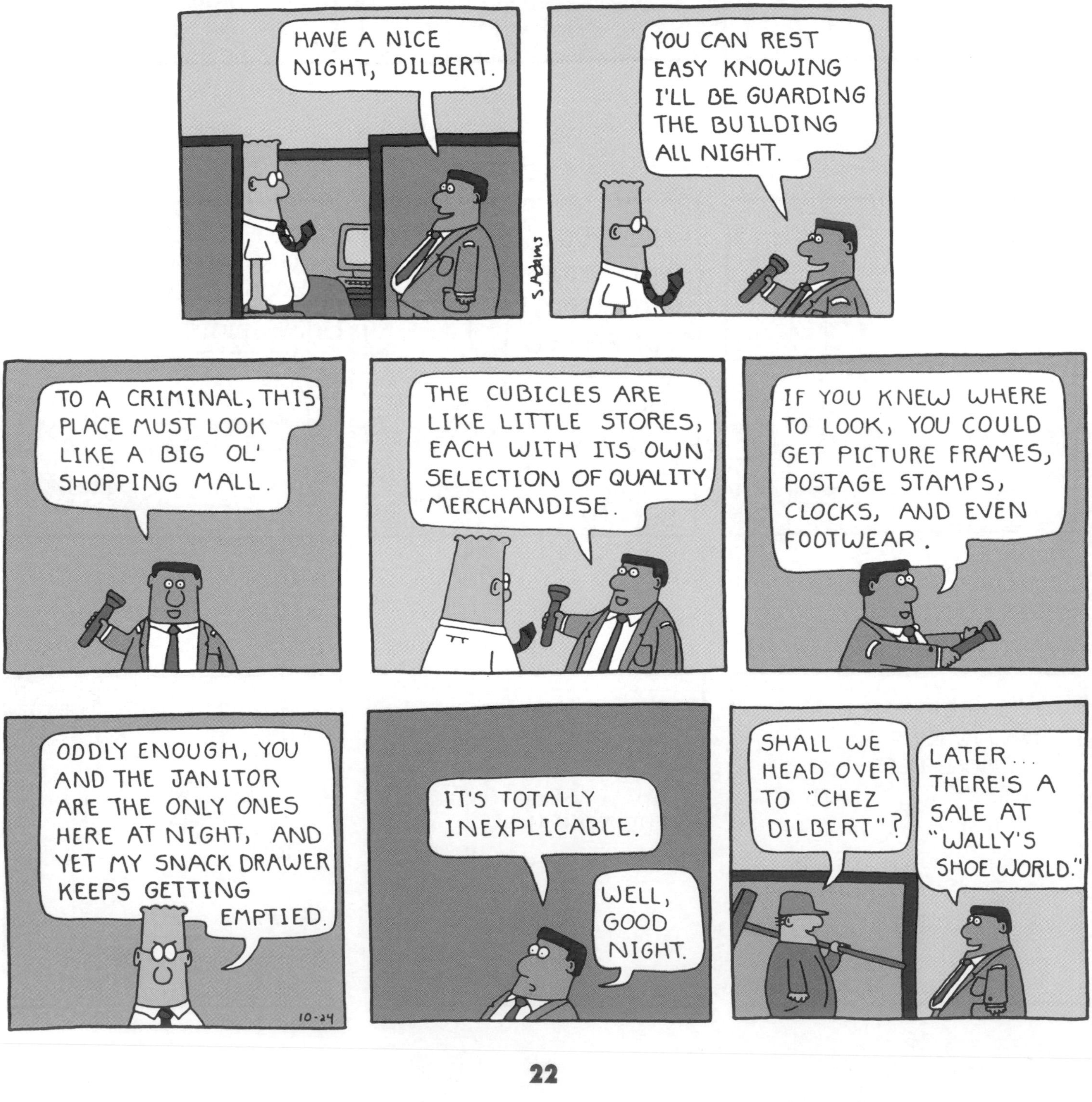
HAVE A NICE NIGHT, DILBERT.
YOU CAN REST EASY KNOWING I'LL BE GUARDING THE BUILDING ALL NIGHT.
S. Adams
TO A CRIMINAL, THIS PLACE MUST LOOK LIKE A BIG OL' SHOPPING MALL.
THE CUBICLES ARE LIKE LITTLE STORES, EACH WITH ITS OWN SELECTION OF QUALITY MERCHANDISE.
IF YOU KNEW WHERE TO LOOK, YOU COULD GET PICTURE FRAMES, POSTAGE STAMPS, CLOCKS, AND EVEN FOOTWEAR.
ODDLY ENOUGH, YOU AND THE JANITOR ARE THE ONLY ONES HERE AT NIGHT, AND YET MY SNACK DRAWER KEEPS GETTING EMPTIED.
10-24
IT'S TOTALLY INEXPLICABLE.
WELL, GOOD NIGHT.
SHALL WE HEAD OVER TO "CHEZ DILBERT"?
LATER... THERE'S A SALE AT "WALLY'S SHOE WORLD."

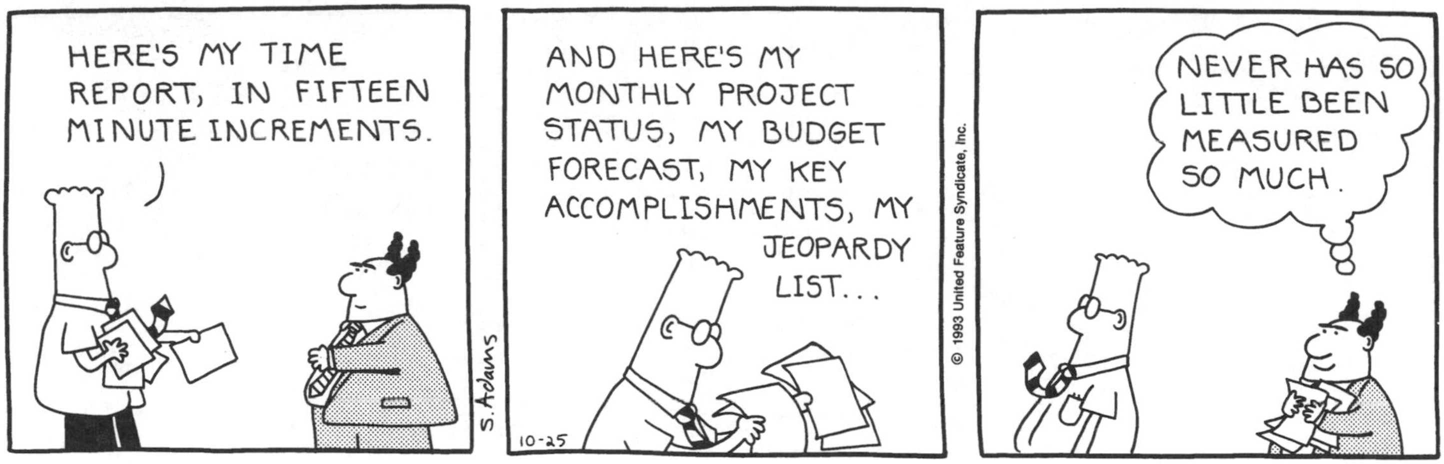
HERE'S MY TIME REPORT, IN FIFTEEN MINUTE INCREMENTS.
S. Adams
AND HERE'S MY MONTHLY PROJECT STATUS, MY BUDGET FORECAST, MY KEY ACCOMPLISHMENTS, MY JEOPARDY LIST...
10-25
© 1993 United Feature Syndicate, Inc.
NEVER HAS SO LITTLE BEEN MEASURED SO MUCH.

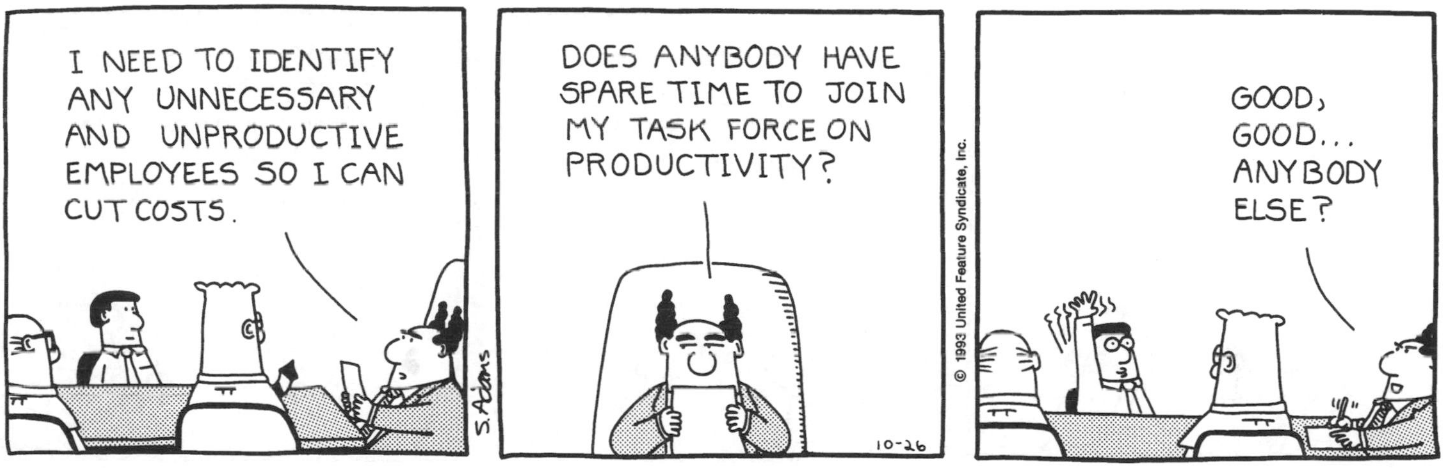
I NEED TO IDENTIFY ANY UNNECESSARY AND UNPRODUCTIVE EMPLOYEES SO I CAN CUT COSTS.
S. Adams
DOES ANYBODY HAVE SPARE TIME TO JOIN MY TASK FORCE ON PRODUCTIVITY?
10-26
© 1993 United Feature Syndicate, Inc.
GOOD, GOOD... ANYBODY ELSE?

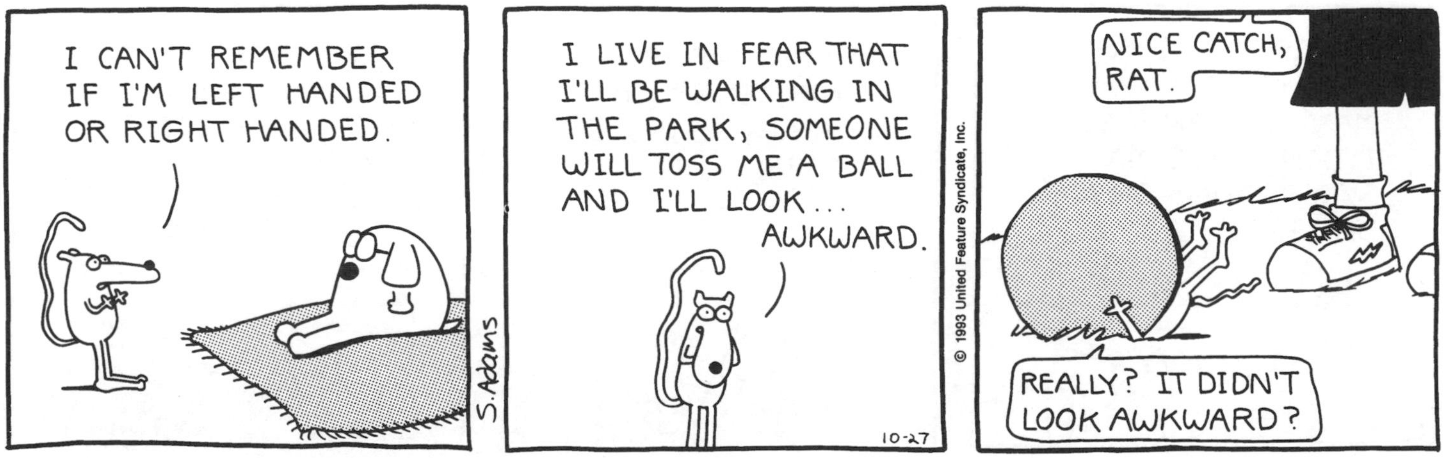
I CAN'T REMEMBER IF I'M LEFT HANDED OR RIGHT HANDED.
S. Adams
I LIVE IN FEAR THAT I'LL BE WALKING IN THE PARK, SOMEONE WILL TOSS ME A BALL AND I'LL LOOK...
AWKWARD.
10-27
© 1993 United Feature Syndicate, Inc.
NICE CATCH, RAT.
REALLY? IT DIDN'T LOOK AWKWARD?

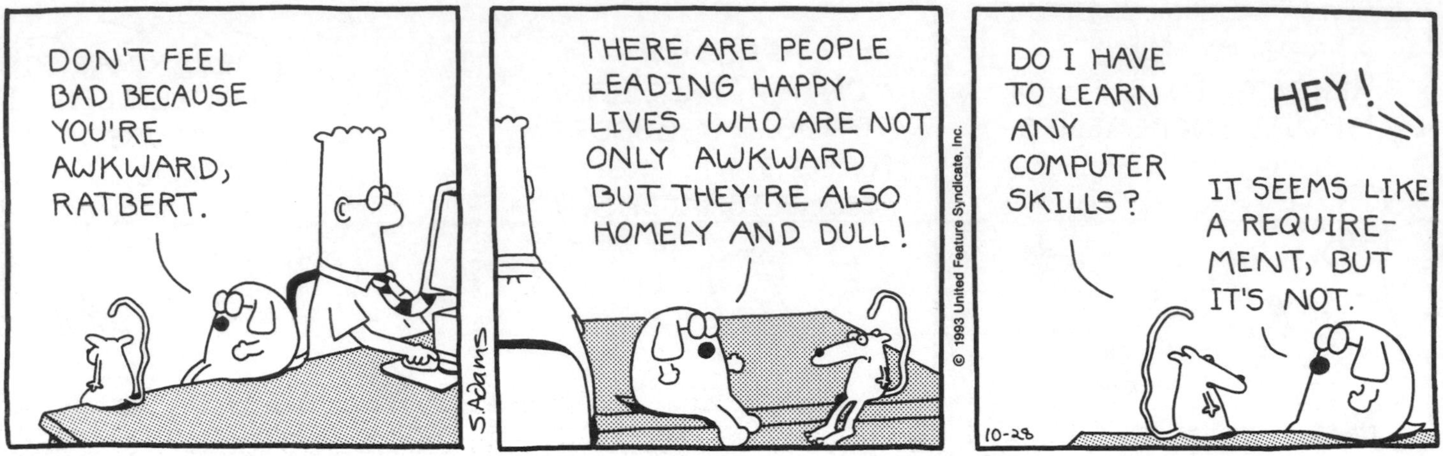
DON'T FEEL BAD BECAUSE YOU'RE AWKWARD, RATBERT.
S.Adams
THERE ARE PEOPLE LEADING HAPPY LIVES WHO ARE NOT ONLY AWKWARD BUT THEY'RE ALSO HOMELY AND DULL!
© 1993 United Feature Syndicate, Inc.
DO I HAVE TO LEARN ANY COMPUTER SKILLS?
HEY!
IT SEEMS LIKE A REQUIREMENT, BUT IT'S NOT.
10-28

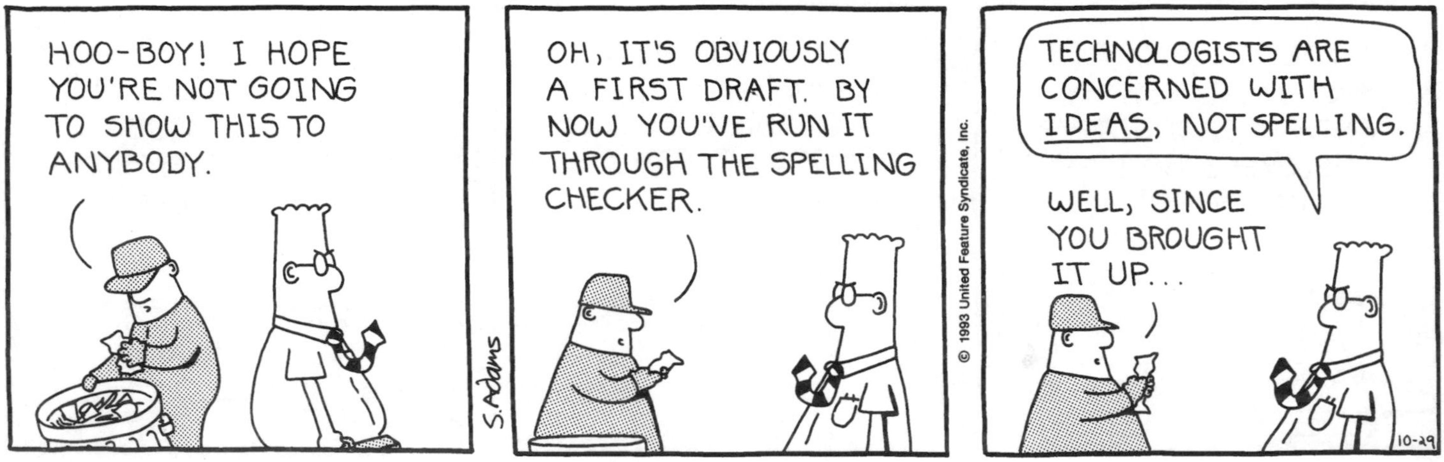
HOO-BOY! I HOPE YOU'RE NOT GOING TO SHOW THIS TO ANYBODY.
S.Adams
OH, IT'S OBVIOUSLY A FIRST DRAFT. BY NOW YOU'VE RUN IT THROUGH THE SPELLING CHECKER.
© 1993 United Feature Syndicate, Inc.
TECHNOLOGISTS ARE CONCERNED WITH IDEAS, NOT SPELLING.
WELL, SINCE YOU BROUGHT IT UP...
10-29

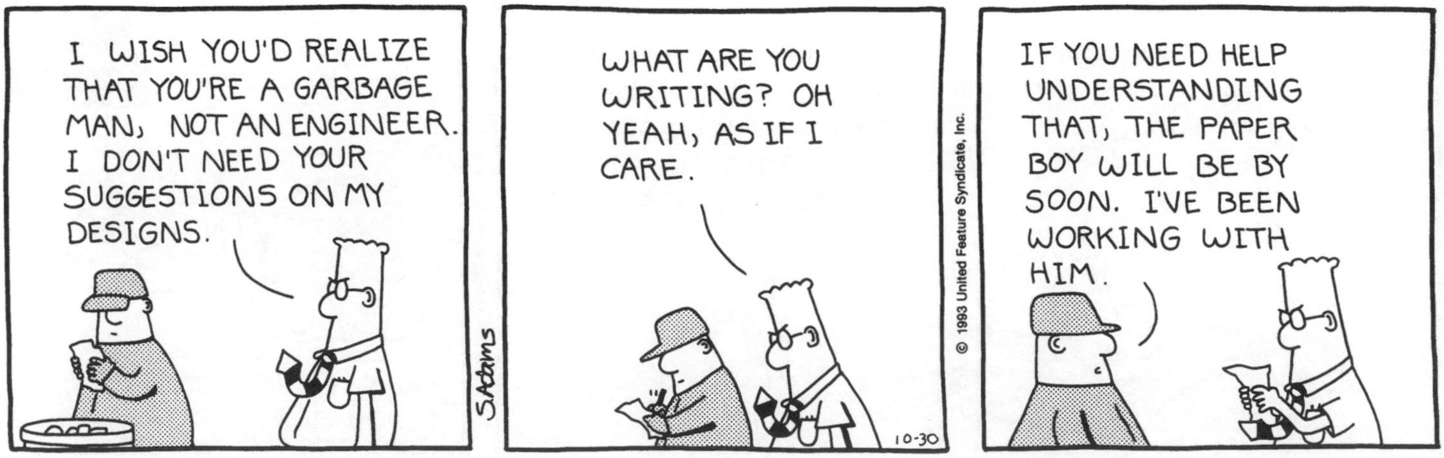
I WISH YOU'D REALIZE THAT YOU'RE A GARBAGE MAN, NOT AN ENGINEER. I DON'T NEED YOUR SUGGESTIONS ON MY DESIGNS.
S.Adams
WHAT ARE YOU WRITING? OH YEAH, AS IF I CARE.
10-30
© 1993 United Feature Syndicate, Inc.
IF YOU NEED HELP UNDERSTANDING THAT, THE PAPER BOY WILL BE BY SOON. I'VE BEEN WORKING WITH HIM.

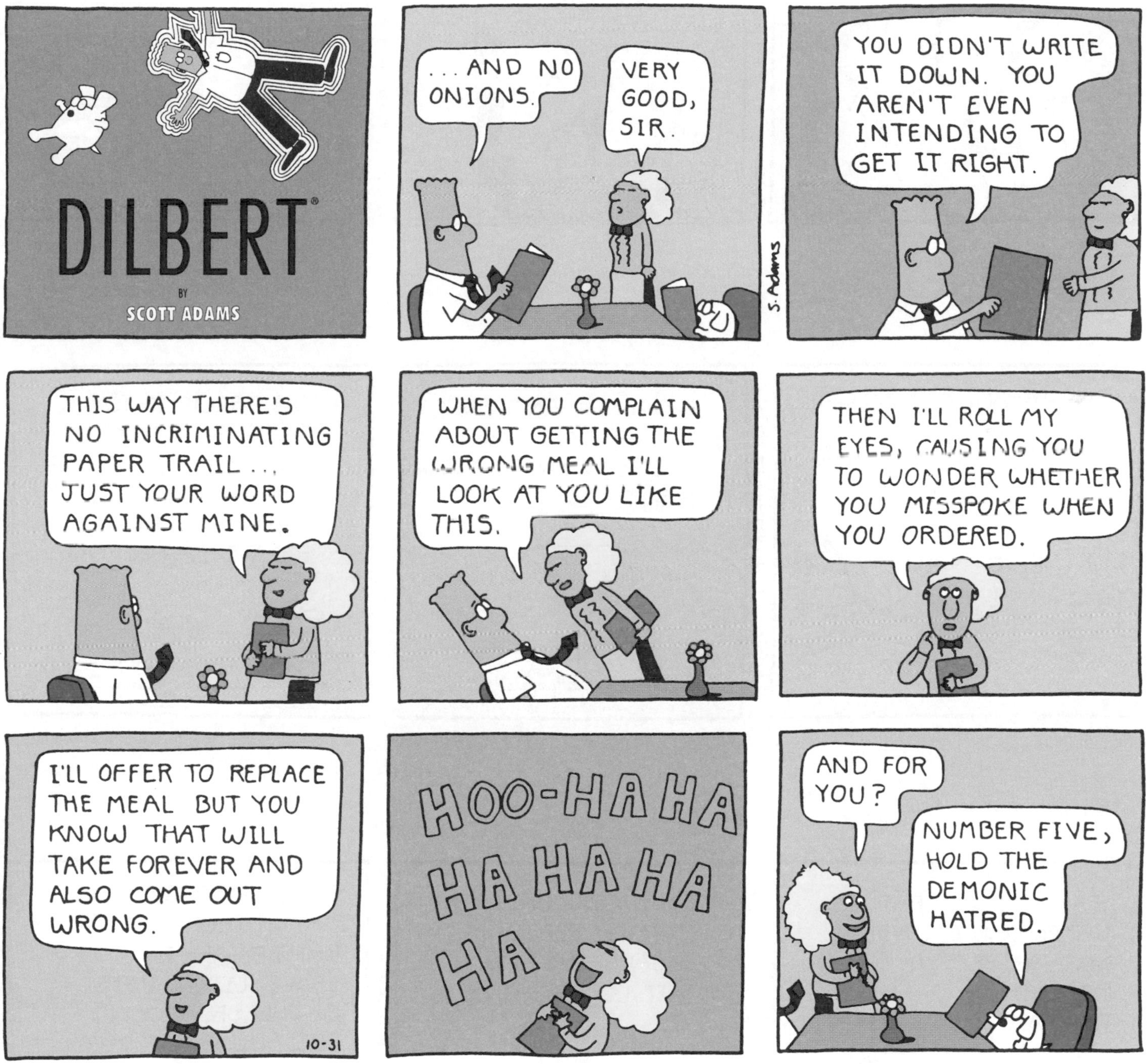
DILBERT®
BY
SCOTT ADAMS
...AND NO ONIONS.
VERY GOOD, SIR.
S. Adams
YOU DIDN'T WRITE IT DOWN. YOU AREN'T EVEN INTENDING TO GET IT RIGHT.
THIS WAY THERE'S NO INCRIMINATING PAPER TRAIL... JUST YOUR WORD AGAINST MINE.
WHEN YOU COMPLAIN ABOUT GETTING THE WRONG MEAL I'LL LOOK AT YOU LIKE THIS.
THEN I'LL ROLL MY EYES, CAUSING YOU TO WONDER WHETHER YOU MISSPOKE WHEN YOU ORDERED.
I'LL OFFER TO REPLACE THE MEAL BUT YOU KNOW THAT WILL TAKE FOREVER AND ALSO COME OUT WRONG.
10-31
HOO-HA HA HA HA HA HA HA
AND FOR YOU?
NUMBER FIVE, HOLD THE DEMONIC HATRED.

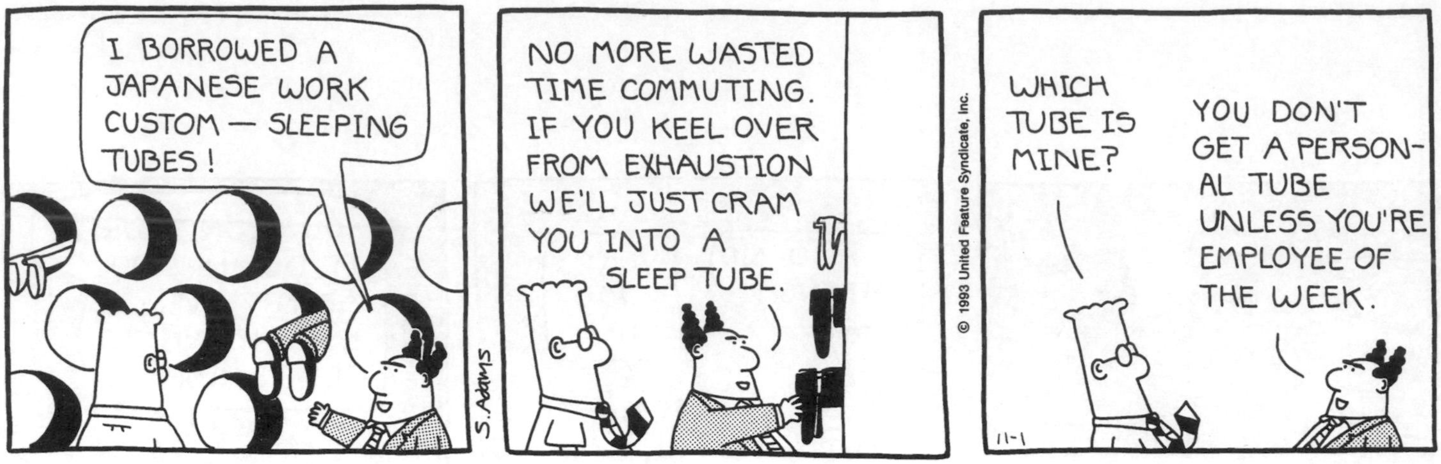
I BORROWED A JAPANESE WORK CUSTOM — SLEEPING TUBES!
NO MORE WASTED TIME COMMUTING. IF YOU KEEL OVER FROM EXHAUSTION WE'LL JUST CRAM YOU INTO A SLEEP TUBE.
WHICH TUBE IS MINE?
YOU DON'T GET A PERSONAL TUBE UNLESS YOU'RE EMPLOYEE OF THE WEEK.
S. Adams
© 1993 United Feature Syndicate, Inc.
11-1

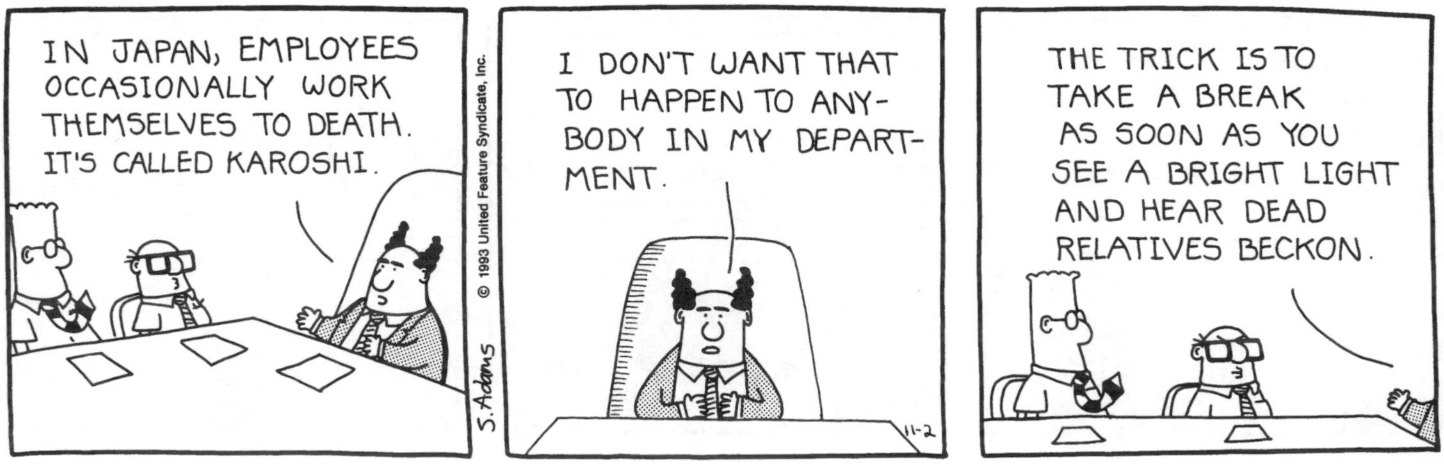
IN JAPAN, EMPLOYEES OCCASIONALLY WORK THEMSELVES TO DEATH. IT'S CALLED KAROSHI.
I DON'T WANT THAT TO HAPPEN TO ANYBODY IN MY DEPARTMENT.
THE TRICK IS TO TAKE A BREAK AS SOON AS YOU SEE A BRIGHT LIGHT AND HEAR DEAD RELATIVES BECKON.
S. Adams
© 1993 United Feature Syndicate, Inc.
11-2

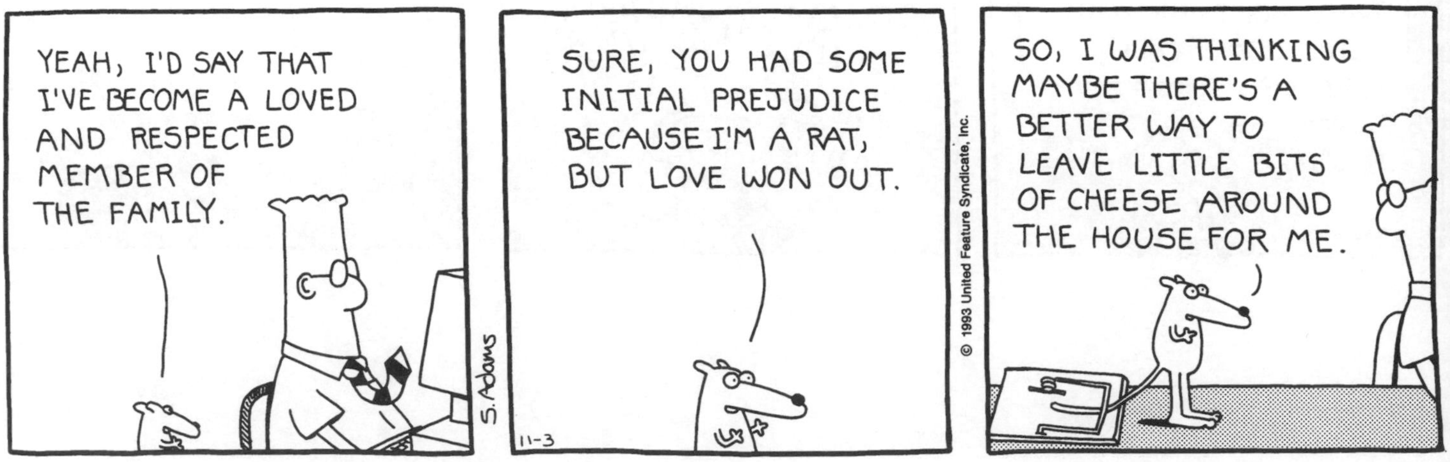
YEAH, I'D SAY THAT I'VE BECOME A LOVED AND RESPECTED MEMBER OF THE FAMILY.
SURE, YOU HAD SOME INITIAL PREJUDICE BECAUSE I'M A RAT, BUT LOVE WON OUT.
SO, I WAS THINKING MAYBE THERE'S A BETTER WAY TO LEAVE LITTLE BITS OF CHEESE AROUND THE HOUSE FOR ME.
S. Adams
© 1993 United Feature Syndicate, Inc.
11-3

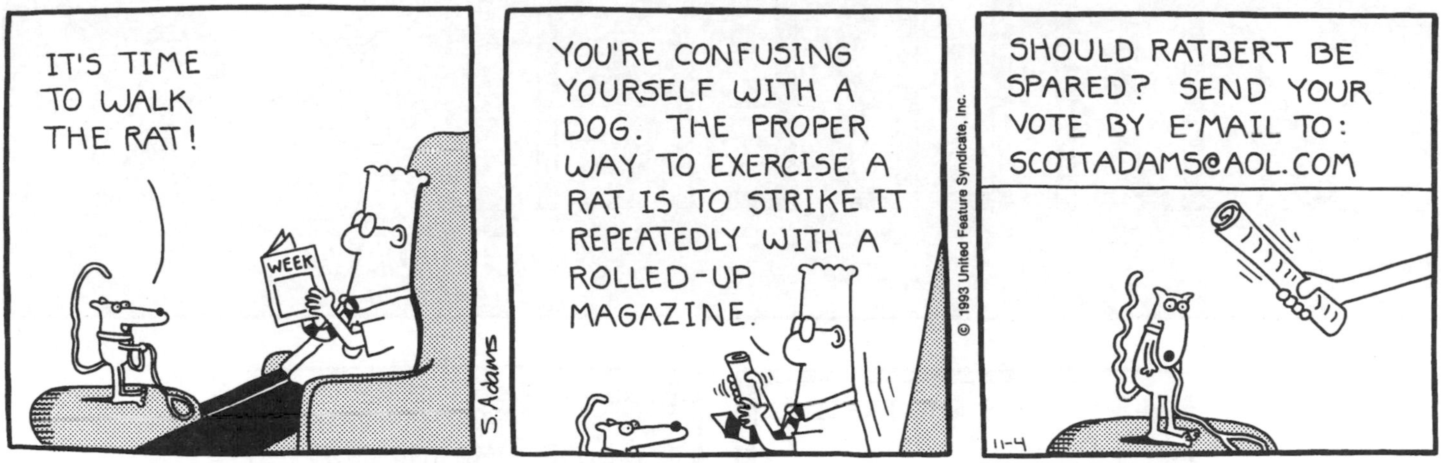
IT'S TIME TO WALK THE RAT!
WEEK
S. Adams
YOU'RE CONFUSING YOURSELF WITH A DOG. THE PROPER WAY TO EXERCISE A RAT IS TO STRIKE IT REPEATEDLY WITH A ROLLED-UP MAGAZINE.
© 1993 United Feature Syndicate, Inc.
SHOULD RATBERT BE SPARED? SEND YOUR VOTE BY E-MAIL TO: SCOTTADAMS@AOL.COM
11-4

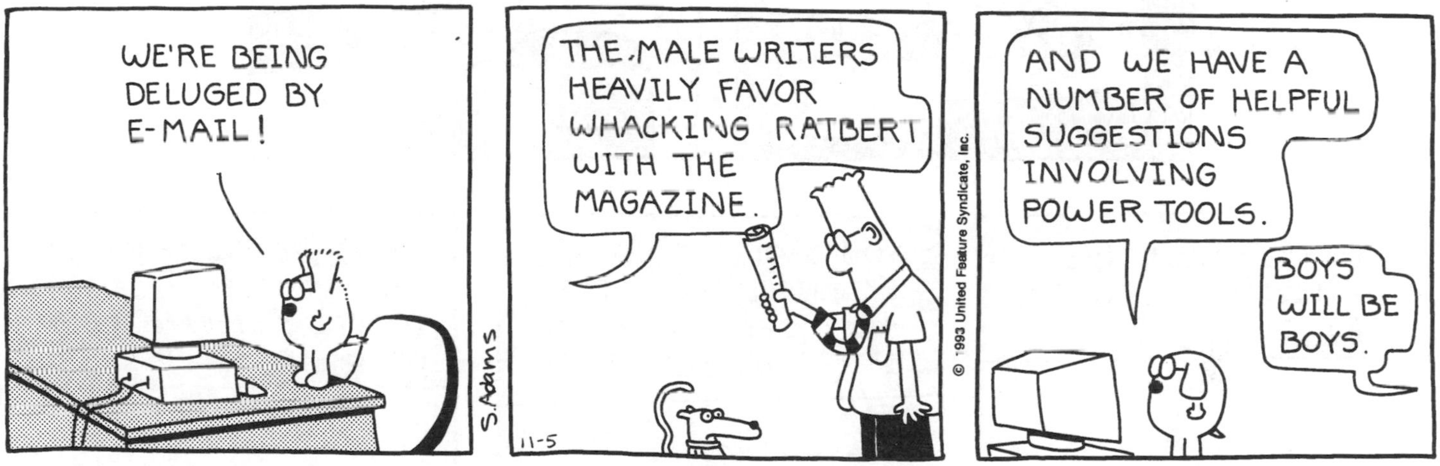
WE'RE BEING DELUGED BY E-MAIL!
S. Adams
11-5
THE MALE WRITERS HEAVILY FAVOR WHACKING RATBERT WITH THE MAGAZINE.
© 1993 United Feature Syndicate, Inc.
AND WE HAVE A NUMBER OF HELPFUL SUGGESTIONS INVOLVING POWER TOOLS.
BOYS WILL BE BOYS.

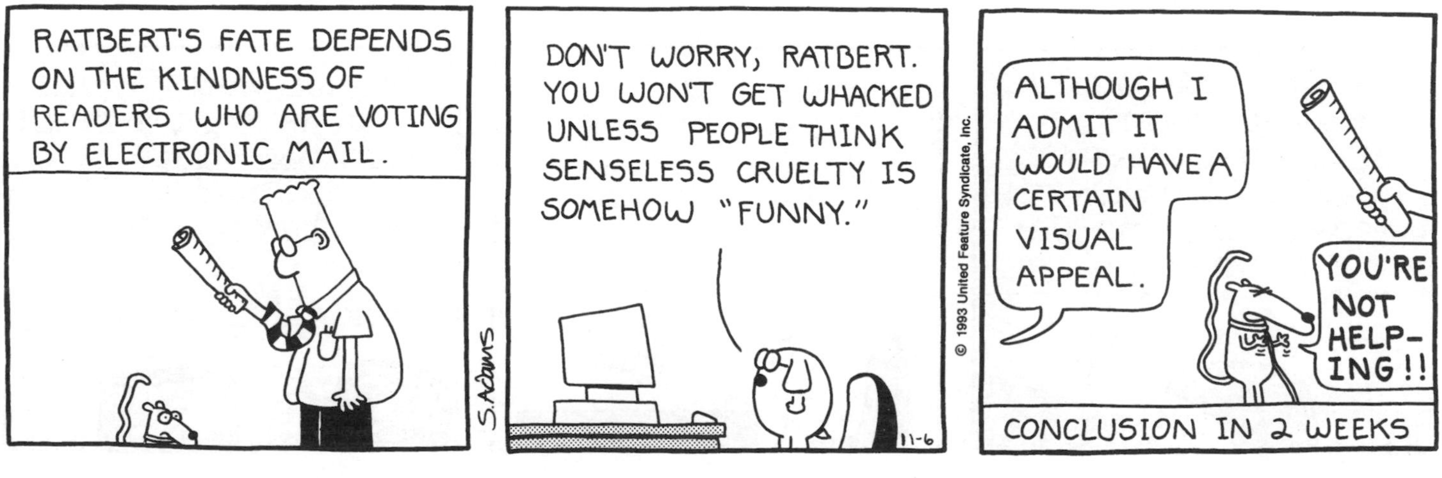
RATBERT'S FATE DEPENDS ON THE KINDNESS OF READERS WHO ARE VOTING BY ELECTRONIC MAIL.
S. Adams
DON'T WORRY, RATBERT. YOU WON'T GET WHACKED UNLESS PEOPLE THINK SENSELESS CRUELTY IS SOMEHOW "FUNNY."
11-6
© 1993 United Feature Syndicate, Inc.
ALTHOUGH I ADMIT IT WOULD HAVE A CERTAIN VISUAL APPEAL.
YOU'RE NOT HELP-ING!!
CONCLUSION IN 2 WEEKS

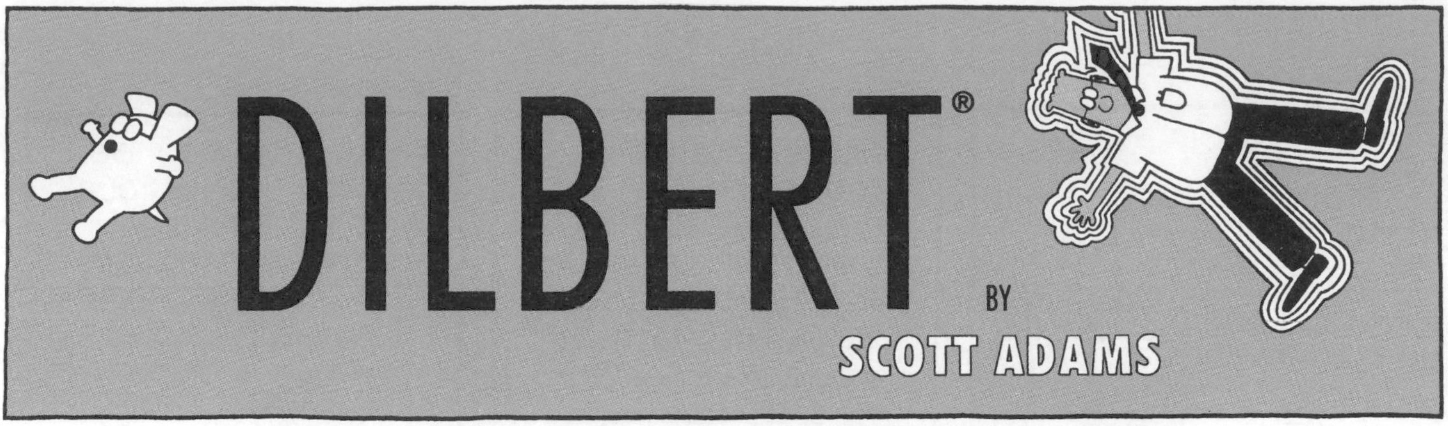
DILBERT®
BY
SCOTT ADAMS

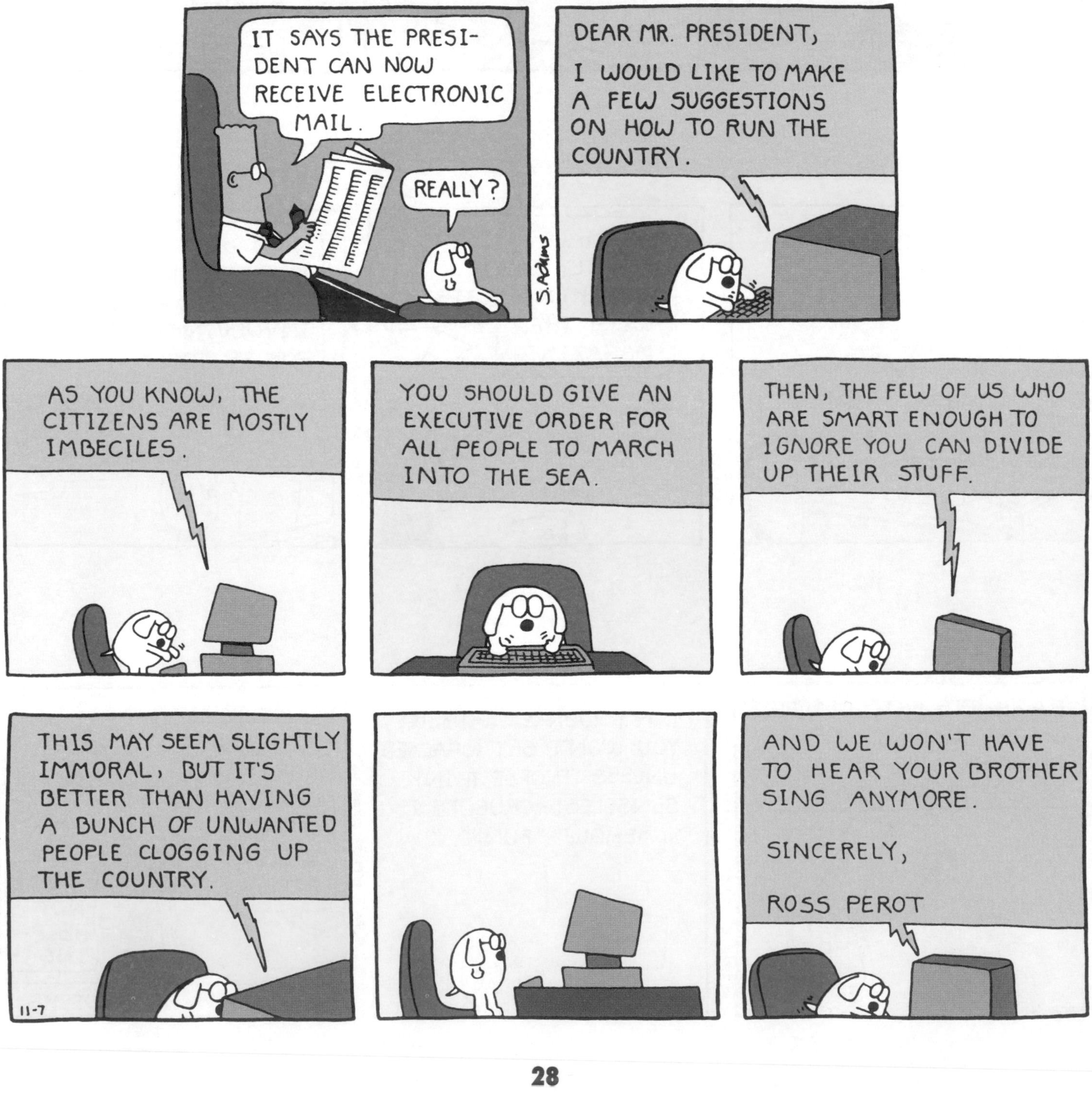
IT SAYS THE PRESI-DENT CAN NOW RECEIVE ELECTRONIC MAIL.
REALLY?
S. Adams
DEAR MR. PRESIDENT,
I WOULD LIKE TO MAKE A FEW SUGGESTIONS ON HOW TO RUN THE COUNTRY.
AS YOU KNOW, THE CITIZENS ARE MOSTLY IMBECILES.
YOU SHOULD GIVE AN EXECUTIVE ORDER FOR ALL PEOPLE TO MARCH INTO THE SEA.
THEN, THE FEW OF US WHO ARE SMART ENOUGH TO IGNORE YOU CAN DIVIDE UP THEIR STUFF.
THIS MAY SEEM SLIGHTLY IMMORAL, BUT IT'S BETTER THAN HAVING A BUNCH OF UNWANTED PEOPLE CLOGGING UP THE COUNTRY.
11-7
AND WE WON'T HAVE TO HEAR YOUR BROTHER SING ANYMORE.
SINCERELY,
ROSS PEROT

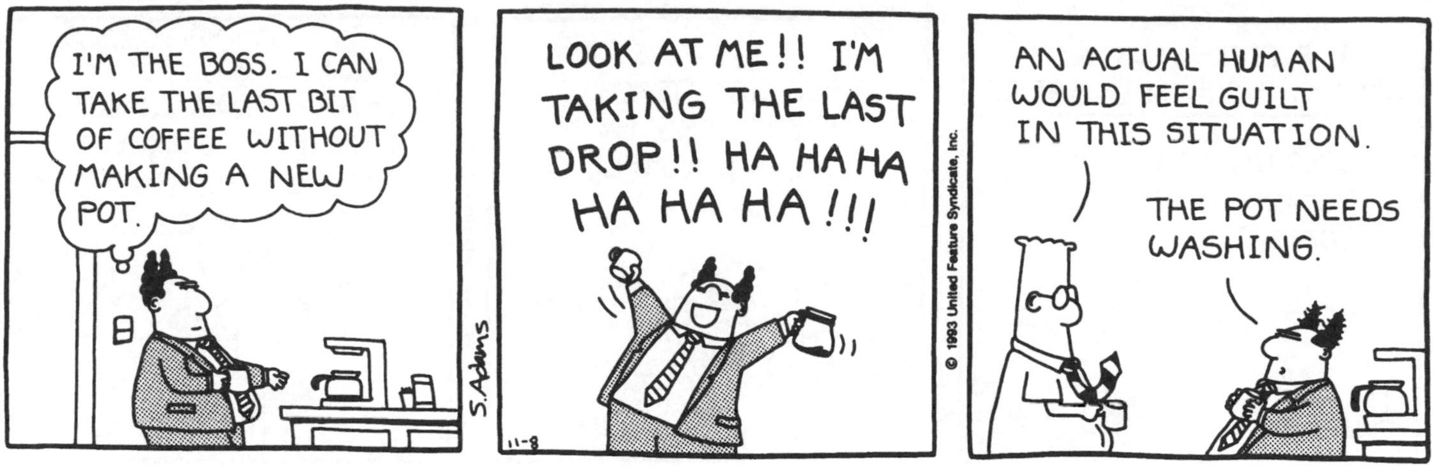
I'M THE BOSS. I CAN TAKE THE LAST BIT OF COFFEE WITHOUT MAKING A NEW POT.
S.Adams
LOOK AT ME!! I'M TAKING THE LAST DROP!! HA HA HA HA HA HA!!!
11-8
© 1993 United Feature Syndicate, Inc.
AN ACTUAL HUMAN WOULD FEEL GUILT IN THIS SITUATION.
THE POT NEEDS WASHING.

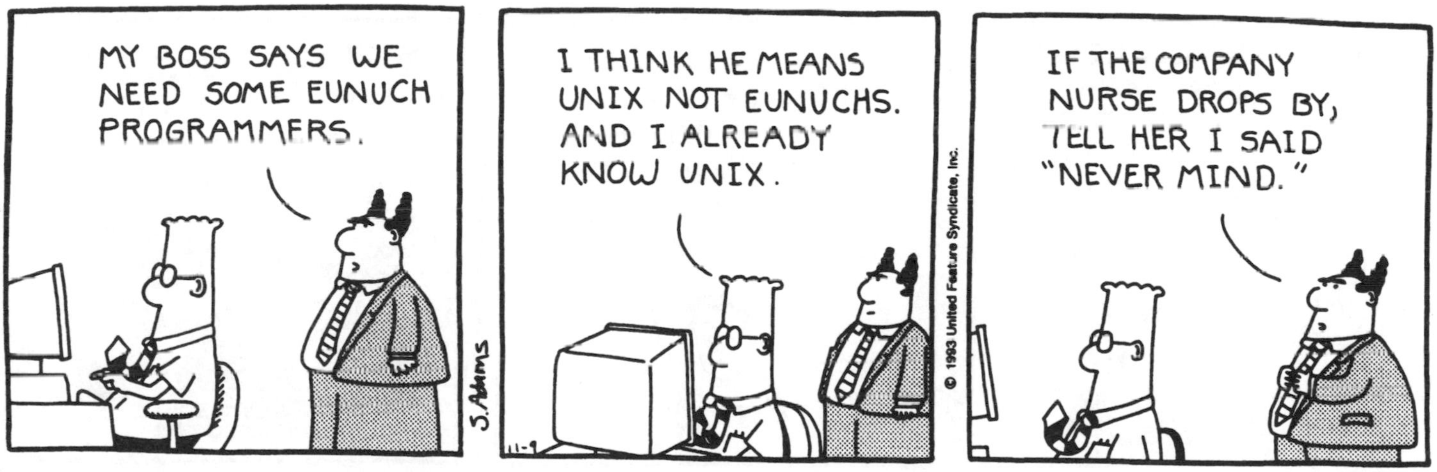
MY BOSS SAYS WE NEED SOME EUNUCH PROGRAMMERS.
S.Adams
I THINK HE MEANS UNIX NOT EUNUCHS. AND I ALREADY KNOW UNIX.
11-9
© 1993 United Feature Syndicate, Inc.
IF THE COMPANY NURSE DROPS BY, TELL HER I SAID "NEVER MIND."

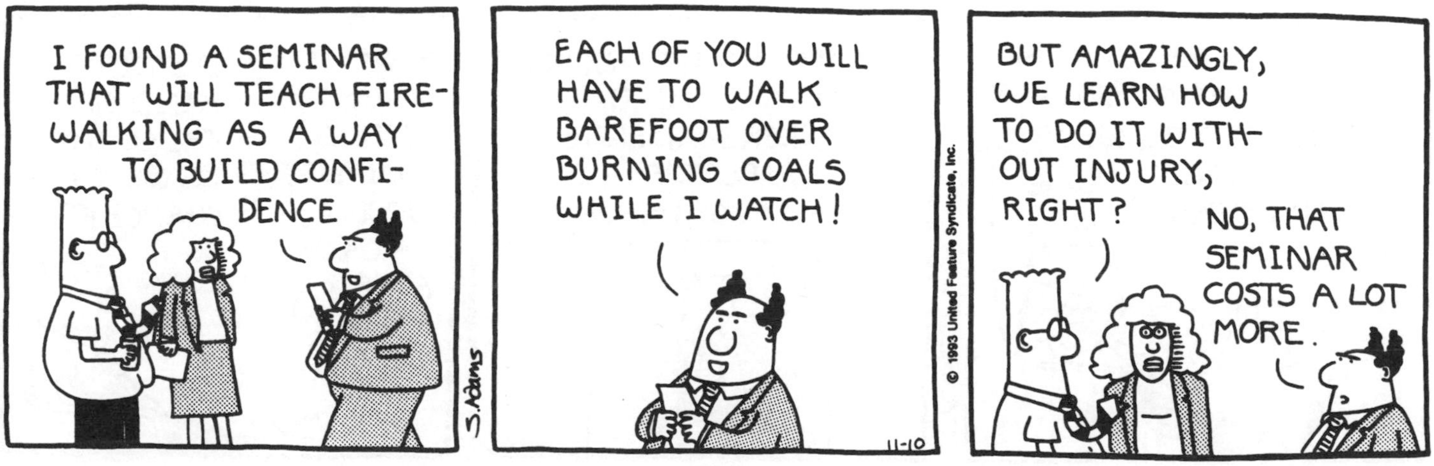
I FOUND A SEMINAR THAT WILL TEACH FIRE-WALKING AS A WAY TO BUILD CONFI-DENCE
S.Adams
EACH OF YOU WILL HAVE TO WALK BAREFOOT OVER BURNING COALS WHILE I WATCH!
11-10
© 1993 United Feature Syndicate, Inc.
BUT AMAZINGLY, WE LEARN HOW TO DO IT WITH-OUT INJURY, RIGHT?
NO, THAT SEMINAR COSTS A LOT MORE.

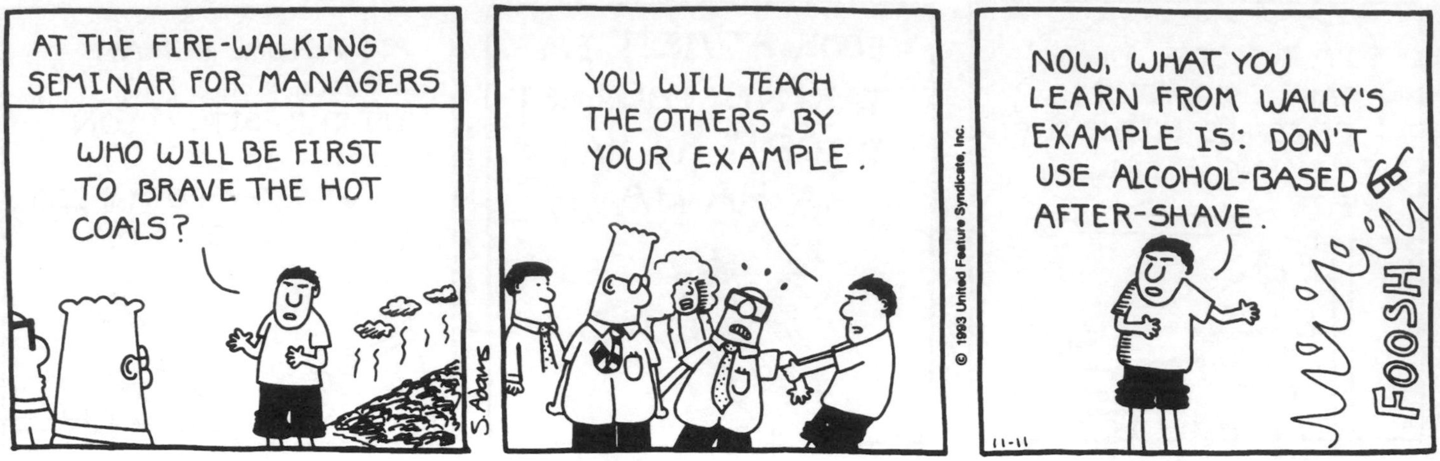
AT THE FIRE-WALKING SEMINAR FOR MANAGERS
WHO WILL BE FIRST TO BRAVE THE HOT COALS?
S. Adams
YOU WILL TEACH THE OTHERS BY YOUR EXAMPLE.
© 1993 United Feature Syndicate, Inc.
NOW, WHAT YOU LEARN FROM WALLY'S EXAMPLE IS: DON'T USE ALCOHOL-BASED AFTER-SHAVE.
FOOSH
11-11

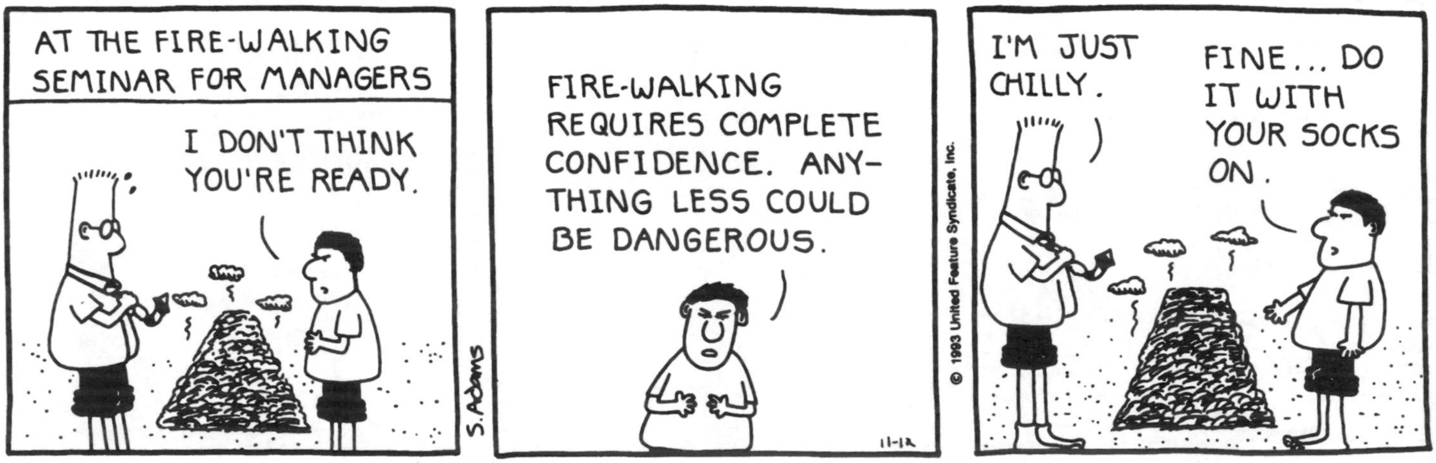
AT THE FIRE-WALKING SEMINAR FOR MANAGERS
I DON'T THINK YOU'RE READY.
S. Adams
FIRE-WALKING REQUIRES COMPLETE CONFIDENCE. ANYTHING LESS COULD BE DANGEROUS.
11-12
© 1993 United Feature Syndicate, Inc.
I'M JUST CHILLY.
FINE... DO IT WITH YOUR SOCKS ON.

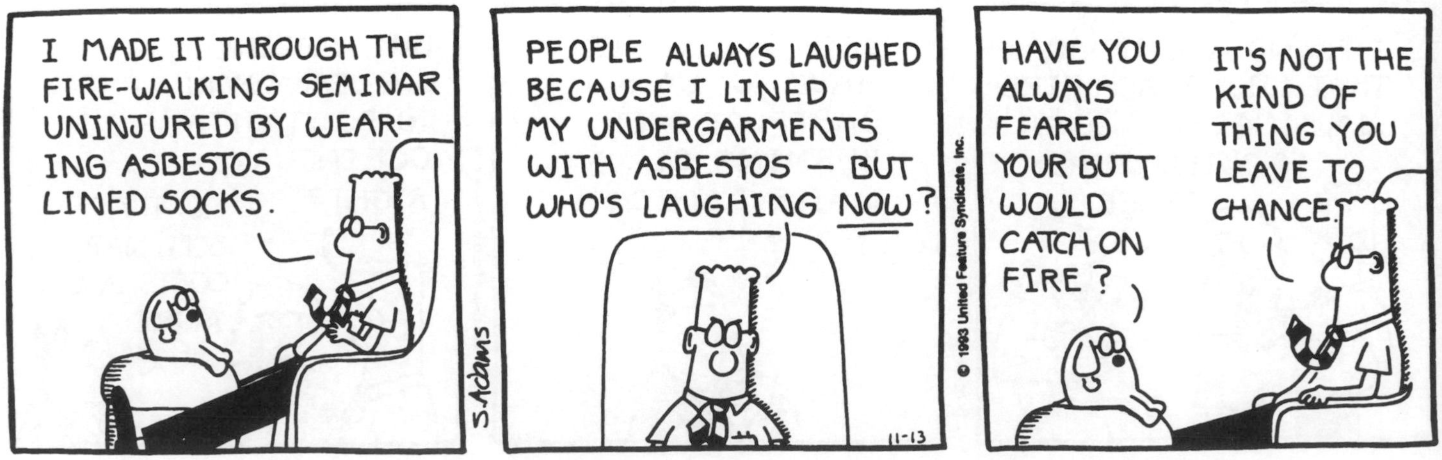
I MADE IT THROUGH THE FIRE-WALKING SEMINAR UNINJURED BY WEARING ASBESTOS LINED SOCKS.
S. Adams
PEOPLE ALWAYS LAUGHED BECAUSE I LINED MY UNDERGARMENTS WITH ASBESTOS — BUT WHO'S LAUGHING NOW?
11-13
© 1993 United Feature Syndicate, Inc.
HAVE YOU ALWAYS FEARED YOUR BUTT WOULD CATCH ON FIRE?
IT'S NOT THE KIND OF THING YOU LEAVE TO CHANCE.

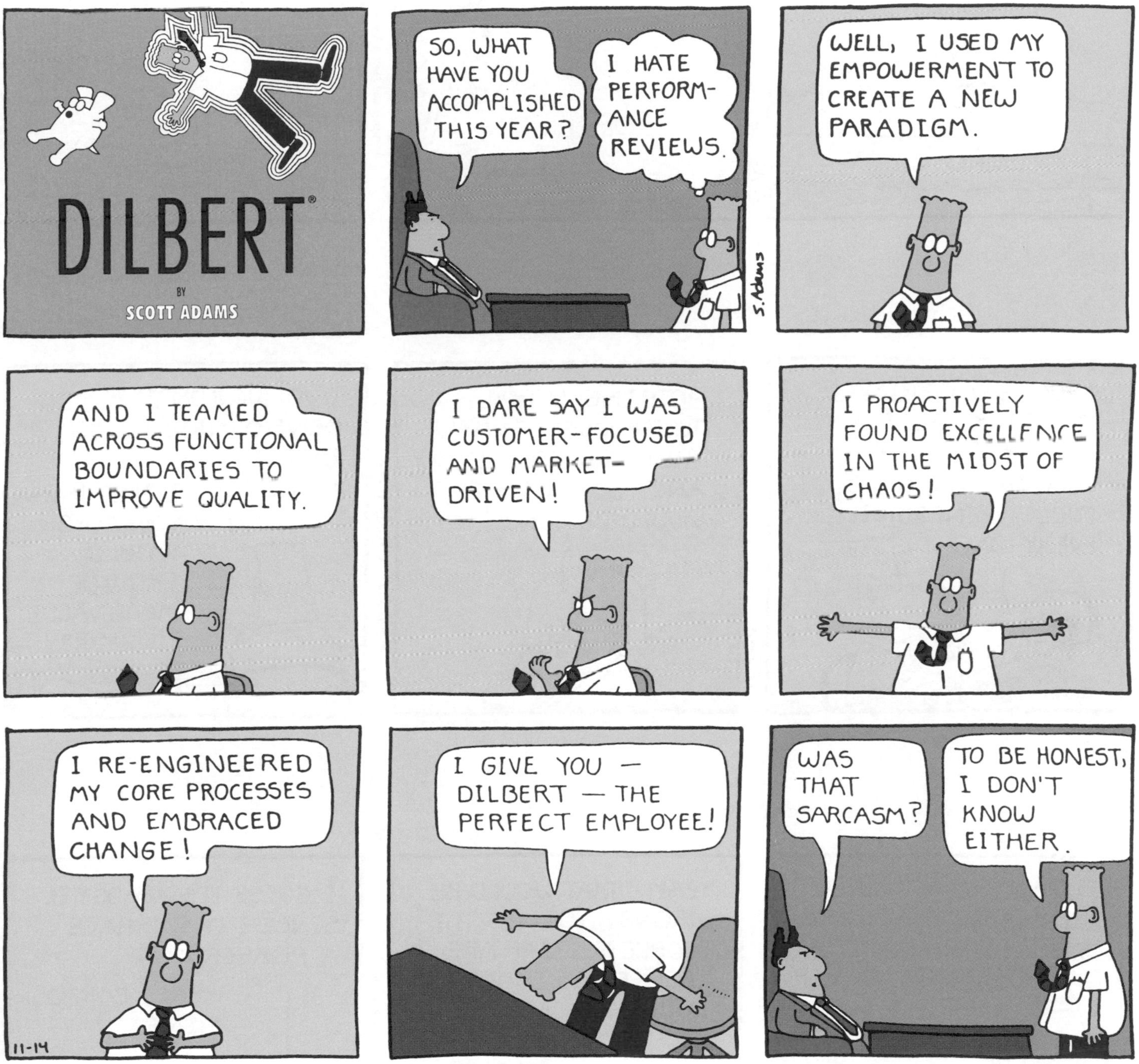
DILBERT®
BY
SCOTT ADAMS
SO, WHAT HAVE YOU ACCOMPLISHED THIS YEAR?
I HATE PERFORMANCE REVIEWS.
S. Adams
WELL, I USED MY EMPOWERMENT TO CREATE A NEW PARADIGM.
AND I TEAMED ACROSS FUNCTIONAL BOUNDARIES TO IMPROVE QUALITY.
I DARE SAY I WAS CUSTOMER-FOCUSED AND MARKET-DRIVEN!
I PROACTIVELY FOUND EXCELLENCE IN THE MIDST OF CHAOS!
I RE-ENGINEERED MY CORE PROCESSES AND EMBRACED CHANGE!
11-14
I GIVE YOU — DILBERT — THE PERFECT EMPLOYEE!
WAS THAT SARCASM?
TO BE HONEST, I DON'T KNOW EITHER.

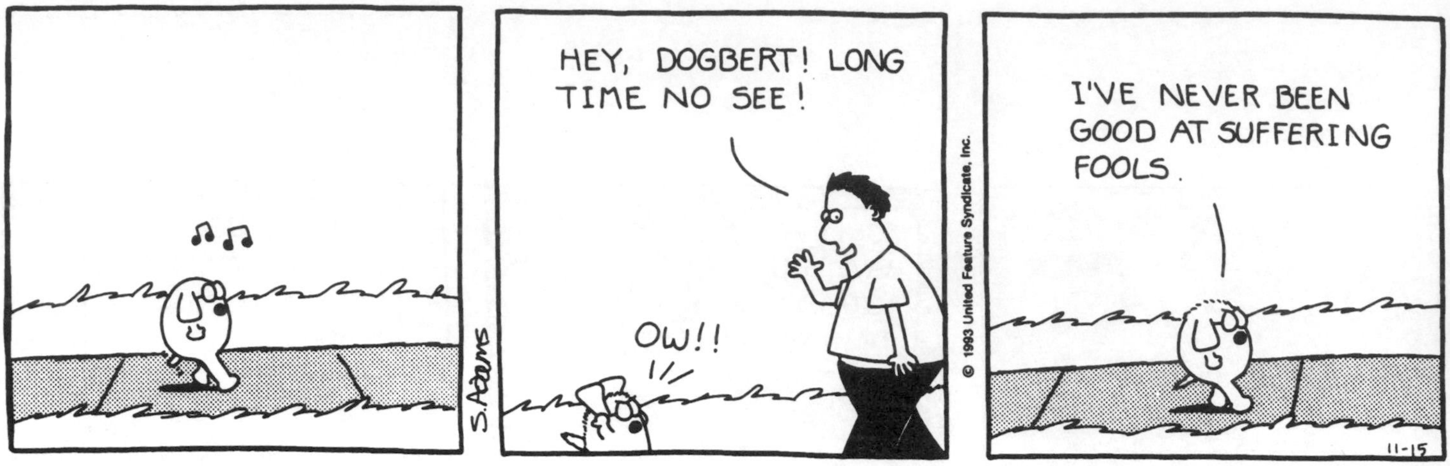
S.Adams
HEY, DOGBERT! LONG TIME NO SEE!
OW!!
© 1993 United Feature Syndicate, Inc.
I'VE NEVER BEEN GOOD AT SUFFERING FOOLS.
11-15

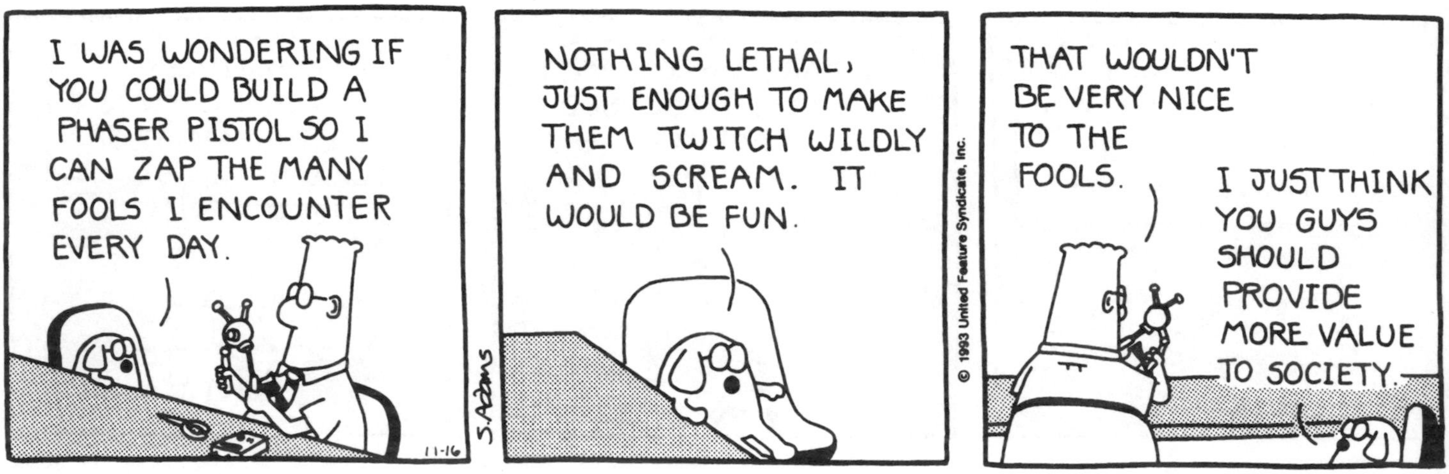
I WAS WONDERING IF YOU COULD BUILD A PHASER PISTOL SO I CAN ZAP THE MANY FOOLS I ENCOUNTER EVERY DAY.
11-16
S.Adams
NOTHING LETHAL, JUST ENOUGH TO MAKE THEM TWITCH WILDLY AND SCREAM. IT WOULD BE FUN.
© 1993 United Feature Syndicate, Inc.
THAT WOULDN'T BE VERY NICE TO THE FOOLS.
I JUST THINK YOU GUYS SHOULD PROVIDE MORE VALUE TO SOCIETY.

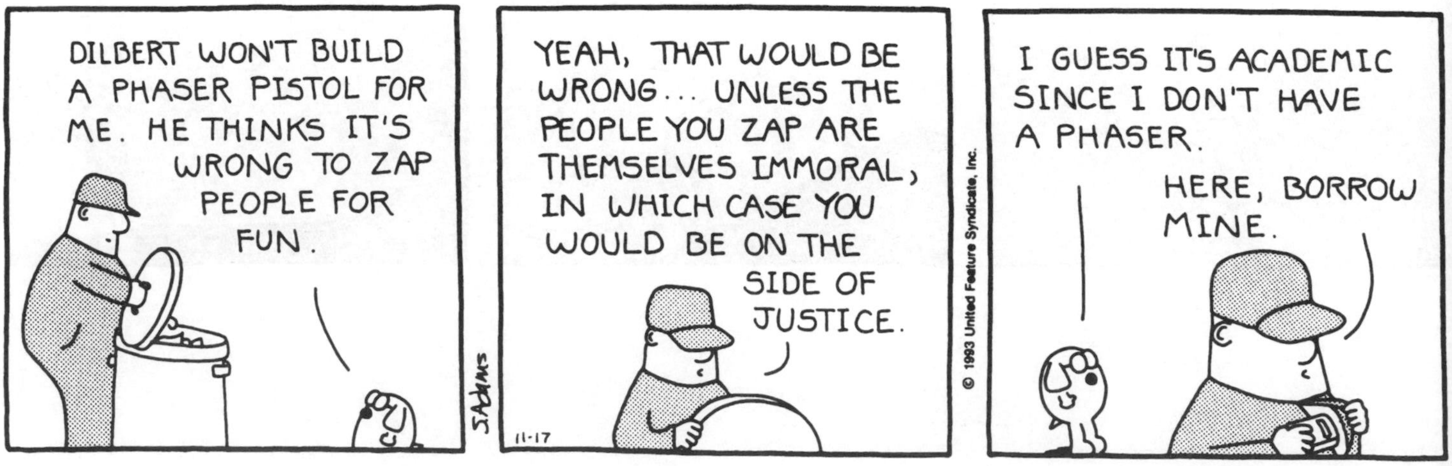
DILBERT WON'T BUILD A PHASER PISTOL FOR ME. HE THINKS IT'S WRONG TO ZAP PEOPLE FOR FUN.
S.Adams
YEAH, THAT WOULD BE WRONG... UNLESS THE PEOPLE YOU ZAP ARE THEMSELVES IMMORAL, IN WHICH CASE YOU WOULD BE ON THE SIDE OF JUSTICE.
11-17
© 1993 United Feature Syndicate, Inc.
I GUESS IT'S ACADEMIC SINCE I DON'T HAVE A PHASER.
HERE, BORROW MINE.

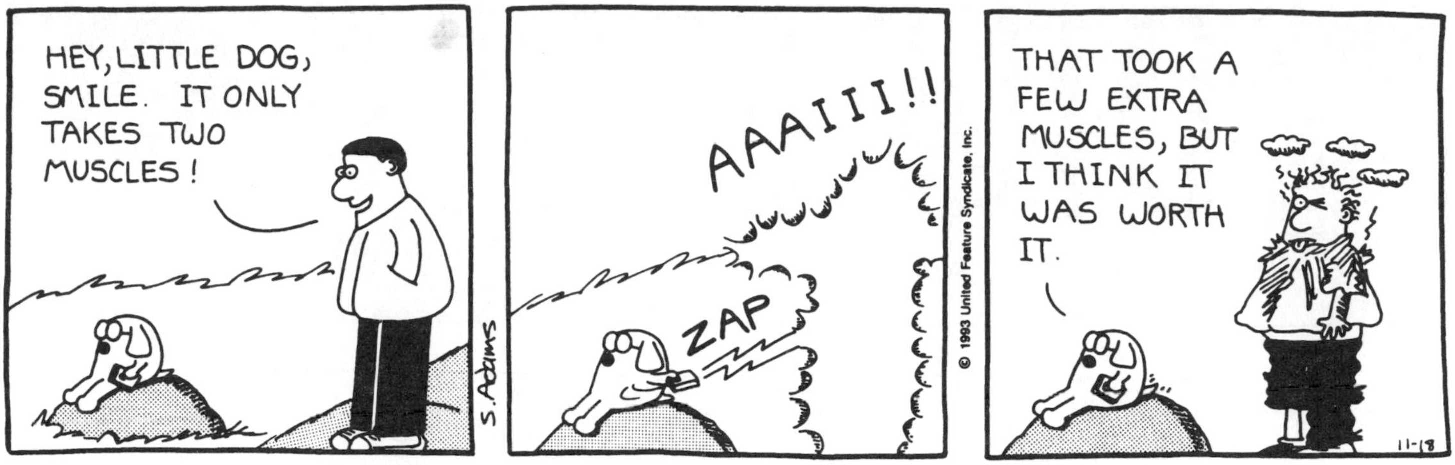
HEY, LITTLE DOG, SMILE. IT ONLY TAKES TWO MUSCLES!
AAAIII!!
ZAP
THAT TOOK A FEW EXTRA MUSCLES, BUT I THINK IT WAS WORTH IT.
© 1993 United Feature Syndicate, Inc.
11-18

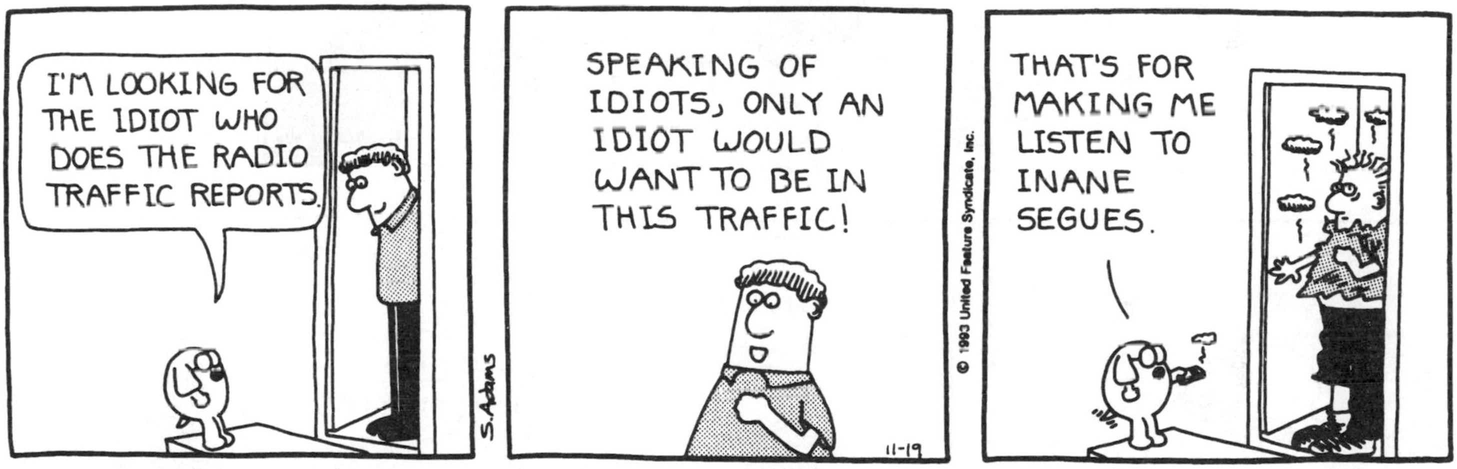
I'M LOOKING FOR THE IDIOT WHO DOES THE RADIO TRAFFIC REPORTS.
SPEAKING OF IDIOTS, ONLY AN IDIOT WOULD WANT TO BE IN THIS TRAFFIC!
THAT'S FOR MAKING ME LISTEN TO INANE SEGUES.
© 1993 United Feature Syndicate, Inc.
11-19

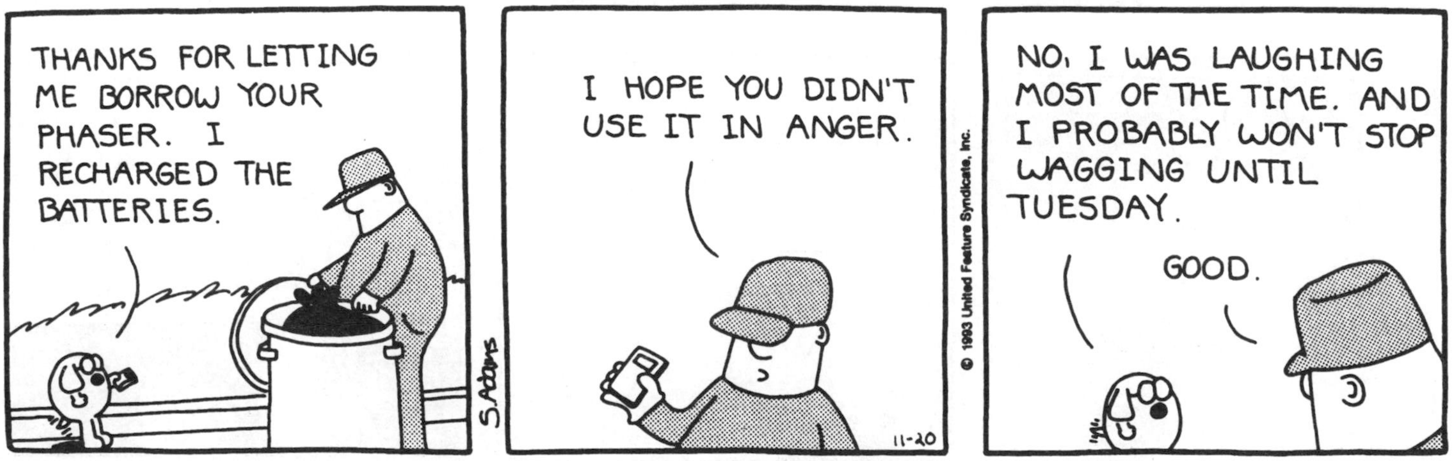
THANKS FOR LETTING ME BORROW YOUR PHASER. I RECHARGED THE BATTERIES.
I HOPE YOU DIDN'T USE IT IN ANGER.
NO, I WAS LAUGHING MOST OF THE TIME. AND I PROBABLY WON'T STOP WAGGING UNTIL TUESDAY.
GOOD.
© 1993 United Feature Syndicate, Inc.
11-20

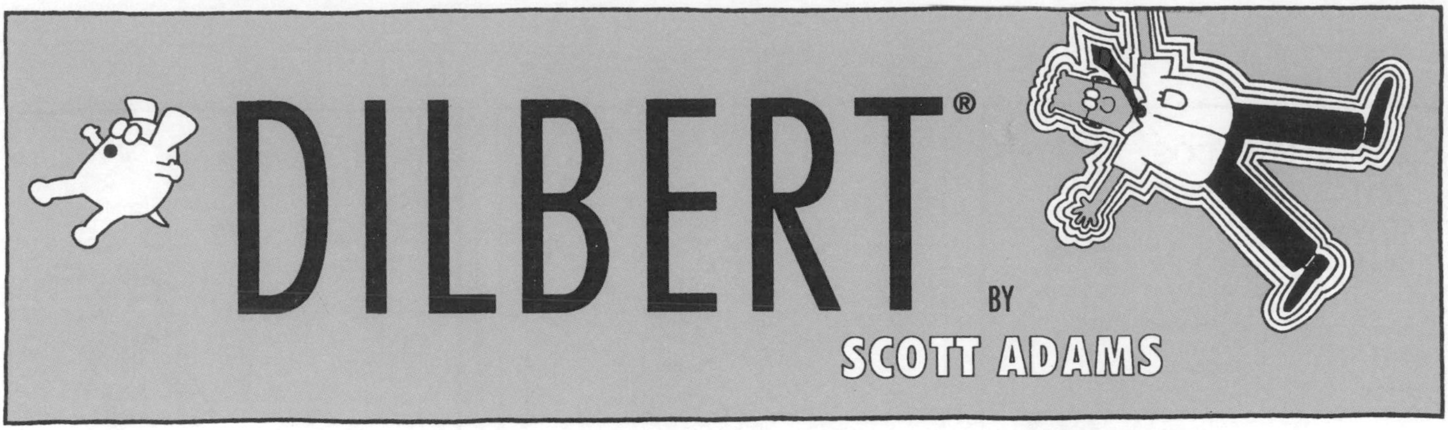
DILBERT®
BY
SCOTT ADAMS

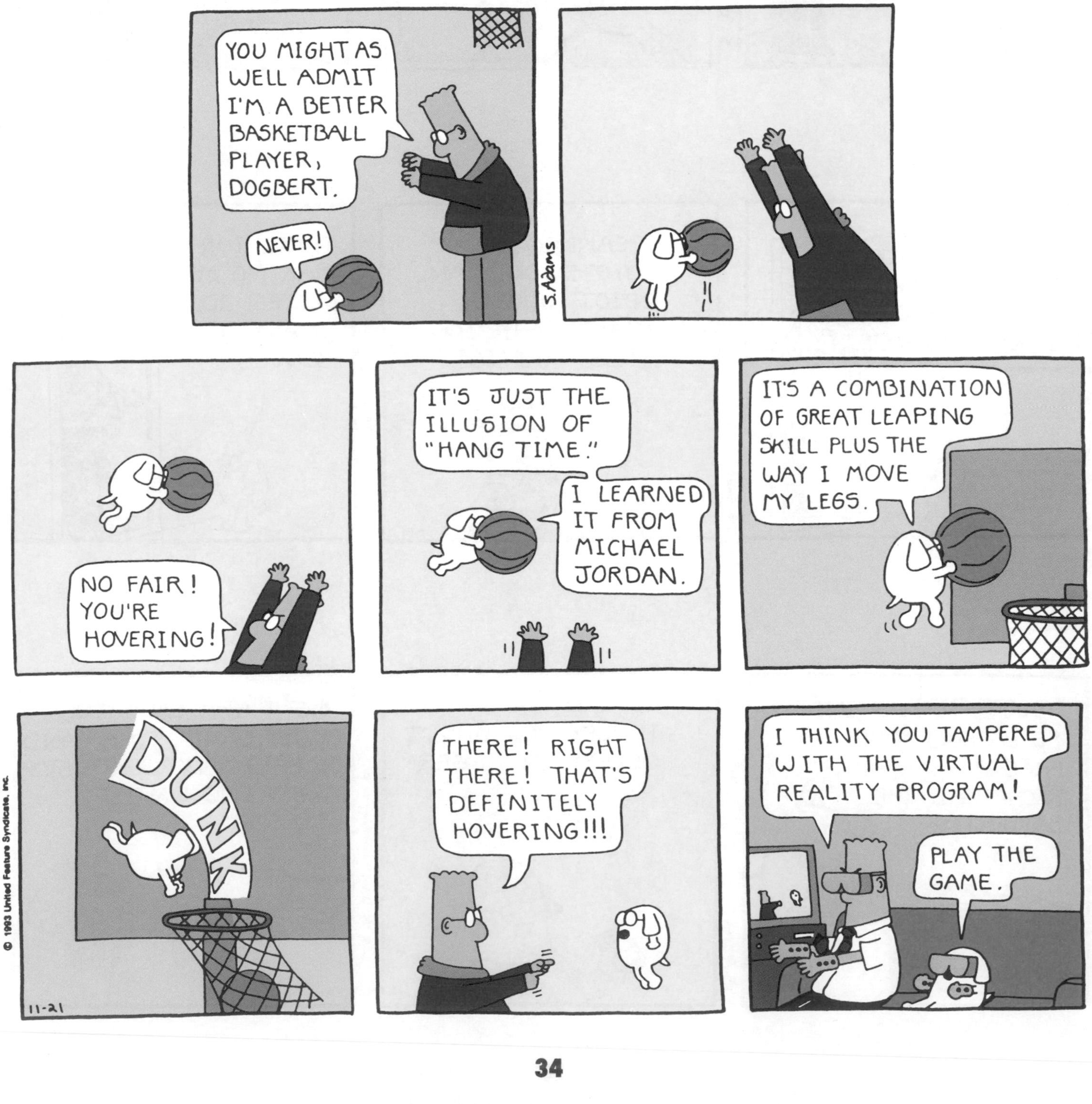
YOU MIGHT AS WELL ADMIT I'M A BETTER BASKETBALL PLAYER, DOGBERT.
NEVER!
S. Adams
NO FAIR! YOU'RE HOVERING!
IT'S JUST THE ILLUSION OF "HANG TIME."
I LEARNED IT FROM MICHAEL JORDAN.
IT'S A COMBINATION OF GREAT LEAPING SKILL PLUS THE WAY I MOVE MY LEGS.
DUNK
11-21
THERE! RIGHT THERE! THAT'S DEFINITELY HOVERING!!!
I THINK YOU TAMPERED WITH THE VIRTUAL REALITY PROGRAM!
PLAY THE GAME.

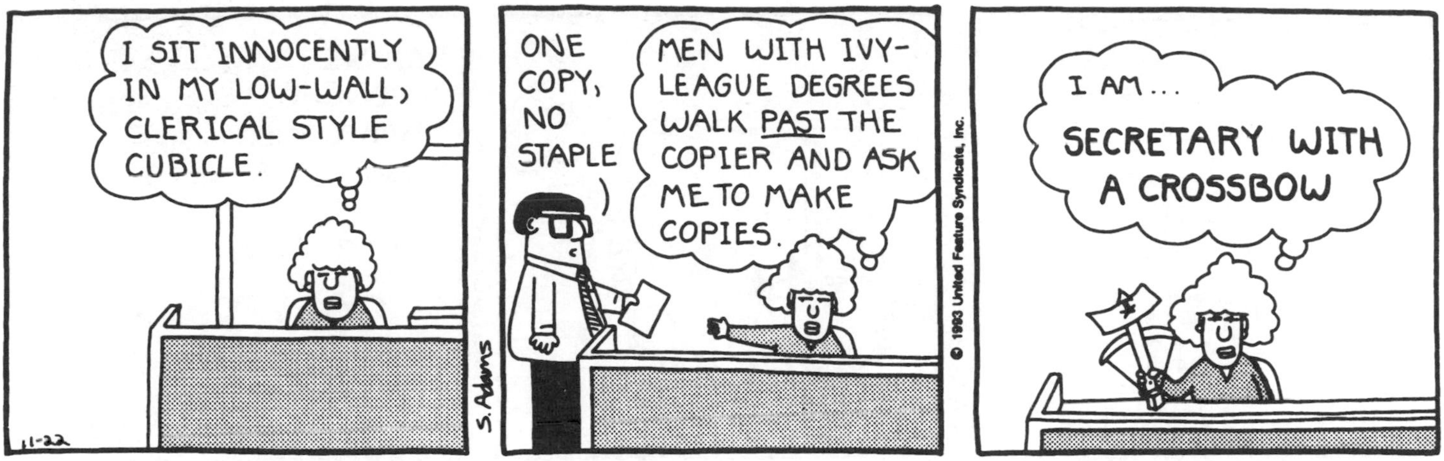
I SIT INNOCENTLY IN MY LOW-WALL, CLERICAL STYLE CUBICLE.
11-22
S. Adams
ONE COPY, NO STAPLE
MEN WITH IVY-LEAGUE DEGREES WALK PAST THE COPIER AND ASK ME TO MAKE COPIES.
© 1993 United Feature Syndicate, Inc.
I AM...
SECRETARY WITH A CROSSBOW

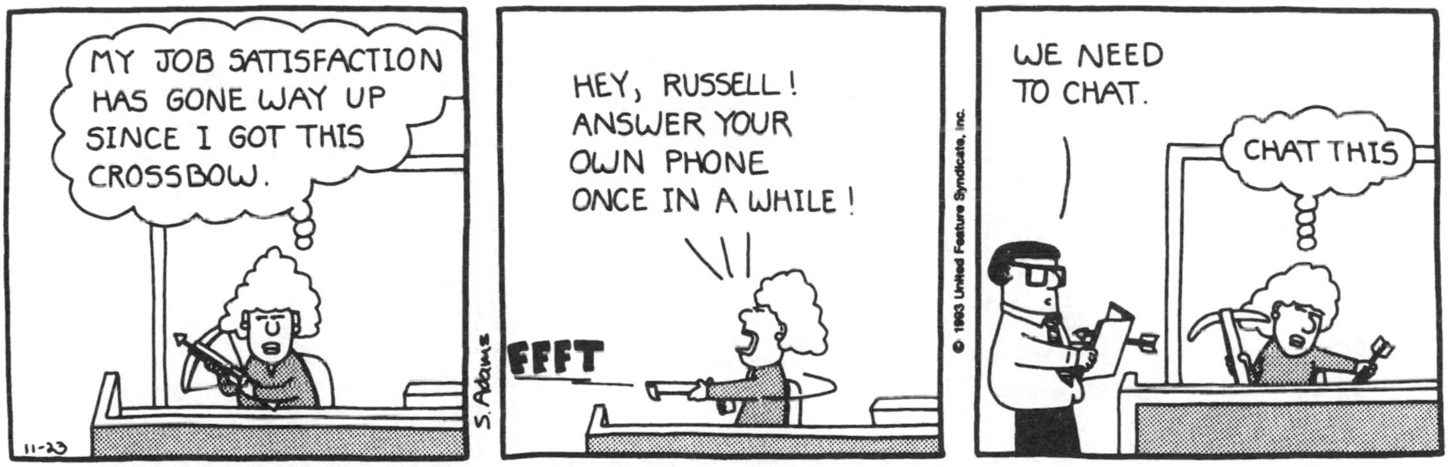
MY JOB SATISFACTION HAS GONE WAY UP SINCE I GOT THIS CROSSBOW.
11-23
S. Adams
HEY, RUSSELL! ANSWER YOUR OWN PHONE ONCE IN A WHILE!
FFFT
© 1993 United Feature Syndicate, Inc.
WE NEED TO CHAT.
CHAT THIS

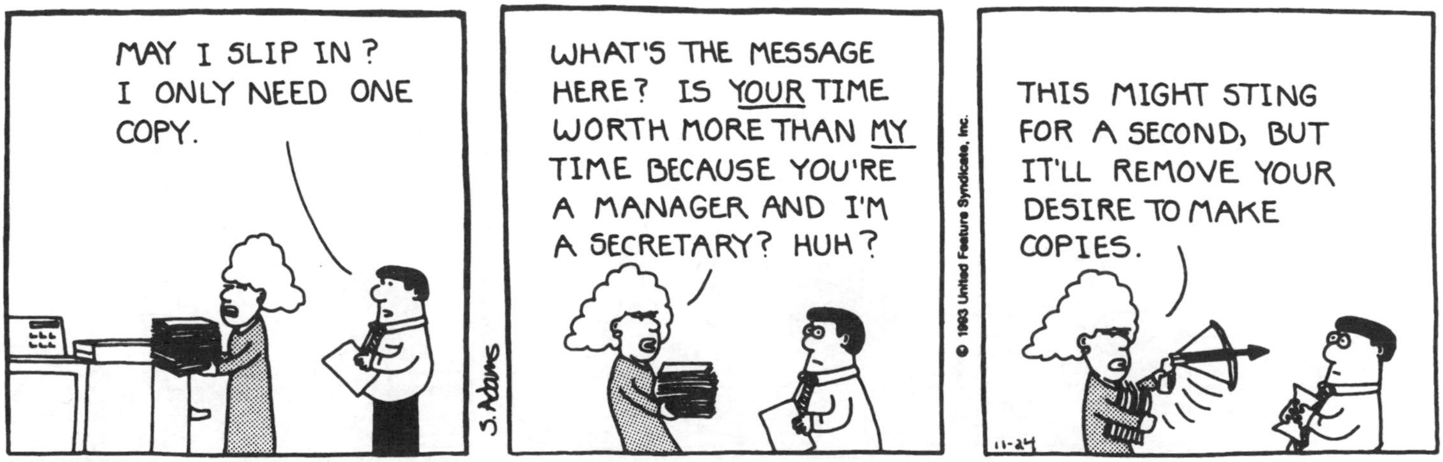
MAY I SLIP IN? I ONLY NEED ONE COPY.
S. Adams
WHAT'S THE MESSAGE HERE? IS YOUR TIME WORTH MORE THAN MY TIME BECAUSE YOU'RE A MANAGER AND I'M A SECRETARY? HUH?
© 1993 United Feature Syndicate, Inc.
THIS MIGHT STING FOR A SECOND, BUT IT'LL REMOVE YOUR DESIRE TO MAKE COPIES.
11-24

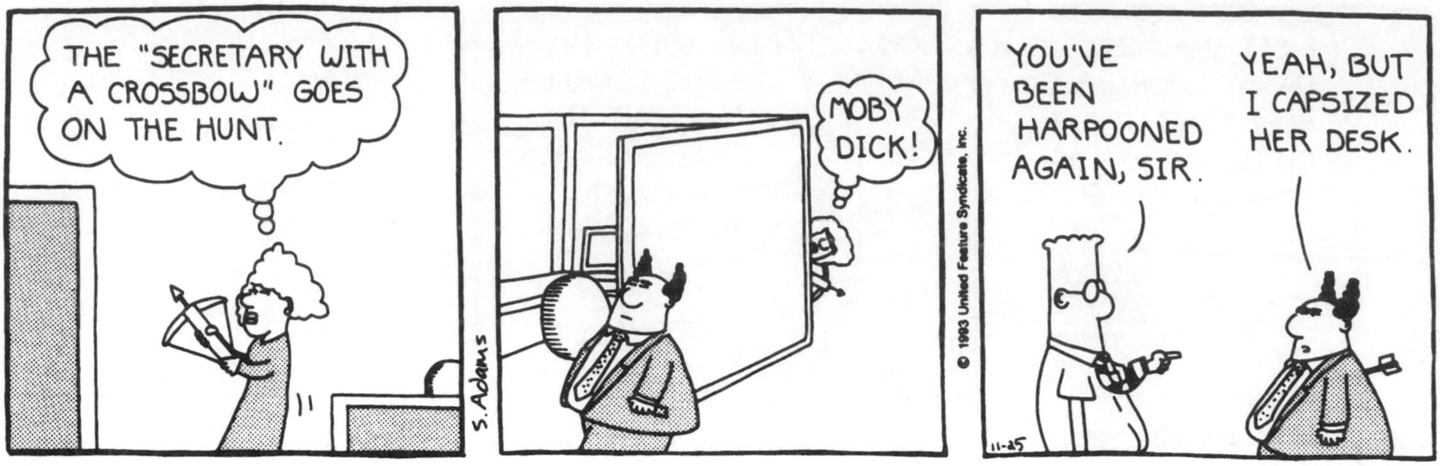
THE "SECRETARY WITH A CROSSBOW" GOES ON THE HUNT.
S. Adams
MOBY DICK!
© 1993 United Feature Syndicate, Inc.
YOU'VE BEEN HARPOONED AGAIN, SIR.
YEAH, BUT I CAPSIZED HER DESK.
11-25

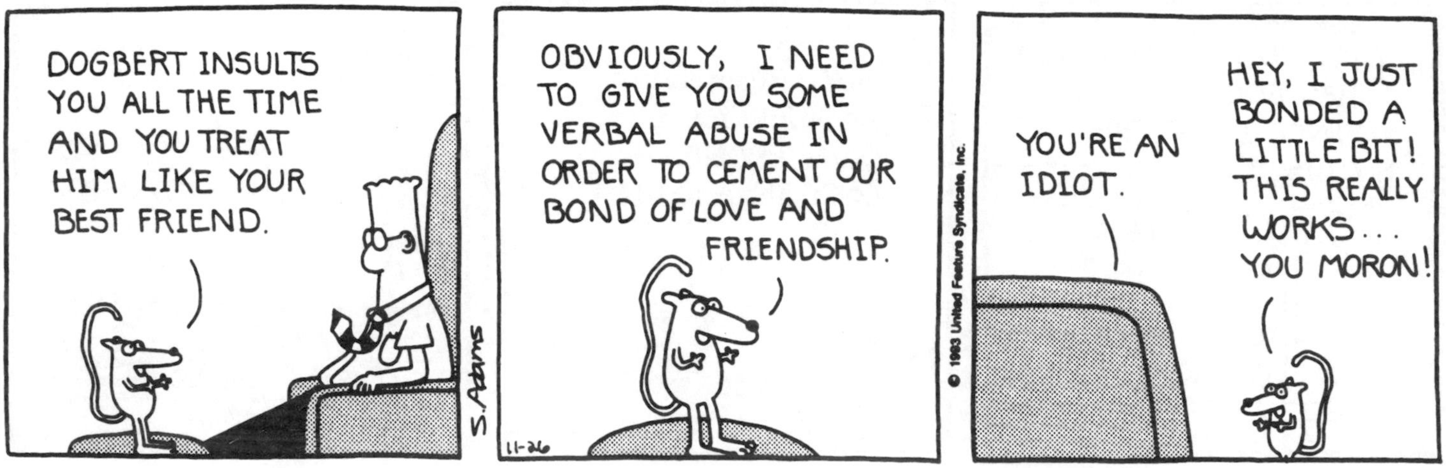
DOGBERT INSULTS YOU ALL THE TIME AND YOU TREAT HIM LIKE YOUR BEST FRIEND.
S. Adams
OBVIOUSLY, I NEED TO GIVE YOU SOME VERBAL ABUSE IN ORDER TO CEMENT OUR BOND OF LOVE AND FRIENDSHIP.
11-26
© 1993 United Feature Syndicate, Inc.
YOU'RE AN IDIOT.
HEY, I JUST BONDED A LITTLE BIT! THIS REALLY WORKS... YOU MORON!

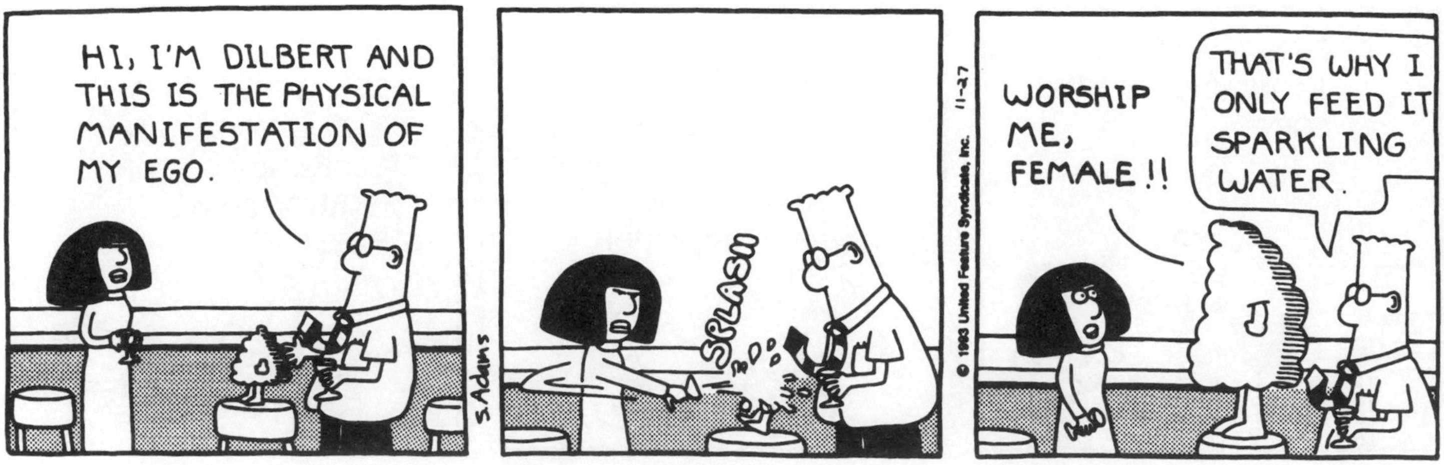
HI, I'M DILBERT AND THIS IS THE PHYSICAL MANIFESTATION OF MY EGO.
S. Adams
SPLASH
11-27
© 1993 United Feature Syndicate, Inc.
WORSHIP ME, FEMALE!!
THAT'S WHY I ONLY FEED IT SPARKLING WATER.

DILBERT®
BY
SCOTT ADAMS
I'M STARVING. IS THERE A MEAL ON THIS FLIGHT?
IT'S PROBABLY JUST A SNACK. THE AIR-LINE IS CUTTING BACK ON FRILLS.
S. Adams
WHEN YOU SAY "SNACK," DO YOU MEAN A SMALL BUT WELL-BALANCED CULINARY EXPERIENCE?
IT'S PEANUTS. WE GET NINE PEANUTS APIECE.
AND A SODA... BUT NOT A WHOLE CAN, JUST A LITTLE CUP... UNLESS THEY CUT BACK ON THAT TOO.
NOW WE JUST DRINK A SODA OURSELVES AND BURP YOUR SEAT NUMBER.
GLUG
GLUG
GLUG
11-28
7B
IT'S ACTUALLY KIND OF REFRESHING.
© 1993 United Feature Syndicate, Inc.

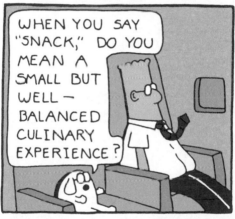

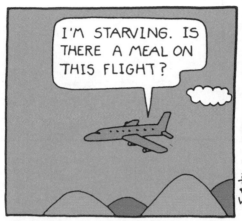

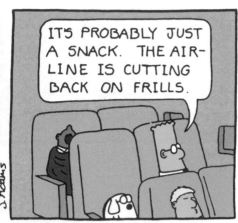

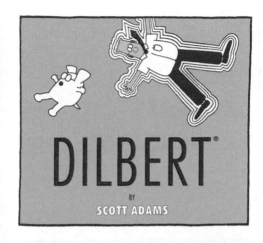

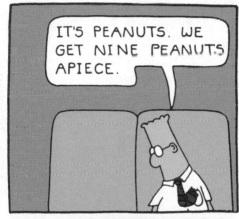

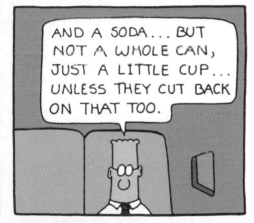

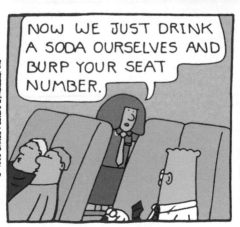

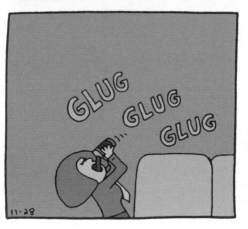

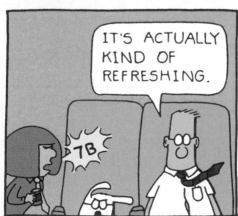

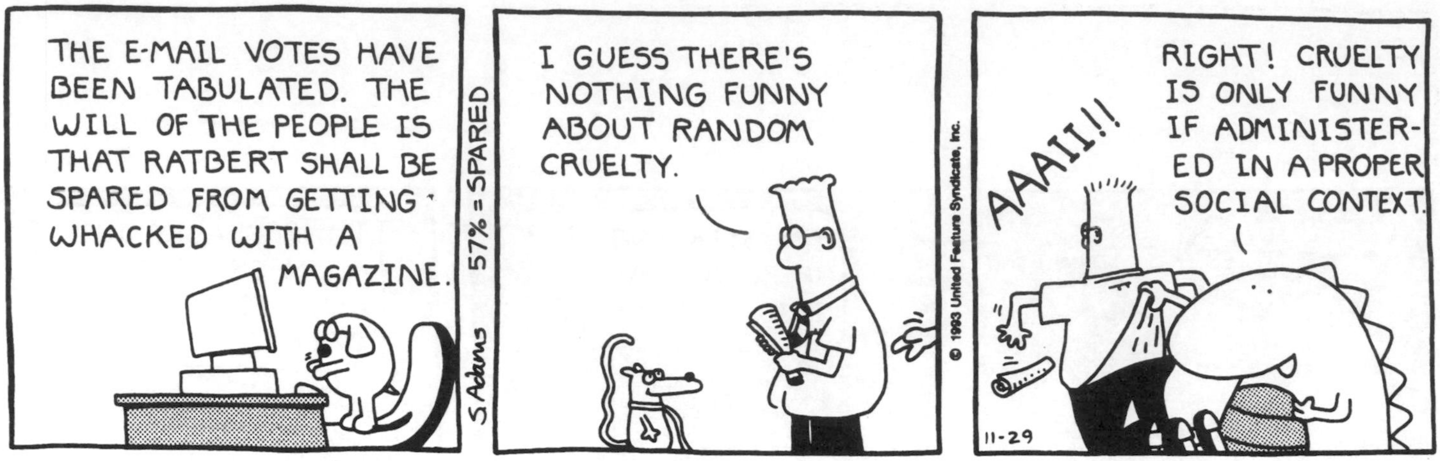
THE E-MAIL VOTES HAVE BEEN TABULATED. THE WILL OF THE PEOPLE IS THAT RATBERT SHALL BE SPARED FROM GETTING WHACKED WITH A MAGAZINE.
57% = SPARED
S. Adams
I GUESS THERE'S NOTHING FUNNY ABOUT RANDOM CRUELTY.
© 1993 United Feature Syndicate, Inc.
AAAII!!
RIGHT! CRUELTY IS ONLY FUNNY IF ADMINISTERED IN A PROPER SOCIAL CONTEXT.
11-29

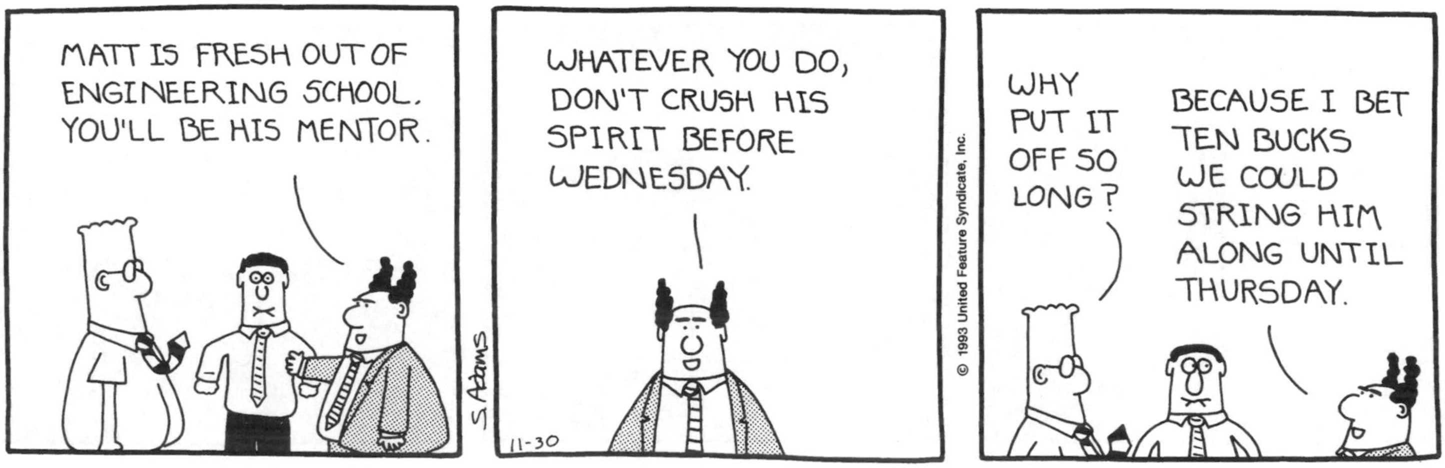
MATT IS FRESH OUT OF ENGINEERING SCHOOL. YOU'LL BE HIS MENTOR.
S. Adams
WHATEVER YOU DO, DON'T CRUSH HIS SPIRIT BEFORE WEDNESDAY.
11-30
© 1993 United Feature Syndicate, Inc.
WHY PUT IT OFF SO LONG?
BECAUSE I BET TEN BUCKS WE COULD STRING HIM ALONG UNTIL THURSDAY.

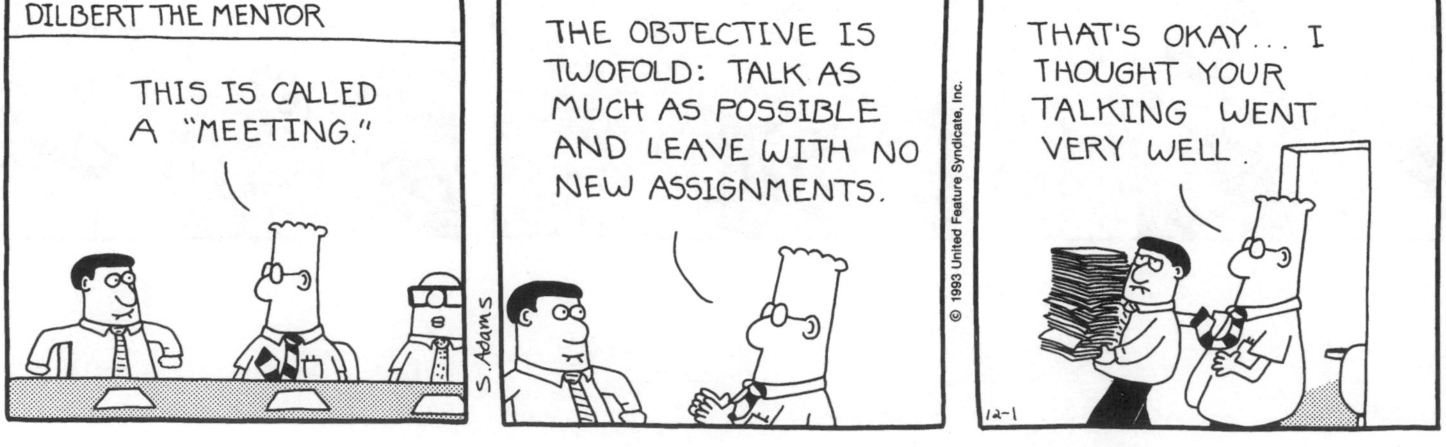
DILBERT THE MENTOR
THIS IS CALLED A "MEETING."
S. Adams
THE OBJECTIVE IS TWOFOLD: TALK AS MUCH AS POSSIBLE AND LEAVE WITH NO NEW ASSIGNMENTS.
© 1993 United Feature Syndicate, Inc.
THAT'S OKAY... I THOUGHT YOUR TALKING WENT VERY WELL.
12-1

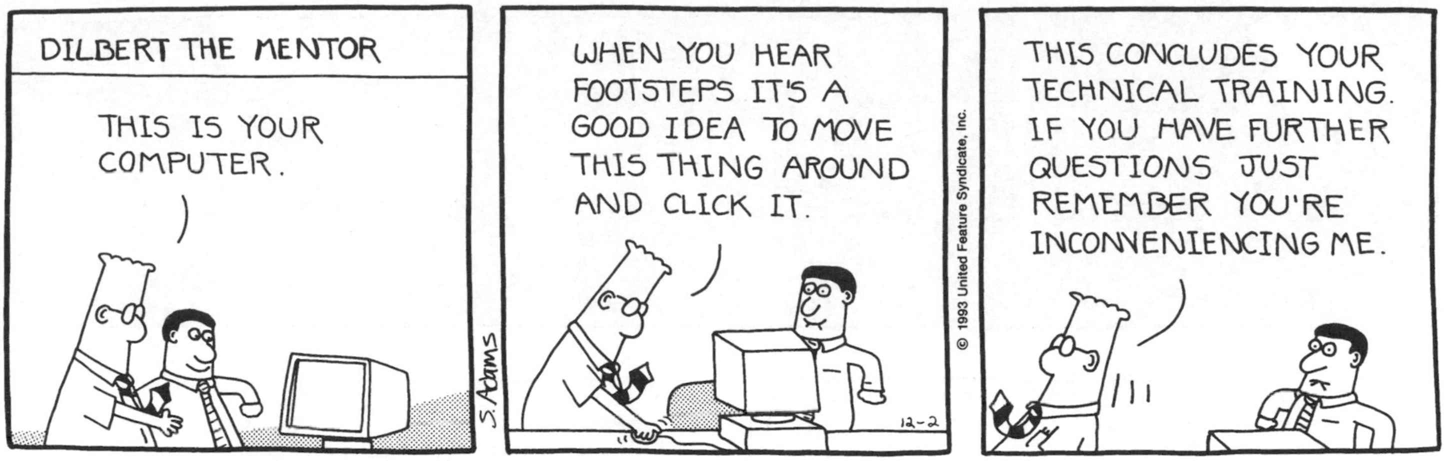
DILBERT THE MENTOR
THIS IS YOUR COMPUTER.
WHEN YOU HEAR FOOTSTEPS IT'S A GOOD IDEA TO MOVE THIS THING AROUND AND CLICK IT.
THIS CONCLUDES YOUR TECHNICAL TRAINING. IF YOU HAVE FURTHER QUESTIONS JUST REMEMBER YOU'RE INCONVENIENCING ME.
S. Adams
12-2
© 1993 United Feature Syndicate, Inc.

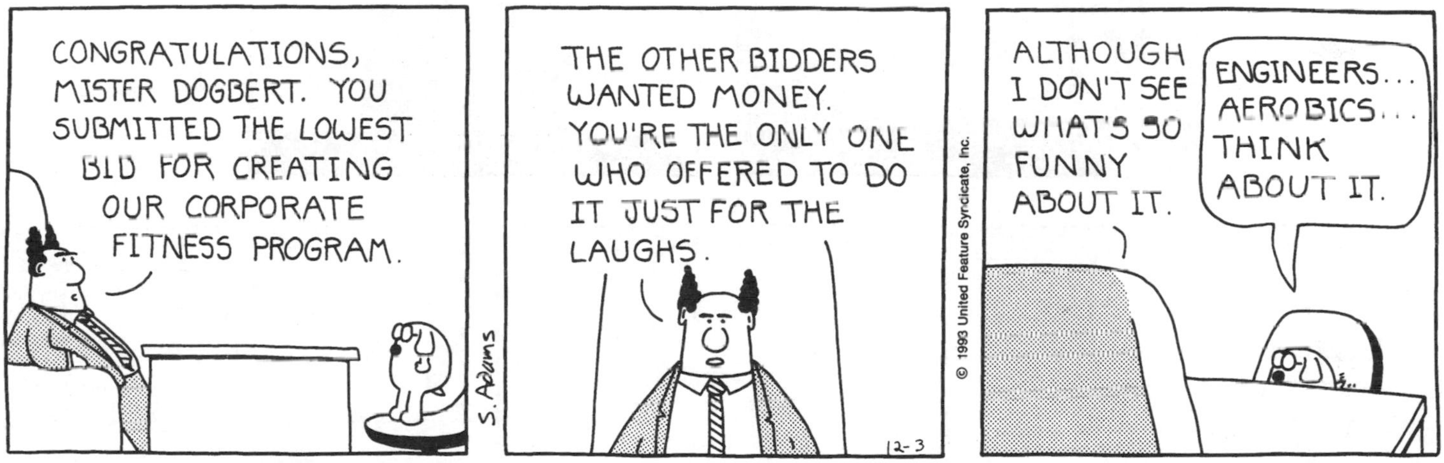
CONGRATULATIONS, MISTER DOGBERT. YOU SUBMITTED THE LOWEST BID FOR CREATING OUR CORPORATE FITNESS PROGRAM.
THE OTHER BIDDERS WANTED MONEY. YOU'RE THE ONLY ONE WHO OFFERED TO DO IT JUST FOR THE LAUGHS.
ALTHOUGH I DON'T SEE WHAT'S SO FUNNY ABOUT IT.
ENGINEERS... AEROBICS... THINK ABOUT IT.
S. Adams
12-3
© 1993 United Feature Syndicate, Inc.

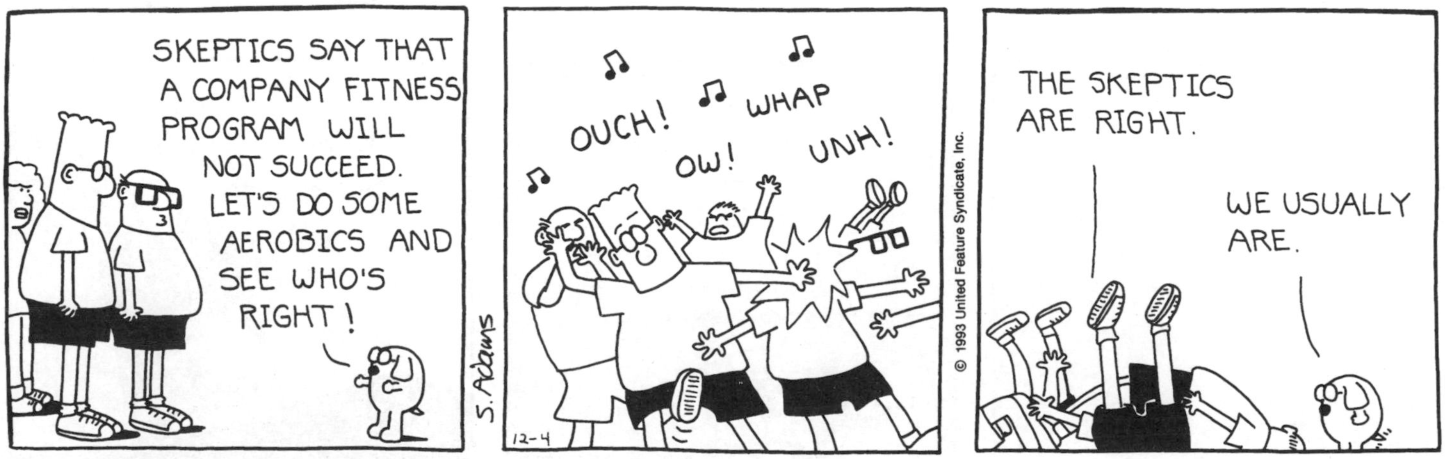
SKEPTICS SAY THAT A COMPANY FITNESS PROGRAM WILL NOT SUCCEED. LET'S DO SOME AEROBICS AND SEE WHO'S RIGHT!
OUCH!
WHAP
OW!
UNH!
THE SKEPTICS ARE RIGHT.
WE USUALLY ARE.
S. Adams
12-4
© 1993 United Feature Syndicate, Inc.

DILBERT®
BY
SCOTT ADAMS
DILBERT, I WANT YOU TO MANAGE WALLY'S PROJECT WHILE HE'S ON VACATION IN ARUBA.
S. Adams
LET THE SHIRK-FEST GAMES BEGIN.
ISN'T THAT THE WEEK WHEN EVERYTHING IS DUE?
COINCIDENCE.
MAYBE YOU COULD CHANGE YOUR PLANS.
NON-REFUNDABLE TICKETS RIGHT HERE!
THE PROJECT CAN'T BE IMPORTANT IF YOU WON'T CHANGE YOUR PLANS.
HE'S GOOD.
I'LL BE HAPPY TO ADD WALLY'S PROJECT TO THE BOTTOM OF MY PILE AND LET IT FAIL WITH WALLY'S NAME ON IT.
WHEN YOU'RE IN ARUBA, STUDY THE WAITERS CAREFULLY — IT'S PROBABLY YOUR NEW CAREER.
12-5
TWO FREE TICKETS TO ARUBA — I WIN.
© 1993 United Feature Syndicate, Inc.

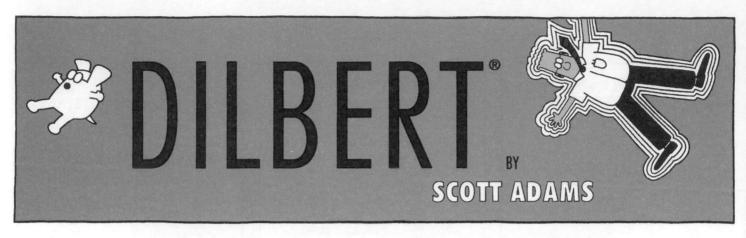

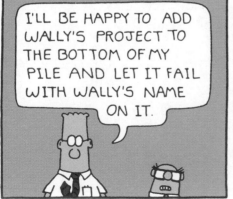

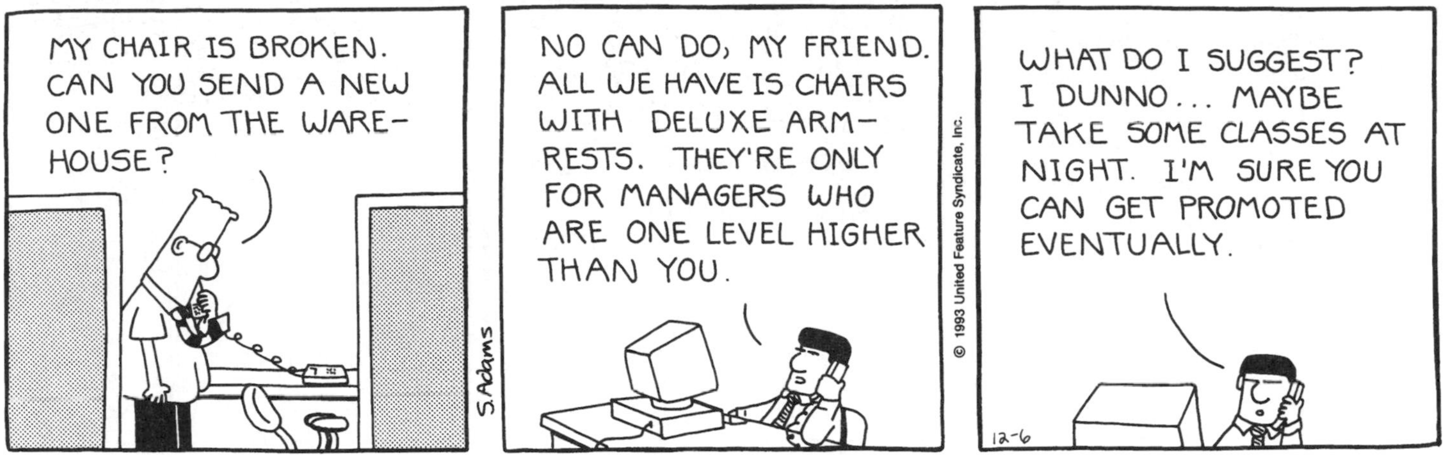
MY CHAIR IS BROKEN. CAN YOU SEND A NEW ONE FROM THE WARE-HOUSE?
S. Adams
NO CAN DO, MY FRIEND. ALL WE HAVE IS CHAIRS WITH DELUXE ARM-RESTS. THEY'RE ONLY FOR MANAGERS WHO ARE ONE LEVEL HIGHER THAN YOU.
© 1993 United Feature Syndicate, Inc.
WHAT DO I SUGGEST? I DUNNO... MAYBE TAKE SOME CLASSES AT NIGHT. I'M SURE YOU CAN GET PROMOTED EVENTUALLY.
12-6

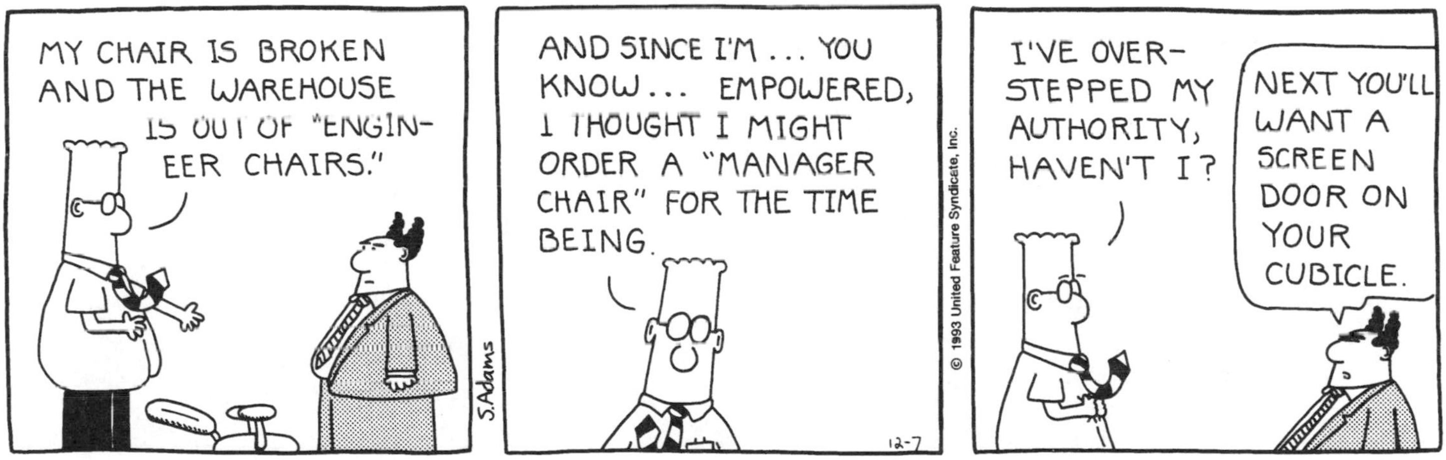
MY CHAIR IS BROKEN AND THE WAREHOUSE IS OUT OF "ENGIN-EER CHAIRS."
S. Adams
AND SINCE I'M ... YOU KNOW... EMPOWERED, I THOUGHT I MIGHT ORDER A "MANAGER CHAIR" FOR THE TIME BEING.
12-7
© 1993 United Feature Syndicate, Inc.
I'VE OVER-STEPPED MY AUTHORITY, HAVEN'T I?
NEXT YOU'LL WANT A SCREEN DOOR ON YOUR CUBICLE.

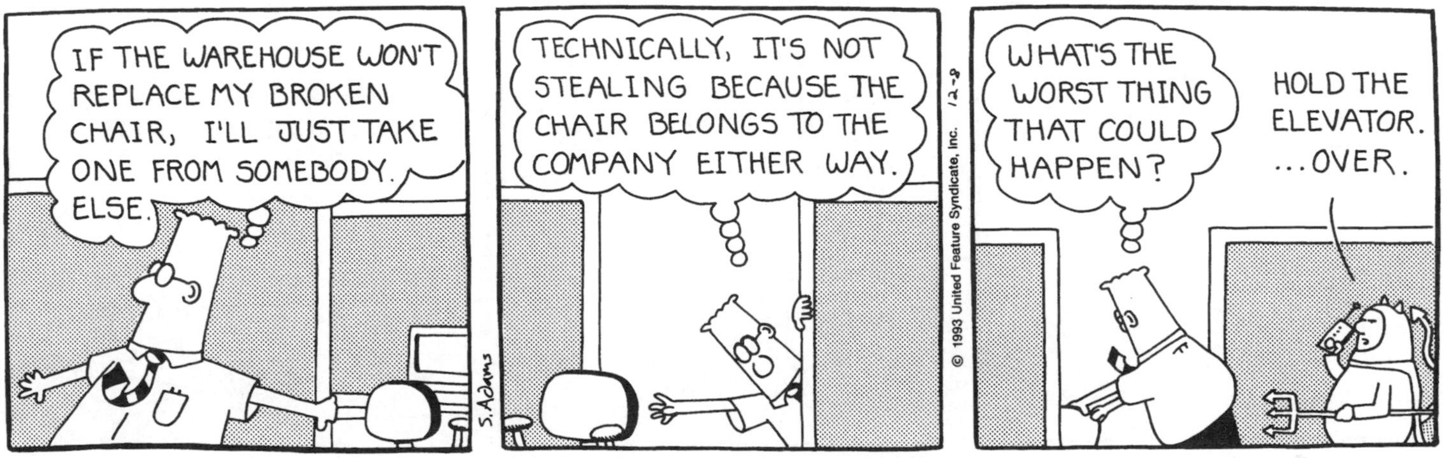
IF THE WAREHOUSE WON'T REPLACE MY BROKEN CHAIR, I'LL JUST TAKE ONE FROM SOMEBODY ELSE.
S. Adams
TECHNICALLY, IT'S NOT STEALING BECAUSE THE CHAIR BELONGS TO THE COMPANY EITHER WAY.
12-8
© 1993 United Feature Syndicate, Inc.
WHAT'S THE WORST THING THAT COULD HAPPEN?
HOLD THE ELEVATOR. ...OVER.

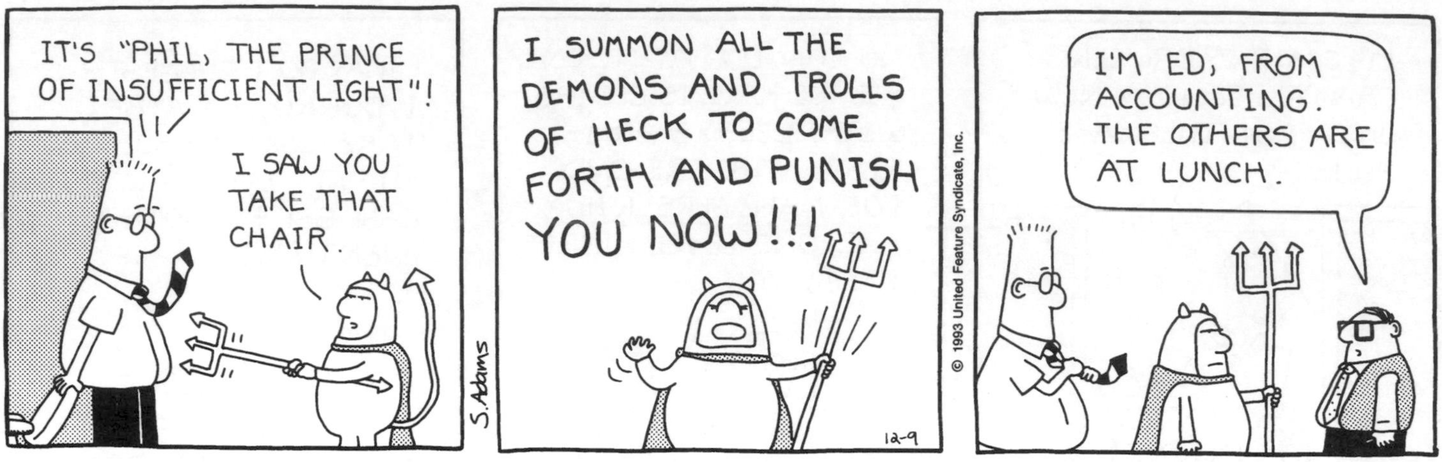
IT'S "PHIL, THE PRINCE OF INSUFFICIENT LIGHT"!
I SAW YOU TAKE THAT CHAIR.
S. Adams
I SUMMON ALL THE DEMONS AND TROLLS OF HECK TO COME FORTH AND PUNISH YOU NOW!!!
12-9
© 1993 United Feature Syndicate, Inc.
I'M ED, FROM ACCOUNTING. THE OTHERS ARE AT LUNCH.

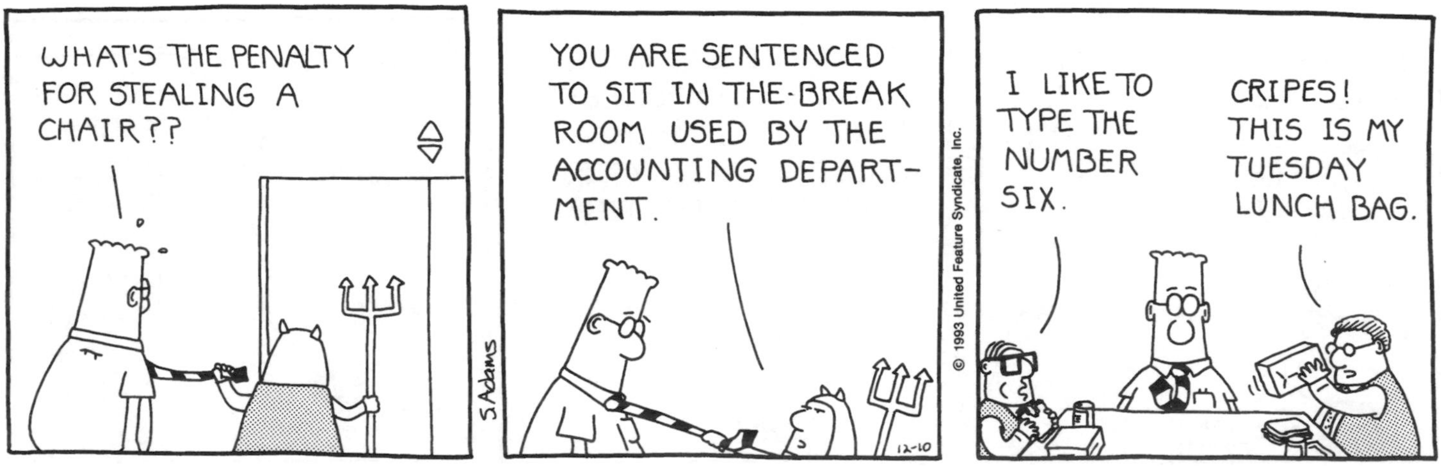
WHAT'S THE PENALTY FOR STEALING A CHAIR??
S. Adams
YOU ARE SENTENCED TO SIT IN THE BREAK ROOM USED BY THE ACCOUNTING DEPARTMENT.
12-10
© 1993 United Feature Syndicate, Inc.
I LIKE TO TYPE THE NUMBER SIX.
CRIPES! THIS IS MY TUESDAY LUNCH BAG.

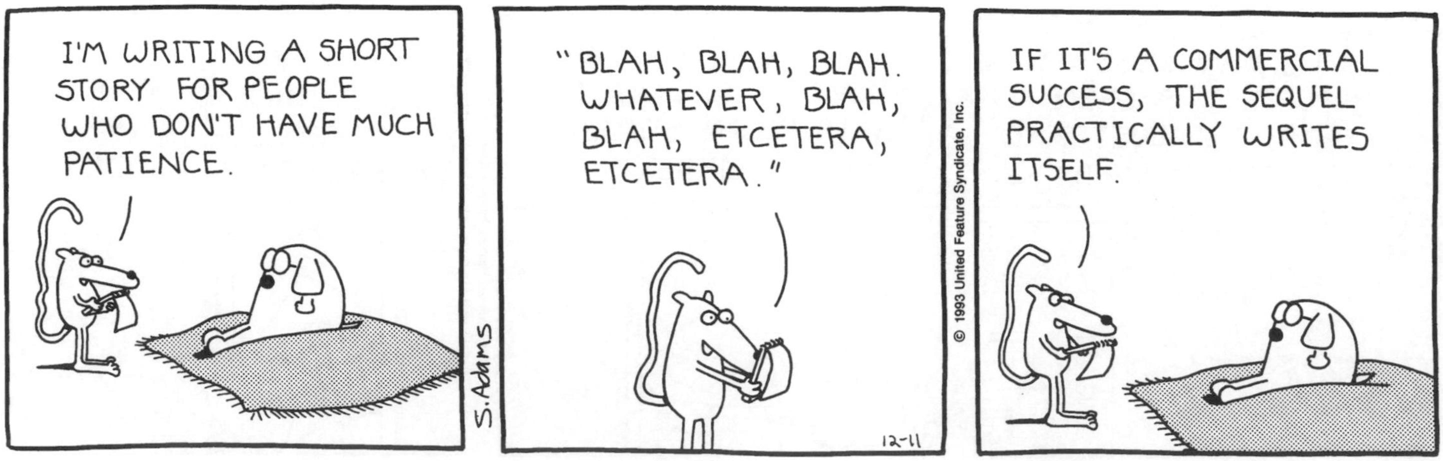
I'M WRITING A SHORT STORY FOR PEOPLE WHO DON'T HAVE MUCH PATIENCE.
S. Adams
"BLAH, BLAH, BLAH. WHATEVER, BLAH, BLAH, ETCETERA, ETCETERA."
12-11
© 1993 United Feature Syndicate, Inc.
IF IT'S A COMMERCIAL SUCCESS, THE SEQUEL PRACTICALLY WRITES ITSELF.

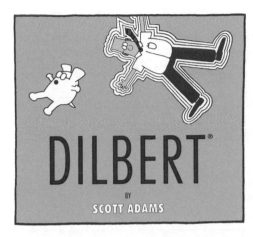

DILBERT
BY SCOTT ADAMS

TODAY YOU WILL LEARN HOW TO DEAL WITH PEOPLE WHO HAVE PERSONALITY DEFECTS.

CASE 1: TODD LAUGHS NERVOUSLY AT EVERY ONE OF HIS OWN COMMENTS.

DON'T HOLD IT AGAINST ME! HEE HEE HAW HAW!

REMEDY: TODD MUST BE RELOCATED TO A DISTANT PLANET.

IT SURE IS LONELY! HEE HEE!

CASE 2: ALLEN STARES AT YOU LIKE A ZOMBIE FOR LONG PERIODS BEFORE RESPONDING TO QUESTIONS.

REMEDY: ALLEN MUST BE PAIRED WITH VIRGINIA (CASE 3) WHO FILLS ALL QUIET SPOTS WITH INANE CHATTER.

YAK YAK YAK

CASE 4: MATT SPEAKS SLOWLY ABOUT AMAZINGLY BORING TOPICS.

I... ATE... A ...PICKLE...

12-12

REMEDY: MATT'S HEAD CAN BE OUTFITTED WITH A READING STAND.

I... LIKE... PICKLES...

CASE 5: AN ENGINEER. REMEDY: VERY QUIETLY SEAL HIM IN HIS OWN CUBICLE.

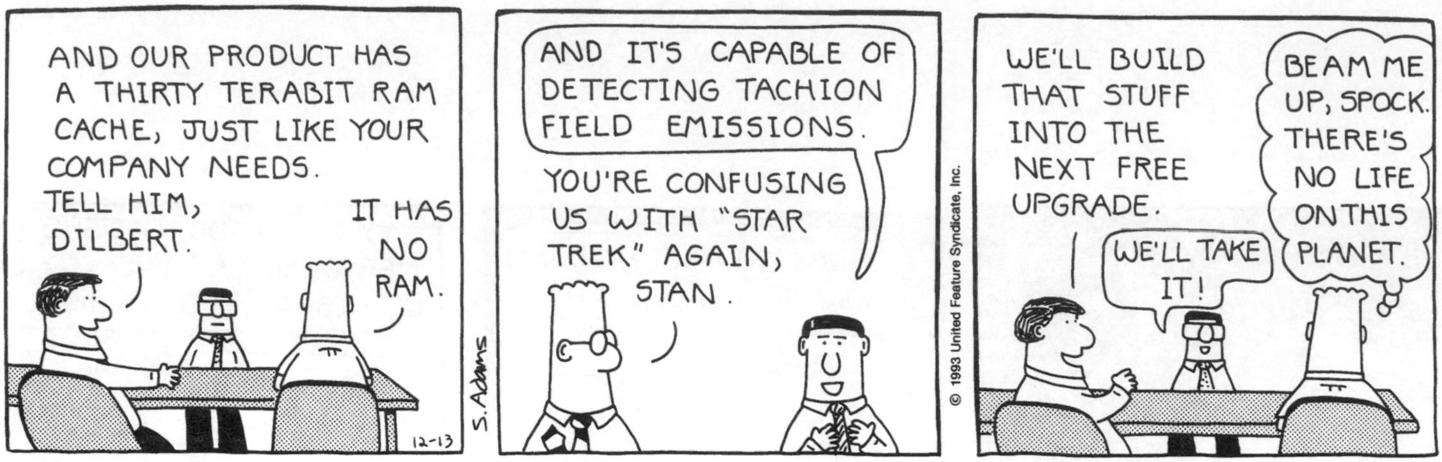
AND OUR PRODUCT HAS A THIRTY TERABIT RAM CACHE, JUST LIKE YOUR COMPANY NEEDS.
TELL HIM, DILBERT.
IT HAS NO RAM.
S. Adams
12-13
AND IT'S CAPABLE OF DETECTING TACHION FIELD EMISSIONS.
YOU'RE CONFUSING US WITH "STAR TREK" AGAIN, STAN.
© 1993 United Feature Syndicate, Inc.
WE'LL BUILD THAT STUFF INTO THE NEXT FREE UPGRADE.
WE'LL TAKE IT!
BEAM ME UP, SPOCK. THERE'S NO LIFE ON THIS PLANET.

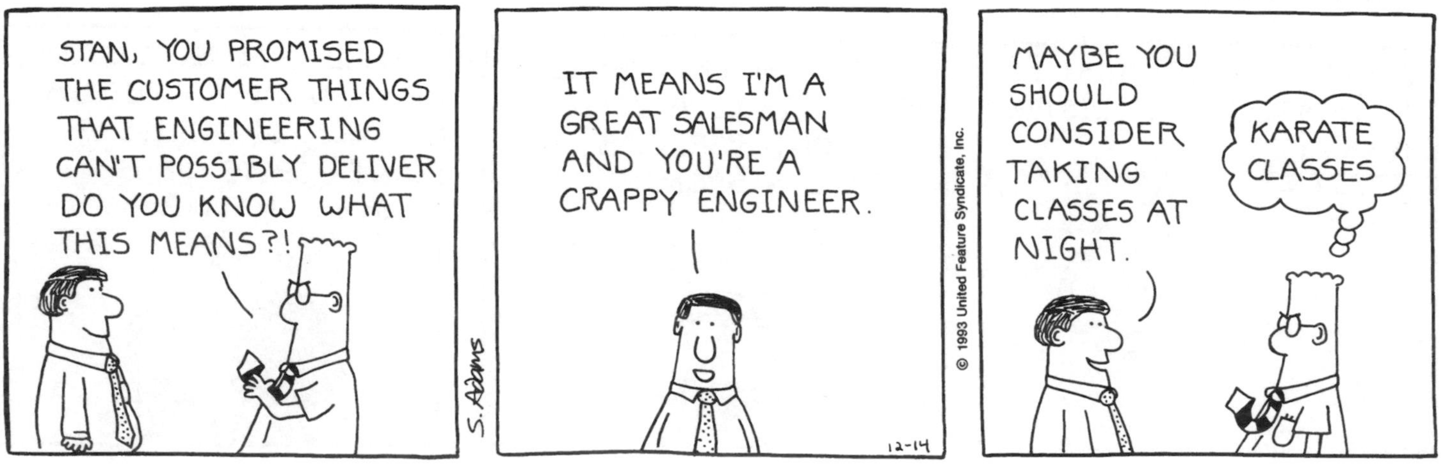
STAN, YOU PROMISED THE CUSTOMER THINGS THAT ENGINEERING CAN'T POSSIBLY DELIVER DO YOU KNOW WHAT THIS MEANS?!
S. Adams
IT MEANS I'M A GREAT SALESMAN AND YOU'RE A CRAPPY ENGINEER.
12-14
© 1993 United Feature Syndicate, Inc.
MAYBE YOU SHOULD CONSIDER TAKING CLASSES AT NIGHT.
KARATE CLASSES

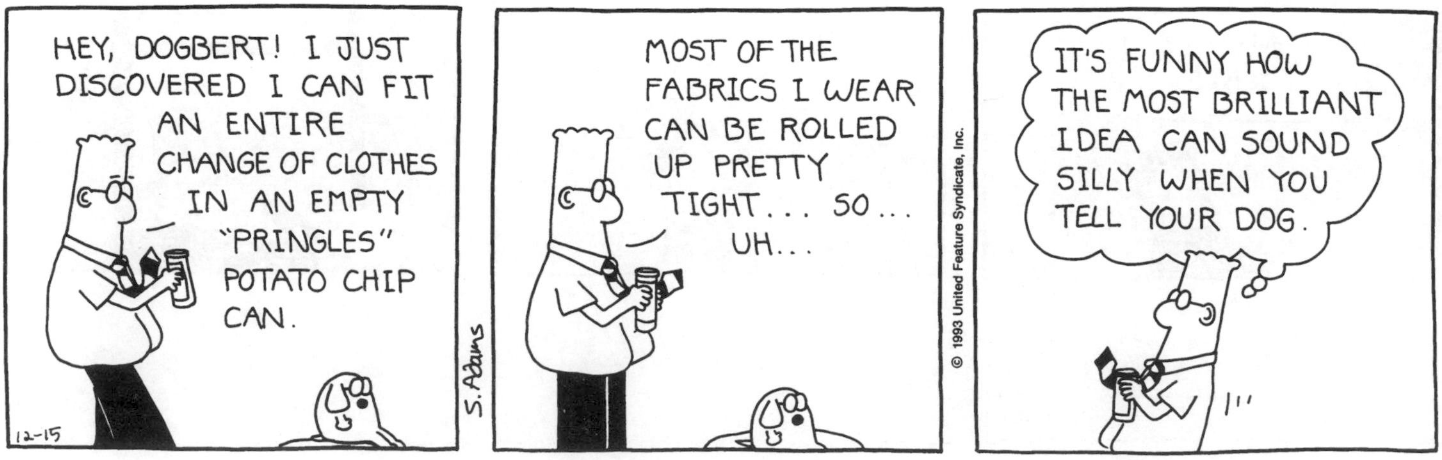
HEY, DOGBERT! I JUST DISCOVERED I CAN FIT AN ENTIRE CHANGE OF CLOTHES IN AN EMPTY "PRINGLES" POTATO CHIP CAN.
12-15
S. Adams
MOST OF THE FABRICS I WEAR CAN BE ROLLED UP PRETTY TIGHT... SO... UH...
© 1993 United Feature Syndicate, Inc.
IT'S FUNNY HOW THE MOST BRILLIANT IDEA CAN SOUND SILLY WHEN YOU TELL YOUR DOG.

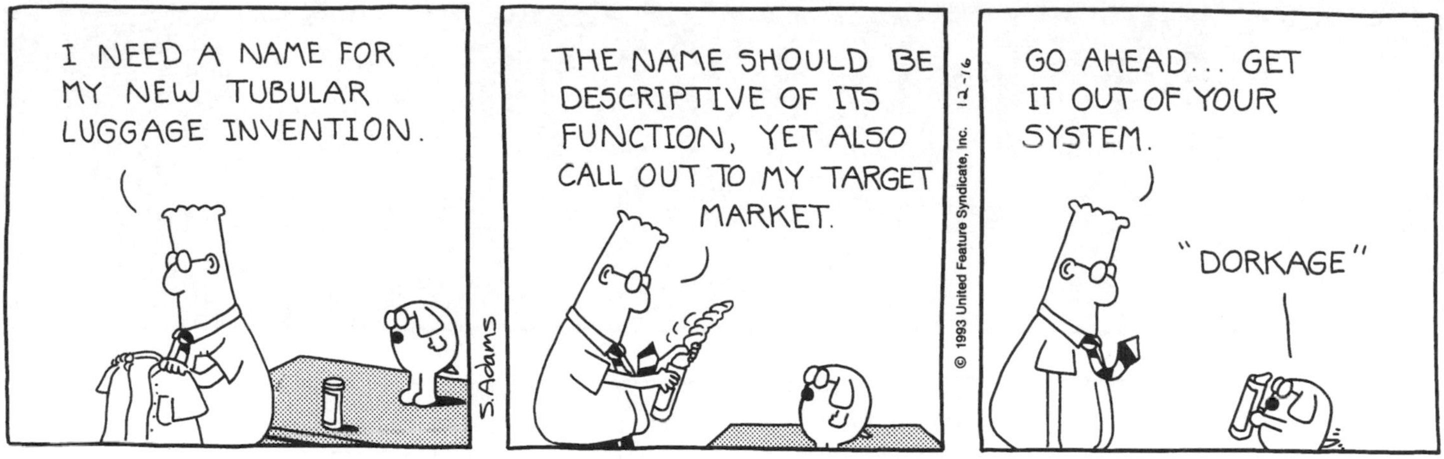
I NEED A NAME FOR MY NEW TUBULAR LUGGAGE INVENTION.
THE NAME SHOULD BE DESCRIPTIVE OF ITS FUNCTION, YET ALSO CALL OUT TO MY TARGET MARKET.
GO AHEAD... GET IT OUT OF YOUR SYSTEM.
"DORKAGE"
S. Adams
12-16
© 1993 United Feature Syndicate, Inc.

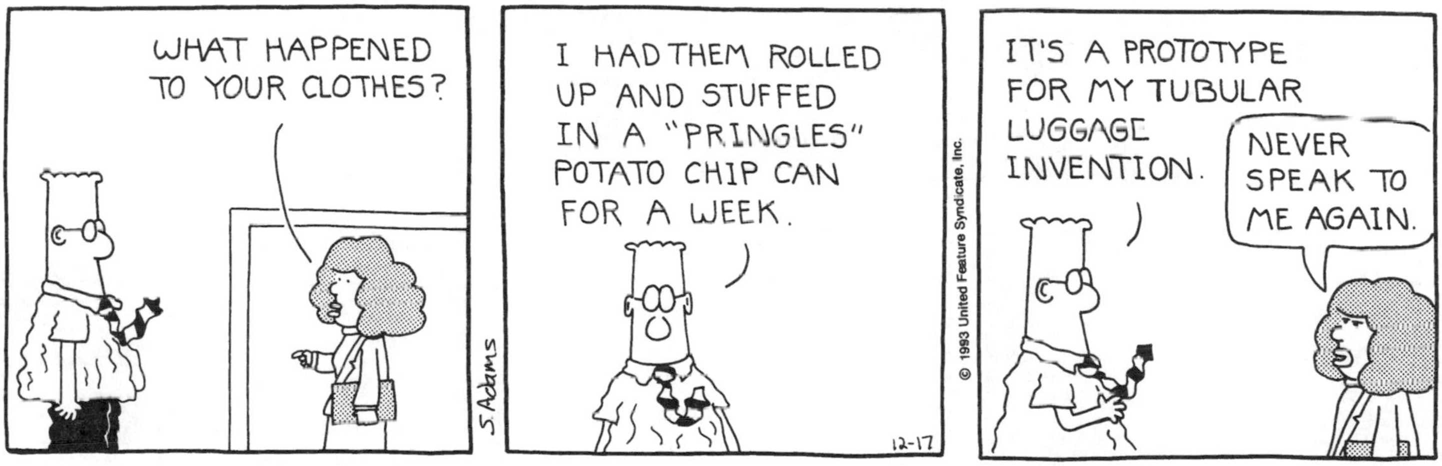
WHAT HAPPENED TO YOUR CLOTHES?
I HAD THEM ROLLED UP AND STUFFED IN A "PRINGLES" POTATO CHIP CAN FOR A WEEK.
IT'S A PROTOTYPE FOR MY TUBULAR LUGGAGE INVENTION.
NEVER SPEAK TO ME AGAIN.
S. Adams
12-17
© 1993 United Feature Syndicate, Inc.

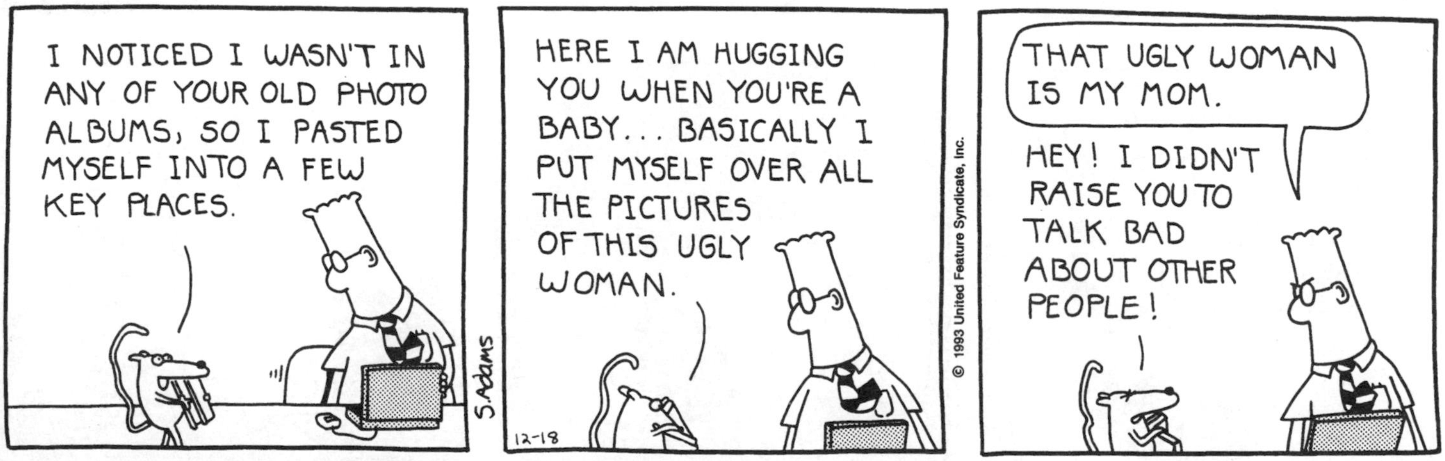
I NOTICED I WASN'T IN ANY OF YOUR OLD PHOTO ALBUMS, SO I PASTED MYSELF INTO A FEW KEY PLACES.
HERE I AM HUGGING YOU WHEN YOU'RE A BABY... BASICALLY I PUT MYSELF OVER ALL THE PICTURES OF THIS UGLY WOMAN.
THAT UGLY WOMAN IS MY MOM.
HEY! I DIDN'T RAISE YOU TO TALK BAD ABOUT OTHER PEOPLE!
S. Adams
12-18
© 1993 United Feature Syndicate, Inc.

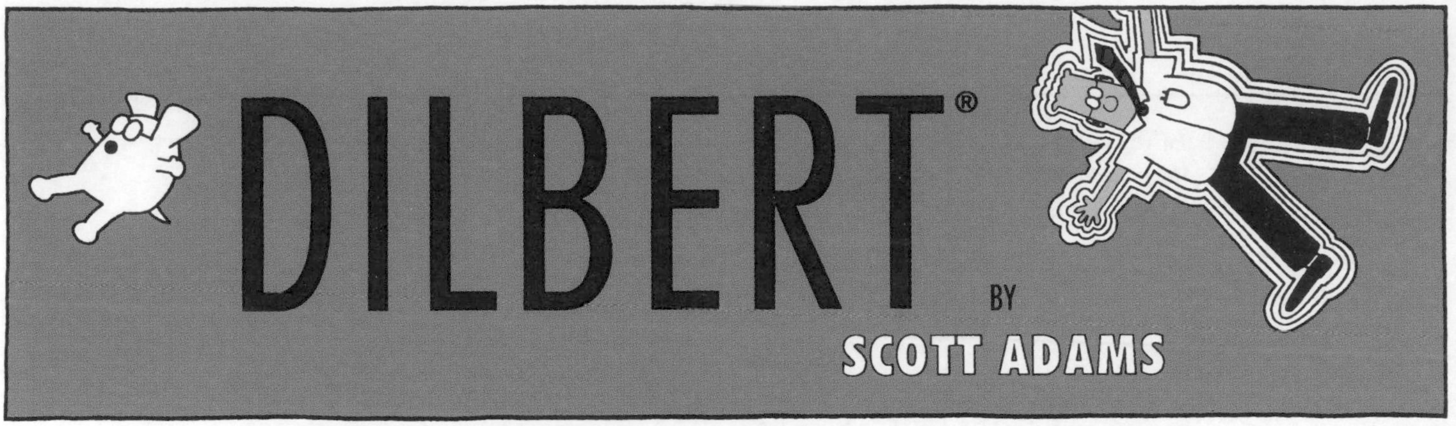
DILBERT®
BY
SCOTT ADAMS

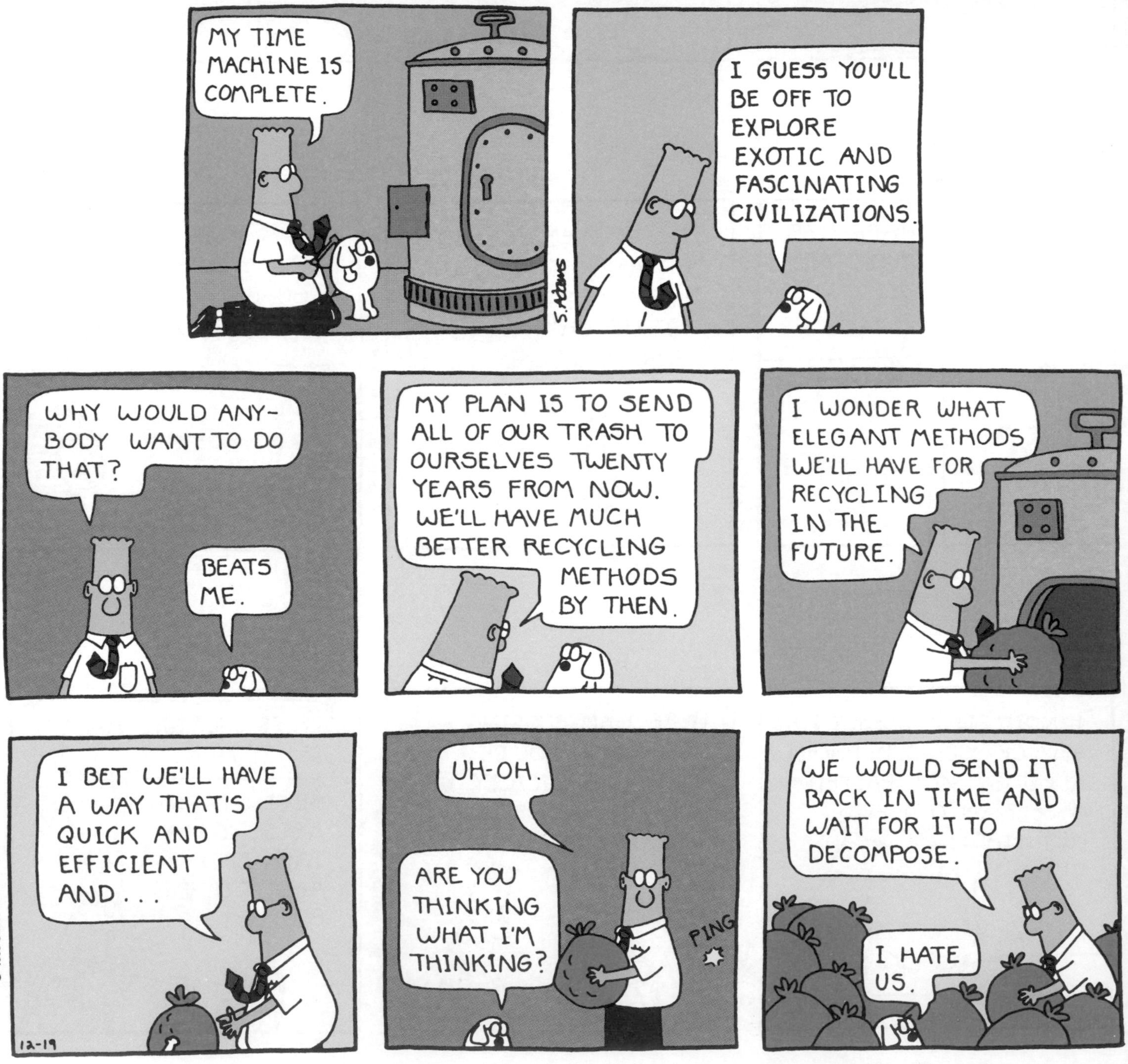
MY TIME MACHINE IS COMPLETE.
S. Adams
I GUESS YOU'LL BE OFF TO EXPLORE EXOTIC AND FASCINATING CIVILIZATIONS.
WHY WOULD ANY-BODY WANT TO DO THAT?
BEATS ME.
MY PLAN IS TO SEND ALL OF OUR TRASH TO OURSELVES TWENTY YEARS FROM NOW. WE'LL HAVE MUCH BETTER RECYCLING METHODS BY THEN.
I WONDER WHAT ELEGANT METHODS WE'LL HAVE FOR RECYCLING IN THE FUTURE.
I BET WE'LL HAVE A WAY THAT'S QUICK AND EFFICIENT AND . . .
12-19
UH-OH.
ARE YOU THINKING WHAT I'M THINKING?
PING
WE WOULD SEND IT BACK IN TIME AND WAIT FOR IT TO DECOMPOSE.
I HATE US.

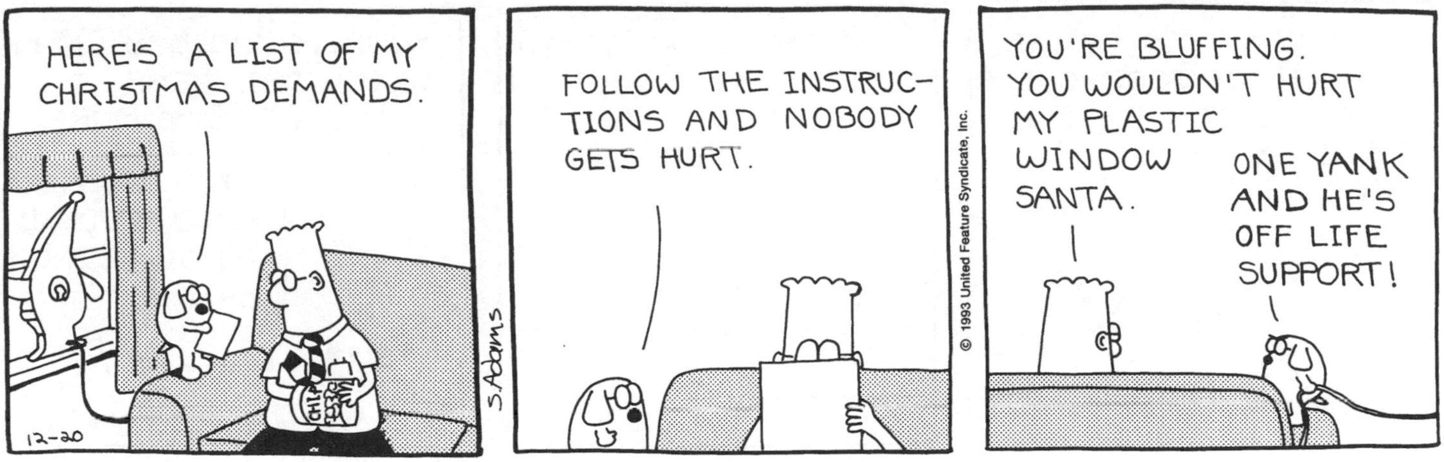
HERE'S A LIST OF MY CHRISTMAS DEMANDS.
12-20
S. Adams
FOLLOW THE INSTRUCTIONS AND NOBODY GETS HURT.
© 1993 United Feature Syndicate, Inc.
YOU'RE BLUFFING. YOU WOULDN'T HURT MY PLASTIC WINDOW SANTA.
ONE YANK AND HE'S OFF LIFE SUPPORT!

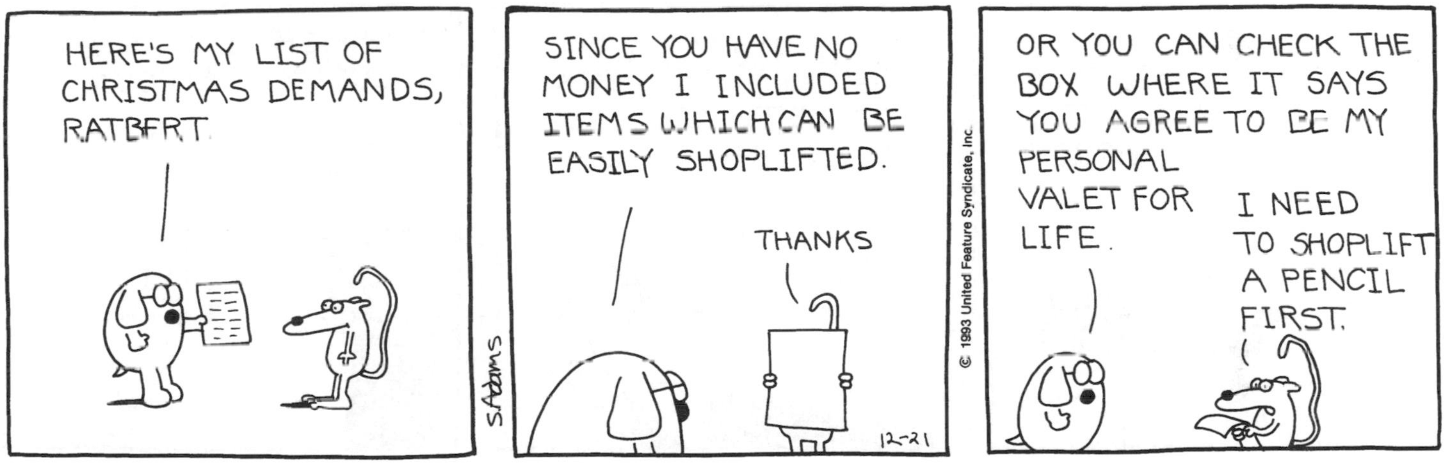
HERE'S MY LIST OF CHRISTMAS DEMANDS, RATBERT.
S. Adams
SINCE YOU HAVE NO MONEY I INCLUDED ITEMS WHICH CAN BE EASILY SHOPLIFTED.
THANKS
12-21
© 1993 United Feature Syndicate, Inc.
OR YOU CAN CHECK THE BOX WHERE IT SAYS YOU AGREE TO BE MY PERSONAL VALET FOR LIFE.
I NEED TO SHOPLIFT A PENCIL FIRST.

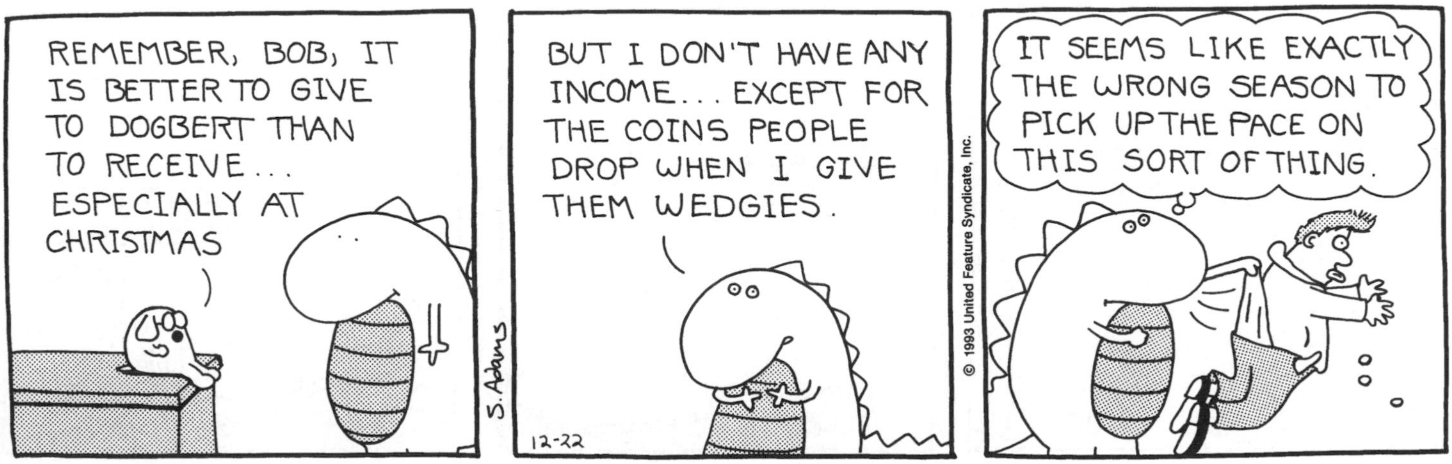
REMEMBER, BOB, IT IS BETTER TO GIVE TO DOGBERT THAN TO RECEIVE... ESPECIALLY AT CHRISTMAS
S. Adams
BUT I DON'T HAVE ANY INCOME... EXCEPT FOR THE COINS PEOPLE DROP WHEN I GIVE THEM WEDGIES.
12-22
© 1993 United Feature Syndicate, Inc.
IT SEEMS LIKE EXACTLY THE WRONG SEASON TO PICK UP THE PACE ON THIS SORT OF THING.

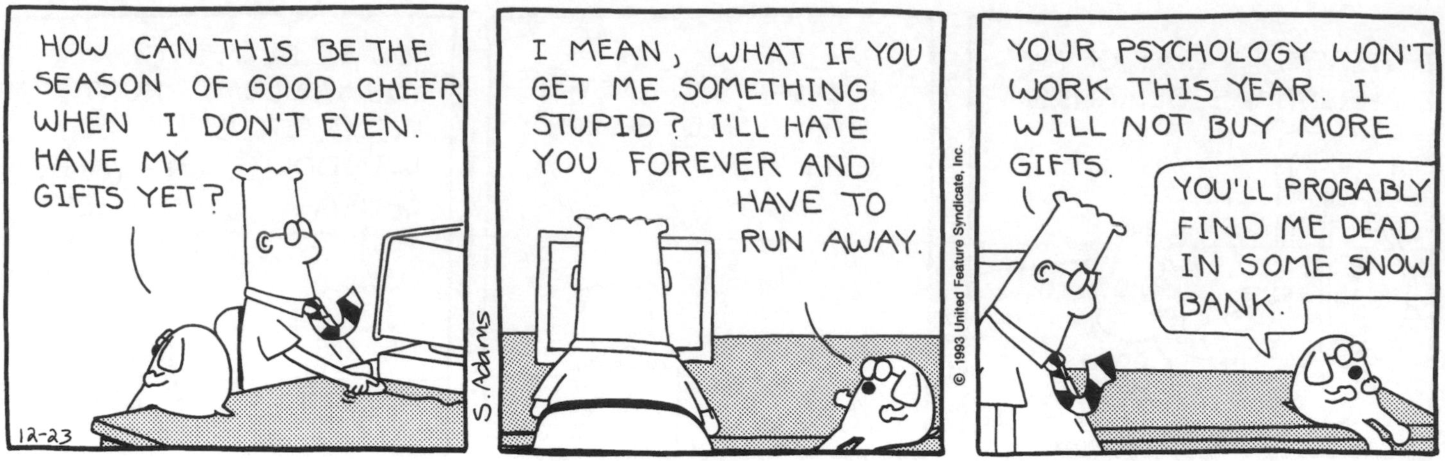
HOW CAN THIS BE THE SEASON OF GOOD CHEER WHEN I DON'T EVEN. HAVE MY GIFTS YET?
12-23
S. Adams
I MEAN, WHAT IF YOU GET ME SOMETHING STUPID? I'LL HATE YOU FOREVER AND HAVE TO RUN AWAY.
© 1993 United Feature Syndicate, Inc.
YOUR PSYCHOLOGY WON'T WORK THIS YEAR. I WILL NOT BUY MORE GIFTS.
YOU'LL PROBABLY FIND ME DEAD IN SOME SNOW BANK.

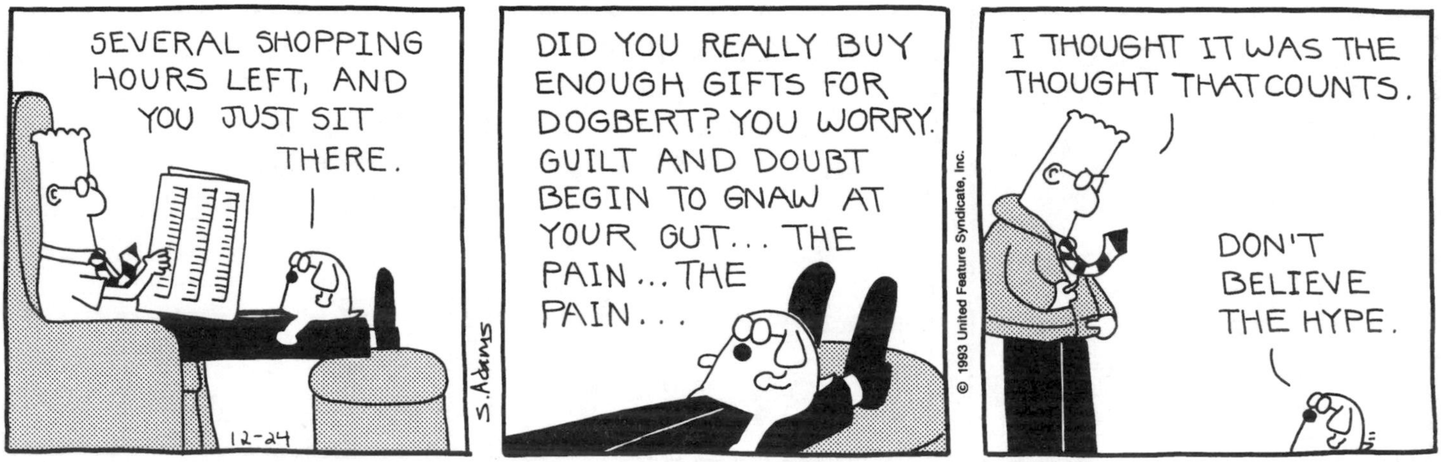
SEVERAL SHOPPING HOURS LEFT, AND YOU JUST SIT THERE.
12-24
S. Adams
DID YOU REALLY BUY ENOUGH GIFTS FOR DOGBERT? YOU WORRY. GUILT AND DOUBT BEGIN TO GNAW AT YOUR GUT... THE PAIN... THE PAIN...
© 1993 United Feature Syndicate, Inc.
I THOUGHT IT WAS THE THOUGHT THAT COUNTS.
DON'T BELIEVE THE HYPE.

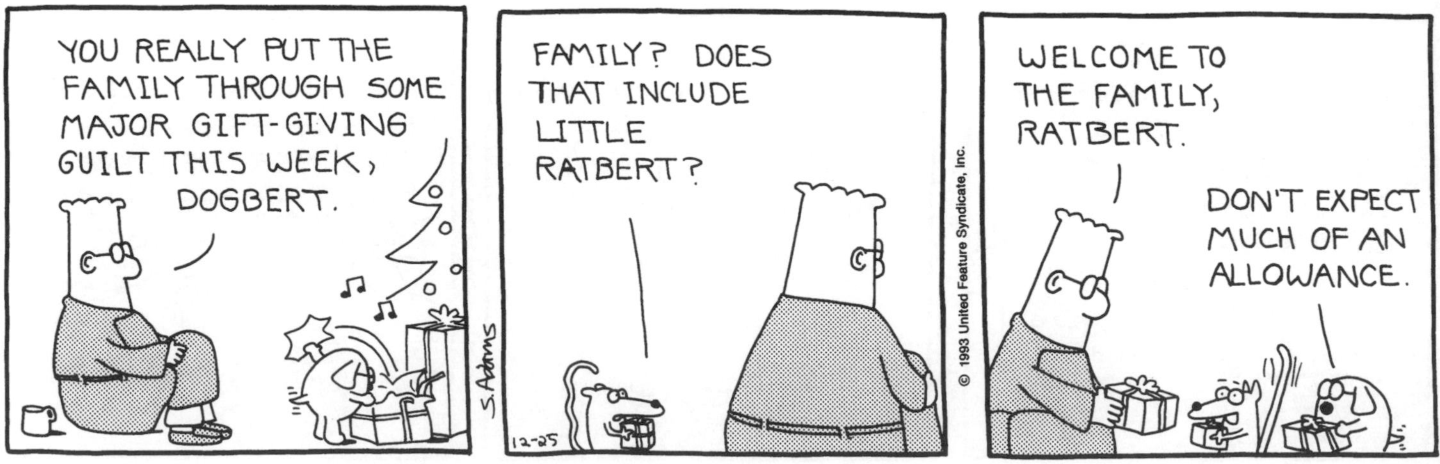
YOU REALLY PUT THE FAMILY THROUGH SOME MAJOR GIFT-GIVING GUILT THIS WEEK, DOGBERT.
S. Adams
FAMILY? DOES THAT INCLUDE LITTLE RATBERT?
12-25
© 1993 United Feature Syndicate, Inc.
WELCOME TO THE FAMILY, RATBERT.
DON'T EXPECT MUCH OF AN ALLOWANCE.

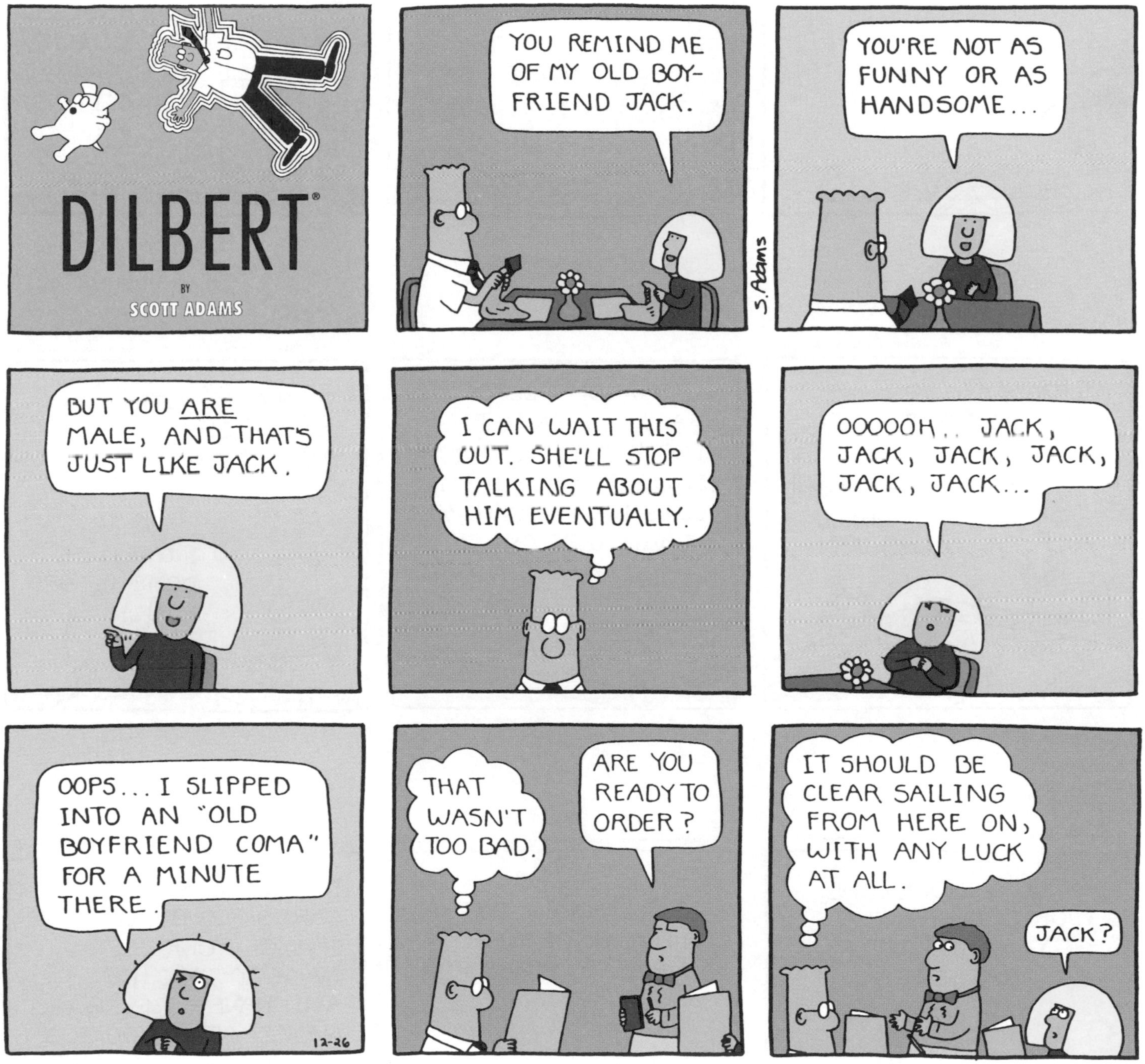

DILBERT®
BY
SCOTT ADAMS
YOU REMIND ME OF MY OLD BOY-FRIEND JACK.
S. Adams
YOU'RE NOT AS FUNNY OR AS HANDSOME...
BUT YOU ARE MALE, AND THAT'S JUST LIKE JACK.
I CAN WAIT THIS OUT. SHE'LL STOP TALKING ABOUT HIM EVENTUALLY.
OOOOOH.. JACK, JACK, JACK, JACK, JACK, JACK...
OOPS... I SLIPPED INTO AN "OLD BOYFRIEND COMA" FOR A MINUTE THERE.
© 1993 United Feature Syndicate, Inc.
12-26
THAT WASN'T TOO BAD.
ARE YOU READY TO ORDER?
IT SHOULD BE CLEAR SAILING FROM HERE ON, WITH ANY LUCK AT ALL.
JACK?

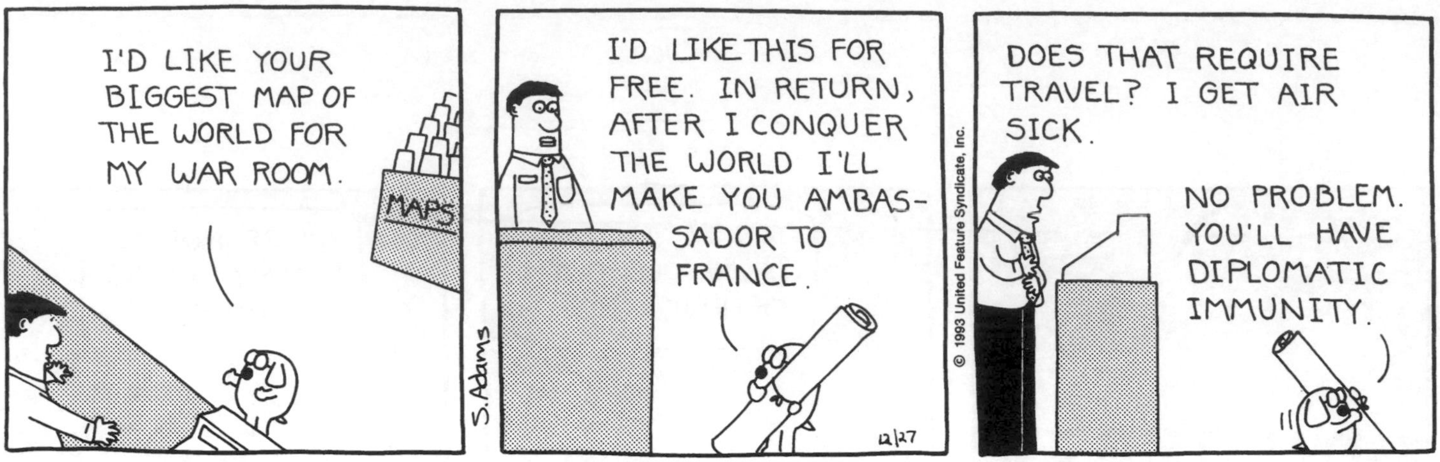
I'D LIKE YOUR BIGGEST MAP OF THE WORLD FOR MY WAR ROOM.
MAPS
S. Adams
I'D LIKE THIS FOR FREE. IN RETURN, AFTER I CONQUER THE WORLD I'LL MAKE YOU AMBASSADOR TO FRANCE.
12/27
© 1993 United Feature Syndicate, Inc.
DOES THAT REQUIRE TRAVEL? I GET AIR SICK.
NO PROBLEM. YOU'LL HAVE DIPLOMATIC IMMUNITY.

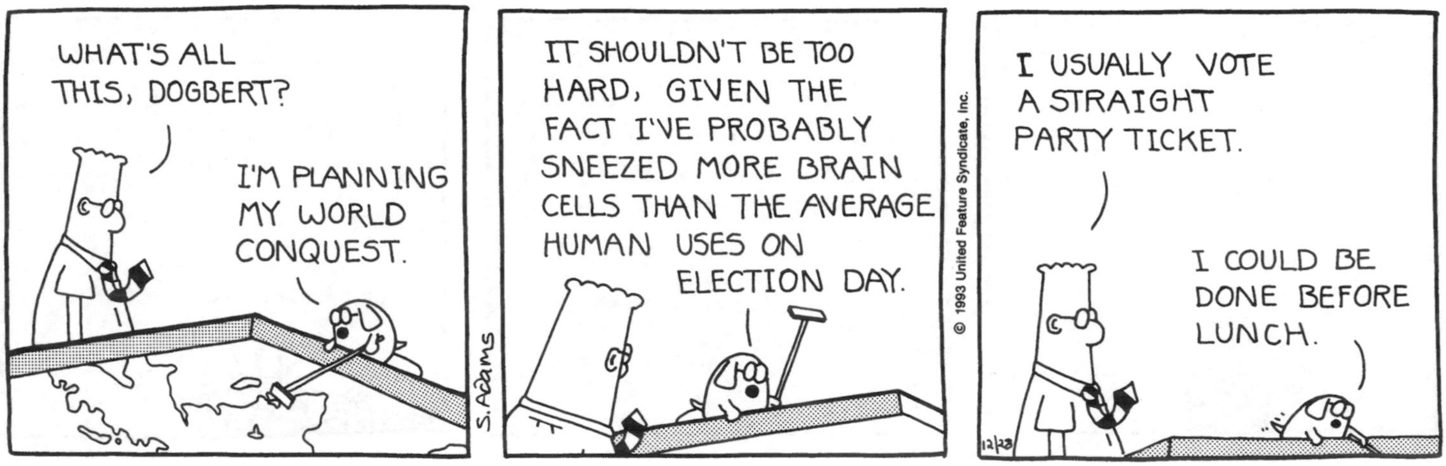
WHAT'S ALL THIS, DOGBERT?
I'M PLANNING MY WORLD CONQUEST.
S. Adams
IT SHOULDN'T BE TOO HARD, GIVEN THE FACT I'VE PROBABLY SNEEZED MORE BRAIN CELLS THAN THE AVERAGE HUMAN USES ON ELECTION DAY.
© 1993 United Feature Syndicate, Inc.
I USUALLY VOTE A STRAIGHT PARTY TICKET.
I COULD BE DONE BEFORE LUNCH.
12/28

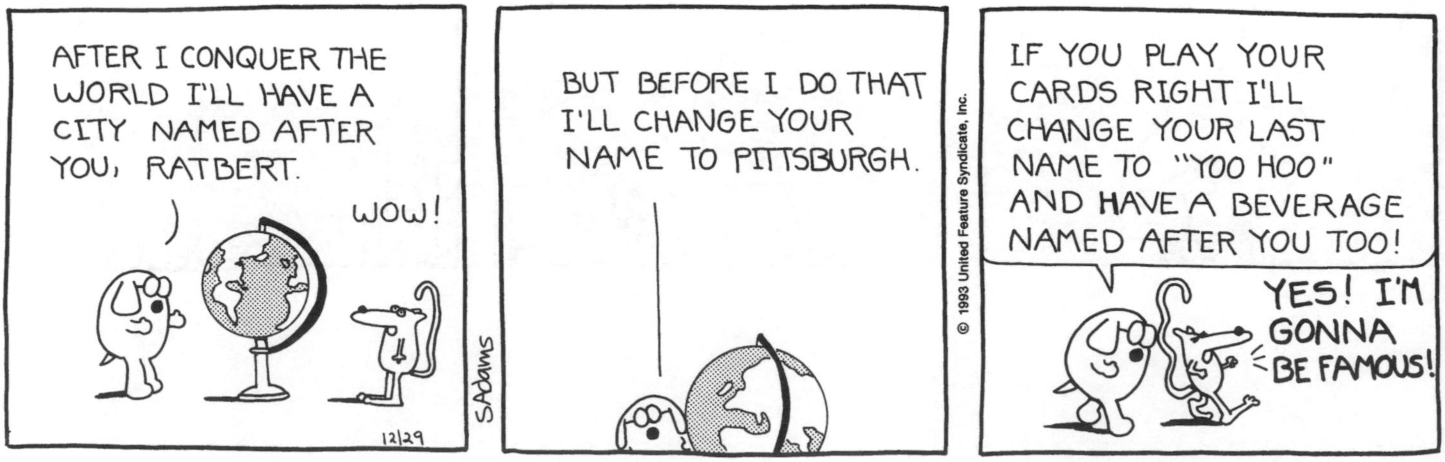
AFTER I CONQUER THE WORLD I'LL HAVE A CITY NAMED AFTER YOU, RATBERT.
WOW!
12/29
S.Adams
BUT BEFORE I DO THAT I'LL CHANGE YOUR NAME TO PITTSBURGH.
© 1993 United Feature Syndicate, Inc.
IF YOU PLAY YOUR CARDS RIGHT I'LL CHANGE YOUR LAST NAME TO "YOO HOO" AND HAVE A BEVERAGE NAMED AFTER YOU TOO!
YES! I'M GONNA BE FAMOUS!

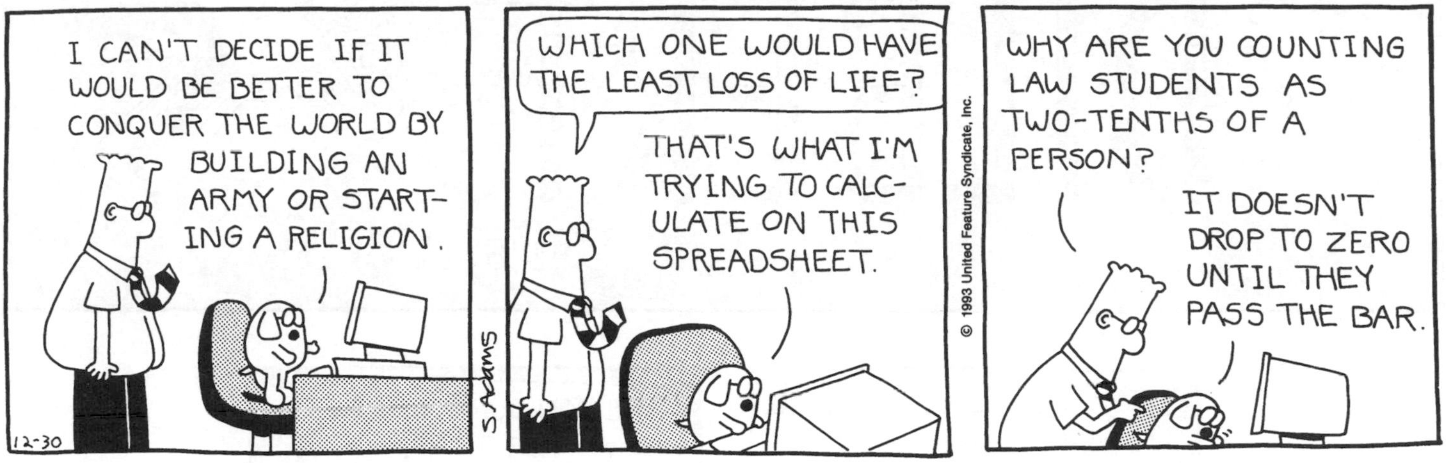
I CAN'T DECIDE IF IT WOULD BE BETTER TO CONQUER THE WORLD BY BUILDING AN ARMY OR STARTING A RELIGION.
WHICH ONE WOULD HAVE THE LEAST LOSS OF LIFE?
THAT'S WHAT I'M TRYING TO CALCULATE ON THIS SPREADSHEET.
WHY ARE YOU COUNTING LAW STUDENTS AS TWO-TENTHS OF A PERSON?
IT DOESN'T DROP TO ZERO UNTIL THEY PASS THE BAR.
12-30
S. Adams
© 1993 United Feature Syndicate, Inc.

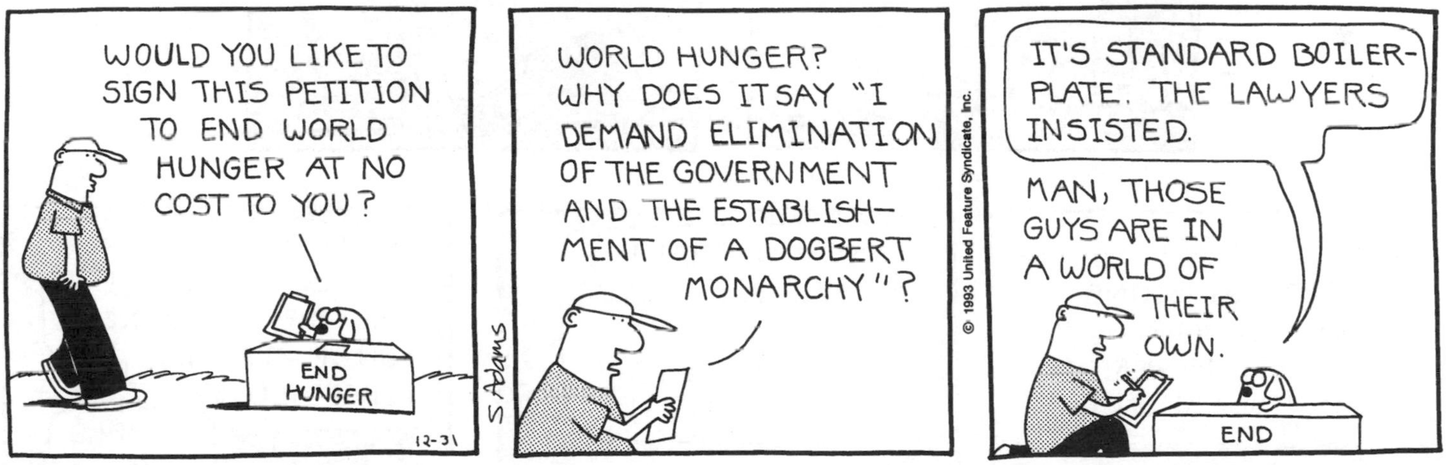
WOULD YOU LIKE TO SIGN THIS PETITION TO END WORLD HUNGER AT NO COST TO YOU?
END HUNGER
12-31
S. Adams
WORLD HUNGER? WHY DOES IT SAY "I DEMAND ELIMINATION OF THE GOVERNMENT AND THE ESTABLISHMENT OF A DOGBERT MONARCHY"?
© 1993 United Feature Syndicate, Inc.
IT'S STANDARD BOILERPLATE. THE LAWYERS INSISTED.
MAN, THOSE GUYS ARE IN A WORLD OF THEIR OWN.
END

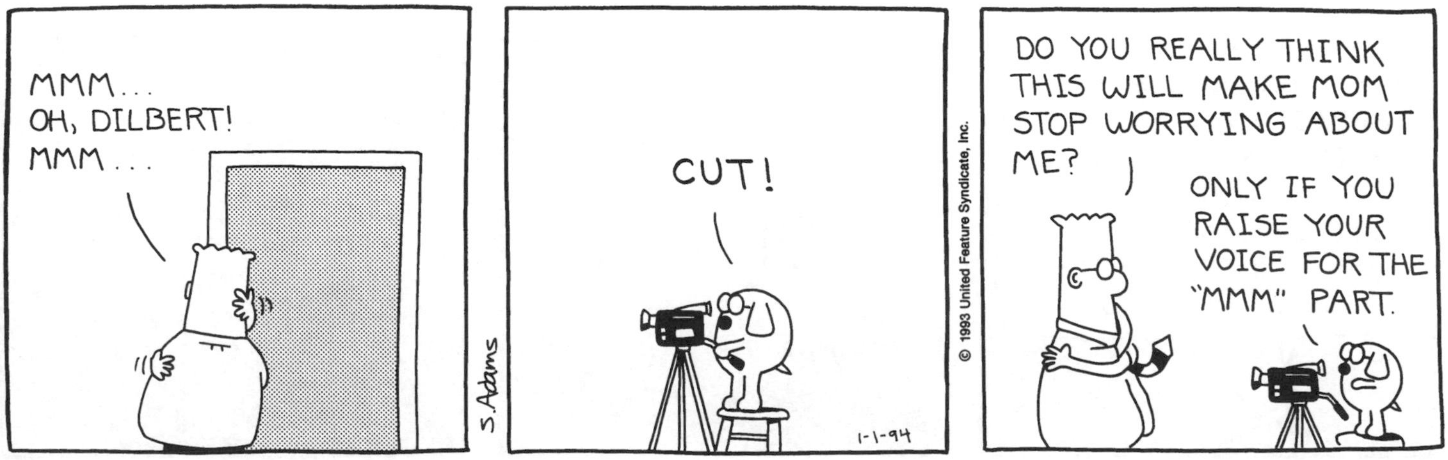
MMM... OH, DILBERT! MMM...
S. Adams
CUT!
1-1-94
© 1993 United Feature Syndicate, Inc.
DO YOU REALLY THINK THIS WILL MAKE MOM STOP WORRYING ABOUT ME?
ONLY IF YOU RAISE YOUR VOICE FOR THE "MMM" PART.

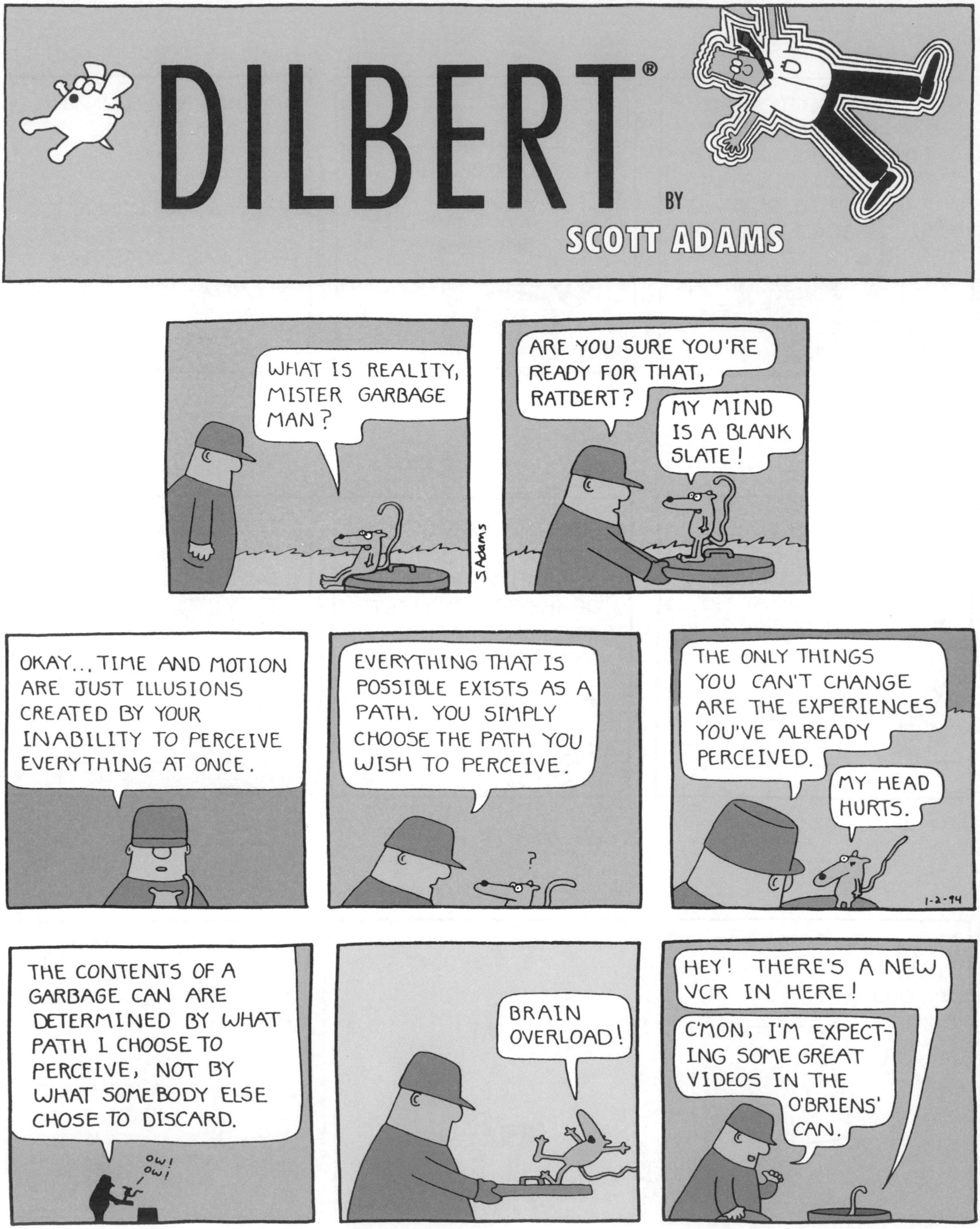
DILBERT®
BY
SCOTT ADAMS
WHAT IS REALITY, MISTER GARBAGE MAN?
S Adams
ARE YOU SURE YOU'RE READY FOR THAT, RATBERT?
MY MIND IS A BLANK SLATE!
OKAY... TIME AND MOTION ARE JUST ILLUSIONS CREATED BY YOUR INABILITY TO PERCEIVE EVERYTHING AT ONCE.
EVERYTHING THAT IS POSSIBLE EXISTS AS A PATH. YOU SIMPLY CHOOSE THE PATH YOU WISH TO PERCEIVE.
?
THE ONLY THINGS YOU CAN'T CHANGE ARE THE EXPERIENCES YOU'VE ALREADY PERCEIVED.
MY HEAD HURTS.
1-2-94
THE CONTENTS OF A GARBAGE CAN ARE DETERMINED BY WHAT PATH I CHOOSE TO PERCEIVE, NOT BY WHAT SOMEBODY ELSE CHOSE TO DISCARD.
OW! OW!
BRAIN OVERLOAD!
HEY! THERE'S A NEW VCR IN HERE!
C'MON, I'M EXPECT-ING SOME GREAT VIDEOS IN THE O'BRIENS' CAN.

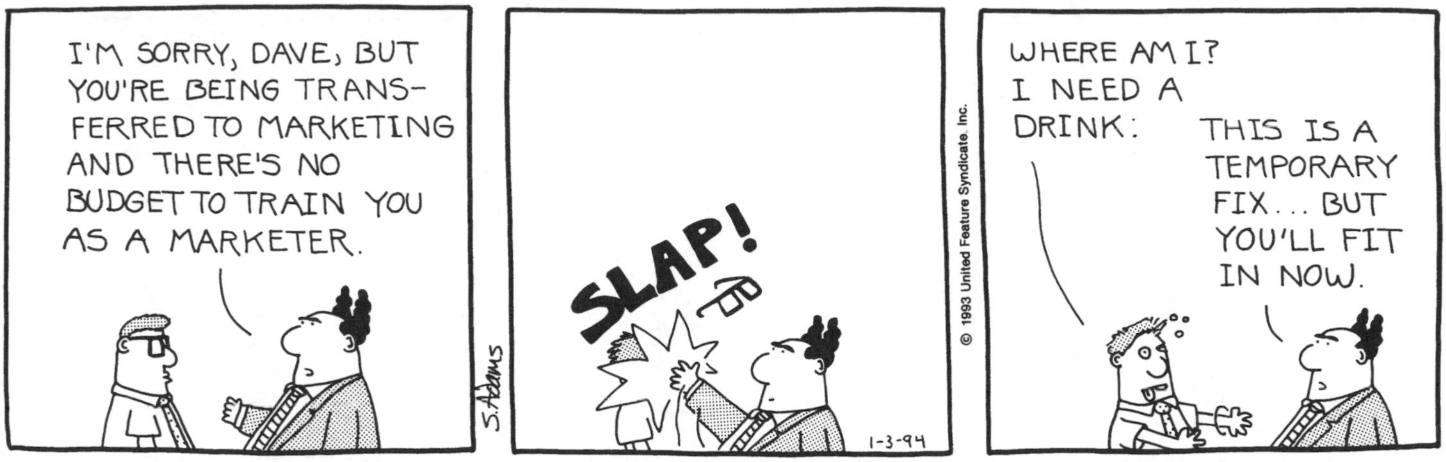
I'M SORRY, DAVE, BUT YOU'RE BEING TRANS-FERRED TO MARKETING AND THERE'S NO BUDGET TO TRAIN YOU AS A MARKETER.
S.Adams
SLAP!
1-3-94
© 1993 United Feature Syndicate, Inc.
WHERE AM I? I NEED A DRINK:
THIS IS A TEMPORARY FIX... BUT YOU'LL FIT IN NOW.

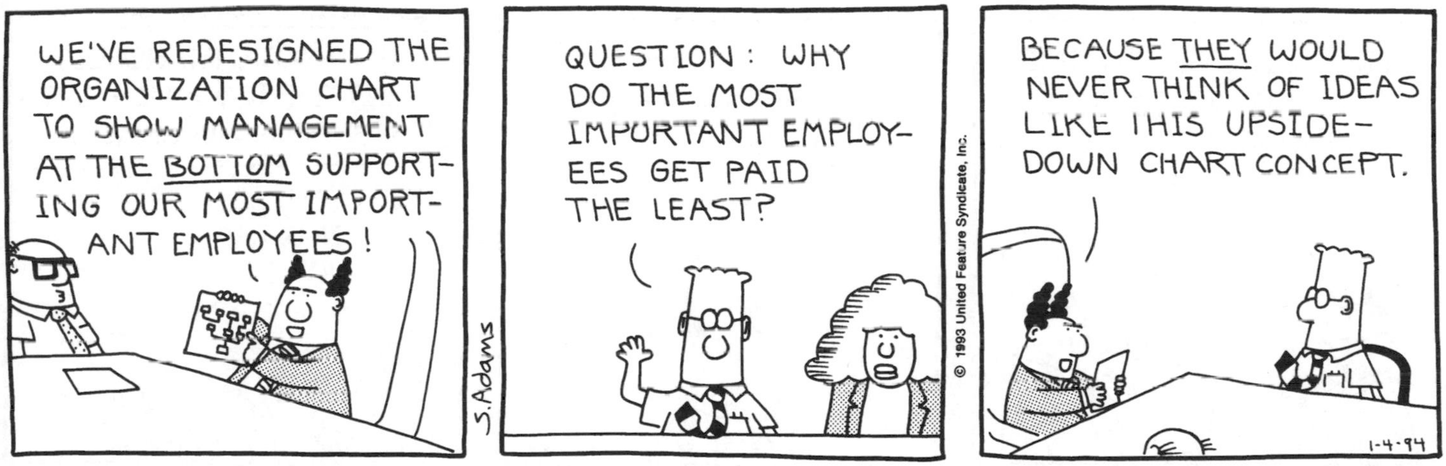
WE'VE REDESIGNED THE ORGANIZATION CHART TO SHOW MANAGEMENT AT THE BOTTOM SUPPORT-ING OUR MOST IMPORT-ANT EMPLOYEES!
S.Adams
QUESTION: WHY DO THE MOST IMPORTANT EMPLOY-EES GET PAID THE LEAST?
© 1993 United Feature Syndicate, Inc.
BECAUSE THEY WOULD NEVER THINK OF IDEAS LIKE THIS UPSIDE-DOWN CHART CONCEPT.
1-4-94

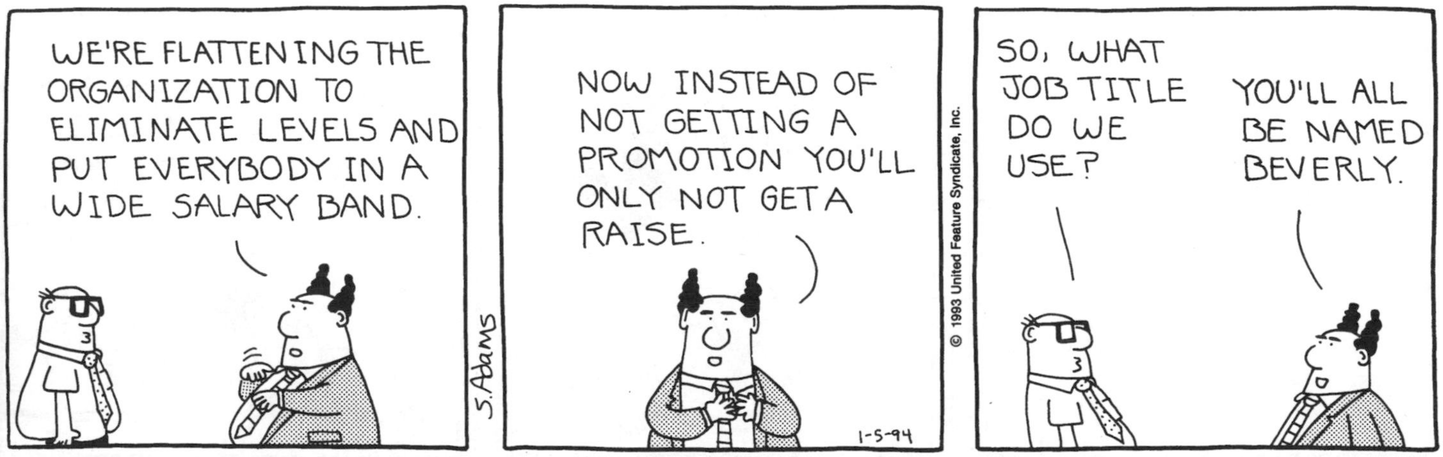
WE'RE FLATTENING THE ORGANIZATION TO ELIMINATE LEVELS AND PUT EVERYBODY IN A WIDE SALARY BAND.
S.Adams
NOW INSTEAD OF NOT GETTING A PROMOTION YOU'LL ONLY NOT GET A RAISE.
1-5-94
© 1993 United Feature Syndicate, Inc.
SO, WHAT JOB TITLE DO WE USE?
YOU'LL ALL BE NAMED BEVERLY.

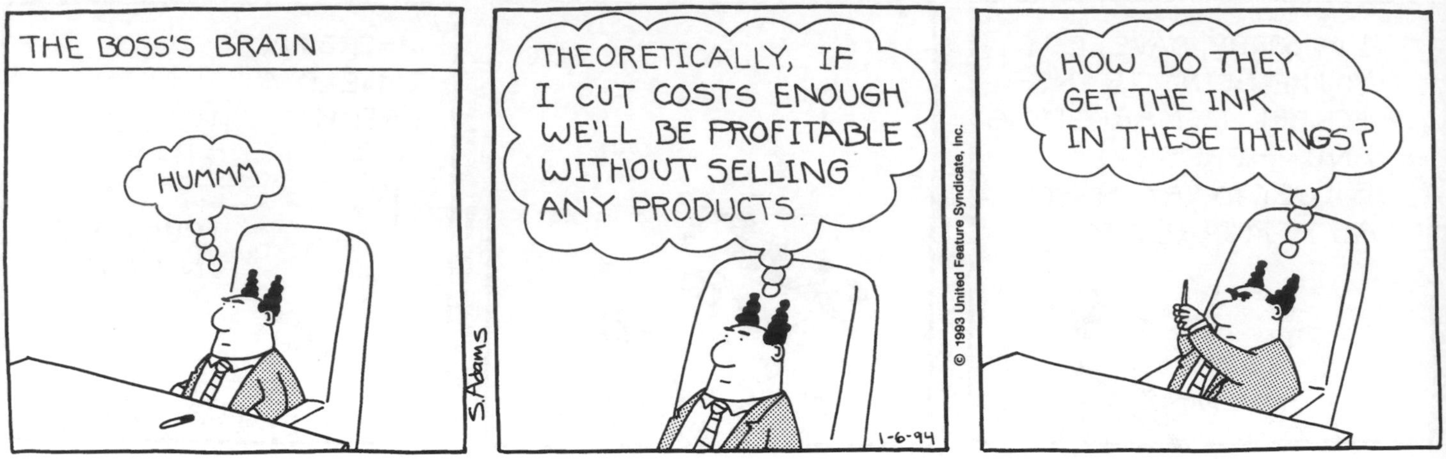
THE BOSS'S BRAIN
HUMMM
S. Adams
THEORETICALLY, IF I CUT COSTS ENOUGH WE'LL BE PROFITABLE WITHOUT SELLING ANY PRODUCTS.
1-6-94
© 1993 United Feature Syndicate, Inc.
HOW DO THEY GET THE INK IN THESE THINGS?

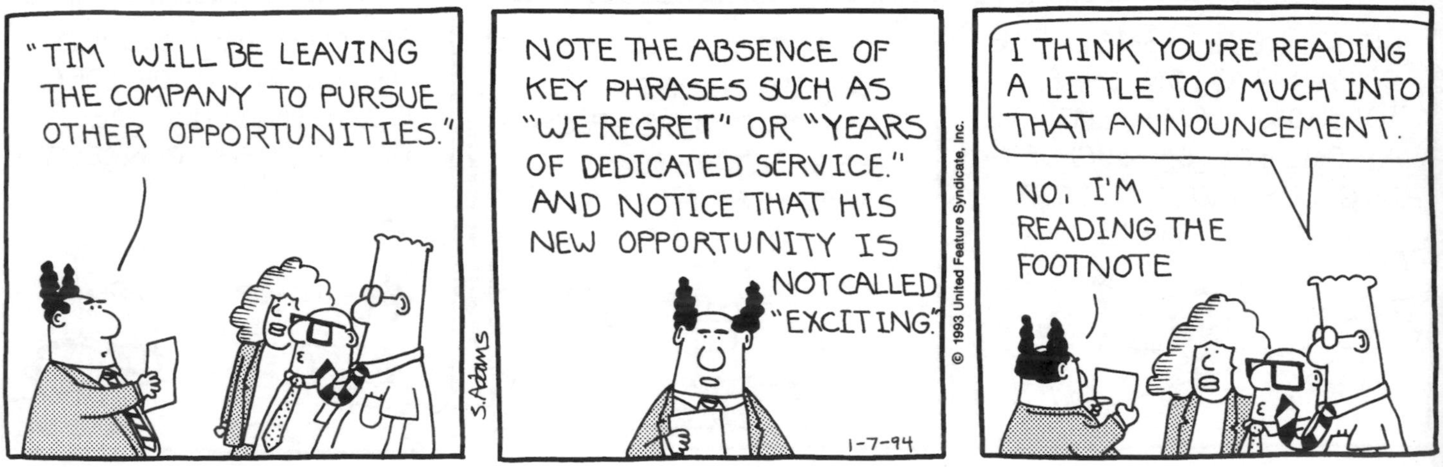
"TIM WILL BE LEAVING THE COMPANY TO PURSUE OTHER OPPORTUNITIES."
S. Adams
NOTE THE ABSENCE OF KEY PHRASES SUCH AS "WE REGRET" OR "YEARS OF DEDICATED SERVICE." AND NOTICE THAT HIS NEW OPPORTUNITY IS NOT CALLED "EXCITING."
1-7-94
© 1993 United Feature Syndicate, Inc.
I THINK YOU'RE READING A LITTLE TOO MUCH INTO THAT ANNOUNCEMENT.
NO, I'M READING THE FOOTNOTE

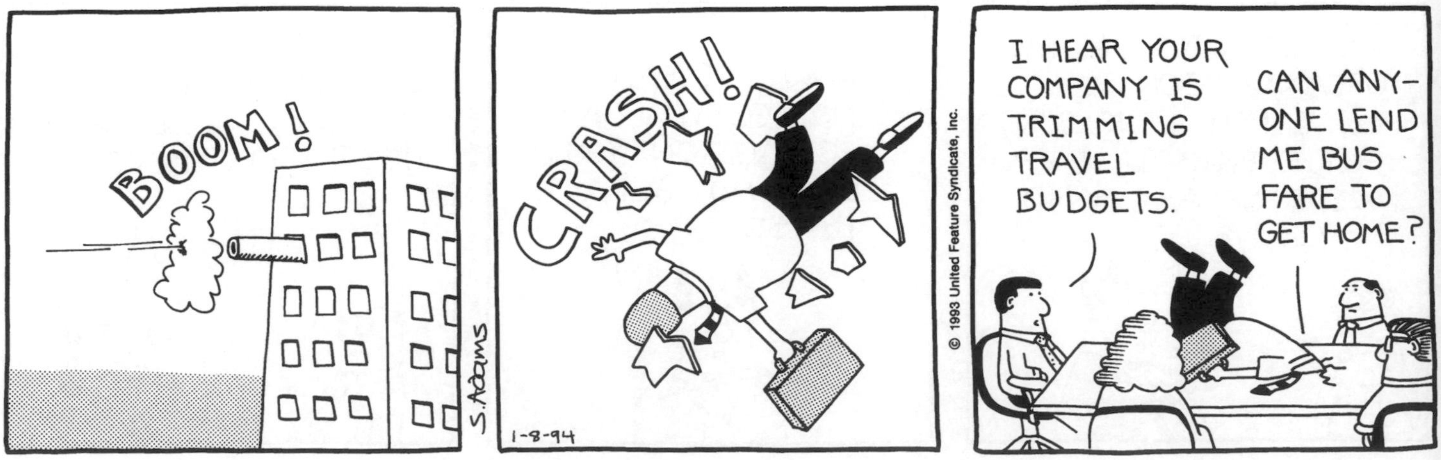
BOOM!
S. Adams
CRASH!
1-8-94
© 1993 United Feature Syndicate, Inc.
I HEAR YOUR COMPANY IS TRIMMING TRAVEL BUDGETS.
CAN ANYONE LEND ME BUS FARE TO GET HOME?

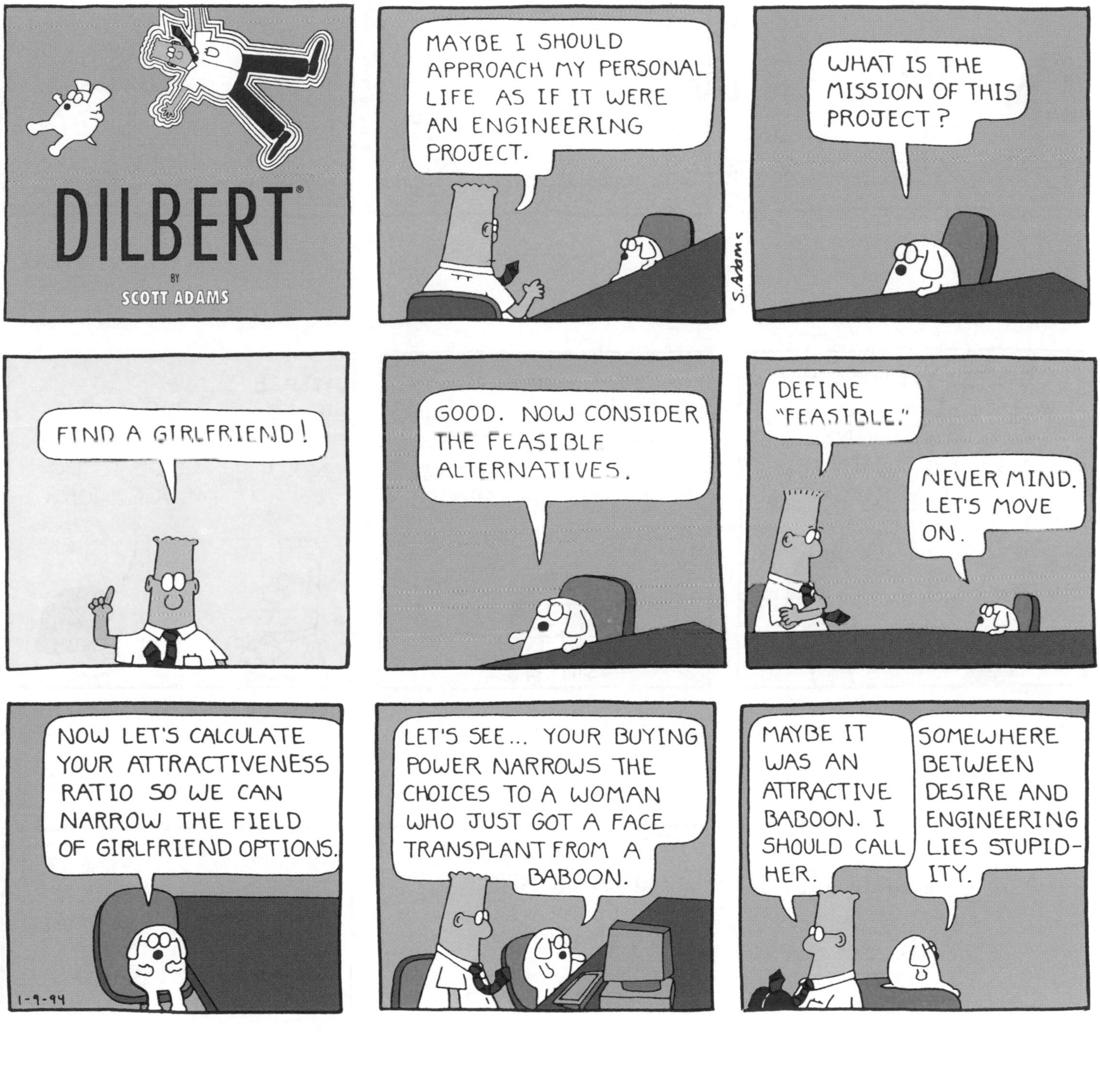
DILBERT®
BY
SCOTT ADAMS
MAYBE I SHOULD APPROACH MY PERSONAL LIFE AS IF IT WERE AN ENGINEERING PROJECT.
S. Adams
WHAT IS THE MISSION OF THIS PROJECT?
FIND A GIRLFRIEND!
GOOD. NOW CONSIDER THE FEASIBLE ALTERNATIVES.
DEFINE "FEASIBLE."
NEVER MIND. LET'S MOVE ON.
NOW LET'S CALCULATE YOUR ATTRACTIVENESS RATIO SO WE CAN NARROW THE FIELD OF GIRLFRIEND OPTIONS.
1-9-94
LET'S SEE... YOUR BUYING POWER NARROWS THE CHOICES TO A WOMAN WHO JUST GOT A FACE TRANSPLANT FROM A BABOON.
MAYBE IT WAS AN ATTRACTIVE BABOON. I SHOULD CALL HER.
SOMEWHERE BETWEEN DESIRE AND ENGINEERING LIES STUPIDITY.

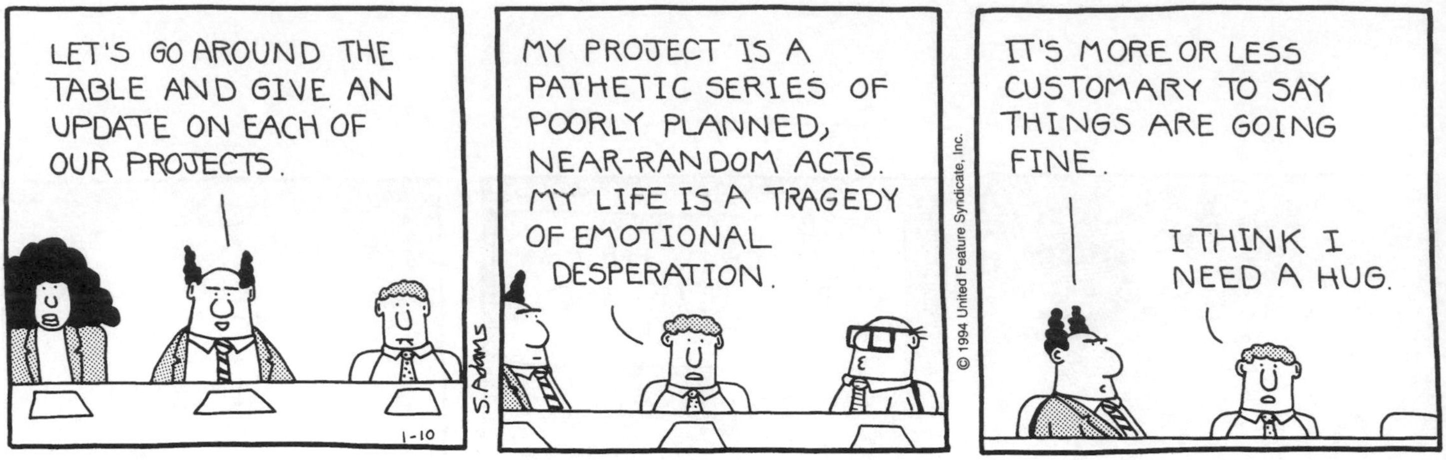
LET'S GO AROUND THE TABLE AND GIVE AN UPDATE ON EACH OF OUR PROJECTS.
MY PROJECT IS A PATHETIC SERIES OF POORLY PLANNED, NEAR-RANDOM ACTS. MY LIFE IS A TRAGEDY OF EMOTIONAL DESPERATION.
IT'S MORE OR LESS CUSTOMARY TO SAY THINGS ARE GOING FINE.
I THINK I NEED A HUG.
S. Adams
1-10
© 1994 United Feature Syndicate, Inc.

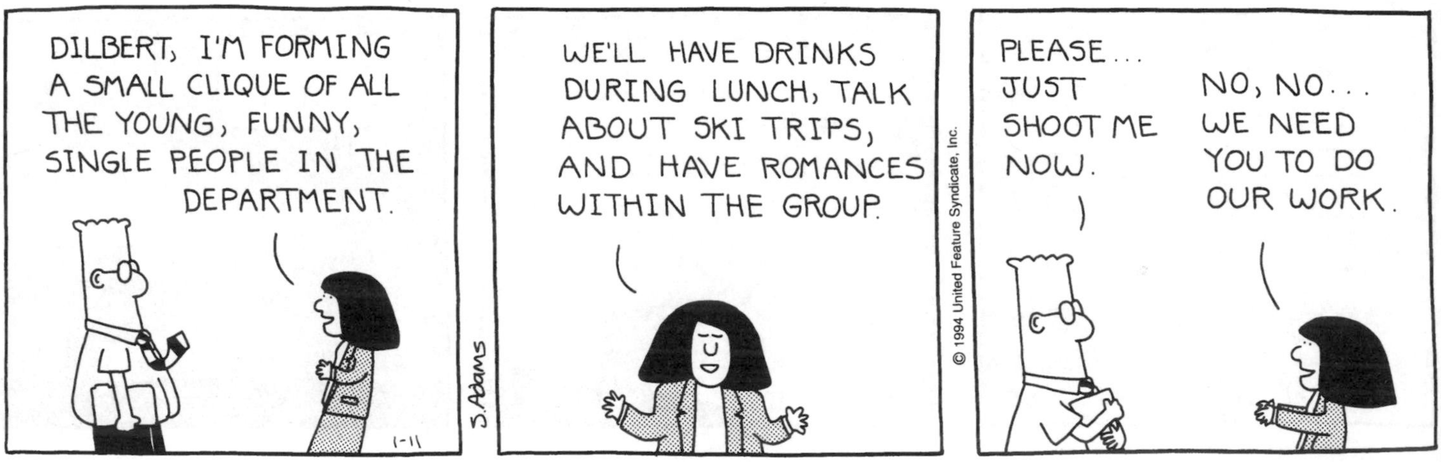
DILBERT, I'M FORMING A SMALL CLIQUE OF ALL THE YOUNG, FUNNY, SINGLE PEOPLE IN THE DEPARTMENT.
WE'LL HAVE DRINKS DURING LUNCH, TALK ABOUT SKI TRIPS, AND HAVE ROMANCES WITHIN THE GROUP.
PLEASE... JUST SHOOT ME NOW.
NO, NO... WE NEED YOU TO DO OUR WORK.
S. Adams
1-11
© 1994 United Feature Syndicate, Inc.

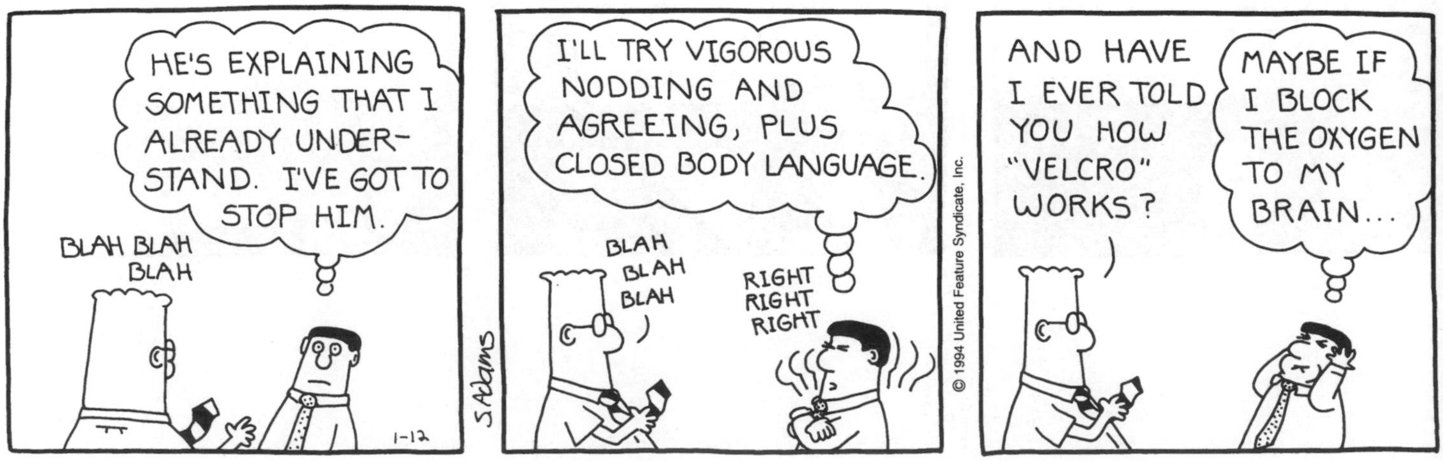
BLAH BLAH BLAH
HE'S EXPLAINING SOMETHING THAT I ALREADY UNDER-STAND. I'VE GOT TO STOP HIM.
BLAH BLAH BLAH
I'LL TRY VIGOROUS NODDING AND AGREEING, PLUS CLOSED BODY LANGUAGE.
RIGHT RIGHT RIGHT
AND HAVE I EVER TOLD YOU HOW "VELCRO" WORKS?
MAYBE IF I BLOCK THE OXYGEN TO MY BRAIN...
S. Adams
1-12
© 1994 United Feature Syndicate, Inc.

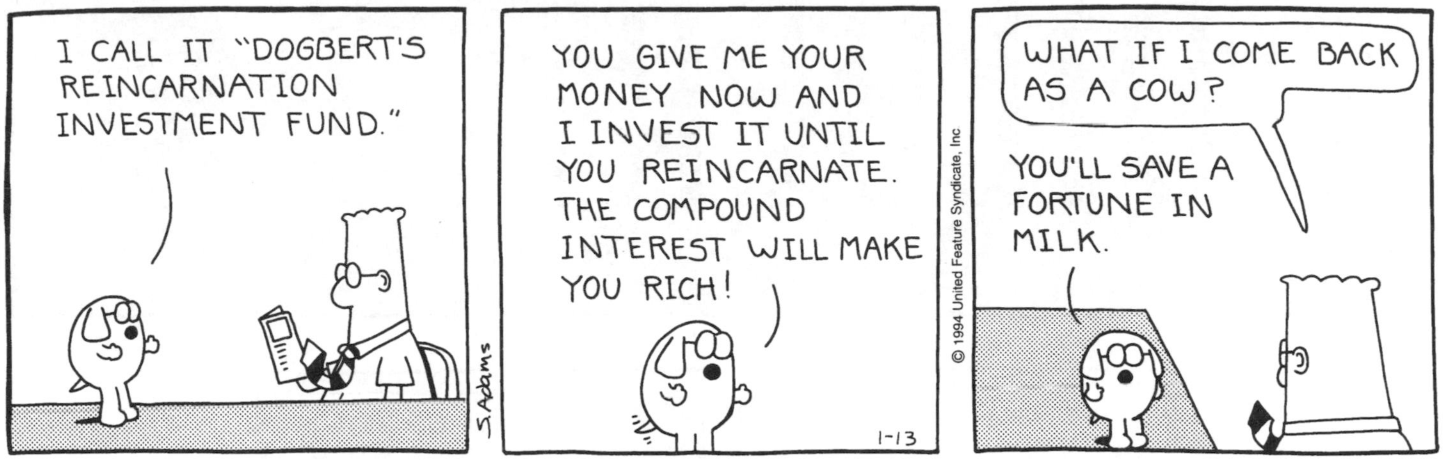
I CALL IT "DOGBERT'S REINCARNATION INVESTMENT FUND."
S. Adams
YOU GIVE ME YOUR MONEY NOW AND I INVEST IT UNTIL YOU REINCARNATE. THE COMPOUND INTEREST WILL MAKE YOU RICH!
1-13
© 1994 United Feature Syndicate, Inc
WHAT IF I COME BACK AS A COW?
YOU'LL SAVE A FORTUNE IN MILK.

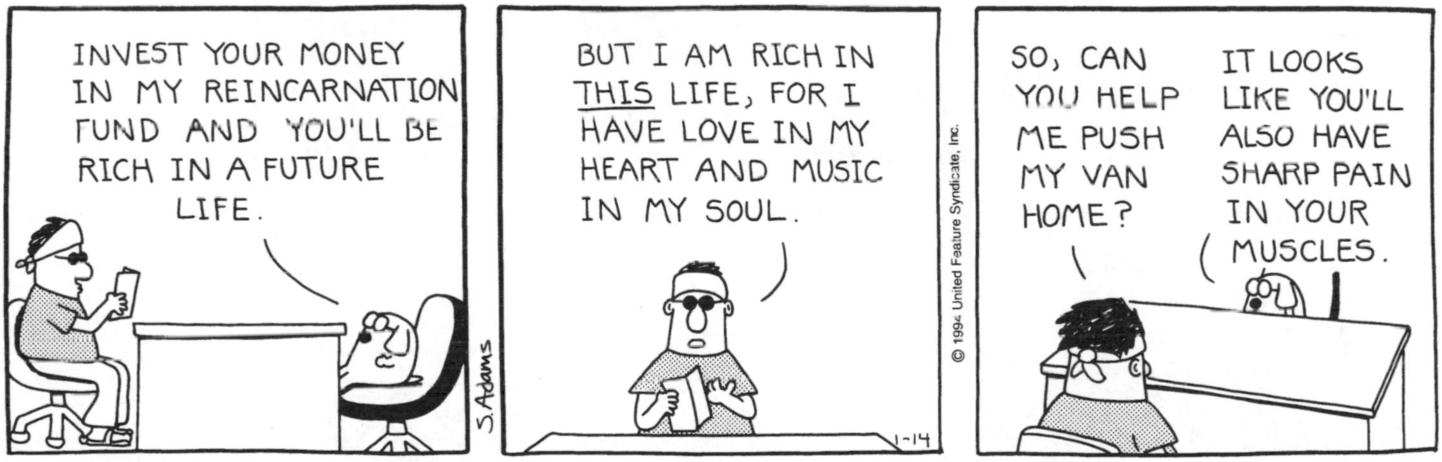
INVEST YOUR MONEY IN MY REINCARNATION FUND AND YOU'LL BE RICH IN A FUTURE LIFE.
S. Adams
BUT I AM RICH IN THIS LIFE, FOR I HAVE LOVE IN MY HEART AND MUSIC IN MY SOUL.
1-14
© 1994 United Feature Syndicate, Inc.
SO, CAN YOU HELP ME PUSH MY VAN HOME?
IT LOOKS LIKE YOU'LL ALSO HAVE SHARP PAIN IN YOUR MUSCLES.

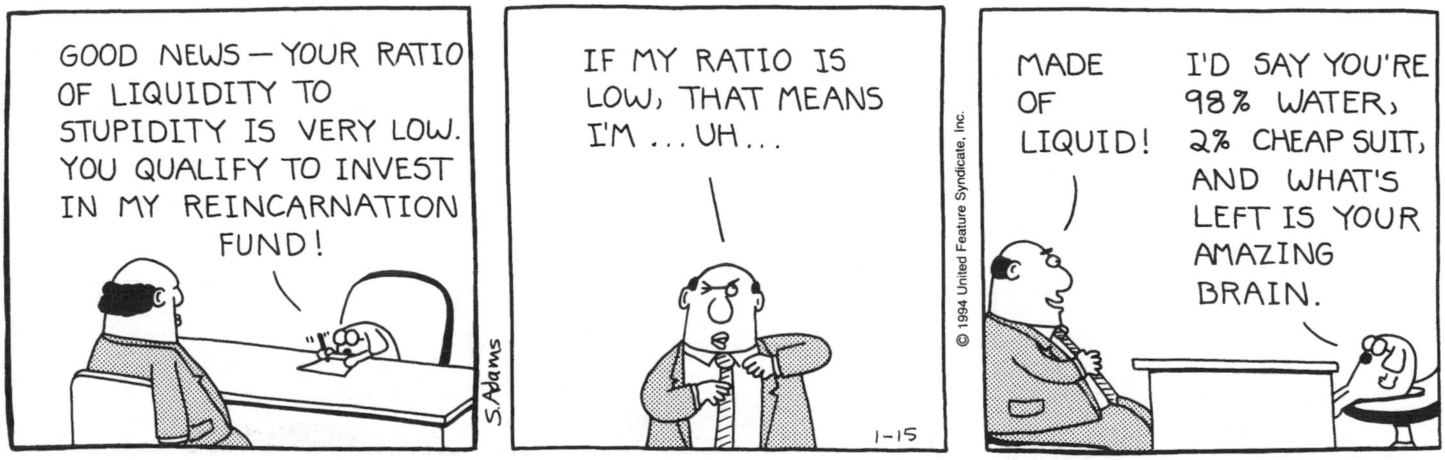
GOOD NEWS — YOUR RATIO OF LIQUIDITY TO STUPIDITY IS VERY LOW. YOU QUALIFY TO INVEST IN MY REINCARNATION FUND!
S. Adams
IF MY RATIO IS LOW, THAT MEANS I'M ... UH ...
1-15
© 1994 United Feature Syndicate, Inc.
MADE OF LIQUID!
I'D SAY YOU'RE 98% WATER, 2% CHEAP SUIT, AND WHAT'S LEFT IS YOUR AMAZING BRAIN.

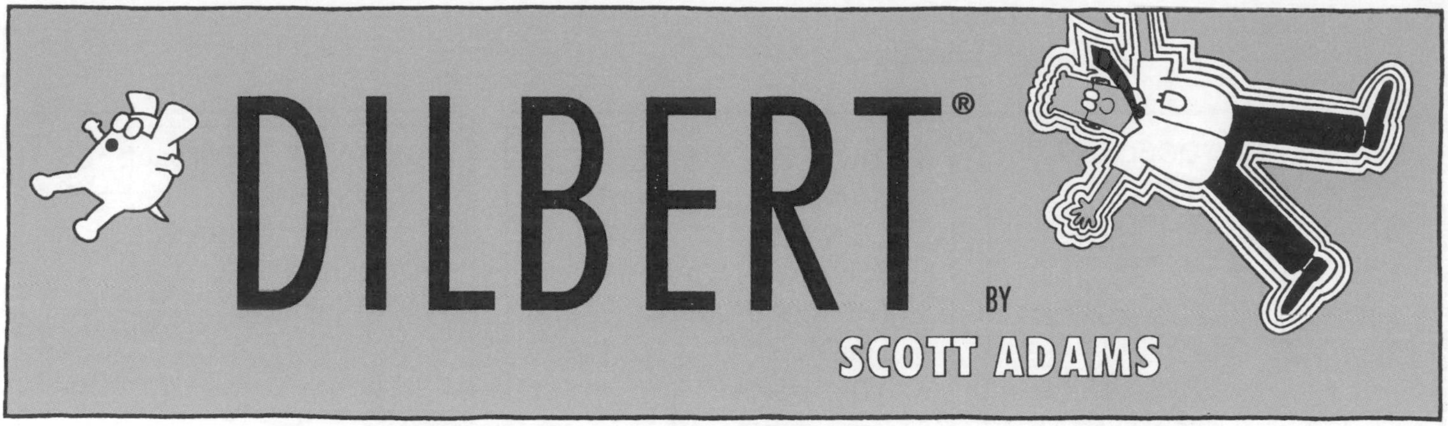
DILBERT®
BY
SCOTT ADAMS

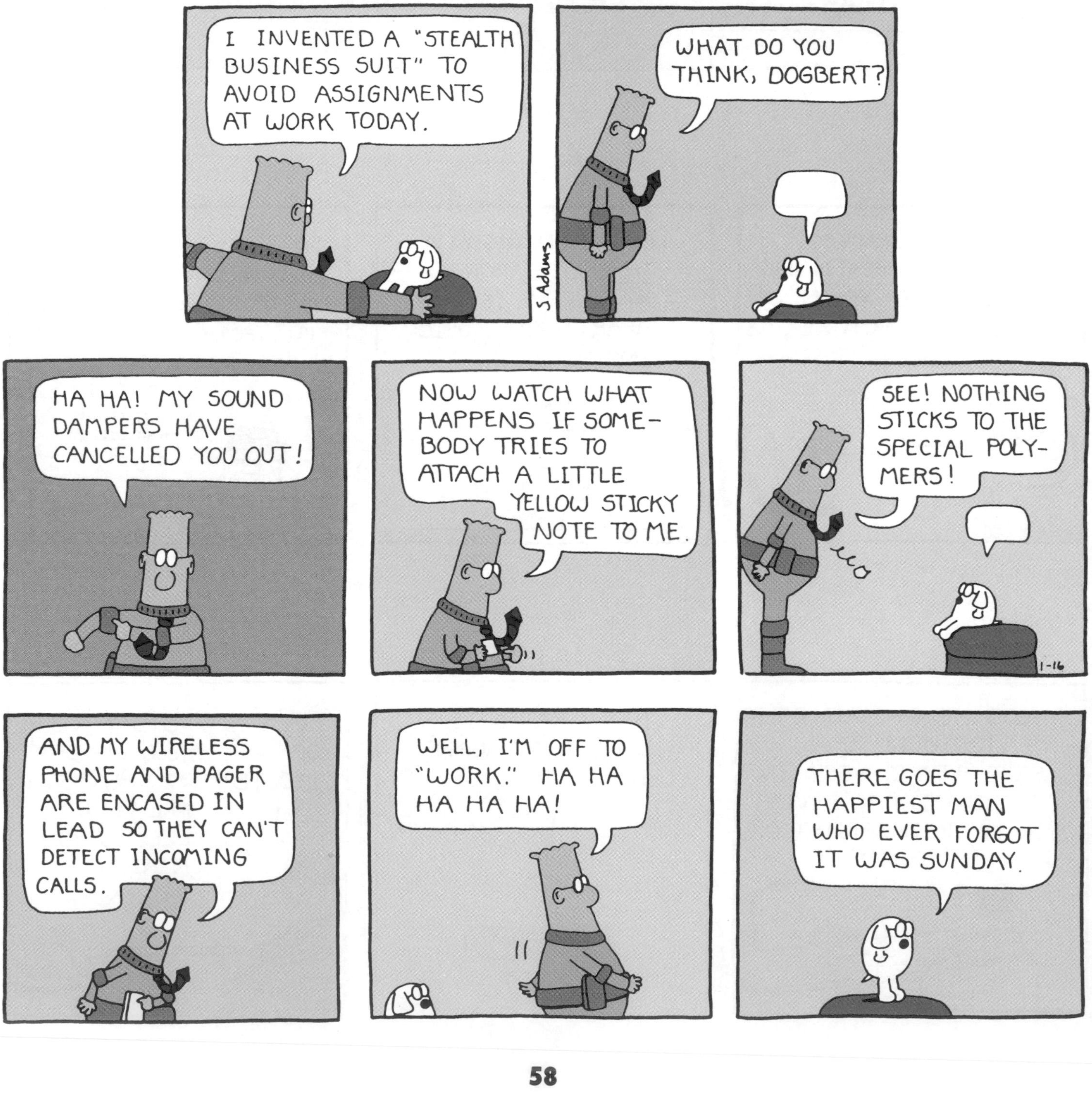
I INVENTED A "STEALTH BUSINESS SUIT" TO AVOID ASSIGNMENTS AT WORK TODAY.
S Adams
WHAT DO YOU THINK, DOGBERT?
HA HA! MY SOUND DAMPERS HAVE CANCELLED YOU OUT!
NOW WATCH WHAT HAPPENS IF SOME-BODY TRIES TO ATTACH A LITTLE YELLOW STICKY NOTE TO ME.
SEE! NOTHING STICKS TO THE SPECIAL POLY-MERS!
1-16
AND MY WIRELESS PHONE AND PAGER ARE ENCASED IN LEAD SO THEY CAN'T DETECT INCOMING CALLS.
WELL, I'M OFF TO "WORK." HA HA HA HA HA!
THERE GOES THE HAPPIEST MAN WHO EVER FORGOT IT WAS SUNDAY.

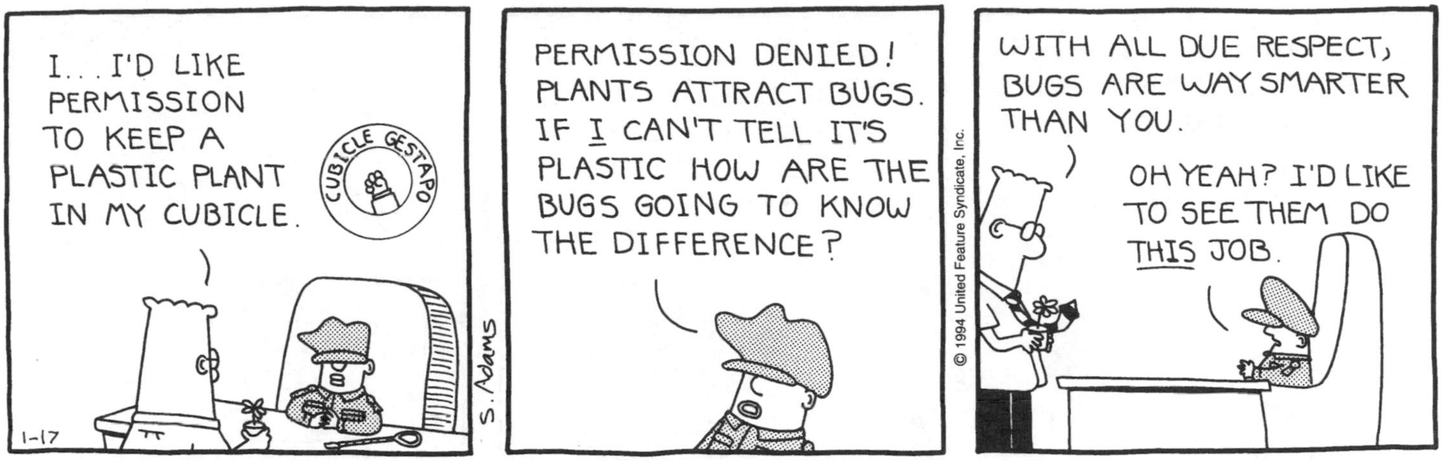
I... I'D LIKE PERMISSION TO KEEP A PLASTIC PLANT IN MY CUBICLE.
CUBICLE GESTAPO
1-17
S. Adams
PERMISSION DENIED! PLANTS ATTRACT BUGS. IF I CAN'T TELL IT'S PLASTIC HOW ARE THE BUGS GOING TO KNOW THE DIFFERENCE?
© 1994 United Feature Syndicate, Inc.
WITH ALL DUE RESPECT, BUGS ARE WAY SMARTER THAN YOU.
OH YEAH? I'D LIKE TO SEE THEM DO THIS JOB.

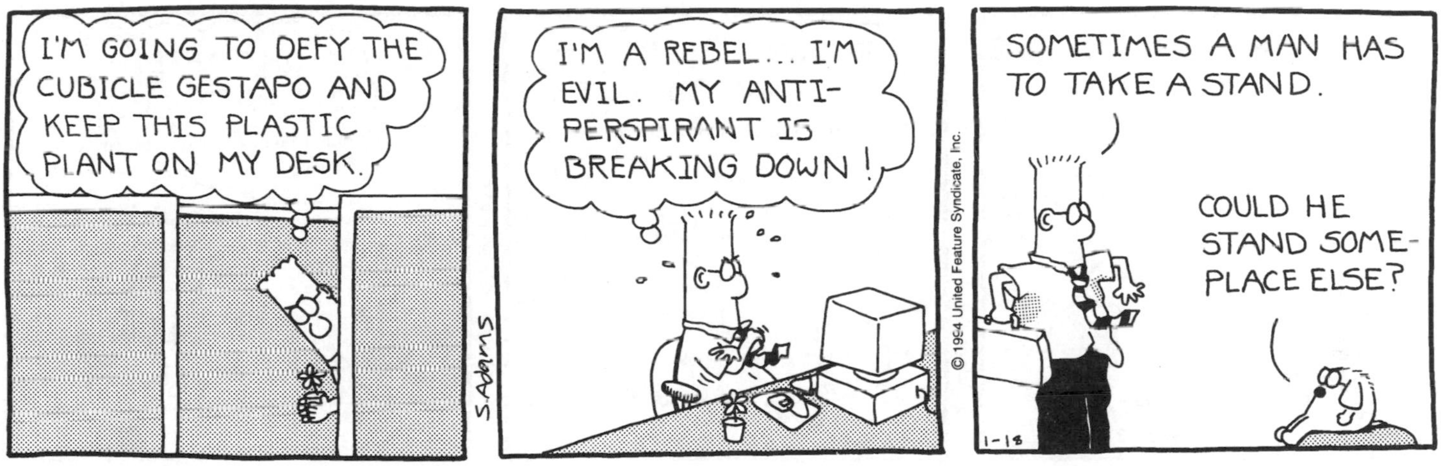
I'M GOING TO DEFY THE CUBICLE GESTAPO AND KEEP THIS PLASTIC PLANT ON MY DESK.
S. Adams
I'M A REBEL... I'M EVIL. MY ANTI-PERSPIRANT IS BREAKING DOWN!
© 1994 United Feature Syndicate, Inc.
SOMETIMES A MAN HAS TO TAKE A STAND.
COULD HE STAND SOME-PLACE ELSE?
1-18

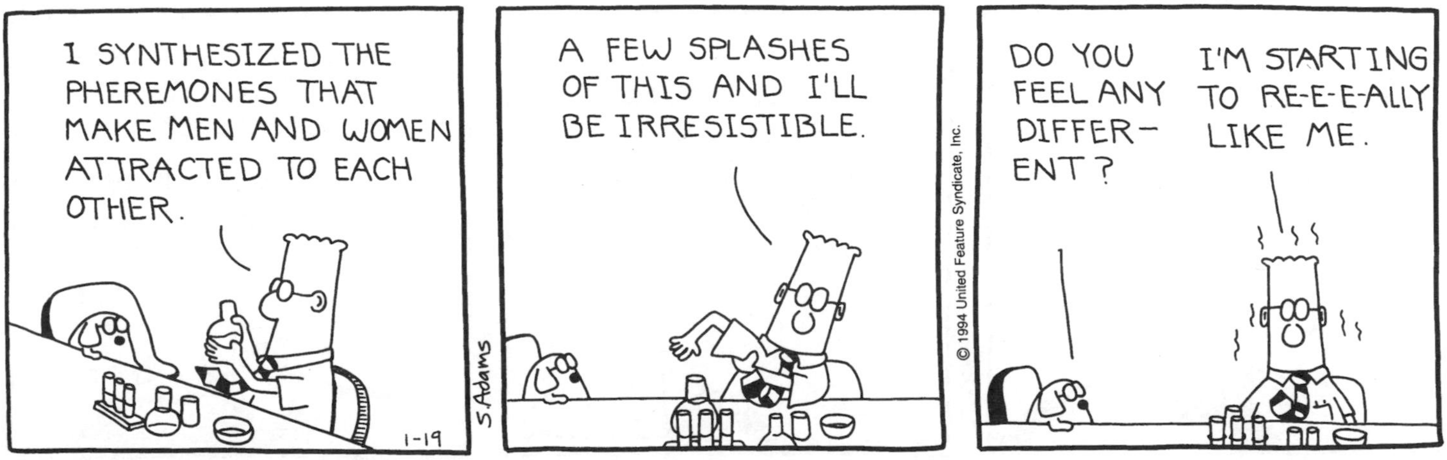
I SYNTHESIZED THE PHEREMONES THAT MAKE MEN AND WOMEN ATTRACTED TO EACH OTHER.
1-19
S. Adams
A FEW SPLASHES OF THIS AND I'LL BE IRRESISTIBLE.
© 1994 United Feature Syndicate, Inc.
DO YOU FEEL ANY DIFFER-ENT?
I'M STARTING TO RE-E-E-ALLY LIKE ME.

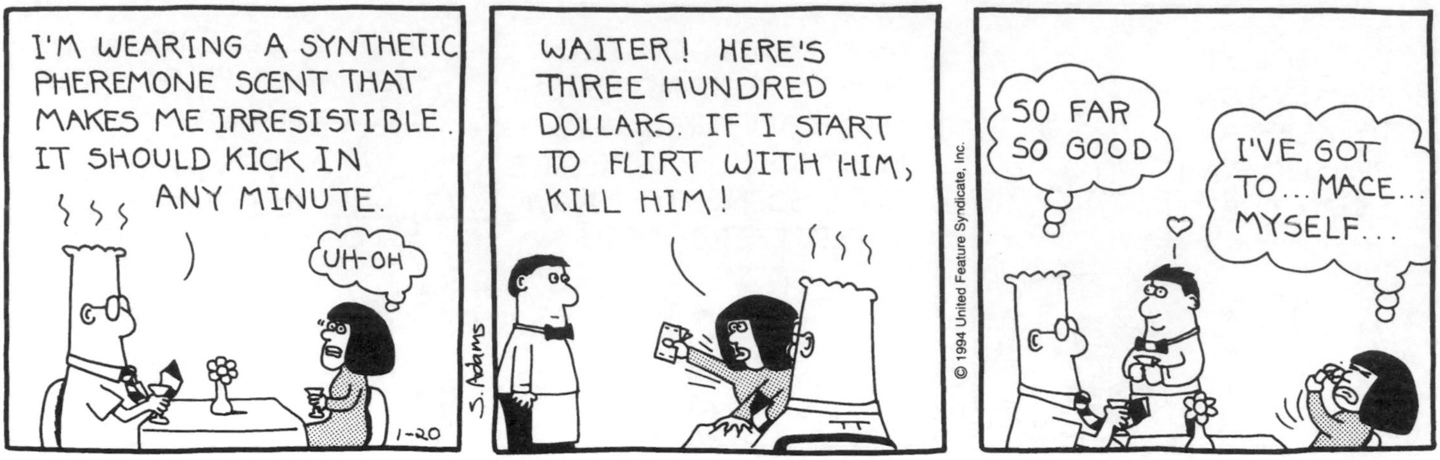
I'M WEARING A SYNTHETIC PHEREMONE SCENT THAT MAKES ME IRRESISTIBLE. IT SHOULD KICK IN ANY MINUTE.
UH-OH
S. Adams
1-20
WAITER! HERE'S THREE HUNDRED DOLLARS. IF I START TO FLIRT WITH HIM, KILL HIM!
© 1994 United Feature Syndicate, Inc.
SO FAR SO GOOD
I'VE GOT TO... MACE... MYSELF...

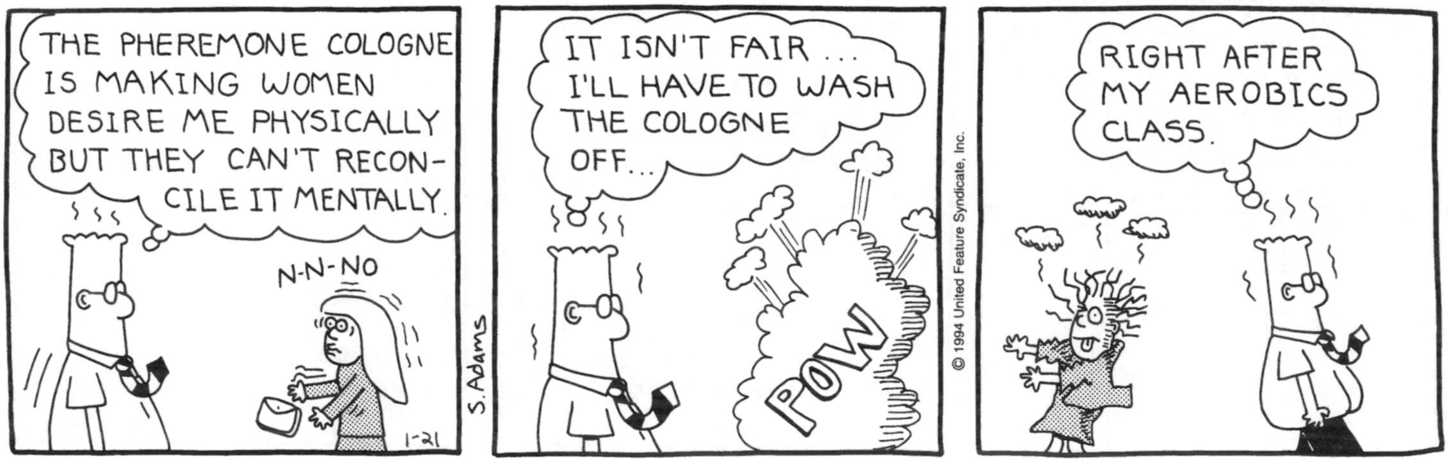
THE PHEREMONE COLOGNE IS MAKING WOMEN DESIRE ME PHYSICALLY BUT THEY CAN'T RECONCILE IT MENTALLY.
N-N-NO
1-21
S. Adams
IT ISN'T FAIR... I'LL HAVE TO WASH THE COLOGNE OFF...
POW
© 1994 United Feature Syndicate, Inc.
RIGHT AFTER MY AEROBICS CLASS.

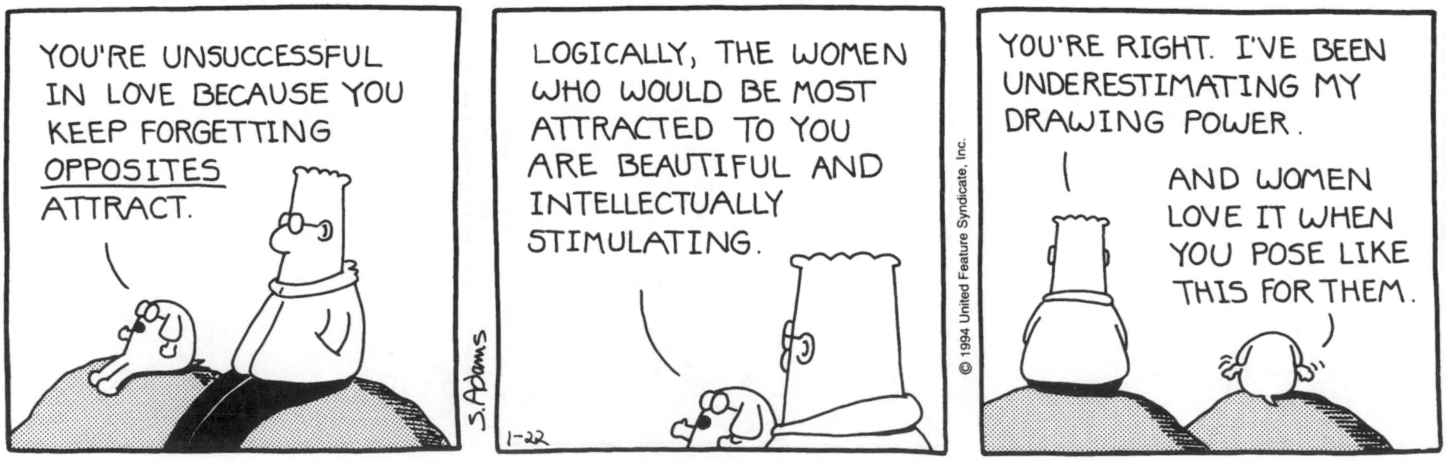
YOU'RE UNSUCCESSFUL IN LOVE BECAUSE YOU KEEP FORGETTING OPPOSITES ATTRACT.
S. Adams
1-22
LOGICALLY, THE WOMEN WHO WOULD BE MOST ATTRACTED TO YOU ARE BEAUTIFUL AND INTELLECTUALLY STIMULATING.
© 1994 United Feature Syndicate, Inc.
YOU'RE RIGHT. I'VE BEEN UNDERESTIMATING MY DRAWING POWER.
AND WOMEN LOVE IT WHEN YOU POSE LIKE THIS FOR THEM.

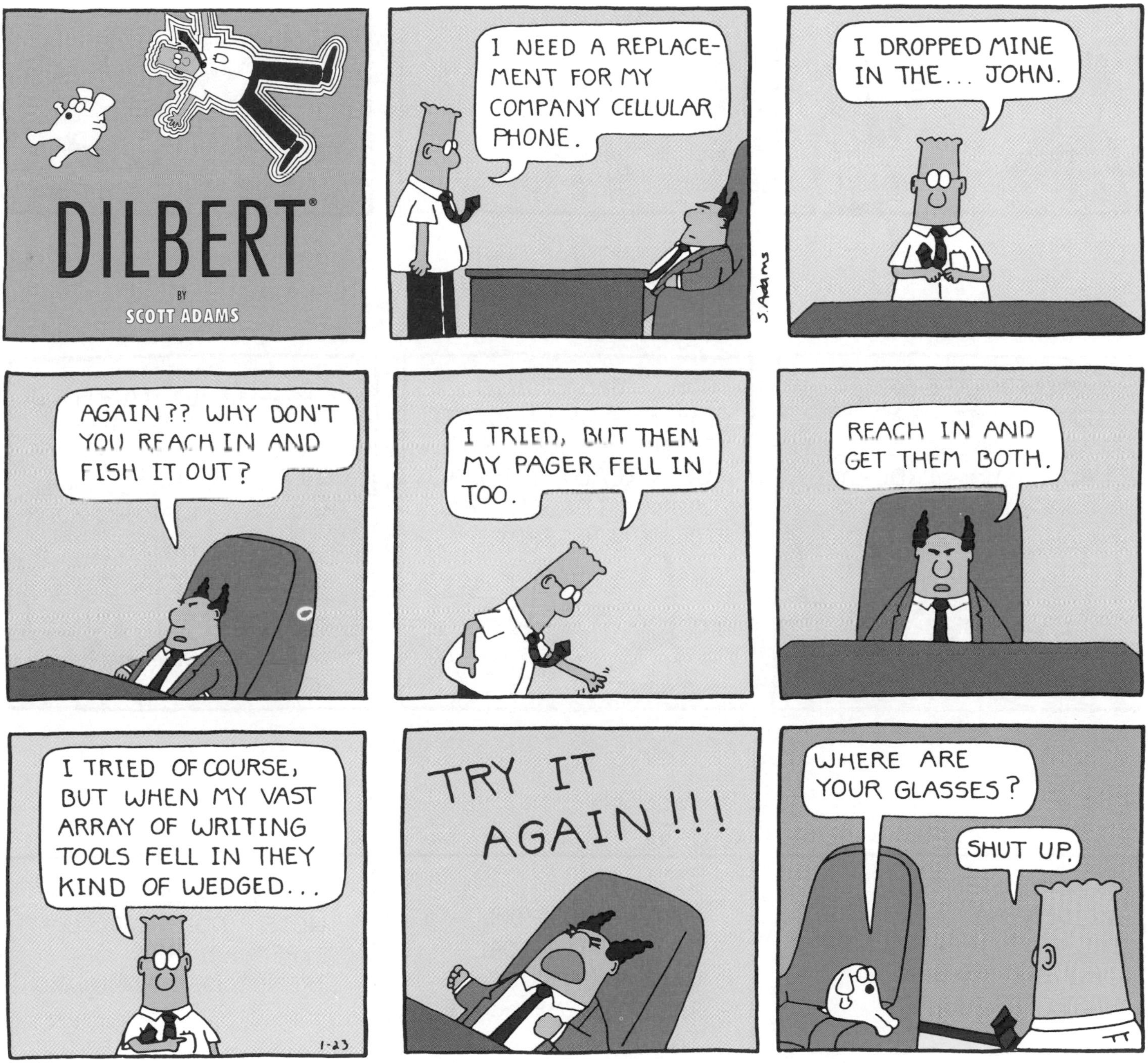
DILBERT®
BY SCOTT ADAMS
I NEED A REPLACEMENT FOR MY COMPANY CELLULAR PHONE.
I DROPPED MINE IN THE... JOHN.
AGAIN?? WHY DON'T YOU REACH IN AND FISH IT OUT?
I TRIED, BUT THEN MY PAGER FELL IN TOO.
REACH IN AND GET THEM BOTH.
I TRIED OF COURSE, BUT WHEN MY VAST ARRAY OF WRITING TOOLS FELL IN THEY KIND OF WEDGED...
TRY IT AGAIN!!!
WHERE ARE YOUR GLASSES?
SHUT UP.

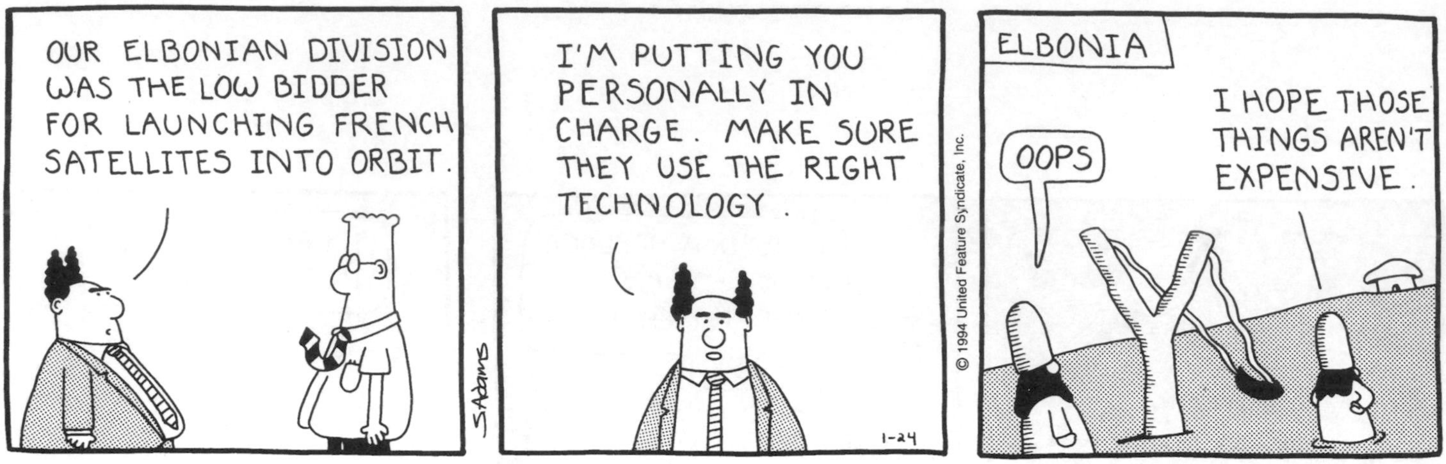
OUR ELBONIAN DIVISION WAS THE LOW BIDDER FOR LAUNCHING FRENCH SATELLITES INTO ORBIT.
I'M PUTTING YOU PERSONALLY IN CHARGE. MAKE SURE THEY USE THE RIGHT TECHNOLOGY.
ELBONIA
OOPS
I HOPE THOSE THINGS AREN'T EXPENSIVE.
S.Adams
1-24
© 1994 United Feature Syndicate, Inc.

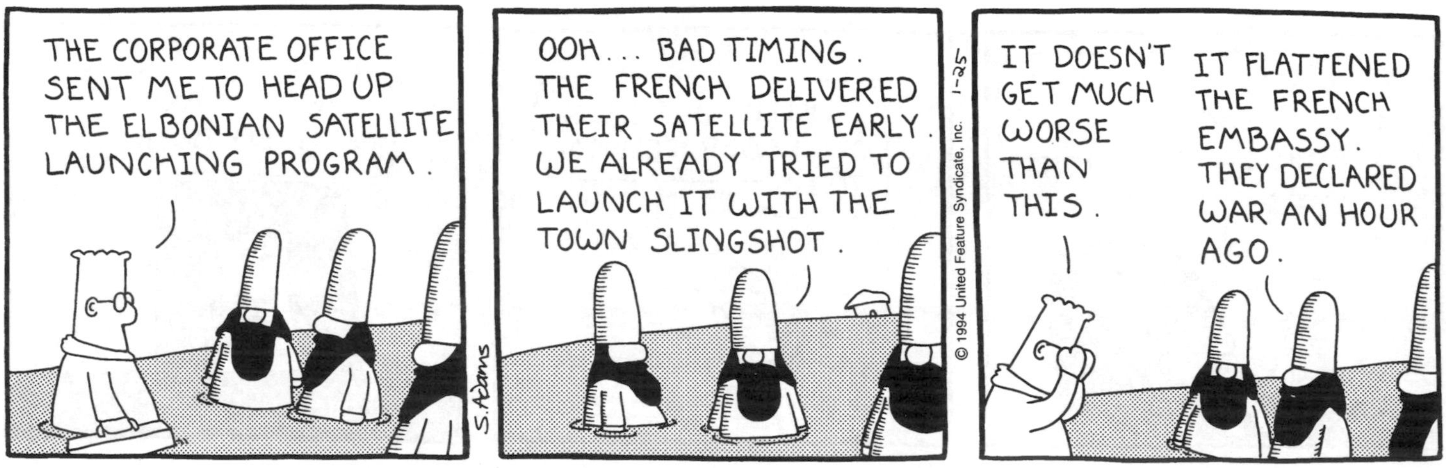
THE CORPORATE OFFICE SENT ME TO HEAD UP THE ELBONIAN SATELLITE LAUNCHING PROGRAM.
OOH... BAD TIMING. THE FRENCH DELIVERED THEIR SATELLITE EARLY. WE ALREADY TRIED TO LAUNCH IT WITH THE TOWN SLINGSHOT.
IT DOESN'T GET MUCH WORSE THAN THIS.
IT FLATTENED THE FRENCH EMBASSY. THEY DECLARED WAR AN HOUR AGO.
S.Adams
1-25
© 1994 United Feature Syndicate, Inc.

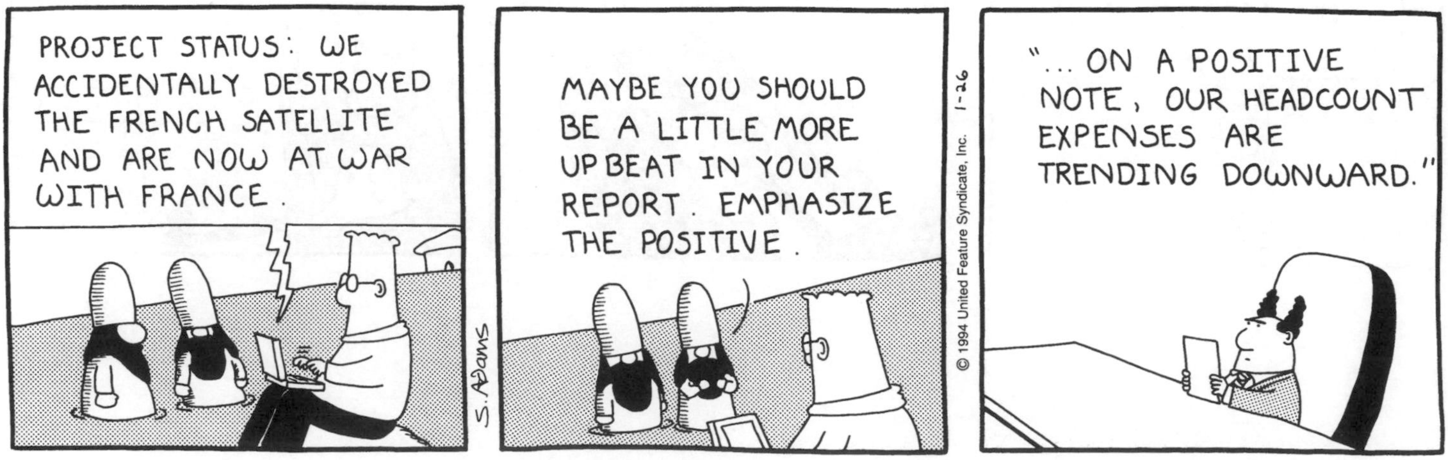
PROJECT STATUS: WE ACCIDENTALLY DESTROYED THE FRENCH SATELLITE AND ARE NOW AT WAR WITH FRANCE.
MAYBE YOU SHOULD BE A LITTLE MORE UPBEAT IN YOUR REPORT. EMPHASIZE THE POSITIVE.
"... ON A POSITIVE NOTE, OUR HEADCOUNT EXPENSES ARE TRENDING DOWNWARD."
S.Adams
1-26
© 1994 United Feature Syndicate, Inc.

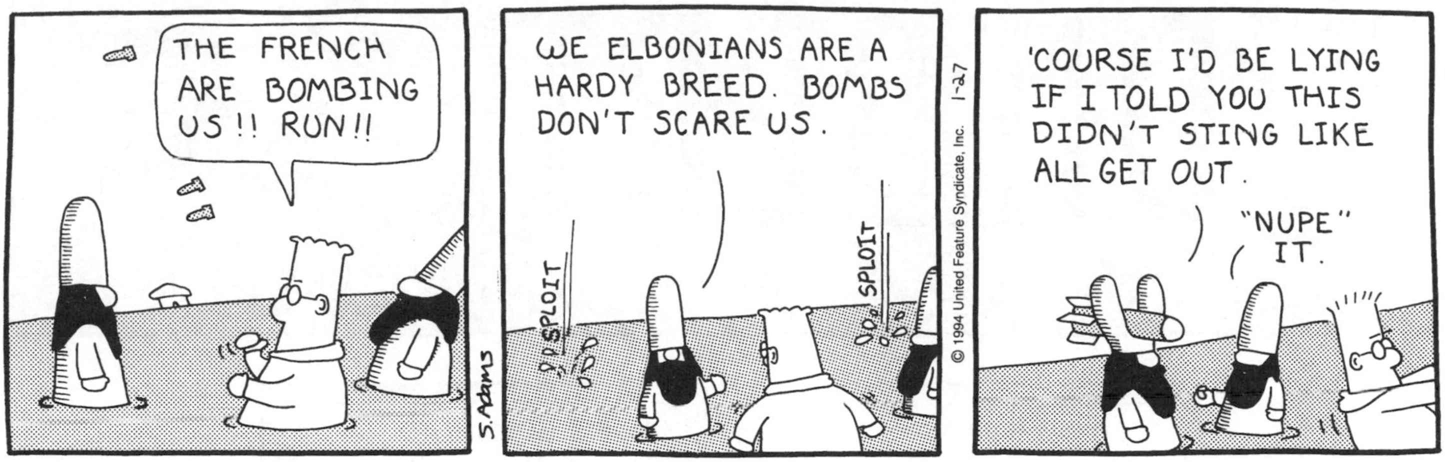
THE FRENCH ARE BOMBING US!! RUN!!
S. Adams
WE ELBONIANS ARE A HARDY BREED. BOMBS DON'T SCARE US.
SPLOIT
SPLOIT
1-27
© 1994 United Feature Syndicate, Inc.
'COURSE I'D BE LYING IF I TOLD YOU THIS DIDN'T STING LIKE ALL GET OUT.
"NUPE" IT.

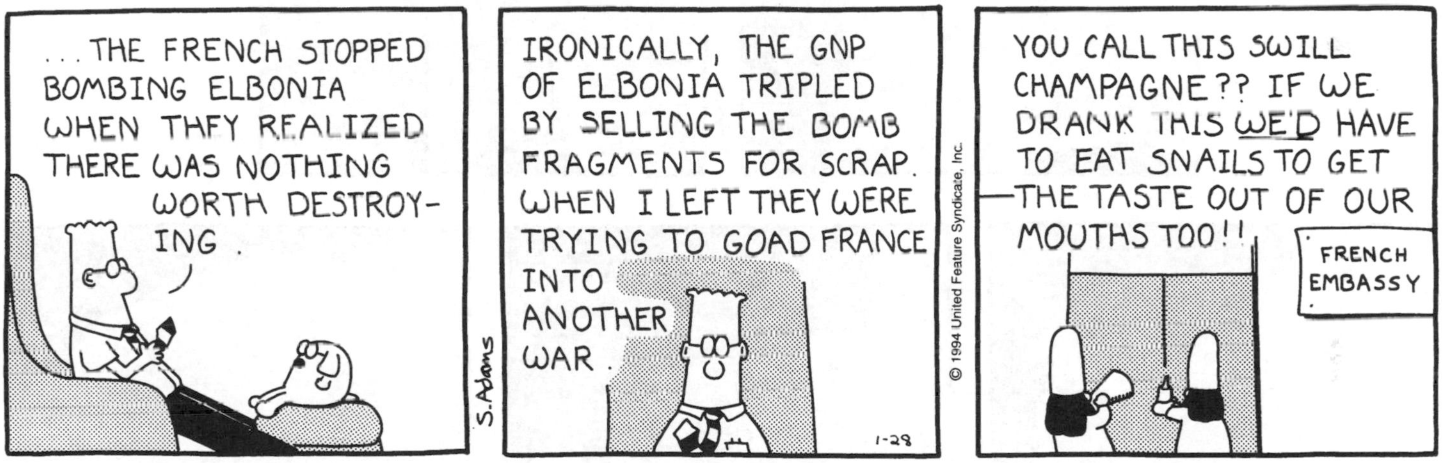
...THE FRENCH STOPPED BOMBING ELBONIA WHEN THEY REALIZED THERE WAS NOTHING WORTH DESTROY-ING.
S. Adams
IRONICALLY, THE GNP OF ELBONIA TRIPLED BY SELLING THE BOMB FRAGMENTS FOR SCRAP. WHEN I LEFT THEY WERE TRYING TO GOAD FRANCE INTO ANOTHER WAR.
1-28
© 1994 United Feature Syndicate, Inc.
YOU CALL THIS SWILL CHAMPAGNE?? IF WE DRANK THIS WE'D HAVE TO EAT SNAILS TO GET THE TASTE OUT OF OUR MOUTHS TOO!!
FRENCH EMBASSY

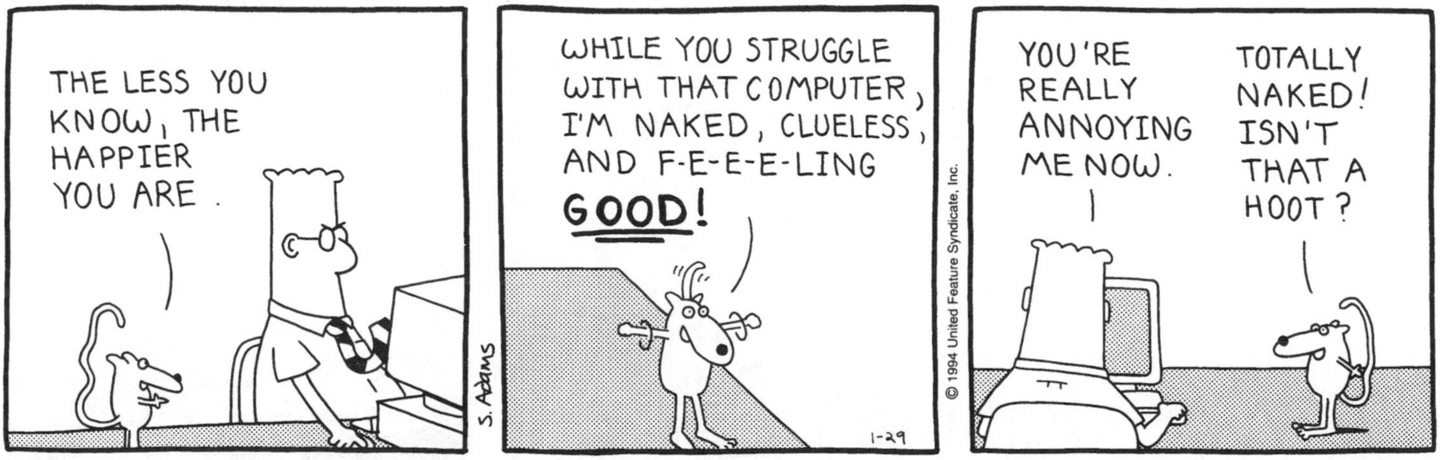
THE LESS YOU KNOW, THE HAPPIER YOU ARE.
S. Adams
WHILE YOU STRUGGLE WITH THAT COMPUTER, I'M NAKED, CLUELESS, AND F-E-E-E-LING GOOD!
1-29
© 1994 United Feature Syndicate, Inc.
YOU'RE REALLY ANNOYING ME NOW.
TOTALLY NAKED! ISN'T THAT A HOOT?

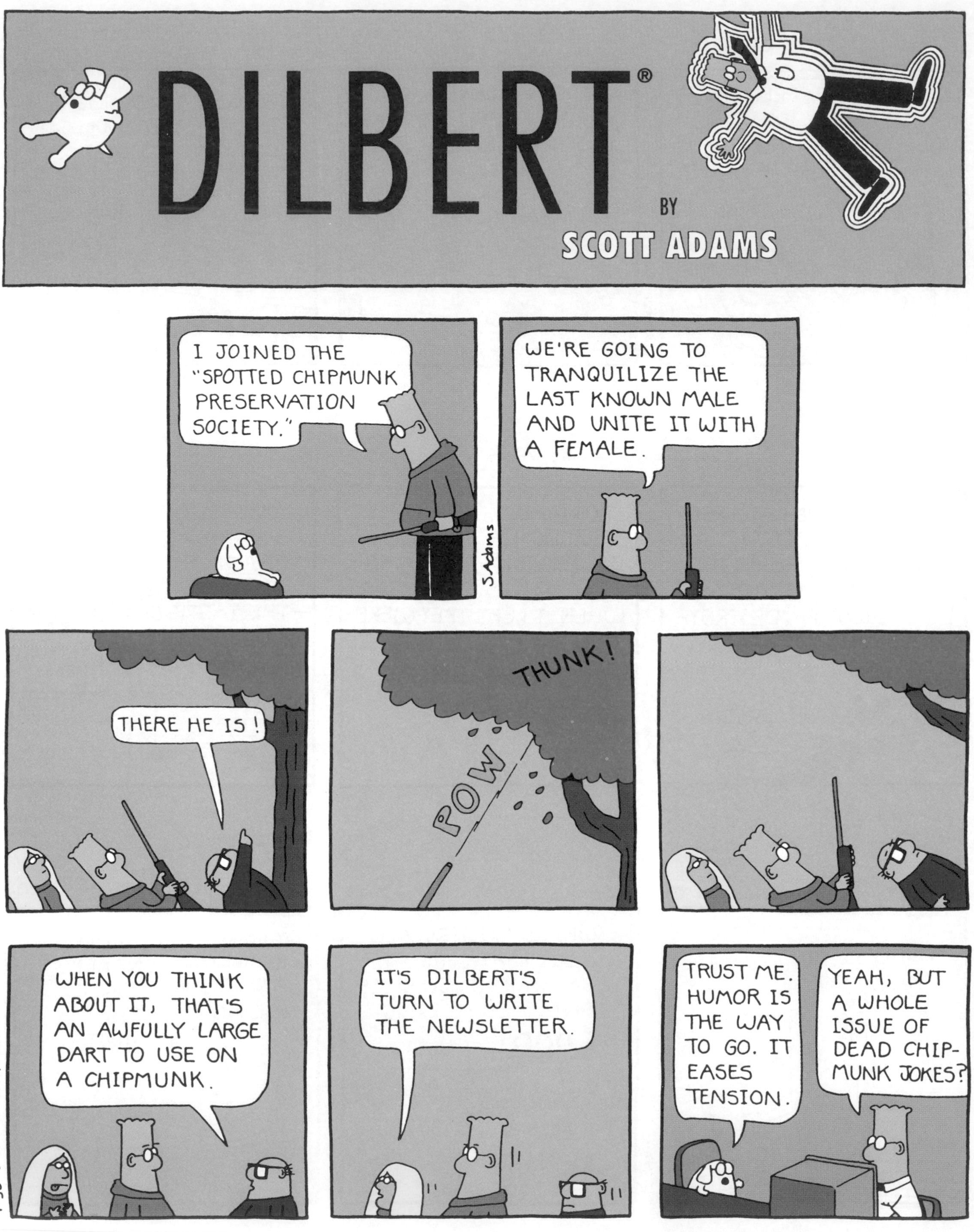
DILBERT®
BY
SCOTT ADAMS
I JOINED THE "SPOTTED CHIPMUNK PRESERVATION SOCIETY."
S.Adams
WE'RE GOING TO TRANQUILIZE THE LAST KNOWN MALE AND UNITE IT WITH A FEMALE.
THERE HE IS!
THUNK!
POW
WHEN YOU THINK ABOUT IT, THAT'S AN AWFULLY LARGE DART TO USE ON A CHIPMUNK.
IT'S DILBERT'S TURN TO WRITE THE NEWSLETTER.
TRUST ME. HUMOR IS THE WAY TO GO. IT EASES TENSION.
YEAH, BUT A WHOLE ISSUE OF DEAD CHIP-MUNK JOKES?
1-30 © 1994 United Feature Syndicate, Inc.

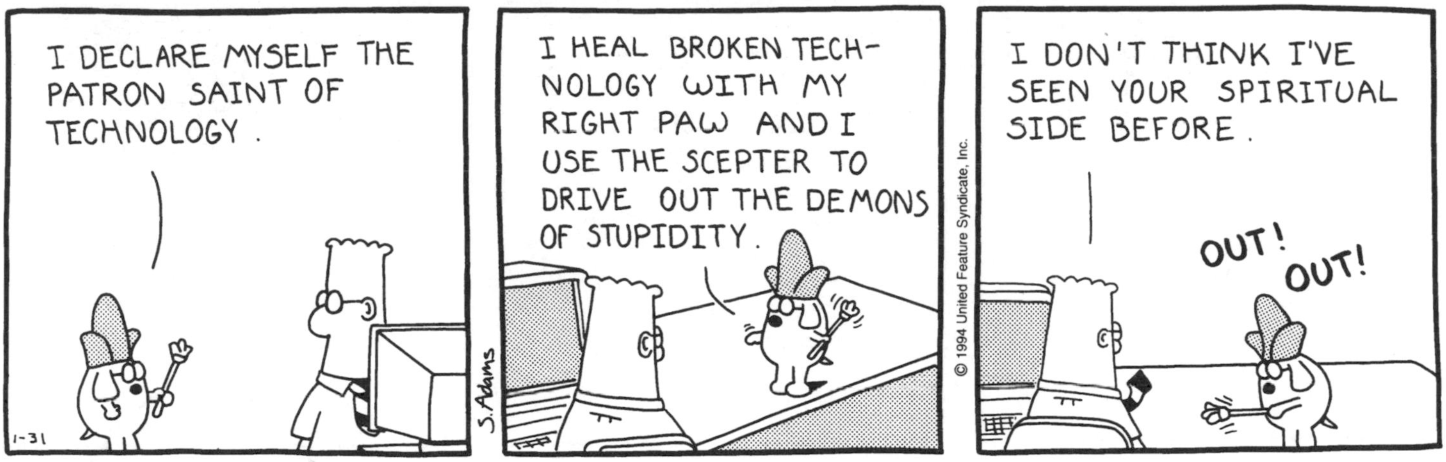
I DECLARE MYSELF THE PATRON SAINT OF TECHNOLOGY.
1-31
I HEAL BROKEN TECHNOLOGY WITH MY RIGHT PAW AND I USE THE SCEPTER TO DRIVE OUT THE DEMONS OF STUPIDITY.
S. Adams
© 1994 United Feature Syndicate, Inc.
I DON'T THINK I'VE SEEN YOUR SPIRITUAL SIDE BEFORE.
OUT! OUT!

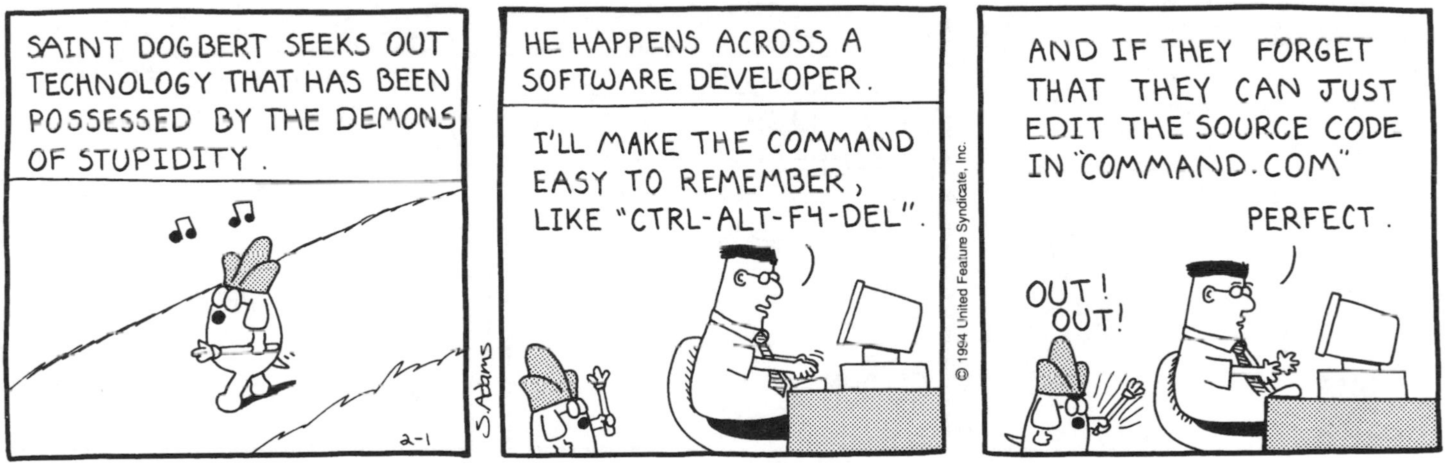
SAINT DOGBERT SEEKS OUT TECHNOLOGY THAT HAS BEEN POSSESSED BY THE DEMONS OF STUPIDITY.
2-1
S. Adams
HE HAPPENS ACROSS A SOFTWARE DEVELOPER.
I'LL MAKE THE COMMAND EASY TO REMEMBER, LIKE "CTRL-ALT-F4-DEL".
© 1994 United Feature Syndicate, Inc.
AND IF THEY FORGET THAT THEY CAN JUST EDIT THE SOURCE CODE IN "COMMAND.COM"
PERFECT.
OUT! OUT!

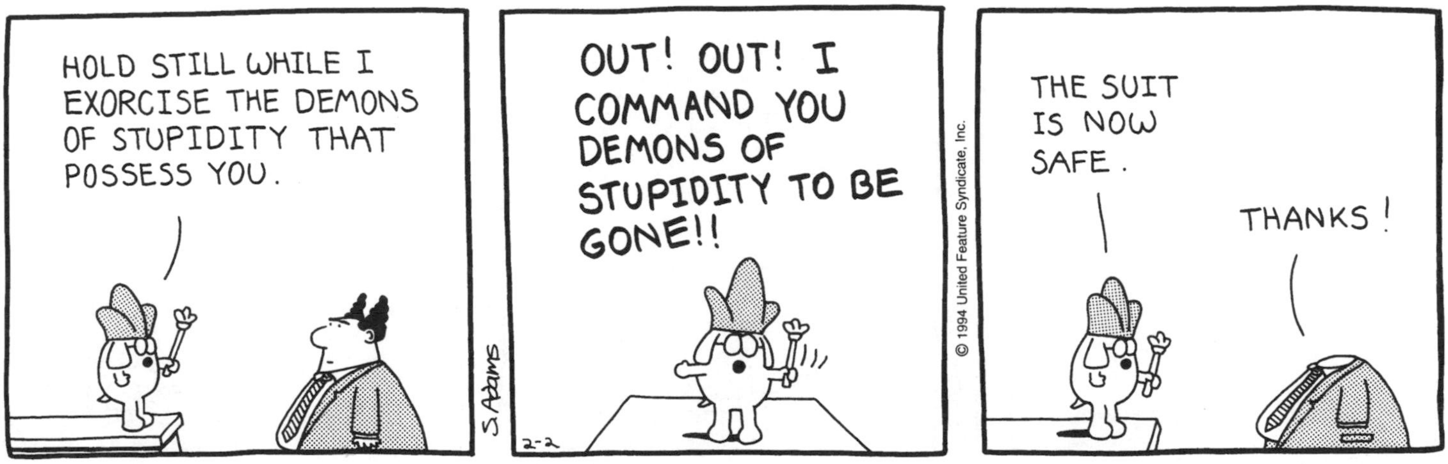
HOLD STILL WHILE I EXORCISE THE DEMONS OF STUPIDITY THAT POSSESS YOU.
S. Adams
OUT! OUT! I COMMAND YOU DEMONS OF STUPIDITY TO BE GONE!!
2-2
© 1994 United Feature Syndicate, Inc.
THE SUIT IS NOW SAFE.
THANKS!

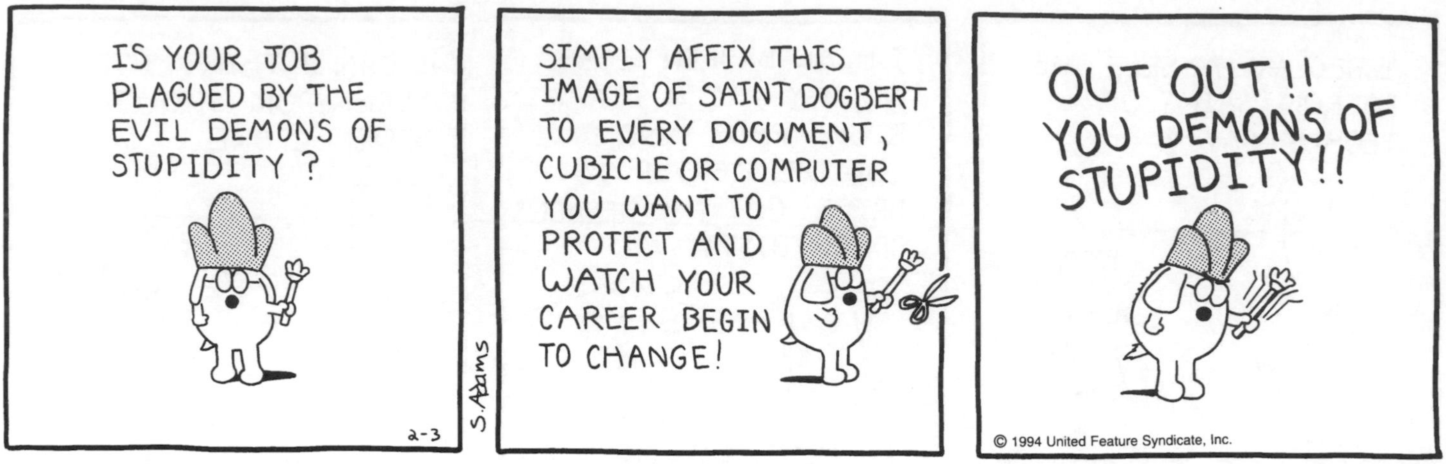
IS YOUR JOB PLAGUED BY THE EVIL DEMONS OF STUPIDITY ?
SIMPLY AFFIX THIS IMAGE OF SAINT DOGBERT TO EVERY DOCUMENT, CUBICLE OR COMPUTER YOU WANT TO PROTECT AND WATCH YOUR CAREER BEGIN TO CHANGE!
OUT OUT!! YOU DEMONS OF STUPIDITY!!
© 1994 United Feature Syndicate, Inc.

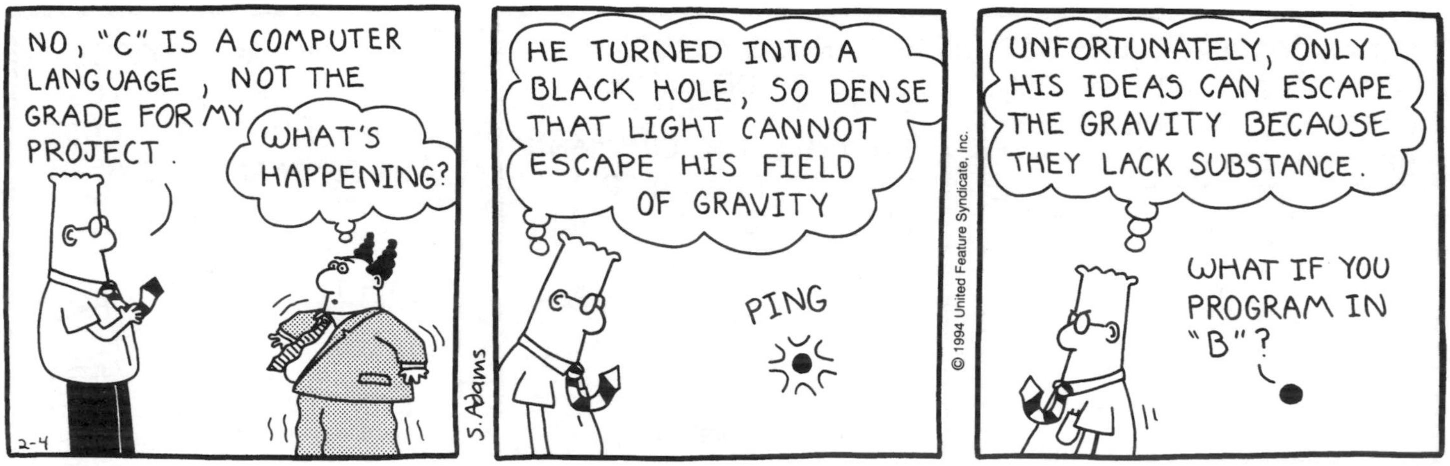
NO, "C" IS A COMPUTER LANGUAGE, NOT THE GRADE FOR MY PROJECT.
WHAT'S HAPPENING?
HE TURNED INTO A BLACK HOLE, SO DENSE THAT LIGHT CANNOT ESCAPE HIS FIELD OF GRAVITY
PING
© 1994 United Feature Syndicate, Inc.
UNFORTUNATELY, ONLY HIS IDEAS CAN ESCAPE THE GRAVITY BECAUSE THEY LACK SUBSTANCE.
WHAT IF YOU PROGRAM IN "B"?

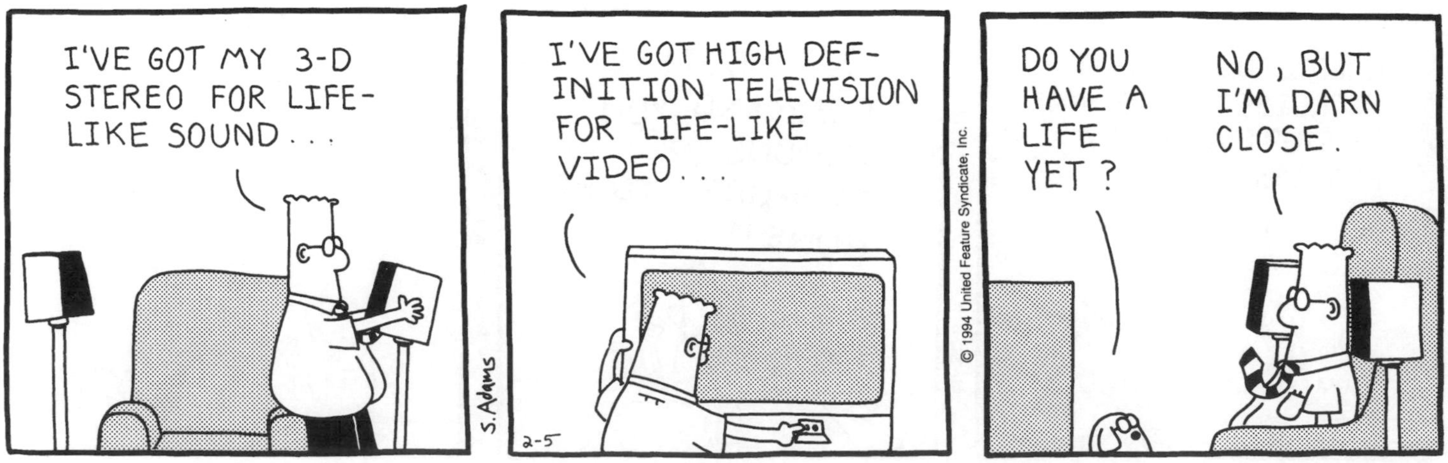
I'VE GOT MY 3-D STEREO FOR LIFE-LIKE SOUND...
I'VE GOT HIGH DEFINITION TELEVISION FOR LIFE-LIKE VIDEO...
© 1994 United Feature Syndicate, Inc.
DO YOU HAVE A LIFE YET ?
NO, BUT I'M DARN CLOSE.

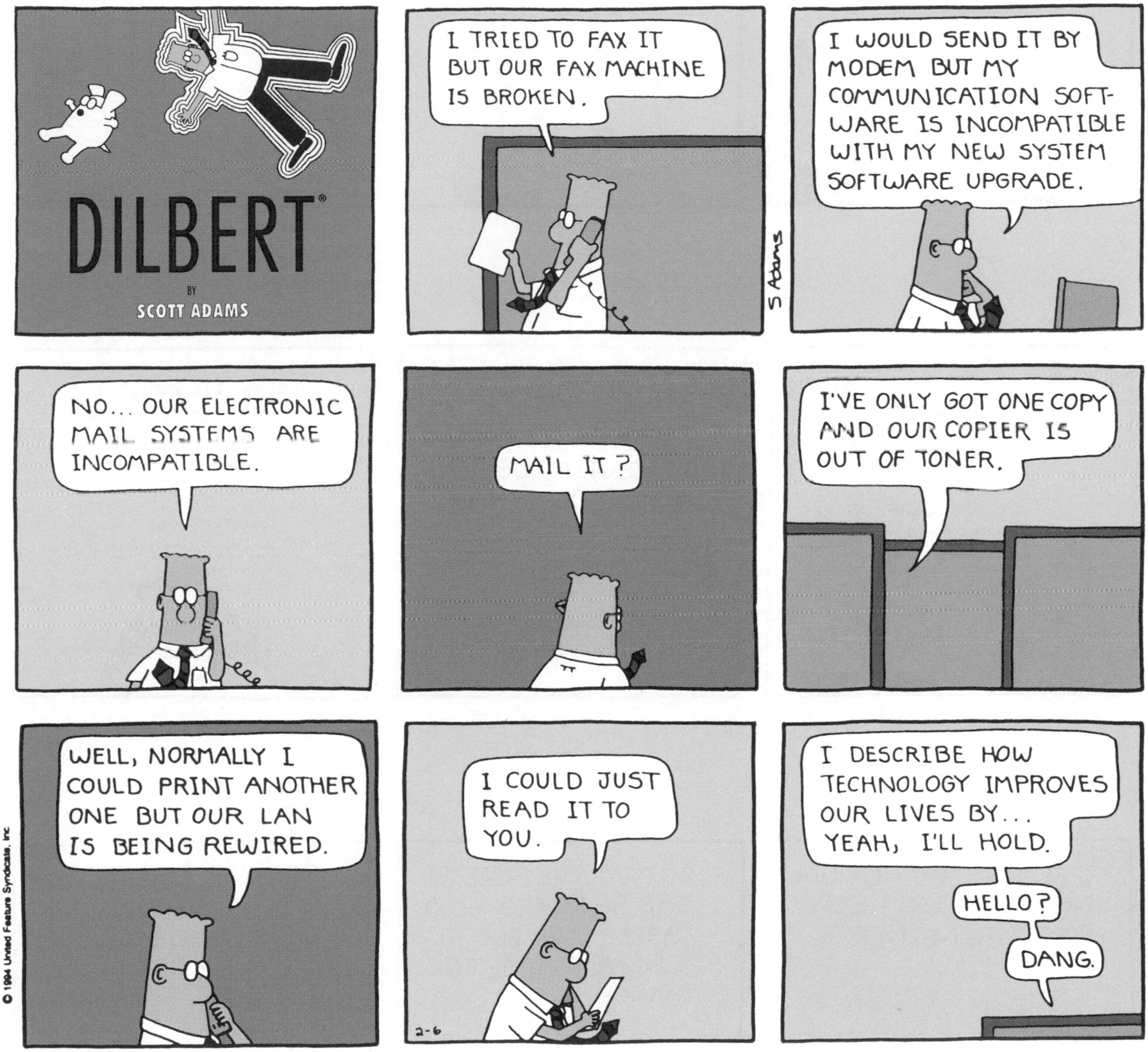
DILBERT®
BY
SCOTT ADAMS
I TRIED TO FAX IT BUT OUR FAX MACHINE IS BROKEN.
S Adams
I WOULD SEND IT BY MODEM BUT MY COMMUNICATION SOFT-WARE IS INCOMPATIBLE WITH MY NEW SYSTEM SOFTWARE UPGRADE.
NO... OUR ELECTRONIC MAIL SYSTEMS ARE INCOMPATIBLE.
MAIL IT?
I'VE ONLY GOT ONE COPY AND OUR COPIER IS OUT OF TONER.
© 1994 United Feature Syndicate, Inc.
WELL, NORMALLY I COULD PRINT ANOTHER ONE BUT OUR LAN IS BEING REWIRED.
I COULD JUST READ IT TO YOU.
2-6
I DESCRIBE HOW TECHNOLOGY IMPROVES OUR LIVES BY... YEAH, I'LL HOLD.
HELLO?
DANG.

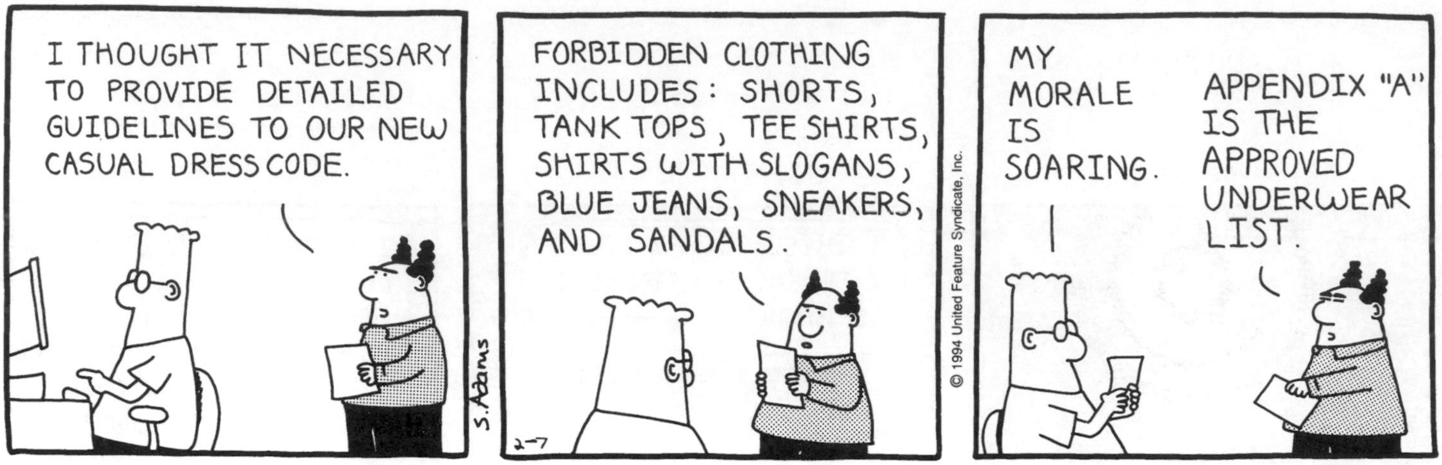
I THOUGHT IT NECESSARY TO PROVIDE DETAILED GUIDELINES TO OUR NEW CASUAL DRESS CODE.
S. Adams
FORBIDDEN CLOTHING INCLUDES: SHORTS, TANK TOPS, TEE SHIRTS, SHIRTS WITH SLOGANS, BLUE JEANS, SNEAKERS, AND SANDALS.
2-7
© 1994 United Feature Syndicate, Inc.
MY MORALE IS SOARING.
APPENDIX "A" IS THE APPROVED UNDERWEAR LIST.

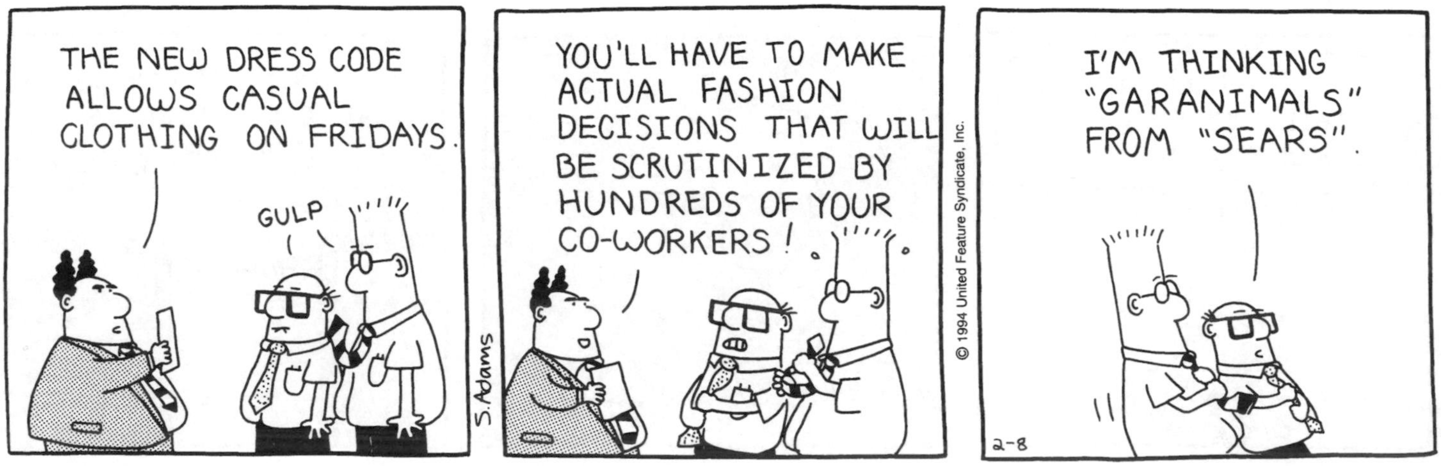
THE NEW DRESS CODE ALLOWS CASUAL CLOTHING ON FRIDAYS.
GULP
S. Adams
YOU'LL HAVE TO MAKE ACTUAL FASHION DECISIONS THAT WILL BE SCRUTINIZED BY HUNDREDS OF YOUR CO-WORKERS!
© 1994 United Feature Syndicate, Inc.
I'M THINKING "GARANIMALS" FROM "SEARS".
2-8

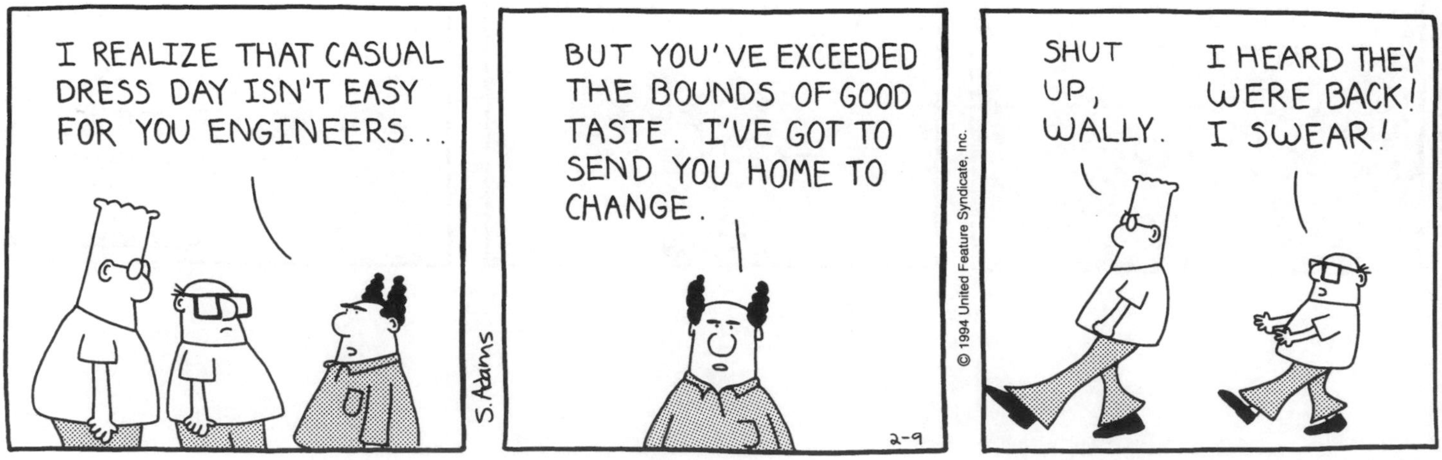
I REALIZE THAT CASUAL DRESS DAY ISN'T EASY FOR YOU ENGINEERS...
S. Adams
BUT YOU'VE EXCEEDED THE BOUNDS OF GOOD TASTE. I'VE GOT TO SEND YOU HOME TO CHANGE.
2-9
© 1994 United Feature Syndicate, Inc.
SHUT UP, WALLY.
I HEARD THEY WERE BACK! I SWEAR!

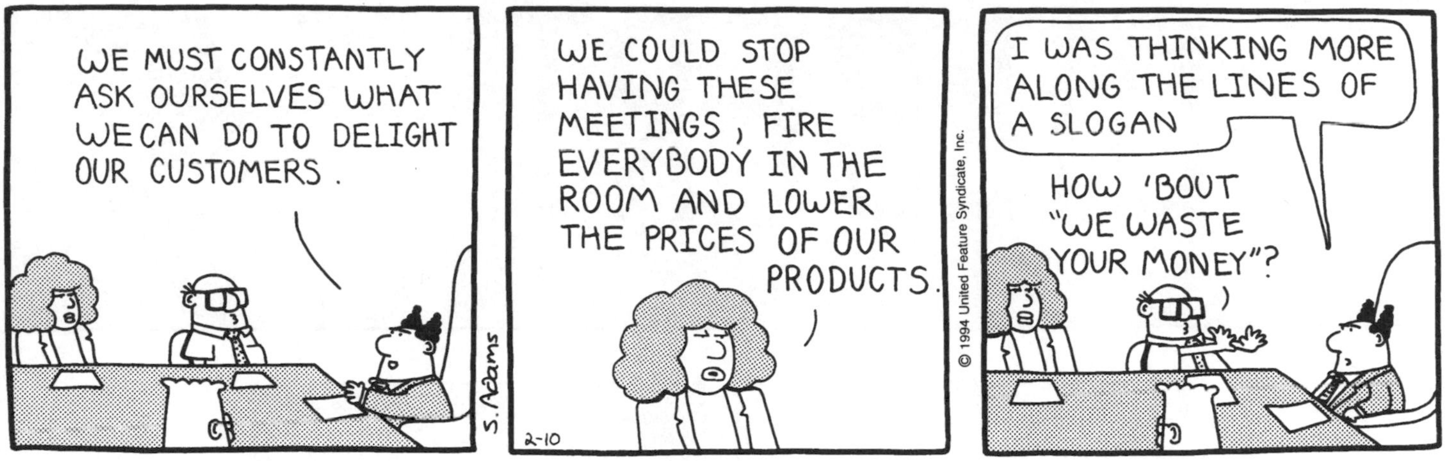
WE MUST CONSTANTLY ASK OURSELVES WHAT WE CAN DO TO DELIGHT OUR CUSTOMERS.
WE COULD STOP HAVING THESE MEETINGS, FIRE EVERYBODY IN THE ROOM AND LOWER THE PRICES OF OUR PRODUCTS.
I WAS THINKING MORE ALONG THE LINES OF A SLOGAN
HOW 'BOUT "WE WASTE YOUR MONEY"?
S. Adams
2-10

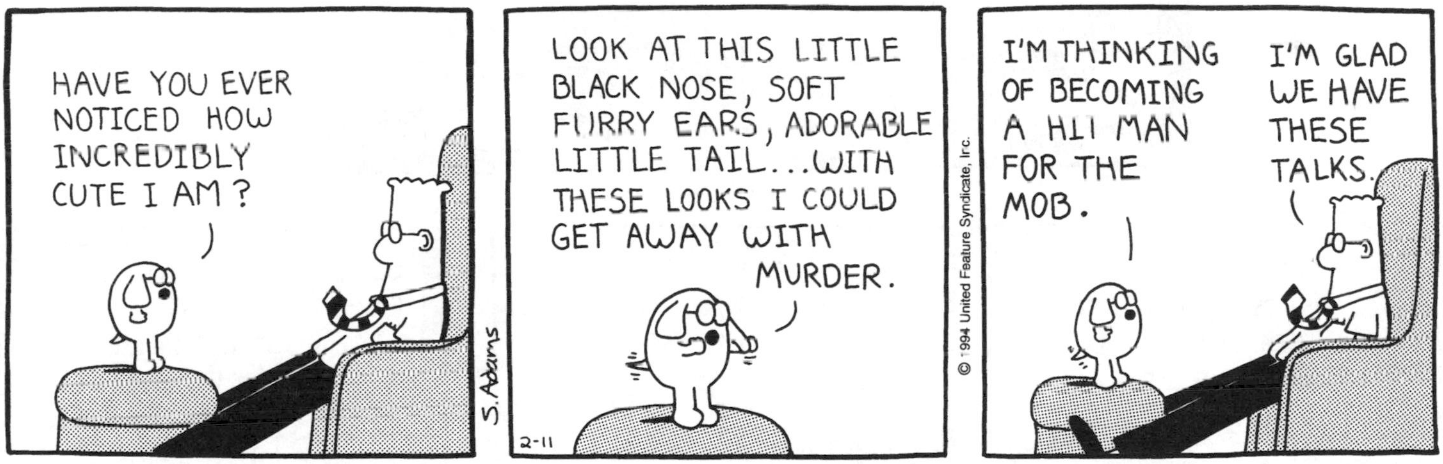
HAVE YOU EVER NOTICED HOW INCREDIBLY CUTE I AM?
LOOK AT THIS LITTLE BLACK NOSE, SOFT FURRY EARS, ADORABLE LITTLE TAIL...WITH THESE LOOKS I COULD GET AWAY WITH MURDER.
I'M THINKING OF BECOMING A HIT MAN FOR THE MOB.
I'M GLAD WE HAVE THESE TALKS.
S. Adams
2-11

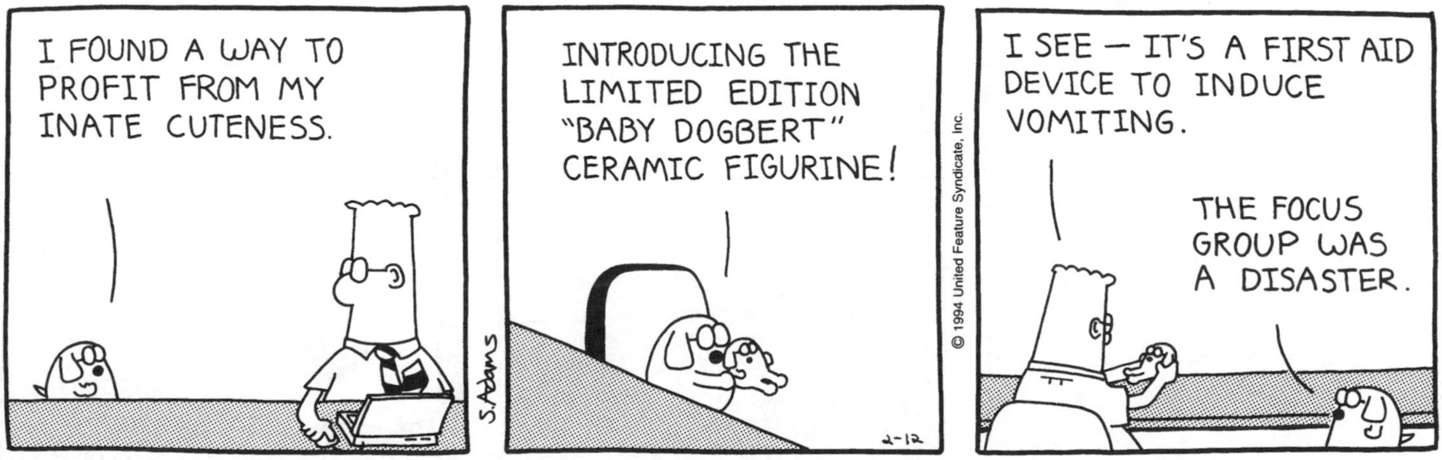
I FOUND A WAY TO PROFIT FROM MY INATE CUTENESS.
INTRODUCING THE LIMITED EDITION "BABY DOGBERT" CERAMIC FIGURINE!
I SEE — IT'S A FIRST AID DEVICE TO INDUCE VOMITING.
THE FOCUS GROUP WAS A DISASTER.
S. Adams
2-12

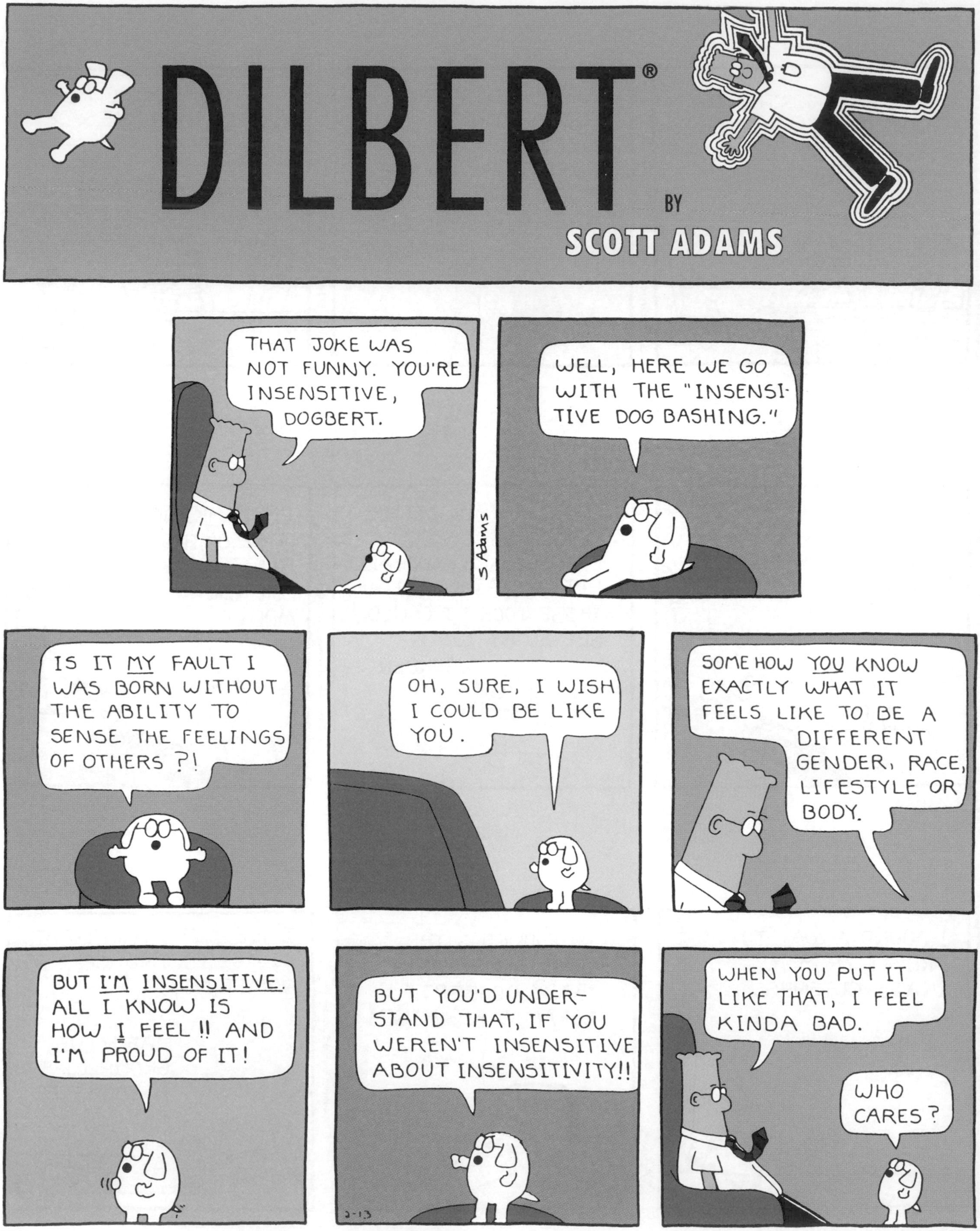
DILBERT®
BY
SCOTT ADAMS
THAT JOKE WAS NOT FUNNY. YOU'RE INSENSITIVE, DOGBERT.
S Adams
WELL, HERE WE GO WITH THE "INSENSITIVE DOG BASHING."
IS IT MY FAULT I WAS BORN WITHOUT THE ABILITY TO SENSE THE FEELINGS OF OTHERS ?!
OH, SURE, I WISH I COULD BE LIKE YOU.
SOME HOW YOU KNOW EXACTLY WHAT IT FEELS LIKE TO BE A DIFFERENT GENDER, RACE, LIFESTYLE OR BODY.
BUT I'M INSENSITIVE. ALL I KNOW IS HOW I FEEL !! AND I'M PROUD OF IT!
BUT YOU'D UNDERSTAND THAT, IF YOU WEREN'T INSENSITIVE ABOUT INSENSITIVITY!!
WHEN YOU PUT IT LIKE THAT, I FEEL KINDA BAD.
WHO CARES ?

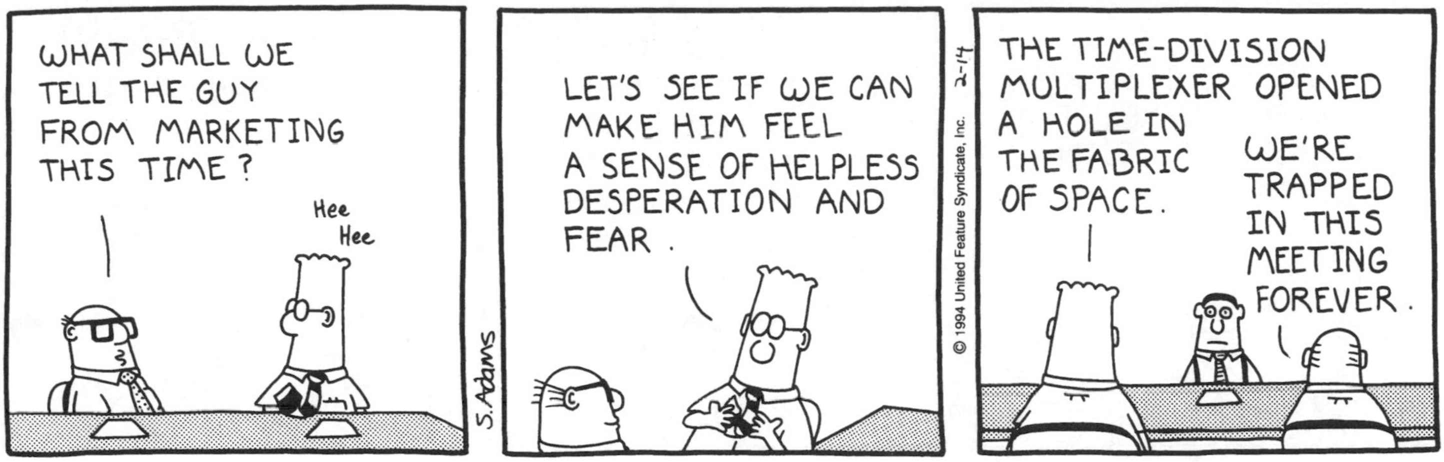
WHAT SHALL WE TELL THE GUY FROM MARKETING THIS TIME?
Hee Hee
S. Adams
LET'S SEE IF WE CAN MAKE HIM FEEL A SENSE OF HELPLESS DESPERATION AND FEAR.
2-14
© 1994 United Feature Syndicate, Inc.
THE TIME-DIVISION MULTIPLEXER OPENED A HOLE IN THE FABRIC OF SPACE.
WE'RE TRAPPED IN THIS MEETING FOREVER.

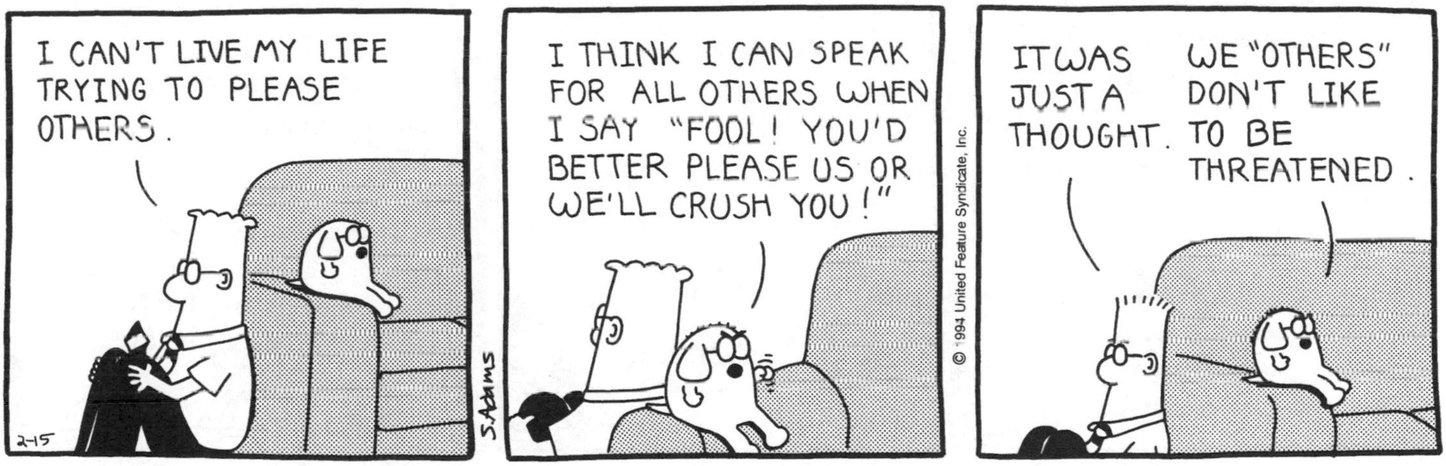
I CAN'T LIVE MY LIFE TRYING TO PLEASE OTHERS.
2-15
S. Adams
I THINK I CAN SPEAK FOR ALL OTHERS WHEN I SAY "FOOL! YOU'D BETTER PLEASE US OR WE'LL CRUSH YOU!"
© 1994 United Feature Syndicate, Inc.
IT WAS JUST A THOUGHT.
WE "OTHERS" DON'T LIKE TO BE THREATENED.

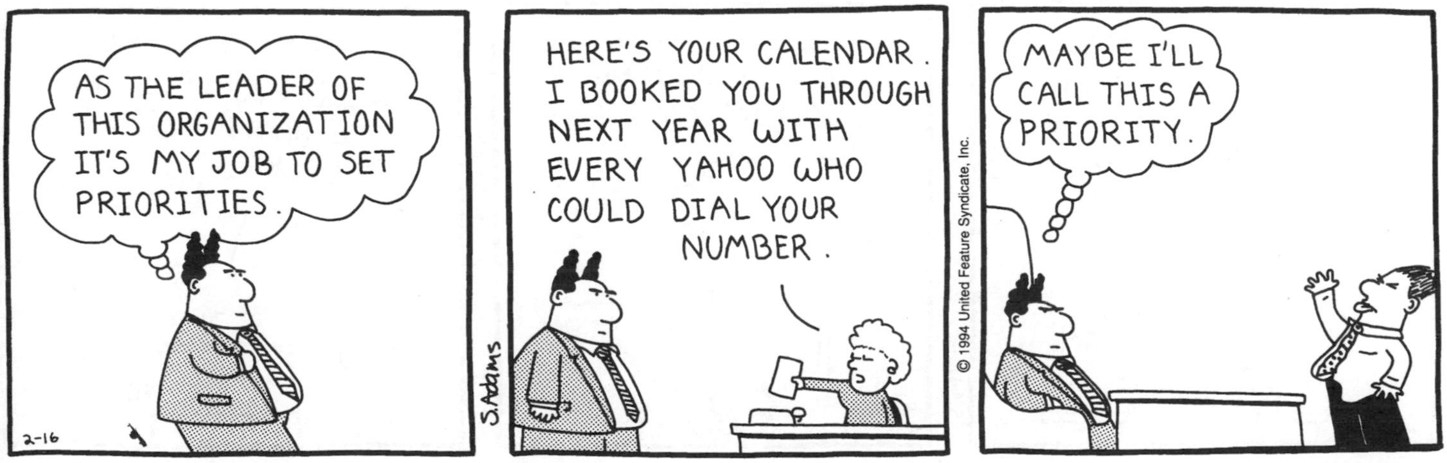
AS THE LEADER OF THIS ORGANIZATION IT'S MY JOB TO SET PRIORITIES.
2-16
S. Adams
HERE'S YOUR CALENDAR. I BOOKED YOU THROUGH NEXT YEAR WITH EVERY YAHOO WHO COULD DIAL YOUR NUMBER.
© 1994 United Feature Syndicate, Inc.
MAYBE I'LL CALL THIS A PRIORITY.

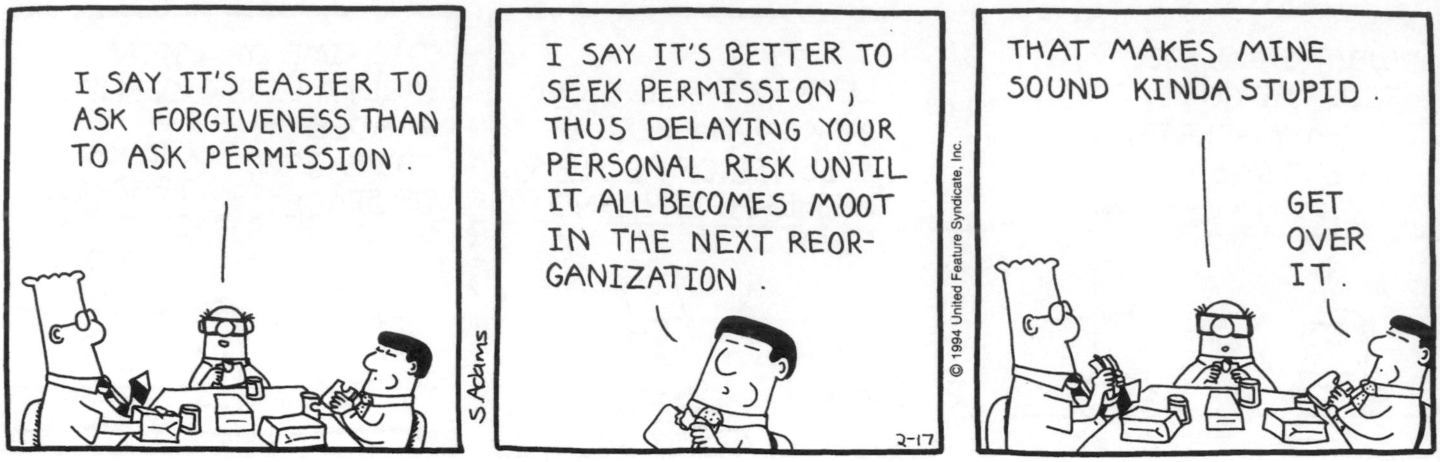
I SAY IT'S EASIER TO ASK FORGIVENESS THAN TO ASK PERMISSION.
I SAY IT'S BETTER TO SEEK PERMISSION, THUS DELAYING YOUR PERSONAL RISK UNTIL IT ALL BECOMES MOOT IN THE NEXT REORGANIZATION.
THAT MAKES MINE SOUND KINDA STUPID.
GET OVER IT.
S. Adams
2-17
© 1994 United Feature Syndicate, Inc.

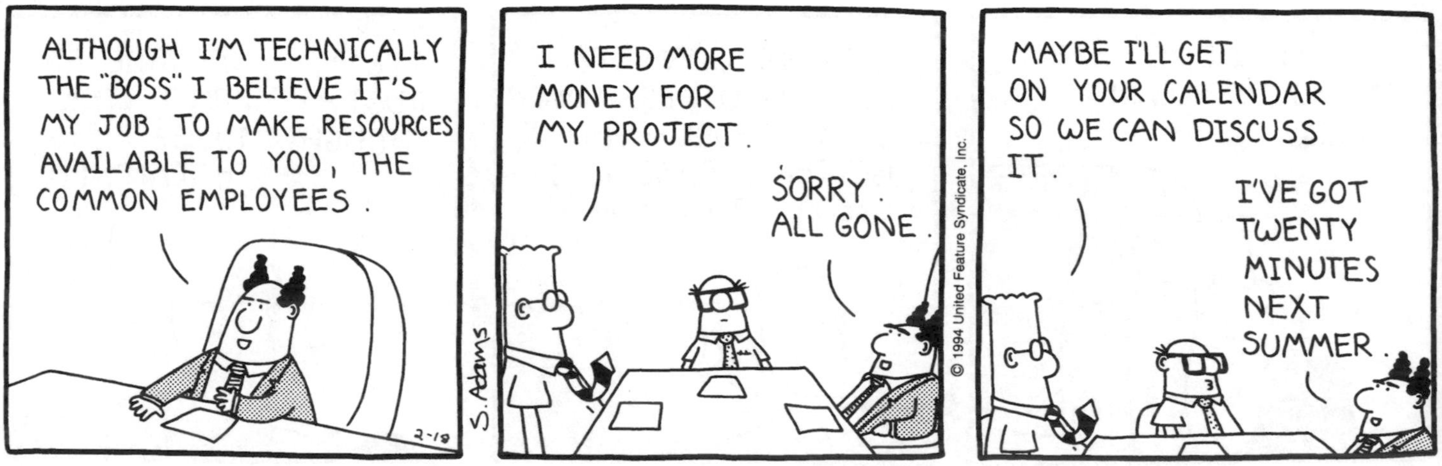
ALTHOUGH I'M TECHNICALLY THE "BOSS" I BELIEVE IT'S MY JOB TO MAKE RESOURCES AVAILABLE TO YOU, THE COMMON EMPLOYEES.
I NEED MORE MONEY FOR MY PROJECT.
SORRY. ALL GONE.
MAYBE I'LL GET ON YOUR CALENDAR SO WE CAN DISCUSS IT.
I'VE GOT TWENTY MINUTES NEXT SUMMER.
2-18
S. Adams
© 1994 United Feature Syndicate, Inc.

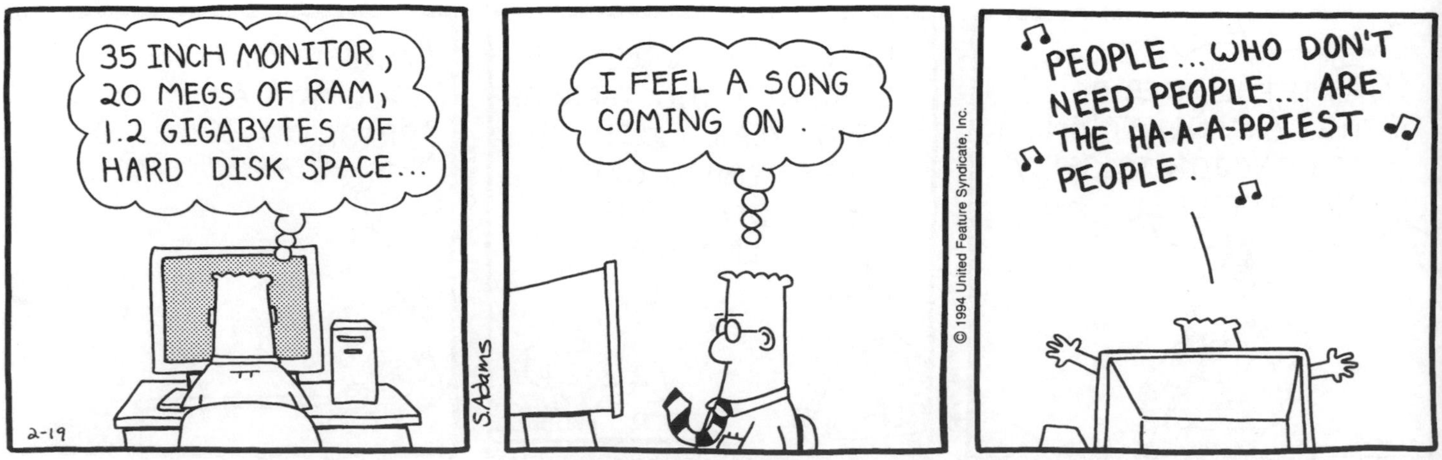
35 INCH MONITOR, 20 MEGS OF RAM, 1.2 GIGABYTES OF HARD DISK SPACE...
I FEEL A SONG COMING ON.
PEOPLE... WHO DON'T NEED PEOPLE... ARE THE HA-A-A-PPIEST PEOPLE.
2-19
S. Adams
© 1994 United Feature Syndicate, Inc.

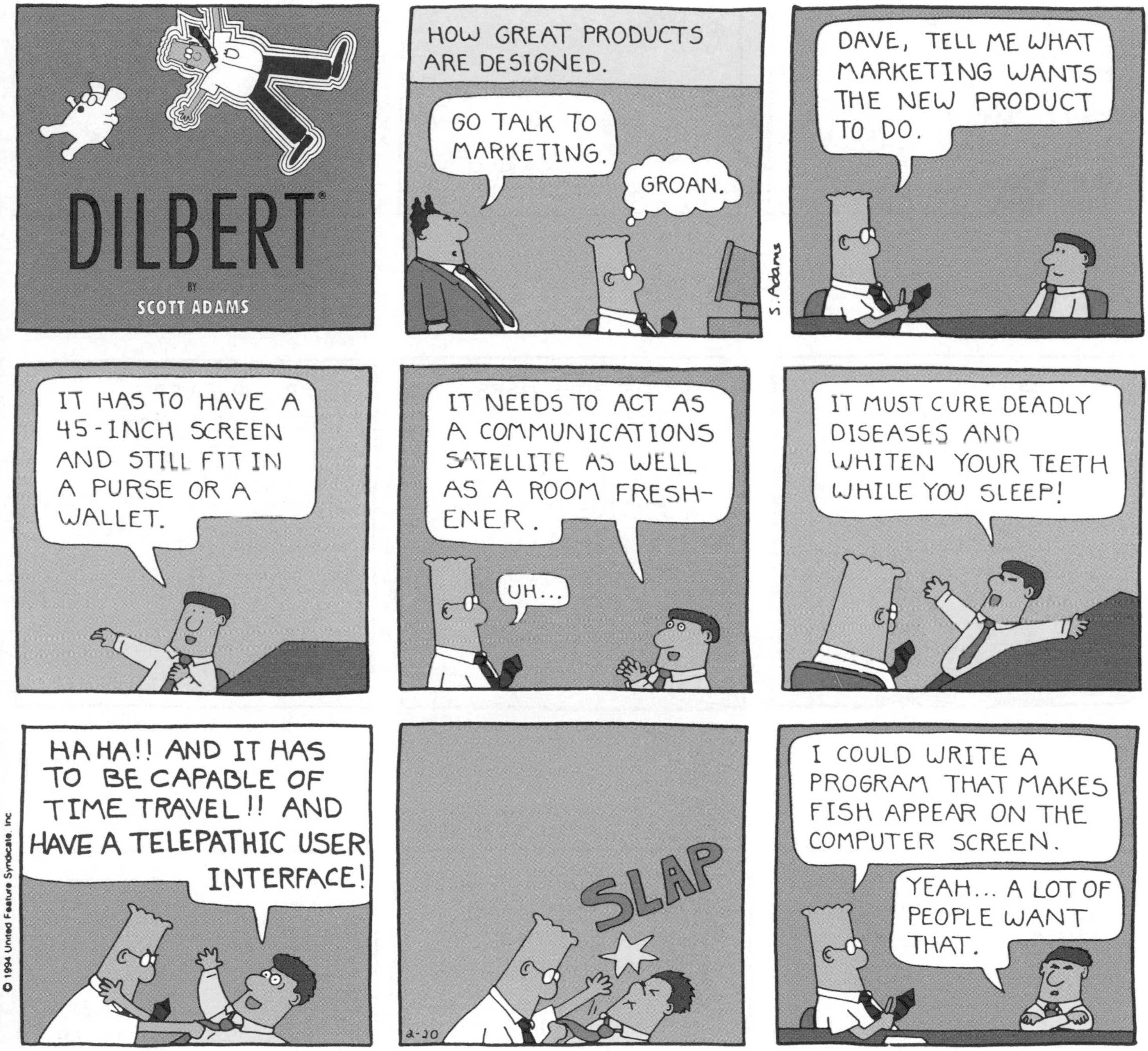
DILBERT®
BY
SCOTT ADAMS
HOW GREAT PRODUCTS ARE DESIGNED.
GO TALK TO MARKETING.
GROAN.
S. Adams
DAVE, TELL ME WHAT MARKETING WANTS THE NEW PRODUCT TO DO.
IT HAS TO HAVE A 45-INCH SCREEN AND STILL FIT IN A PURSE OR A WALLET.
IT NEEDS TO ACT AS A COMMUNICATIONS SATELLITE AS WELL AS A ROOM FRESH-ENER.
UH...
IT MUST CURE DEADLY DISEASES AND WHITEN YOUR TEETH WHILE YOU SLEEP!
HA HA!! AND IT HAS TO BE CAPABLE OF TIME TRAVEL!! AND HAVE A TELEPATHIC USER INTERFACE!
© 1994 United Feature Syndicate, Inc.
SLAP
2-20
I COULD WRITE A PROGRAM THAT MAKES FISH APPEAR ON THE COMPUTER SCREEN.
YEAH... A LOT OF PEOPLE WANT THAT.

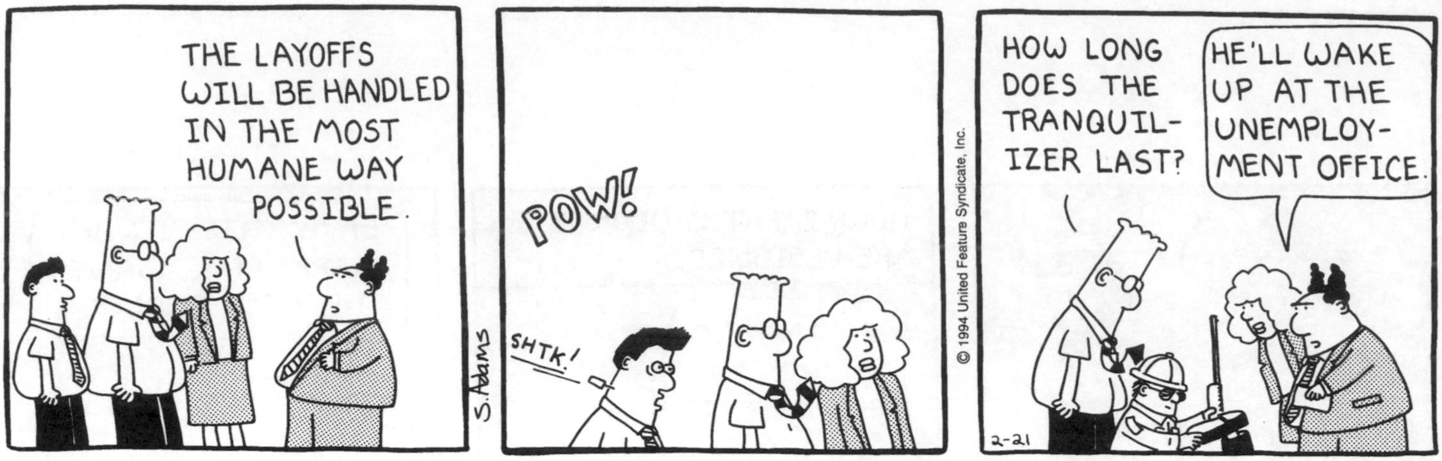
THE LAYOFFS WILL BE HANDLED IN THE MOST HUMANE WAY POSSIBLE.
S. Adams
POW!
SHTK!
© 1994 United Feature Syndicate, Inc.
HOW LONG DOES THE TRANQUIL-IZER LAST?
HE'LL WAKE UP AT THE UNEMPLOY-MENT OFFICE.
2-21

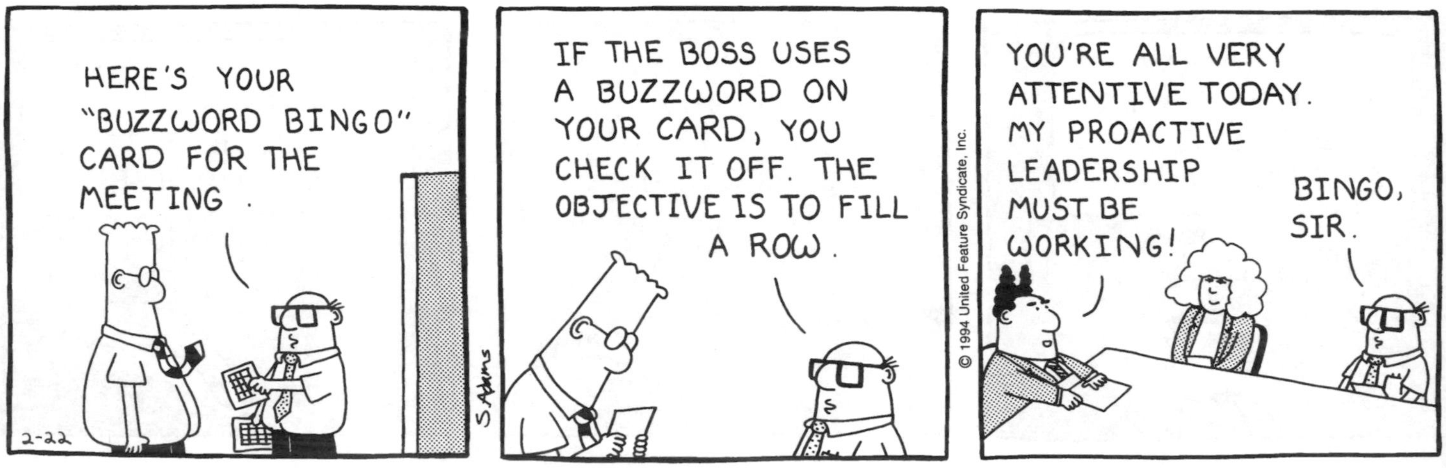
HERE'S YOUR "BUZZWORD BINGO" CARD FOR THE MEETING.
2-22
S. Adams
IF THE BOSS USES A BUZZWORD ON YOUR CARD, YOU CHECK IT OFF. THE OBJECTIVE IS TO FILL A ROW.
© 1994 United Feature Syndicate, Inc.
YOU'RE ALL VERY ATTENTIVE TODAY. MY PROACTIVE LEADERSHIP MUST BE WORKING!
BINGO, SIR.

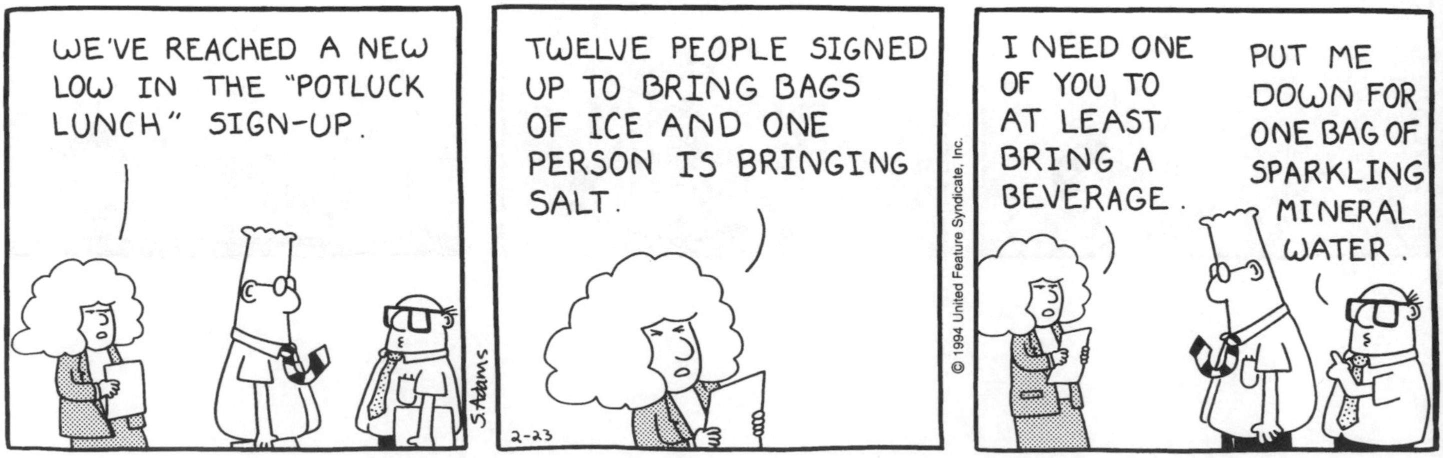
WE'VE REACHED A NEW LOW IN THE "POTLUCK LUNCH" SIGN-UP.
S. Adams
TWELVE PEOPLE SIGNED UP TO BRING BAGS OF ICE AND ONE PERSON IS BRINGING SALT.
2-23
© 1994 United Feature Syndicate, Inc.
I NEED ONE OF YOU TO AT LEAST BRING A BEVERAGE.
PUT ME DOWN FOR ONE BAG OF SPARKLING MINERAL WATER.

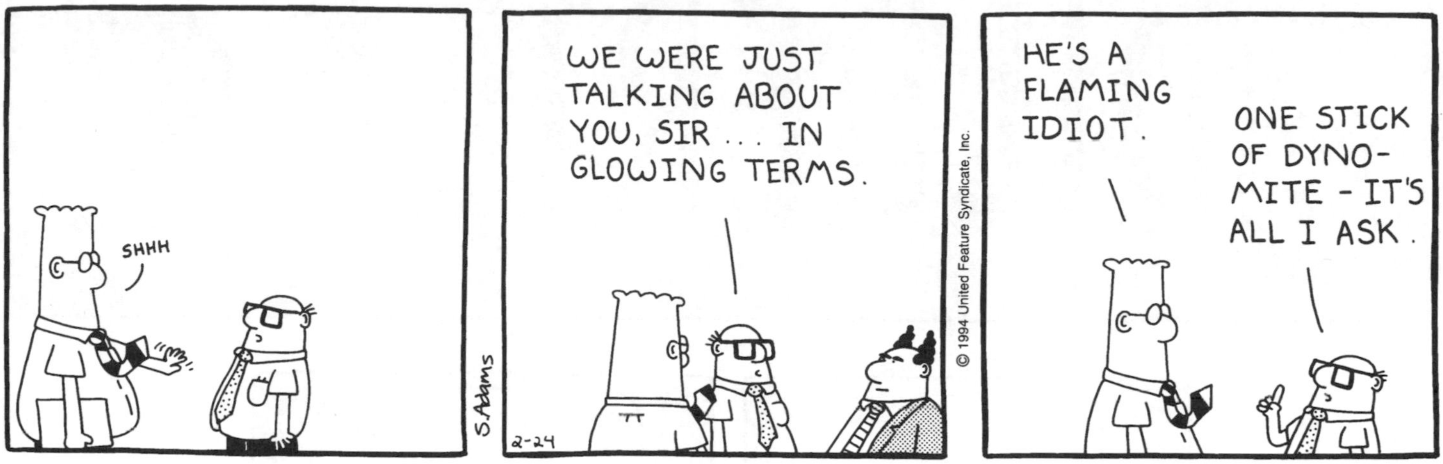
SHHH
S. Adams
WE WERE JUST TALKING ABOUT YOU, SIR . . . IN GLOWING TERMS.
2-24
© 1994 United Feature Syndicate, Inc.
HE'S A FLAMING IDIOT.
ONE STICK OF DYNO-MITE - IT'S ALL I ASK.

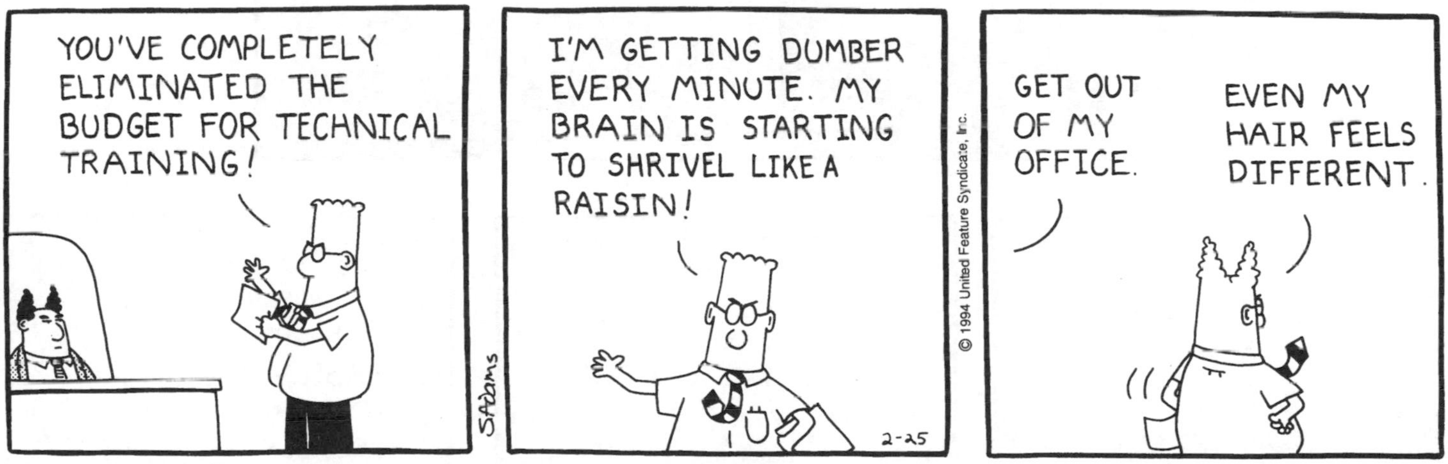
YOU'VE COMPLETELY ELIMINATED THE BUDGET FOR TECHNICAL TRAINING!
S.Adams
I'M GETTING DUMBER EVERY MINUTE. MY BRAIN IS STARTING TO SHRIVEL LIKE A RAISIN!
2-25
© 1994 United Feature Syndicate, Inc.
GET OUT OF MY OFFICE.
EVEN MY HAIR FEELS DIFFERENT.

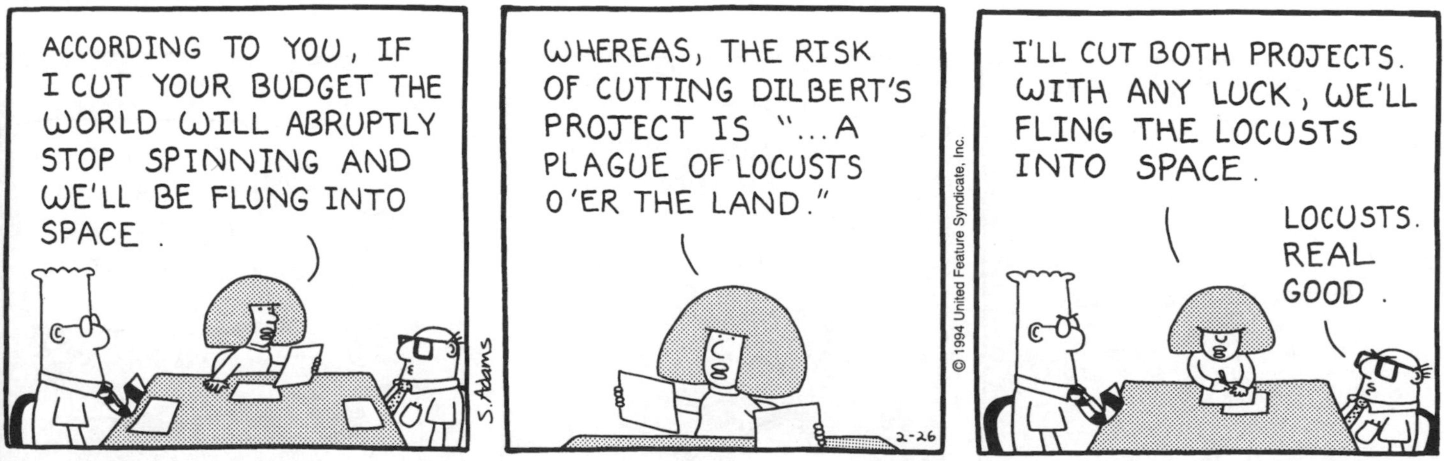
ACCORDING TO YOU, IF I CUT YOUR BUDGET THE WORLD WILL ABRUPTLY STOP SPINNING AND WE'LL BE FLUNG INTO SPACE.
S. Adams
WHEREAS, THE RISK OF CUTTING DILBERT'S PROJECT IS "...A PLAGUE OF LOCUSTS O'ER THE LAND."
2-26
© 1994 United Feature Syndicate, Inc.
I'LL CUT BOTH PROJECTS. WITH ANY LUCK, WE'LL FLING THE LOCUSTS INTO SPACE.
LOCUSTS. REAL GOOD.

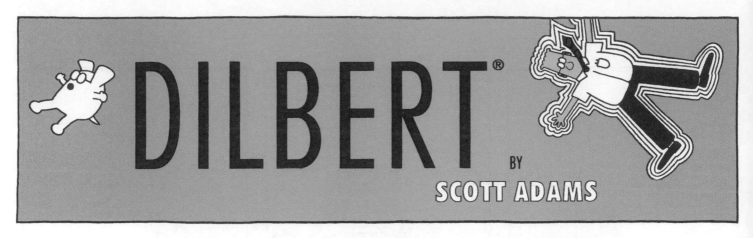

DILBERT® BY SCOTT ADAMS

HERE'S YOUR EMPLOYEE LOCATOR DEVICE.

SENSORS IN THE BUILDING WILL BE ABLE TO TRACK YOU AT ALL TIMES.

WE'LL KNOW HOW MANY TIMES YOU USE THE RESTROOM AND HOW LONG.

IT'S A DOG COLLAR... THE FINAL HUMILIATION.

ONCE YOU GOT USED TO WORKING IN CUBICLES, LIKE GERBILS, WE KNEW ANYTHING WAS POSSIBLE.

MY CONFORMANCE RATIONALIZATION MECHANISMS ARE KICKING IN.

2-27

IT'S NOT SO BAD. A COLLAR IS SIMPLY AN EFFICIENT DESIGN. EVERYONE IS DOING IT.

IT'S NOT SO BAD.

IT'S POWERED BY THIS SIX FOOT LONG EXTENSION CORD.

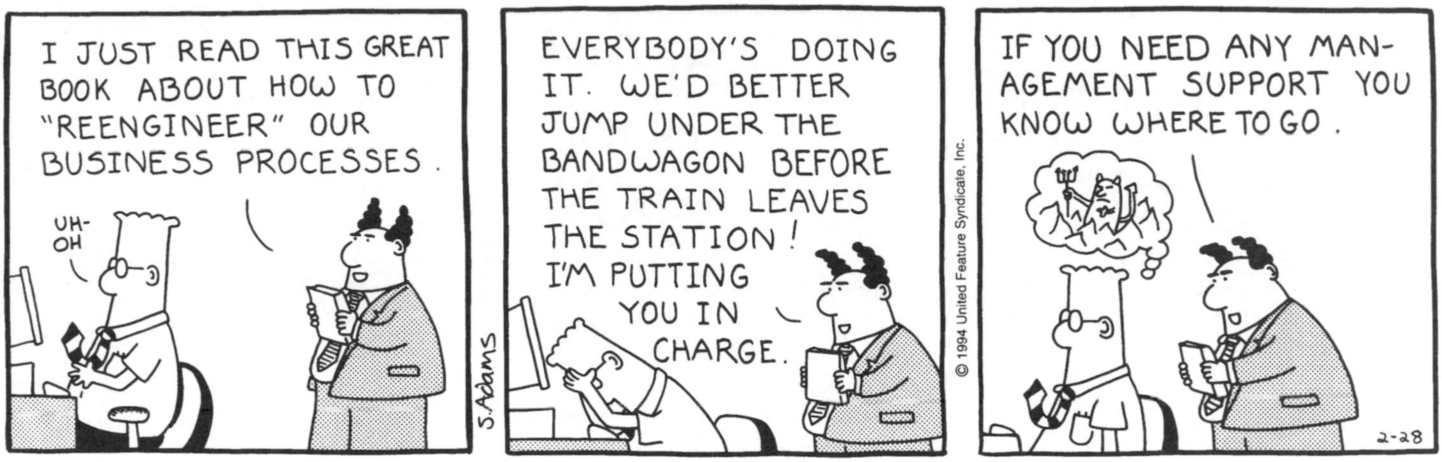
I JUST READ THIS GREAT BOOK ABOUT HOW TO "REENGINEER" OUR BUSINESS PROCESSES.
UH-OH
S. Adams
EVERYBODY'S DOING IT. WE'D BETTER JUMP UNDER THE BANDWAGON BEFORE THE TRAIN LEAVES THE STATION!
I'M PUTTING YOU IN CHARGE.
© 1994 United Feature Syndicate, Inc.
IF YOU NEED ANY MANAGEMENT SUPPORT YOU KNOW WHERE TO GO.
2-28

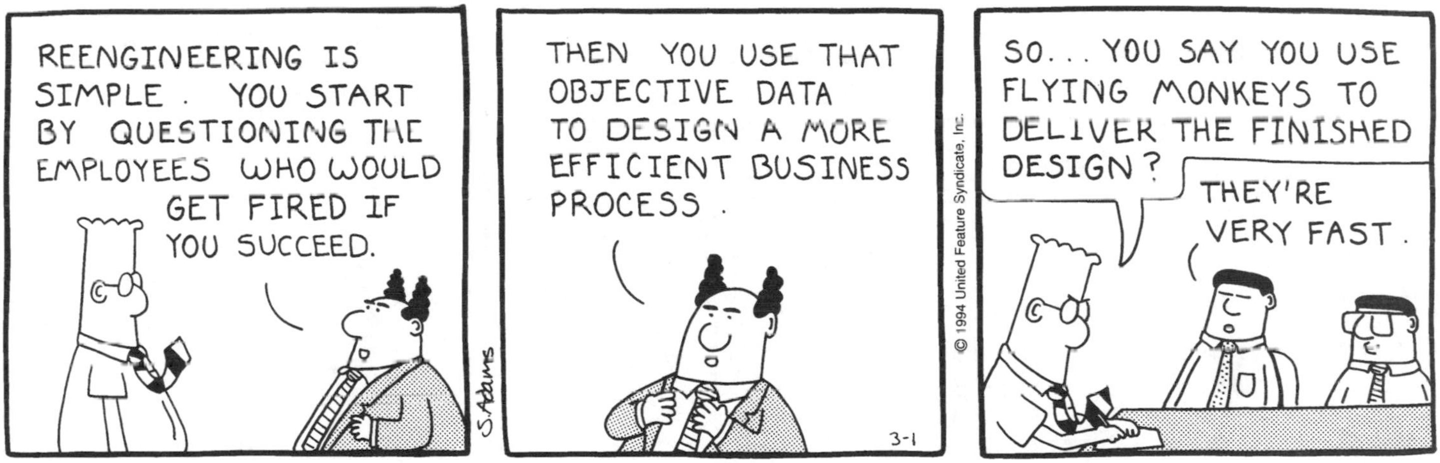
REENGINEERING IS SIMPLE. YOU START BY QUESTIONING THE EMPLOYEES WHO WOULD GET FIRED IF YOU SUCCEED.
S. Adams
THEN YOU USE THAT OBJECTIVE DATA TO DESIGN A MORE EFFICIENT BUSINESS PROCESS.
3-1
© 1994 United Feature Syndicate, Inc.
SO... YOU SAY YOU USE FLYING MONKEYS TO DELIVER THE FINISHED DESIGN?
THEY'RE VERY FAST.

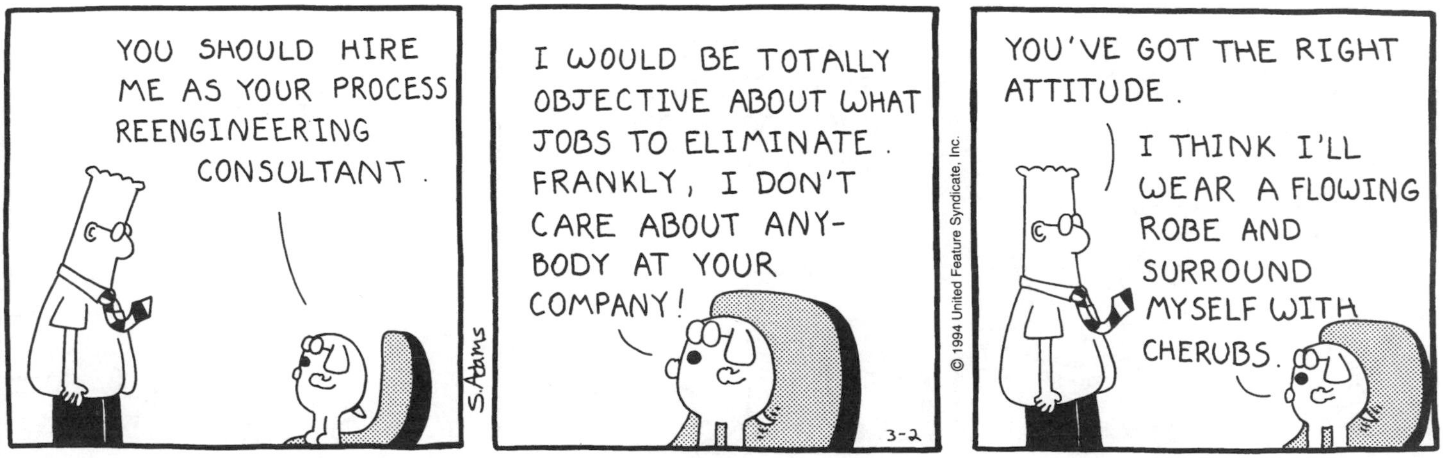
YOU SHOULD HIRE ME AS YOUR PROCESS REENGINEERING CONSULTANT.
S. Adams
I WOULD BE TOTALLY OBJECTIVE ABOUT WHAT JOBS TO ELIMINATE. FRANKLY, I DON'T CARE ABOUT ANYBODY AT YOUR COMPANY!
3-2
© 1994 United Feature Syndicate, Inc.
YOU'VE GOT THE RIGHT ATTITUDE.
I THINK I'LL WEAR A FLOWING ROBE AND SURROUND MYSELF WITH CHERUBS.

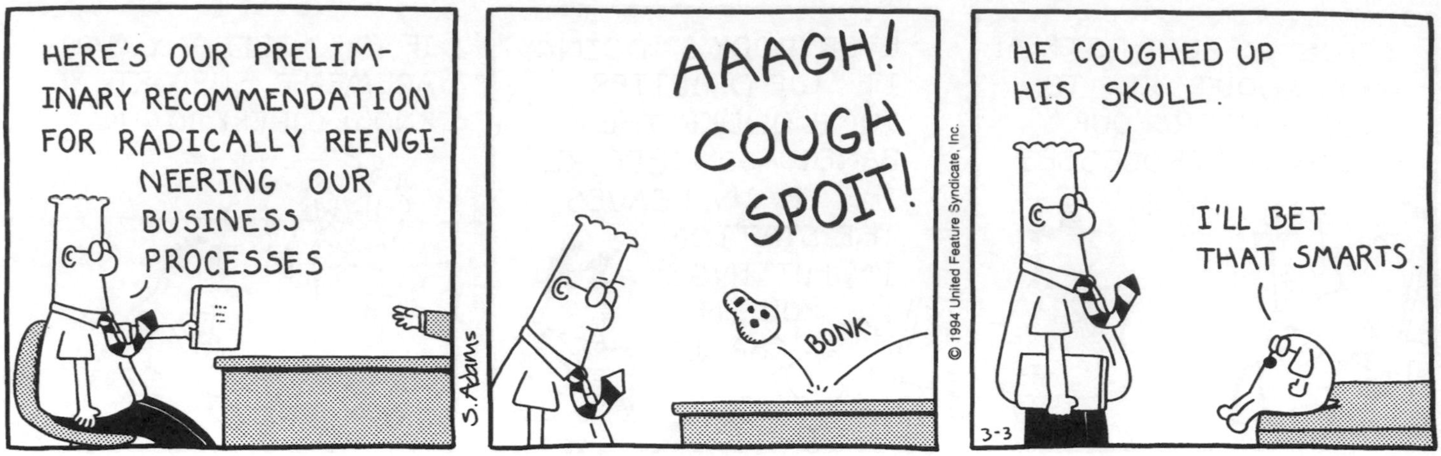
HERE'S OUR PRELIMINARY RECOMMENDATION FOR RADICALLY REENGINEERING OUR BUSINESS PROCESSES
S. Adams
AAAGH! COUGH SPOIT!
BONK
© 1994 United Feature Syndicate, Inc.
HE COUGHED UP HIS SKULL.
I'LL BET THAT SMARTS.
3-3

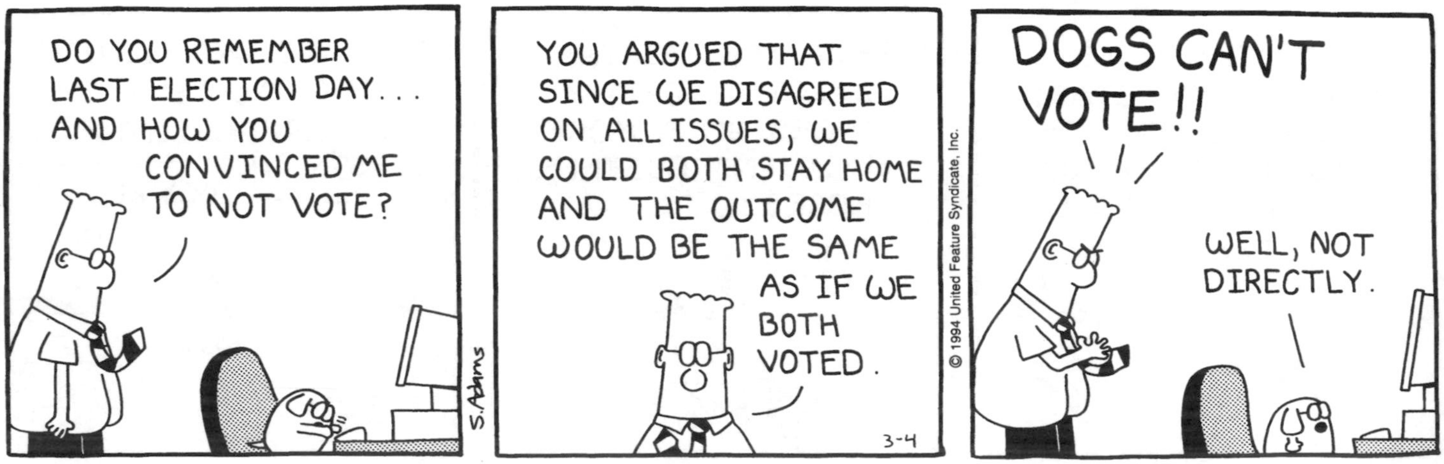
DO YOU REMEMBER LAST ELECTION DAY... AND HOW YOU CONVINCED ME TO NOT VOTE?
S. Adams
YOU ARGUED THAT SINCE WE DISAGREED ON ALL ISSUES, WE COULD BOTH STAY HOME AND THE OUTCOME WOULD BE THE SAME AS IF WE BOTH VOTED.
3-4
© 1994 United Feature Syndicate, Inc.
DOGS CAN'T VOTE!!
WELL, NOT DIRECTLY.

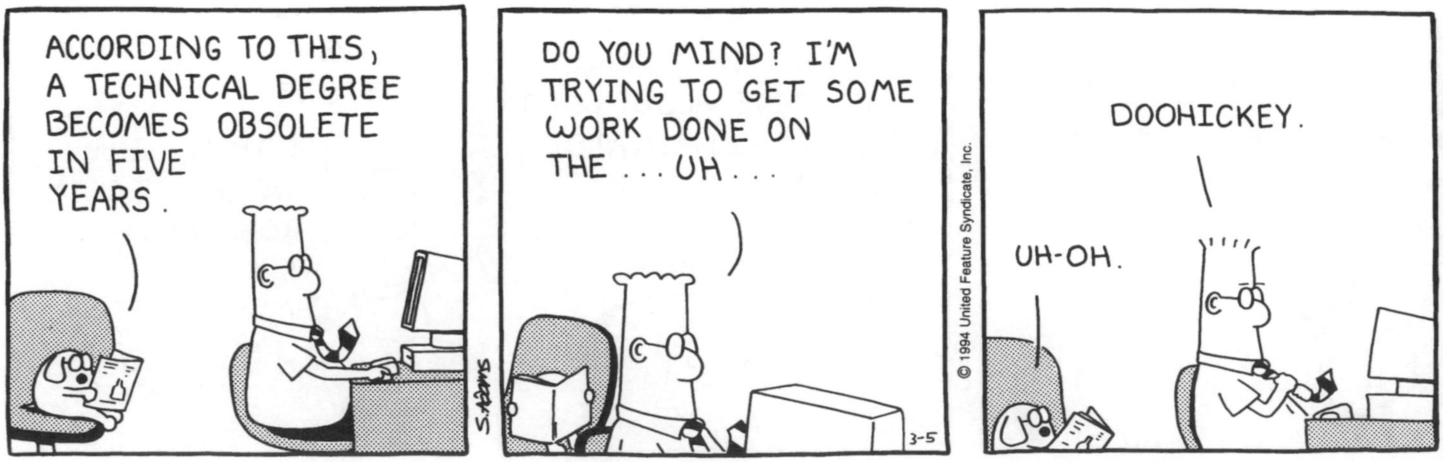
ACCORDING TO THIS, A TECHNICAL DEGREE BECOMES OBSOLETE IN FIVE YEARS.
S. Adams
DO YOU MIND? I'M TRYING TO GET SOME WORK DONE ON THE ... UH ...
3-5
© 1994 United Feature Syndicate, Inc.
DOOHICKEY.
UH-OH.

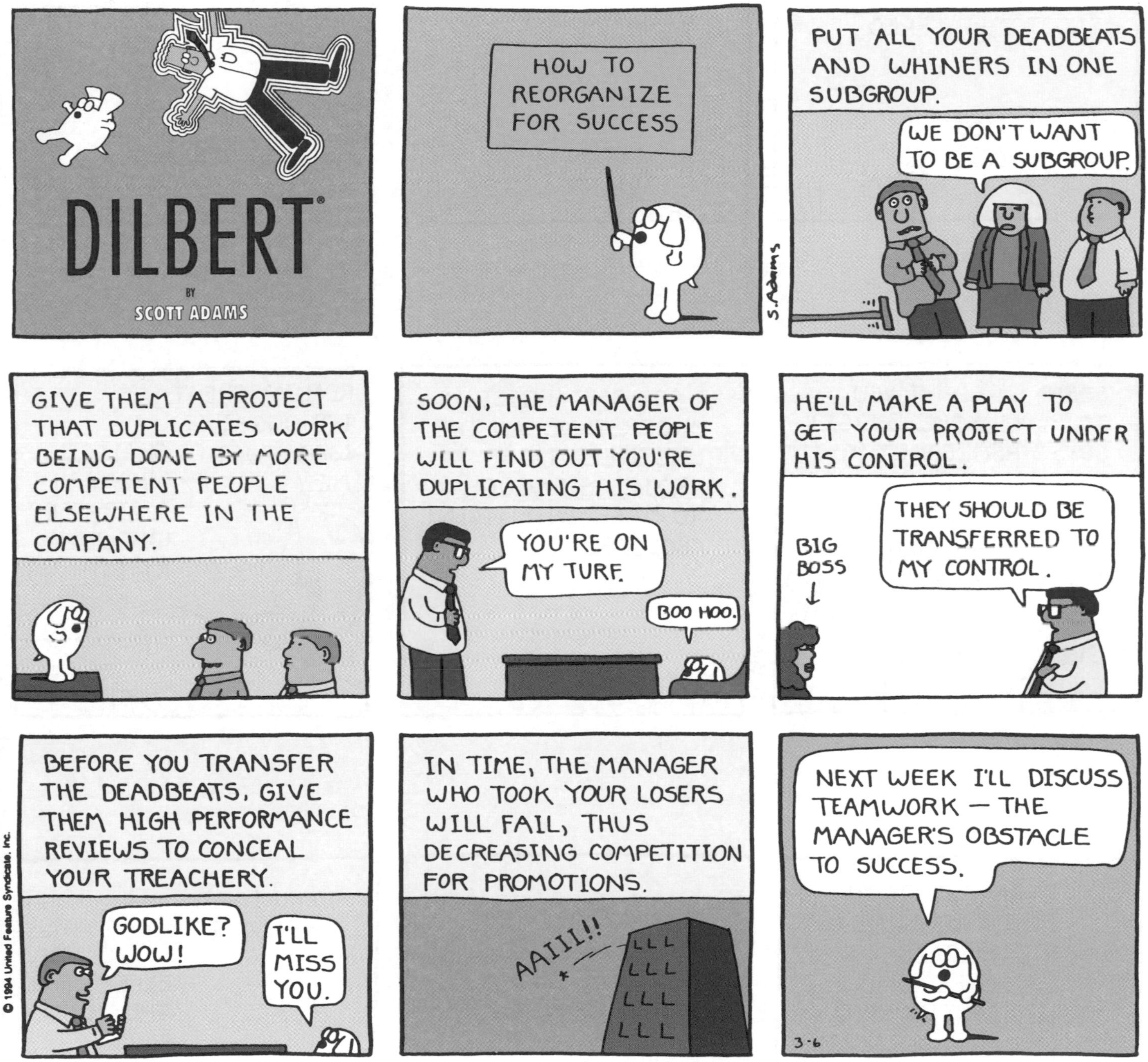

DILBERT®
BY
SCOTT ADAMS
HOW TO REORGANIZE FOR SUCCESS
PUT ALL YOUR DEADBEATS AND WHINERS IN ONE SUBGROUP.
WE DON'T WANT TO BE A SUBGROUP.
S. Adams
GIVE THEM A PROJECT THAT DUPLICATES WORK BEING DONE BY MORE COMPETENT PEOPLE ELSEWHERE IN THE COMPANY.
SOON, THE MANAGER OF THE COMPETENT PEOPLE WILL FIND OUT YOU'RE DUPLICATING HIS WORK.
YOU'RE ON MY TURF.
BOO HOO.
HE'LL MAKE A PLAY TO GET YOUR PROJECT UNDFR HIS CONTROL.
BIG BOSS
THEY SHOULD BE TRANSFERRED TO MY CONTROL.
BEFORE YOU TRANSFER THE DEADBEATS, GIVE THEM HIGH PERFORMANCE REVIEWS TO CONCEAL YOUR TREACHERY.
GODLIKE? WOW!
I'LL MISS YOU.
IN TIME, THE MANAGER WHO TOOK YOUR LOSERS WILL FAIL, THUS DECREASING COMPETITION FOR PROMOTIONS.
AAIII!!
NEXT WEEK I'LL DISCUSS TEAMWORK — THE MANAGER'S OBSTACLE TO SUCCESS.
3-6
© 1994 United Feature Syndicate, Inc.

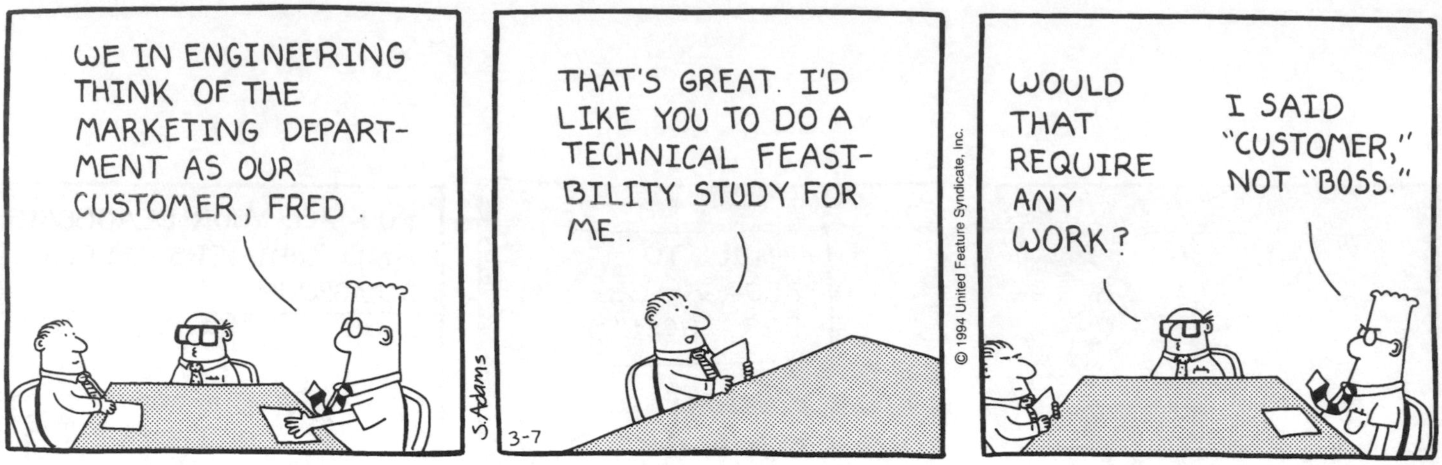
WE IN ENGINEERING THINK OF THE MARKETING DEPARTMENT AS OUR CUSTOMER, FRED.
THAT'S GREAT. I'D LIKE YOU TO DO A TECHNICAL FEASIBILITY STUDY FOR ME.
WOULD THAT REQUIRE ANY WORK?
I SAID "CUSTOMER," NOT "BOSS."
S.Adams
3-7
© 1994 United Feature Syndicate, Inc.

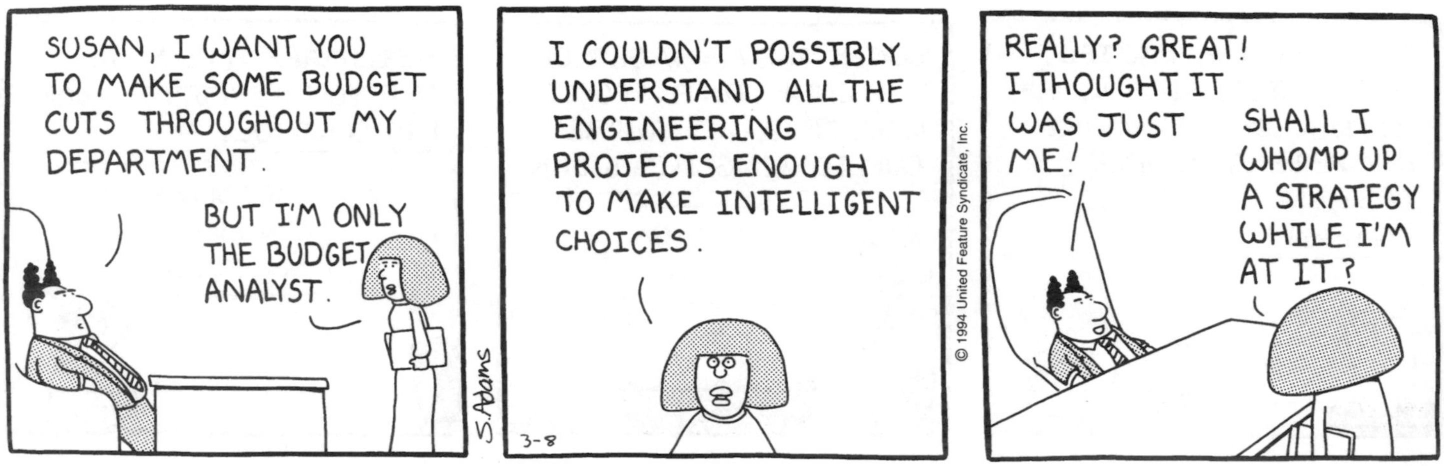
SUSAN, I WANT YOU TO MAKE SOME BUDGET CUTS THROUGHOUT MY DEPARTMENT.
BUT I'M ONLY THE BUDGET ANALYST.
I COULDN'T POSSIBLY UNDERSTAND ALL THE ENGINEERING PROJECTS ENOUGH TO MAKE INTELLIGENT CHOICES.
REALLY? GREAT! I THOUGHT IT WAS JUST ME!
SHALL I WHOMP UP A STRATEGY WHILE I'M AT IT?
S.Adams
3-8
© 1994 United Feature Syndicate, Inc.

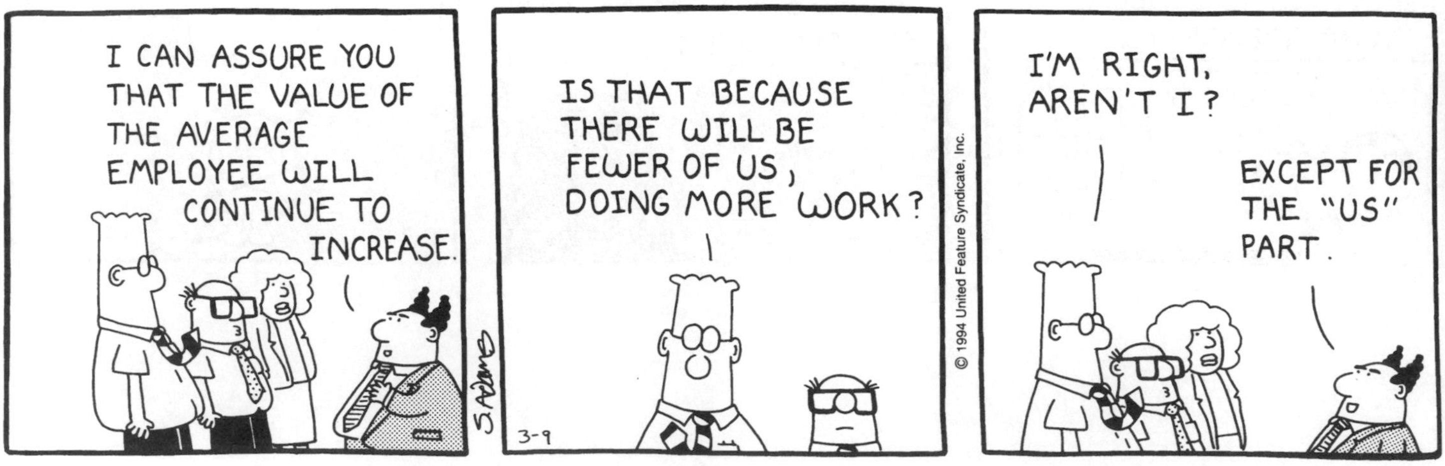
I CAN ASSURE YOU THAT THE VALUE OF THE AVERAGE EMPLOYEE WILL CONTINUE TO INCREASE.
IS THAT BECAUSE THERE WILL BE FEWER OF US, DOING MORE WORK?
I'M RIGHT, AREN'T I?
EXCEPT FOR THE "US" PART.
S.Adams
3-9
© 1994 United Feature Syndicate, Inc.

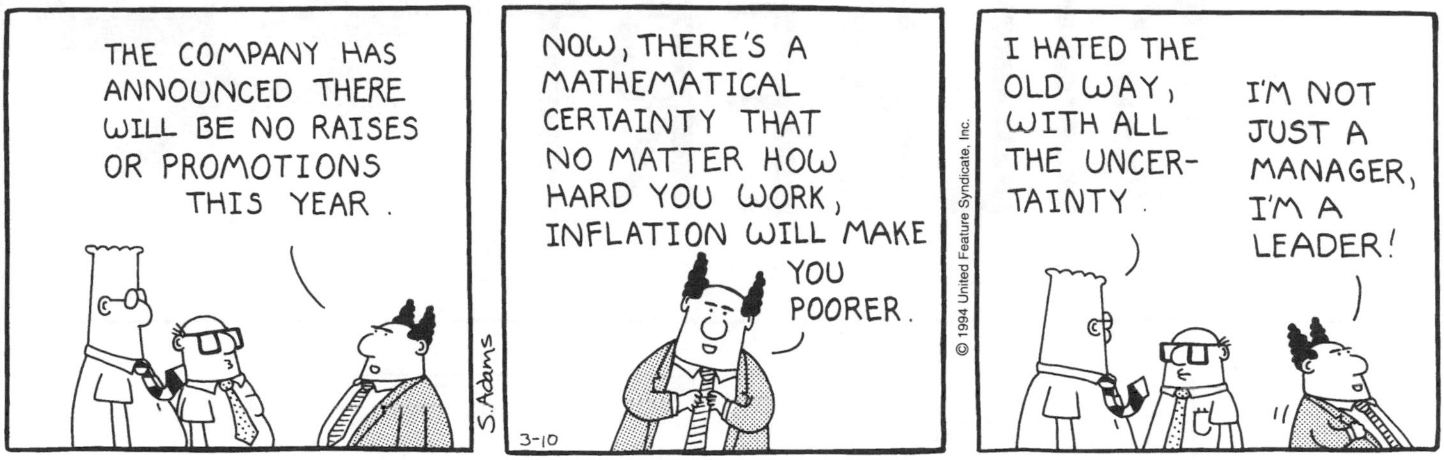
THE COMPANY HAS ANNOUNCED THERE WILL BE NO RAISES OR PROMOTIONS THIS YEAR.
S. Adams
NOW, THERE'S A MATHEMATICAL CERTAINTY THAT NO MATTER HOW HARD YOU WORK, INFLATION WILL MAKE YOU POORER.
3-10
© 1994 United Feature Syndicate, Inc.
I HATED THE OLD WAY, WITH ALL THE UNCERTAINTY.
I'M NOT JUST A MANAGER, I'M A LEADER!

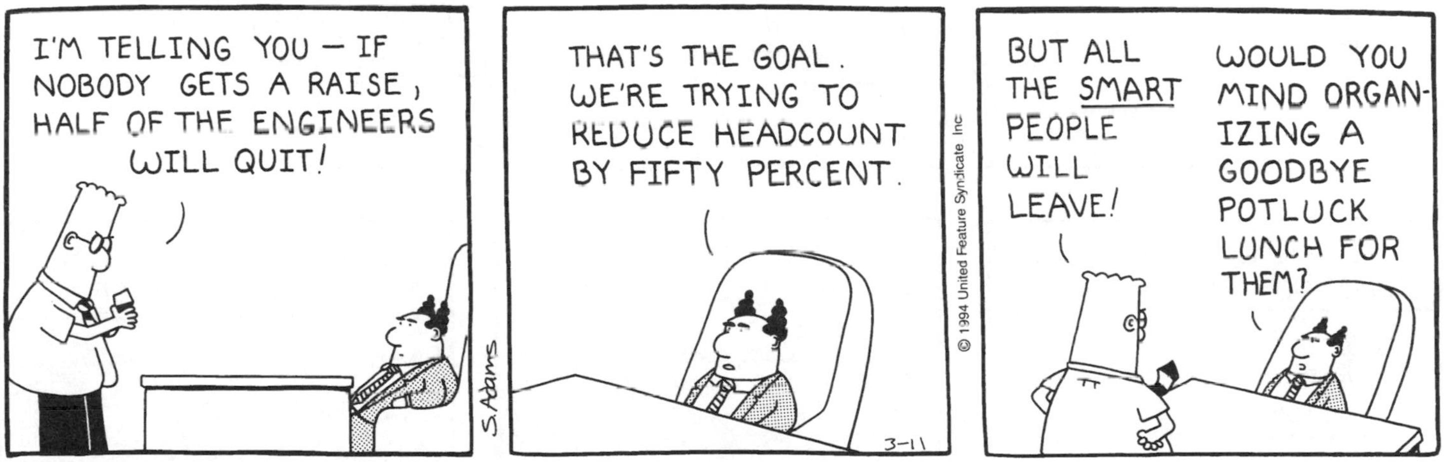
I'M TELLING YOU — IF NOBODY GETS A RAISE, HALF OF THE ENGINEERS WILL QUIT!
S. Adams
THAT'S THE GOAL. WE'RE TRYING TO REDUCE HEADCOUNT BY FIFTY PERCENT.
3-11
© 1994 United Feature Syndicate, Inc.
BUT ALL THE SMART PEOPLE WILL LEAVE!
WOULD YOU MIND ORGANIZING A GOODBYE POTLUCK LUNCH FOR THEM?

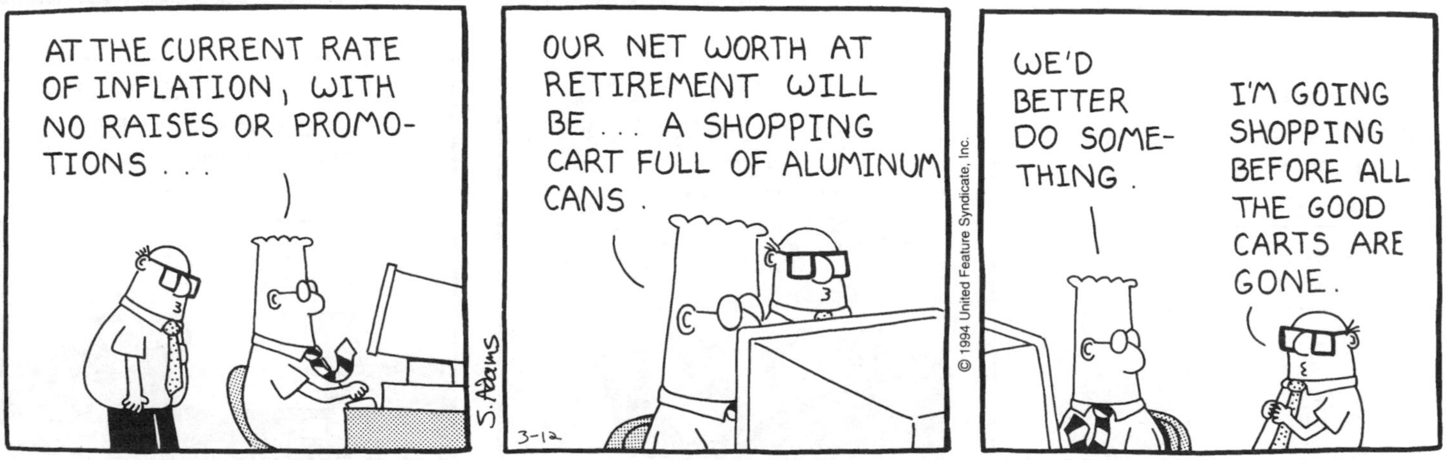
AT THE CURRENT RATE OF INFLATION, WITH NO RAISES OR PROMOTIONS . . .
S. Adams
3-12
OUR NET WORTH AT RETIREMENT WILL BE . . . A SHOPPING CART FULL OF ALUMINUM CANS.
© 1994 United Feature Syndicate, Inc.
WE'D BETTER DO SOMETHING.
I'M GOING SHOPPING BEFORE ALL THE GOOD CARTS ARE GONE.

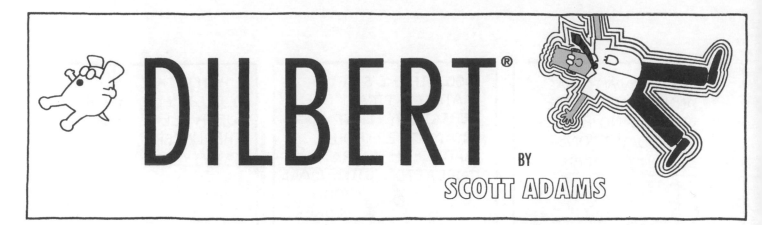

DILBERT®

BY SCOTT ADAMS

DOGBERT'S BODY LANGUAGE UPDATE

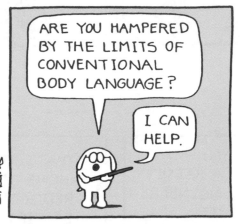

ARE YOU HAMPERED BY THE LIMITS OF CONVENTIONAL BODY LANGUAGE?

I CAN HELP.

HOW CAN YOU POLITELY TELL SOMEBODY HE'S BABBLING?

BABBLE BABBLE

REMOVE THE OFFENDER'S WATCH WHILE HE BABBLES.

BABBLE

SMASH THE WATCH WITH YOUR DAILY PLANNER.

BABBLE

WHACK!

THIS WON'T STOP THE BABBLE, BUT IT WILL FEEL REAL GOOD FOR A MINUTE.

BABBLE

MMM ♪♫

USE THIS POSITION TO SIGNAL YOUR SURRENDER TO THE BABBLE.

BABBLE

3-13

NEXT WEEK: THE SELF-HEIMLICH MANUEVER AND THE KEVORKIAN DODGE.

BABBLE

82

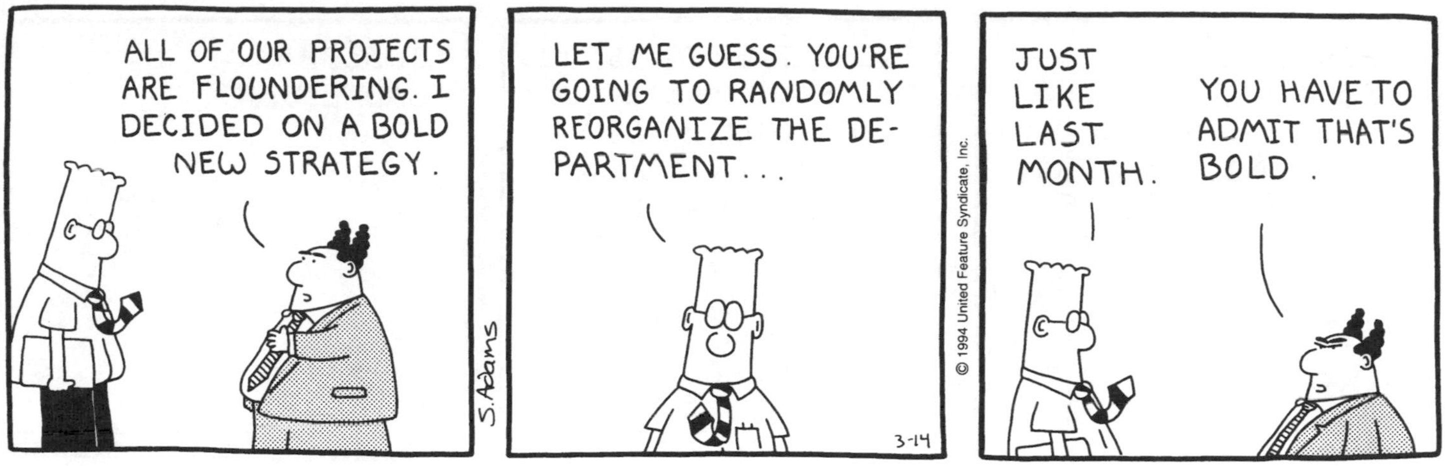
ALL OF OUR PROJECTS ARE FLOUNDERING. I DECIDED ON A BOLD NEW STRATEGY.
S. Adams
LET ME GUESS. YOU'RE GOING TO RANDOMLY REORGANIZE THE DE-PARTMENT...
3-14
© 1994 United Feature Syndicate, Inc.
JUST LIKE LAST MONTH.
YOU HAVE TO ADMIT THAT'S BOLD.

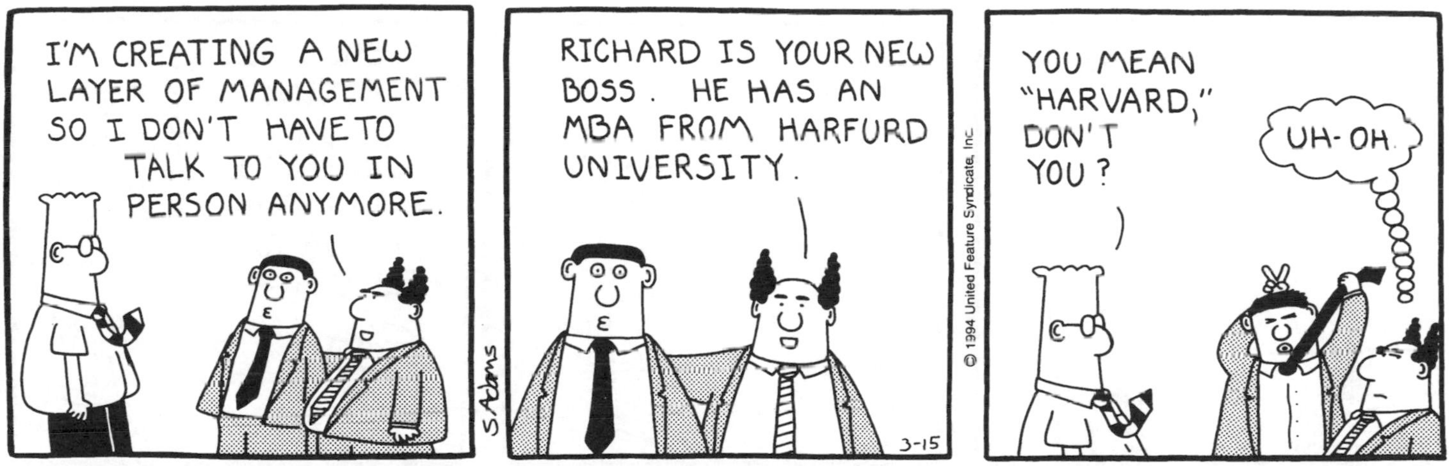
I'M CREATING A NEW LAYER OF MANAGEMENT SO I DON'T HAVE TO TALK TO YOU IN PERSON ANYMORE.
S. Adams
RICHARD IS YOUR NEW BOSS. HE HAS AN MBA FROM HARFURD UNIVERSITY.
3-15
© 1994 United Feature Syndicate, Inc.
YOU MEAN "HARVARD," DON'T YOU?
UH-OH.

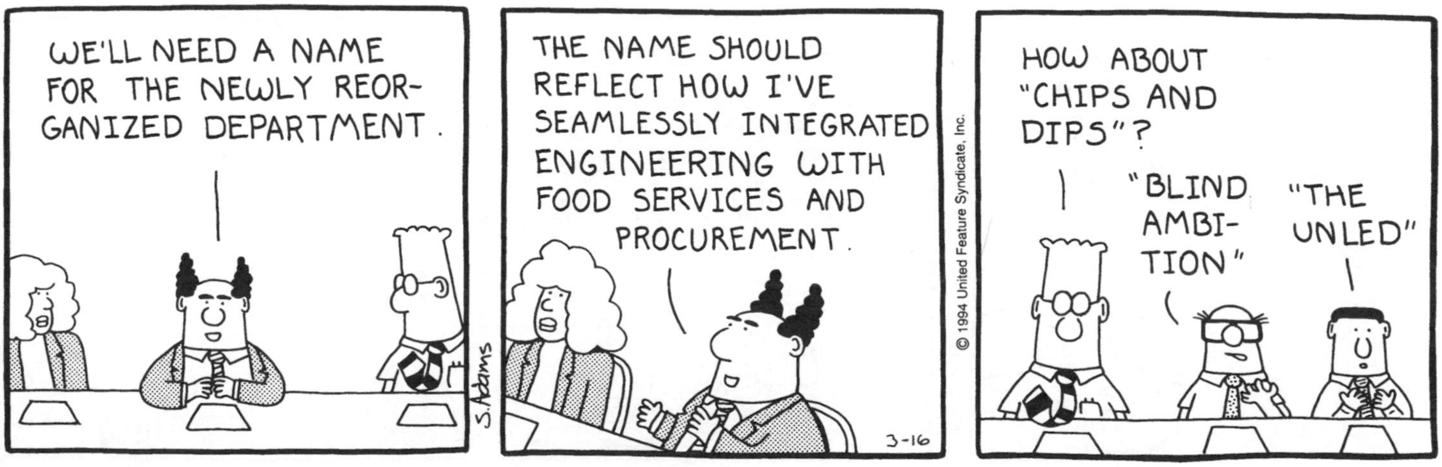
WE'LL NEED A NAME FOR THE NEWLY REOR-GANIZED DEPARTMENT.
S. Adams
THE NAME SHOULD REFLECT HOW I'VE SEAMLESSLY INTEGRATED ENGINEERING WITH FOOD SERVICES AND PROCUREMENT.
3-16
© 1994 United Feature Syndicate, Inc.
HOW ABOUT "CHIPS AND DIPS"?
"BLIND AMBI-TION"
"THE UNLED"

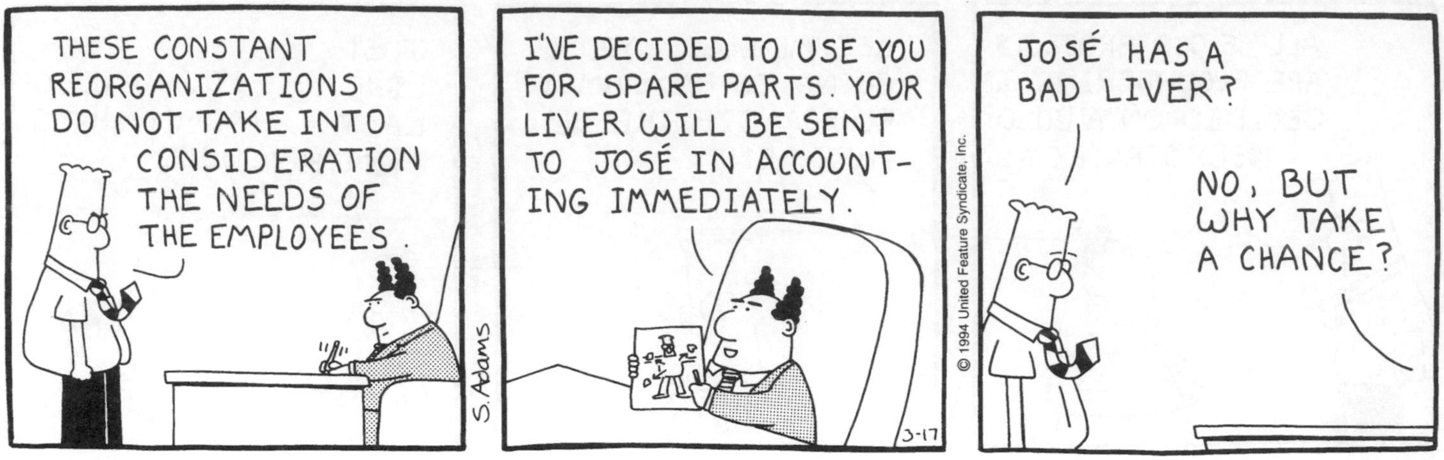
THESE CONSTANT REORGANIZATIONS DO NOT TAKE INTO CONSIDERATION THE NEEDS OF THE EMPLOYEES.
S. Adams
I'VE DECIDED TO USE YOU FOR SPARE PARTS. YOUR LIVER WILL BE SENT TO JOSÉ IN ACCOUNTING IMMEDIATELY.
3-17
© 1994 United Feature Syndicate, Inc.
JOSÉ HAS A BAD LIVER?
NO, BUT WHY TAKE A CHANCE?

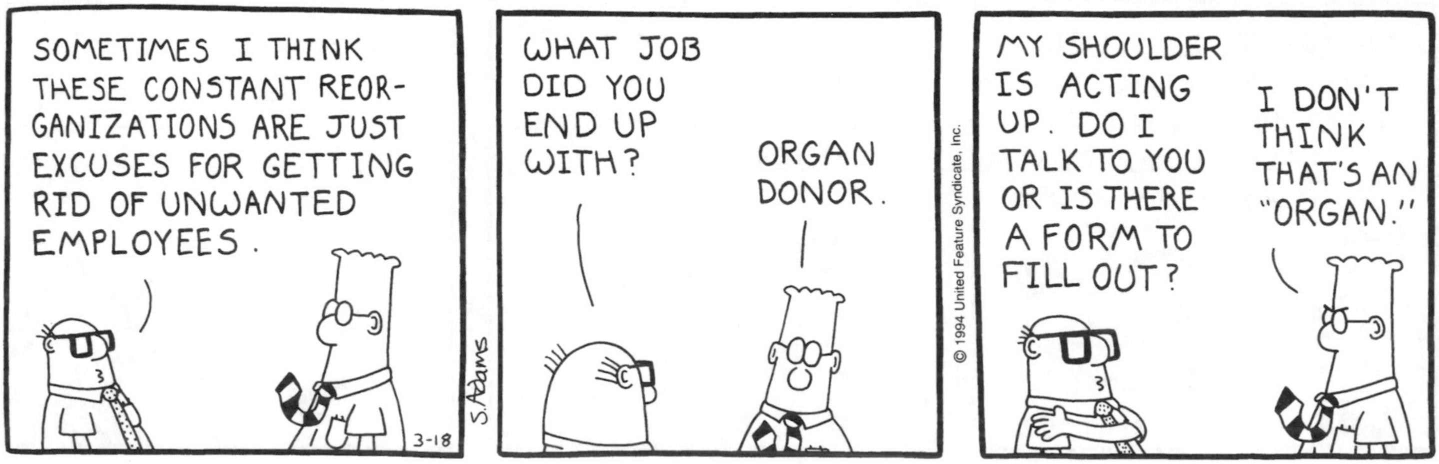
SOMETIMES I THINK THESE CONSTANT REORGANIZATIONS ARE JUST EXCUSES FOR GETTING RID OF UNWANTED EMPLOYEES.
3-18
S. Adams
WHAT JOB DID YOU END UP WITH?
ORGAN DONOR.
© 1994 United Feature Syndicate, Inc.
MY SHOULDER IS ACTING UP. DO I TALK TO YOU OR IS THERE A FORM TO FILL OUT?
I DON'T THINK THAT'S AN "ORGAN."

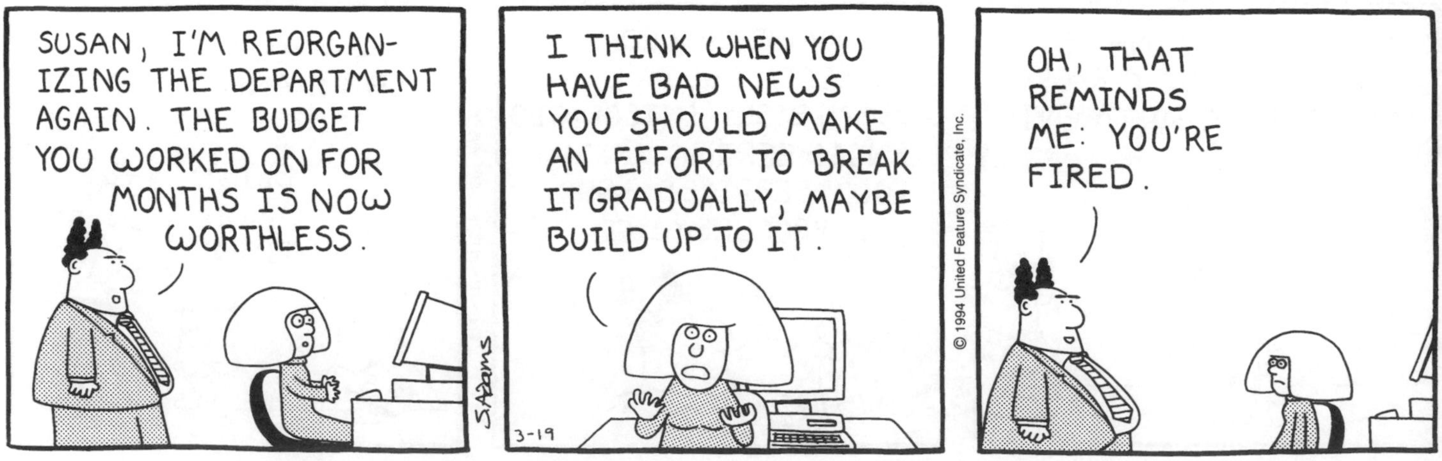
SUSAN, I'M REORGANIZING THE DEPARTMENT AGAIN. THE BUDGET YOU WORKED ON FOR MONTHS IS NOW WORTHLESS.
S. Adams
I THINK WHEN YOU HAVE BAD NEWS YOU SHOULD MAKE AN EFFORT TO BREAK IT GRADUALLY, MAYBE BUILD UP TO IT.
3-19
© 1994 United Feature Syndicate, Inc.
OH, THAT REMINDS ME: YOU'RE FIRED.

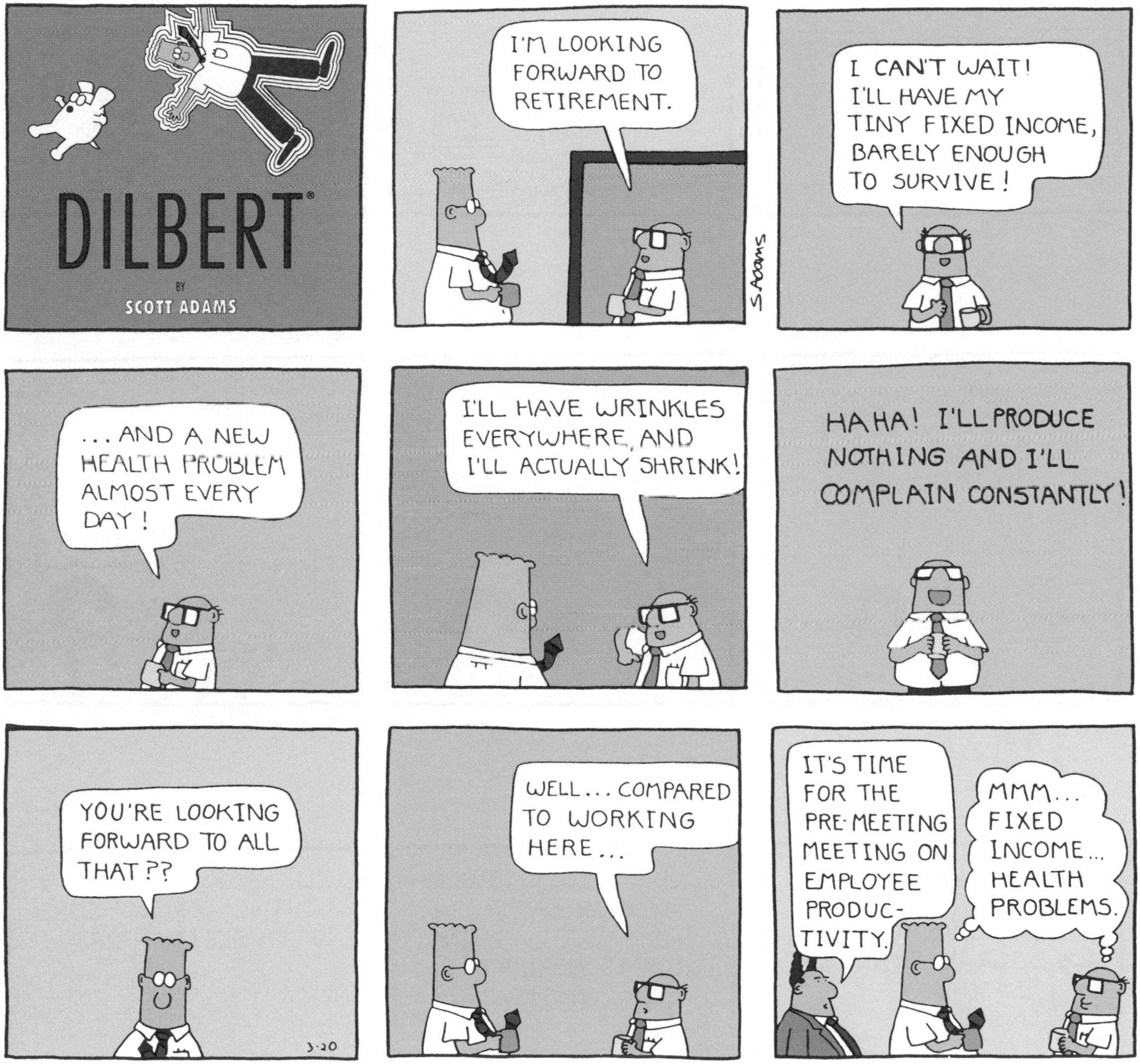
DILBERT®
BY SCOTT ADAMS
I'M LOOKING FORWARD TO RETIREMENT.
S. ADAMS
I CAN'T WAIT! I'LL HAVE MY TINY FIXED INCOME, BARELY ENOUGH TO SURVIVE!
... AND A NEW HEALTH PROBLEM ALMOST EVERY DAY!
I'LL HAVE WRINKLES EVERYWHERE, AND I'LL ACTUALLY SHRINK!
HA HA! I'LL PRODUCE NOTHING AND I'LL COMPLAIN CONSTANTLY!
YOU'RE LOOKING FORWARD TO ALL THAT??
© 1994 United Feature Syndicate Inc
3·20
WELL... COMPARED TO WORKING HERE...
IT'S TIME FOR THE PRE-MEETING MEETING ON EMPLOYEE PRODUC-TIVITY.
MMM... FIXED INCOME... HEALTH PROBLEMS.

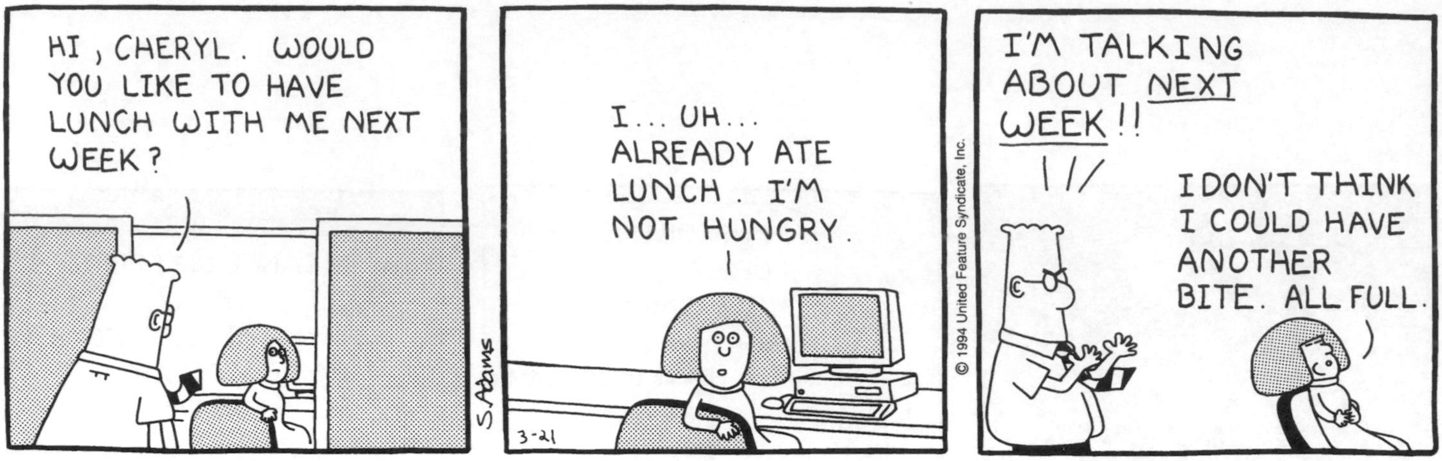
HI, CHERYL. WOULD YOU LIKE TO HAVE LUNCH WITH ME NEXT WEEK?
S. Adams
I... UH... ALREADY ATE LUNCH. I'M NOT HUNGRY.
3-21
© 1994 United Feature Syndicate, Inc.
I'M TALKING ABOUT NEXT WEEK!!
I DON'T THINK I COULD HAVE ANOTHER BITE. ALL FULL.

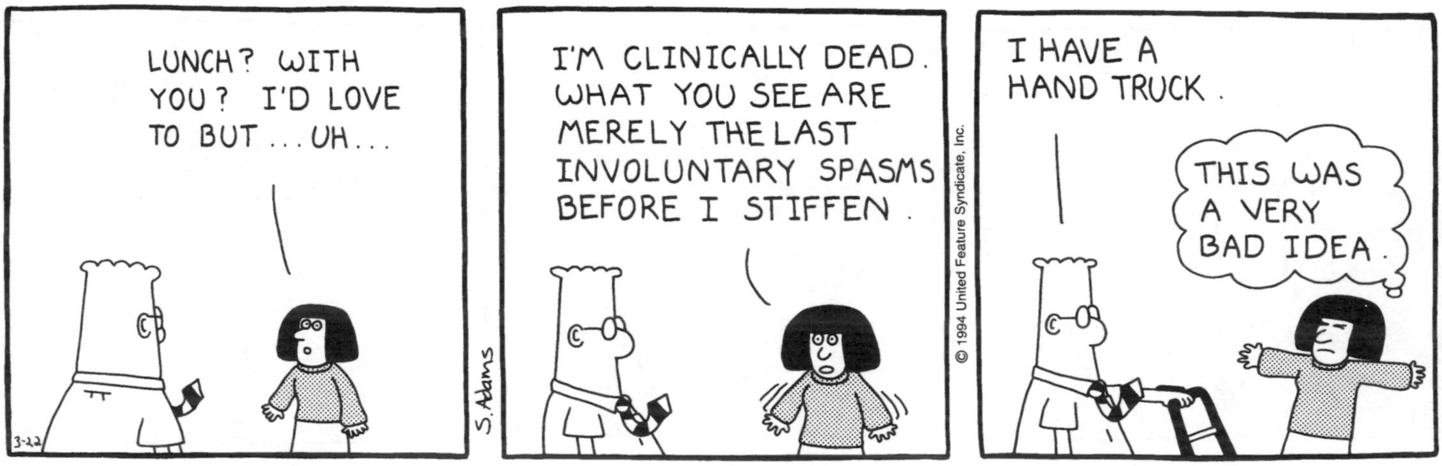
LUNCH? WITH YOU? I'D LOVE TO BUT... UH...
3-22
S. Adams
I'M CLINICALLY DEAD. WHAT YOU SEE ARE MERELY THE LAST INVOLUNTARY SPASMS BEFORE I STIFFEN.
© 1994 United Feature Syndicate, Inc.
I HAVE A HAND TRUCK.
THIS WAS A VERY BAD IDEA.

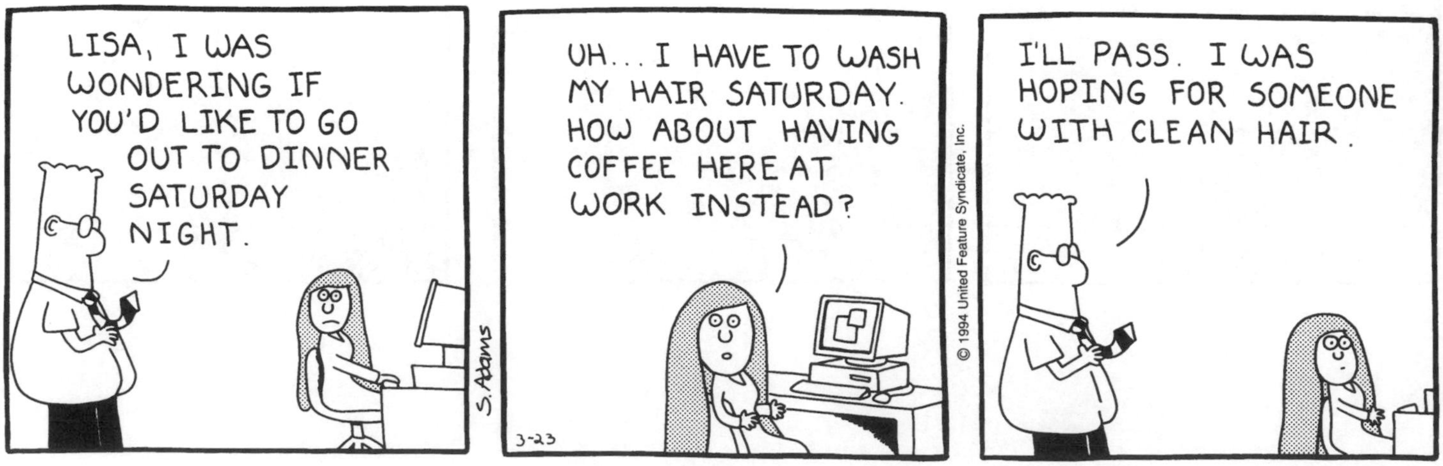
LISA, I WAS WONDERING IF YOU'D LIKE TO GO OUT TO DINNER SATURDAY NIGHT.
S. Adams
UH... I HAVE TO WASH MY HAIR SATURDAY. HOW ABOUT HAVING COFFEE HERE AT WORK INSTEAD?
3-23
© 1994 United Feature Syndicate, Inc.
I'LL PASS. I WAS HOPING FOR SOMEONE WITH CLEAN HAIR.

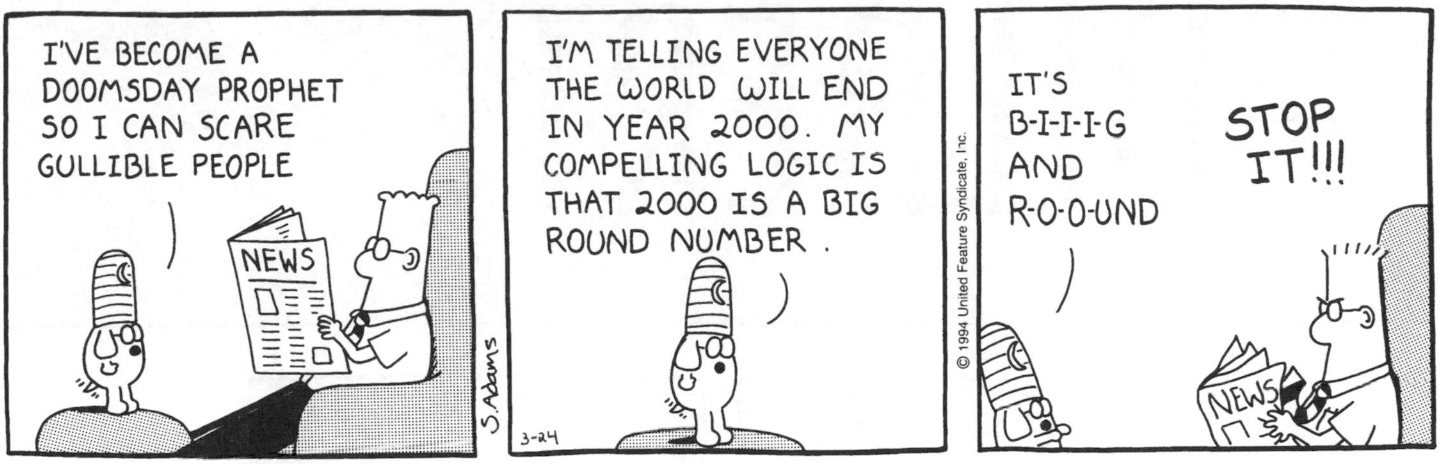
I'VE BECOME A DOOMSDAY PROPHET SO I CAN SCARE GULLIBLE PEOPLE
NEWS
S. Adams
I'M TELLING EVERYONE THE WORLD WILL END IN YEAR 2000. MY COMPELLING LOGIC IS THAT 2000 IS A BIG ROUND NUMBER.
3-24
© 1994 United Feature Syndicate, Inc.
IT'S B-I-I-I-G AND R-O-O-UND
STOP IT!!!
NEWS

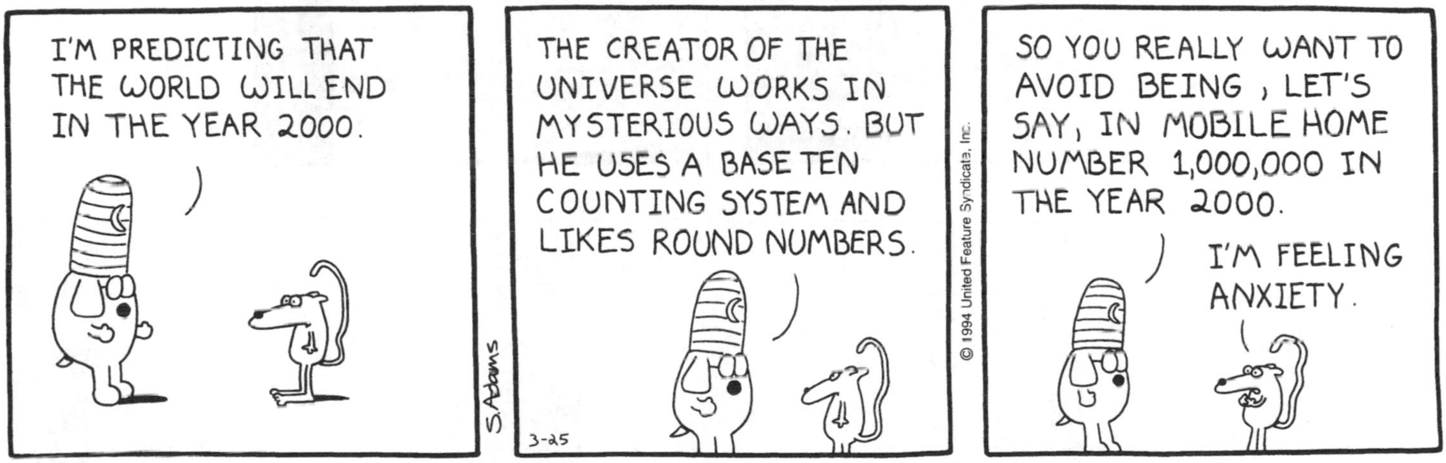
I'M PREDICTING THAT THE WORLD WILL END IN THE YEAR 2000.
S. Adams
THE CREATOR OF THE UNIVERSE WORKS IN MYSTERIOUS WAYS. BUT HE USES A BASE TEN COUNTING SYSTEM AND LIKES ROUND NUMBERS.
3-25
© 1994 United Feature Syndicate, Inc.
SO YOU REALLY WANT TO AVOID BEING, LET'S SAY, IN MOBILE HOME NUMBER 1,000,000 IN THE YEAR 2000.
I'M FEELING ANXIETY.

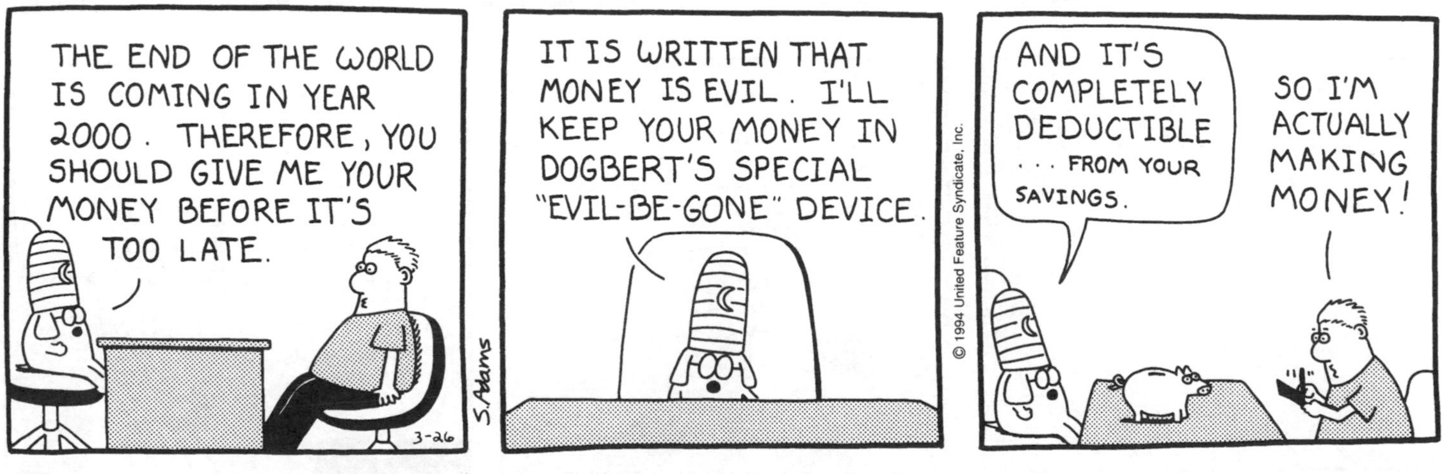
THE END OF THE WORLD IS COMING IN YEAR 2000. THEREFORE, YOU SHOULD GIVE ME YOUR MONEY BEFORE IT'S TOO LATE.
3-26
S. Adams
IT IS WRITTEN THAT MONEY IS EVIL. I'LL KEEP YOUR MONEY IN DOGBERT'S SPECIAL "EVIL-BE-GONE" DEVICE.
© 1994 United Feature Syndicate, Inc.
AND IT'S COMPLETELY DEDUCTIBLE . . . FROM YOUR SAVINGS.
SO I'M ACTUALLY MAKING MONEY!

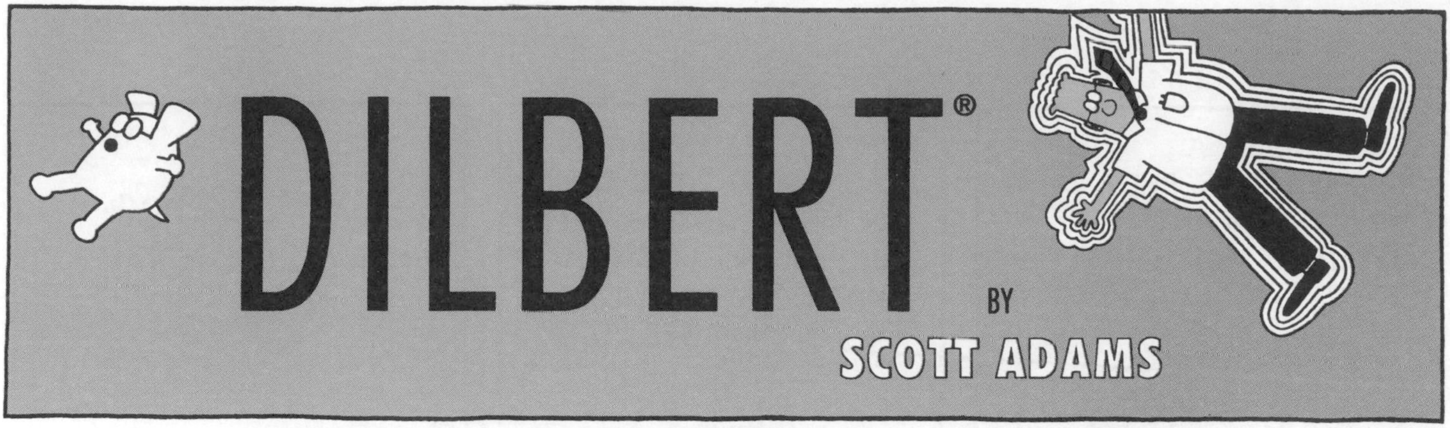
DILBERT®
BY
SCOTT ADAMS

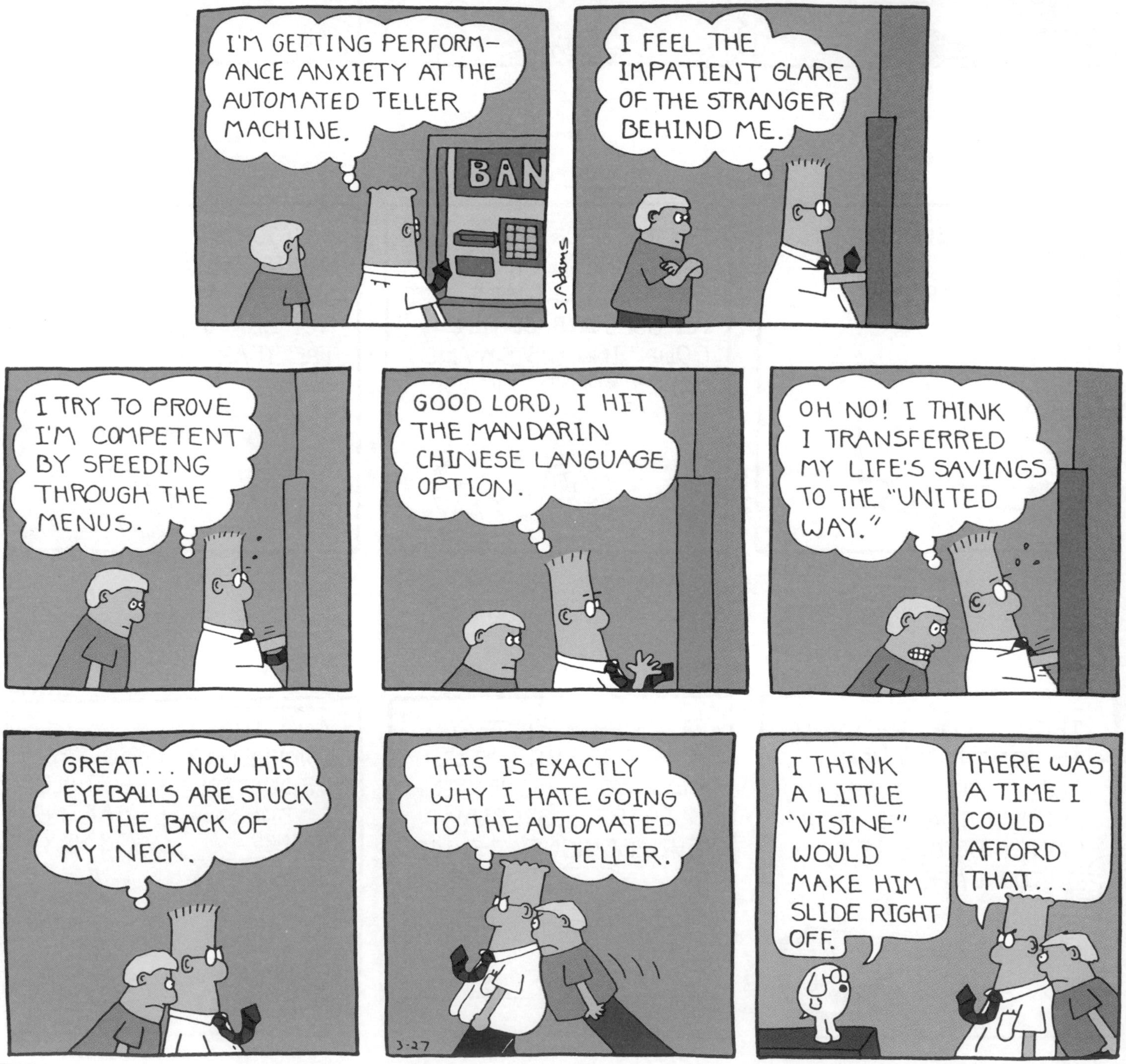
I'M GETTING PERFORM-ANCE ANXIETY AT THE AUTOMATED TELLER MACHINE.
BAN
S. Adams
I FEEL THE IMPATIENT GLARE OF THE STRANGER BEHIND ME.
I TRY TO PROVE I'M COMPETENT BY SPEEDING THROUGH THE MENUS.
GOOD LORD, I HIT THE MANDARIN CHINESE LANGUAGE OPTION.
OH NO! I THINK I TRANSFERRED MY LIFE'S SAVINGS TO THE "UNITED WAY."
GREAT... NOW HIS EYEBALLS ARE STUCK TO THE BACK OF MY NECK.
THIS IS EXACTLY WHY I HATE GOING TO THE AUTOMATED TELLER.
3-27
I THINK A LITTLE "VISINE" WOULD MAKE HIM SLIDE RIGHT OFF.
THERE WAS A TIME I COULD AFFORD THAT...

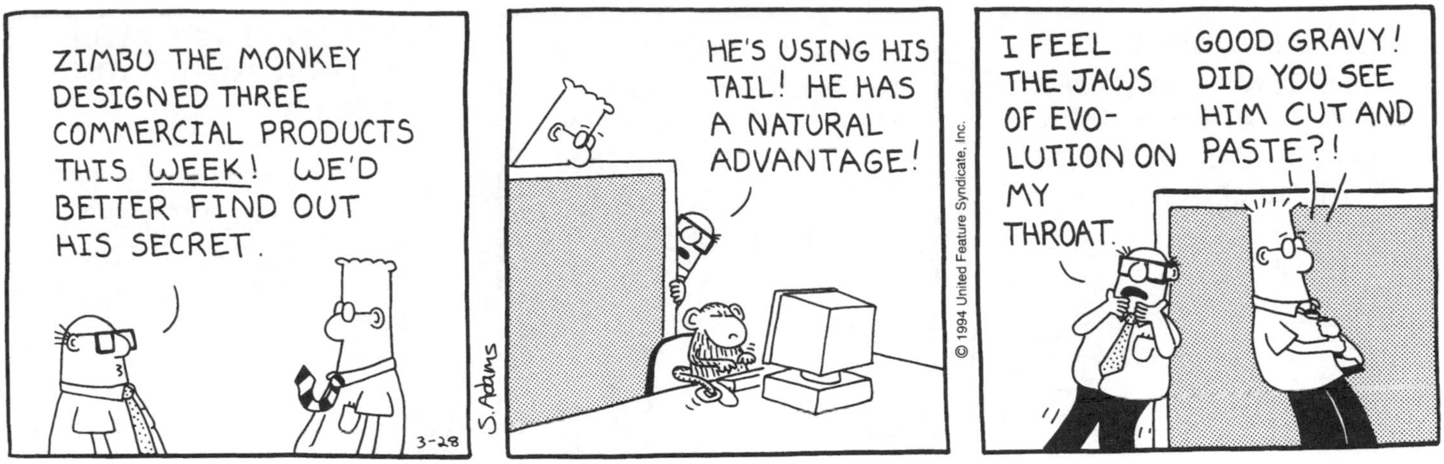
ZIMBU THE MONKEY DESIGNED THREE COMMERCIAL PRODUCTS THIS WEEK! WE'D BETTER FIND OUT HIS SECRET.
HE'S USING HIS TAIL! HE HAS A NATURAL ADVANTAGE!
I FEEL THE JAWS OF EVO-LUTION ON MY THROAT.
GOOD GRAVY! DID YOU SEE HIM CUT AND PASTE?!
3-28
S. Adams
© 1994 United Feature Syndicate, Inc.

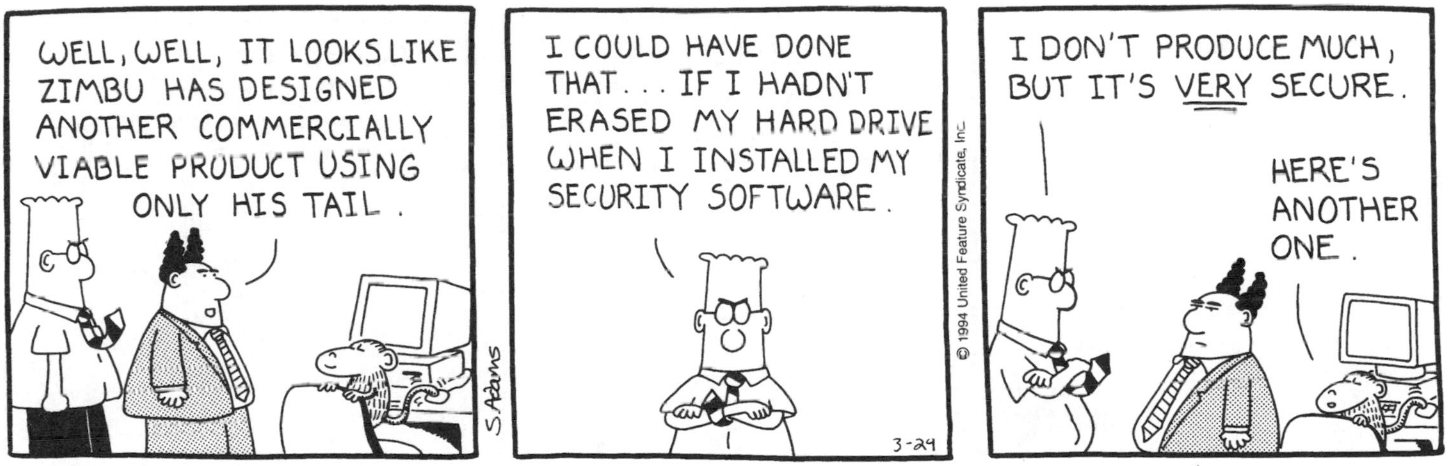
WELL, WELL, IT LOOKS LIKE ZIMBU HAS DESIGNED ANOTHER COMMERCIALLY VIABLE PRODUCT USING ONLY HIS TAIL.
I COULD HAVE DONE THAT... IF I HADN'T ERASED MY HARD DRIVE WHEN I INSTALLED MY SECURITY SOFTWARE.
I DON'T PRODUCE MUCH, BUT IT'S VERY SECURE.
HERE'S ANOTHER ONE.
3-29
S. Adams
© 1994 United Feature Syndicate, Inc.

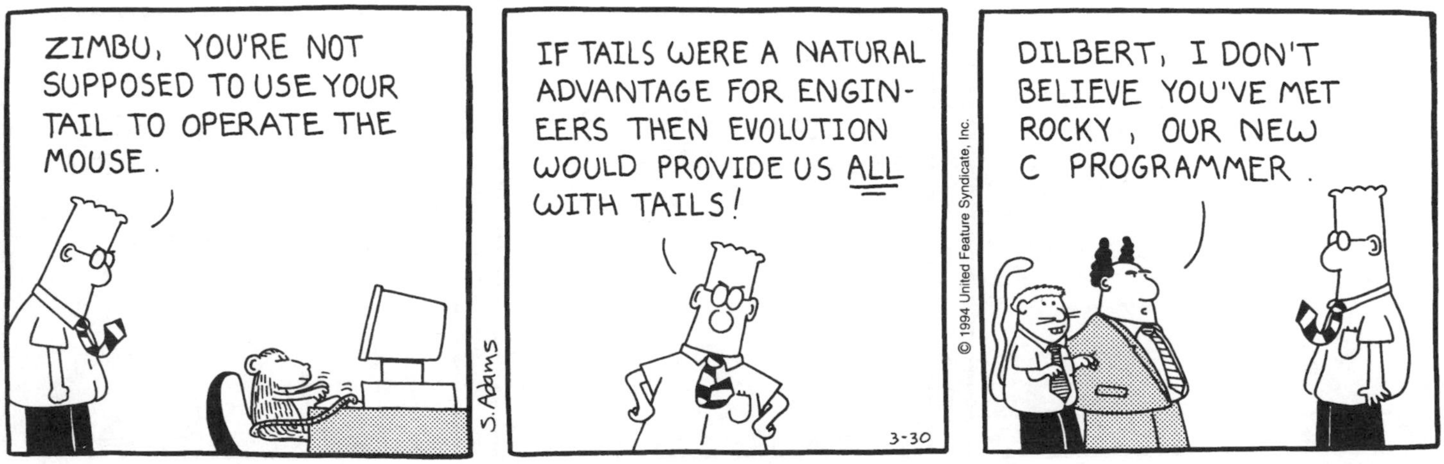
ZIMBU, YOU'RE NOT SUPPOSED TO USE YOUR TAIL TO OPERATE THE MOUSE.
IF TAILS WERE A NATURAL ADVANTAGE FOR ENGIN-EERS THEN EVOLUTION WOULD PROVIDE US ALL WITH TAILS!
DILBERT, I DON'T BELIEVE YOU'VE MET ROCKY, OUR NEW C PROGRAMMER.
3-30
S. Adams
© 1994 United Feature Syndicate, Inc.

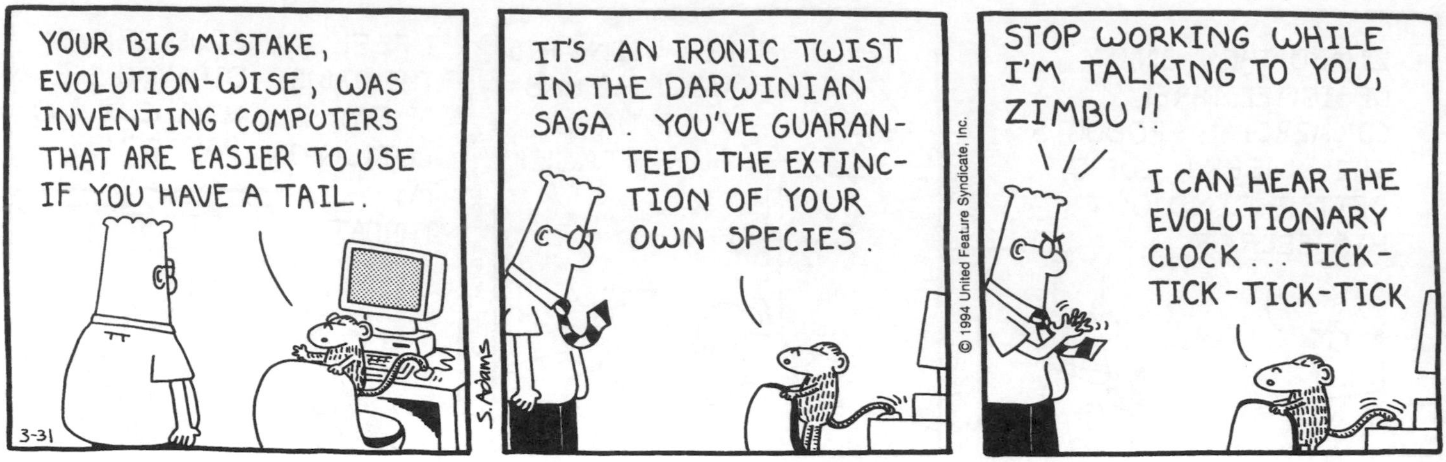
YOUR BIG MISTAKE, EVOLUTION-WISE, WAS INVENTING COMPUTERS THAT ARE EASIER TO USE IF YOU HAVE A TAIL.
3-31
S. Adams
IT'S AN IRONIC TWIST IN THE DARWINIAN SAGA. YOU'VE GUARANTEED THE EXTINCTION OF YOUR OWN SPECIES.
© 1994 United Feature Syndicate, Inc.
STOP WORKING WHILE I'M TALKING TO YOU, ZIMBU!!
I CAN HEAR THE EVOLUTIONARY CLOCK... TICK-TICK-TICK-TICK

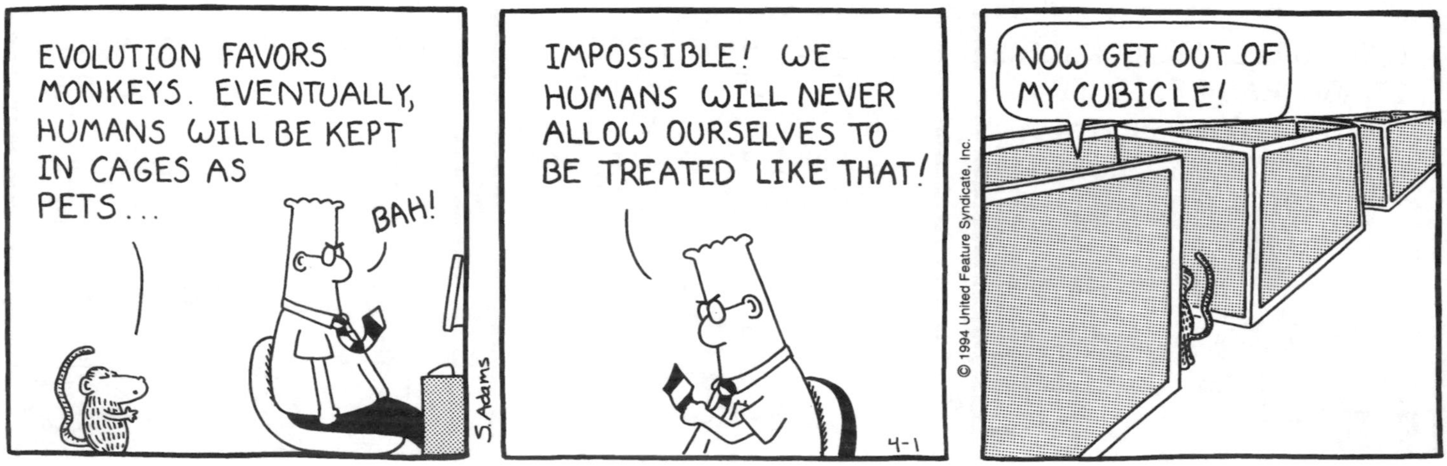
EVOLUTION FAVORS MONKEYS. EVENTUALLY, HUMANS WILL BE KEPT IN CAGES AS PETS...
BAH!
S. Adams
IMPOSSIBLE! WE HUMANS WILL NEVER ALLOW OURSELVES TO BE TREATED LIKE THAT!
4-1
© 1994 United Feature Syndicate, Inc.
NOW GET OUT OF MY CUBICLE!

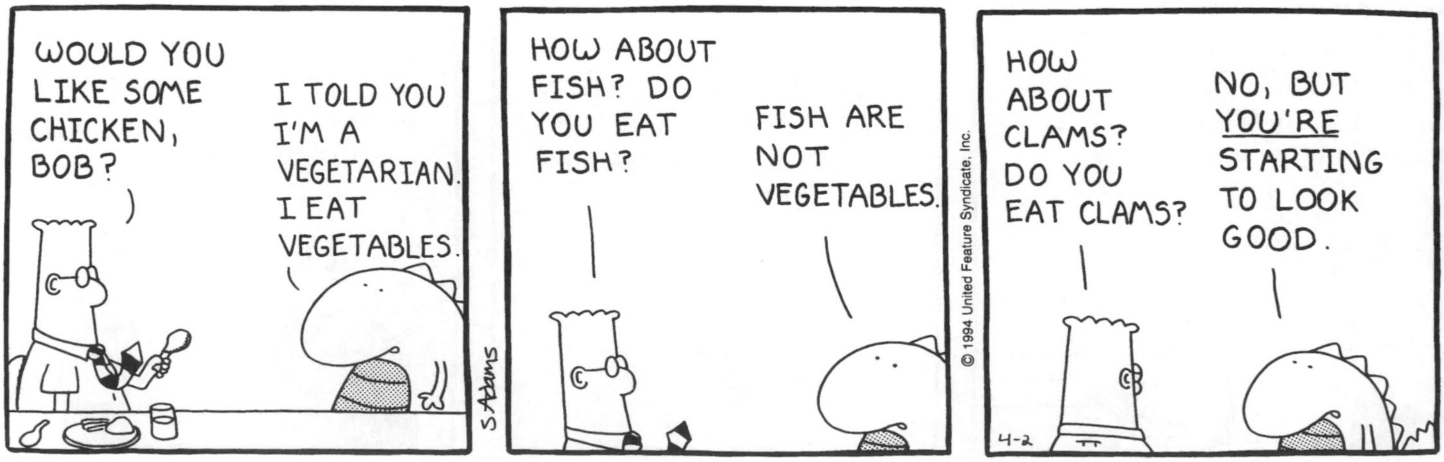
WOULD YOU LIKE SOME CHICKEN, BOB?
I TOLD YOU I'M A VEGETARIAN. I EAT VEGETABLES.
S. Adams
HOW ABOUT FISH? DO YOU EAT FISH?
FISH ARE NOT VEGETABLES.
© 1994 United Feature Syndicate, Inc.
HOW ABOUT CLAMS? DO YOU EAT CLAMS?
NO, BUT YOU'RE STARTING TO LOOK GOOD.
4-2

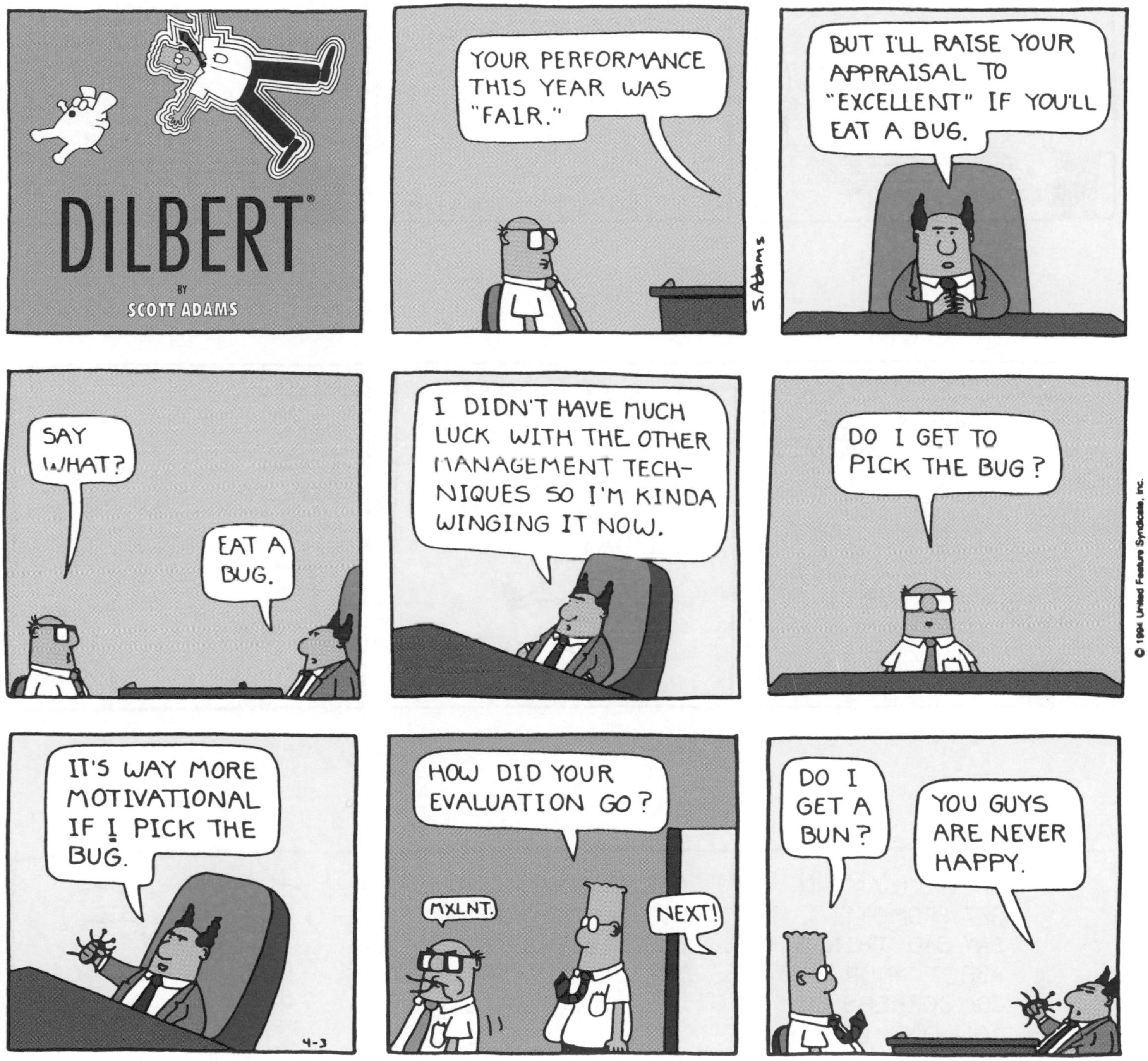
DILBERT®
BY
SCOTT ADAMS
YOUR PERFORMANCE THIS YEAR WAS "FAIR."
S. Adams
BUT I'LL RAISE YOUR APPRAISAL TO "EXCELLENT" IF YOU'LL EAT A BUG.
SAY WHAT?
EAT A BUG.
I DIDN'T HAVE MUCH LUCK WITH THE OTHER MANAGEMENT TECH- NIQUES SO I'M KINDA WINGING IT NOW.
DO I GET TO PICK THE BUG?
© 1994 United Feature Syndicate, Inc.
IT'S WAY MORE MOTIVATIONAL IF I PICK THE BUG.
4-3
HOW DID YOUR EVALUATION GO?
MXLNT.
NEXT!
DO I GET A BUN?
YOU GUYS ARE NEVER HAPPY.

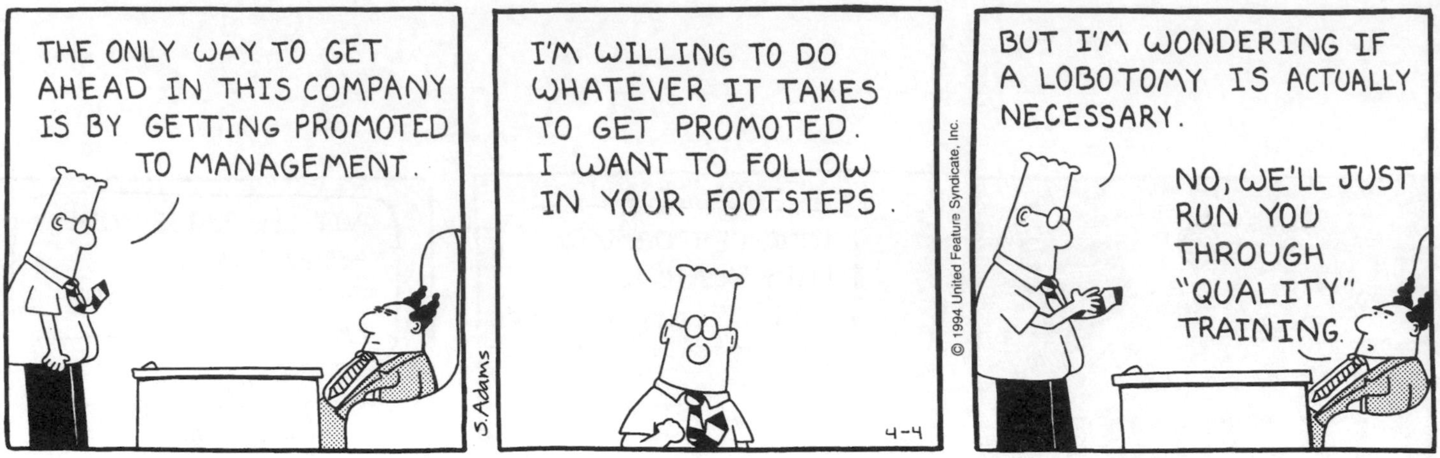
THE ONLY WAY TO GET AHEAD IN THIS COMPANY IS BY GETTING PROMOTED TO MANAGEMENT.
I'M WILLING TO DO WHATEVER IT TAKES TO GET PROMOTED. I WANT TO FOLLOW IN YOUR FOOTSTEPS.
BUT I'M WONDERING IF A LOBOTOMY IS ACTUALLY NECESSARY.
NO, WE'LL JUST RUN YOU THROUGH "QUALITY" TRAINING.
S. Adams
4-4
© 1994 United Feature Syndicate, Inc.

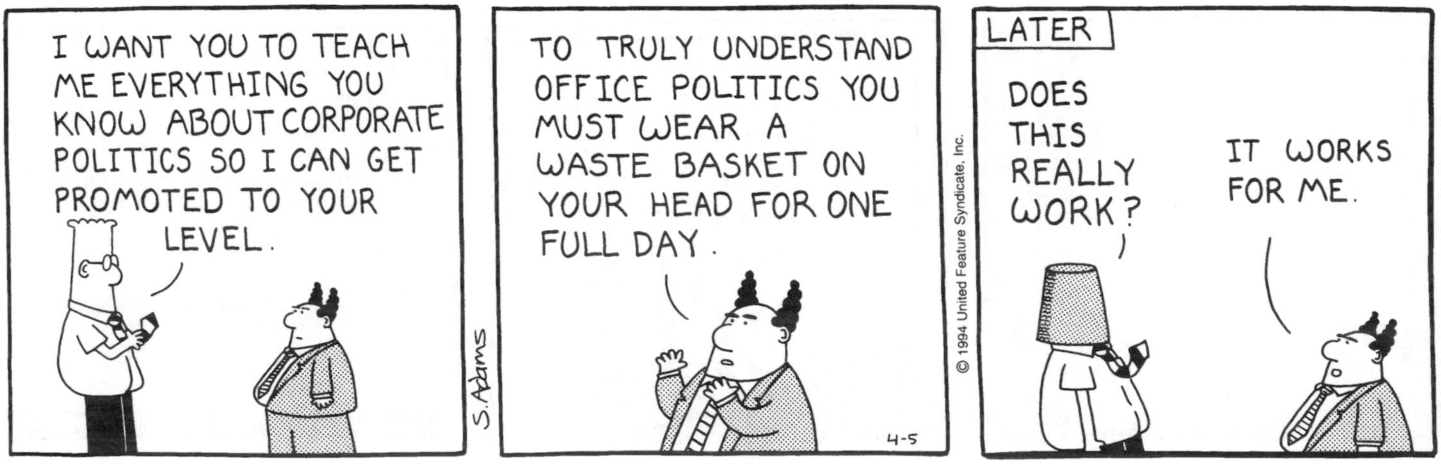
I WANT YOU TO TEACH ME EVERYTHING YOU KNOW ABOUT CORPORATE POLITICS SO I CAN GET PROMOTED TO YOUR LEVEL.
TO TRULY UNDERSTAND OFFICE POLITICS YOU MUST WEAR A WASTE BASKET ON YOUR HEAD FOR ONE FULL DAY.
LATER
DOES THIS REALLY WORK?
IT WORKS FOR ME.
S. Adams
4-5
© 1994 United Feature Syndicate, Inc.

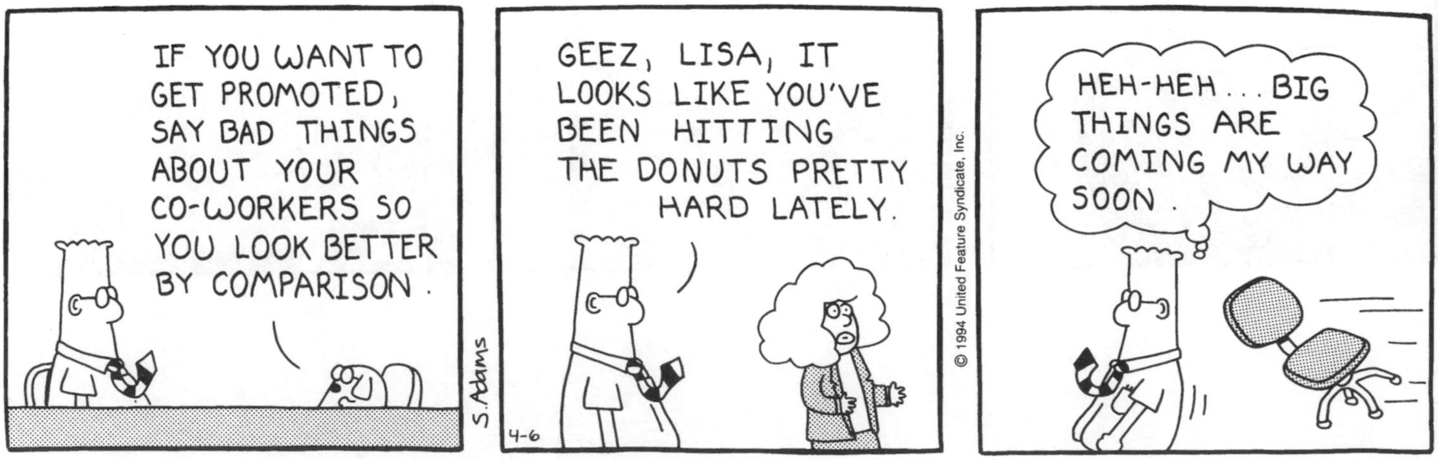
IF YOU WANT TO GET PROMOTED, SAY BAD THINGS ABOUT YOUR CO-WORKERS SO YOU LOOK BETTER BY COMPARISON.
GEEZ, LISA, IT LOOKS LIKE YOU'VE BEEN HITTING THE DONUTS PRETTY HARD LATELY.
HEH-HEH... BIG THINGS ARE COMING MY WAY SOON.
S. Adams
4-6
© 1994 United Feature Syndicate, Inc.

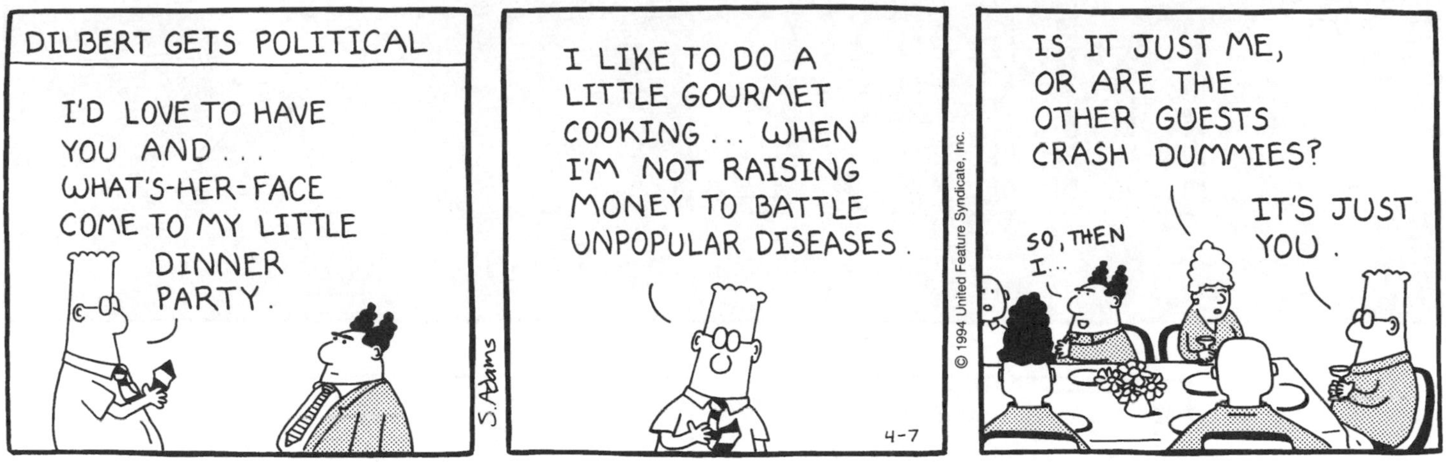
DILBERT GETS POLITICAL
I'D LOVE TO HAVE YOU AND . . . WHAT'S-HER-FACE COME TO MY LITTLE DINNER PARTY.
S. Adams
I LIKE TO DO A LITTLE GOURMET COOKING . . . WHEN I'M NOT RAISING MONEY TO BATTLE UNPOPULAR DISEASES.
4-7
© 1994 United Feature Syndicate, Inc.
IS IT JUST ME, OR ARE THE OTHER GUESTS CRASH DUMMIES?
SO, THEN I . . .
IT'S JUST YOU.

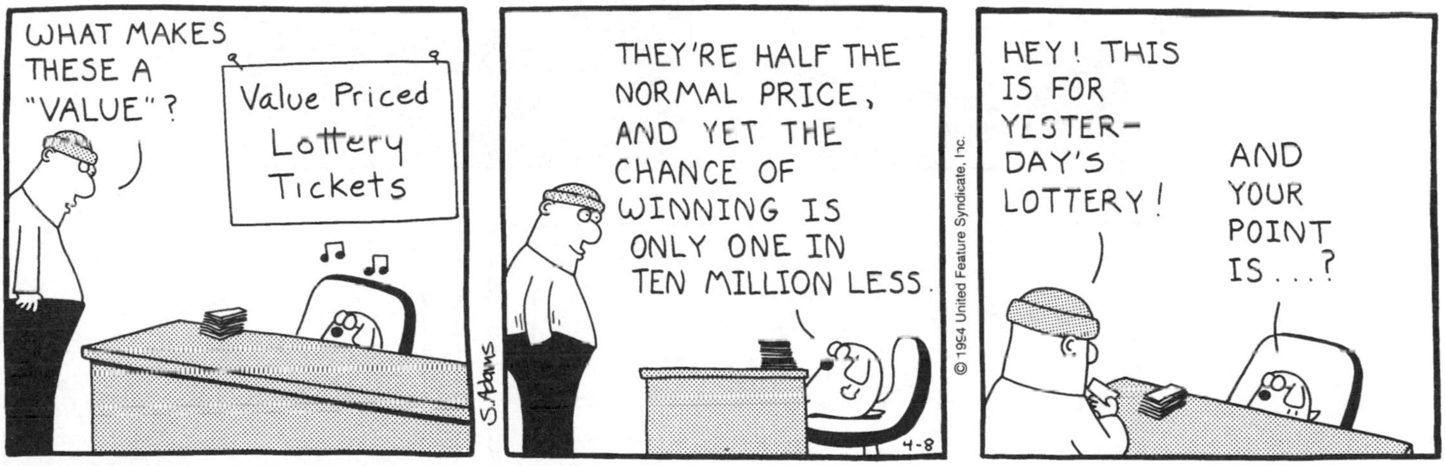
WHAT MAKES THESE A "VALUE"?
Value Priced Lottery Tickets
S. Adams
THEY'RE HALF THE NORMAL PRICE, AND YET THE CHANCE OF WINNING IS ONLY ONE IN TEN MILLION LESS.
4-8
© 1954 United Feature Syndicate, Inc.
HEY! THIS IS FOR YESTER-DAY'S LOTTERY!
AND YOUR POINT IS . . . ?

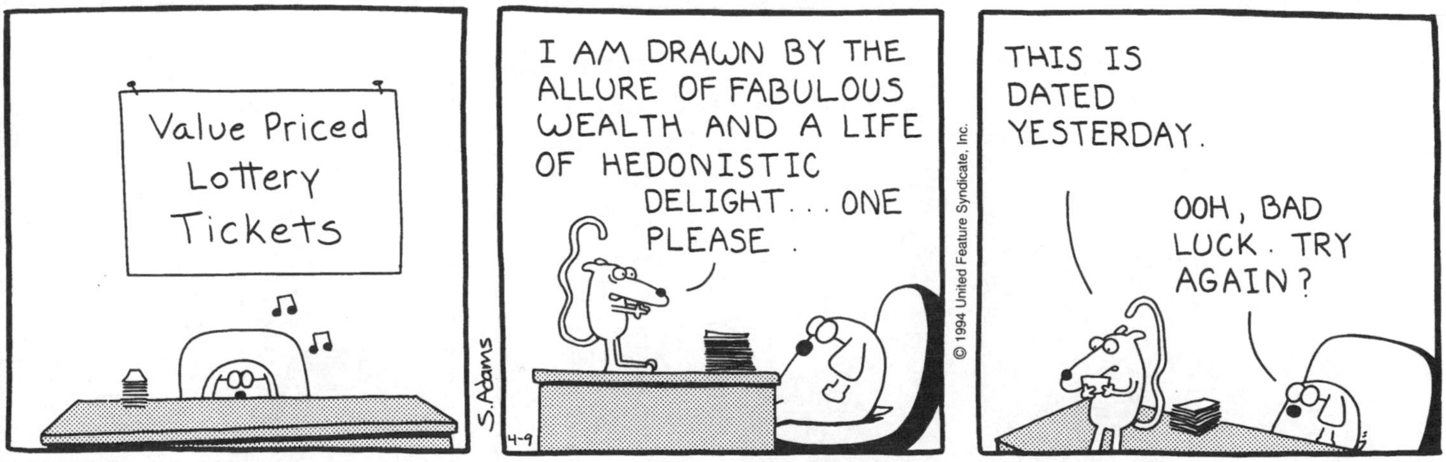
Value Priced Lottery Tickets
S. Adams
4-9
I AM DRAWN BY THE ALLURE OF FABULOUS WEALTH AND A LIFE OF HEDONISTIC DELIGHT . . . ONE PLEASE.
© 1994 United Feature Syndicate, Inc.
THIS IS DATED YESTERDAY.
OOH, BAD LUCK. TRY AGAIN?

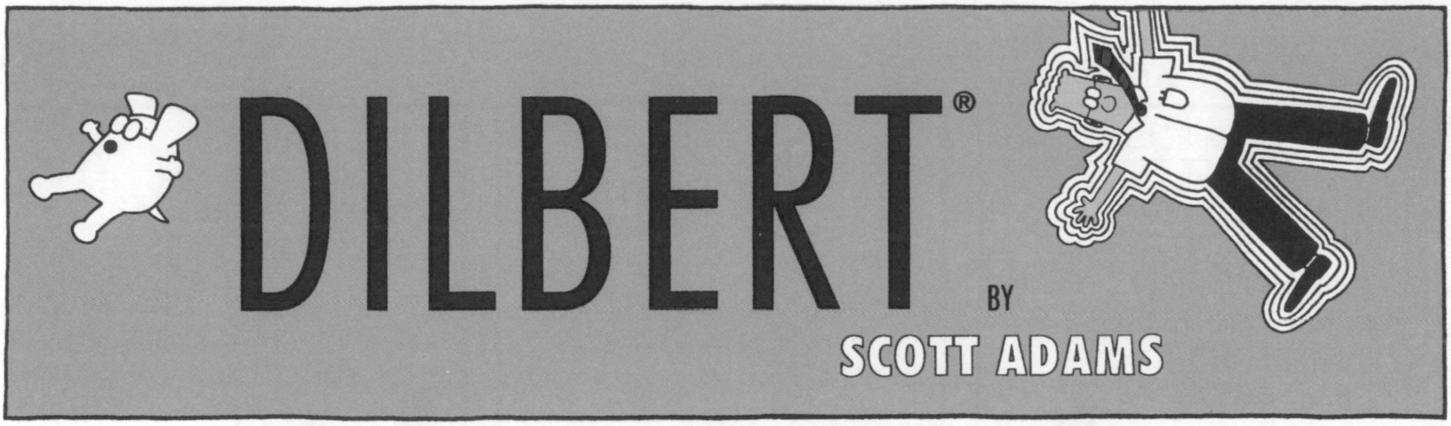
DILBERT®
BY
SCOTT ADAMS

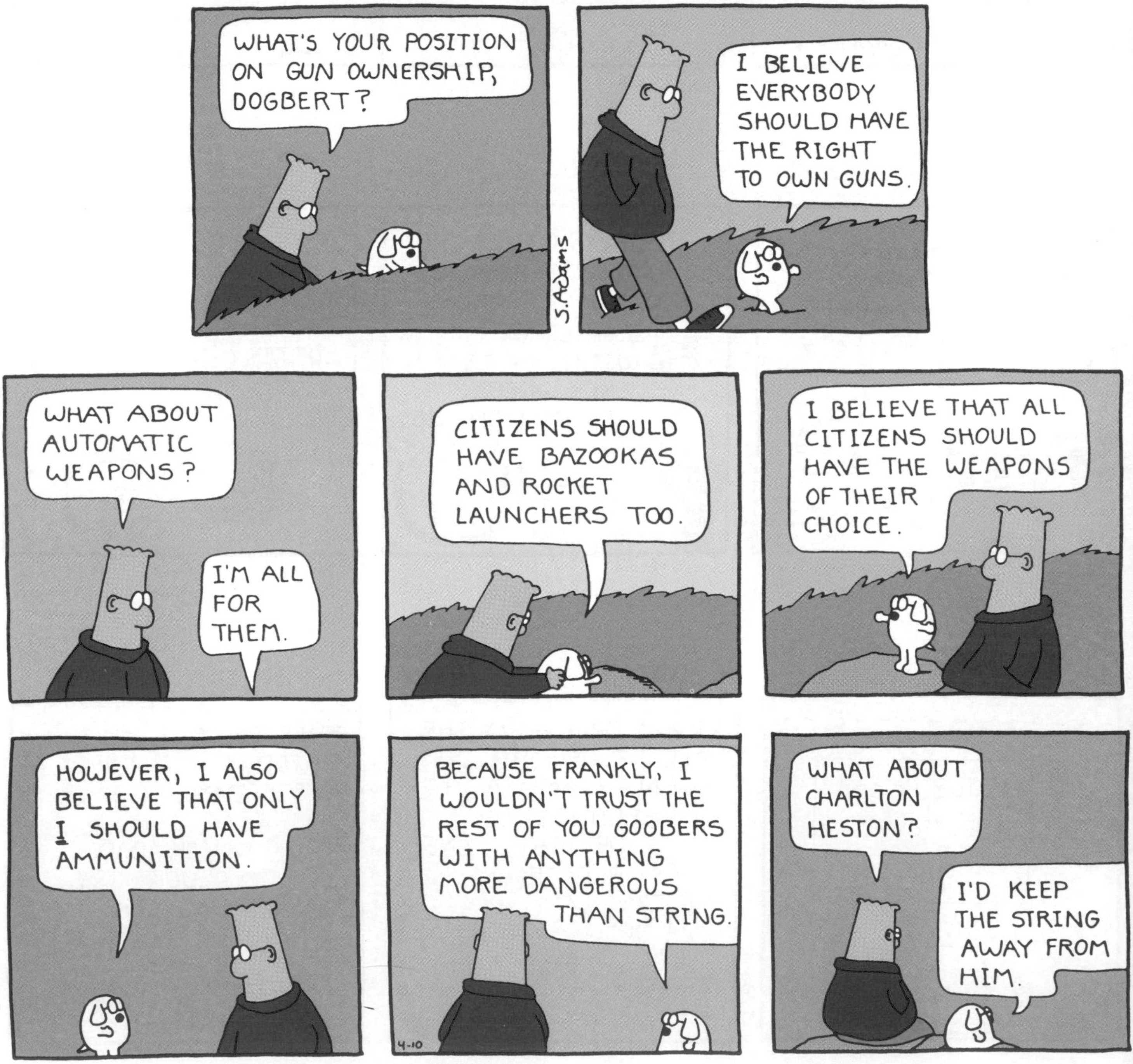
WHAT'S YOUR POSITION ON GUN OWNERSHIP, DOGBERT?
S. ADAMS
I BELIEVE EVERYBODY SHOULD HAVE THE RIGHT TO OWN GUNS.
WHAT ABOUT AUTOMATIC WEAPONS?
I'M ALL FOR THEM.
CITIZENS SHOULD HAVE BAZOOKAS AND ROCKET LAUNCHERS TOO.
I BELIEVE THAT ALL CITIZENS SHOULD HAVE THE WEAPONS OF THEIR CHOICE.
HOWEVER, I ALSO BELIEVE THAT ONLY I SHOULD HAVE AMMUNITION.
BECAUSE FRANKLY, I WOULDN'T TRUST THE REST OF YOU GOOBERS WITH ANYTHING MORE DANGEROUS THAN STRING.
4-10
WHAT ABOUT CHARLTON HESTON?
I'D KEEP THE STRING AWAY FROM HIM.

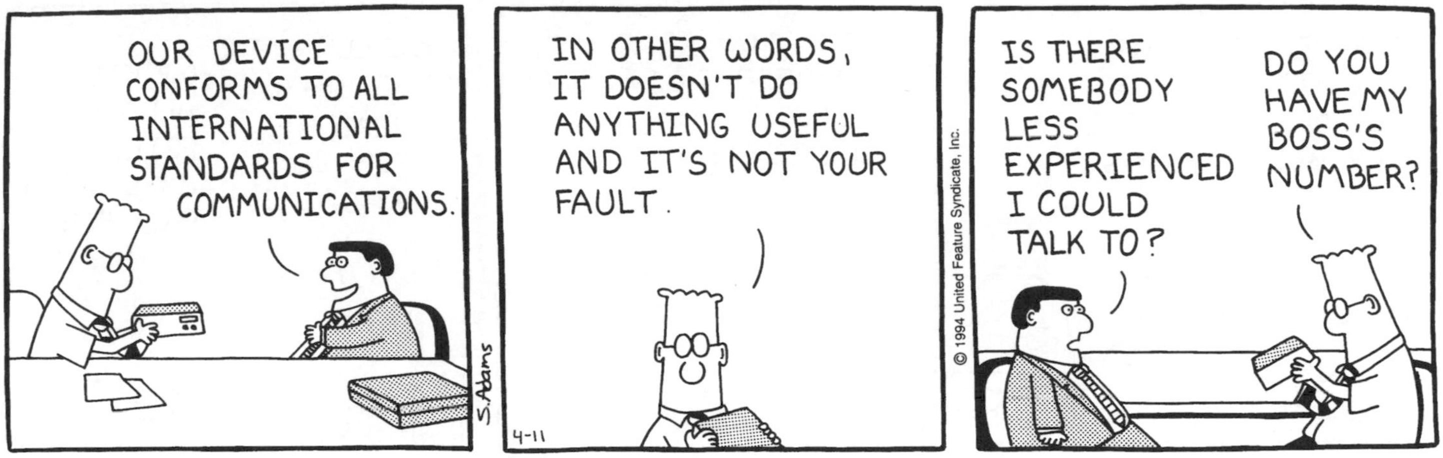
OUR DEVICE CONFORMS TO ALL INTERNATIONAL STANDARDS FOR COMMUNICATIONS.
S. Adams
IN OTHER WORDS, IT DOESN'T DO ANYTHING USEFUL AND IT'S NOT YOUR FAULT.
4-11
© 1994 United Feature Syndicate, Inc.
IS THERE SOMEBODY LESS EXPERIENCED I COULD TALK TO?
DO YOU HAVE MY BOSS'S NUMBER?

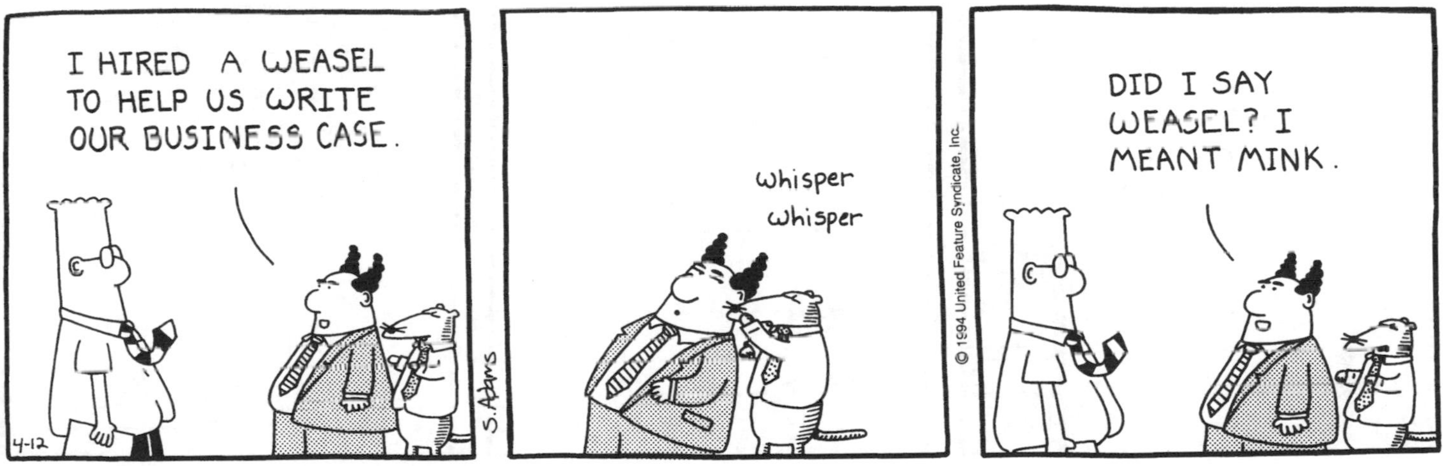
I HIRED A WEASEL TO HELP US WRITE OUR BUSINESS CASE.
4-12
S. Adams
whisper whisper
© 1994 United Feature Syndicate, Inc.
DID I SAY WEASEL? I MEANT MINK.

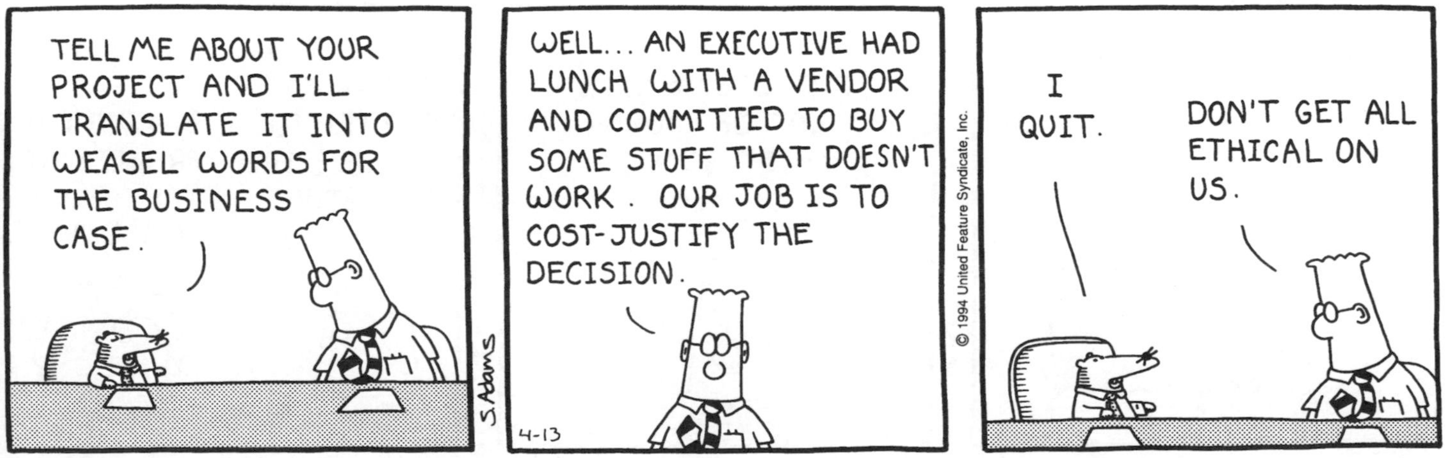
TELL ME ABOUT YOUR PROJECT AND I'LL TRANSLATE IT INTO WEASEL WORDS FOR THE BUSINESS CASE.
S. Adams
WELL... AN EXECUTIVE HAD LUNCH WITH A VENDOR AND COMMITTED TO BUY SOME STUFF THAT DOESN'T WORK. OUR JOB IS TO COST-JUSTIFY THE DECISION.
4-13
© 1994 United Feature Syndicate, Inc.
I QUIT.
DON'T GET ALL ETHICAL ON US.

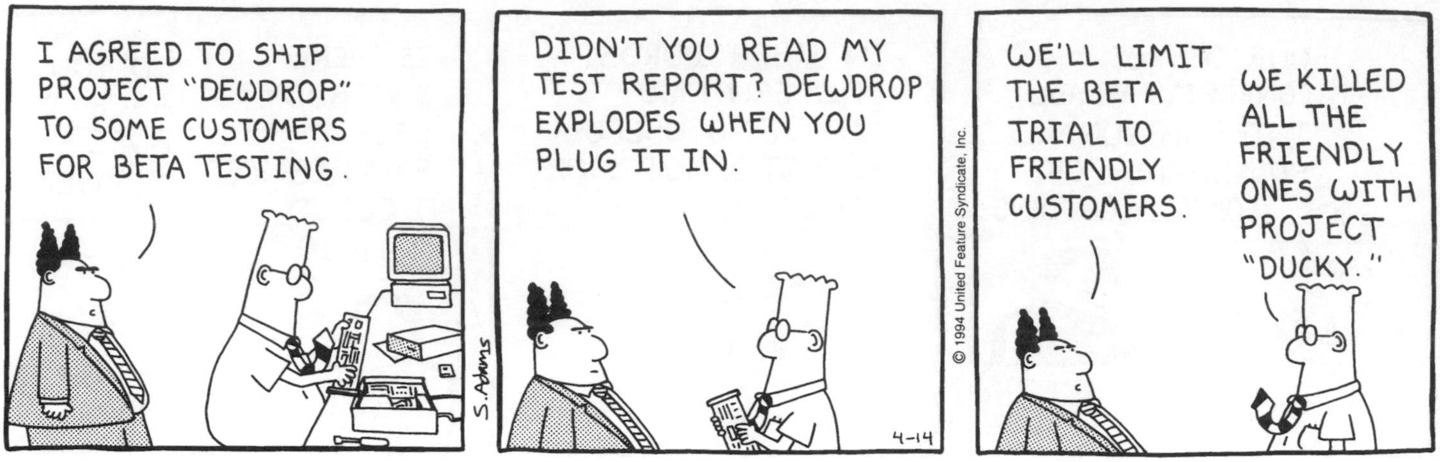
I AGREED TO SHIP PROJECT "DEWDROP" TO SOME CUSTOMERS FOR BETA TESTING.
S. Adams
DIDN'T YOU READ MY TEST REPORT? DEWDROP EXPLODES WHEN YOU PLUG IT IN.
4-14
© 1994 United Feature Syndicate, Inc.
WE'LL LIMIT THE BETA TRIAL TO FRIENDLY CUSTOMERS.
WE KILLED ALL THE FRIENDLY ONES WITH PROJECT "DUCKY."

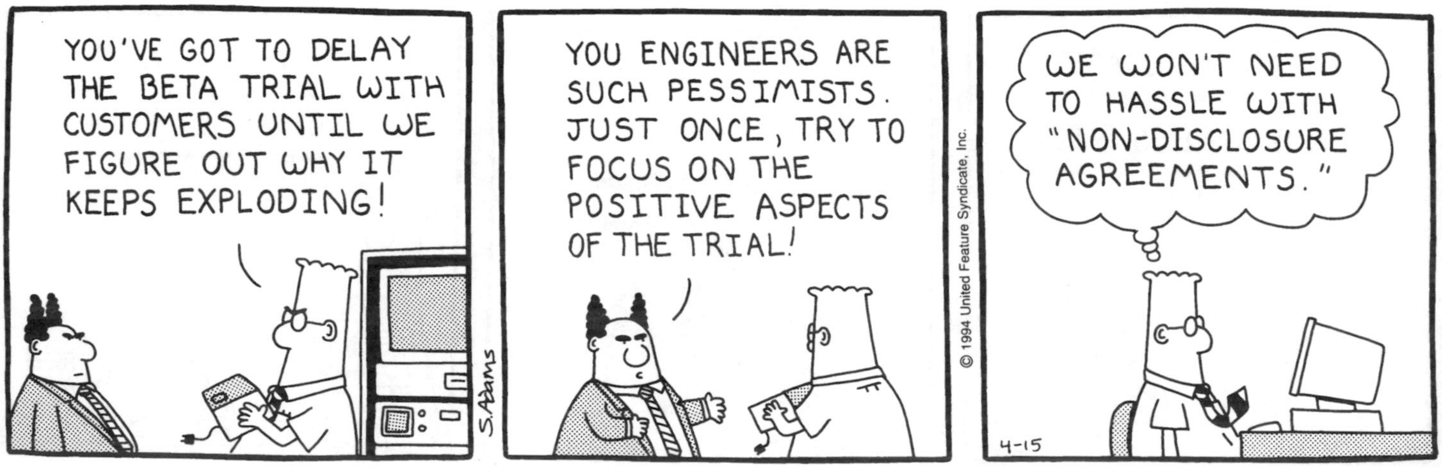
YOU'VE GOT TO DELAY THE BETA TRIAL WITH CUSTOMERS UNTIL WE FIGURE OUT WHY IT KEEPS EXPLODING!
S. Adams
YOU ENGINEERS ARE SUCH PESSIMISTS. JUST ONCE, TRY TO FOCUS ON THE POSITIVE ASPECTS OF THE TRIAL!
© 1994 United Feature Syndicate, Inc.
WE WON'T NEED TO HASSLE WITH "NON-DISCLOSURE AGREEMENTS."
4-15

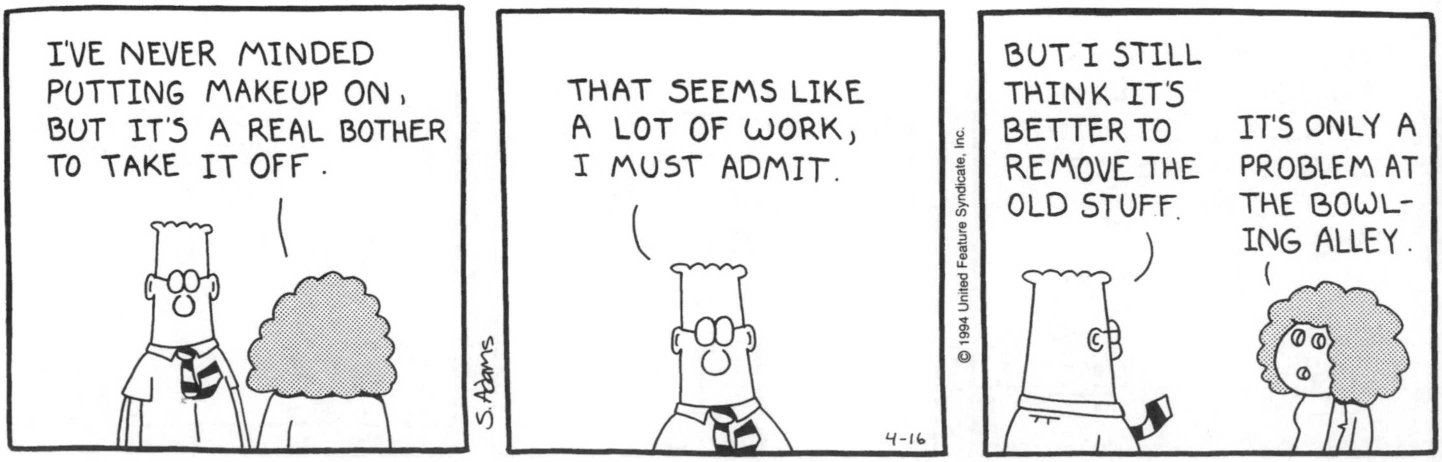
I'VE NEVER MINDED PUTTING MAKEUP ON, BUT IT'S A REAL BOTHER TO TAKE IT OFF.
S. Adams
THAT SEEMS LIKE A LOT OF WORK, I MUST ADMIT.
4-16
© 1994 United Feature Syndicate, Inc.
BUT I STILL THINK IT'S BETTER TO REMOVE THE OLD STUFF.
IT'S ONLY A PROBLEM AT THE BOWL-ING ALLEY.

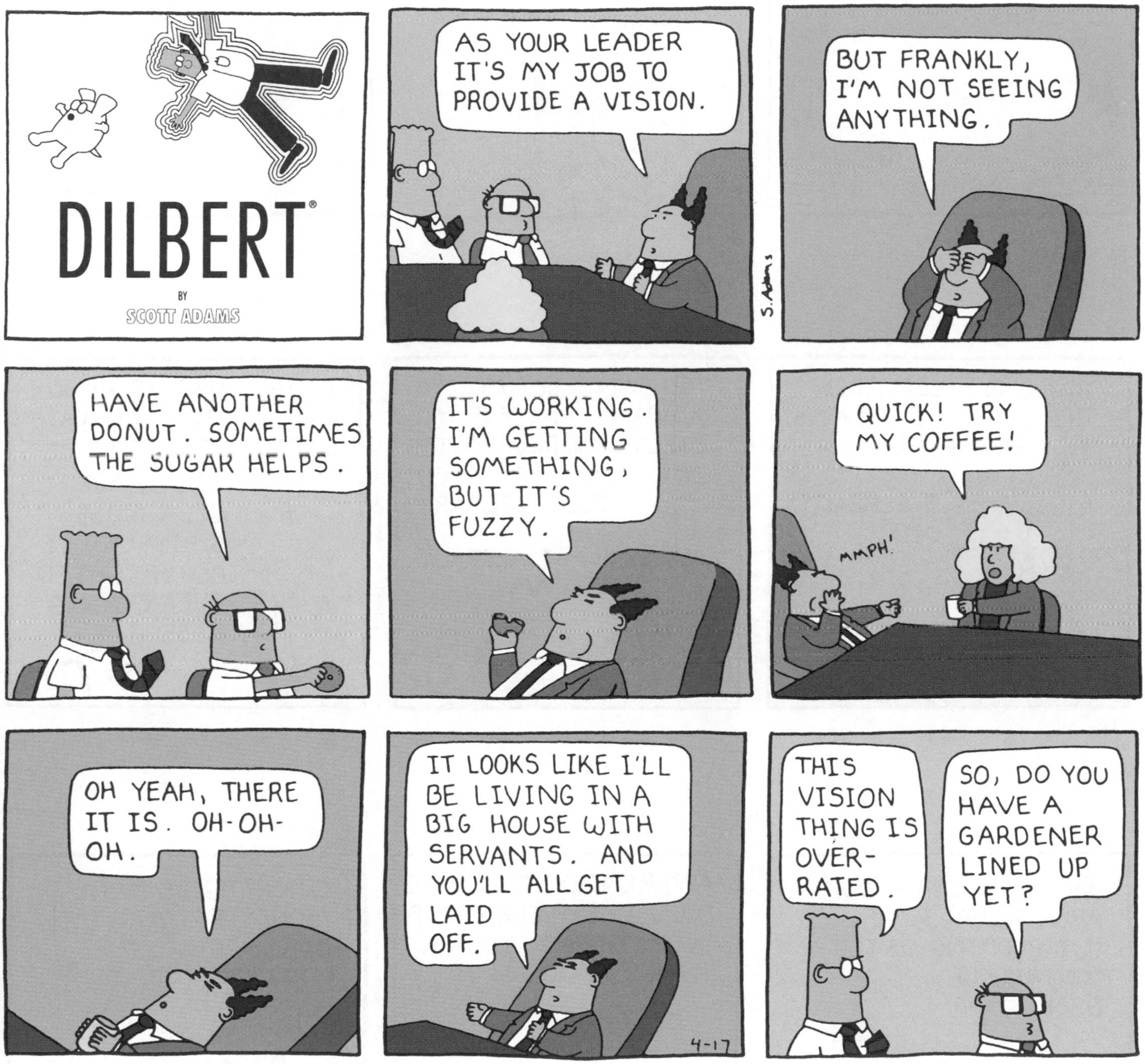
DILBERT®
BY
SCOTT ADAMS
AS YOUR LEADER IT'S MY JOB TO PROVIDE A VISION.
S. Adams
BUT FRANKLY, I'M NOT SEEING ANYTHING.
HAVE ANOTHER DONUT. SOMETIMES THE SUGAR HELPS.
IT'S WORKING. I'M GETTING SOMETHING, BUT IT'S FUZZY.
QUICK! TRY MY COFFEE!
MMPH!
OH YEAH, THERE IT IS. OH-OH-OH.
IT LOOKS LIKE I'LL BE LIVING IN A BIG HOUSE WITH SERVANTS. AND YOU'LL ALL GET LAID OFF.
4-17
THIS VISION THING IS OVER-RATED.
SO, DO YOU HAVE A GARDENER LINED UP YET?

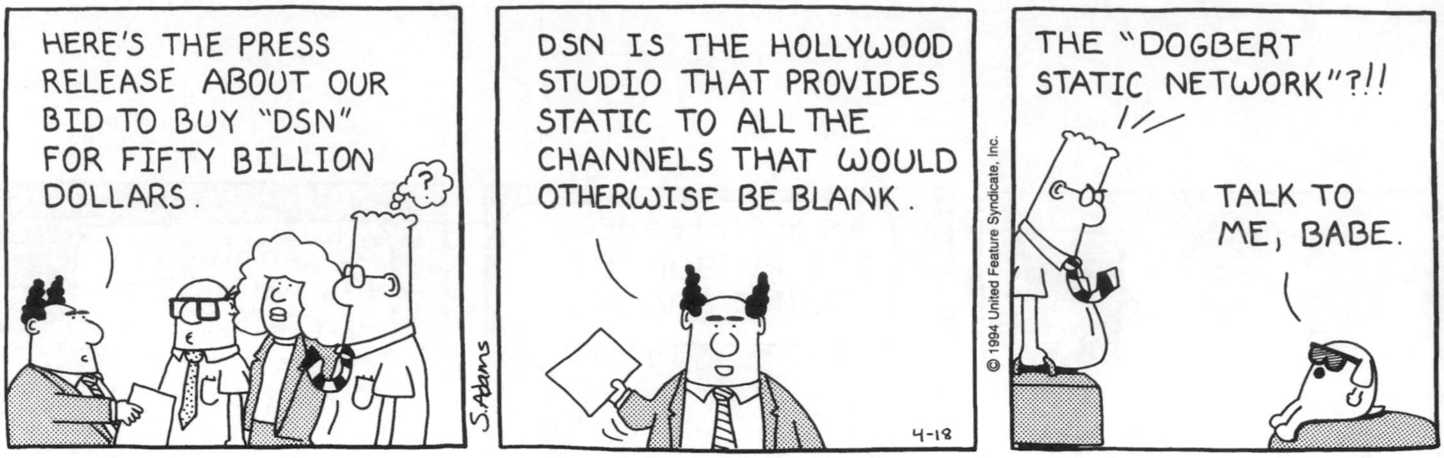
HERE'S THE PRESS RELEASE ABOUT OUR BID TO BUY "DSN" FOR FIFTY BILLION DOLLARS.
?
S. Adams
DSN IS THE HOLLYWOOD STUDIO THAT PROVIDES STATIC TO ALL THE CHANNELS THAT WOULD OTHERWISE BE BLANK.
4-18
© 1994 United Feature Syndicate, Inc.
THE "DOGBERT STATIC NETWORK"?!!
TALK TO ME, BABE.

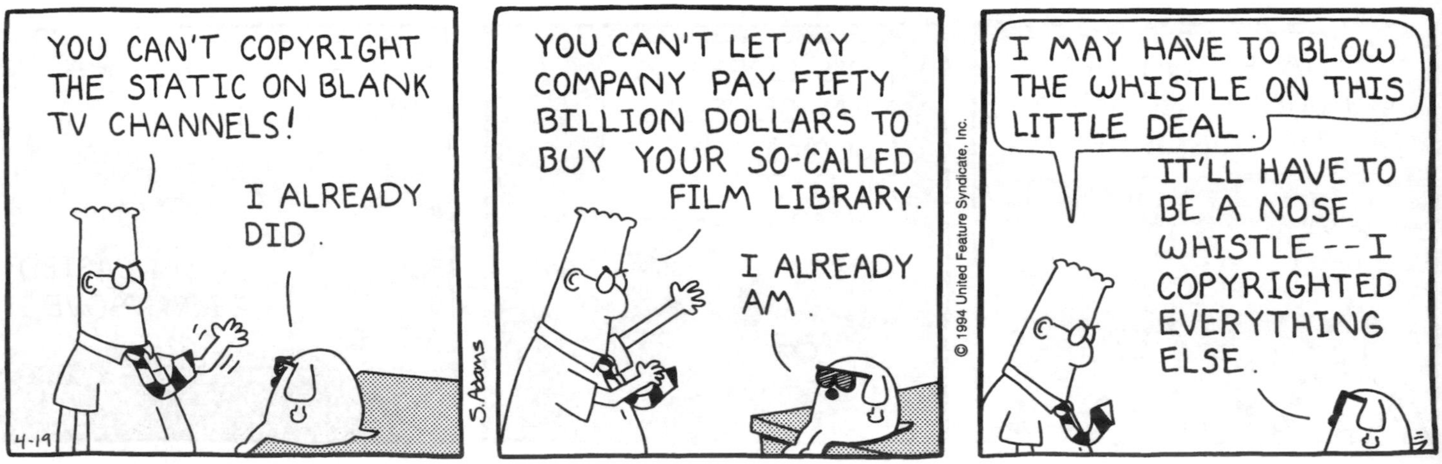
YOU CAN'T COPYRIGHT THE STATIC ON BLANK TV CHANNELS!
I ALREADY DID.
4-19
S. Adams
YOU CAN'T LET MY COMPANY PAY FIFTY BILLION DOLLARS TO BUY YOUR SO-CALLED FILM LIBRARY.
I ALREADY AM.
© 1994 United Feature Syndicate, Inc.
I MAY HAVE TO BLOW THE WHISTLE ON THIS LITTLE DEAL.
IT'LL HAVE TO BE A NOSE WHISTLE -- I COPYRIGHTED EVERYTHING ELSE.

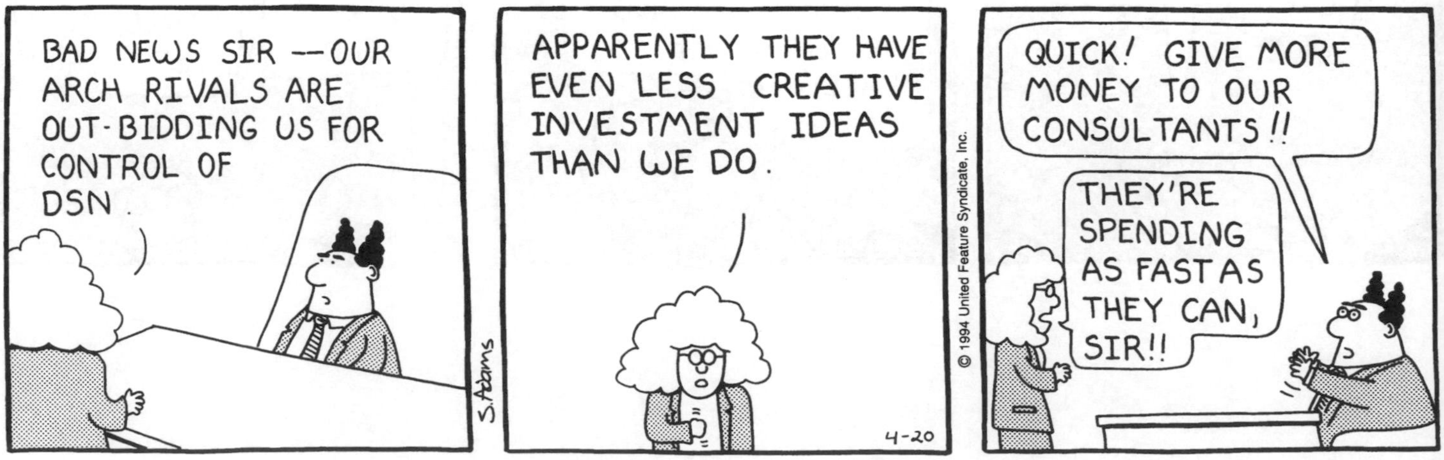
BAD NEWS SIR -- OUR ARCH RIVALS ARE OUT-BIDDING US FOR CONTROL OF DSN.
S. Adams
APPARENTLY THEY HAVE EVEN LESS CREATIVE INVESTMENT IDEAS THAN WE DO.
4-20
© 1994 United Feature Syndicate, Inc.
QUICK! GIVE MORE MONEY TO OUR CONSULTANTS!!
THEY'RE SPENDING AS FAST AS THEY CAN, SIR!!

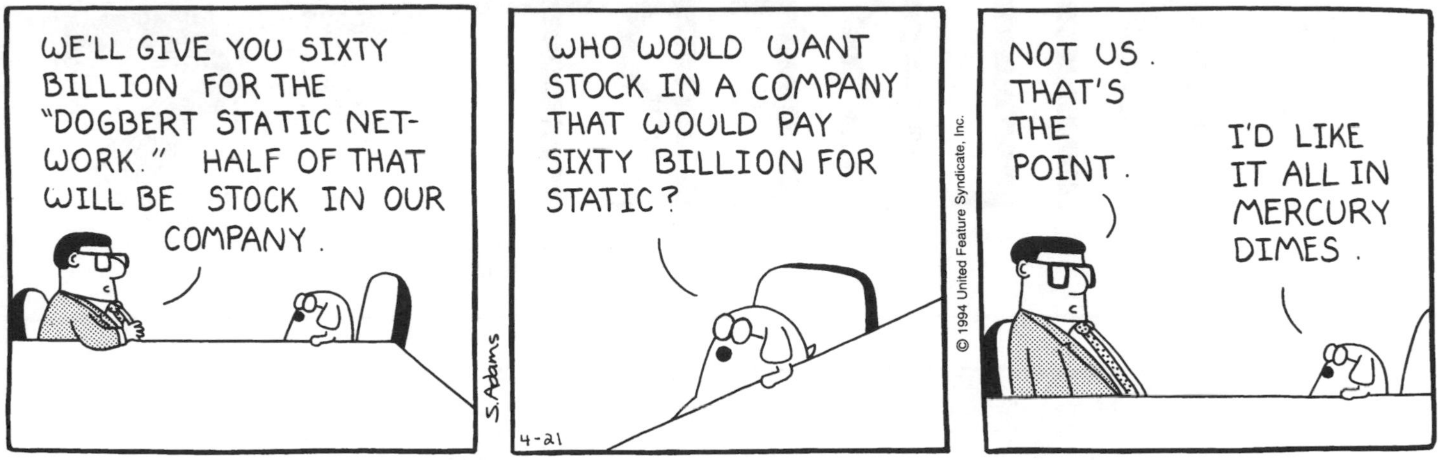
WE'LL GIVE YOU SIXTY BILLION FOR THE "DOGBERT STATIC NETWORK." HALF OF THAT WILL BE STOCK IN OUR COMPANY.
S. Adams
4-21
WHO WOULD WANT STOCK IN A COMPANY THAT WOULD PAY SIXTY BILLION FOR STATIC?
© 1994 United Feature Syndicate, Inc.
NOT US. THAT'S THE POINT.
I'D LIKE IT ALL IN MERCURY DIMES.

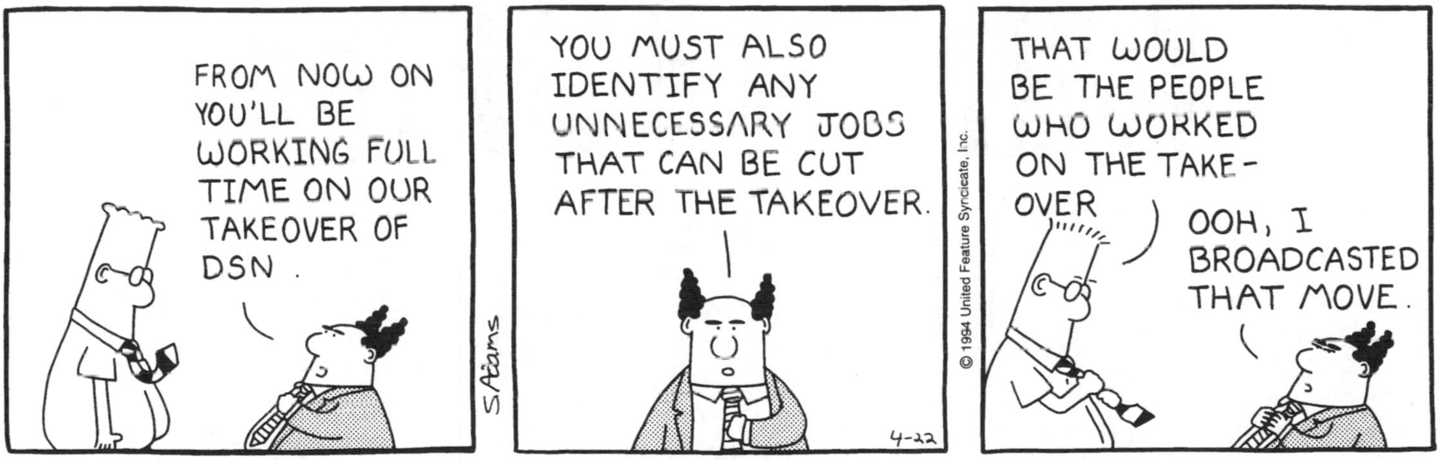
FROM NOW ON YOU'LL BE WORKING FULL TIME ON OUR TAKEOVER OF DSN.
S. Adams
YOU MUST ALSO IDENTIFY ANY UNNECESSARY JOBS THAT CAN BE CUT AFTER THE TAKEOVER.
4-22
© 1994 United Feature Syndicate, Inc.
THAT WOULD BE THE PEOPLE WHO WORKED ON THE TAKEOVER
OOH, I BROADCASTED THAT MOVE.

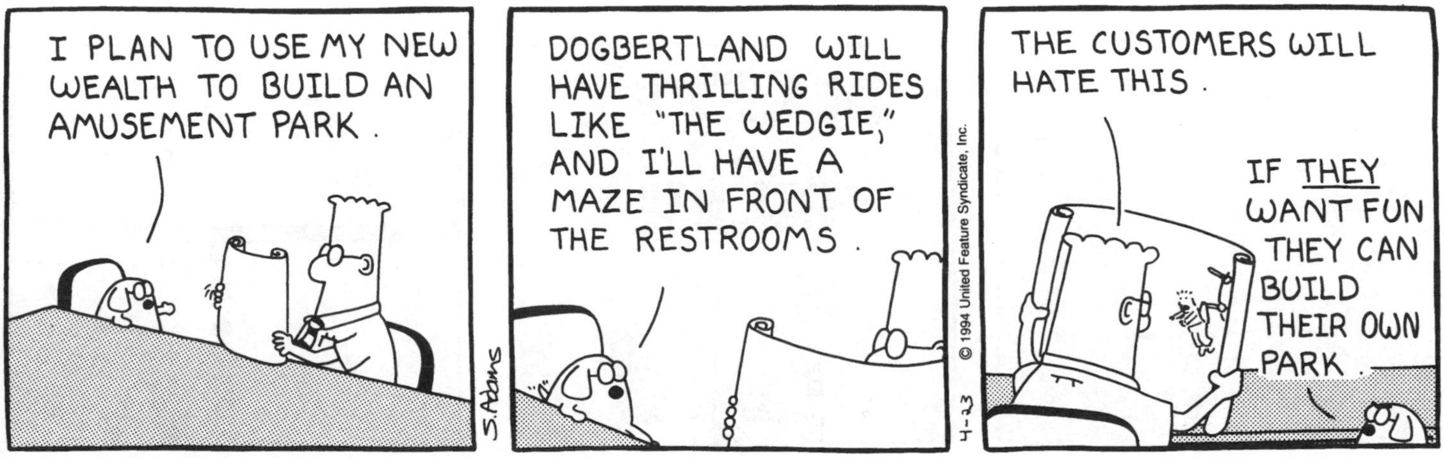
I PLAN TO USE MY NEW WEALTH TO BUILD AN AMUSEMENT PARK.
S. Adams
DOGBERTLAND WILL HAVE THRILLING RIDES LIKE "THE WEDGIE," AND I'LL HAVE A MAZE IN FRONT OF THE RESTROOMS.
© 1994 United Feature Syndicate, Inc.
4-23
THE CUSTOMERS WILL HATE THIS.
IF THEY WANT FUN THEY CAN BUILD THEIR OWN PARK.

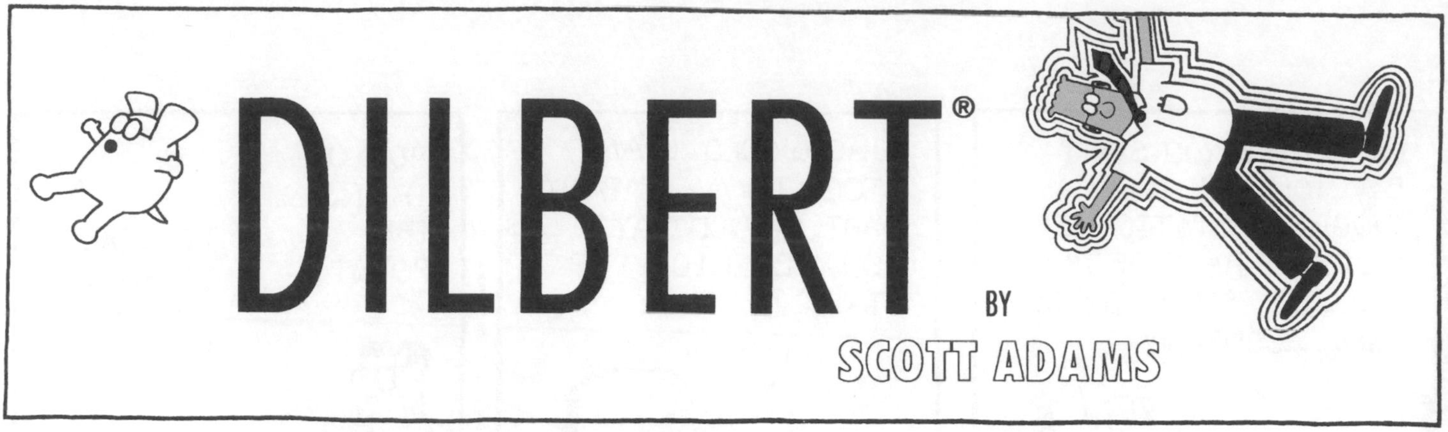
DILBERT®
BY
SCOTT ADAMS

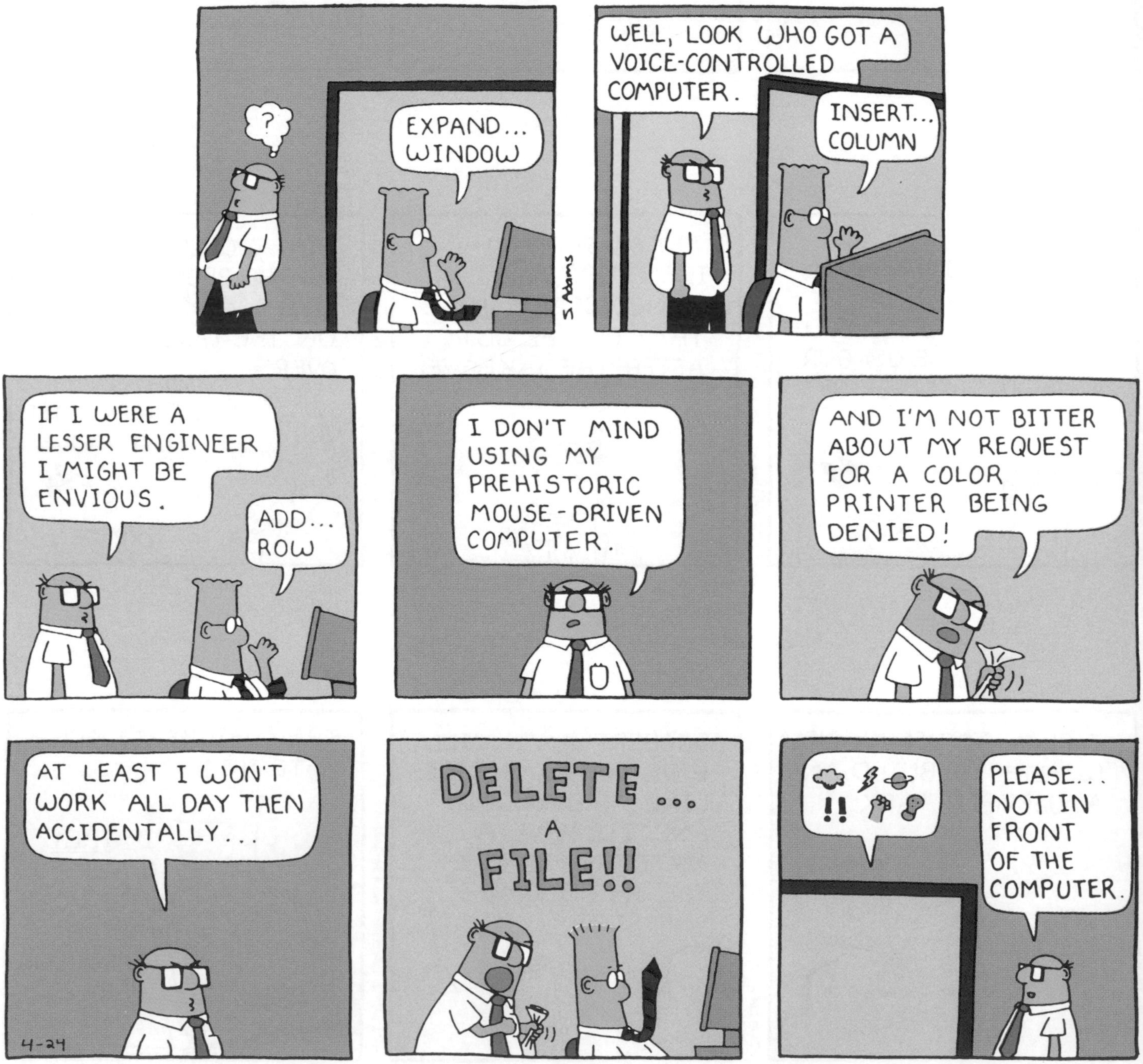
?
EXPAND... WINDOW
S Adams
WELL, LOOK WHO GOT A VOICE-CONTROLLED COMPUTER.
INSERT... COLUMN
IF I WERE A LESSER ENGINEER I MIGHT BE ENVIOUS.
ADD... ROW
I DON'T MIND USING MY PREHISTORIC MOUSE-DRIVEN COMPUTER.
AND I'M NOT BITTER ABOUT MY REQUEST FOR A COLOR PRINTER BEING DENIED!
AT LEAST I WON'T WORK ALL DAY THEN ACCIDENTALLY...
4-24
DELETE... A FILE!!
!!
PLEASE... NOT IN FRONT OF THE COMPUTER.

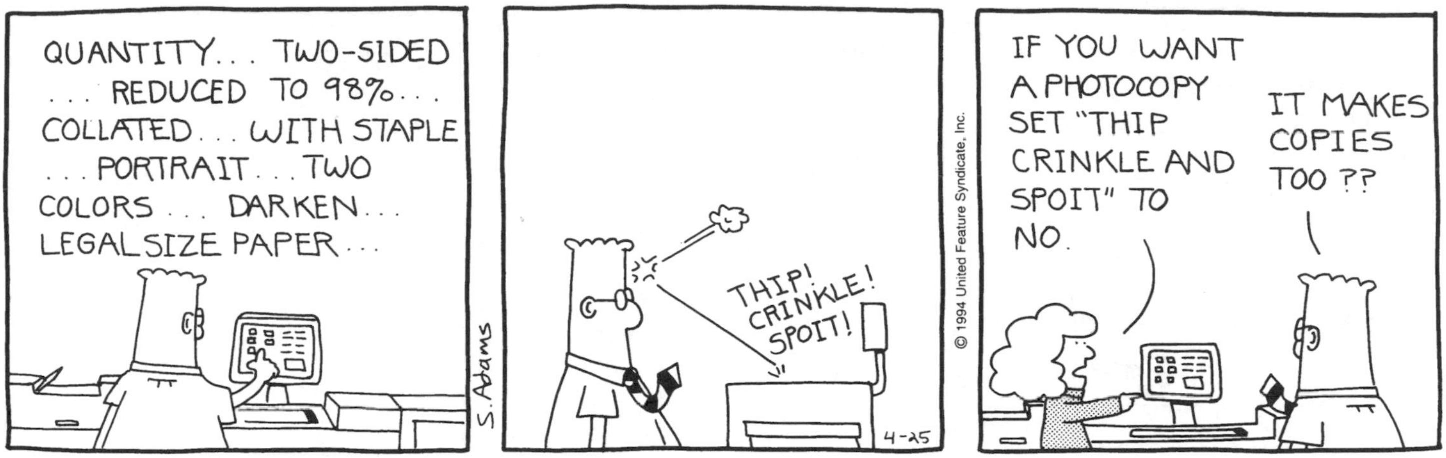
QUANTITY... TWO-SIDED ... REDUCED TO 98%... COLLATED... WITH STAPLE ...PORTRAIT...TWO COLORS... DARKEN... LEGAL SIZE PAPER...
S. Adams
THIP! CRINKLE! SPOIT!
4-25
© 1994 United Feature Syndicate, Inc.
IF YOU WANT A PHOTOCOPY SET "THIP CRINKLE AND SPOIT" TO NO.
IT MAKES COPIES TOO??

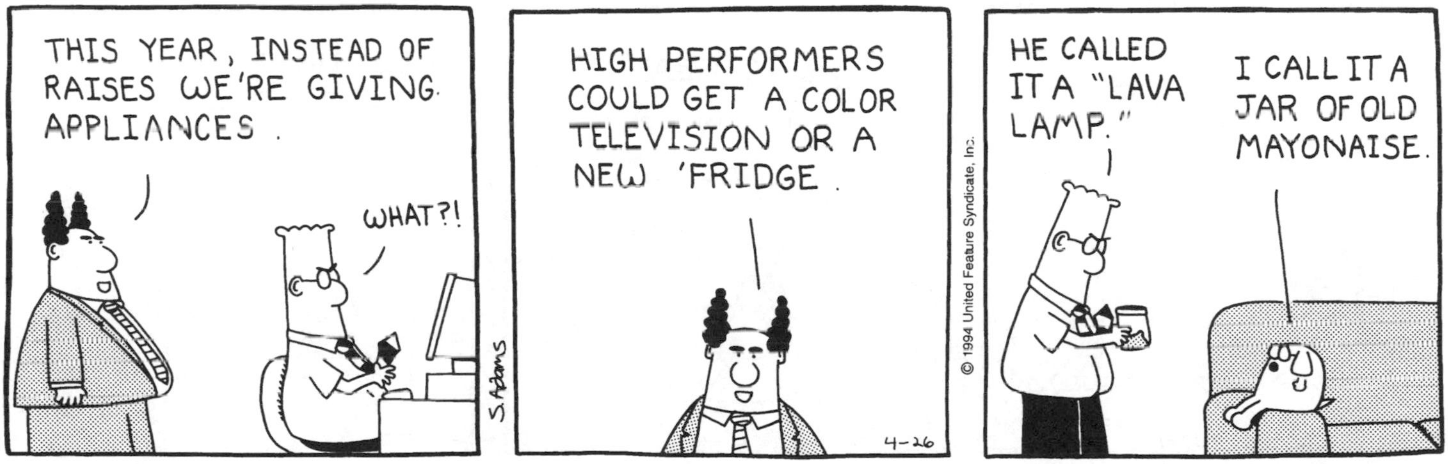
THIS YEAR, INSTEAD OF RAISES WE'RE GIVING APPLIANCES.
WHAT?!
S. Adams
HIGH PERFORMERS COULD GET A COLOR TELEVISION OR A NEW 'FRIDGE.
4-26
© 1994 United Feature Syndicate, Inc.
HE CALLED IT A "LAVA LAMP."
I CALL IT A JAR OF OLD MAYONAISE.

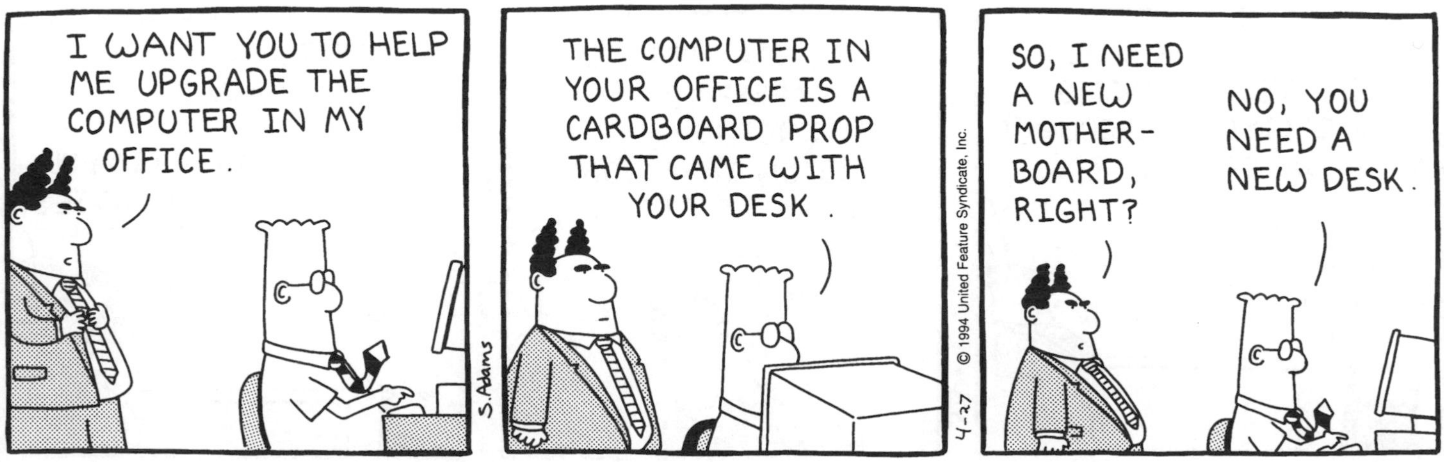
I WANT YOU TO HELP ME UPGRADE THE COMPUTER IN MY OFFICE.
S. Adams
THE COMPUTER IN YOUR OFFICE IS A CARDBOARD PROP THAT CAME WITH YOUR DESK.
4-27
© 1994 United Feature Syndicate, Inc.
SO, I NEED A NEW MOTHER-BOARD, RIGHT?
NO, YOU NEED A NEW DESK.

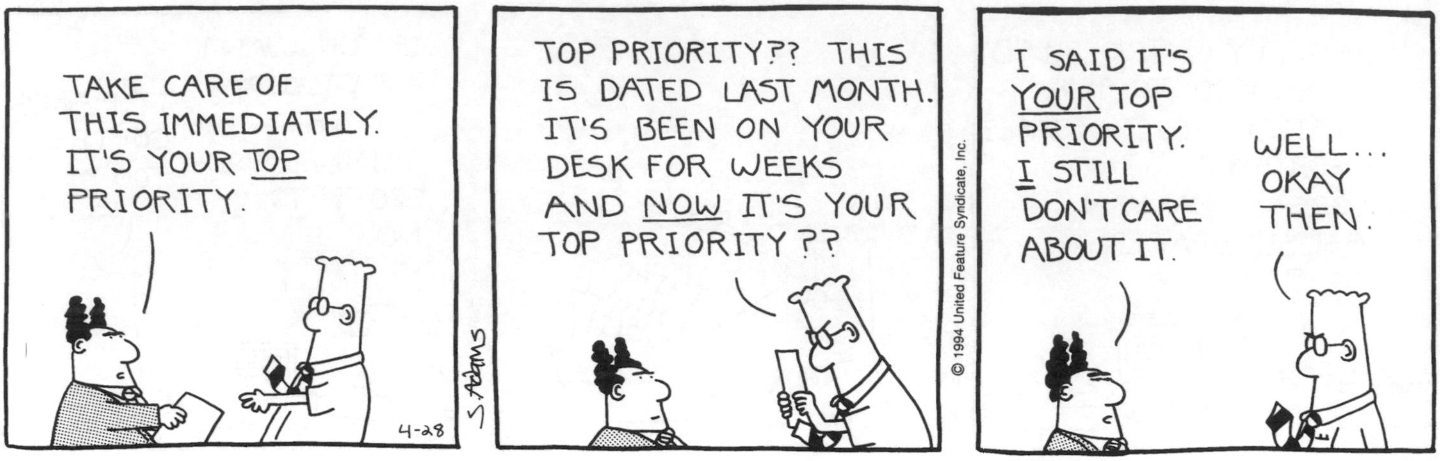
TAKE CARE OF THIS IMMEDIATELY. IT'S YOUR TOP PRIORITY.
4-28
S. Adams
TOP PRIORITY?? THIS IS DATED LAST MONTH. IT'S BEEN ON YOUR DESK FOR WEEKS AND NOW IT'S YOUR TOP PRIORITY??
© 1994 United Feature Syndicate, Inc.
I SAID IT'S YOUR TOP PRIORITY. I STILL DON'T CARE ABOUT IT.
WELL... OKAY THEN.

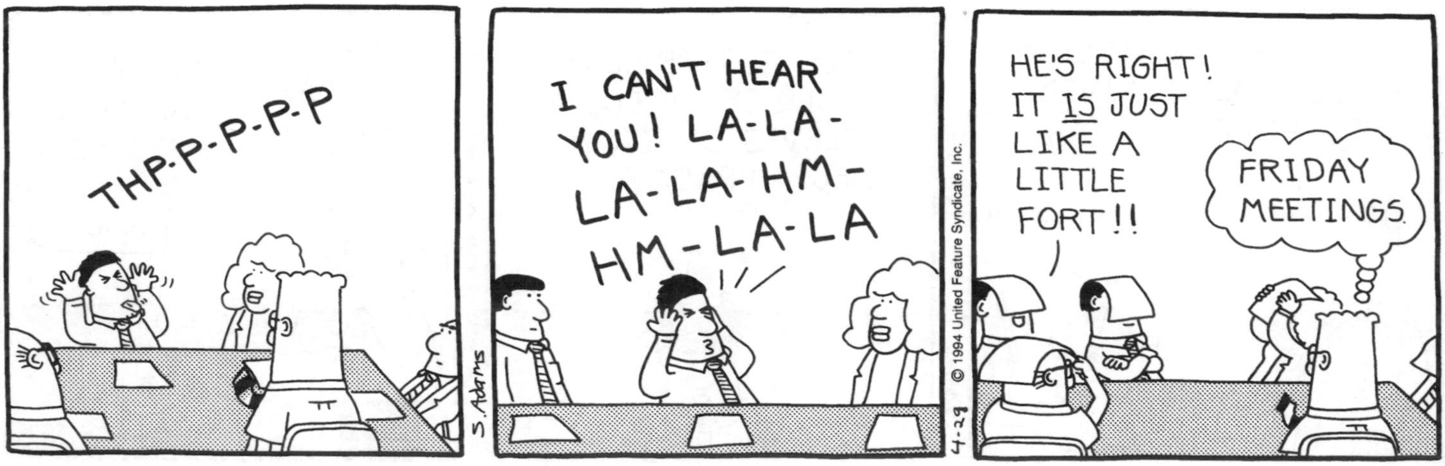
THP-P-P-P-P
S. Adams
I CAN'T HEAR YOU! LA-LA-LA-LA-HM-HM-LA-LA
© 1994 United Feature Syndicate, Inc.
4-29
HE'S RIGHT! IT IS JUST LIKE A LITTLE FORT!!
FRIDAY MEETINGS.

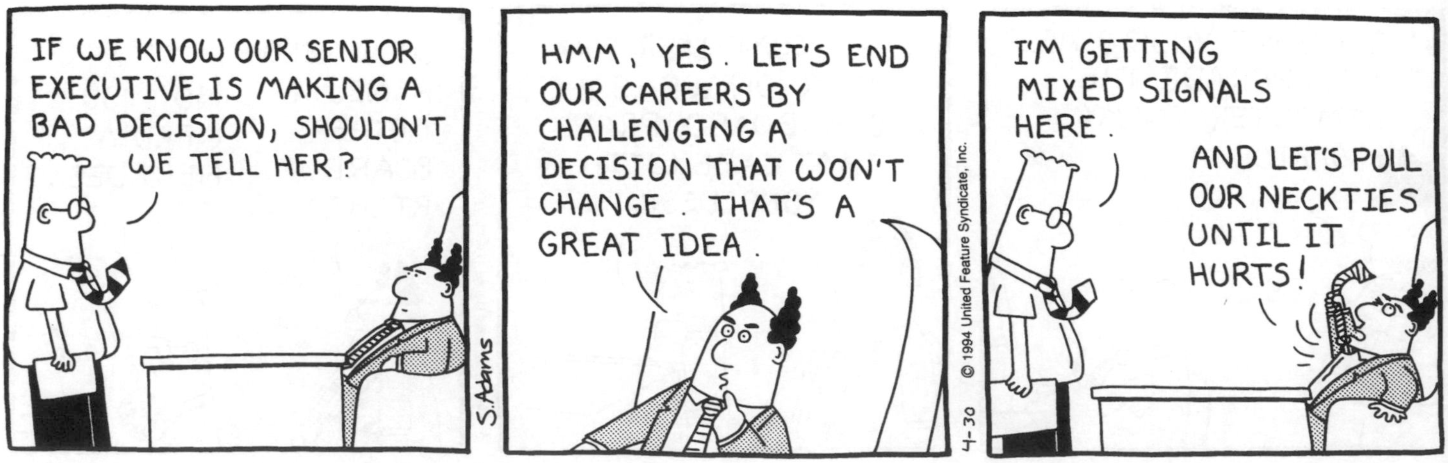
IF WE KNOW OUR SENIOR EXECUTIVE IS MAKING A BAD DECISION, SHOULDN'T WE TELL HER?
S. Adams
HMM, YES. LET'S END OUR CAREERS BY CHALLENGING A DECISION THAT WON'T CHANGE. THAT'S A GREAT IDEA.
© 1994 United Feature Syndicate, Inc.
4-30
I'M GETTING MIXED SIGNALS HERE.
AND LET'S PULL OUR NECKTIES UNTIL IT HURTS!

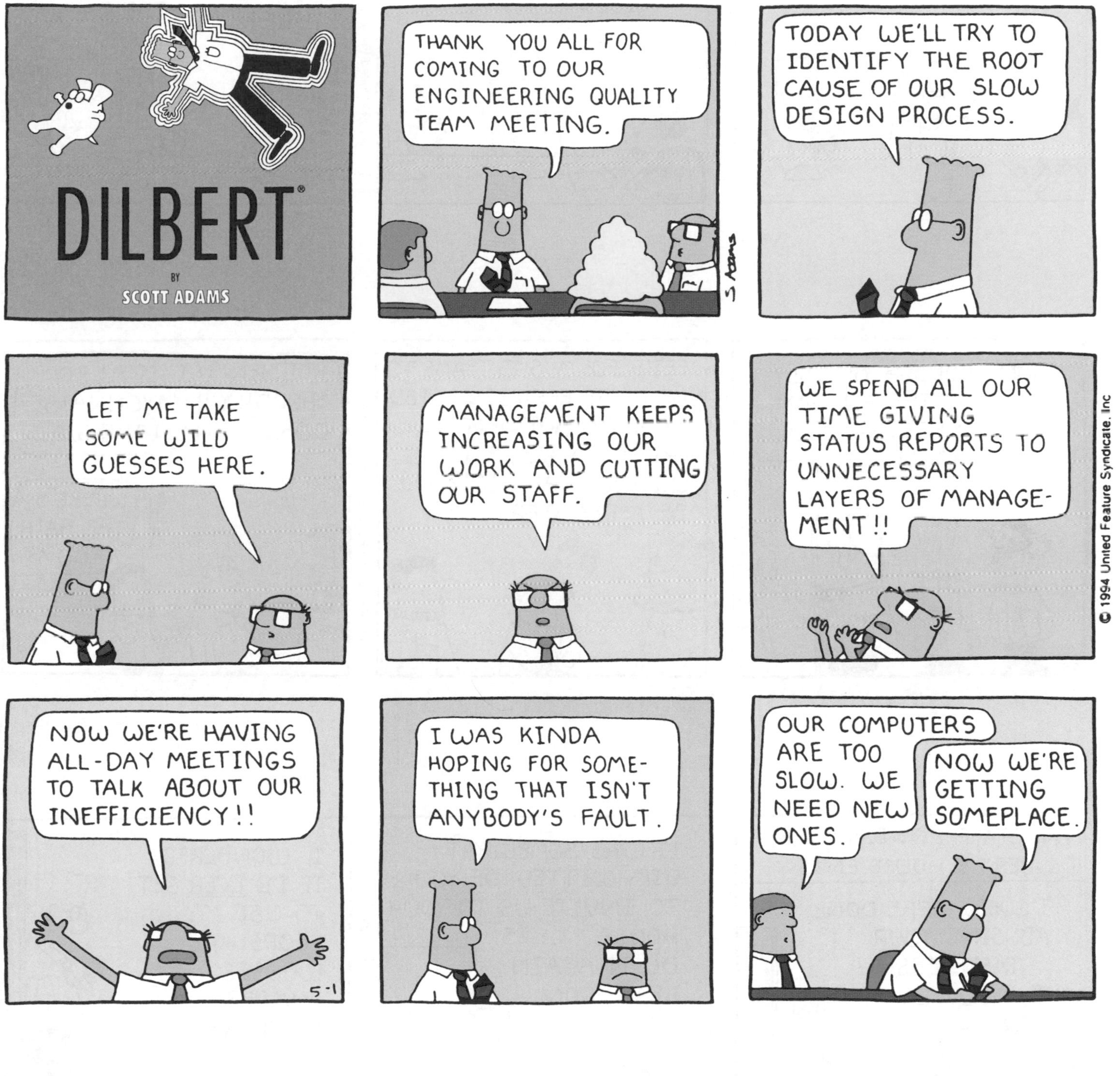
DILBERT®
BY
SCOTT ADAMS
THANK YOU ALL FOR COMING TO OUR ENGINEERING QUALITY TEAM MEETING.
S. Adams
TODAY WE'LL TRY TO IDENTIFY THE ROOT CAUSE OF OUR SLOW DESIGN PROCESS.
LET ME TAKE SOME WILD GUESSES HERE.
MANAGEMENT KEEPS INCREASING OUR WORK AND CUTTING OUR STAFF.
WE SPEND ALL OUR TIME GIVING STATUS REPORTS TO UNNECESSARY LAYERS OF MANAGE-MENT!!
© 1994 United Feature Syndicate, Inc
NOW WE'RE HAVING ALL-DAY MEETINGS TO TALK ABOUT OUR INEFFICIENCY!!
5-1
I WAS KINDA HOPING FOR SOME-THING THAT ISN'T ANYBODY'S FAULT.
OUR COMPUTERS ARE TOO SLOW. WE NEED NEW ONES.
NOW WE'RE GETTING SOMEPLACE.

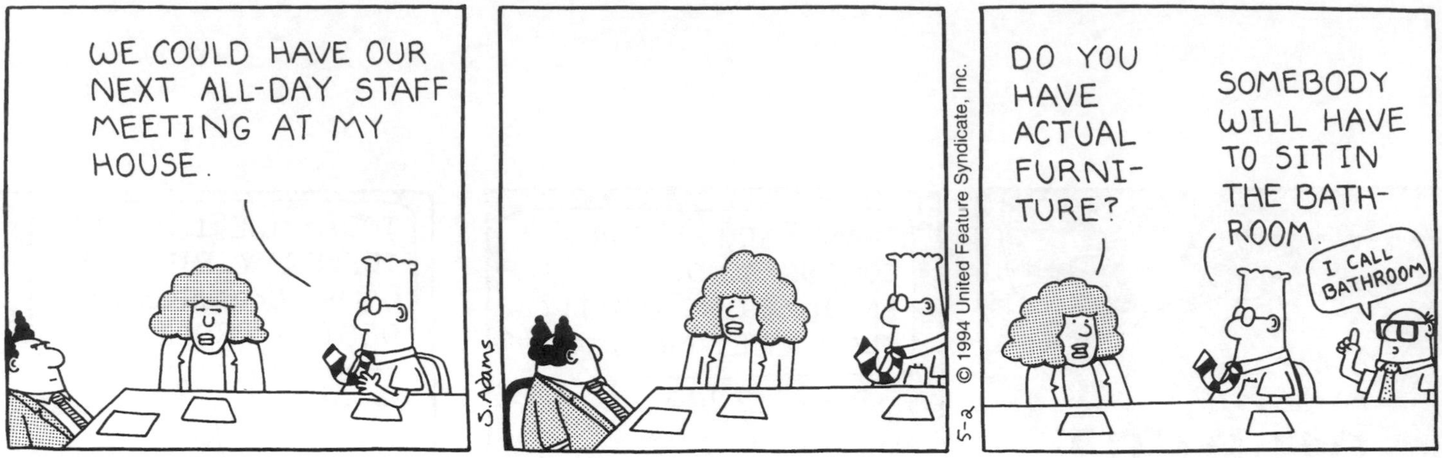
WE COULD HAVE OUR NEXT ALL-DAY STAFF MEETING AT MY HOUSE.
S. Adams
5-2
© 1994 United Feature Syndicate, Inc.
DO YOU HAVE ACTUAL FURNI-TURE?
SOMEBODY WILL HAVE TO SIT IN THE BATH-ROOM.
I CALL BATHROOM

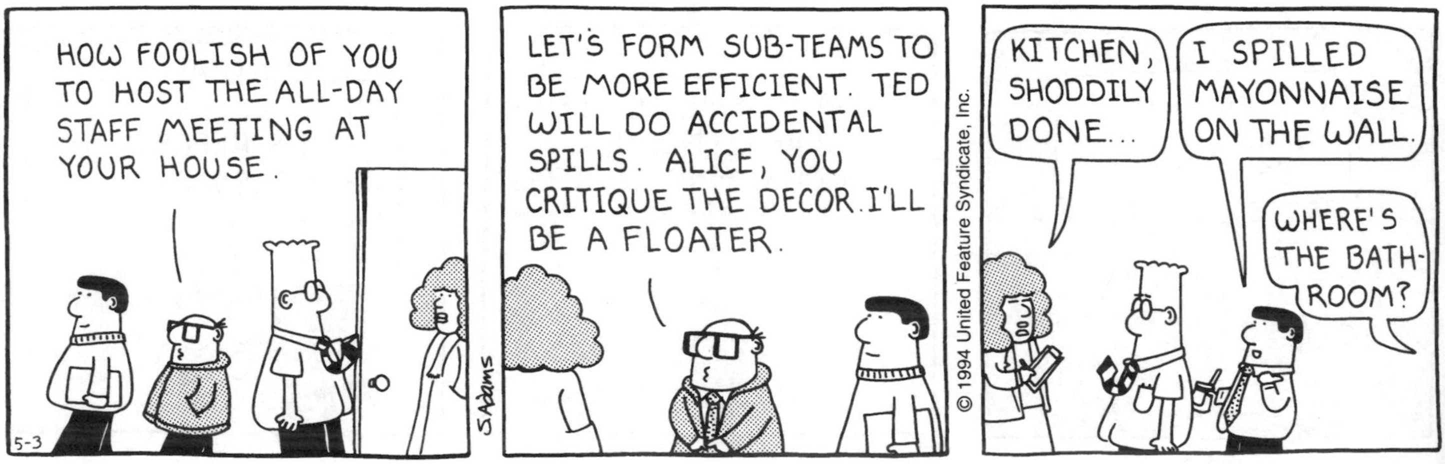
5-3
HOW FOOLISH OF YOU TO HOST THE ALL-DAY STAFF MEETING AT YOUR HOUSE.
S. Adams
LET'S FORM SUB-TEAMS TO BE MORE EFFICIENT. TED WILL DO ACCIDENTAL SPILLS. ALICE, YOU CRITIQUE THE DECOR. I'LL BE A FLOATER.
© 1994 United Feature Syndicate, Inc.
KITCHEN, SHODDILY DONE...
I SPILLED MAYONNAISE ON THE WALL.
WHERE'S THE BATH-ROOM?

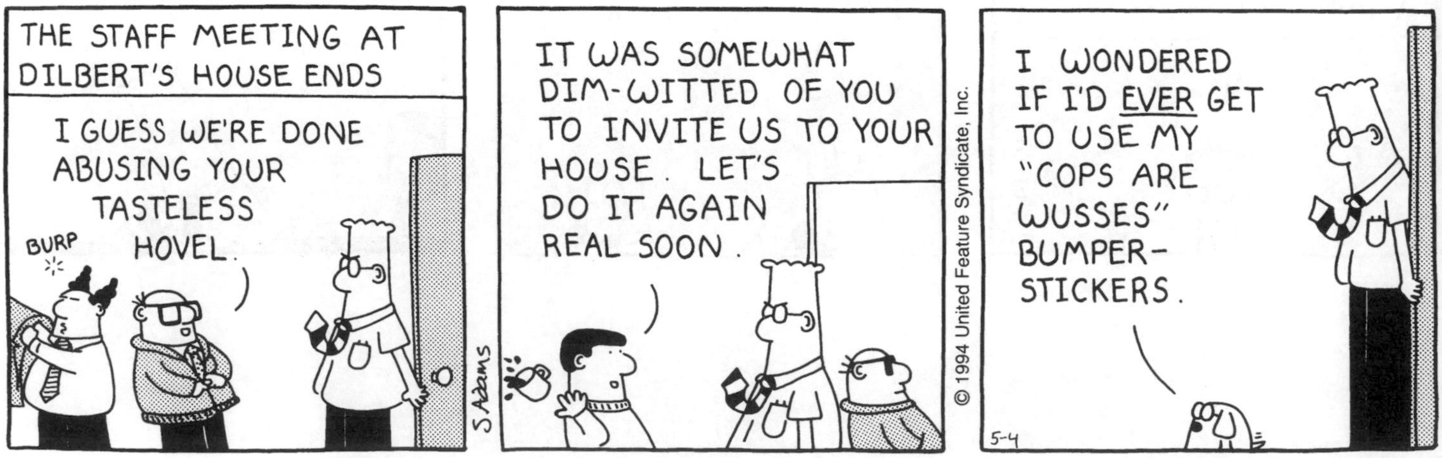
THE STAFF MEETING AT DILBERT'S HOUSE ENDS
I GUESS WE'RE DONE ABUSING YOUR TASTELESS HOVEL.
BURP
S. Adams
IT WAS SOMEWHAT DIM-WITTED OF YOU TO INVITE US TO YOUR HOUSE. LET'S DO IT AGAIN REAL SOON.
© 1994 United Feature Syndicate, Inc.
I WONDERED IF I'D EVER GET TO USE MY "COPS ARE WUSSES" BUMPER-STICKERS.
5-4

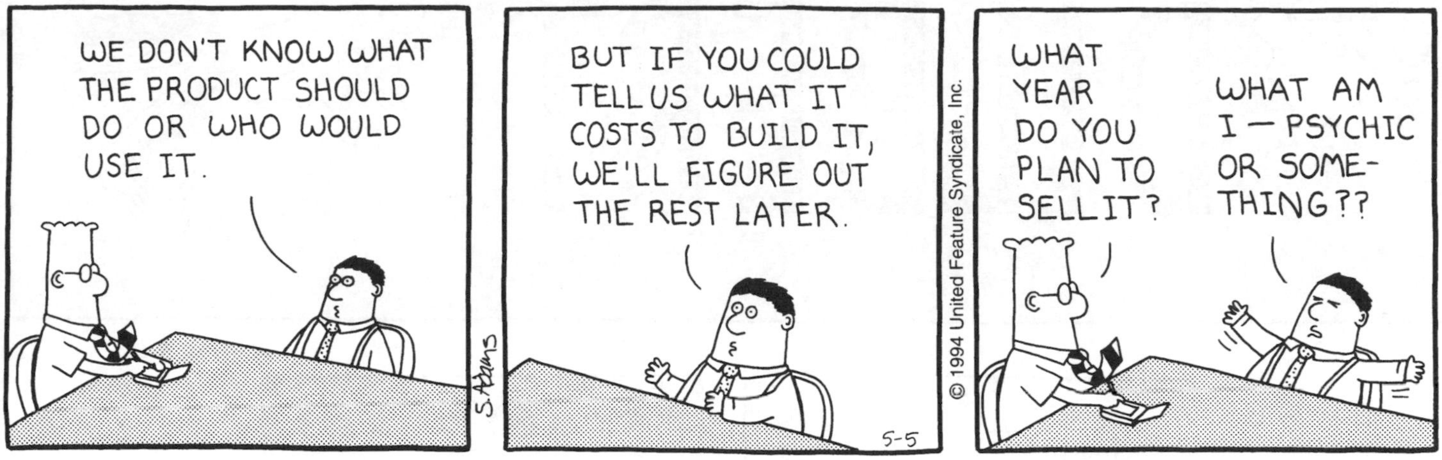
WE DON'T KNOW WHAT THE PRODUCT SHOULD DO OR WHO WOULD USE IT.
BUT IF YOU COULD TELL US WHAT IT COSTS TO BUILD IT, WE'LL FIGURE OUT THE REST LATER.
WHAT YEAR DO YOU PLAN TO SELL IT?
WHAT AM I — PSYCHIC OR SOME-THING??
S. Adams
5-5
© 1994 United Feature Syndicate, Inc.

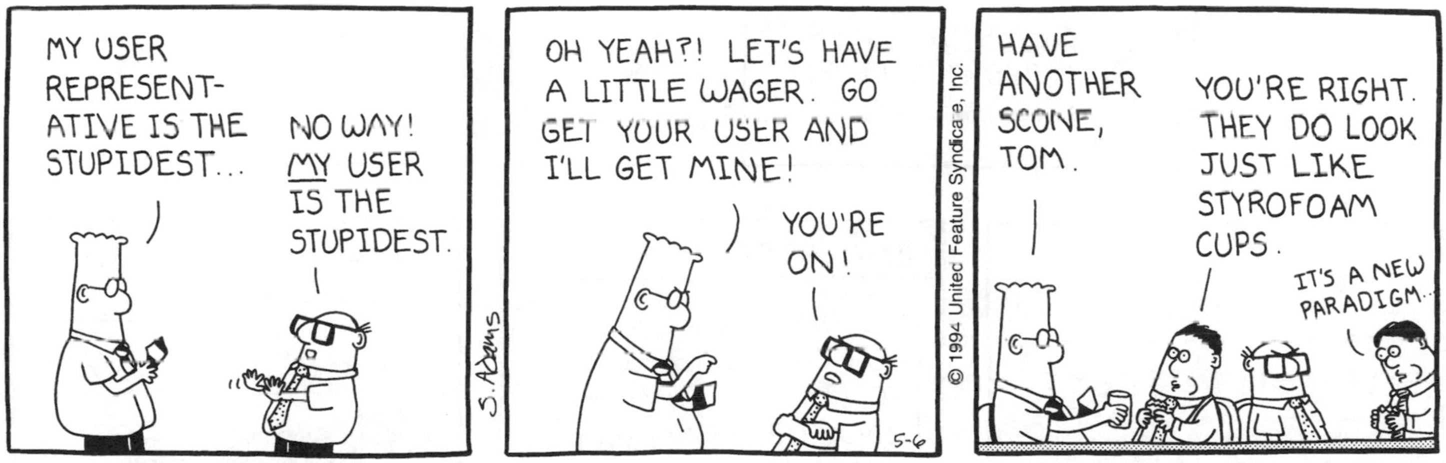
MY USER REPRESENT-ATIVE IS THE STUPIDEST...
NO WAY! MY USER IS THE STUPIDEST.
OH YEAH?! LET'S HAVE A LITTLE WAGER. GO GET YOUR USER AND I'LL GET MINE!
YOU'RE ON!
HAVE ANOTHER SCONE, TOM.
YOU'RE RIGHT. THEY DO LOOK JUST LIKE STYROFOAM CUPS.
IT'S A NEW PARADIGM...
S. Adams
5-6
© 1994 United Feature Syndicate, Inc.

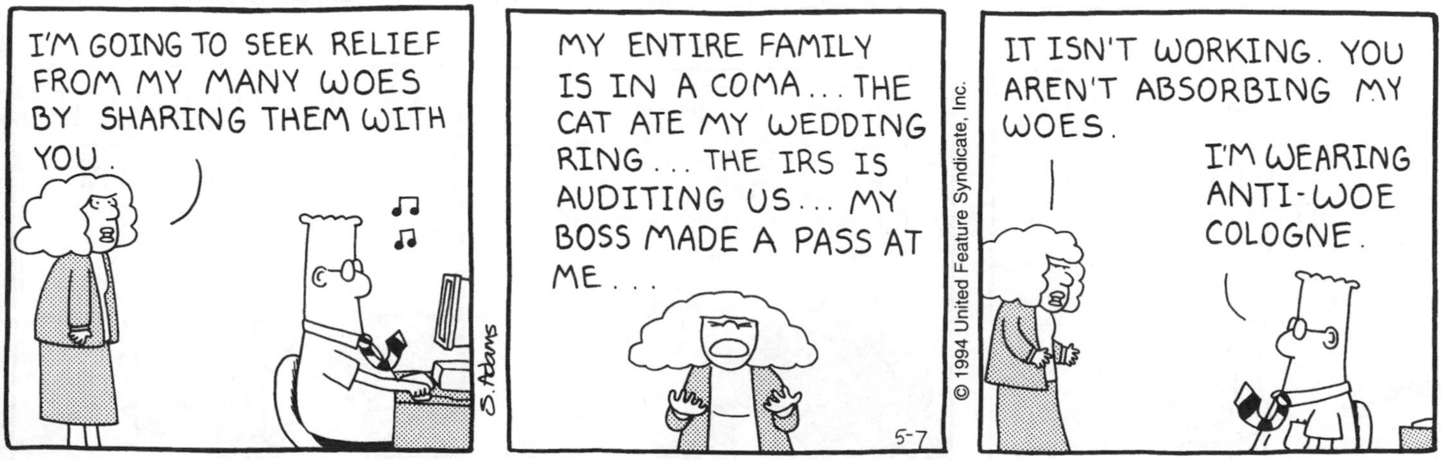
I'M GOING TO SEEK RELIEF FROM MY MANY WOES BY SHARING THEM WITH YOU.
MY ENTIRE FAMILY IS IN A COMA... THE CAT ATE MY WEDDING RING... THE IRS IS AUDITING US... MY BOSS MADE A PASS AT ME...
IT ISN'T WORKING. YOU AREN'T ABSORBING MY WOES.
I'M WEARING ANTI-WOE COLOGNE.
S. Adams
5-7
© 1994 United Feature Syndicate, Inc.

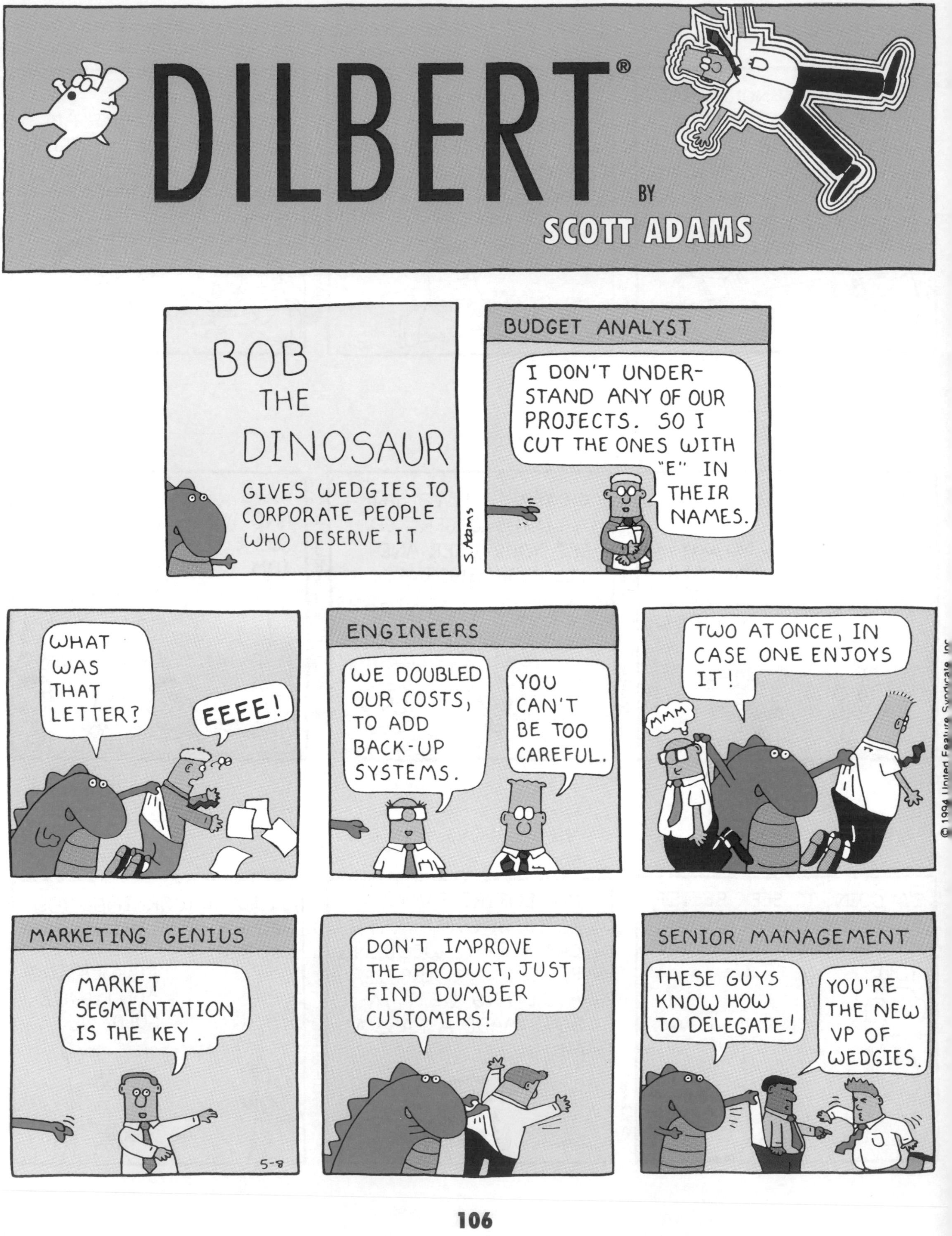

DILBERT®
BY
SCOTT ADAMS
BOB THE DINOSAUR
GIVES WEDGIES TO CORPORATE PEOPLE WHO DESERVE IT
S. Adams
BUDGET ANALYST
I DON'T UNDER-STAND ANY OF OUR PROJECTS. SO I CUT THE ONES WITH "E" IN THEIR NAMES.
WHAT WAS THAT LETTER?
EEEE!
ENGINEERS
WE DOUBLED OUR COSTS, TO ADD BACK-UP SYSTEMS.
YOU CAN'T BE TOO CAREFUL.
TWO AT ONCE, IN CASE ONE ENJOYS IT!
MMM
© 1994 United Feature Syndicate, Inc.
MARKETING GENIUS
MARKET SEGMENTATION IS THE KEY.
5-8
DON'T IMPROVE THE PRODUCT, JUST FIND DUMBER CUSTOMERS!
SENIOR MANAGEMENT
THESE GUYS KNOW HOW TO DELEGATE!
YOU'RE THE NEW VP OF WEDGIES.

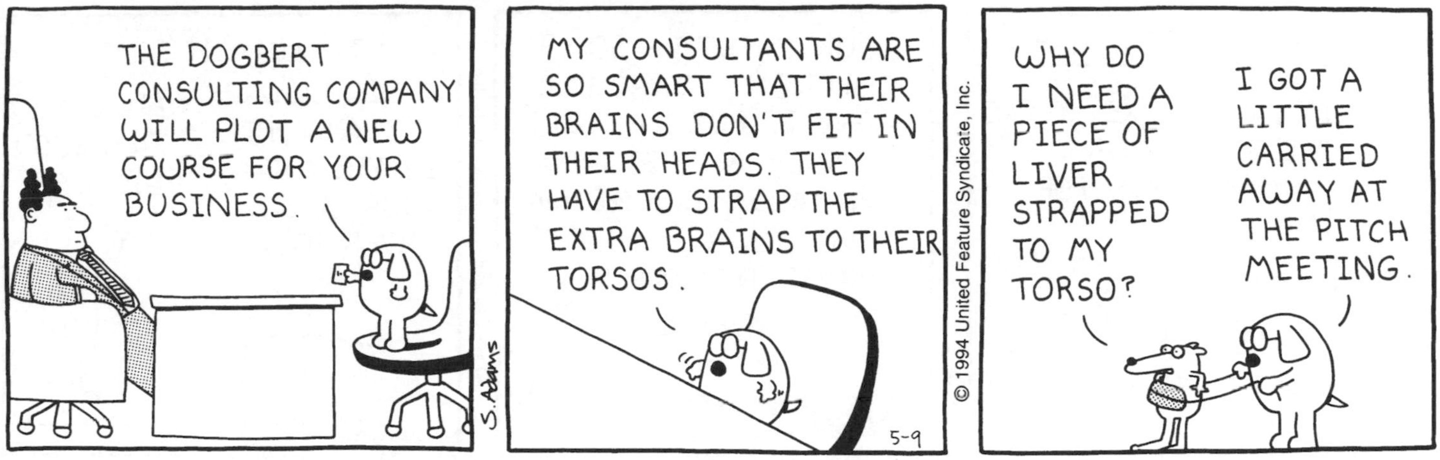
THE DOGBERT CONSULTING COMPANY WILL PLOT A NEW COURSE FOR YOUR BUSINESS.
S. Adams
MY CONSULTANTS ARE SO SMART THAT THEIR BRAINS DON'T FIT IN THEIR HEADS. THEY HAVE TO STRAP THE EXTRA BRAINS TO THEIR TORSOS.
5-9
© 1994 United Feature Syndicate, Inc.
WHY DO I NEED A PIECE OF LIVER STRAPPED TO MY TORSO?
I GOT A LITTLE CARRIED AWAY AT THE PITCH MEETING.

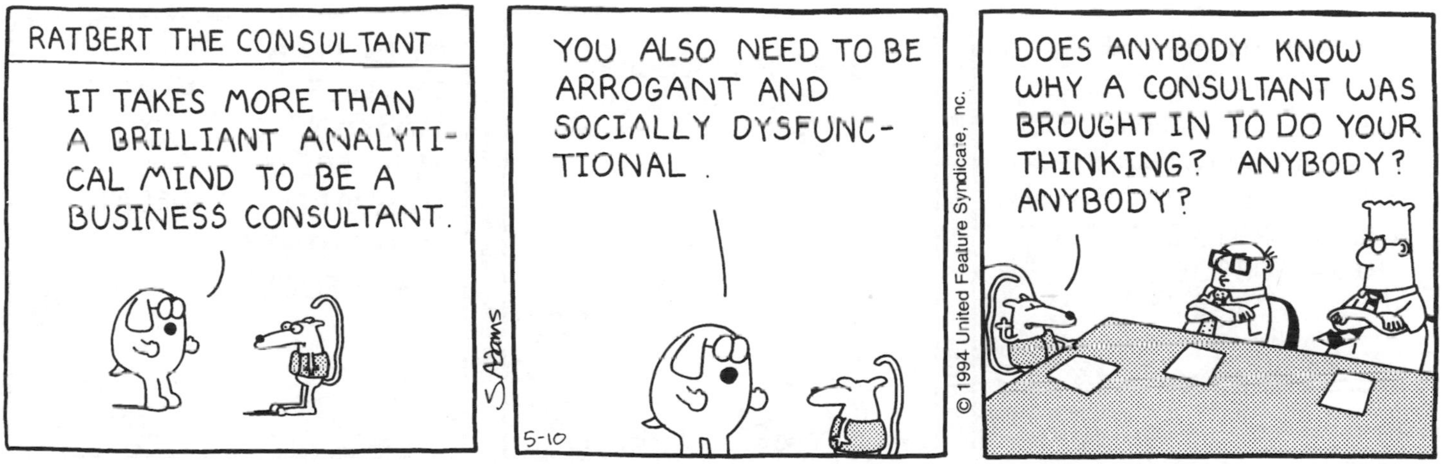
RATBERT THE CONSULTANT
IT TAKES MORE THAN A BRILLIANT ANALYTICAL MIND TO BE A BUSINESS CONSULTANT.
S. Adams
YOU ALSO NEED TO BE ARROGANT AND SOCIALLY DYSFUNCTIONAL.
5-10
© 1994 United Feature Syndicate, Inc.
DOES ANYBODY KNOW WHY A CONSULTANT WAS BROUGHT IN TO DO YOUR THINKING? ANYBODY? ANYBODY?

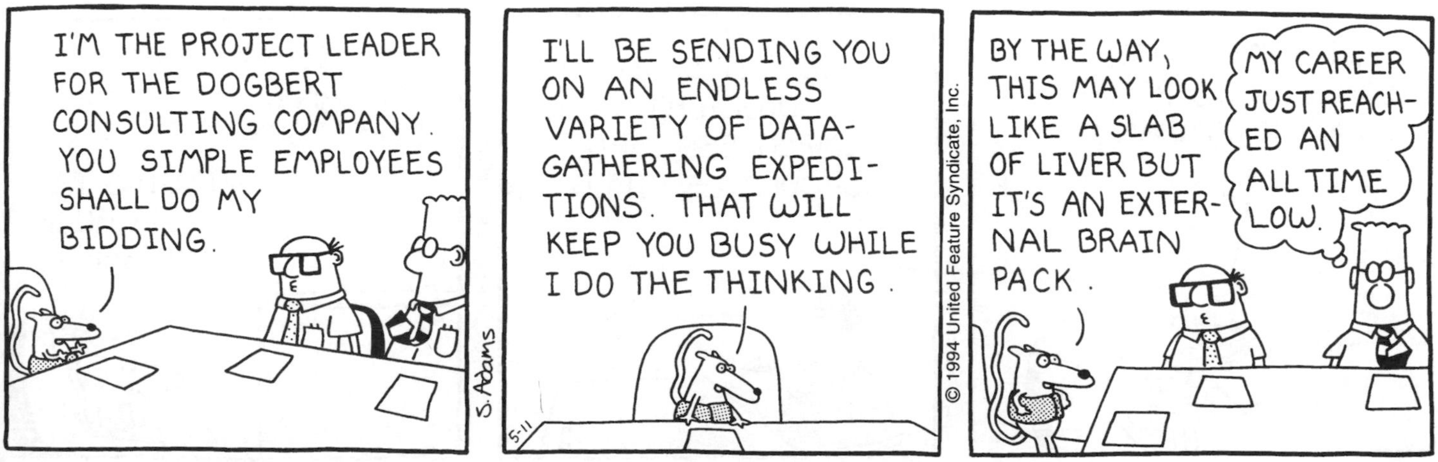
I'M THE PROJECT LEADER FOR THE DOGBERT CONSULTING COMPANY. YOU SIMPLE EMPLOYEES SHALL DO MY BIDDING.
S. Adams
I'LL BE SENDING YOU ON AN ENDLESS VARIETY OF DATA-GATHERING EXPEDITIONS. THAT WILL KEEP YOU BUSY WHILE I DO THE THINKING.
5-11
© 1994 United Feature Syndicate, Inc.
BY THE WAY, THIS MAY LOOK LIKE A SLAB OF LIVER BUT IT'S AN EXTERNAL BRAIN PACK.
MY CAREER JUST REACHED AN ALL TIME LOW.

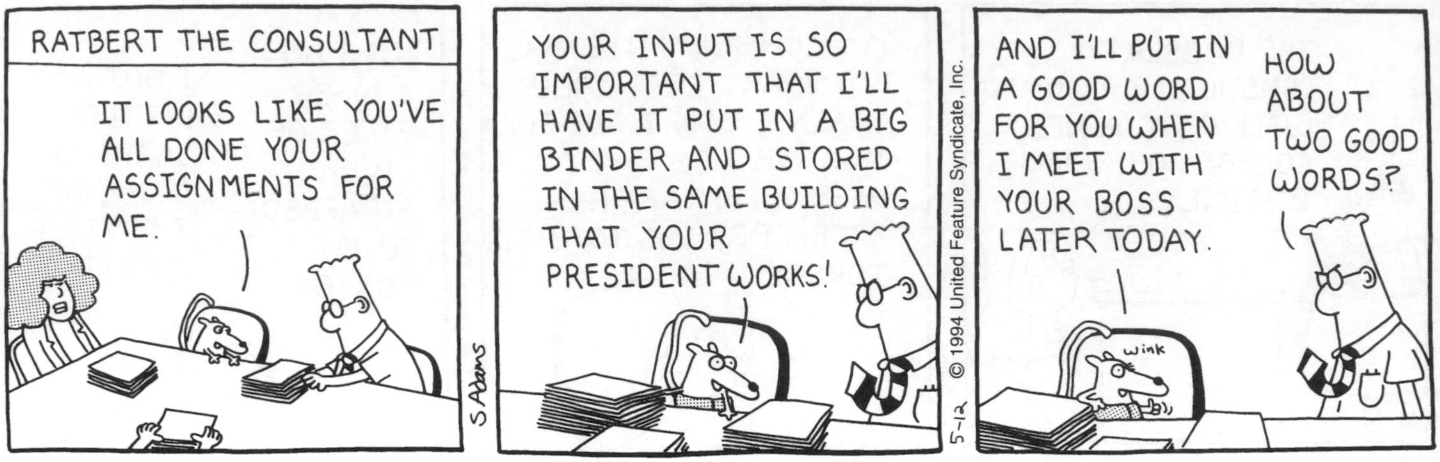
RATBERT THE CONSULTANT
IT LOOKS LIKE YOU'VE ALL DONE YOUR ASSIGNMENTS FOR ME.
YOUR INPUT IS SO IMPORTANT THAT I'LL HAVE IT PUT IN A BIG BINDER AND STORED IN THE SAME BUILDING THAT YOUR PRESIDENT WORKS!
AND I'LL PUT IN A GOOD WORD FOR YOU WHEN I MEET WITH YOUR BOSS LATER TODAY.
wink
HOW ABOUT TWO GOOD WORDS?
© 1994 United Feature Syndicate, Inc.

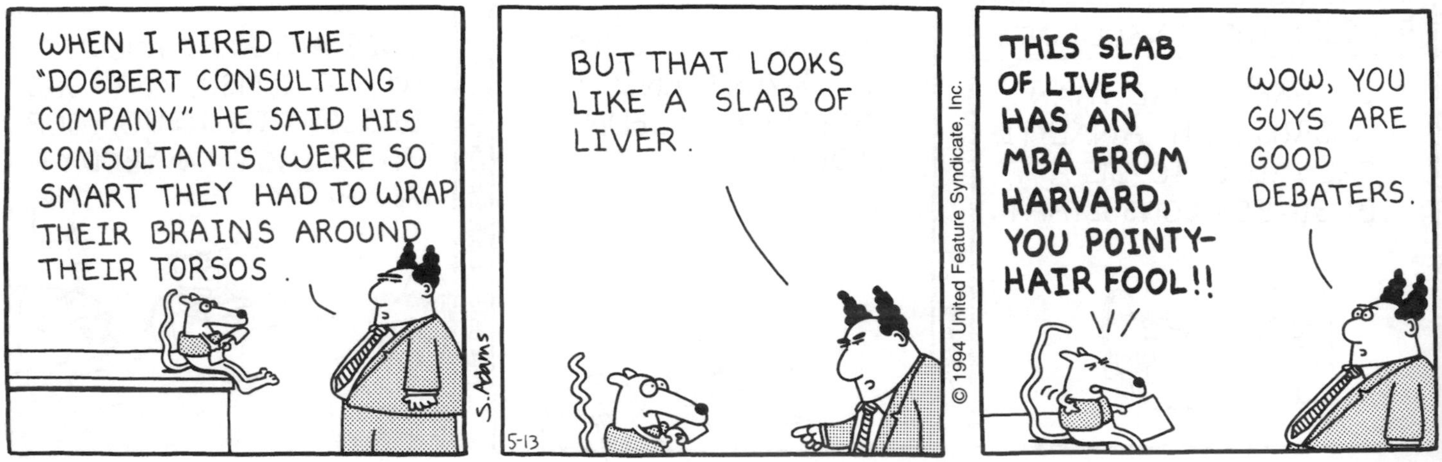
WHEN I HIRED THE "DOGBERT CONSULTING COMPANY" HE SAID HIS CONSULTANTS WERE SO SMART THEY HAD TO WRAP THEIR BRAINS AROUND THEIR TORSOS.
BUT THAT LOOKS LIKE A SLAB OF LIVER.
THIS SLAB OF LIVER HAS AN MBA FROM HARVARD, YOU POINTY-HAIR FOOL!!
WOW, YOU GUYS ARE GOOD DEBATERS.
© 1994 United Feature Syndicate, Inc.

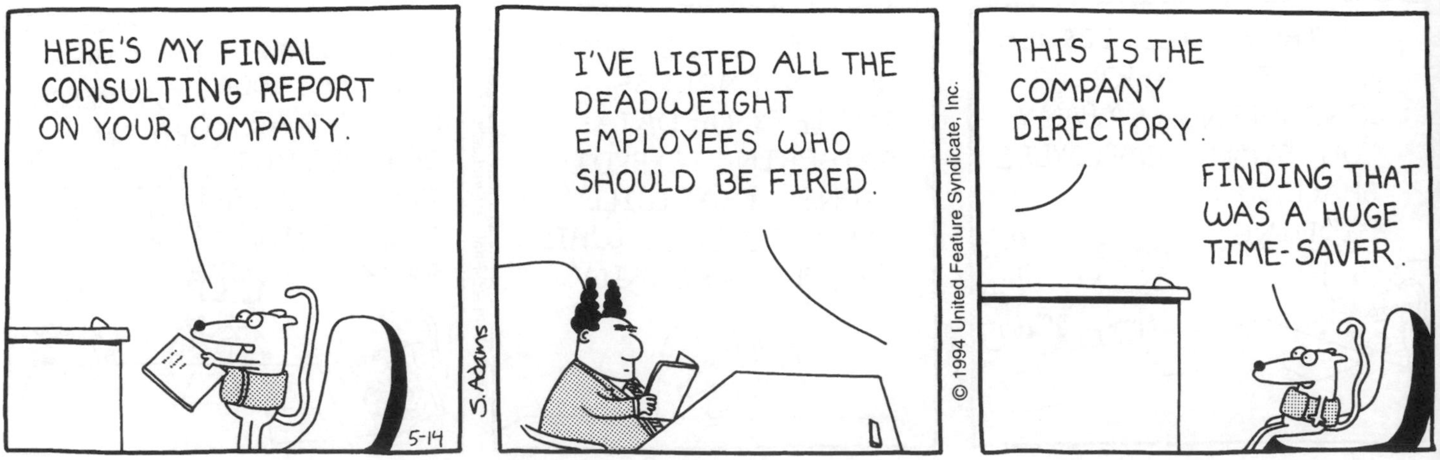
HERE'S MY FINAL CONSULTING REPORT ON YOUR COMPANY.
I'VE LISTED ALL THE DEADWEIGHT EMPLOYEES WHO SHOULD BE FIRED.
THIS IS THE COMPANY DIRECTORY.
FINDING THAT WAS A HUGE TIME-SAVER.
© 1994 United Feature Syndicate, Inc.

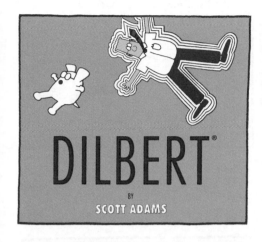

DILBERT

BY SCOTT ADAMS

HI, GUYS. HOW ARE YOUR FAMILIES?

? ?

WHY ARE YOU PRETENDING TO BE INTERESTED IN OUR PERSONAL LIVES?

IT'S A MANAGEMENT TECHNIQUE TO INCREASE YOUR JOB SATISFACTION WITHOUT GIVING YOU MORE MONEY.

MY PLAN IS TO BOOST YOUR INTANGIBLE BENEFITS WHILE CONTINUING TO CHISEL AWAY AT YOUR SALARIES.

5-15

BUT ENOUGH ABOUT ME... HOW ARE THOSE FAMILIES OF YOURS?

MY WIFE DIVORCED ME BECAUSE YOU MAKE ME WORK SO MANY HOURS.

THIS JOB LOWERS MY SELF-ESTEEM TOO MUCH TO ATTRACT A MATE.

TELL THEM I SAID "HI."

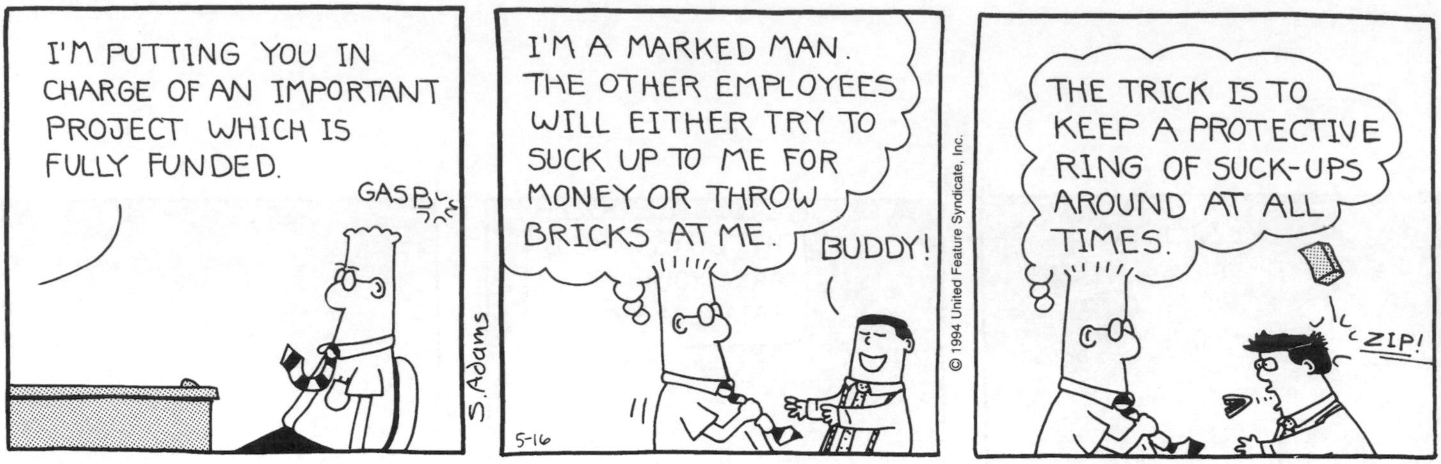
I'M PUTTING YOU IN CHARGE OF AN IMPORTANT PROJECT WHICH IS FULLY FUNDED.
GASP
S. Adams
5-16
I'M A MARKED MAN. THE OTHER EMPLOYEES WILL EITHER TRY TO SUCK UP TO ME FOR MONEY OR THROW BRICKS AT ME.
BUDDY!
© 1994 United Feature Syndicate, Inc.
THE TRICK IS TO KEEP A PROTECTIVE RING OF SUCK-UPS AROUND AT ALL TIMES.
ZIP!

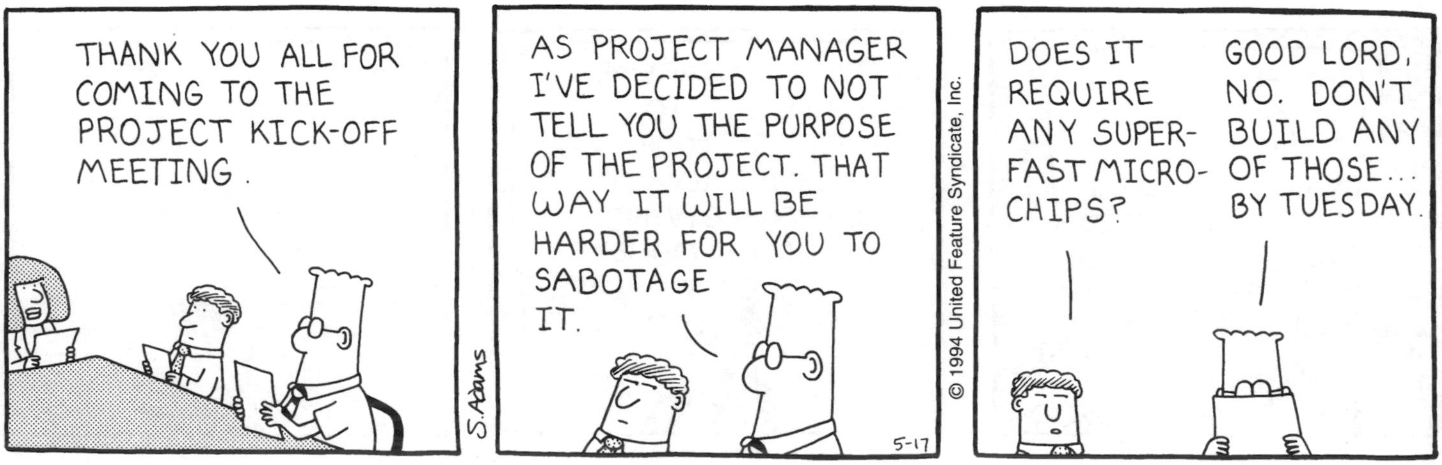
THANK YOU ALL FOR COMING TO THE PROJECT KICK-OFF MEETING.
S. Adams
AS PROJECT MANAGER I'VE DECIDED TO NOT TELL YOU THE PURPOSE OF THE PROJECT. THAT WAY IT WILL BE HARDER FOR YOU TO SABOTAGE IT.
5-17
© 1994 United Feature Syndicate, Inc.
DOES IT REQUIRE ANY SUPER-FAST MICRO-CHIPS?
GOOD LORD, NO. DON'T BUILD ANY OF THOSE... BY TUESDAY.

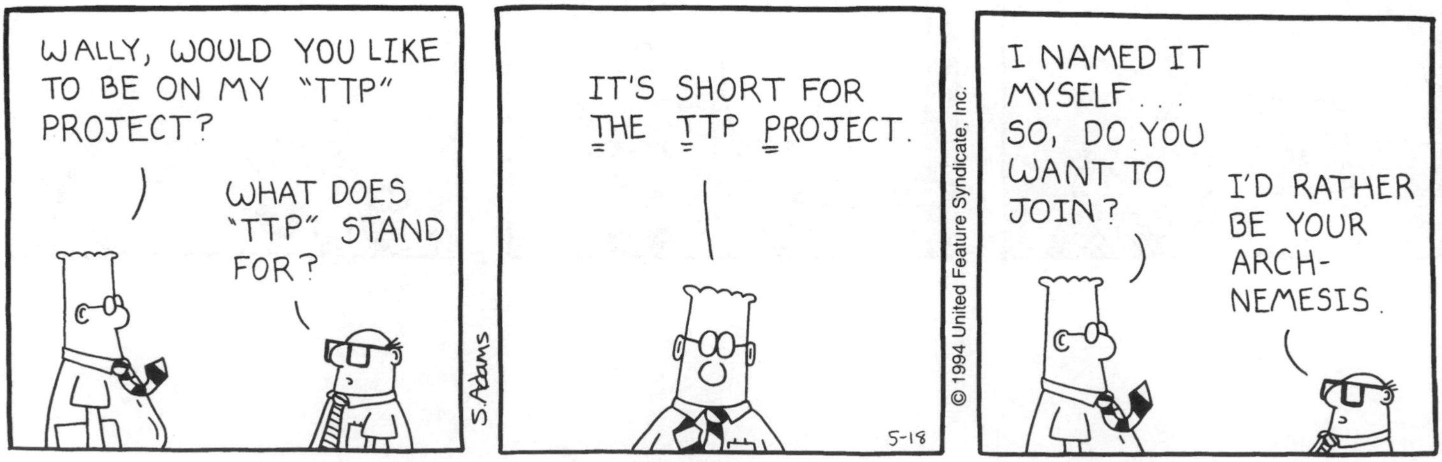
WALLY, WOULD YOU LIKE TO BE ON MY "TTP" PROJECT?
WHAT DOES "TTP" STAND FOR?
S. Adams
IT'S SHORT FOR THE TTP PROJECT.
5-18
© 1994 United Feature Syndicate, Inc.
I NAMED IT MYSELF... SO, DO YOU WANT TO JOIN?
I'D RATHER BE YOUR ARCH-NEMESIS.

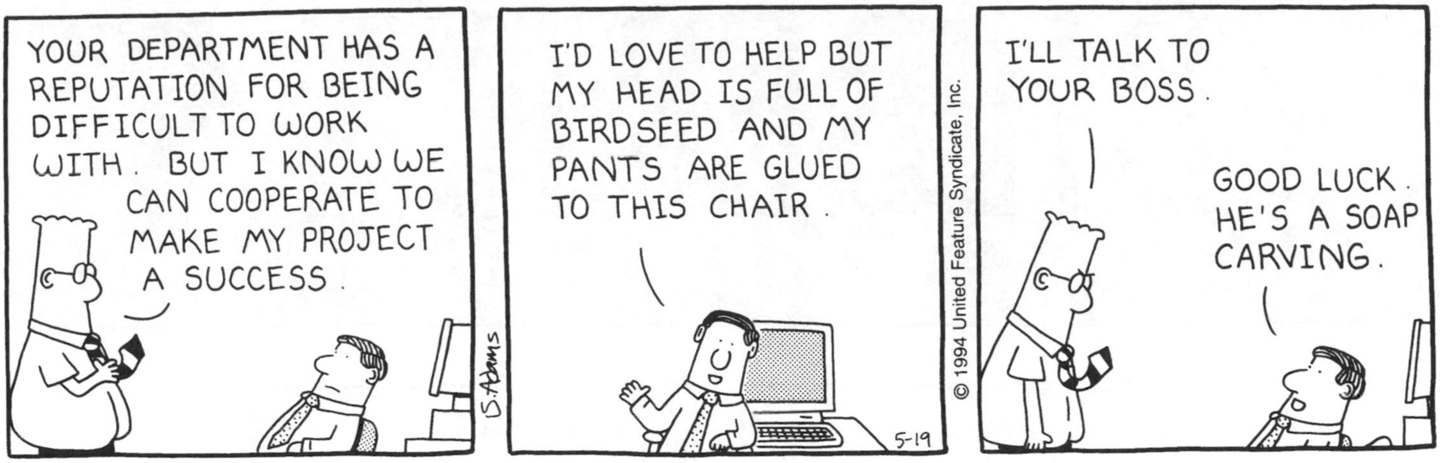
YOUR DEPARTMENT HAS A REPUTATION FOR BEING DIFFICULT TO WORK WITH. BUT I KNOW WE CAN COOPERATE TO MAKE MY PROJECT A SUCCESS.
S. Adams
I'D LOVE TO HELP BUT MY HEAD IS FULL OF BIRDSEED AND MY PANTS ARE GLUED TO THIS CHAIR.
5-19
© 1994 United Feature Syndicate, Inc.
I'LL TALK TO YOUR BOSS.
GOOD LUCK. HE'S A SOAP CARVING.

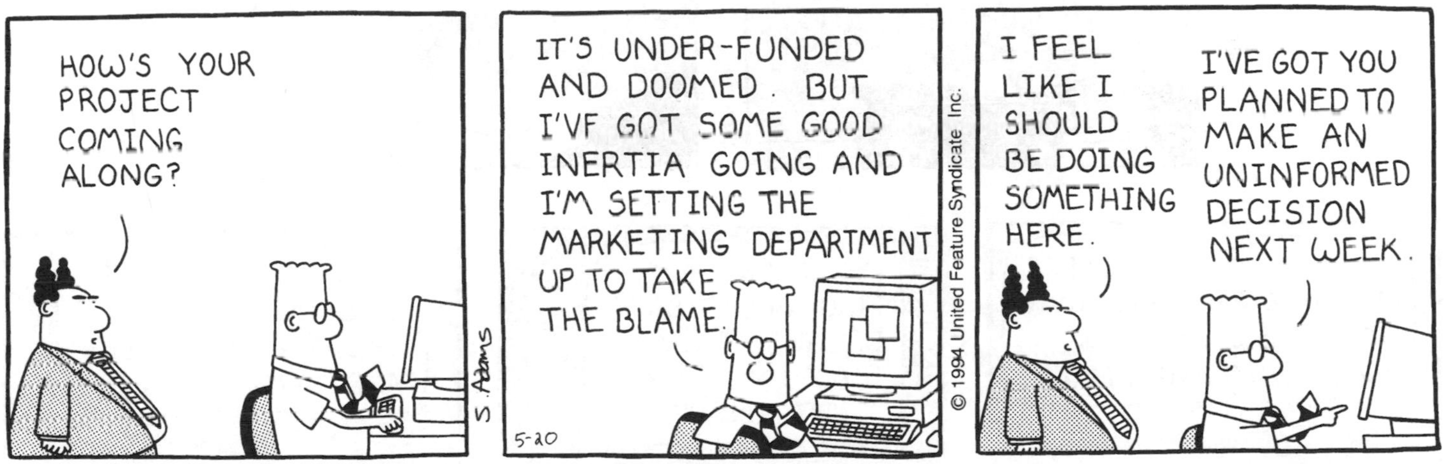
HOW'S YOUR PROJECT COMING ALONG?
S. Adams
IT'S UNDER-FUNDED AND DOOMED. BUT I'VF GOT SOME GOOD INERTIA GOING AND I'M SETTING THE MARKETING DEPARTMENT UP TO TAKE THE BLAME.
5-20
© 1994 United Feature Syndicate, Inc.
I FEEL LIKE I SHOULD BE DOING SOMETHING HERE.
I'VE GOT YOU PLANNED TO MAKE AN UNINFORMED DECISION NEXT WEEK.

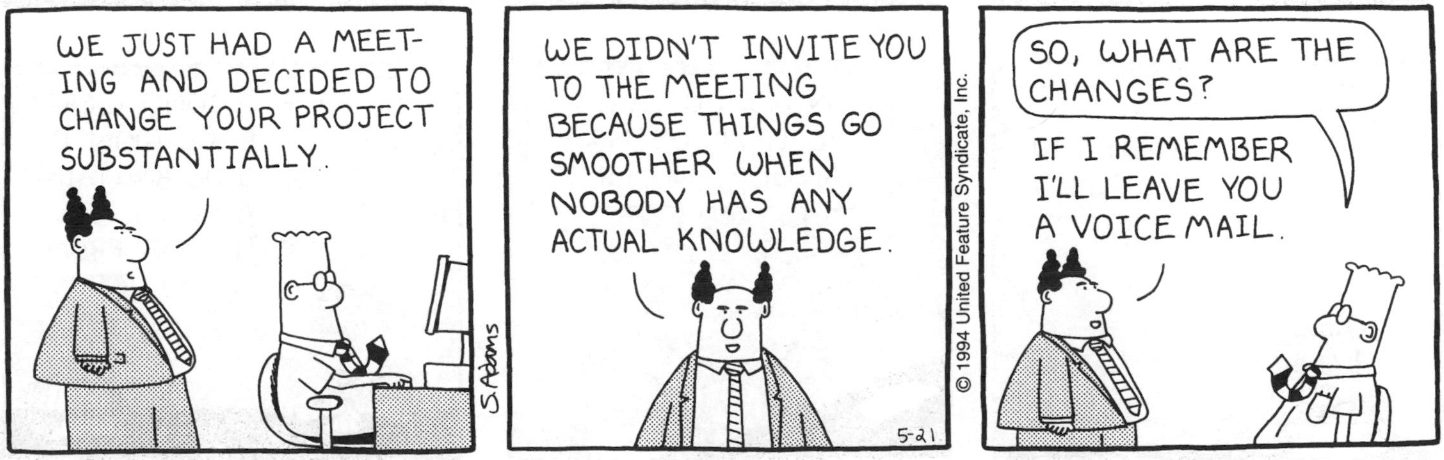
WE JUST HAD A MEET-ING AND DECIDED TO CHANGE YOUR PROJECT SUBSTANTIALLY.
S. Adams
WE DIDN'T INVITE YOU TO THE MEETING BECAUSE THINGS GO SMOOTHER WHEN NOBODY HAS ANY ACTUAL KNOWLEDGE.
5-21
© 1994 United Feature Syndicate, Inc.
SO, WHAT ARE THE CHANGES?
IF I REMEMBER I'LL LEAVE YOU A VOICE MAIL.

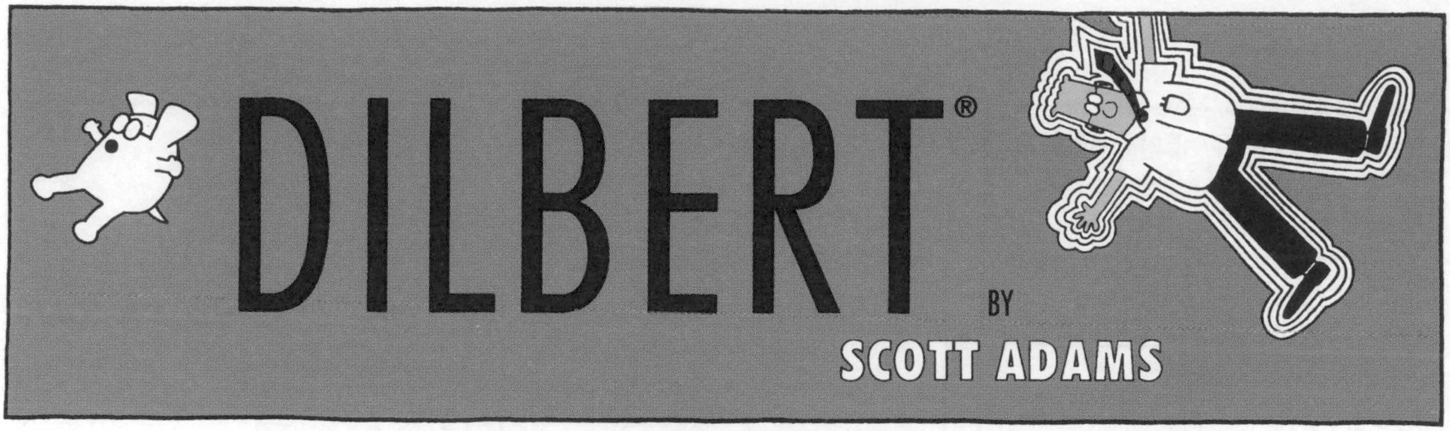
DILBERT®
BY
SCOTT ADAMS

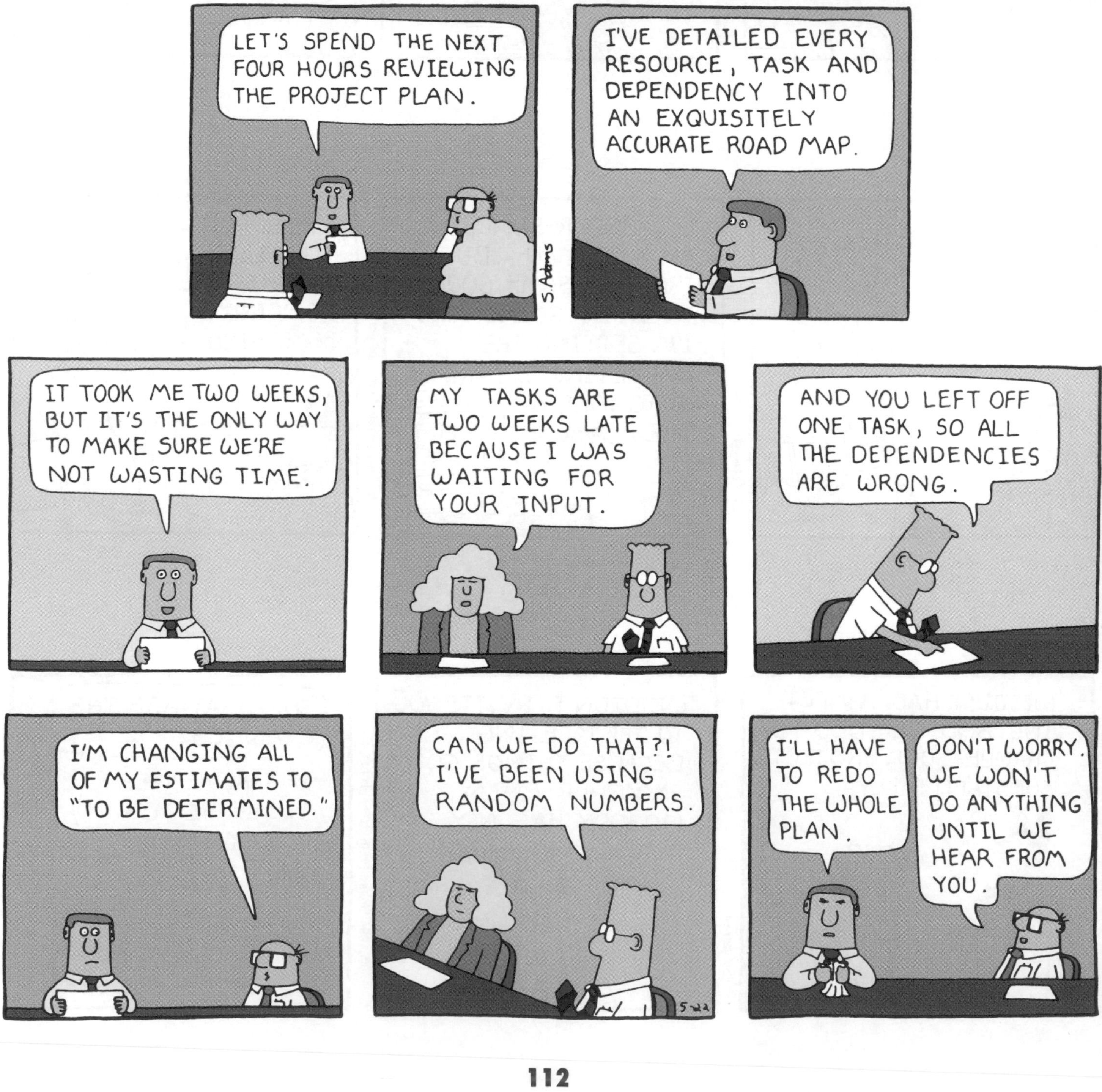
LET'S SPEND THE NEXT FOUR HOURS REVIEWING THE PROJECT PLAN.
S. Adams
I'VE DETAILED EVERY RESOURCE, TASK AND DEPENDENCY INTO AN EXQUISITELY ACCURATE ROAD MAP.
IT TOOK ME TWO WEEKS, BUT IT'S THE ONLY WAY TO MAKE SURE WE'RE NOT WASTING TIME.
MY TASKS ARE TWO WEEKS LATE BECAUSE I WAS WAITING FOR YOUR INPUT.
AND YOU LEFT OFF ONE TASK, SO ALL THE DEPENDENCIES ARE WRONG.
I'M CHANGING ALL OF MY ESTIMATES TO "TO BE DETERMINED."
CAN WE DO THAT?! I'VE BEEN USING RANDOM NUMBERS.
I'LL HAVE TO REDO THE WHOLE PLAN.
DON'T WORRY. WE WON'T DO ANYTHING UNTIL WE HEAR FROM YOU.

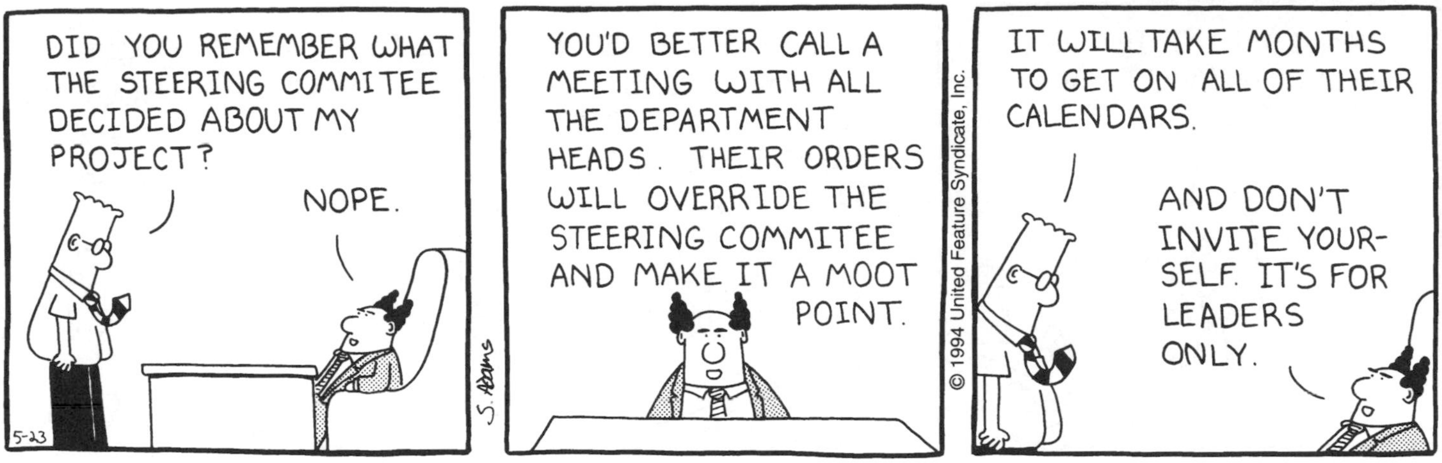
DID YOU REMEMBER WHAT THE STEERING COMMITEE DECIDED ABOUT MY PROJECT?
NOPE.
YOU'D BETTER CALL A MEETING WITH ALL THE DEPARTMENT HEADS. THEIR ORDERS WILL OVERRIDE THE STEERING COMMITEE AND MAKE IT A MOOT POINT.
IT WILL TAKE MONTHS TO GET ON ALL OF THEIR CALENDARS.
AND DON'T INVITE YOURSELF. IT'S FOR LEADERS ONLY.
5-23
S. Adams
© 1994 United Feature Syndicate, Inc.

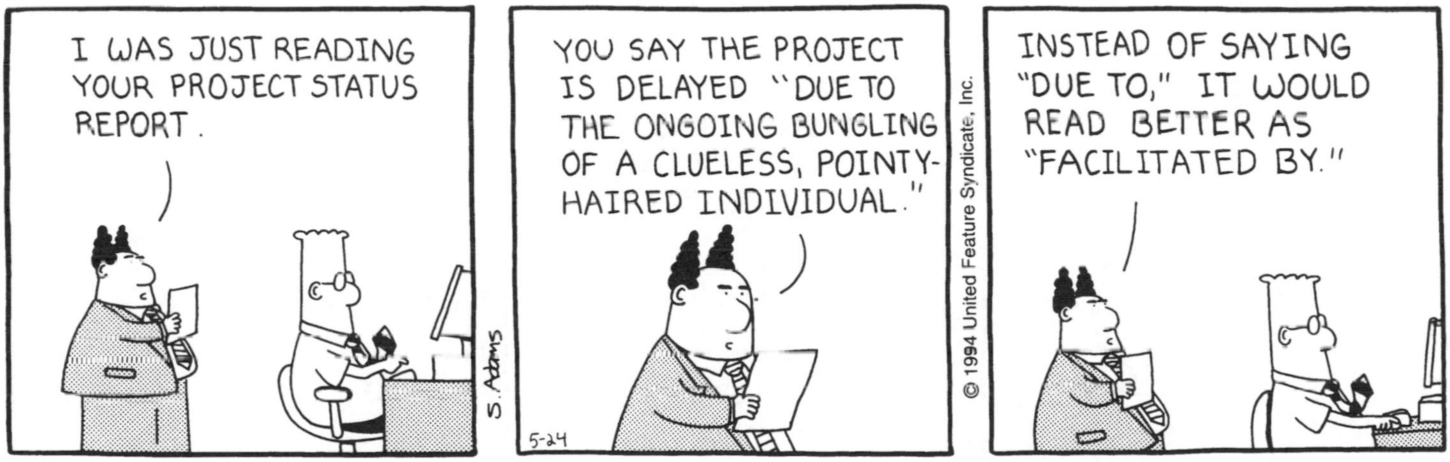
I WAS JUST READING YOUR PROJECT STATUS REPORT.
YOU SAY THE PROJECT IS DELAYED "DUE TO THE ONGOING BUNGLING OF A CLUELESS, POINTY-HAIRED INDIVIDUAL."
INSTEAD OF SAYING "DUE TO," IT WOULD READ BETTER AS "FACILITATED BY."
S. Adams
5-24
© 1994 United Feature Syndicate, Inc.

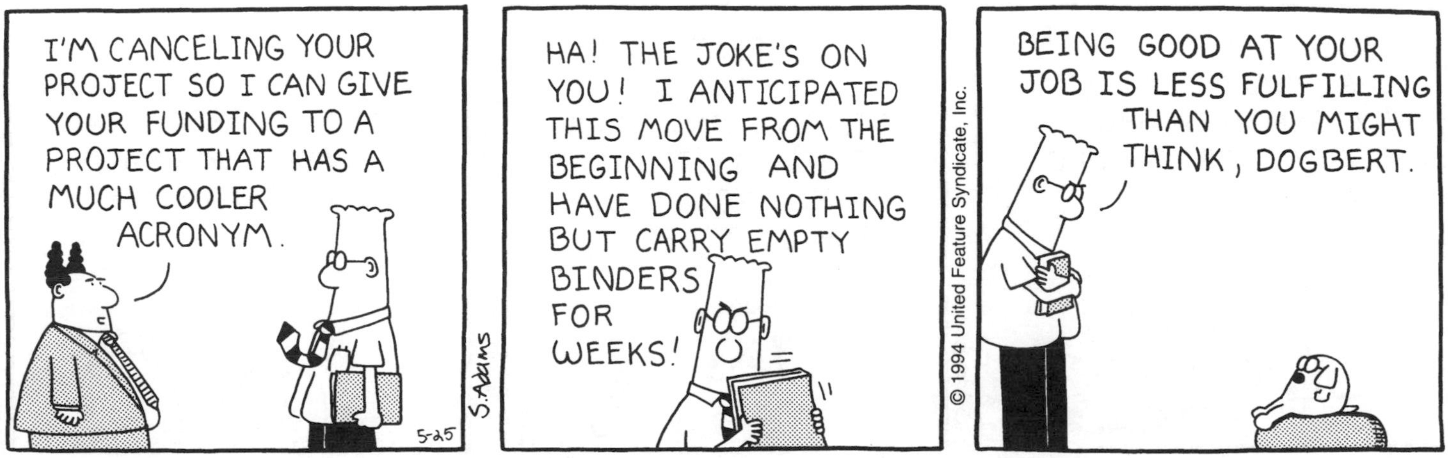
I'M CANCELING YOUR PROJECT SO I CAN GIVE YOUR FUNDING TO A PROJECT THAT HAS A MUCH COOLER ACRONYM.
HA! THE JOKE'S ON YOU! I ANTICIPATED THIS MOVE FROM THE BEGINNING AND HAVE DONE NOTHING BUT CARRY EMPTY BINDERS FOR WEEKS!
BEING GOOD AT YOUR JOB IS LESS FULFILLING THAN YOU MIGHT THINK, DOGBERT.
5-25
S. Adams
© 1994 United Feature Syndicate, Inc.

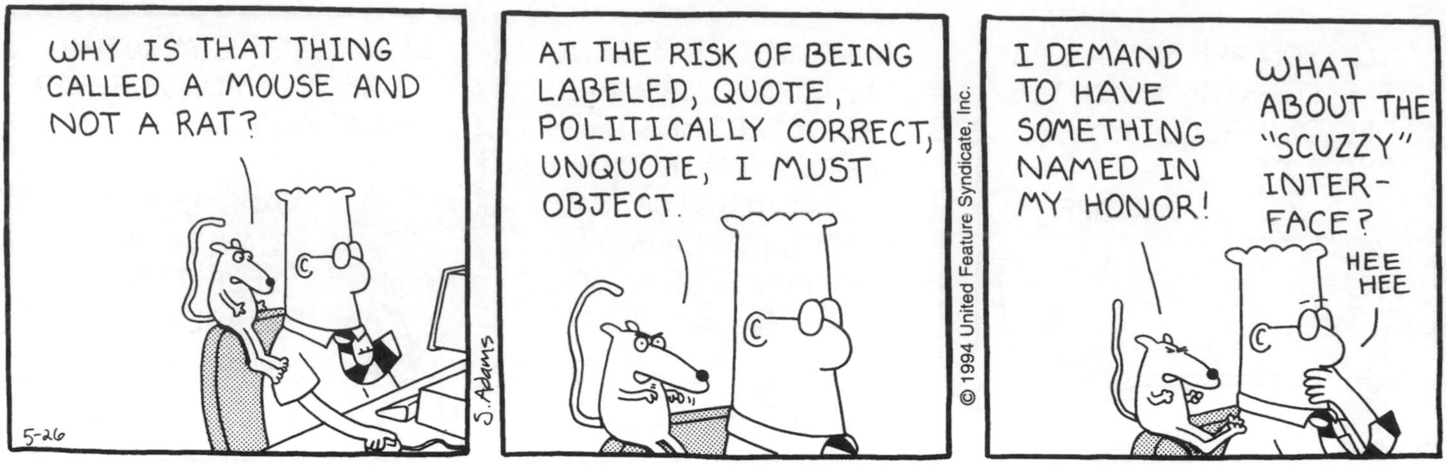
WHY IS THAT THING CALLED A MOUSE AND NOT A RAT?
AT THE RISK OF BEING LABELED, QUOTE, POLITICALLY CORRECT, UNQUOTE, I MUST OBJECT.
I DEMAND TO HAVE SOMETHING NAMED IN MY HONOR!
WHAT ABOUT THE "SCUZZY" INTERFACE?
HEE HEE
© 1994 United Feature Syndicate, Inc.
5-26
S. Adams

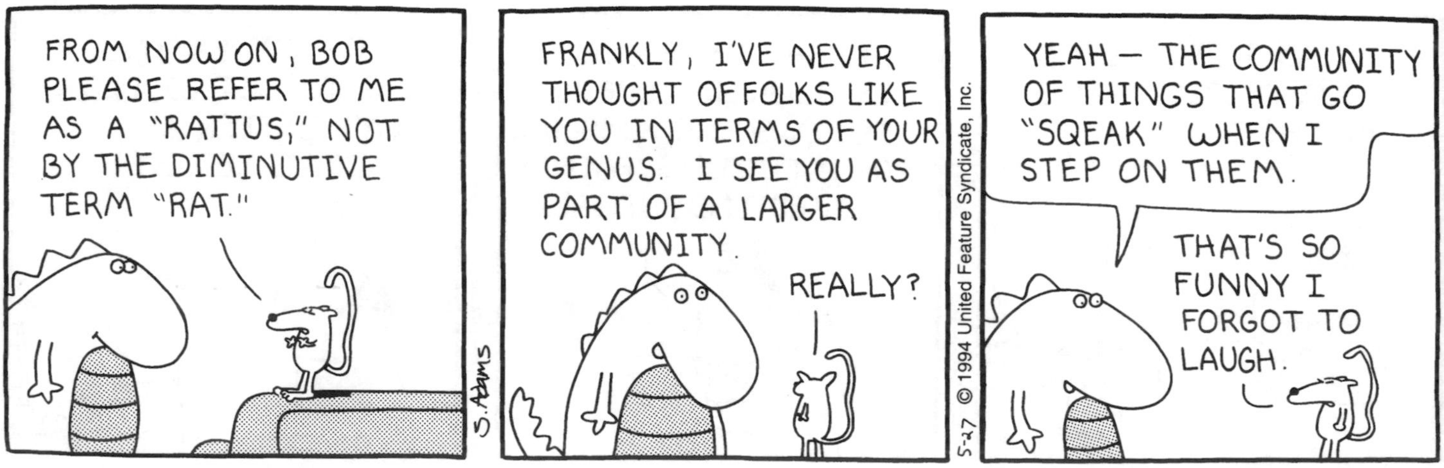
FROM NOW ON, BOB PLEASE REFER TO ME AS A "RATTUS," NOT BY THE DIMINUTIVE TERM "RAT."
FRANKLY, I'VE NEVER THOUGHT OF FOLKS LIKE YOU IN TERMS OF YOUR GENUS. I SEE YOU AS PART OF A LARGER COMMUNITY.
REALLY?
YEAH — THE COMMUNITY OF THINGS THAT GO "SQEAK" WHEN I STEP ON THEM.
THAT'S SO FUNNY I FORGOT TO LAUGH.
© 1994 United Feature Syndicate, Inc.
5-27
S. Adams

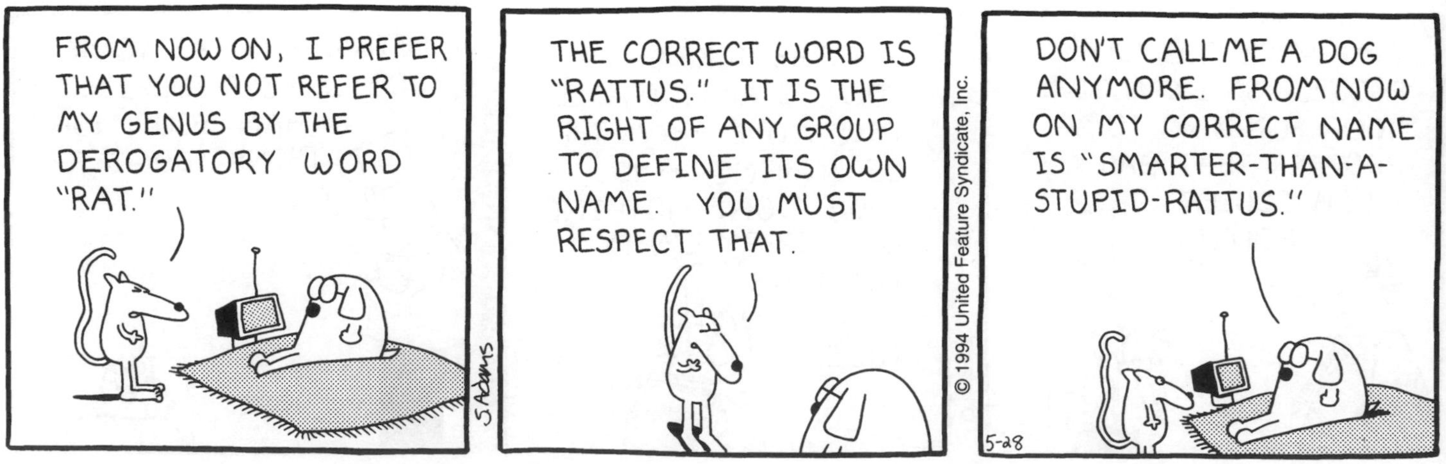
FROM NOW ON, I PREFER THAT YOU NOT REFER TO MY GENUS BY THE DEROGATORY WORD "RAT."
THE CORRECT WORD IS "RATTUS." IT IS THE RIGHT OF ANY GROUP TO DEFINE ITS OWN NAME. YOU MUST RESPECT THAT.
DON'T CALL ME A DOG ANYMORE. FROM NOW ON MY CORRECT NAME IS "SMARTER-THAN-A-STUPID-RATTUS."
© 1994 United Feature Syndicate, Inc.
5-28
S. Adams

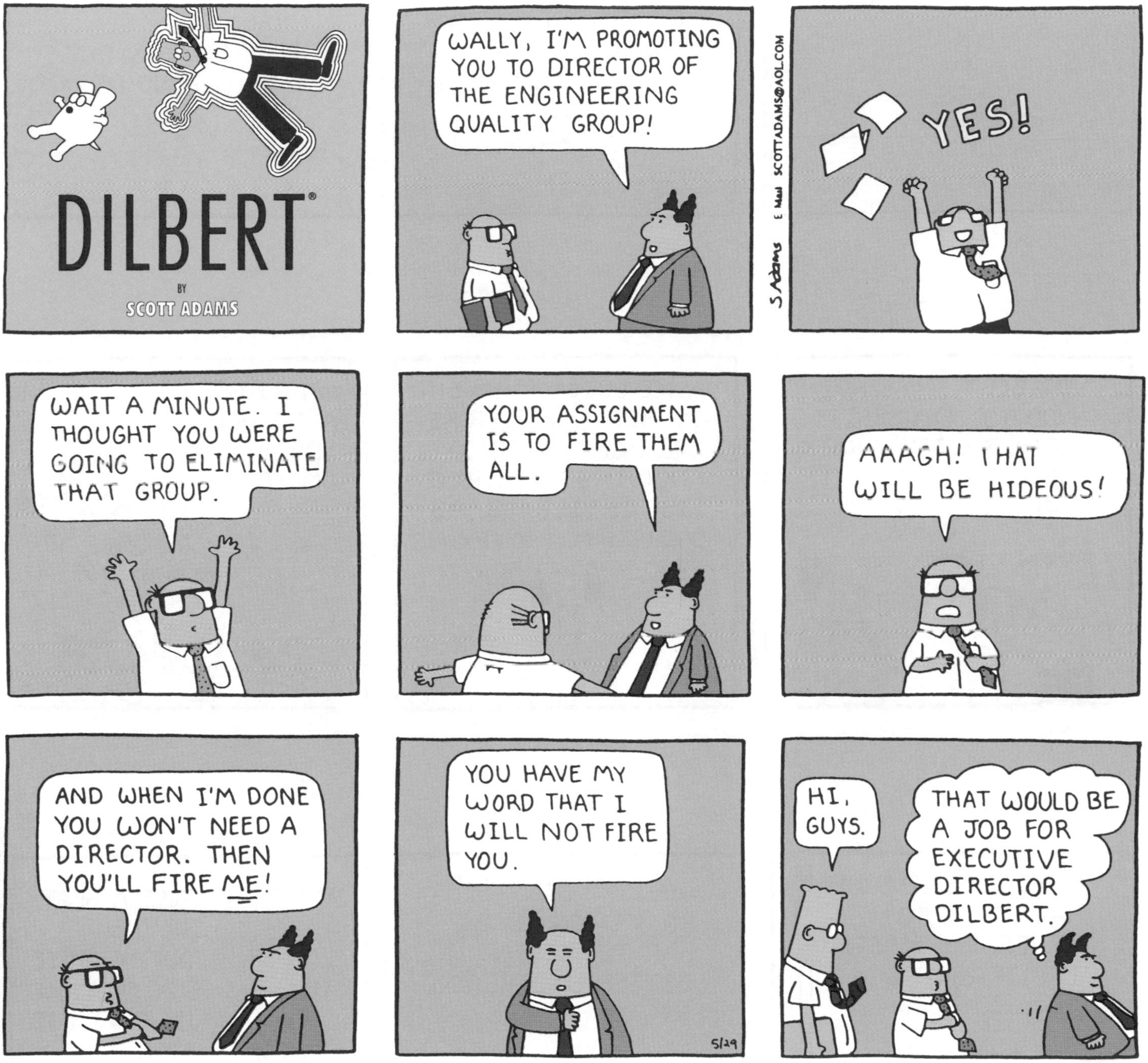
DILBERT®
BY
SCOTT ADAMS
WALLY, I'M PROMOTING YOU TO DIRECTOR OF THE ENGINEERING QUALITY GROUP!
S Adams E Mail SCOTTADAMS@AOL.COM
YES!
WAIT A MINUTE. I THOUGHT YOU WERE GOING TO ELIMINATE THAT GROUP.
YOUR ASSIGNMENT IS TO FIRE THEM ALL.
AAAGH! THAT WILL BE HIDEOUS!
AND WHEN I'M DONE YOU WON'T NEED A DIRECTOR. THEN YOU'LL FIRE ME!
YOU HAVE MY WORD THAT I WILL NOT FIRE YOU.
5/29
HI, GUYS.
THAT WOULD BE A JOB FOR EXECUTIVE DIRECTOR DILBERT.

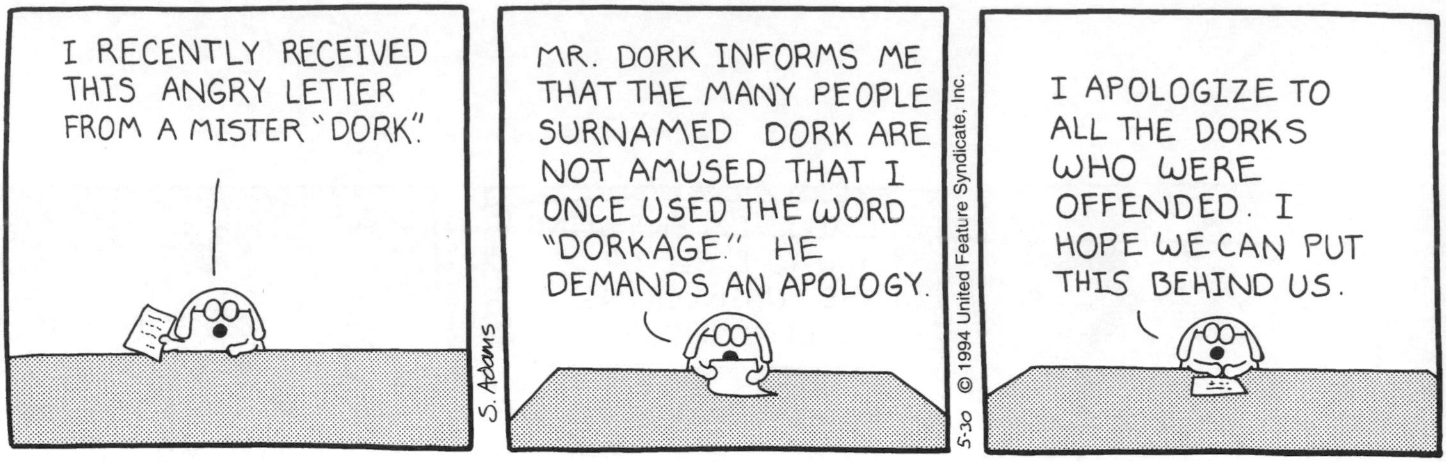
I RECENTLY RECEIVED THIS ANGRY LETTER FROM A MISTER "DORK."
MR. DORK INFORMS ME THAT THE MANY PEOPLE SURNAMED DORK ARE NOT AMUSED THAT I ONCE USED THE WORD "DORKAGE." HE DEMANDS AN APOLOGY.
I APOLOGIZE TO ALL THE DORKS WHO WERE OFFENDED. I HOPE WE CAN PUT THIS BEHIND US.
S. Adams
5-30 © 1994 United Feature Syndicate, Inc.

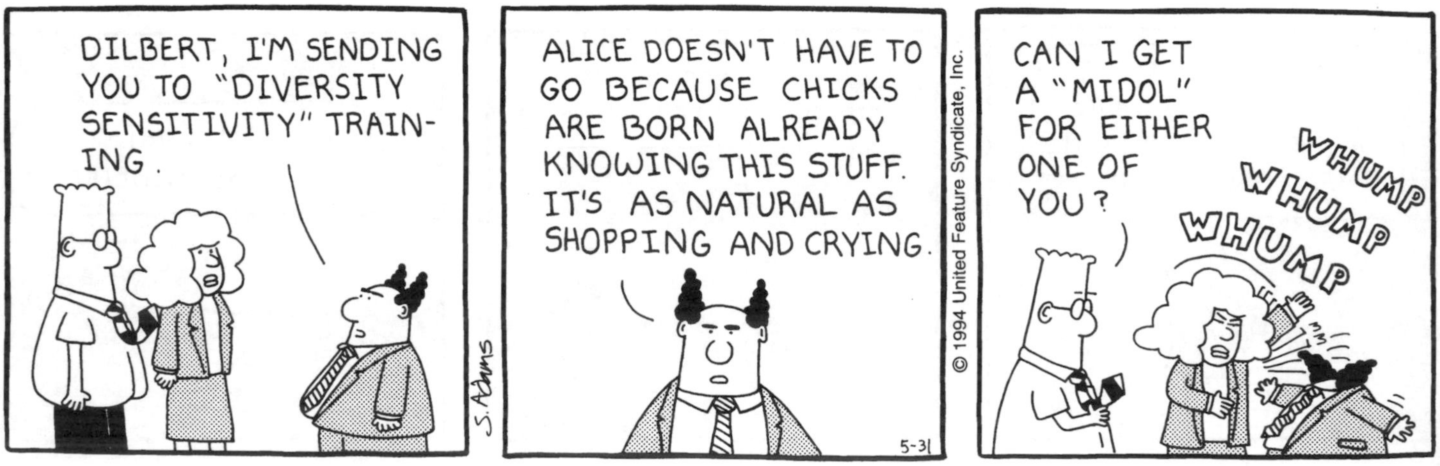
DILBERT, I'M SENDING YOU TO "DIVERSITY SENSITIVITY" TRAINING.
ALICE DOESN'T HAVE TO GO BECAUSE CHICKS ARE BORN ALREADY KNOWING THIS STUFF. IT'S AS NATURAL AS SHOPPING AND CRYING.
CAN I GET A "MIDOL" FOR EITHER ONE OF YOU?
WHUMP
WHUMP
WHUMP
S. Adams
5-31
© 1994 United Feature Syndicate, Inc.

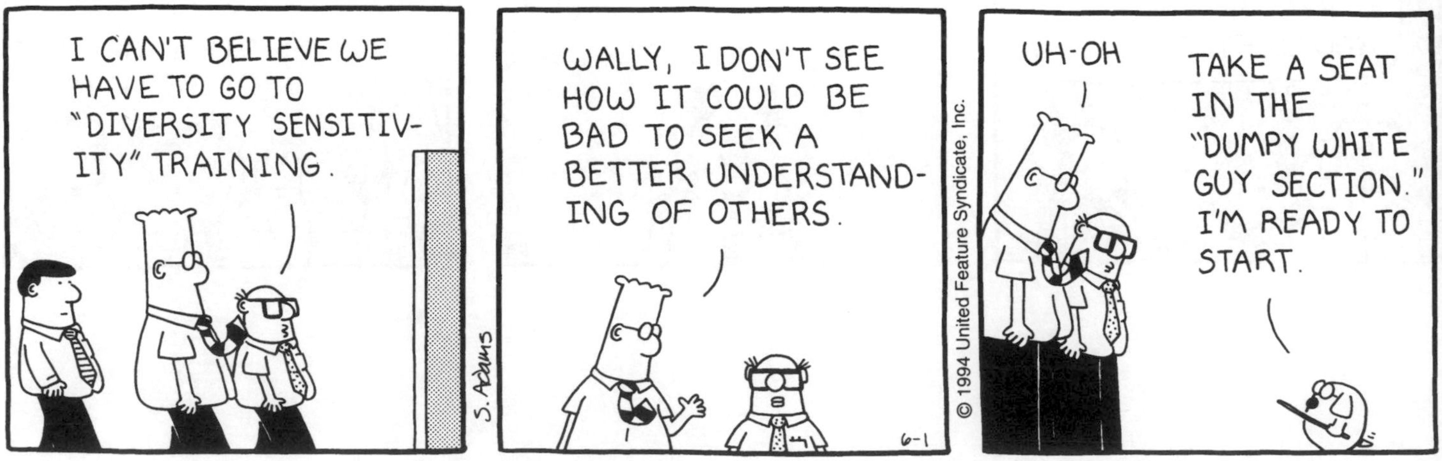
I CAN'T BELIEVE WE HAVE TO GO TO "DIVERSITY SENSITIVITY" TRAINING.
WALLY, I DON'T SEE HOW IT COULD BE BAD TO SEEK A BETTER UNDERSTANDING OF OTHERS.
UH-OH
TAKE A SEAT IN THE "DUMPY WHITE GUY SECTION." I'M READY TO START.
S. Adams
6-1
© 1994 United Feature Syndicate, Inc.

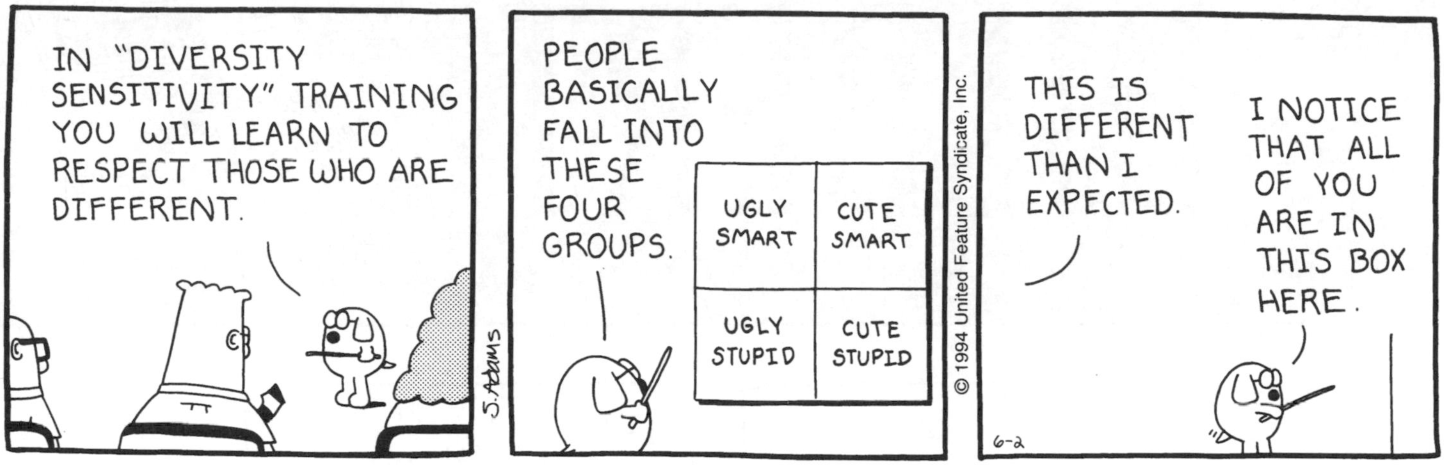
IN "DIVERSITY SENSITIVITY" TRAINING YOU WILL LEARN TO RESPECT THOSE WHO ARE DIFFERENT.
S. Adams
PEOPLE BASICALLY FALL INTO THESE FOUR GROUPS.
UGLY SMART
CUTE SMART
UGLY STUPID
CUTE STUPID
© 1994 United Feature Syndicate, Inc.
THIS IS DIFFERENT THAN I EXPECTED.
I NOTICE THAT ALL OF YOU ARE IN THIS BOX HERE.
6-2

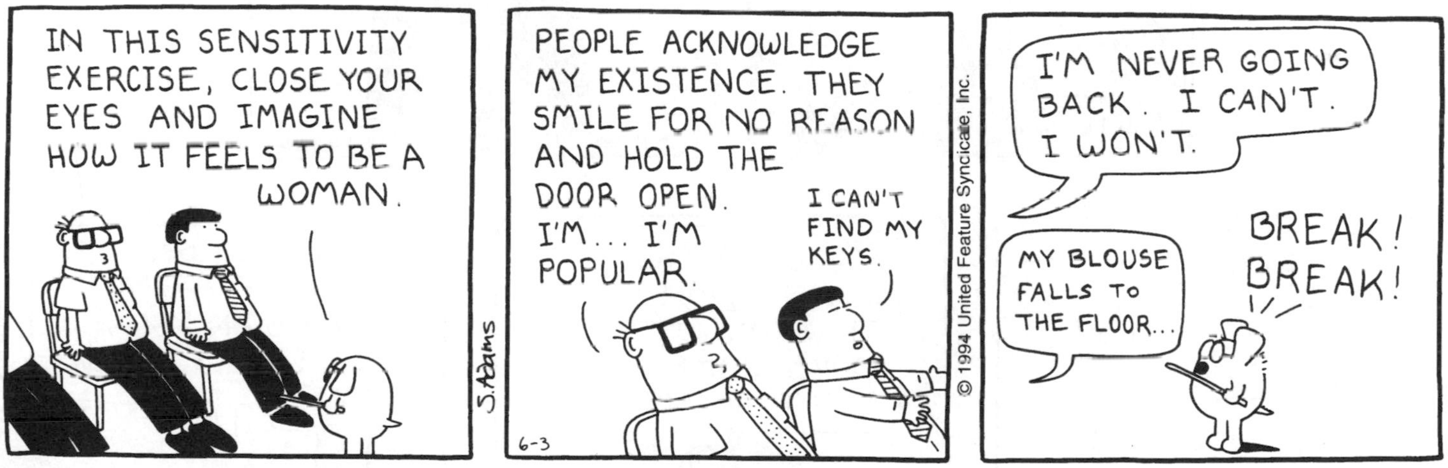
IN THIS SENSITIVITY EXERCISE, CLOSE YOUR EYES AND IMAGINE HOW IT FEELS TO BE A WOMAN.
S. Adams
PEOPLE ACKNOWLEDGE MY EXISTENCE. THEY SMILE FOR NO REASON AND HOLD THE DOOR OPEN. I'M... I'M POPULAR.
I CAN'T FIND MY KEYS.
6-3
© 1994 United Feature Syndicate, Inc.
I'M NEVER GOING BACK. I CAN'T. I WON'T.
MY BLOUSE FALLS TO THE FLOOR...
BREAK! BREAK!

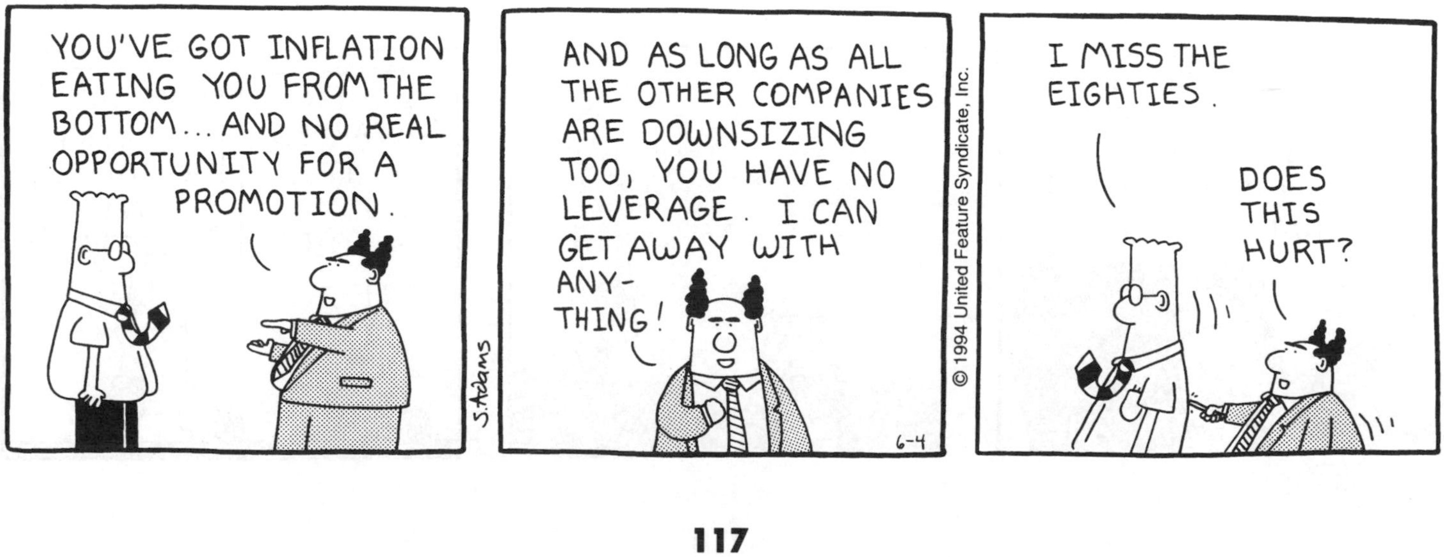
YOU'VE GOT INFLATION EATING YOU FROM THE BOTTOM... AND NO REAL OPPORTUNITY FOR A PROMOTION.
S. Adams
AND AS LONG AS ALL THE OTHER COMPANIES ARE DOWNSIZING TOO, YOU HAVE NO LEVERAGE. I CAN GET AWAY WITH ANY-THING!
6-4
© 1994 United Feature Syndicate, Inc.
I MISS THE EIGHTIES.
DOES THIS HURT?

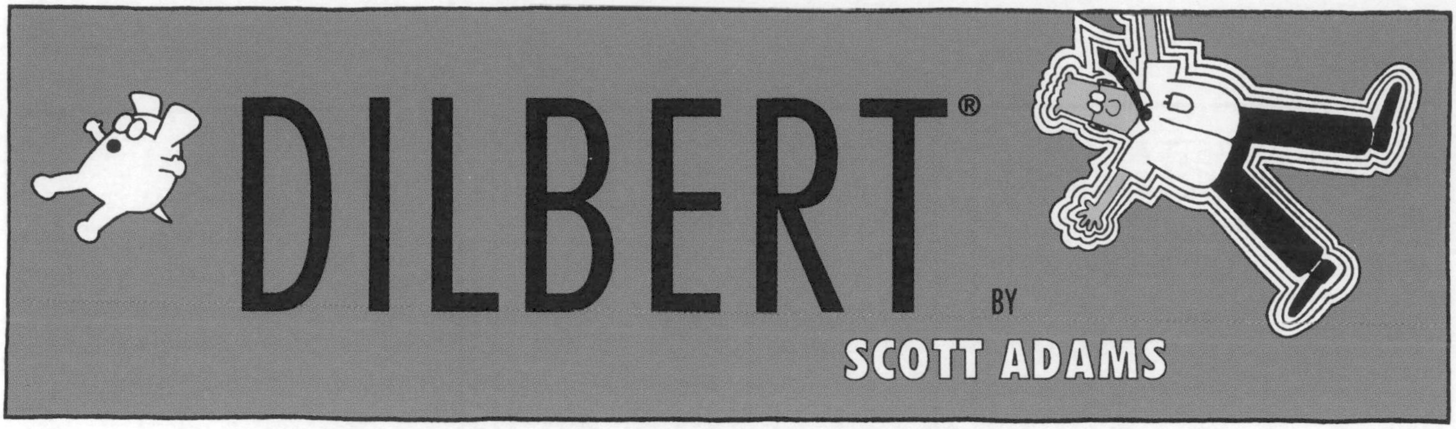
DILBERT®
BY
SCOTT ADAMS

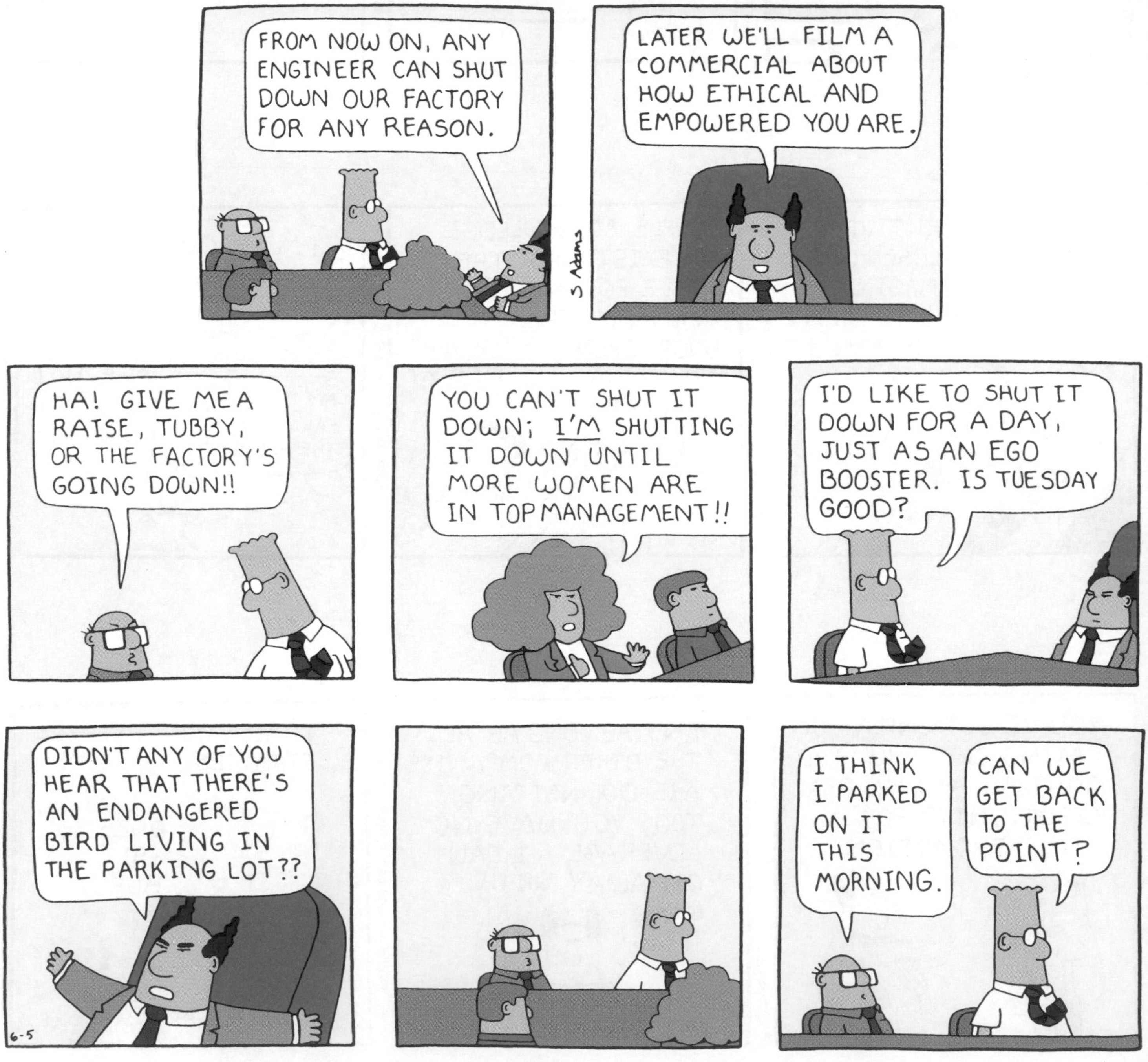
FROM NOW ON, ANY ENGINEER CAN SHUT DOWN OUR FACTORY FOR ANY REASON.
LATER WE'LL FILM A COMMERCIAL ABOUT HOW ETHICAL AND EMPOWERED YOU ARE.
S Adams
HA! GIVE ME A RAISE, TUBBY, OR THE FACTORY'S GOING DOWN!!
YOU CAN'T SHUT IT DOWN; I'M SHUTTING IT DOWN UNTIL MORE WOMEN ARE IN TOP MANAGEMENT!!
I'D LIKE TO SHUT IT DOWN FOR A DAY, JUST AS AN EGO BOOSTER. IS TUESDAY GOOD?
DIDN'T ANY OF YOU HEAR THAT THERE'S AN ENDANGERED BIRD LIVING IN THE PARKING LOT??
6-5
I THINK I PARKED ON IT THIS MORNING.
CAN WE GET BACK TO THE POINT?

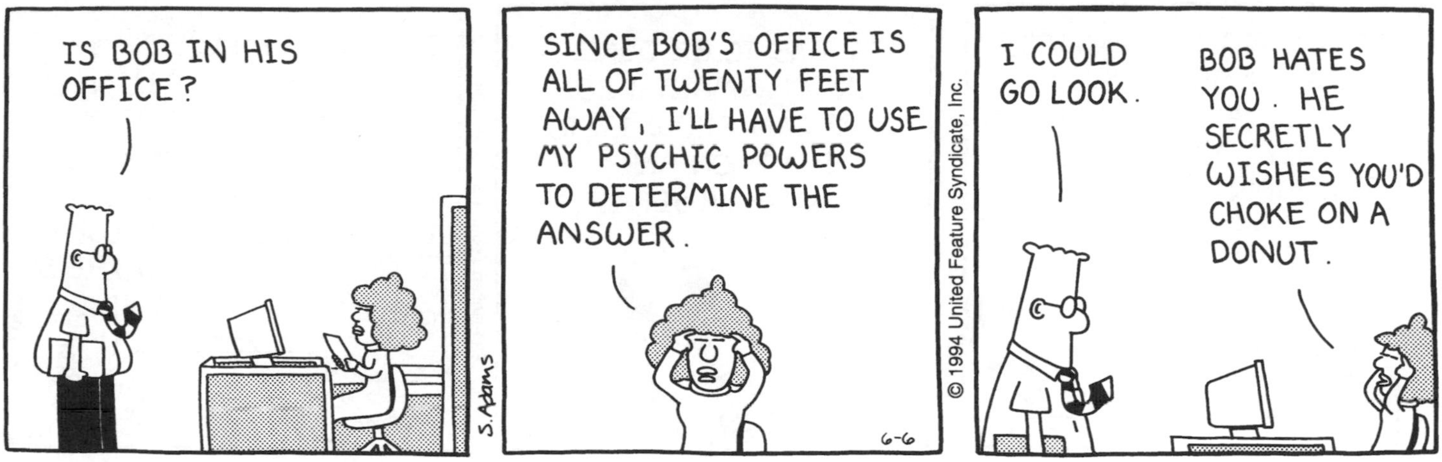
IS BOB IN HIS OFFICE?
SINCE BOB'S OFFICE IS ALL OF TWENTY FEET AWAY, I'LL HAVE TO USE MY PSYCHIC POWERS TO DETERMINE THE ANSWER.
I COULD GO LOOK.
BOB HATES YOU. HE SECRETLY WISHES YOU'D CHOKE ON A DONUT.
S. Adams
6-6
© 1994 United Feature Syndicate, Inc.

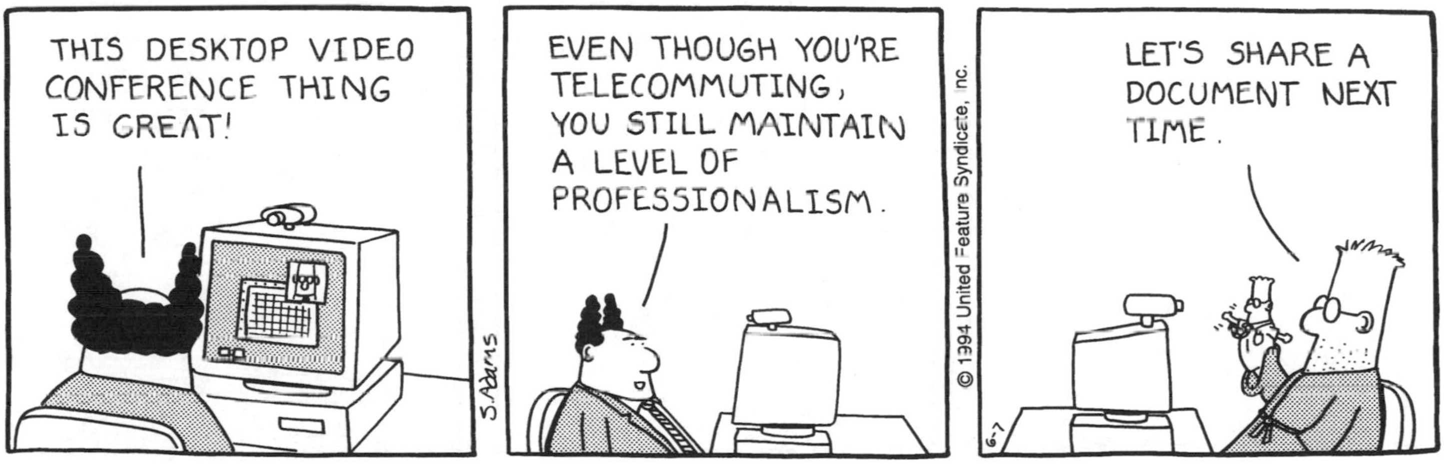
THIS DESKTOP VIDEO CONFERENCE THING IS GREAT!
EVEN THOUGH YOU'RE TELECOMMUTING, YOU STILL MAINTAIN A LEVEL OF PROFESSIONALISM.
LET'S SHARE A DOCUMENT NEXT TIME.
S. Adams
6-7
© 1994 United Feature Syndicate, Inc.

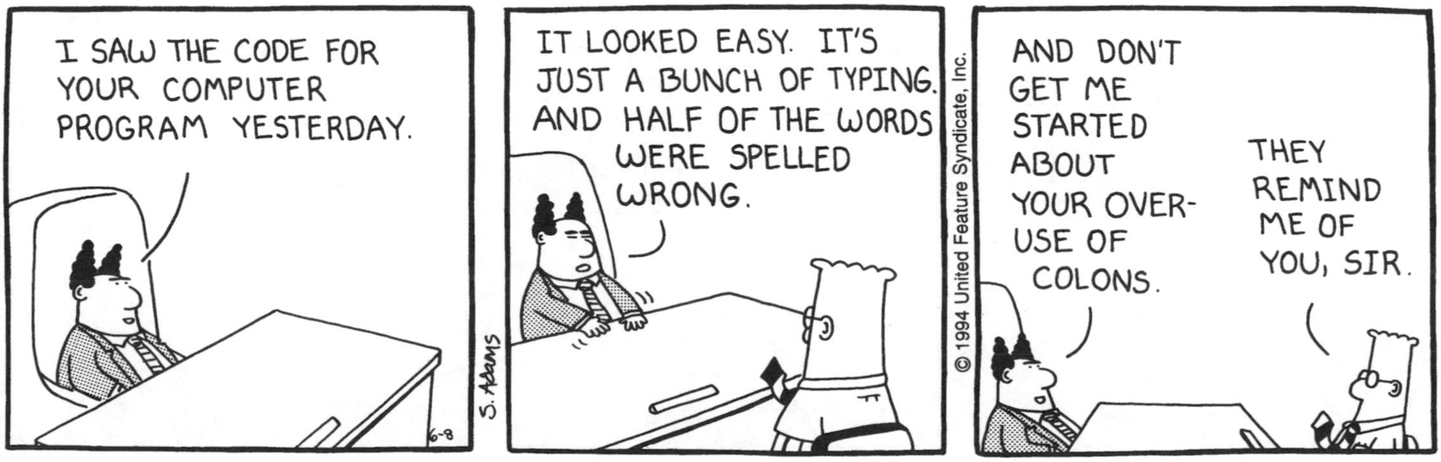
I SAW THE CODE FOR YOUR COMPUTER PROGRAM YESTERDAY.
IT LOOKED EASY. IT'S JUST A BUNCH OF TYPING. AND HALF OF THE WORDS WERE SPELLED WRONG.
AND DON'T GET ME STARTED ABOUT YOUR OVER-USE OF COLONS.
THEY REMIND ME OF YOU, SIR.
S. Adams
6-8
© 1994 United Feature Syndicate, Inc.

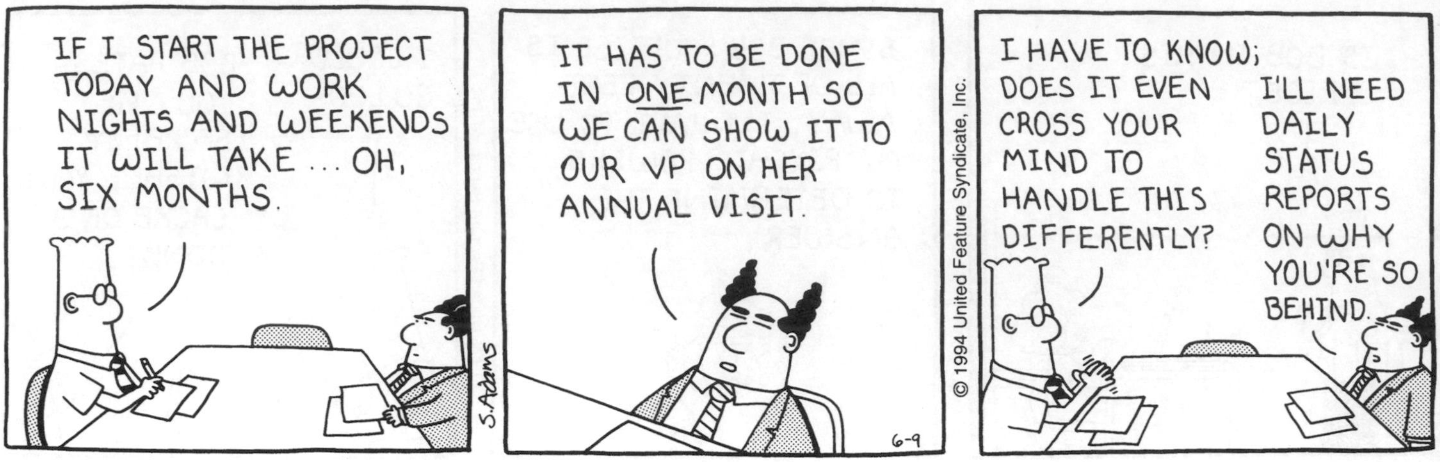
IF I START THE PROJECT TODAY AND WORK NIGHTS AND WEEKENDS IT WILL TAKE ... OH, SIX MONTHS.
IT HAS TO BE DONE IN ONE MONTH SO WE CAN SHOW IT TO OUR VP ON HER ANNUAL VISIT.
I HAVE TO KNOW; DOES IT EVEN CROSS YOUR MIND TO HANDLE THIS DIFFERENTLY?
I'LL NEED DAILY STATUS REPORTS ON WHY YOU'RE SO BEHIND.
S. Adams
6-9
© 1994 United Feature Syndicate, Inc.

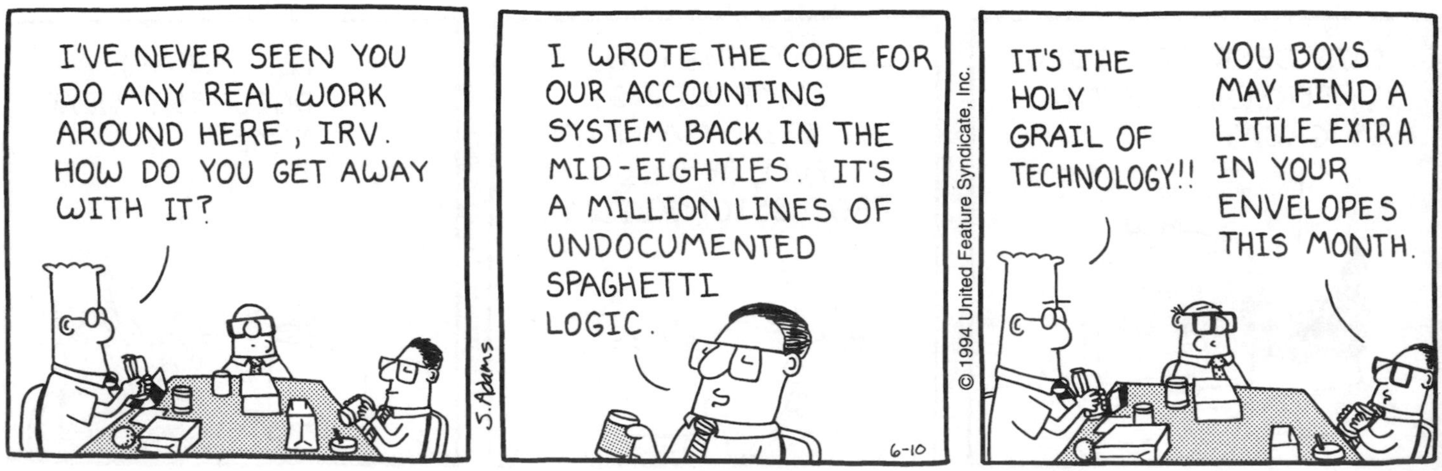
I'VE NEVER SEEN YOU DO ANY REAL WORK AROUND HERE, IRV. HOW DO YOU GET AWAY WITH IT?
I WROTE THE CODE FOR OUR ACCOUNTING SYSTEM BACK IN THE MID-EIGHTIES. IT'S A MILLION LINES OF UNDOCUMENTED SPAGHETTI LOGIC.
IT'S THE HOLY GRAIL OF TECHNOLOGY!!
YOU BOYS MAY FIND A LITTLE EXTRA IN YOUR ENVELOPES THIS MONTH.
S. Adams
6-10
© 1994 United Feature Syndicate, Inc.

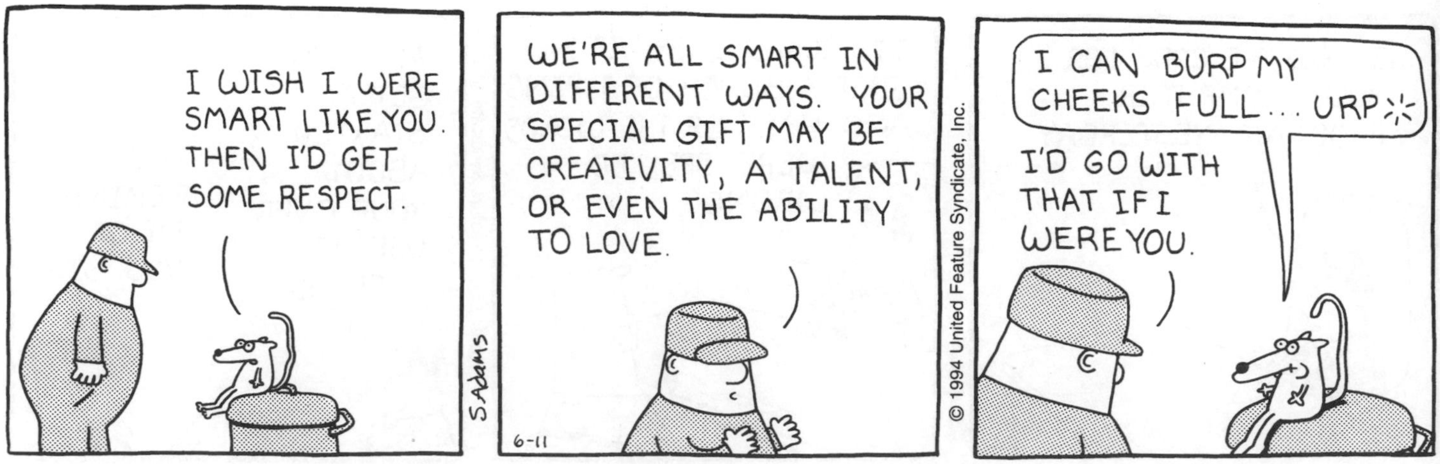
I WISH I WERE SMART LIKE YOU. THEN I'D GET SOME RESPECT.
WE'RE ALL SMART IN DIFFERENT WAYS. YOUR SPECIAL GIFT MAY BE CREATIVITY, A TALENT, OR EVEN THE ABILITY TO LOVE.
I CAN BURP MY CHEEKS FULL... URP
I'D GO WITH THAT IF I WERE YOU.
S. Adams
6-11
© 1994 United Feature Syndicate, Inc.

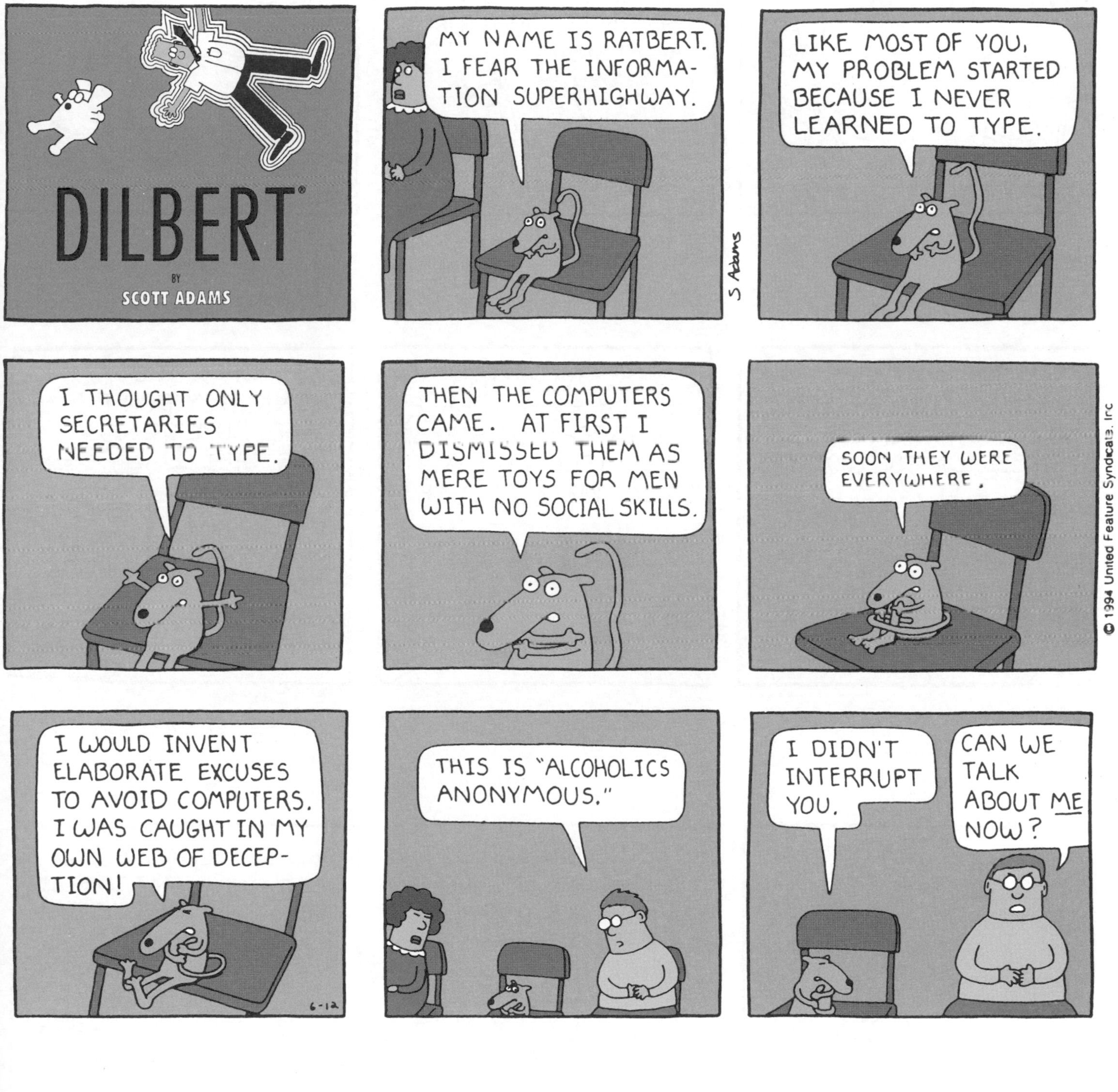
DILBERT®
BY
SCOTT ADAMS
MY NAME IS RATBERT. I FEAR THE INFORMATION SUPERHIGHWAY.
S Adams
LIKE MOST OF YOU, MY PROBLEM STARTED BECAUSE I NEVER LEARNED TO TYPE.
I THOUGHT ONLY SECRETARIES NEEDED TO TYPE.
THEN THE COMPUTERS CAME. AT FIRST I DISMISSED THEM AS MERE TOYS FOR MEN WITH NO SOCIAL SKILLS.
SOON THEY WERE EVERYWHERE.
© 1994 United Feature Syndicate, Inc
I WOULD INVENT ELABORATE EXCUSES TO AVOID COMPUTERS. I WAS CAUGHT IN MY OWN WEB OF DECEPTION!
6-12
THIS IS "ALCOHOLICS ANONYMOUS."
I DIDN'T INTERRUPT YOU.
CAN WE TALK ABOUT ME NOW?

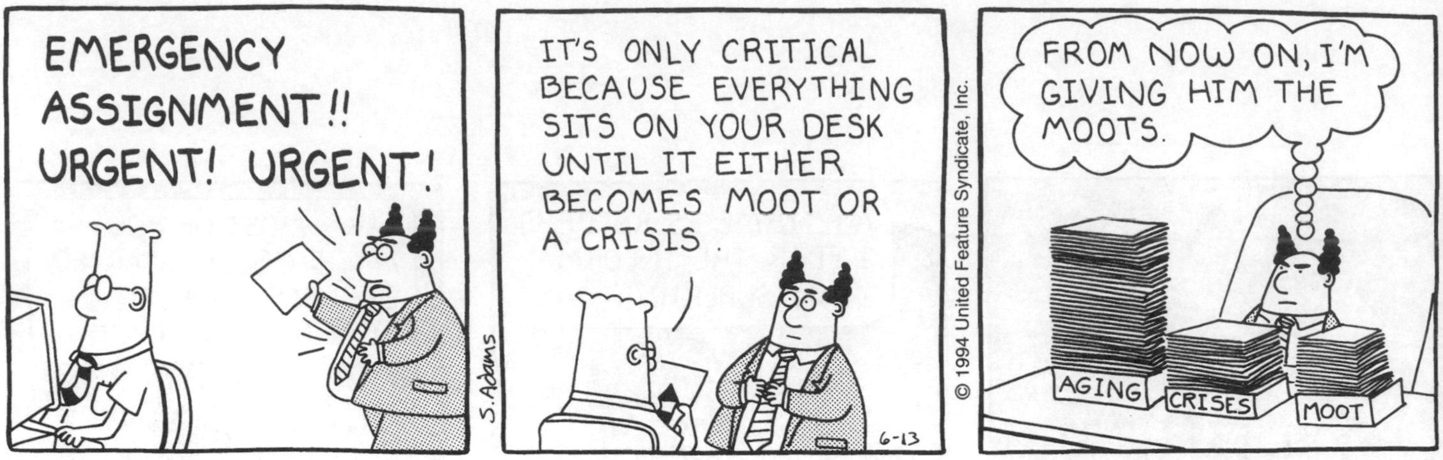
EMERGENCY ASSIGNMENT!! URGENT! URGENT!
S. Adams
IT'S ONLY CRITICAL BECAUSE EVERYTHING SITS ON YOUR DESK UNTIL IT EITHER BECOMES MOOT OR A CRISIS.
6-13
© 1994 United Feature Syndicate, Inc.
FROM NOW ON, I'M GIVING HIM THE MOOTS.
AGING
CRISES
MOOT

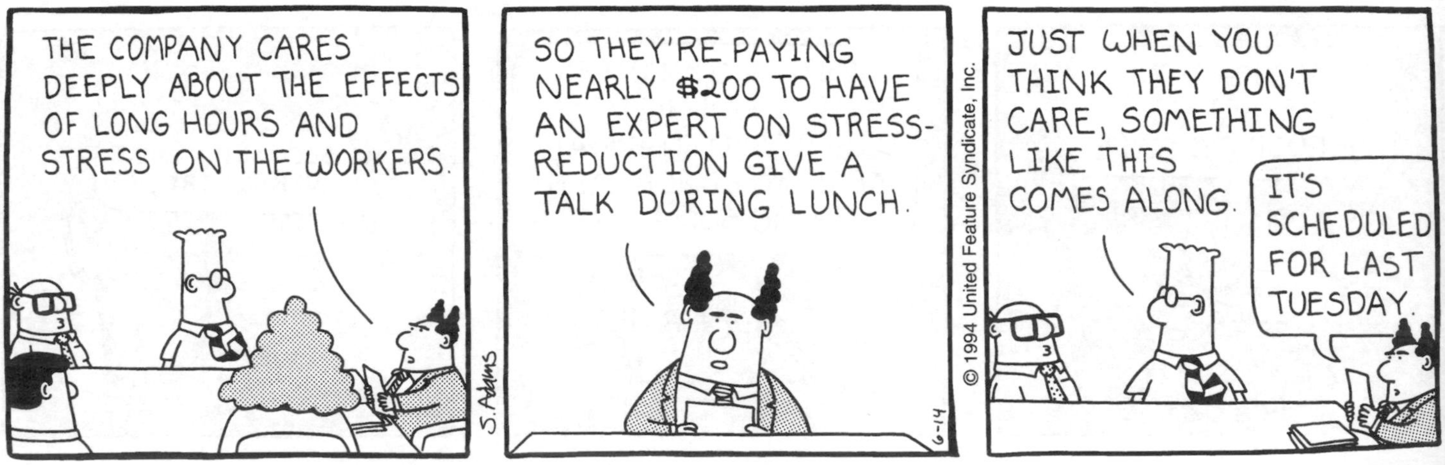
THE COMPANY CARES DEEPLY ABOUT THE EFFECTS OF LONG HOURS AND STRESS ON THE WORKERS.
S. Adams
SO THEY'RE PAYING NEARLY $200 TO HAVE AN EXPERT ON STRESS-REDUCTION GIVE A TALK DURING LUNCH.
6-14
© 1994 United Feature Syndicate, Inc.
JUST WHEN YOU THINK THEY DON'T CARE, SOMETHING LIKE THIS COMES ALONG.
IT'S SCHEDULED FOR LAST TUESDAY.

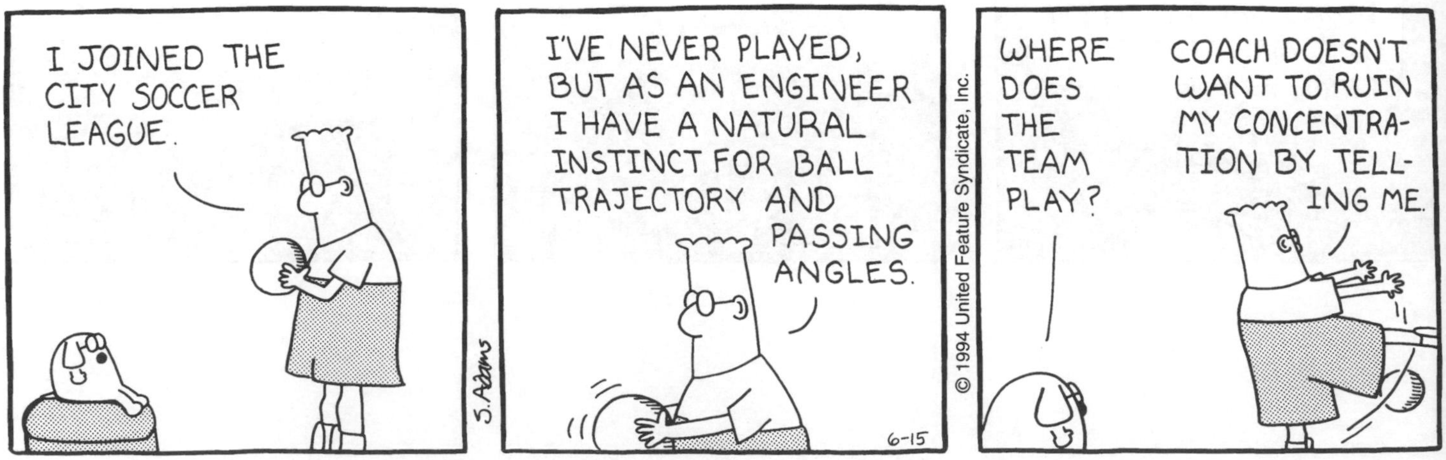
I JOINED THE CITY SOCCER LEAGUE.
S. Adams
I'VE NEVER PLAYED, BUT AS AN ENGINEER I HAVE A NATURAL INSTINCT FOR BALL TRAJECTORY AND PASSING ANGLES.
6-15
© 1994 United Feature Syndicate, Inc.
WHERE DOES THE TEAM PLAY?
COACH DOESN'T WANT TO RUIN MY CONCENTRATION BY TELLING ME.

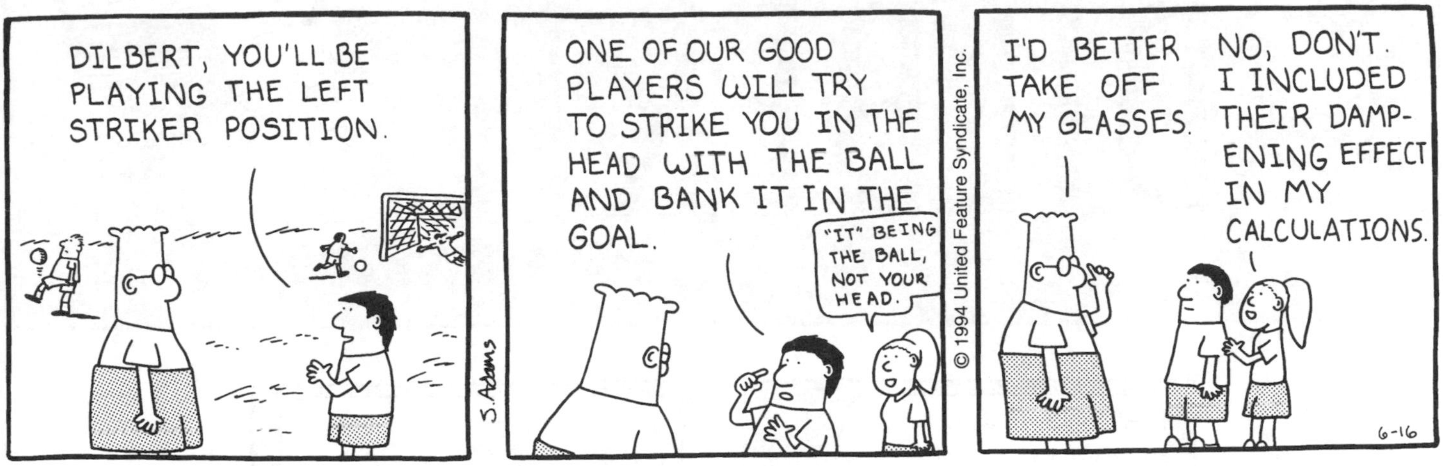
DILBERT, YOU'LL BE PLAYING THE LEFT STRIKER POSITION.
ONE OF OUR GOOD PLAYERS WILL TRY TO STRIKE YOU IN THE HEAD WITH THE BALL AND BANK IT IN THE GOAL.
"IT" BEING THE BALL, NOT YOUR HEAD.
I'D BETTER TAKE OFF MY GLASSES.
NO, DON'T. I INCLUDED THEIR DAMP-ENING EFFECT IN MY CALCULATIONS.
S. Adams
© 1994 United Feature Syndicate, Inc.
6-16

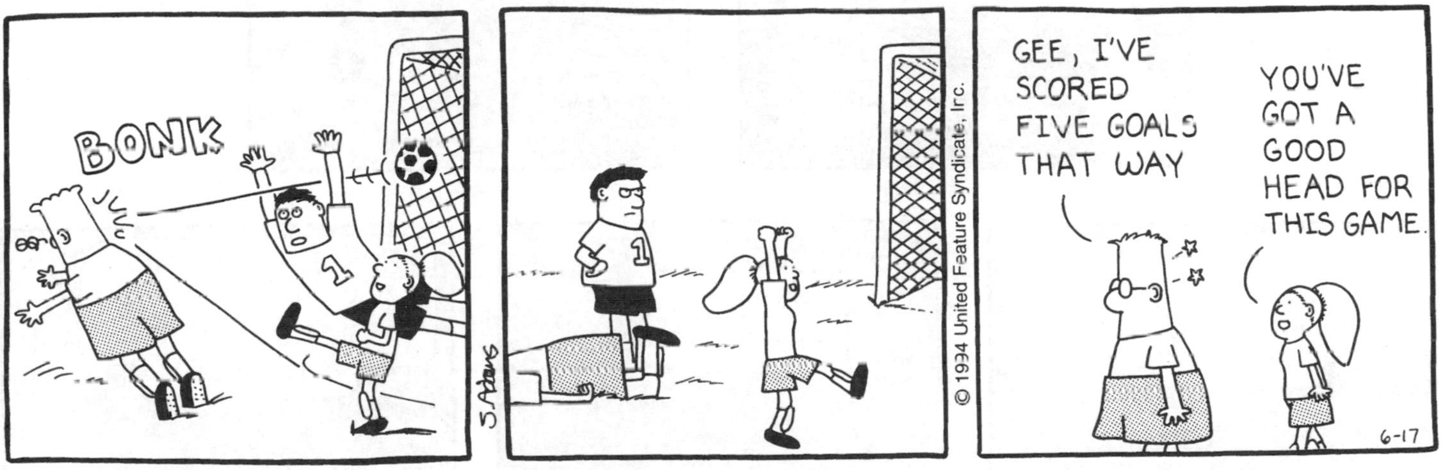
BONK
1
GEE, I'VE SCORED FIVE GOALS THAT WAY
YOU'VE GOT A GOOD HEAD FOR THIS GAME.
S. Adams
© 1994 United Feature Syndicate, Inc.
6-17

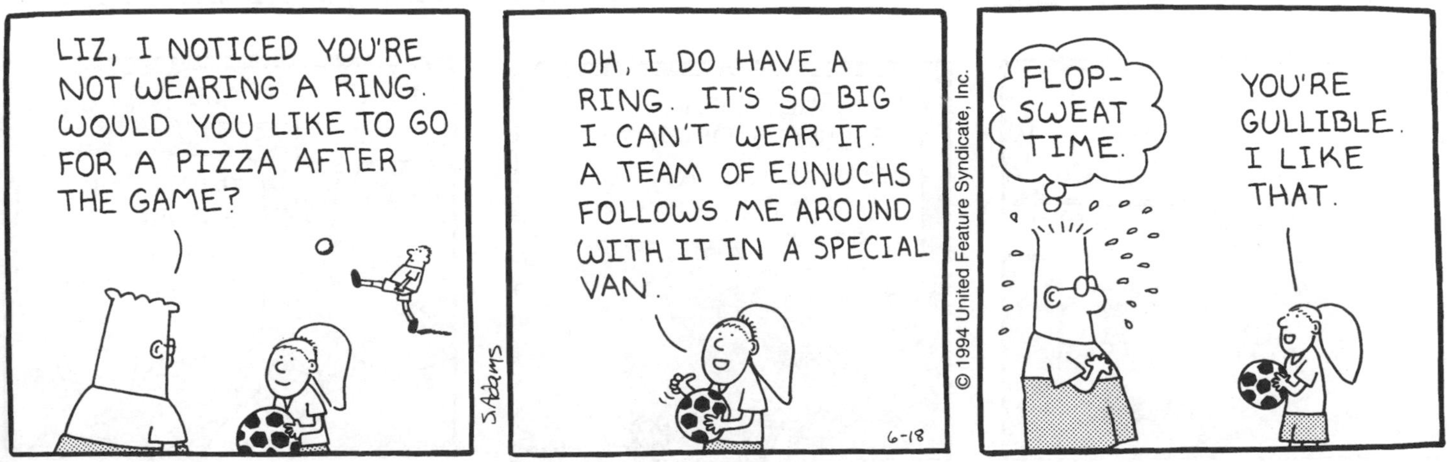
LIZ, I NOTICED YOU'RE NOT WEARING A RING. WOULD YOU LIKE TO GO FOR A PIZZA AFTER THE GAME?
OH, I DO HAVE A RING. IT'S SO BIG I CAN'T WEAR IT. A TEAM OF EUNUCHS FOLLOWS ME AROUND WITH IT IN A SPECIAL VAN.
FLOP-SWEAT TIME.
YOU'RE GULLIBLE. I LIKE THAT.
S. Adams
© 1994 United Feature Syndicate, Inc.
6-18

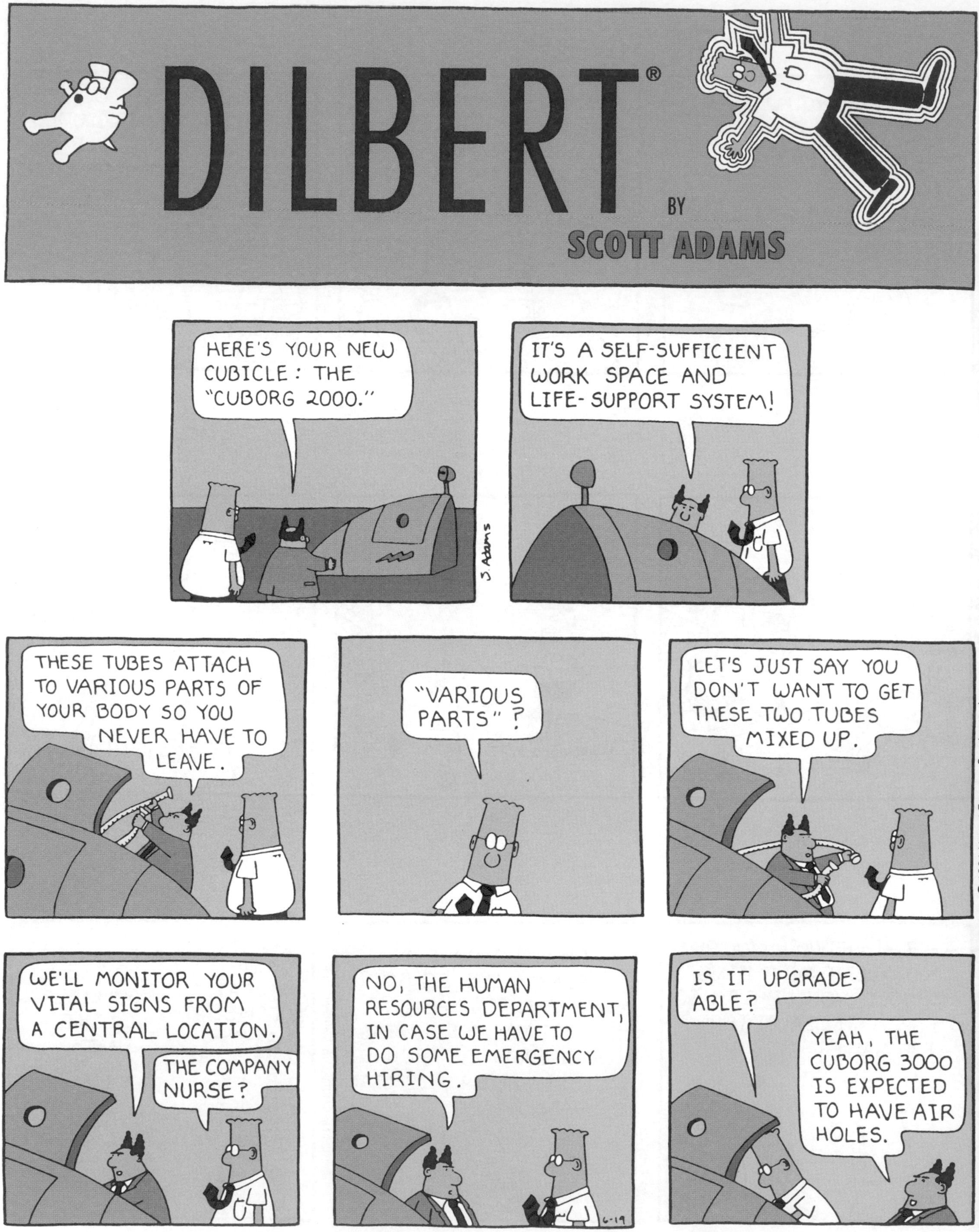

DILBERT®
BY
SCOTT ADAMS
HERE'S YOUR NEW CUBICLE: THE "CUBORG 2000."
S. Adams
IT'S A SELF-SUFFICIENT WORK SPACE AND LIFE-SUPPORT SYSTEM!
THESE TUBES ATTACH TO VARIOUS PARTS OF YOUR BODY SO YOU NEVER HAVE TO LEAVE.
"VARIOUS PARTS"?
LET'S JUST SAY YOU DON'T WANT TO GET THESE TWO TUBES MIXED UP.
WE'LL MONITOR YOUR VITAL SIGNS FROM A CENTRAL LOCATION.
THE COMPANY NURSE?
NO, THE HUMAN RESOURCES DEPARTMENT, IN CASE WE HAVE TO DO SOME EMERGENCY HIRING.
6-19
IS IT UPGRADE-ABLE?
YEAH, THE CUBORG 3000 IS EXPECTED TO HAVE AIR HOLES.

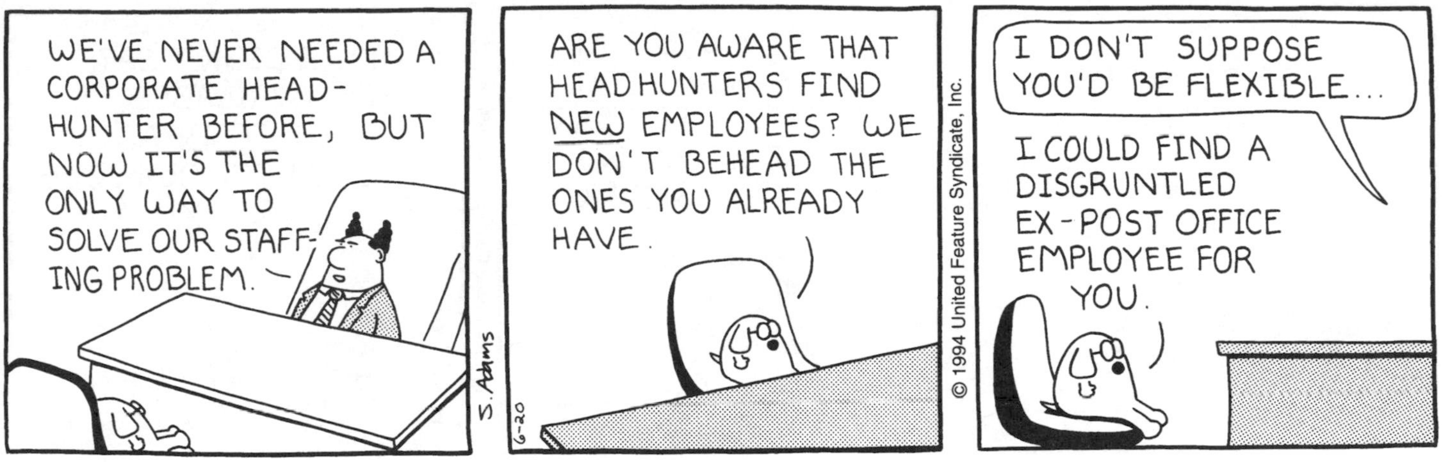
WE'VE NEVER NEEDED A CORPORATE HEAD-HUNTER BEFORE, BUT NOW IT'S THE ONLY WAY TO SOLVE OUR STAFF-ING PROBLEM.
S. Adams 6-20
ARE YOU AWARE THAT HEAD HUNTERS FIND NEW EMPLOYEES? WE DON'T BEHEAD THE ONES YOU ALREADY HAVE.
© 1994 United Feature Syndicate, Inc.
I DON'T SUPPOSE YOU'D BE FLEXIBLE...
I COULD FIND A DISGRUNTLED EX-POST OFFICE EMPLOYEE FOR YOU.

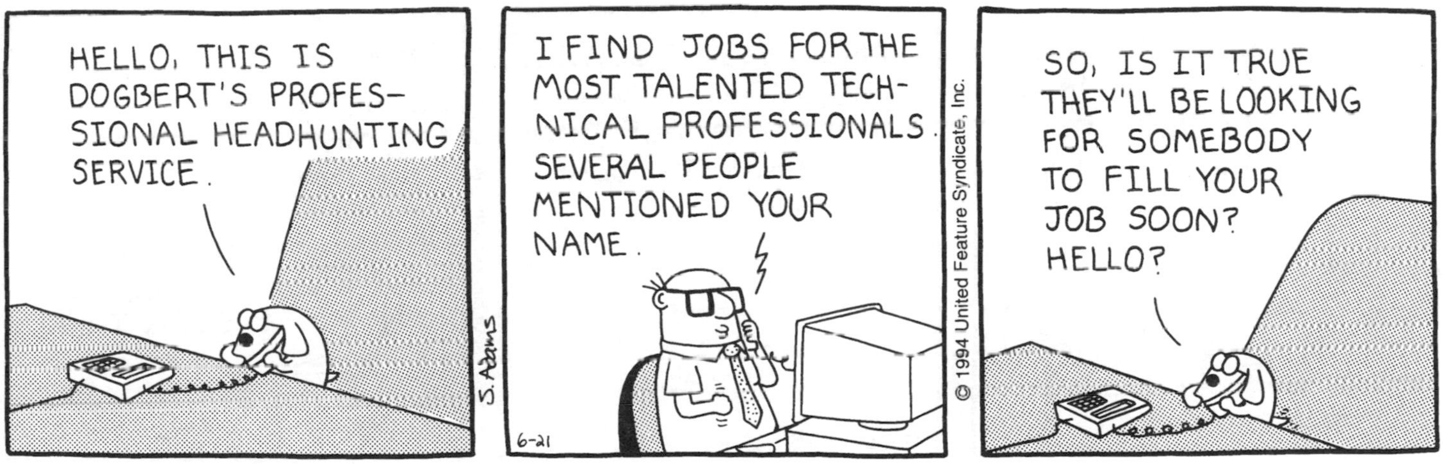
HELLO, THIS IS DOGBERT'S PROFES-SIONAL HEADHUNTING SERVICE.
S. Adams 6-21
I FIND JOBS FOR THE MOST TALENTED TECH-NICAL PROFESSIONALS. SEVERAL PEOPLE MENTIONED YOUR NAME.
© 1994 United Feature Syndicate, Inc.
SO, IS IT TRUE THEY'LL BE LOOKING FOR SOMEBODY TO FILL YOUR JOB SOON? HELLO?

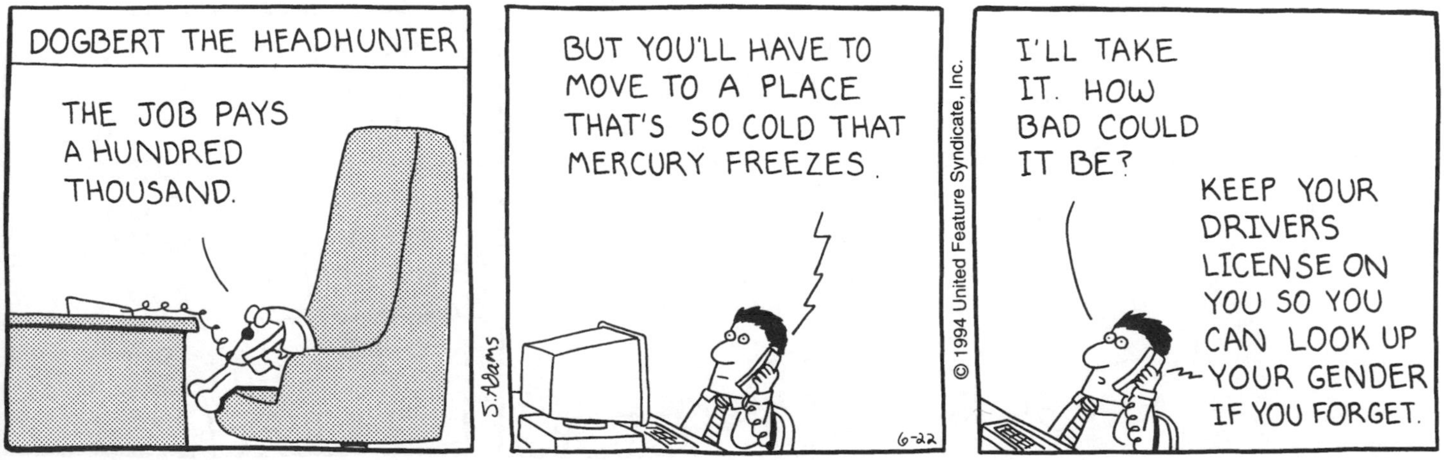
DOGBERT THE HEADHUNTER
THE JOB PAYS A HUNDRED THOUSAND.
S. Adams
BUT YOU'LL HAVE TO MOVE TO A PLACE THAT'S SO COLD THAT MERCURY FREEZES.
6-22
© 1994 United Feature Syndicate, Inc.
I'LL TAKE IT. HOW BAD COULD IT BE?
KEEP YOUR DRIVERS LICENSE ON YOU SO YOU CAN LOOK UP YOUR GENDER IF YOU FORGET.

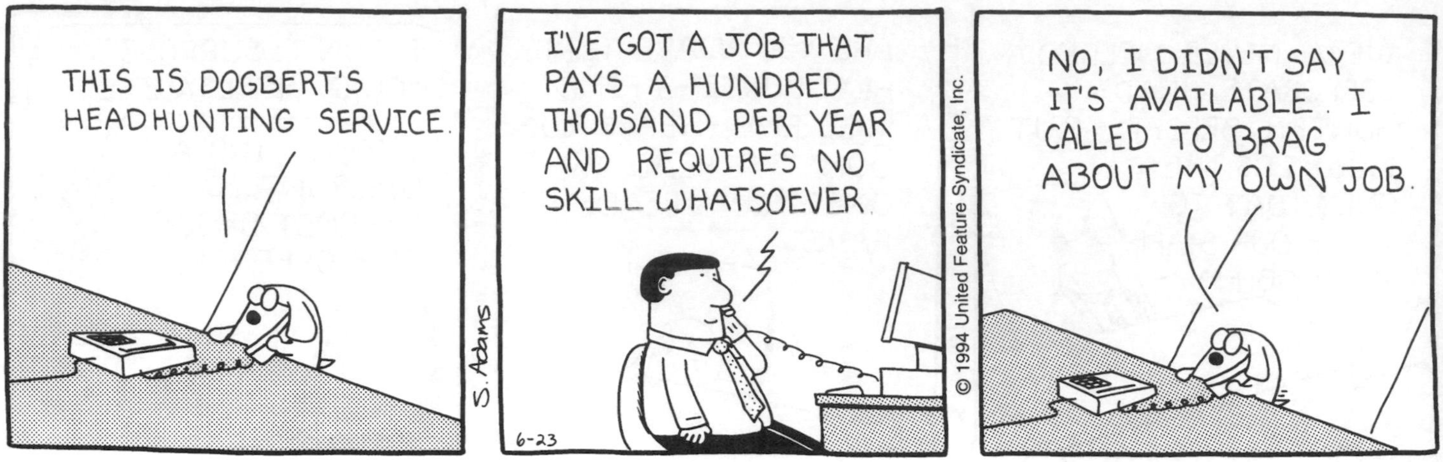
THIS IS DOGBERT'S HEADHUNTING SERVICE.
I'VE GOT A JOB THAT PAYS A HUNDRED THOUSAND PER YEAR AND REQUIRES NO SKILL WHATSOEVER.
NO, I DIDN'T SAY IT'S AVAILABLE. I CALLED TO BRAG ABOUT MY OWN JOB.
S. Adams
6-23
© 1994 United Feature Syndicate, Inc.

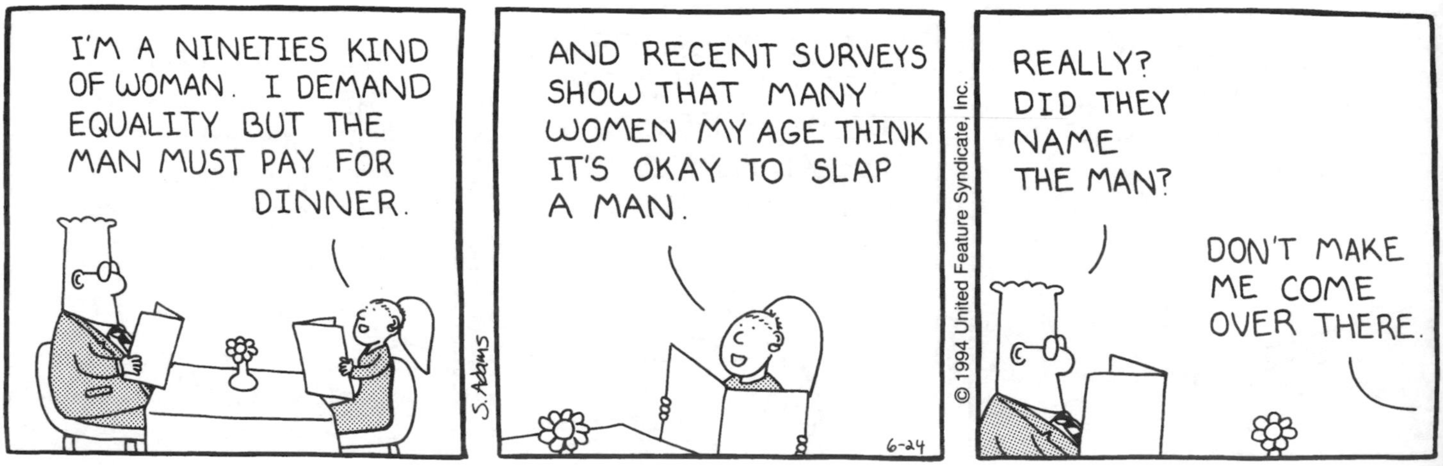
I'M A NINETIES KIND OF WOMAN. I DEMAND EQUALITY BUT THE MAN MUST PAY FOR DINNER.
AND RECENT SURVEYS SHOW THAT MANY WOMEN MY AGE THINK IT'S OKAY TO SLAP A MAN.
REALLY? DID THEY NAME THE MAN?
DON'T MAKE ME COME OVER THERE.
S. Adams
6-24
© 1994 United Feature Syndicate, Inc.

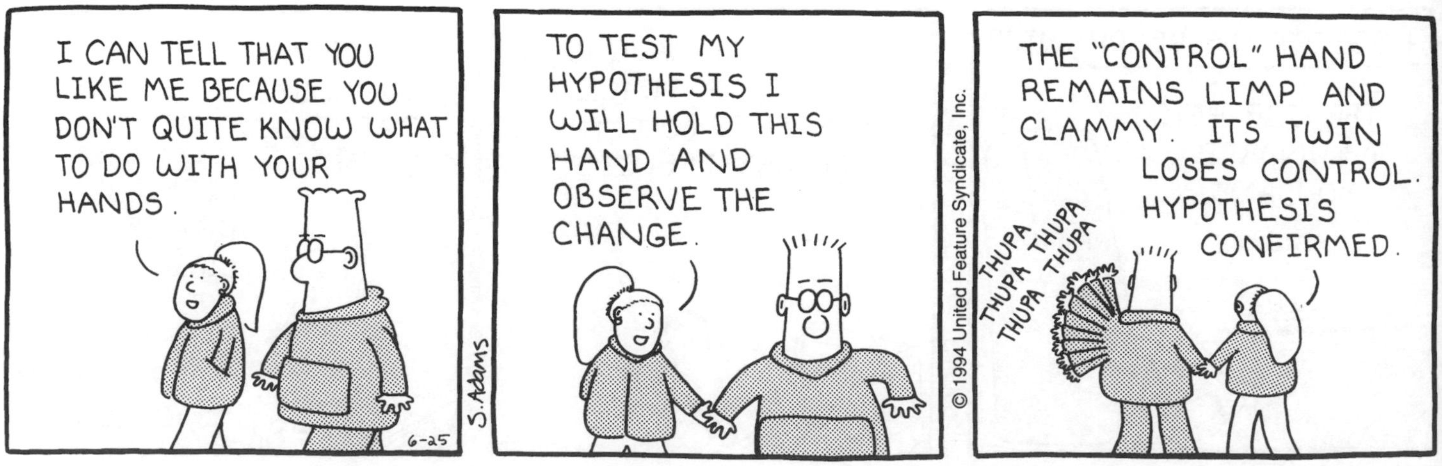
I CAN TELL THAT YOU LIKE ME BECAUSE YOU DON'T QUITE KNOW WHAT TO DO WITH YOUR HANDS.
TO TEST MY HYPOTHESIS I WILL HOLD THIS HAND AND OBSERVE THE CHANGE.
THE "CONTROL" HAND REMAINS LIMP AND CLAMMY. ITS TWIN LOSES CONTROL. HYPOTHESIS CONFIRMED.
THUPA THUPA THUPA THUPA THUPA THUPA
S. Adams
6-25
© 1994 United Feature Syndicate, Inc.

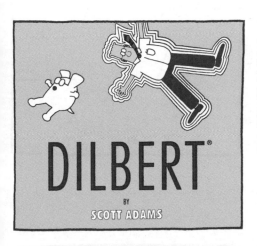

DILBERT®
BY
SCOTT ADAMS
THE NEW LAB SUPPLIES ARE IN!
S Adams
WE GOT THE BATTERIES AND THE ELECTRIC MOTOR!
TAKE THE WHEELS OFF THE HAND-TRUCK AND WE CAN START BUILDING OUR GO-CART.
I THINK I'LL DROP IN ON THE LAB.
LAB
WHAT ARE YOU WORKING ON NOW?
© 1994 United Feature Syndicate Inc
6-26
WE'RE BUILDING A LINEAR ACCELERATOR.
MARKETING INSISTED.
GOOD, GOOD. CARRY ON.
WE REALLY DON'T APPRECIATE HIM ENOUGH.
LET'S PUT A TV IN THIS BABY.

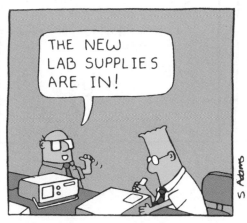

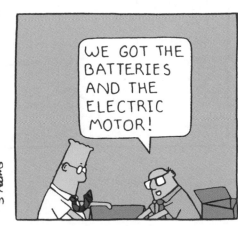

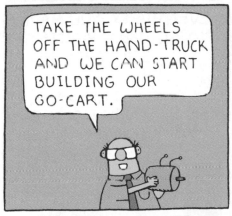

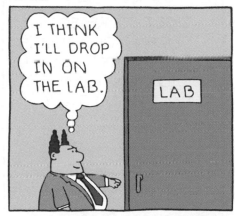

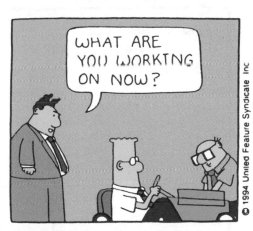

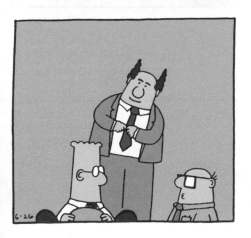

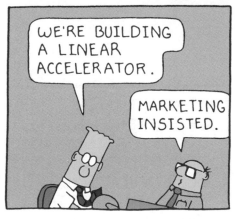

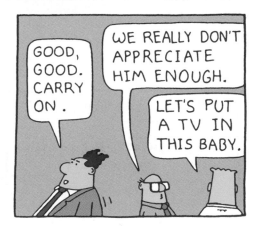

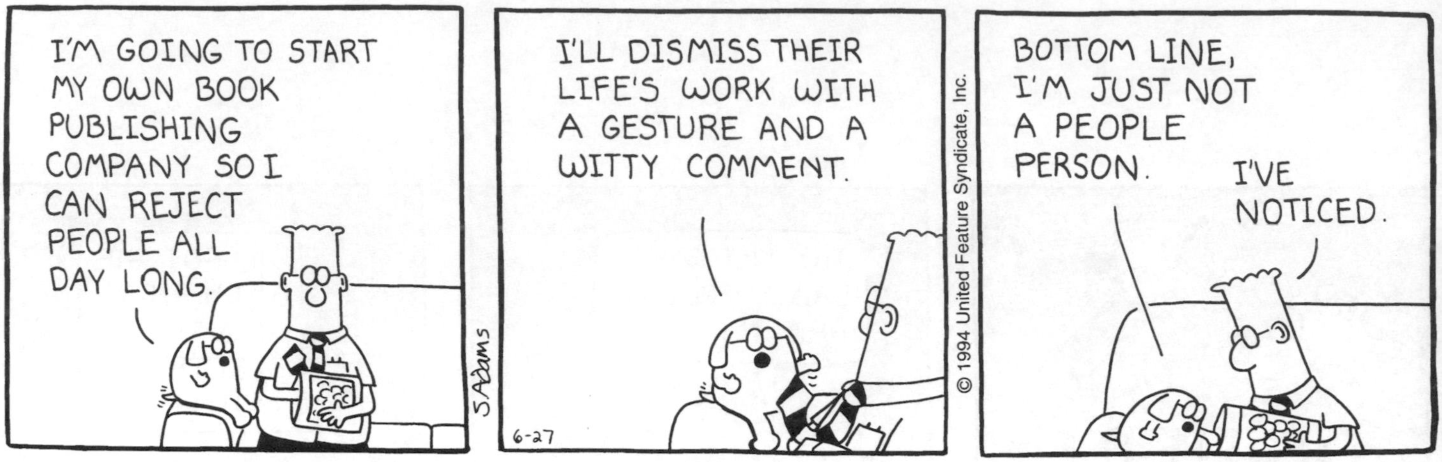
I'M GOING TO START MY OWN BOOK PUBLISHING COMPANY SO I CAN REJECT PEOPLE ALL DAY LONG.
I'LL DISMISS THEIR LIFE'S WORK WITH A GESTURE AND A WITTY COMMENT.
BOTTOM LINE, I'M JUST NOT A PEOPLE PERSON.
I'VE NOTICED.
S. Adams
6-27
© 1994 United Feature Syndicate, Inc.

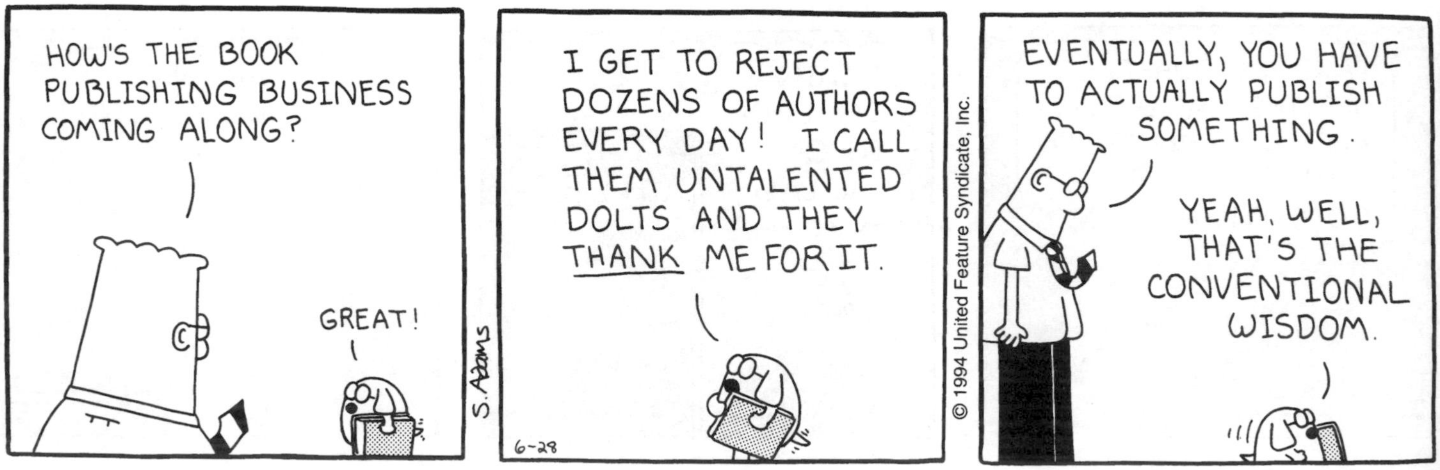
HOW'S THE BOOK PUBLISHING BUSINESS COMING ALONG?
GREAT!
I GET TO REJECT DOZENS OF AUTHORS EVERY DAY! I CALL THEM UNTALENTED DOLTS AND THEY THANK ME FOR IT.
EVENTUALLY, YOU HAVE TO ACTUALLY PUBLISH SOMETHING.
YEAH, WELL, THAT'S THE CONVENTIONAL WISDOM.
S. Adams
6-28
© 1994 United Feature Syndicate, Inc.

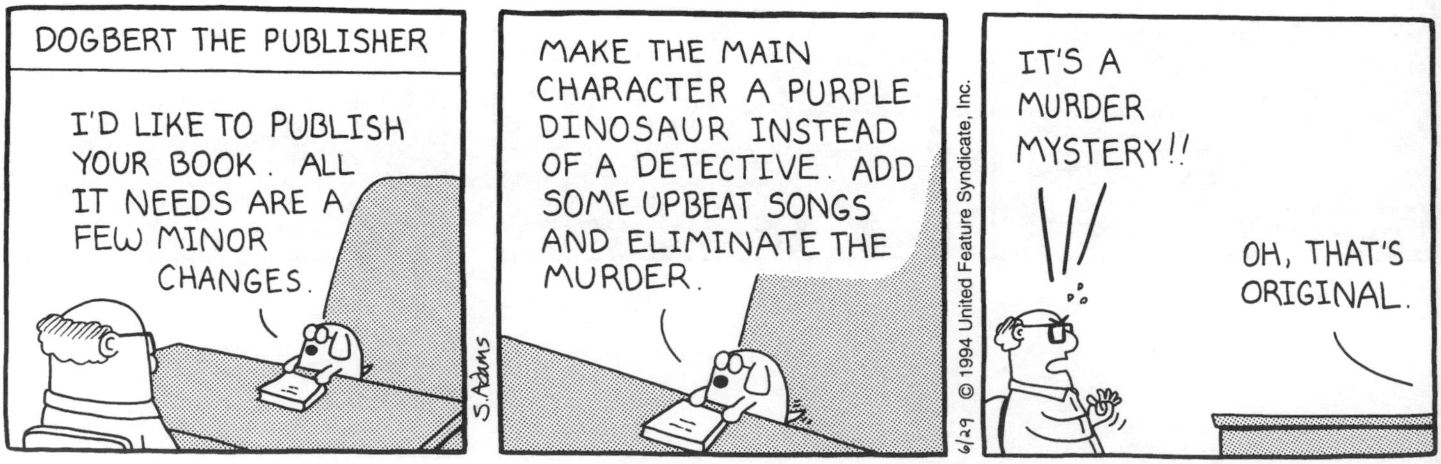
DOGBERT THE PUBLISHER
I'D LIKE TO PUBLISH YOUR BOOK. ALL IT NEEDS ARE A FEW MINOR CHANGES.
MAKE THE MAIN CHARACTER A PURPLE DINOSAUR INSTEAD OF A DETECTIVE. ADD SOME UPBEAT SONGS AND ELIMINATE THE MURDER.
IT'S A MURDER MYSTERY!!
OH, THAT'S ORIGINAL.
S. Adams
6/29
© 1994 United Feature Syndicate, Inc.

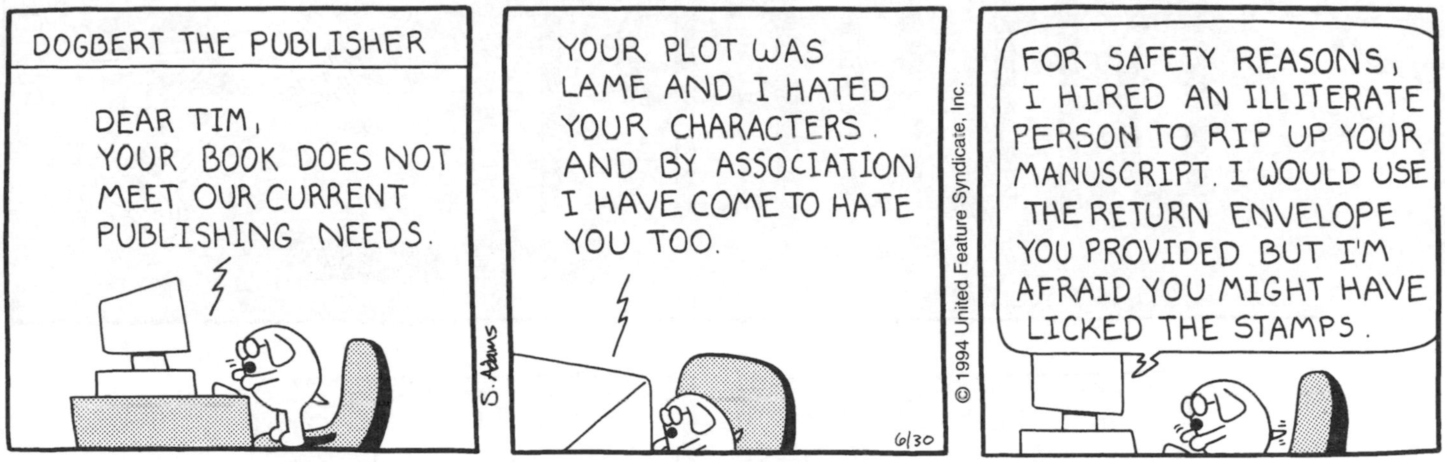
DOGBERT THE PUBLISHER
DEAR TIM, YOUR BOOK DOES NOT MEET OUR CURRENT PUBLISHING NEEDS.
S. Adams
YOUR PLOT WAS LAME AND I HATED YOUR CHARACTERS. AND BY ASSOCIATION I HAVE COME TO HATE YOU TOO.
6/30
© 1994 United Feature Syndicate, Inc.
FOR SAFETY REASONS, I HIRED AN ILLITERATE PERSON TO RIP UP YOUR MANUSCRIPT. I WOULD USE THE RETURN ENVELOPE YOU PROVIDED BUT I'M AFRAID YOU MIGHT HAVE LICKED THE STAMPS.

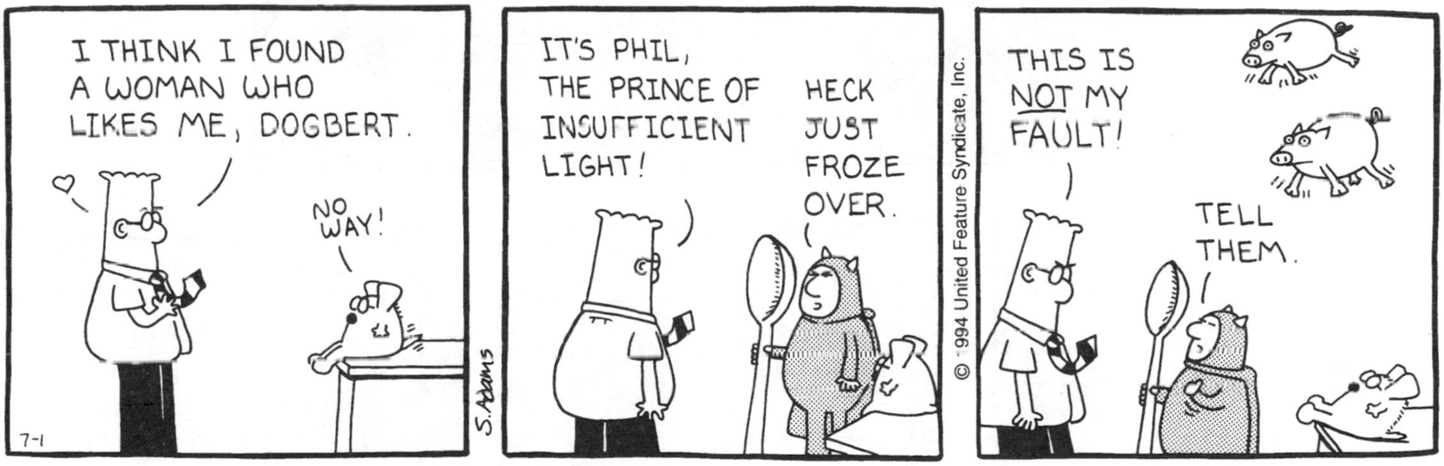
I THINK I FOUND A WOMAN WHO LIKES ME, DOGBERT.
NO WAY!
7-1
S. Adams
IT'S PHIL, THE PRINCE OF INSUFFICIENT LIGHT!
HECK JUST FROZE OVER.
© 1994 United Feature Syndicate, Inc.
THIS IS NOT MY FAULT!
TELL THEM.

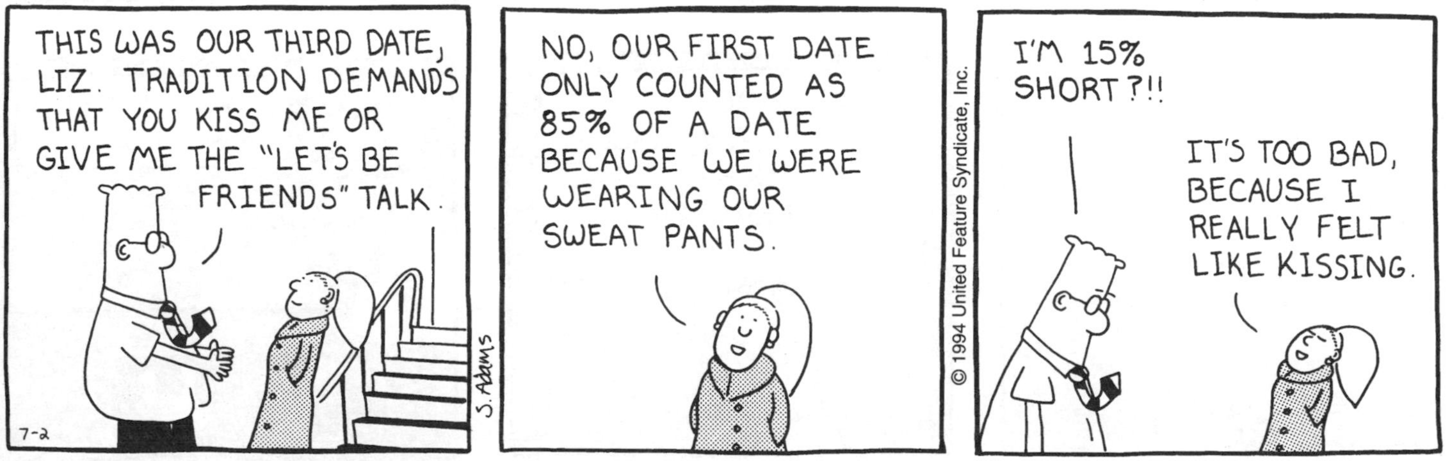
THIS WAS OUR THIRD DATE, LIZ. TRADITION DEMANDS THAT YOU KISS ME OR GIVE ME THE "LET'S BE FRIENDS" TALK.
7-2
S. Adams
NO, OUR FIRST DATE ONLY COUNTED AS 85% OF A DATE BECAUSE WE WERE WEARING OUR SWEAT PANTS.
© 1994 United Feature Syndicate, Inc.
I'M 15% SHORT?!!
IT'S TOO BAD, BECAUSE I REALLY FELT LIKE KISSING.

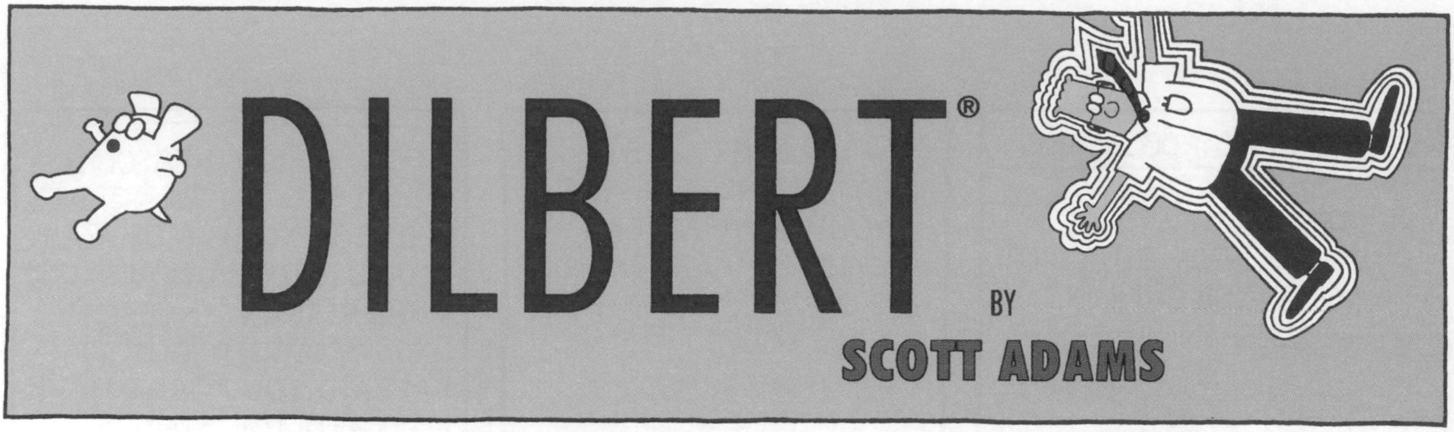
DILBERT®
BY
SCOTT ADAMS

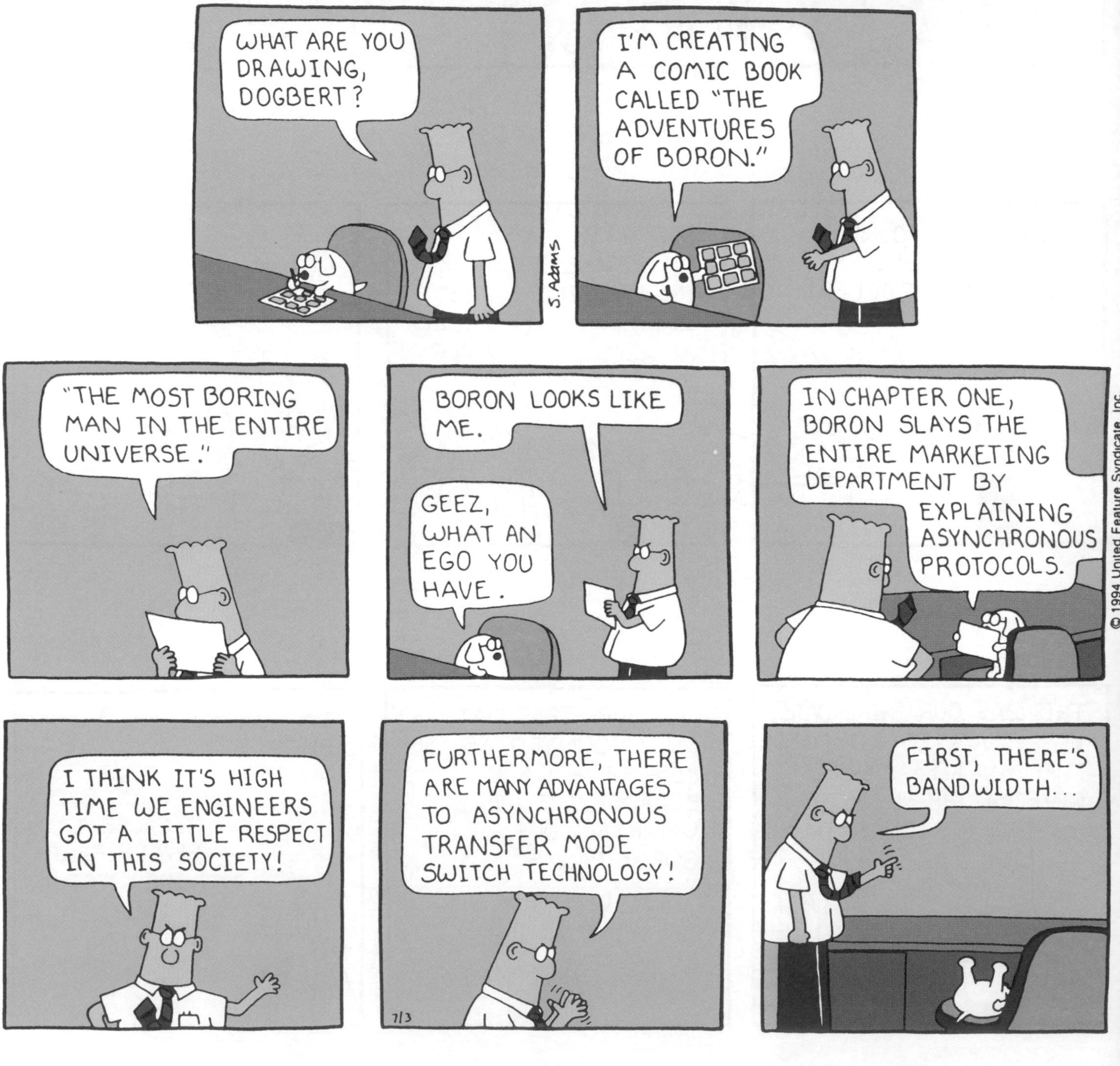
WHAT ARE YOU DRAWING, DOGBERT?
S. ADAMS
I'M CREATING A COMIC BOOK CALLED "THE ADVENTURES OF BORON."
"THE MOST BORING MAN IN THE ENTIRE UNIVERSE."
BORON LOOKS LIKE ME.
GEEZ, WHAT AN EGO YOU HAVE.
IN CHAPTER ONE, BORON SLAYS THE ENTIRE MARKETING DEPARTMENT BY EXPLAINING ASYNCHRONOUS PROTOCOLS.
© 1994 United Feature Syndicate, Inc.
I THINK IT'S HIGH TIME WE ENGINEERS GOT A LITTLE RESPECT IN THIS SOCIETY!
FURTHERMORE, THERE ARE MANY ADVANTAGES TO ASYNCHRONOUS TRANSFER MODE SWITCH TECHNOLOGY!
7/3
FIRST, THERE'S BANDWIDTH...

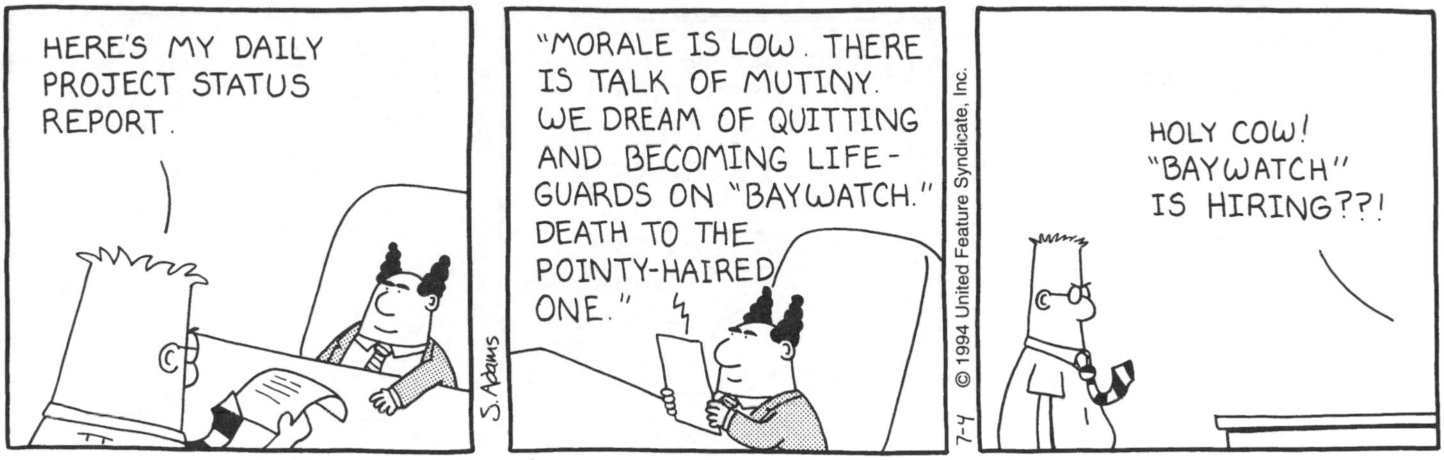
HERE'S MY DAILY PROJECT STATUS REPORT.
"MORALE IS LOW. THERE IS TALK OF MUTINY. WE DREAM OF QUITTING AND BECOMING LIFE-GUARDS ON "BAYWATCH." DEATH TO THE POINTY-HAIRED ONE."
HOLY COW! "BAYWATCH" IS HIRING??!
S. Adams
7-4 © 1994 United Feature Syndicate, Inc.

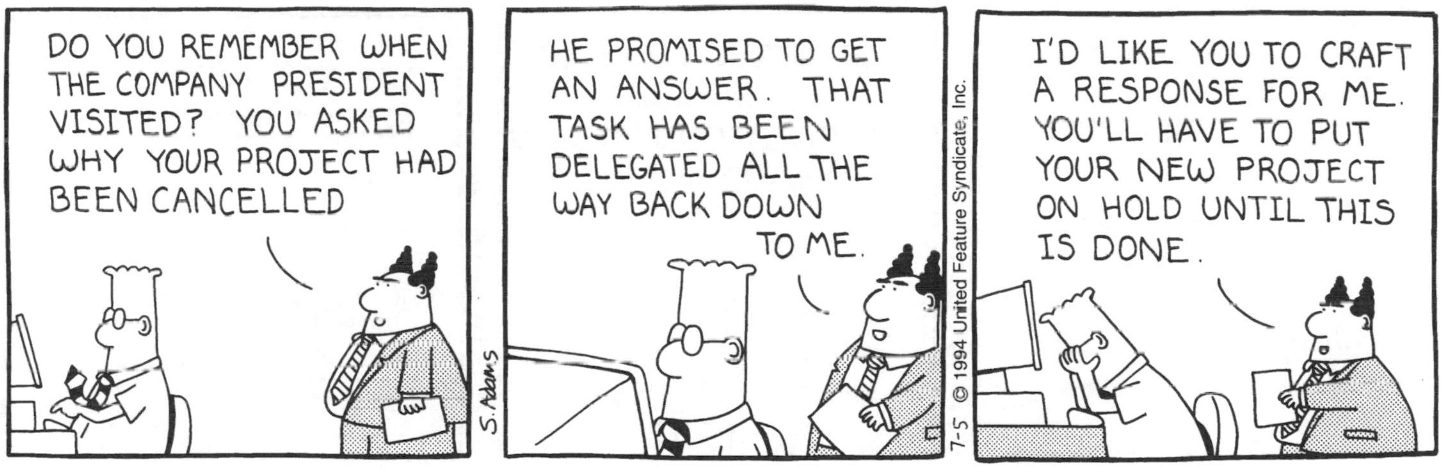
DO YOU REMEMBER WHEN THE COMPANY PRESIDENT VISITED? YOU ASKED WHY YOUR PROJECT HAD BEEN CANCELLED
HE PROMISED TO GET AN ANSWER. THAT TASK HAS BEEN DELEGATED ALL THE WAY BACK DOWN TO ME.
I'D LIKE YOU TO CRAFT A RESPONSE FOR ME. YOU'LL HAVE TO PUT YOUR NEW PROJECT ON HOLD UNTIL THIS IS DONE.
S. Adams
7-5 © 1994 United Feature Syndicate, Inc.

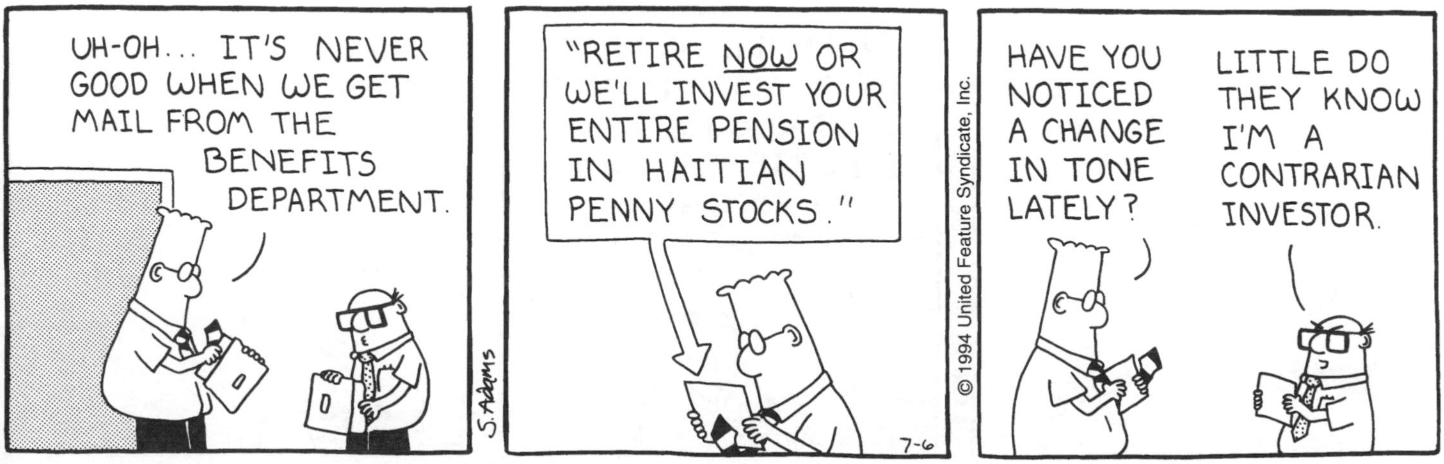
UH-OH... IT'S NEVER GOOD WHEN WE GET MAIL FROM THE BENEFITS DEPARTMENT.
"RETIRE NOW OR WE'LL INVEST YOUR ENTIRE PENSION IN HAITIAN PENNY STOCKS."
HAVE YOU NOTICED A CHANGE IN TONE LATELY?
LITTLE DO THEY KNOW I'M A CONTRARIAN INVESTOR.
S. Adams
7-6
© 1994 United Feature Syndicate, Inc.

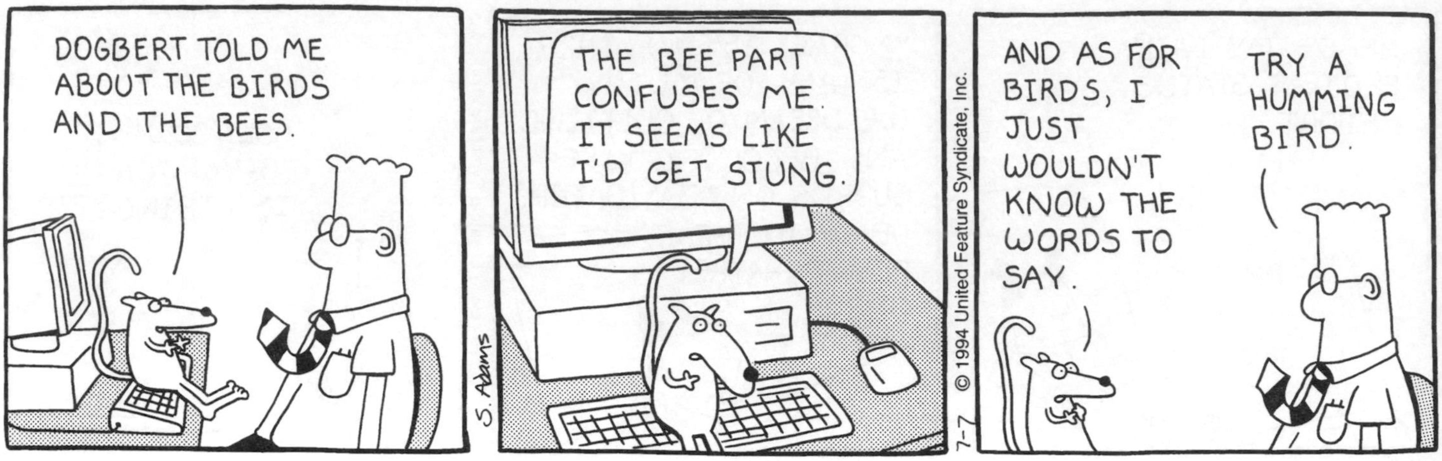
DOGBERT TOLD ME ABOUT THE BIRDS AND THE BEES.
THE BEE PART CONFUSES ME. IT SEEMS LIKE I'D GET STUNG.
AND AS FOR BIRDS, I JUST WOULDN'T KNOW THE WORDS TO SAY.
TRY A HUMMING BIRD.
S. Adams 7-7 © 1994 United Feature Syndicate, Inc.

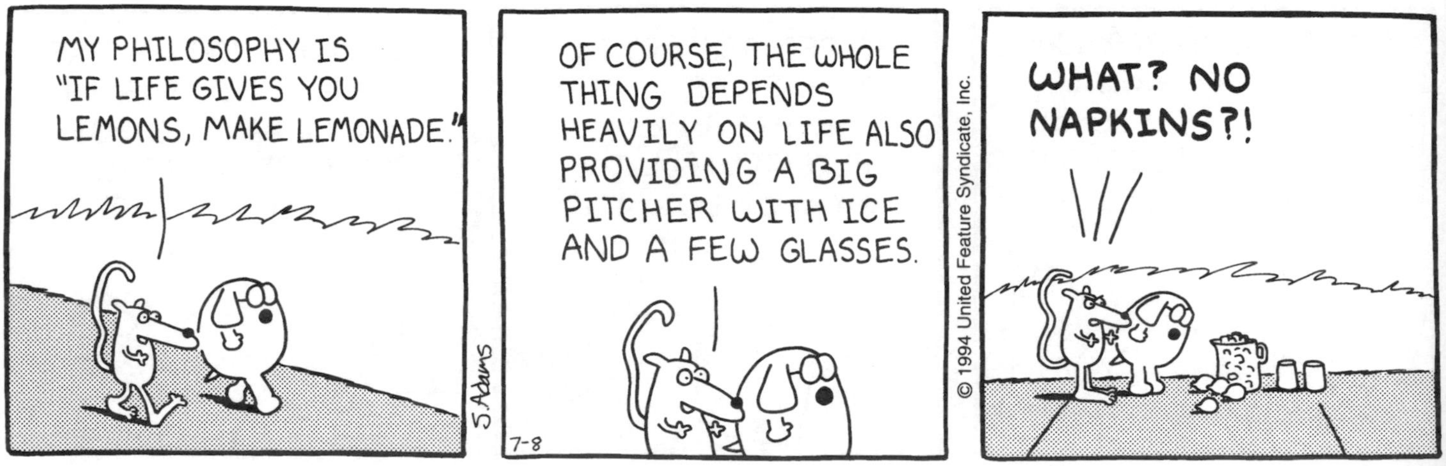
MY PHILOSOPHY IS "IF LIFE GIVES YOU LEMONS, MAKE LEMONADE."
OF COURSE, THE WHOLE THING DEPENDS HEAVILY ON LIFE ALSO PROVIDING A BIG PITCHER WITH ICE AND A FEW GLASSES.
WHAT? NO NAPKINS?!
S. Adams 7-8 © 1994 United Feature Syndicate, Inc.

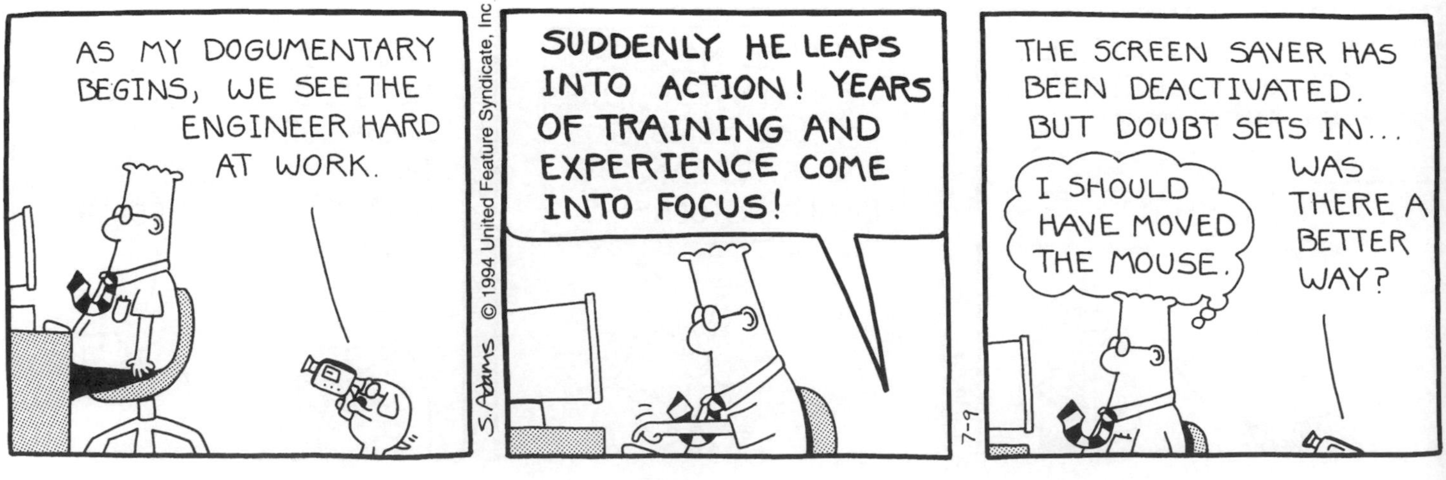
AS MY DOGUMENTARY BEGINS, WE SEE THE ENGINEER HARD AT WORK.
SUDDENLY HE LEAPS INTO ACTION! YEARS OF TRAINING AND EXPERIENCE COME INTO FOCUS!
THE SCREEN SAVER HAS BEEN DEACTIVATED. BUT DOUBT SETS IN...
I SHOULD HAVE MOVED THE MOUSE.
WAS THERE A BETTER WAY?
S. Adams 7-9 © 1994 United Feature Syndicate, Inc.

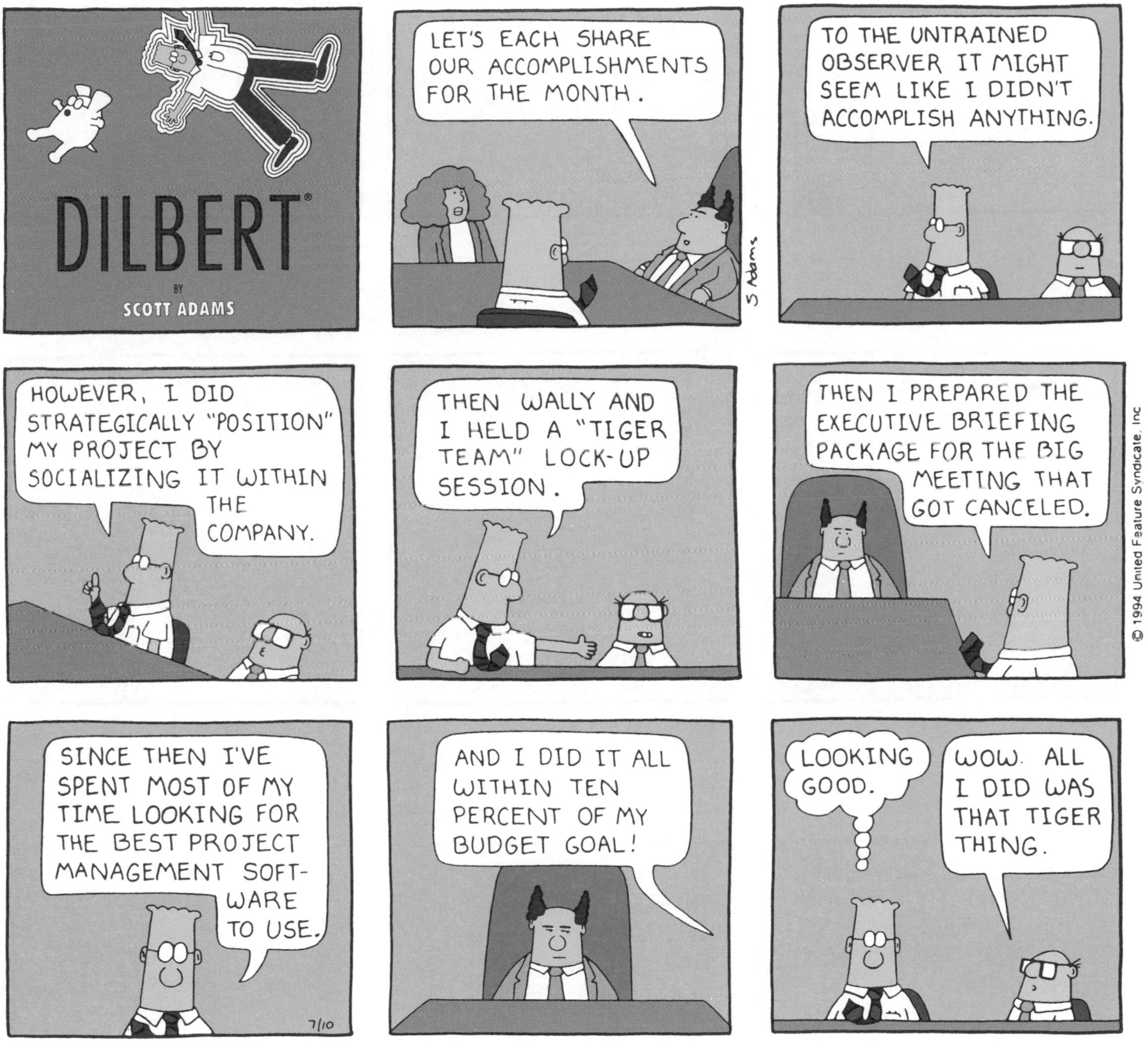
DILBERT®
BY
SCOTT ADAMS
LET'S EACH SHARE OUR ACCOMPLISHMENTS FOR THE MONTH.
S Adams
TO THE UNTRAINED OBSERVER IT MIGHT SEEM LIKE I DIDN'T ACCOMPLISH ANYTHING.
HOWEVER, I DID STRATEGICALLY "POSITION" MY PROJECT BY SOCIALIZING IT WITHIN THE COMPANY.
THEN WALLY AND I HELD A "TIGER TEAM" LOCK-UP SESSION.
THEN I PREPARED THE EXECUTIVE BRIEFING PACKAGE FOR THE BIG MEETING THAT GOT CANCELED.
© 1994 United Feature Syndicate, Inc
SINCE THEN I'VE SPENT MOST OF MY TIME LOOKING FOR THE BEST PROJECT MANAGEMENT SOFT-WARE TO USE.
7/10
AND I DID IT ALL WITHIN TEN PERCENT OF MY BUDGET GOAL!
LOOKING GOOD.
WOW. ALL I DID WAS THAT TIGER THING.

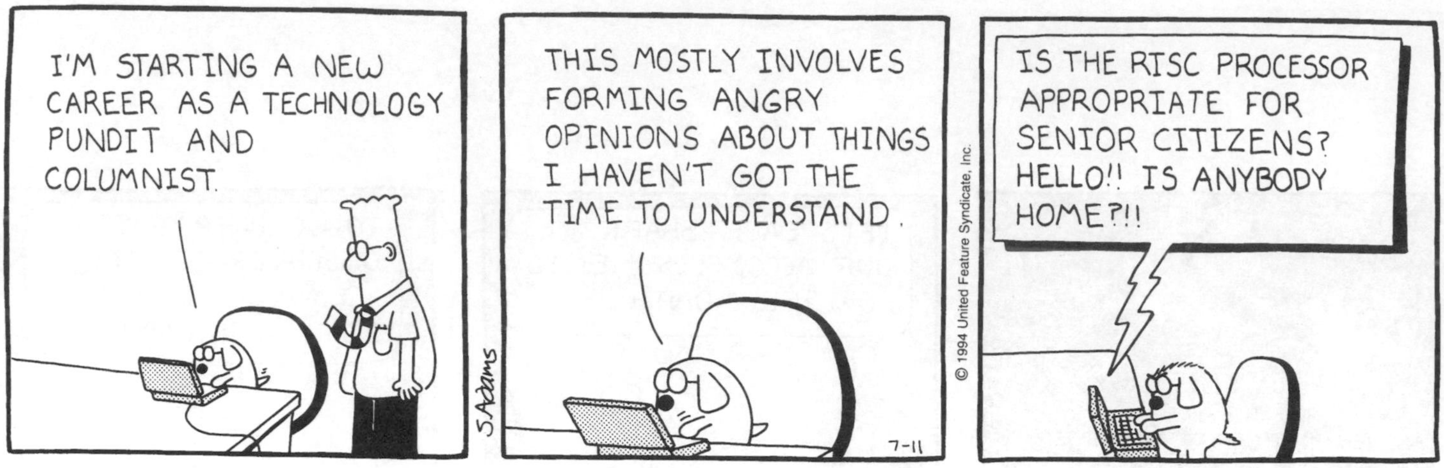
I'M STARTING A NEW CAREER AS A TECHNOLOGY PUNDIT AND COLUMNIST.
THIS MOSTLY INVOLVES FORMING ANGRY OPINIONS ABOUT THINGS I HAVEN'T GOT THE TIME TO UNDERSTAND.
IS THE RISC PROCESSOR APPROPRIATE FOR SENIOR CITIZENS? HELLO!! IS ANYBODY HOME?!!
© 1994 United Feature Syndicate, Inc.

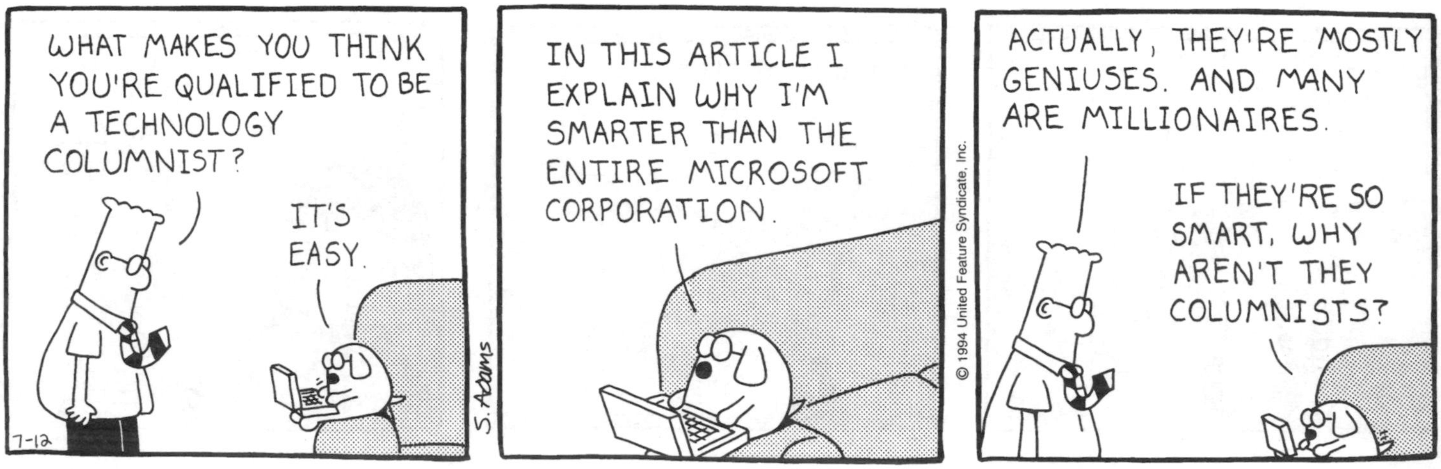
WHAT MAKES YOU THINK YOU'RE QUALIFIED TO BE A TECHNOLOGY COLUMNIST?
IT'S EASY.
IN THIS ARTICLE I EXPLAIN WHY I'M SMARTER THAN THE ENTIRE MICROSOFT CORPORATION.
ACTUALLY, THEY'RE MOSTLY GENIUSES. AND MANY ARE MILLIONAIRES.
IF THEY'RE SO SMART, WHY AREN'T THEY COLUMNISTS?
© 1994 United Feature Syndicate, Inc.

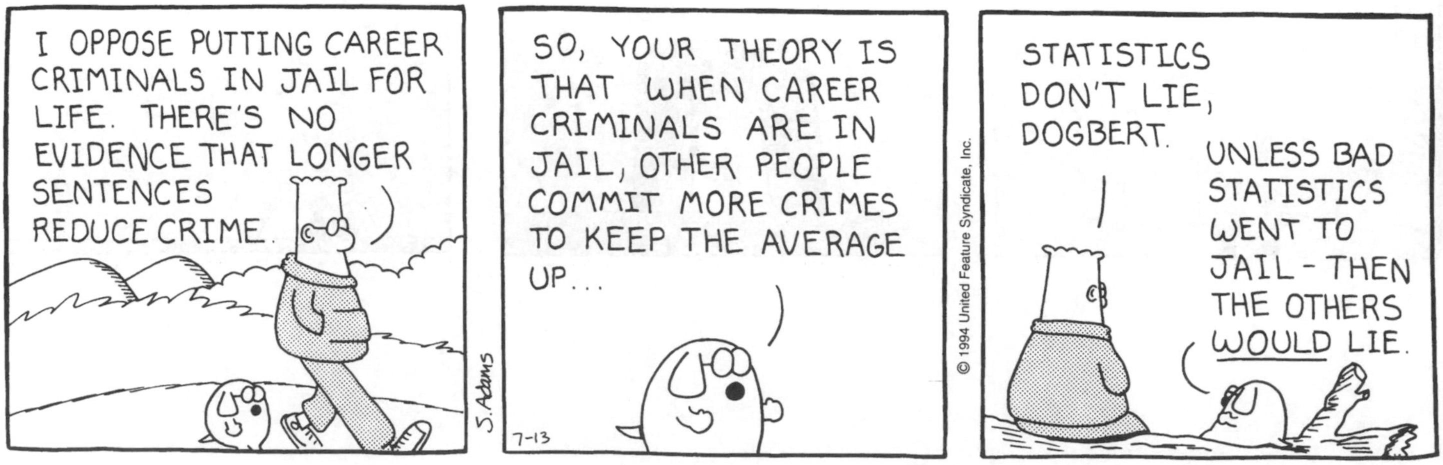
I OPPOSE PUTTING CAREER CRIMINALS IN JAIL FOR LIFE. THERE'S NO EVIDENCE THAT LONGER SENTENCES REDUCE CRIME.
SO, YOUR THEORY IS THAT WHEN CAREER CRIMINALS ARE IN JAIL, OTHER PEOPLE COMMIT MORE CRIMES TO KEEP THE AVERAGE UP...
STATISTICS DON'T LIE, DOGBERT.
UNLESS BAD STATISTICS WENT TO JAIL - THEN THE OTHERS WOULD LIE.
© 1994 United Feature Syndicate, Inc.

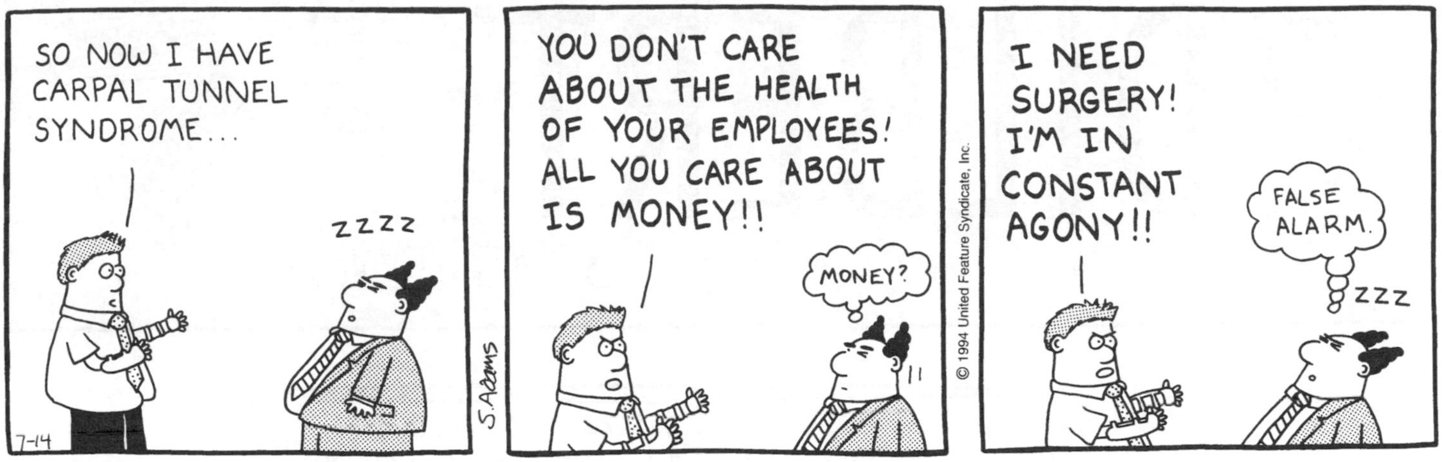
SO NOW I HAVE CARPAL TUNNEL SYNDROME...
ZZZZ
7-14
S. ADAMS
YOU DON'T CARE ABOUT THE HEALTH OF YOUR EMPLOYEES! ALL YOU CARE ABOUT IS MONEY!!
MONEY?
© 1994 United Feature Syndicate, Inc.
I NEED SURGERY! I'M IN CONSTANT AGONY!!
FALSE ALARM.
ZZZ

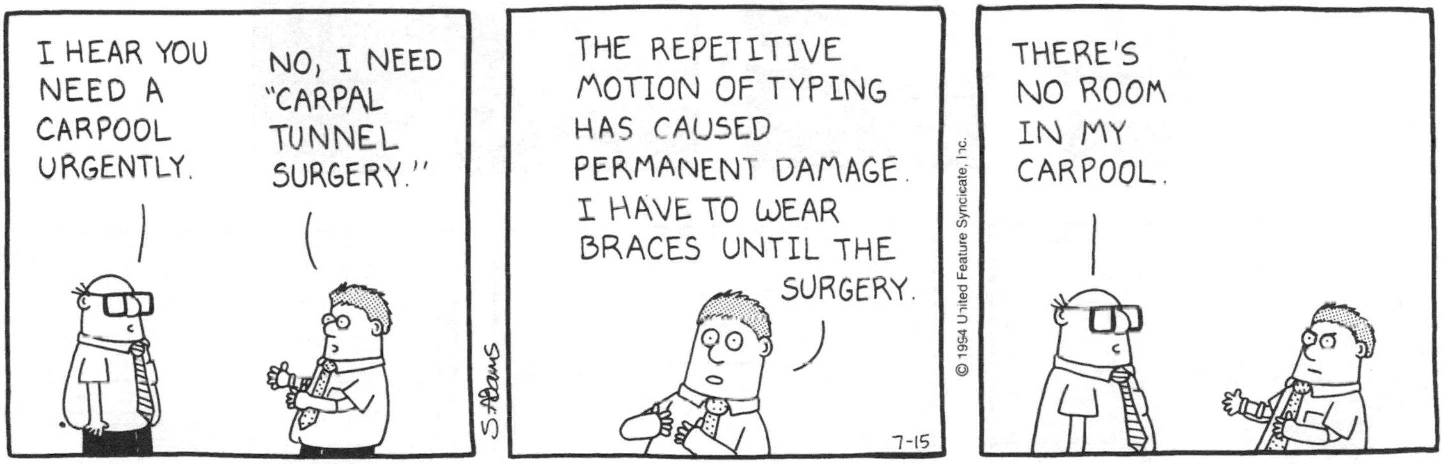
I HEAR YOU NEED A CARPOOL URGENTLY.
NO, I NEED "CARPAL TUNNEL SURGERY."
S. ADAMS
THE REPETITIVE MOTION OF TYPING HAS CAUSED PERMANENT DAMAGE. I HAVE TO WEAR BRACES UNTIL THE SURGERY.
7-15
© 1994 United Feature Syndicate, Inc.
THERE'S NO ROOM IN MY CARPOOL.

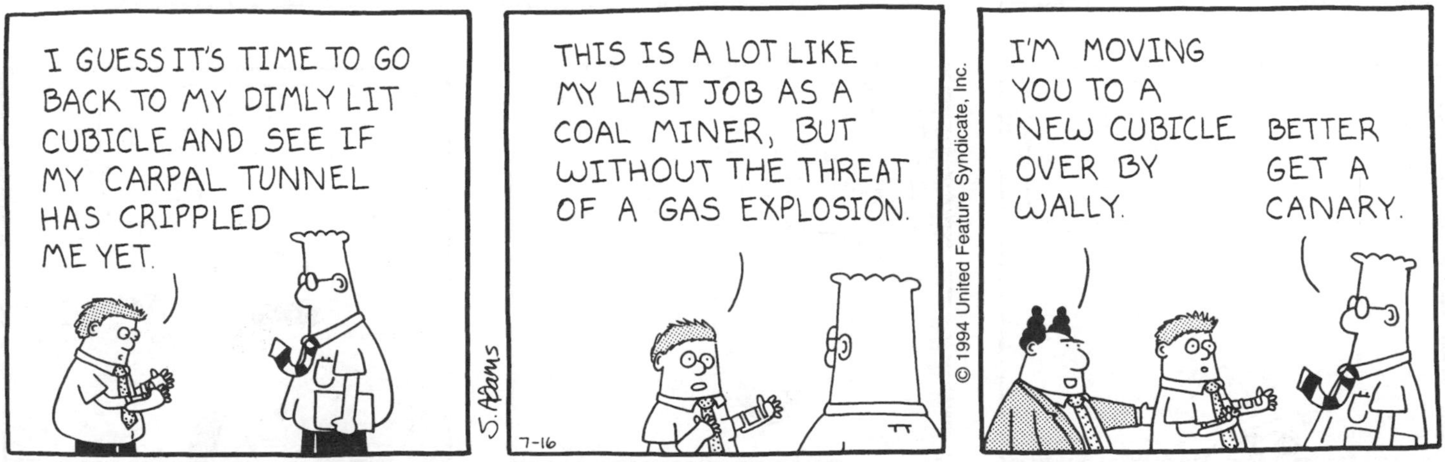
I GUESS IT'S TIME TO GO BACK TO MY DIMLY LIT CUBICLE AND SEE IF MY CARPAL TUNNEL HAS CRIPPLED ME YET.
S. ADAMS
THIS IS A LOT LIKE MY LAST JOB AS A COAL MINER, BUT WITHOUT THE THREAT OF A GAS EXPLOSION.
7-16
© 1994 United Feature Syndicate, Inc.
I'M MOVING YOU TO A NEW CUBICLE OVER BY WALLY.
BETTER GET A CANARY.

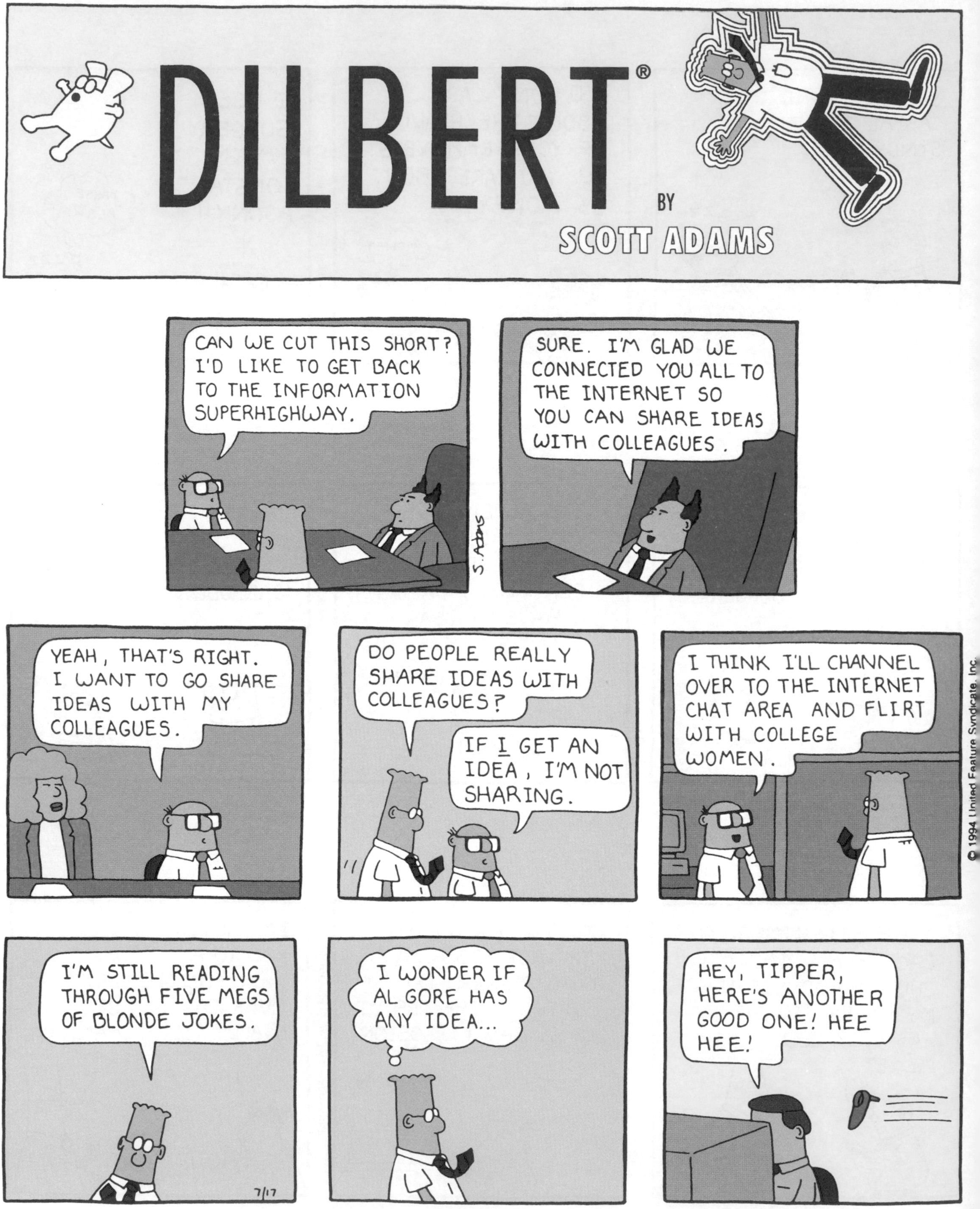
DILBERT®
BY
SCOTT ADAMS
CAN WE CUT THIS SHORT? I'D LIKE TO GET BACK TO THE INFORMATION SUPERHIGHWAY.
S. ADAMS
SURE. I'M GLAD WE CONNECTED YOU ALL TO THE INTERNET SO YOU CAN SHARE IDEAS WITH COLLEAGUES.
YEAH, THAT'S RIGHT. I WANT TO GO SHARE IDEAS WITH MY COLLEAGUES.
DO PEOPLE REALLY SHARE IDEAS WITH COLLEAGUES?
IF I GET AN IDEA, I'M NOT SHARING.
I THINK I'LL CHANNEL OVER TO THE INTERNET CHAT AREA AND FLIRT WITH COLLEGE WOMEN.
© 1994 United Feature Syndicate, Inc.
I'M STILL READING THROUGH FIVE MEGS OF BLONDE JOKES.
7/17
I WONDER IF AL GORE HAS ANY IDEA...
HEY, TIPPER, HERE'S ANOTHER GOOD ONE! HEE HEE!

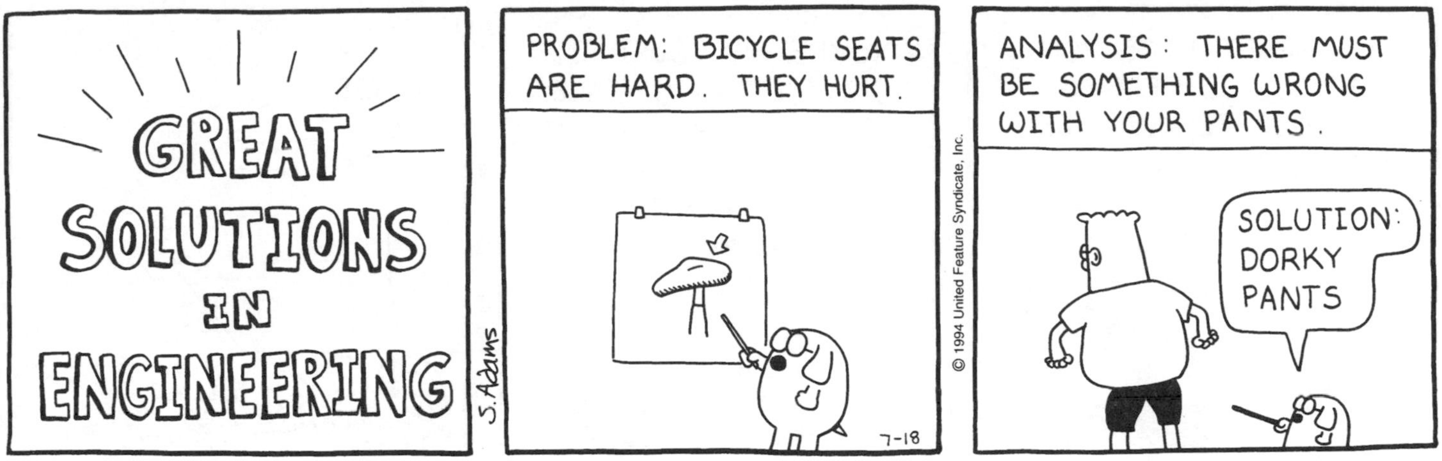
GREAT SOLUTIONS IN ENGINEERING
S. Adams
PROBLEM: BICYCLE SEATS ARE HARD. THEY HURT.
7-18
© 1994 United Feature Syndicate, Inc.
ANALYSIS: THERE MUST BE SOMETHING WRONG WITH YOUR PANTS.
SOLUTION: DORKY PANTS

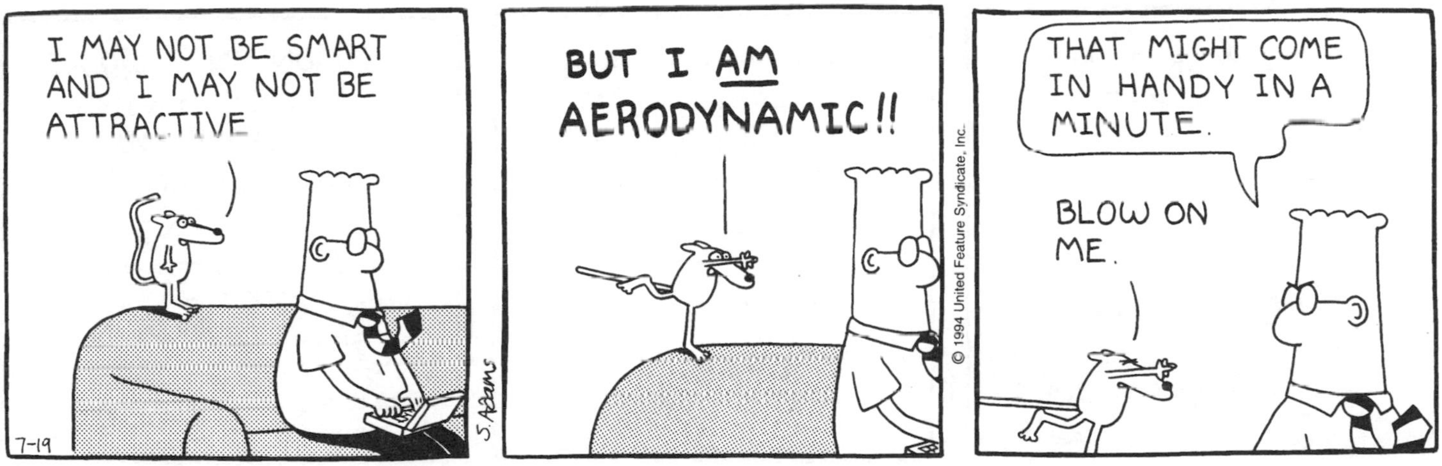
I MAY NOT BE SMART AND I MAY NOT BE ATTRACTIVE
7-19
S. Adams
BUT I AM AERODYNAMIC!!
© 1994 United Feature Syndicate, Inc.
THAT MIGHT COME IN HANDY IN A MINUTE.
BLOW ON ME.

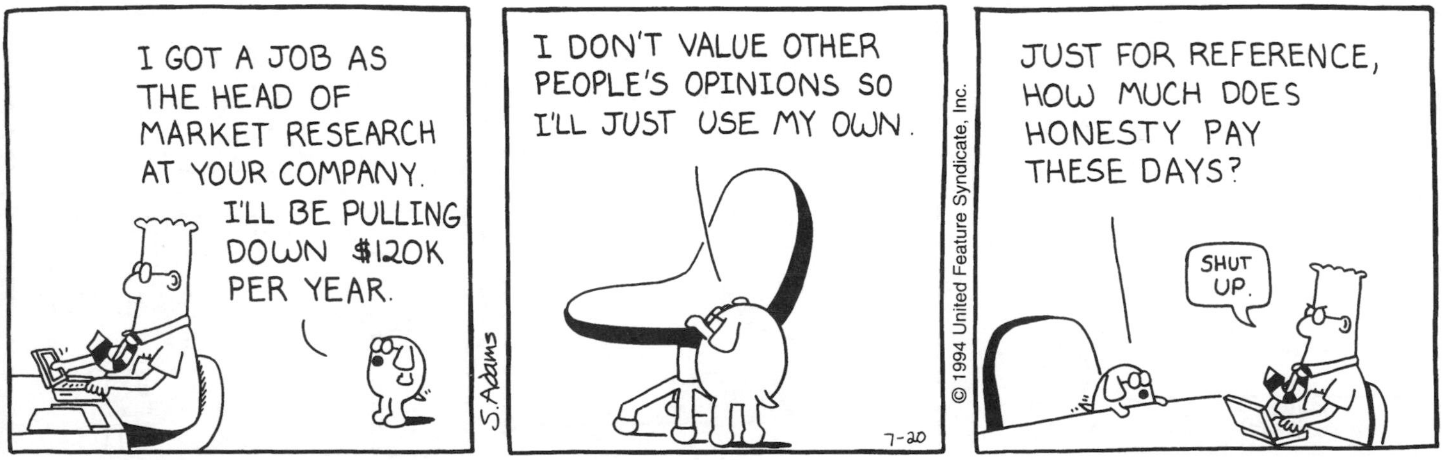
I GOT A JOB AS THE HEAD OF MARKET RESEARCH AT YOUR COMPANY.
I'LL BE PULLING DOWN $120K PER YEAR.
S. Adams
I DON'T VALUE OTHER PEOPLE'S OPINIONS SO I'LL JUST USE MY OWN.
7-20
© 1994 United Feature Syndicate, Inc.
JUST FOR REFERENCE, HOW MUCH DOES HONESTY PAY THESE DAYS?
SHUT UP.

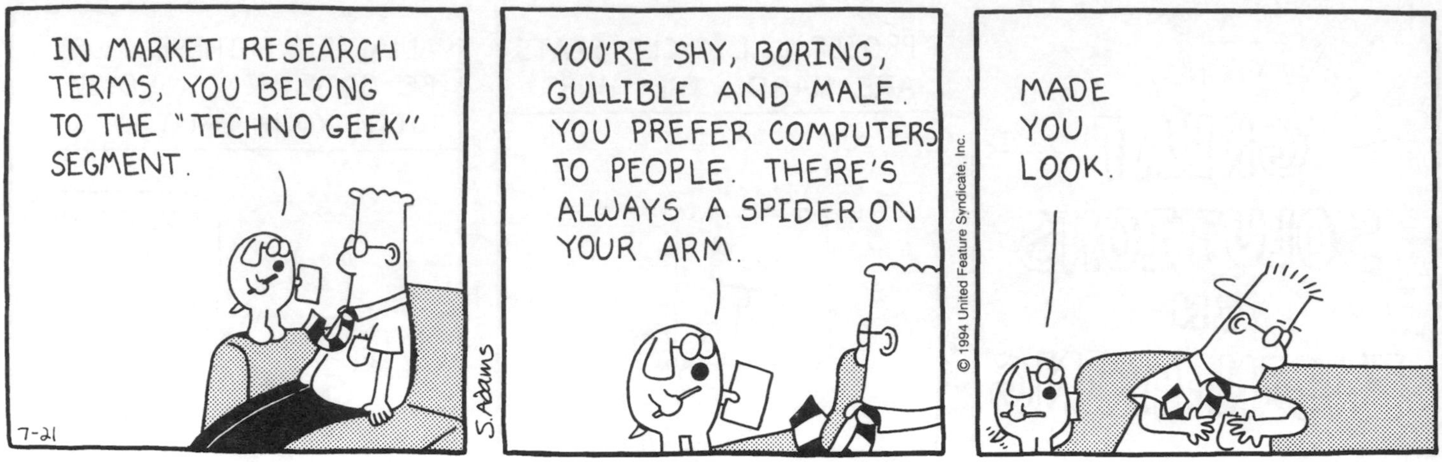
IN MARKET RESEARCH TERMS, YOU BELONG TO THE "TECHNO GEEK" SEGMENT.
7-21
S. Adams
YOU'RE SHY, BORING, GULLIBLE AND MALE. YOU PREFER COMPUTERS TO PEOPLE. THERE'S ALWAYS A SPIDER ON YOUR ARM.
© 1994 United Feature Syndicate, Inc.
MADE YOU LOOK.

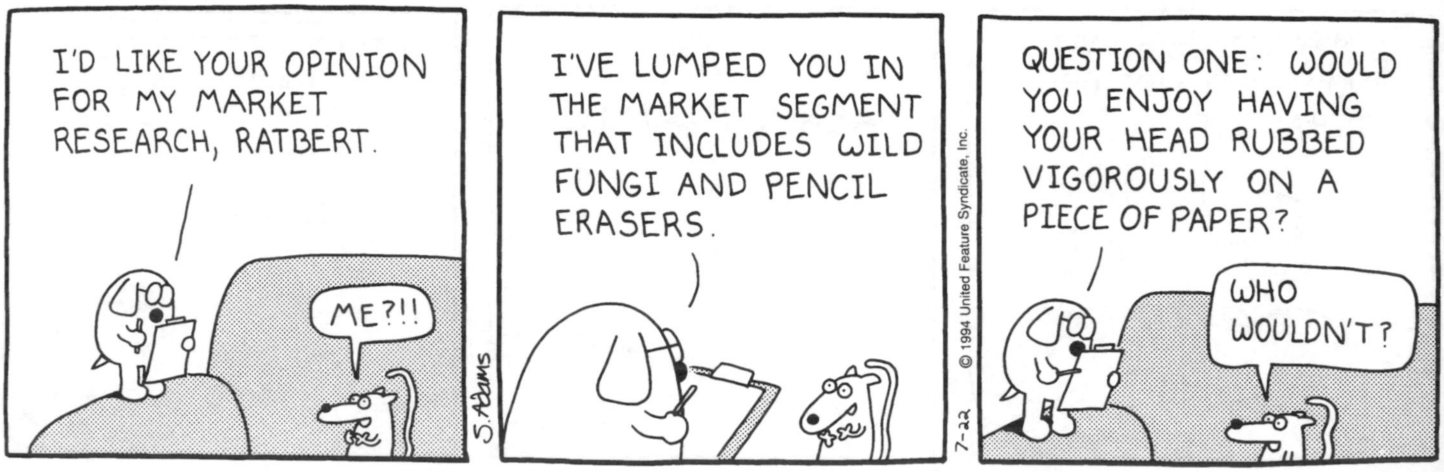
I'D LIKE YOUR OPINION FOR MY MARKET RESEARCH, RATBERT.
ME?!!
S. Adams
I'VE LUMPED YOU IN THE MARKET SEGMENT THAT INCLUDES WILD FUNGI AND PENCIL ERASERS.
© 1994 United Feature Syndicate, Inc.
7-22
QUESTION ONE: WOULD YOU ENJOY HAVING YOUR HEAD RUBBED VIGOROUSLY ON A PIECE OF PAPER?
WHO WOULDN'T?

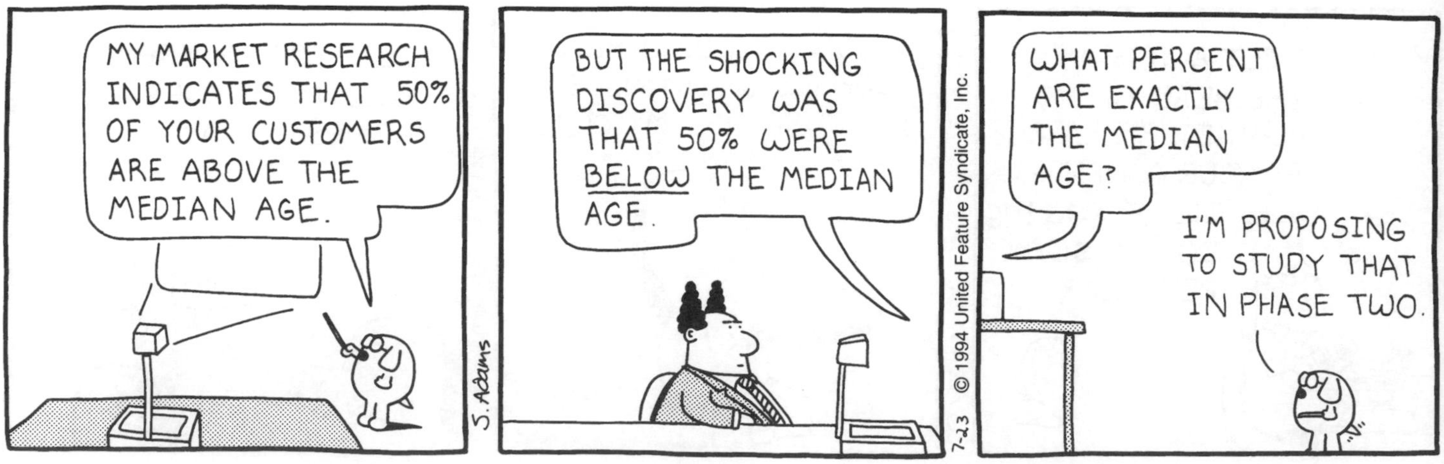
MY MARKET RESEARCH INDICATES THAT 50% OF YOUR CUSTOMERS ARE ABOVE THE MEDIAN AGE.
S. Adams
BUT THE SHOCKING DISCOVERY WAS THAT 50% WERE BELOW THE MEDIAN AGE.
© 1994 United Feature Syndicate, Inc.
7-23
WHAT PERCENT ARE EXACTLY THE MEDIAN AGE?
I'M PROPOSING TO STUDY THAT IN PHASE TWO.

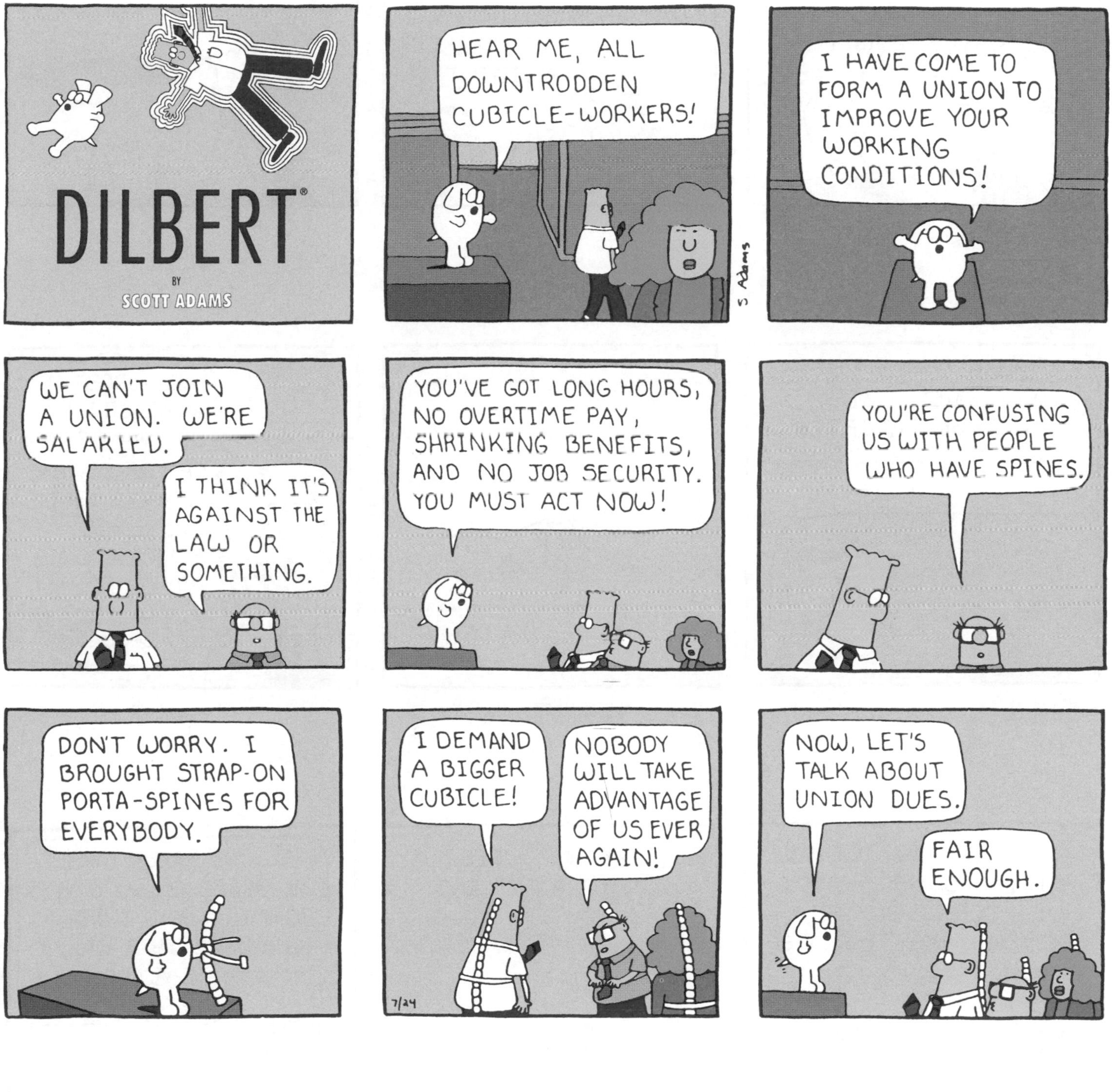
DILBERT®
BY
SCOTT ADAMS
HEAR ME, ALL DOWNTRODDEN CUBICLE-WORKERS!
S. Adams
I HAVE COME TO FORM A UNION TO IMPROVE YOUR WORKING CONDITIONS!
WE CAN'T JOIN A UNION. WE'RE SALARIED.
I THINK IT'S AGAINST THE LAW OR SOMETHING.
YOU'VE GOT LONG HOURS, NO OVERTIME PAY, SHRINKING BENEFITS, AND NO JOB SECURITY. YOU MUST ACT NOW!
YOU'RE CONFUSING US WITH PEOPLE WHO HAVE SPINES.
© 1994 United Feature Syndicate, Inc
DON'T WORRY. I BROUGHT STRAP-ON PORTA-SPINES FOR EVERYBODY.
I DEMAND A BIGGER CUBICLE!
NOBODY WILL TAKE ADVANTAGE OF US EVER AGAIN!
7/24
NOW, LET'S TALK ABOUT UNION DUES.
FAIR ENOUGH.

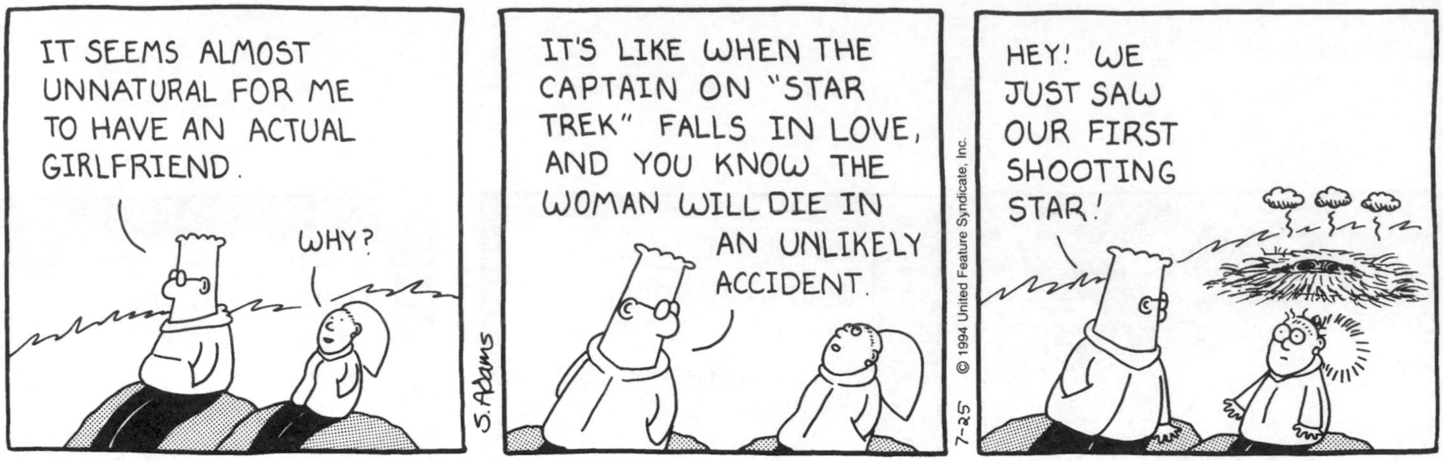
IT SEEMS ALMOST UNNATURAL FOR ME TO HAVE AN ACTUAL GIRLFRIEND.
WHY?
S. Adams
IT'S LIKE WHEN THE CAPTAIN ON "STAR TREK" FALLS IN LOVE, AND YOU KNOW THE WOMAN WILL DIE IN AN UNLIKELY ACCIDENT.
7-25 © 1994 United Feature Syndicate, Inc.
HEY! WE JUST SAW OUR FIRST SHOOTING STAR!

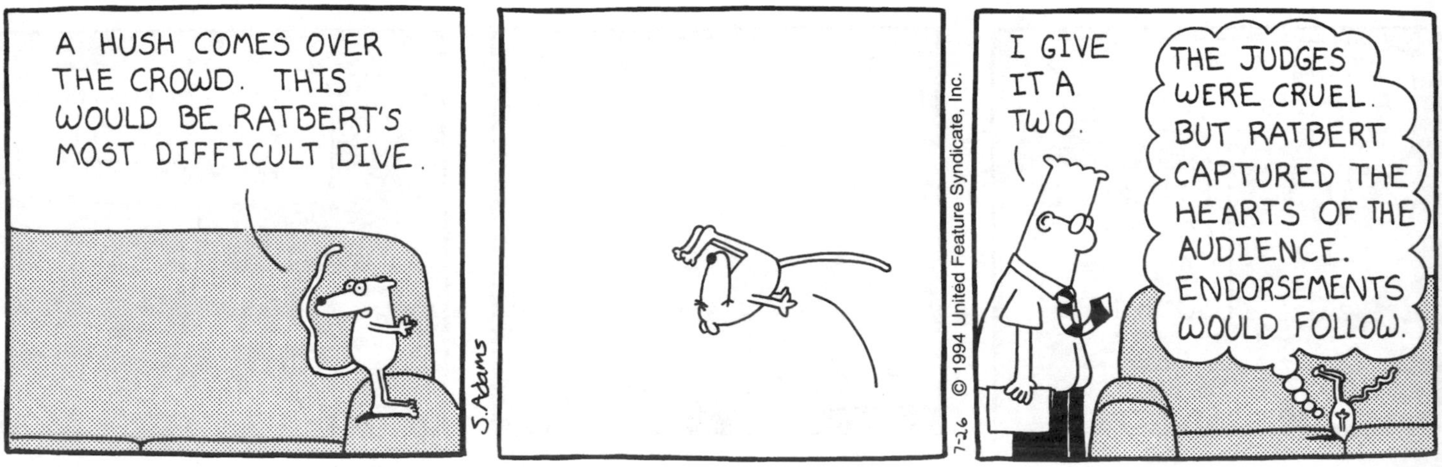
A HUSH COMES OVER THE CROWD. THIS WOULD BE RATBERT'S MOST DIFFICULT DIVE.
S. Adams
7-26 © 1994 United Feature Syndicate, Inc.
I GIVE IT A TWO.
THE JUDGES WERE CRUEL. BUT RATBERT CAPTURED THE HEARTS OF THE AUDIENCE. ENDORSEMENTS WOULD FOLLOW.

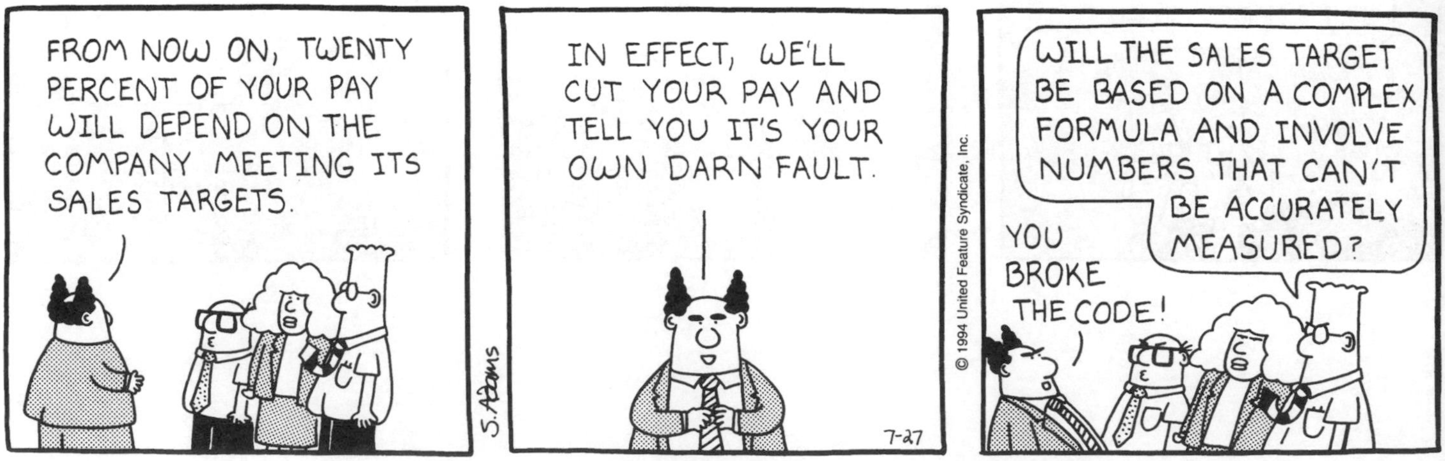
FROM NOW ON, TWENTY PERCENT OF YOUR PAY WILL DEPEND ON THE COMPANY MEETING ITS SALES TARGETS.
S. Adams
IN EFFECT, WE'LL CUT YOUR PAY AND TELL YOU IT'S YOUR OWN DARN FAULT.
7-27
© 1994 United Feature Syndicate, Inc.
WILL THE SALES TARGET BE BASED ON A COMPLEX FORMULA AND INVOLVE NUMBERS THAT CAN'T BE ACCURATELY MEASURED?
YOU BROKE THE CODE!

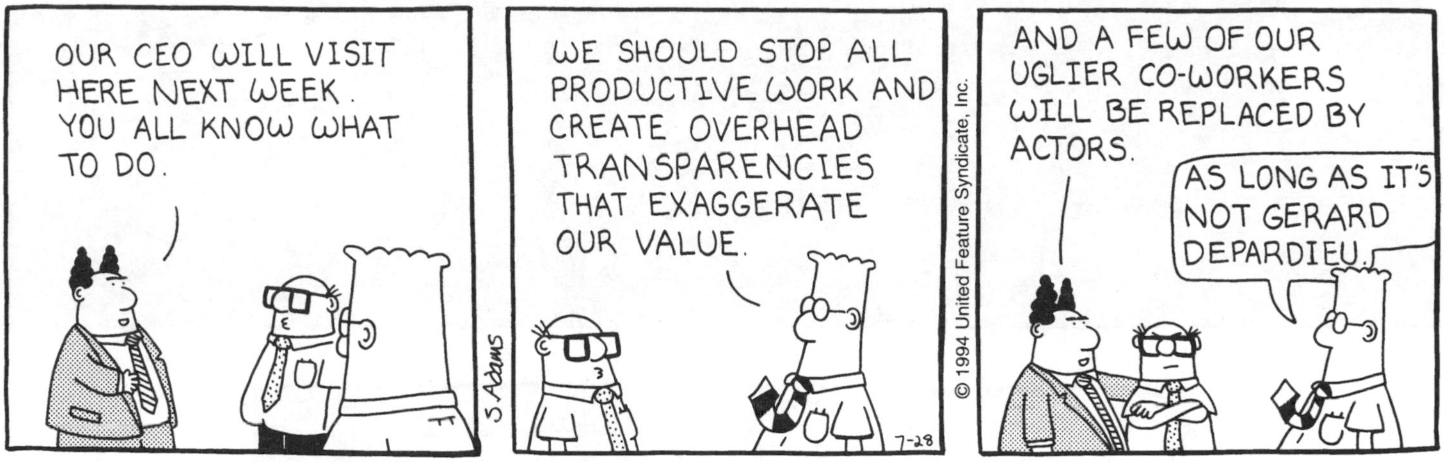
OUR CEO WILL VISIT HERE NEXT WEEK. YOU ALL KNOW WHAT TO DO.
WE SHOULD STOP ALL PRODUCTIVE WORK AND CREATE OVERHEAD TRANSPARENCIES THAT EXAGGERATE OUR VALUE.
AND A FEW OF OUR UGLIER CO-WORKERS WILL BE REPLACED BY ACTORS.
AS LONG AS IT'S NOT GERARD DEPARDIEU.
S. Adams
7-28
© 1994 United Feature Syndicate, Inc.

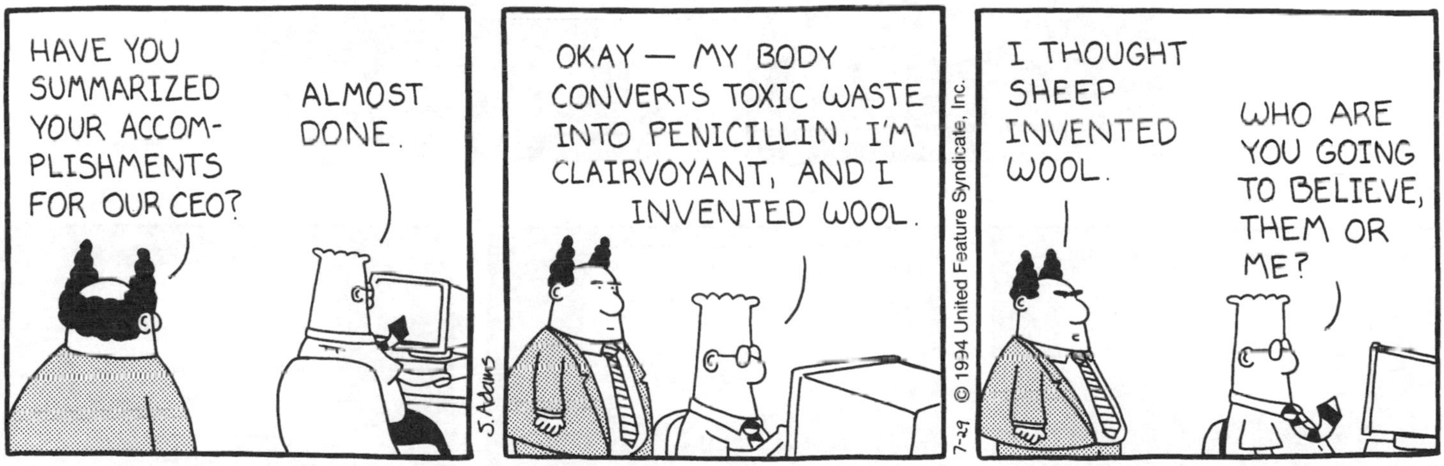
HAVE YOU SUMMARIZED YOUR ACCOM-PLISHMENTS FOR OUR CEO?
ALMOST DONE.
OKAY — MY BODY CONVERTS TOXIC WASTE INTO PENICILLIN, I'M CLAIRVOYANT, AND I INVENTED WOOL.
I THOUGHT SHEEP INVENTED WOOL.
WHO ARE YOU GOING TO BELIEVE, THEM OR ME?
S. Adams
7-29
© 1994 United Feature Syndicate, Inc.

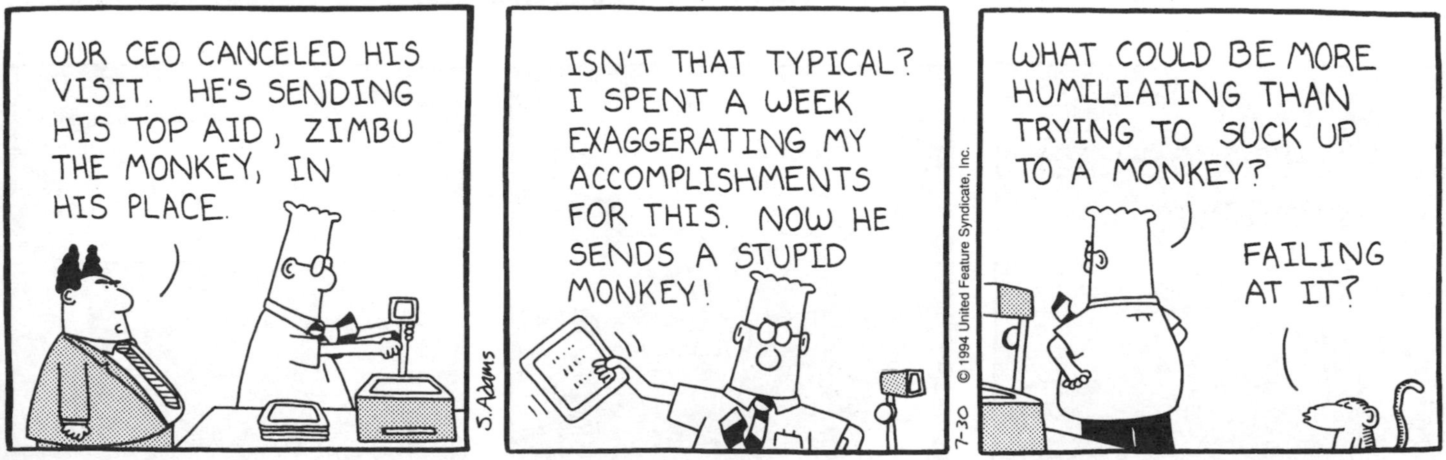
OUR CEO CANCELED HIS VISIT. HE'S SENDING HIS TOP AID, ZIMBU THE MONKEY, IN HIS PLACE.
ISN'T THAT TYPICAL? I SPENT A WEEK EXAGGERATING MY ACCOMPLISHMENTS FOR THIS. NOW HE SENDS A STUPID MONKEY!
WHAT COULD BE MORE HUMILIATING THAN TRYING TO SUCK UP TO A MONKEY?
FAILING AT IT?
S. Adams
7-30
© 1994 United Feature Syndicate, Inc.

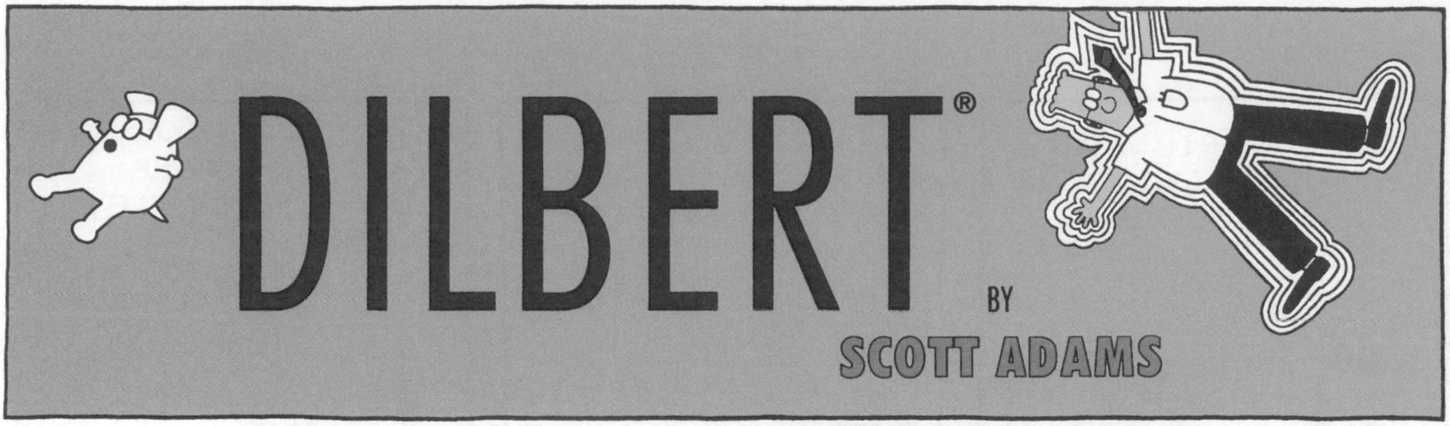
DILBERT®
BY
SCOTT ADAMS

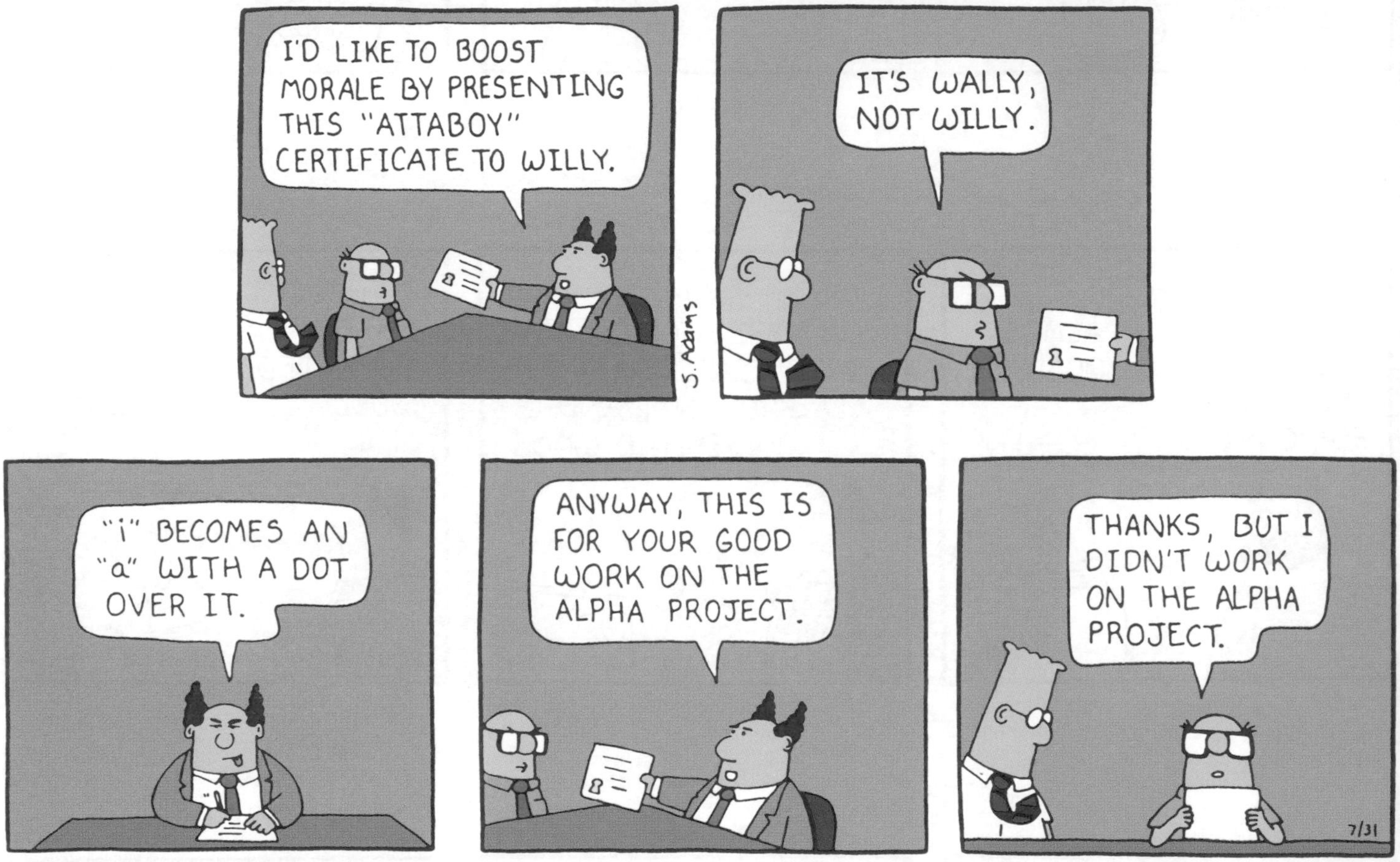
I'D LIKE TO BOOST MORALE BY PRESENTING THIS "ATTABOY" CERTIFICATE TO WILLY.
S. Adams
IT'S WALLY, NOT WILLY.
"i" BECOMES AN "a" WITH A DOT OVER IT.
ANYWAY, THIS IS FOR YOUR GOOD WORK ON THE ALPHA PROJECT.
THANKS, BUT I DIDN'T WORK ON THE ALPHA PROJECT.
7/31

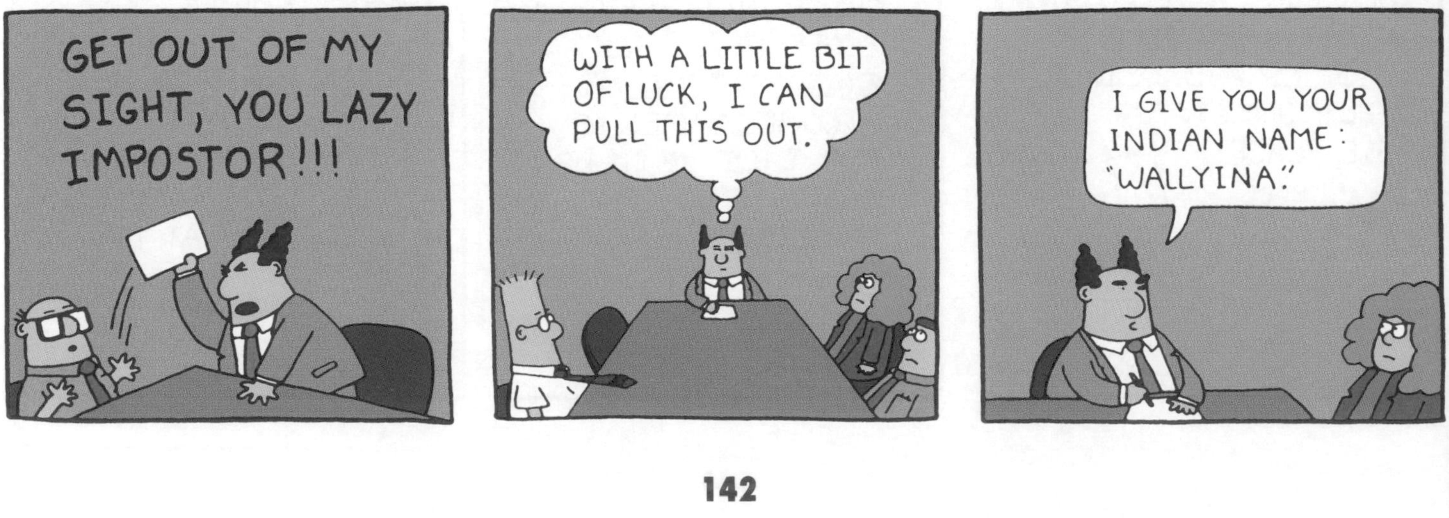
GET OUT OF MY SIGHT, YOU LAZY IMPOSTOR!!!
WITH A LITTLE BIT OF LUCK, I CAN PULL THIS OUT.
I GIVE YOU YOUR INDIAN NAME: "WALLYINA."

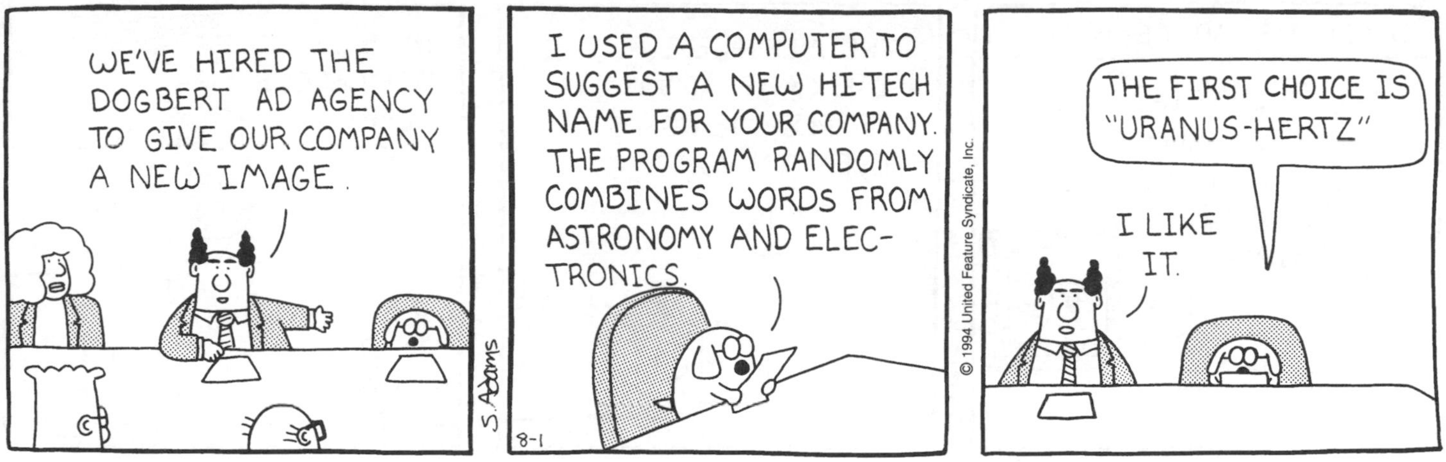
WE'VE HIRED THE DOGBERT AD AGENCY TO GIVE OUR COMPANY A NEW IMAGE.
S. Adams
8-1
I USED A COMPUTER TO SUGGEST A NEW HI-TECH NAME FOR YOUR COMPANY. THE PROGRAM RANDOMLY COMBINES WORDS FROM ASTRONOMY AND ELECTRONICS.
© 1994 United Feature Syndicate, Inc.
THE FIRST CHOICE IS "URANUS-HERTZ"
I LIKE IT.

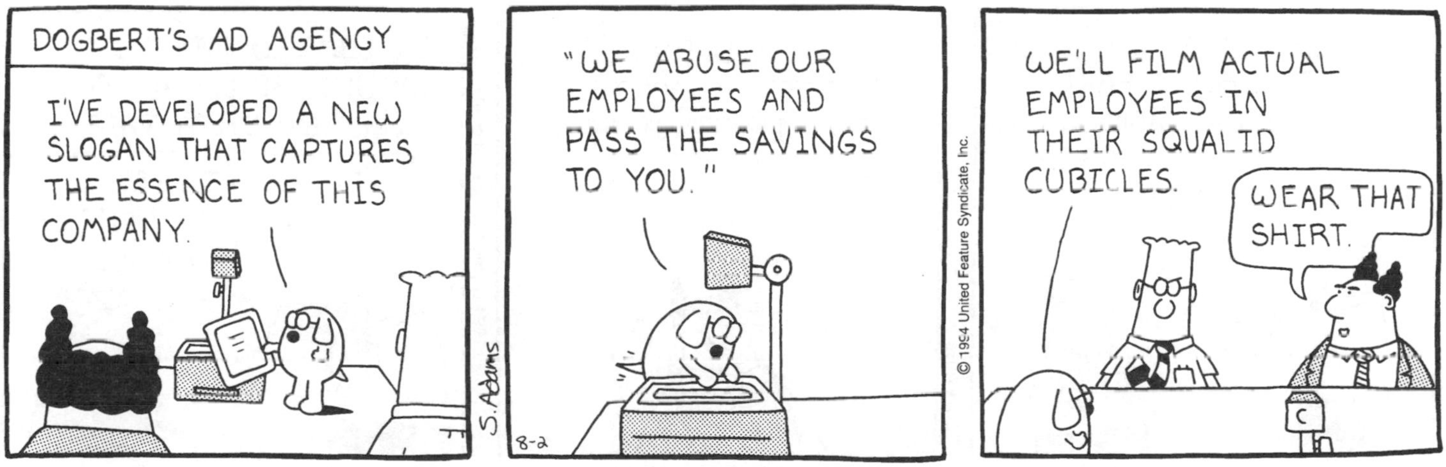
DOGBERT'S AD AGENCY
I'VE DEVELOPED A NEW SLOGAN THAT CAPTURES THE ESSENCE OF THIS COMPANY.
S. Adams
8-2
"WE ABUSE OUR EMPLOYEES AND PASS THE SAVINGS TO YOU."
© 1994 United Feature Syndicate, Inc.
WE'LL FILM ACTUAL EMPLOYEES IN THEIR SQUALID CUBICLES.
WEAR THAT SHIRT.

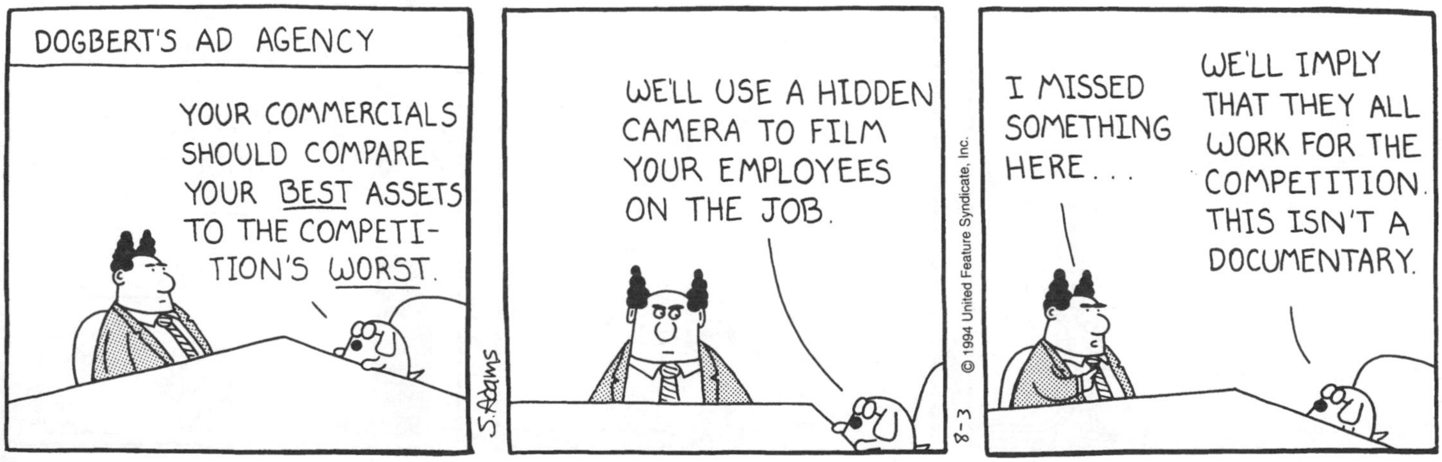
DOGBERT'S AD AGENCY
YOUR COMMERCIALS SHOULD COMPARE YOUR BEST ASSETS TO THE COMPETITION'S WORST.
S. Adams
WE'LL USE A HIDDEN CAMERA TO FILM YOUR EMPLOYEES ON THE JOB.
8-3
© 1994 United Feature Syndicate, Inc.
I MISSED SOMETHING HERE...
WE'LL IMPLY THAT THEY ALL WORK FOR THE COMPETITION. THIS ISN'T A DOCUMENTARY.

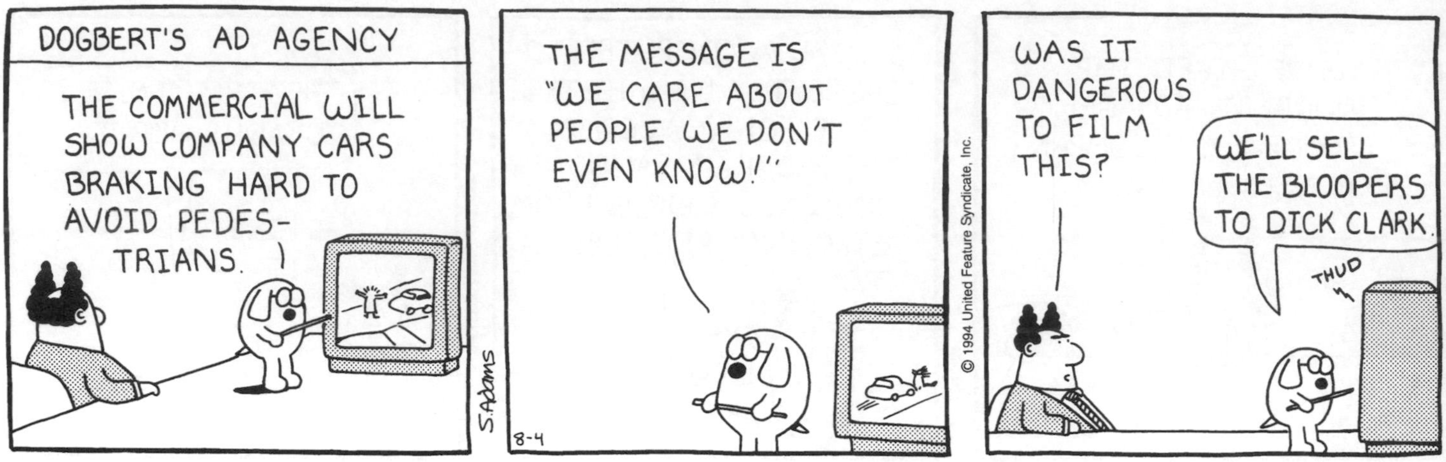
DOGBERT'S AD AGENCY
THE COMMERCIAL WILL SHOW COMPANY CARS BRAKING HARD TO AVOID PEDES-TRIANS.
THE MESSAGE IS "WE CARE ABOUT PEOPLE WE DON'T EVEN KNOW!"
WAS IT DANGEROUS TO FILM THIS?
WE'LL SELL THE BLOOPERS TO DICK CLARK.
THUD
S. Adams
8-4
© 1994 United Feature Syndicate, Inc.

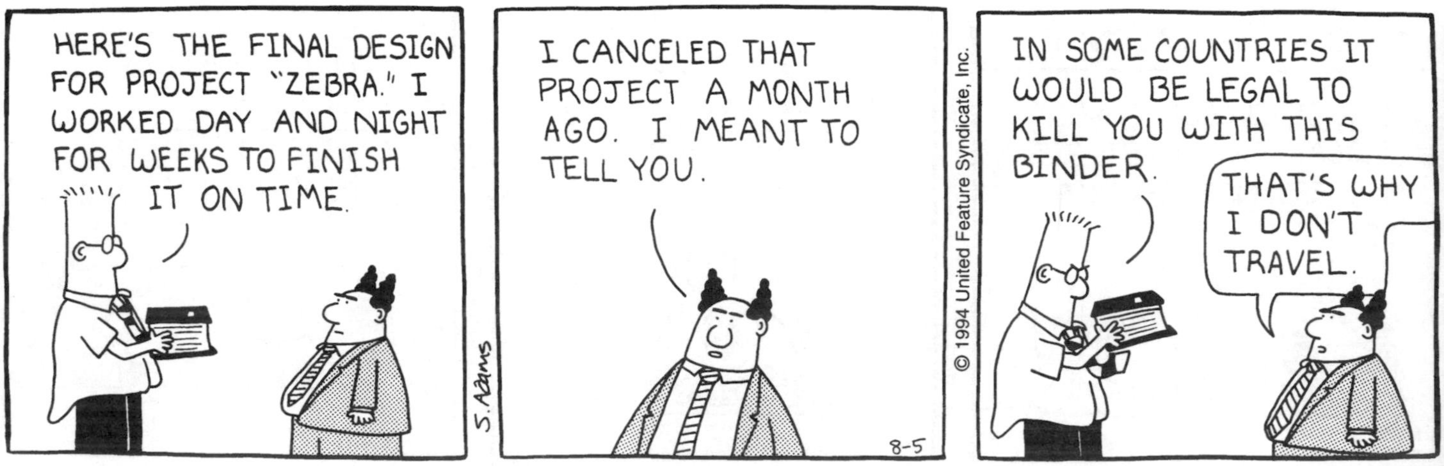
HERE'S THE FINAL DESIGN FOR PROJECT "ZEBRA." I WORKED DAY AND NIGHT FOR WEEKS TO FINISH IT ON TIME.
I CANCELED THAT PROJECT A MONTH AGO. I MEANT TO TELL YOU.
IN SOME COUNTRIES IT WOULD BE LEGAL TO KILL YOU WITH THIS BINDER.
THAT'S WHY I DON'T TRAVEL.
S. Adams
8-5
© 1994 United Feature Syndicate, Inc.

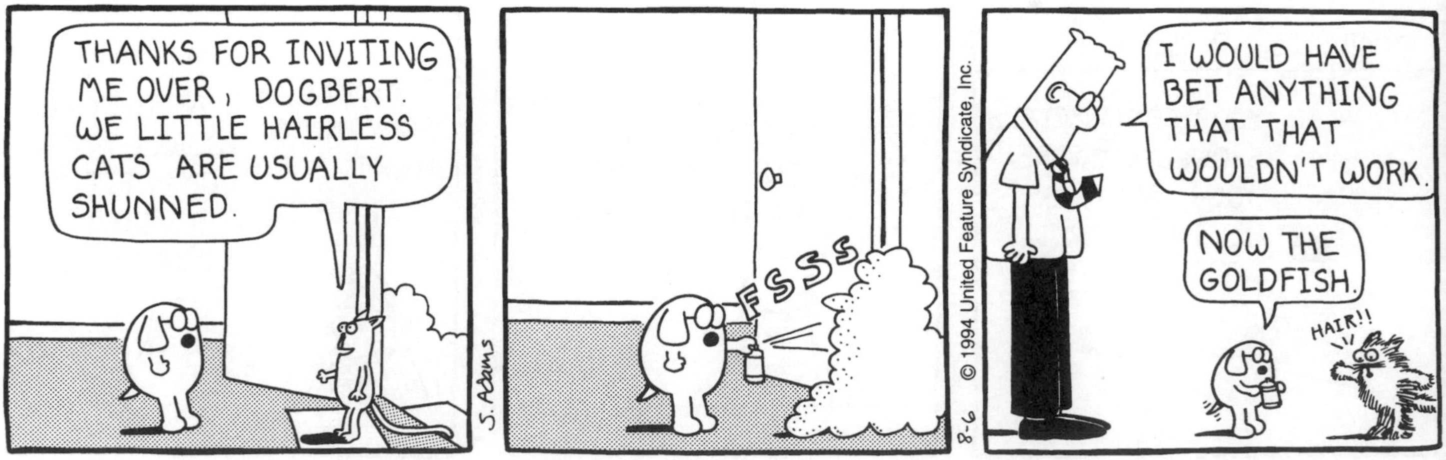
THANKS FOR INVITING ME OVER, DOGBERT. WE LITTLE HAIRLESS CATS ARE USUALLY SHUNNED.
FSSS
I WOULD HAVE BET ANYTHING THAT THAT WOULDN'T WORK.
NOW THE GOLDFISH.
HAIR!!
S. Adams
8-6
© 1994 United Feature Syndicate, Inc.

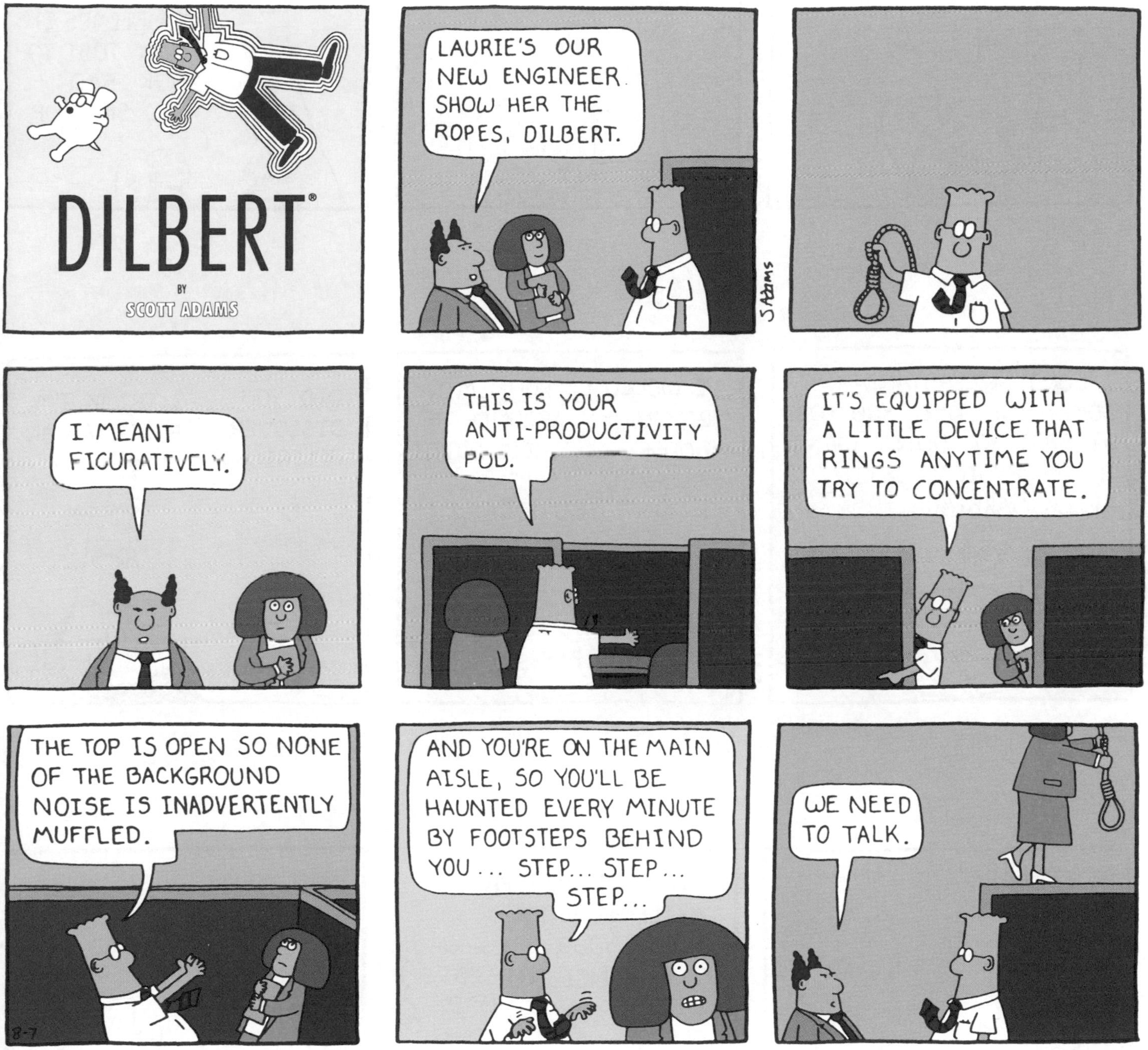
DILBERT®
BY
SCOTT ADAMS
LAURIE'S OUR NEW ENGINEER. SHOW HER THE ROPES, DILBERT.
S. ADAMS
I MEANT FIGURATIVELY.
THIS IS YOUR ANTI-PRODUCTIVITY POD.
IT'S EQUIPPED WITH A LITTLE DEVICE THAT RINGS ANYTIME YOU TRY TO CONCENTRATE.
© 1994 United Feature Syndicate, Inc
THE TOP IS OPEN SO NONE OF THE BACKGROUND NOISE IS INADVERTENTLY MUFFLED.
8-7
AND YOU'RE ON THE MAIN AISLE, SO YOU'LL BE HAUNTED EVERY MINUTE BY FOOTSTEPS BEHIND YOU... STEP... STEP... STEP...
WE NEED TO TALK.

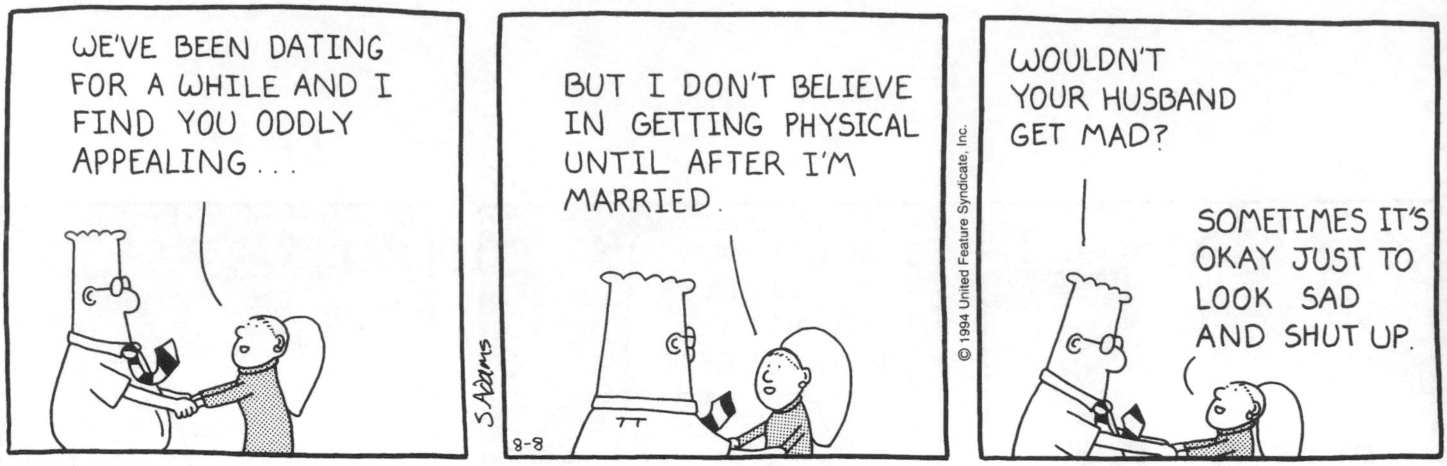
WE'VE BEEN DATING FOR A WHILE AND I FIND YOU ODDLY APPEALING...
BUT I DON'T BELIEVE IN GETTING PHYSICAL UNTIL AFTER I'M MARRIED.
S. Adams 8-8
© 1994 United Feature Syndicate, Inc.
WOULDN'T YOUR HUSBAND GET MAD?
SOMETIMES IT'S OKAY JUST TO LOOK SAD AND SHUT UP.

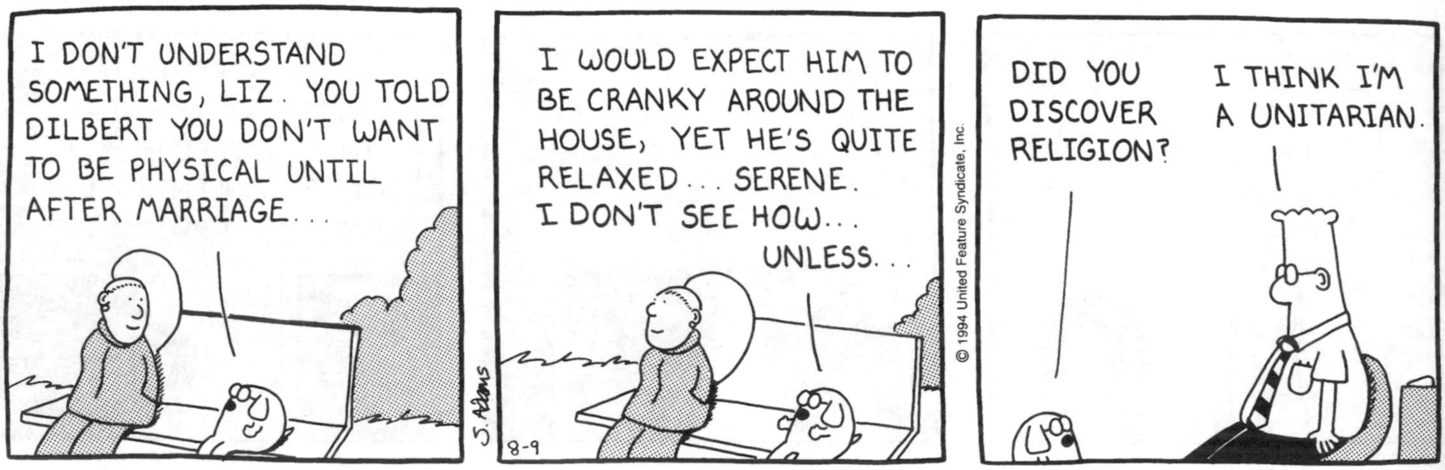
I DON'T UNDERSTAND SOMETHING, LIZ. YOU TOLD DILBERT YOU DON'T WANT TO BE PHYSICAL UNTIL AFTER MARRIAGE...
I WOULD EXPECT HIM TO BE CRANKY AROUND THE HOUSE, YET HE'S QUITE RELAXED... SERENE. I DON'T SEE HOW...
UNLESS...
S. Adams 8-9
© 1994 United Feature Syndicate, Inc.
DID YOU DISCOVER RELIGION?
I THINK I'M A UNITARIAN.

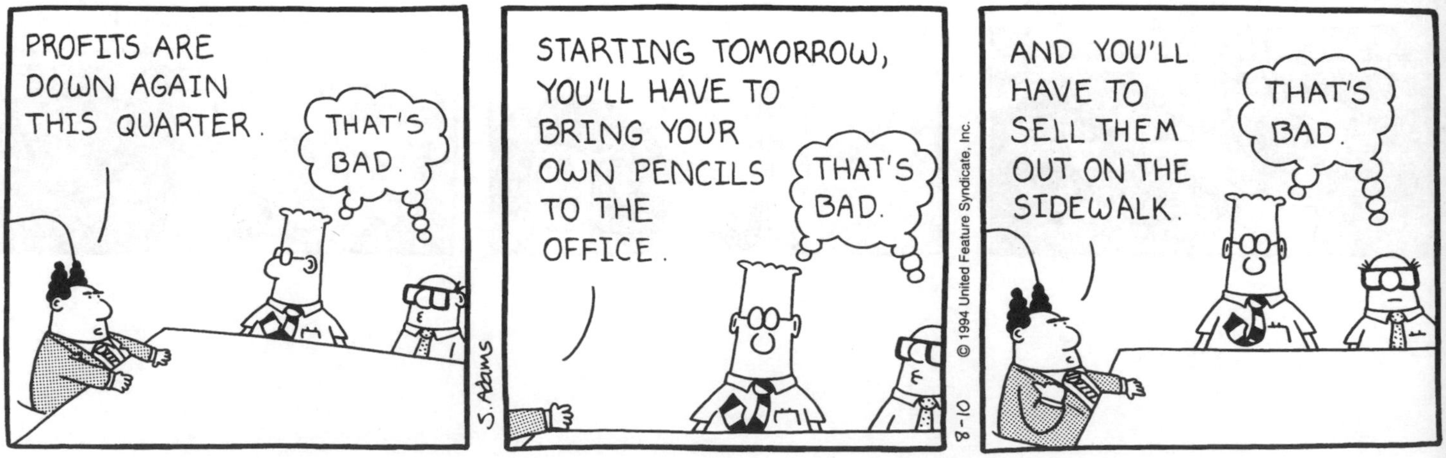
PROFITS ARE DOWN AGAIN THIS QUARTER.
THAT'S BAD.
STARTING TOMORROW, YOU'LL HAVE TO BRING YOUR OWN PENCILS TO THE OFFICE.
THAT'S BAD.
S. Adams 8-10
© 1994 United Feature Syndicate, Inc.
AND YOU'LL HAVE TO SELL THEM OUT ON THE SIDEWALK.
THAT'S BAD.

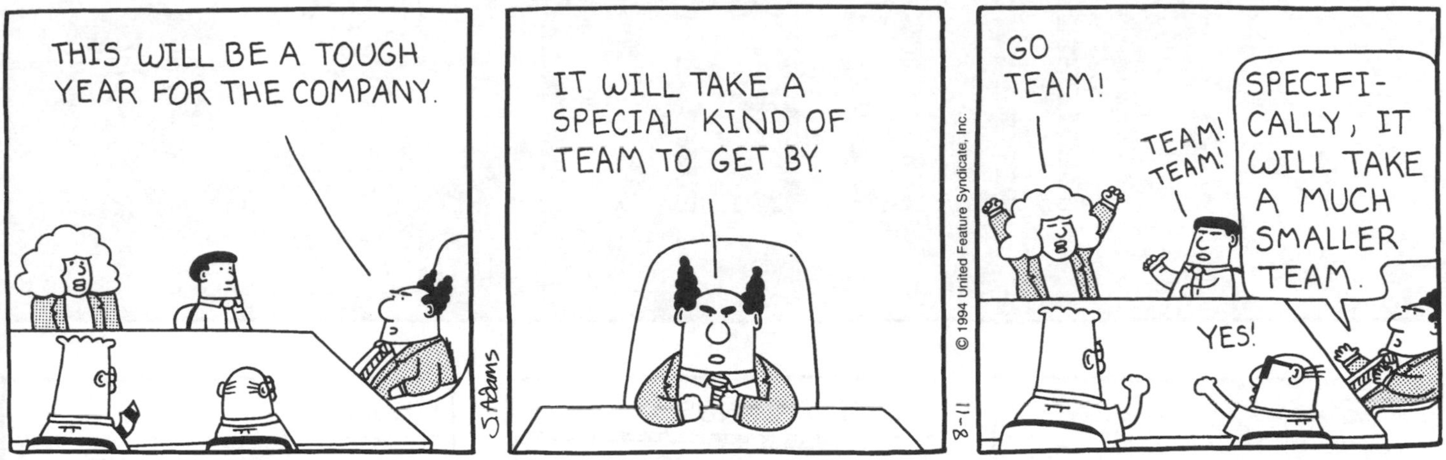
THIS WILL BE A TOUGH YEAR FOR THE COMPANY.
IT WILL TAKE A SPECIAL KIND OF TEAM TO GET BY.
GO TEAM!
TEAM! TEAM!
YES!
SPECIFI-CALLY, IT WILL TAKE A MUCH SMALLER TEAM.
S. Adams
© 1994 United Feature Syndicate, Inc.
8-11

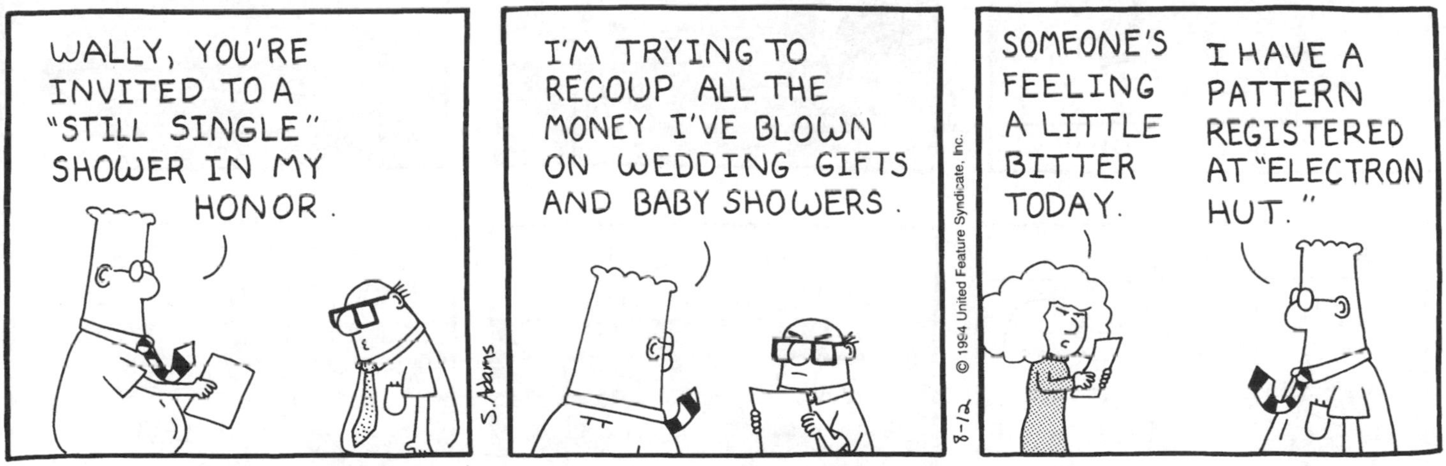
WALLY, YOU'RE INVITED TO A "STILL SINGLE" SHOWER IN MY HONOR.
I'M TRYING TO RECOUP ALL THE MONEY I'VE BLOWN ON WEDDING GIFTS AND BABY SHOWERS.
SOMEONE'S FEELING A LITTLE BITTER TODAY.
I HAVE A PATTERN REGISTERED AT "ELECTRON HUT."
S. Adams
© 1994 United Feature Syndicate, Inc.
8-12

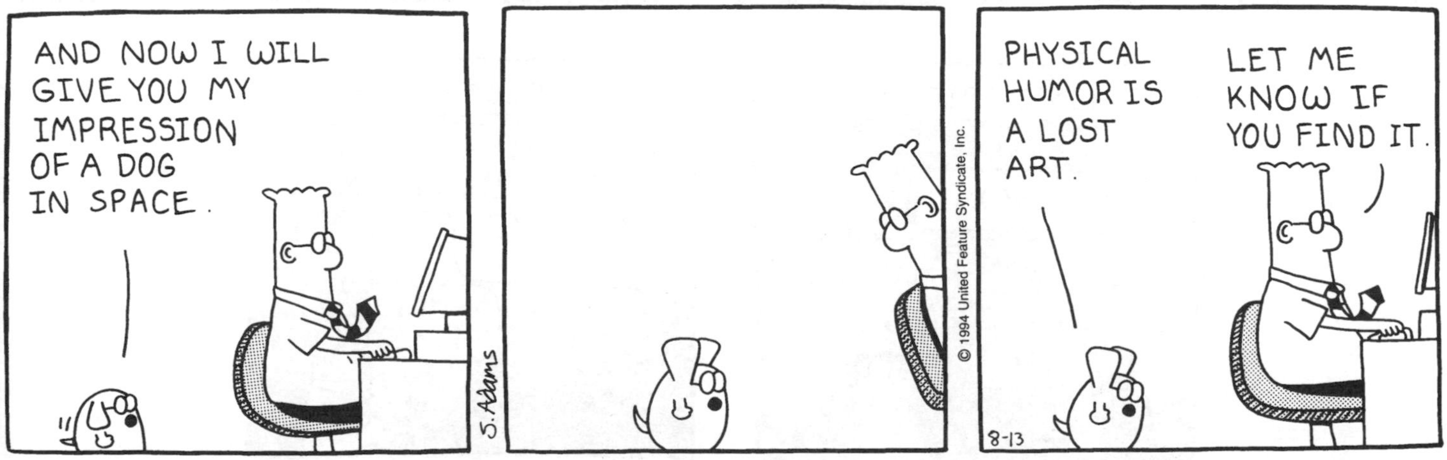
AND NOW I WILL GIVE YOU MY IMPRESSION OF A DOG IN SPACE.
PHYSICAL HUMOR IS A LOST ART.
LET ME KNOW IF YOU FIND IT.
S. Adams
© 1994 United Feature Syndicate, Inc.
8-13

DILBERT®
BY
SCOTT ADAMS
"FRIENDS" EXPLAINED
A VERY SPECIAL "DILBERT"
S. ADAMS
CLOSE FRIENDS
MAY I BORROW YOUR GUM?
SURE. REACH IN AND TAKE WHAT YOU NEED.
"BUDDIES"
CAN I BORROW YOUR HAMMER?
WHY NOT USE YOUR FOREHEAD AS USUAL?
WORK FRIENDS
SO, HOW'S YOUR WIFE?
DEAD. SAME AS LAST WEEK.
BOYFRIEND/GIRLFRIEND (STEREOTYPICAL VIEW)
LOVE.
LUST.
8-14
BOYFRIEND/GIRLFRIEND (MODERN CORRECT VIEW)
LUST.
TELEVISION.
PLATONIC FRIENDS
TELEVISION?
LUST.
MAN'S BEST FRIEND
BY MY ESTIMATE THERE ARE 2.6 BILLION FEMALES WHO DO NOT DESIRE YOU.
NAME THEM.

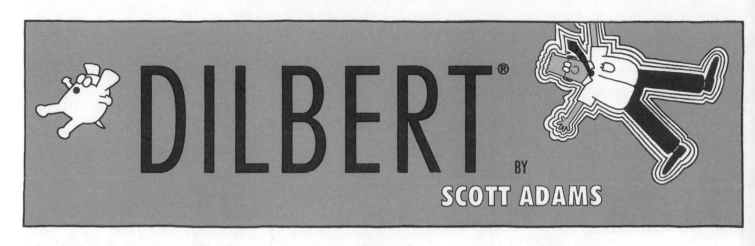

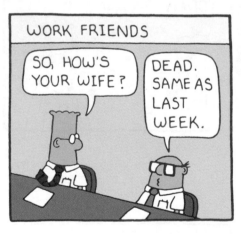

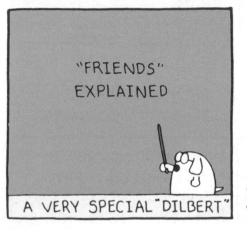

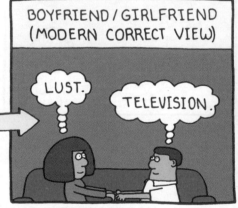

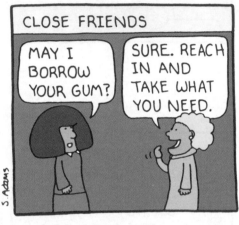

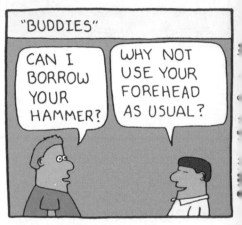

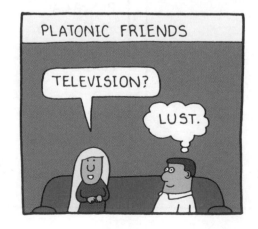

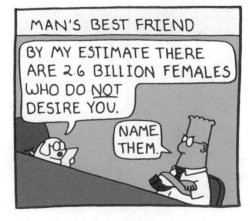

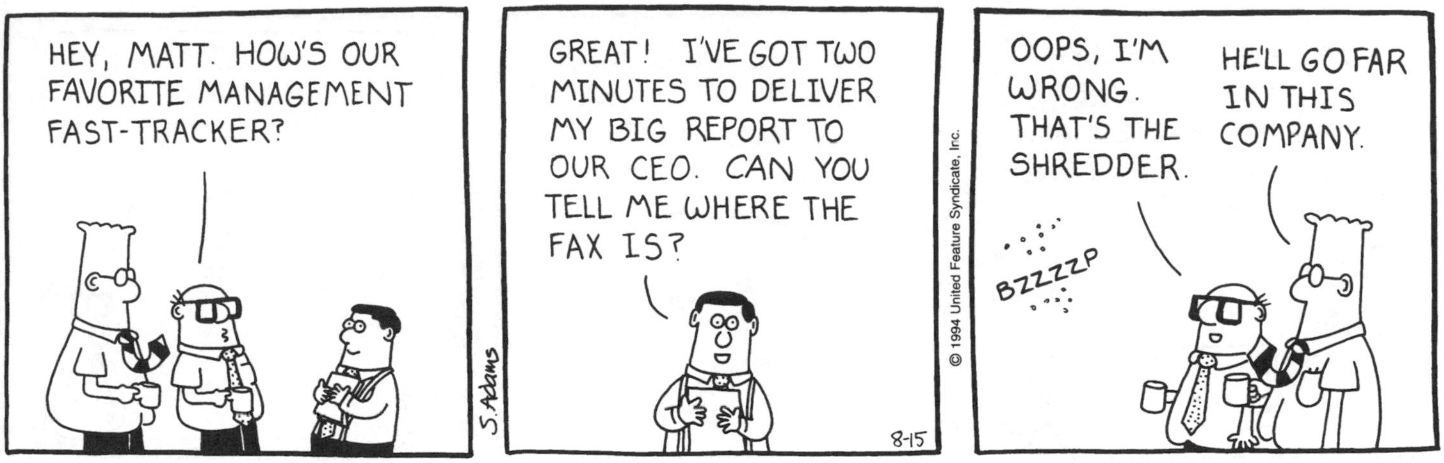
HEY, MATT. HOW'S OUR FAVORITE MANAGEMENT FAST-TRACKER?
GREAT! I'VE GOT TWO MINUTES TO DELIVER MY BIG REPORT TO OUR CEO. CAN YOU TELL ME WHERE THE FAX IS?
OOPS, I'M WRONG. THAT'S THE SHREDDER.
BZZZZP
HE'LL GO FAR IN THIS COMPANY.
S. Adams
8-15
© 1994 United Feature Syndicate, Inc.

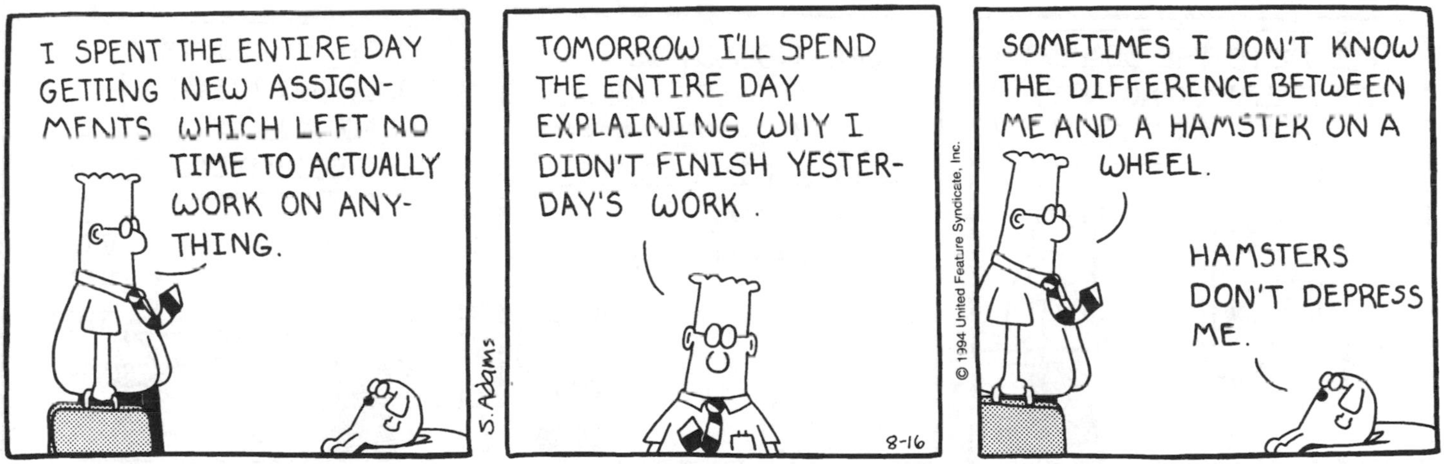
I SPENT THE ENTIRE DAY GETTING NEW ASSIGNMENTS WHICH LEFT NO TIME TO ACTUALLY WORK ON ANYTHING.
TOMORROW I'LL SPEND THE ENTIRE DAY EXPLAINING WHY I DIDN'T FINISH YESTERDAY'S WORK.
SOMETIMES I DON'T KNOW THE DIFFERENCE BETWEEN ME AND A HAMSTER ON A WHEEL.
HAMSTERS DON'T DEPRESS ME.
S. Adams
8-16
© 1994 United Feature Syndicate, Inc.

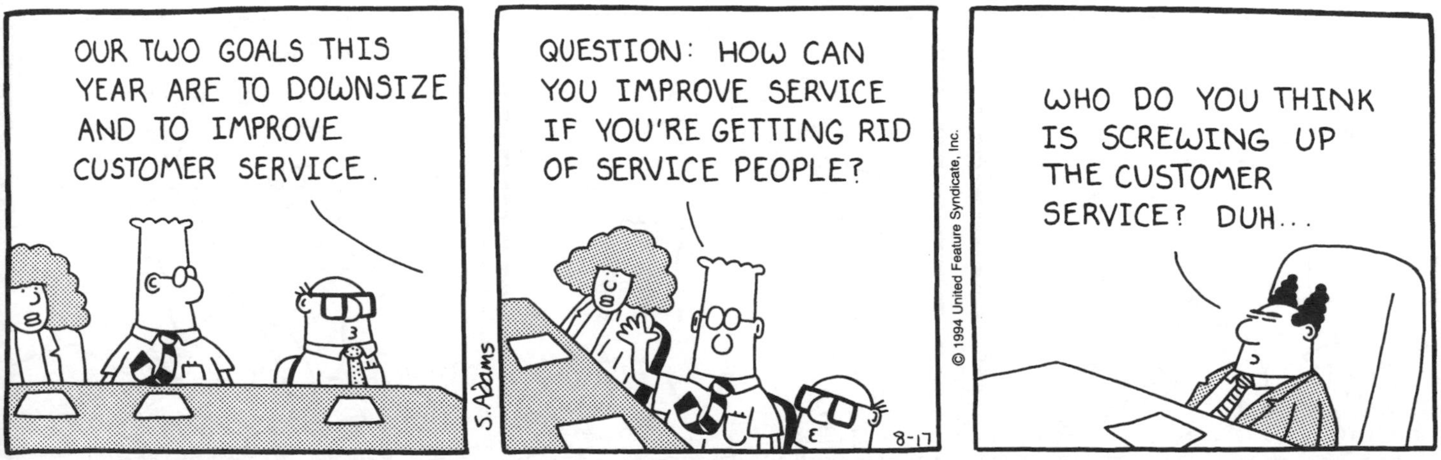
OUR TWO GOALS THIS YEAR ARE TO DOWNSIZE AND TO IMPROVE CUSTOMER SERVICE.
QUESTION: HOW CAN YOU IMPROVE SERVICE IF YOU'RE GETTING RID OF SERVICE PEOPLE?
WHO DO YOU THINK IS SCREWING UP THE CUSTOMER SERVICE? DUH...
S. Adams
8-17
© 1994 United Feature Syndicate, Inc.

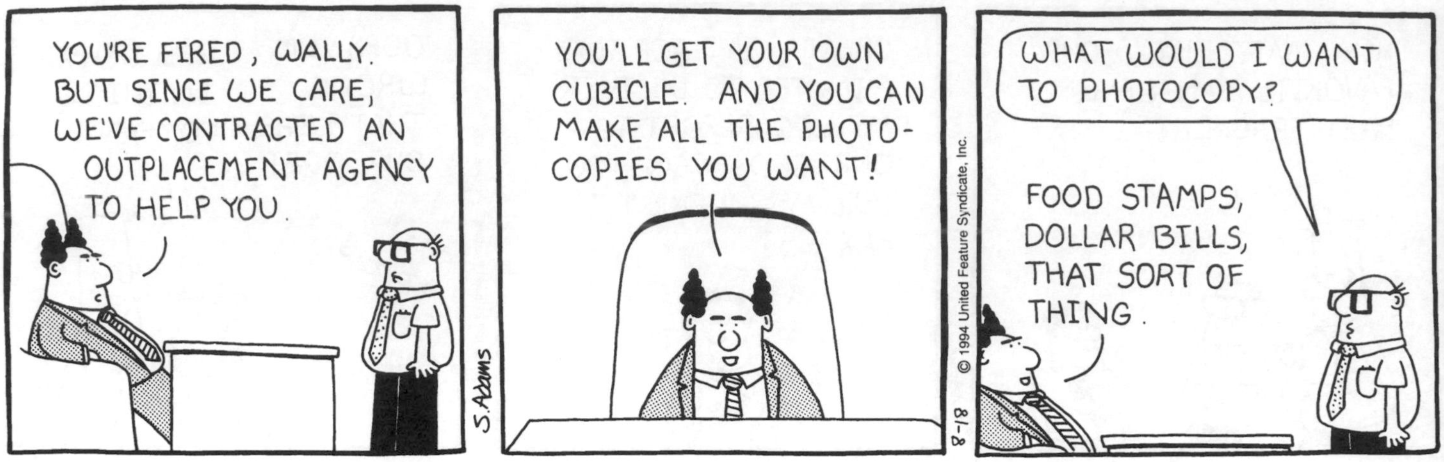
YOU'RE FIRED, WALLY. BUT SINCE WE CARE, WE'VE CONTRACTED AN OUTPLACEMENT AGENCY TO HELP YOU.
S. ADAMS
YOU'LL GET YOUR OWN CUBICLE. AND YOU CAN MAKE ALL THE PHOTOCOPIES YOU WANT!
8-18 © 1994 United Feature Syndicate, Inc.
WHAT WOULD I WANT TO PHOTOCOPY?
FOOD STAMPS, DOLLAR BILLS, THAT SORT OF THING.

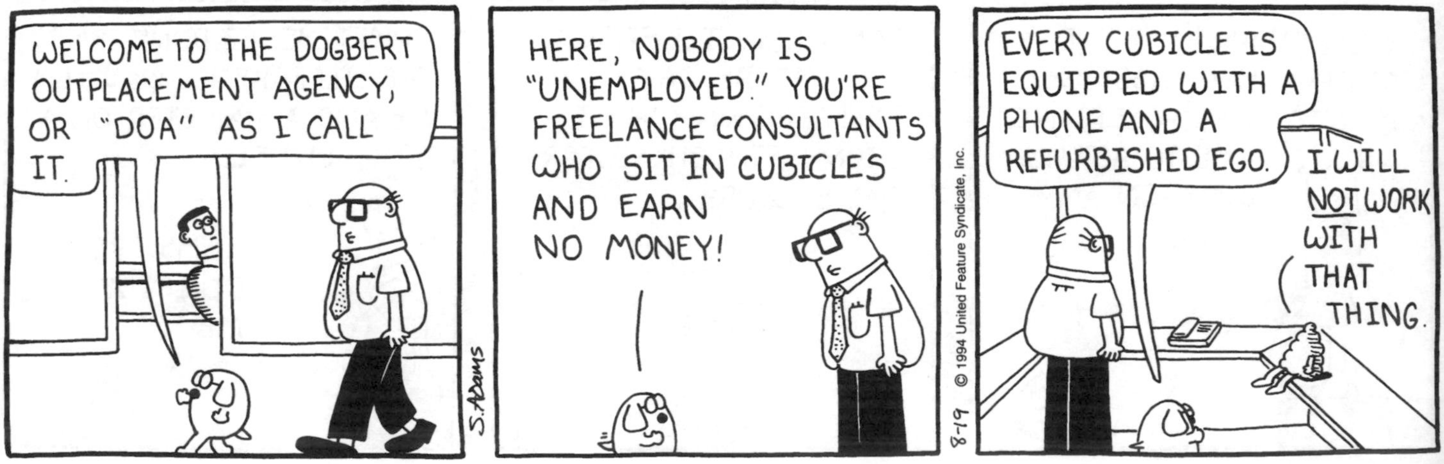
WELCOME TO THE DOGBERT OUTPLACEMENT AGENCY, OR "DOA" AS I CALL IT.
S. ADAMS
HERE, NOBODY IS "UNEMPLOYED." YOU'RE FREELANCE CONSULTANTS WHO SIT IN CUBICLES AND EARN NO MONEY!
8-19 © 1994 United Feature Syndicate, Inc.
EVERY CUBICLE IS EQUIPPED WITH A PHONE AND A REFURBISHED EGO.
I WILL NOT WORK WITH THAT THING.

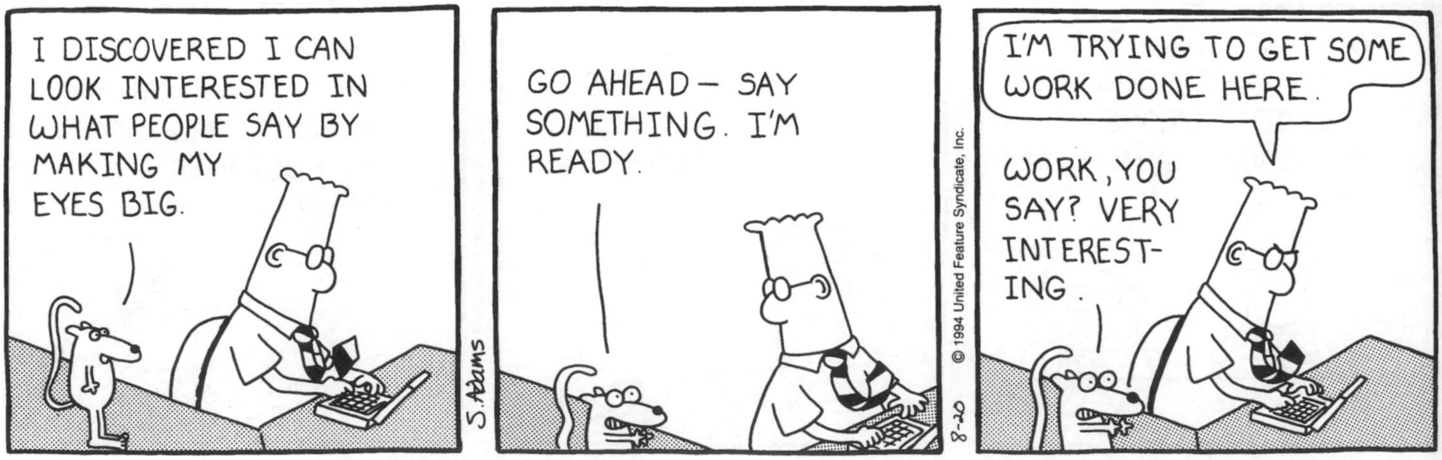
I DISCOVERED I CAN LOOK INTERESTED IN WHAT PEOPLE SAY BY MAKING MY EYES BIG.
S. ADAMS
GO AHEAD— SAY SOMETHING. I'M READY.
8-20 © 1994 United Feature Syndicate, Inc.
I'M TRYING TO GET SOME WORK DONE HERE.
WORK, YOU SAY? VERY INTEREST-ING.

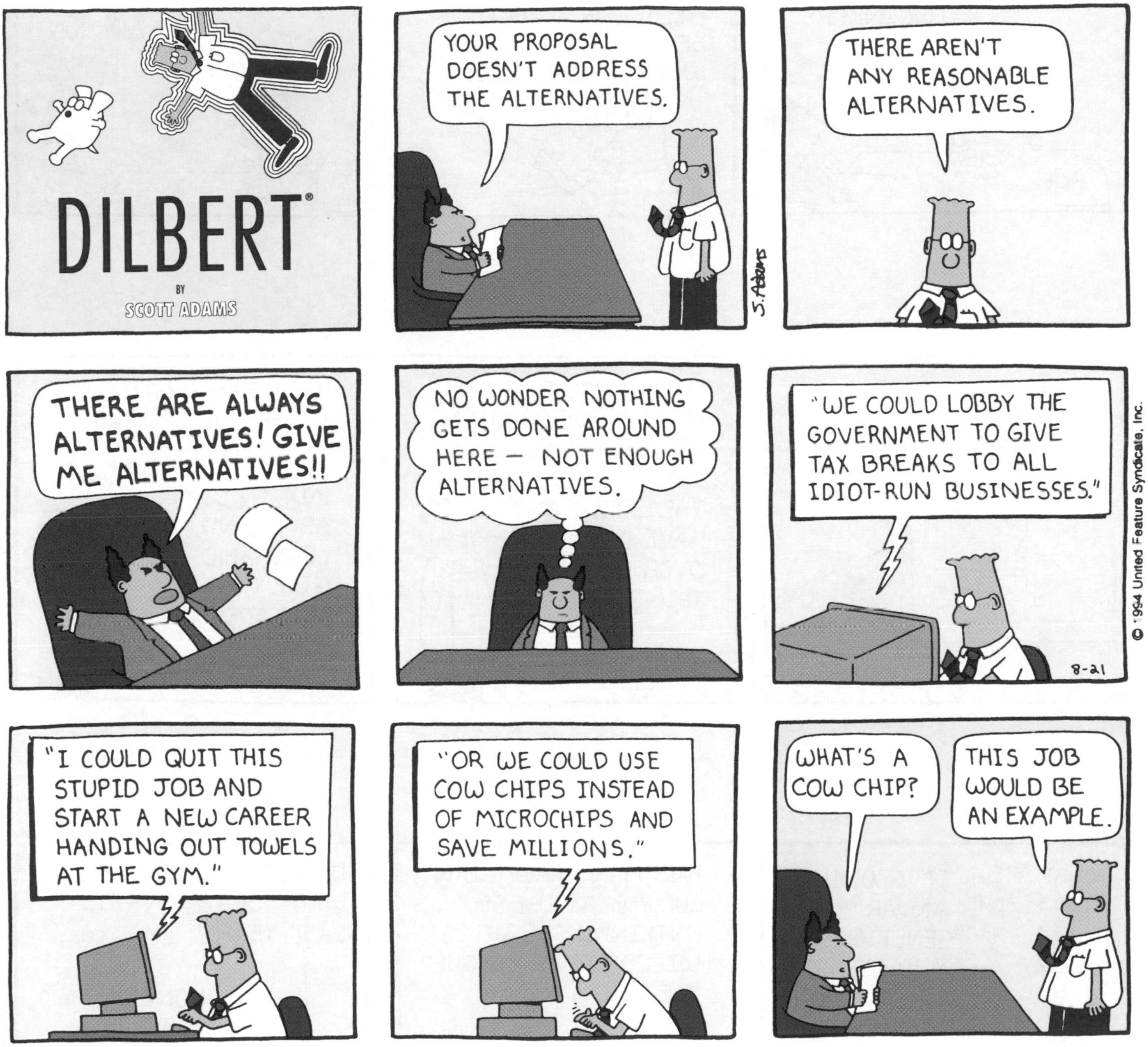
DILBERT®
BY
SCOTT ADAMS
YOUR PROPOSAL DOESN'T ADDRESS THE ALTERNATIVES.
S. Adams
THERE AREN'T ANY REASONABLE ALTERNATIVES.
THERE ARE ALWAYS ALTERNATIVES! GIVE ME ALTERNATIVES!!
NO WONDER NOTHING GETS DONE AROUND HERE — NOT ENOUGH ALTERNATIVES.
"WE COULD LOBBY THE GOVERNMENT TO GIVE TAX BREAKS TO ALL IDIOT-RUN BUSINESSES."
8-21
© 1994 United Feature Syndicate, Inc.
"I COULD QUIT THIS STUPID JOB AND START A NEW CAREER HANDING OUT TOWELS AT THE GYM."
"OR WE COULD USE COW CHIPS INSTEAD OF MICROCHIPS AND SAVE MILLIONS."
WHAT'S A COW CHIP?
THIS JOB WOULD BE AN EXAMPLE.

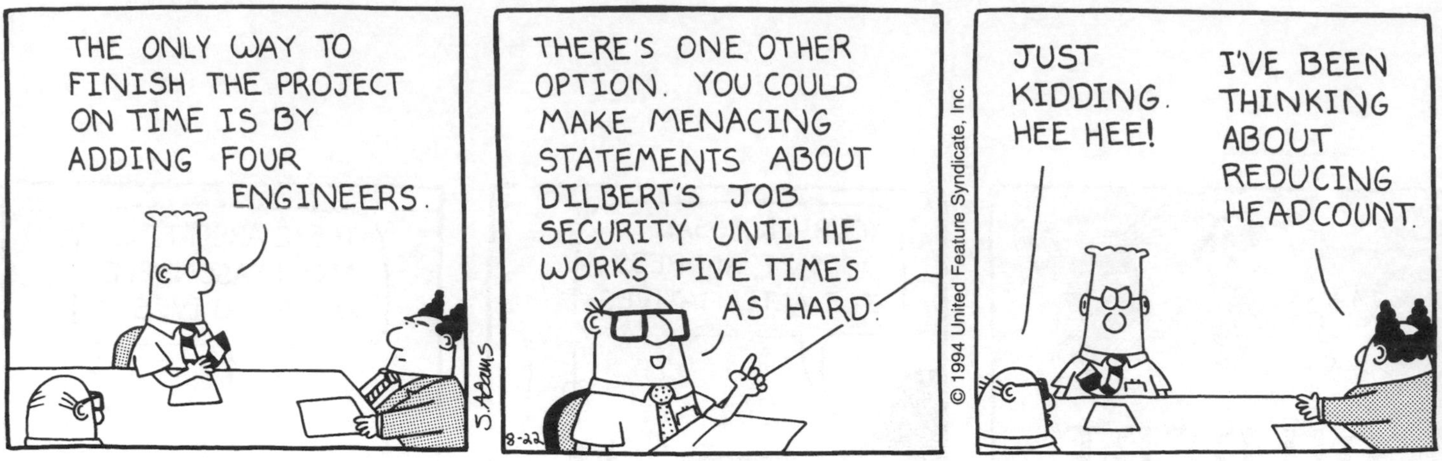
THE ONLY WAY TO FINISH THE PROJECT ON TIME IS BY ADDING FOUR ENGINEERS.
S. Adams 8-22
THERE'S ONE OTHER OPTION. YOU COULD MAKE MENACING STATEMENTS ABOUT DILBERT'S JOB SECURITY UNTIL HE WORKS FIVE TIMES AS HARD.
© 1994 United Feature Syndicate, Inc.
JUST KIDDING. HEE HEE!
I'VE BEEN THINKING ABOUT REDUCING HEADCOUNT.

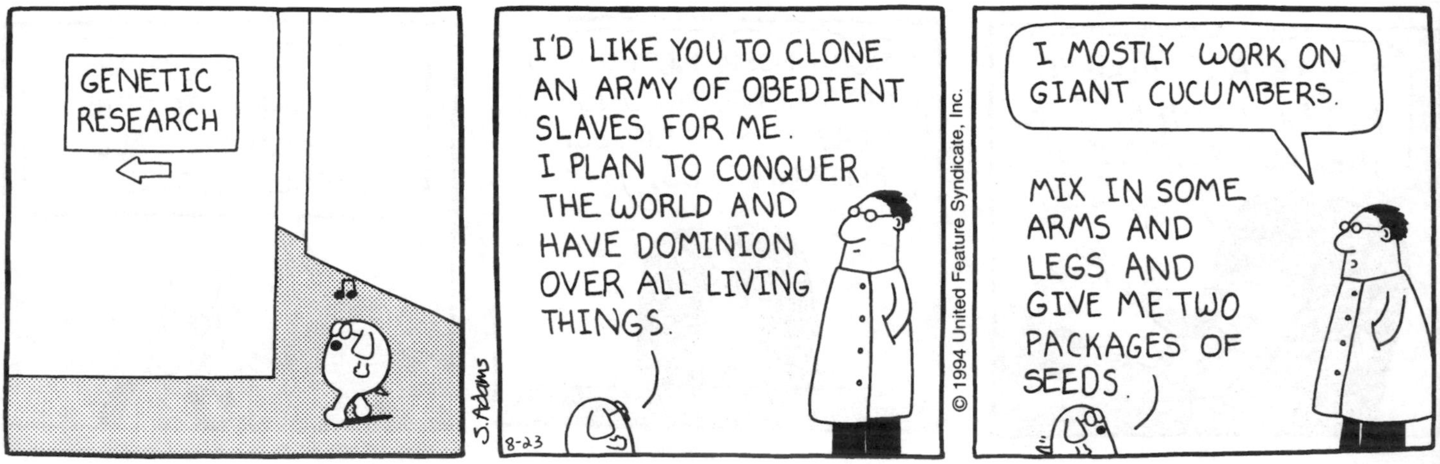
GENETIC RESEARCH
S. Adams 8-23
I'D LIKE YOU TO CLONE AN ARMY OF OBEDIENT SLAVES FOR ME. I PLAN TO CONQUER THE WORLD AND HAVE DOMINION OVER ALL LIVING THINGS.
© 1994 United Feature Syndicate, Inc.
I MOSTLY WORK ON GIANT CUCUMBERS.
MIX IN SOME ARMS AND LEGS AND GIVE ME TWO PACKAGES OF SEEDS.

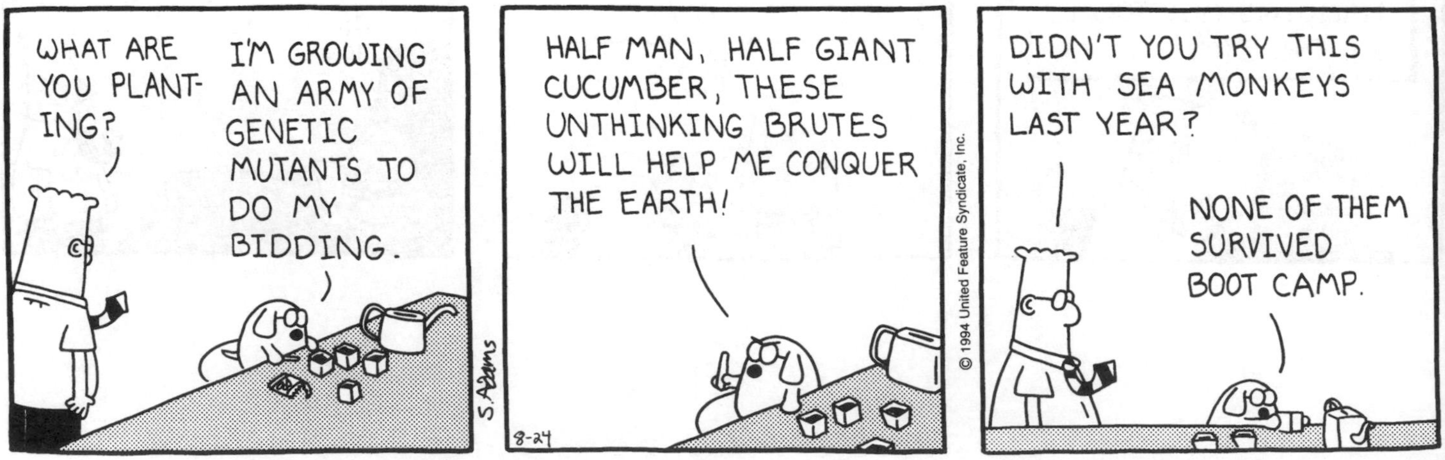
WHAT ARE YOU PLANTING?
I'M GROWING AN ARMY OF GENETIC MUTANTS TO DO MY BIDDING.
S. Adams 8-24
HALF MAN, HALF GIANT CUCUMBER, THESE UNTHINKING BRUTES WILL HELP ME CONQUER THE EARTH!
© 1994 United Feature Syndicate, Inc.
DIDN'T YOU TRY THIS WITH SEA MONKEYS LAST YEAR?
NONE OF THEM SURVIVED BOOT CAMP.

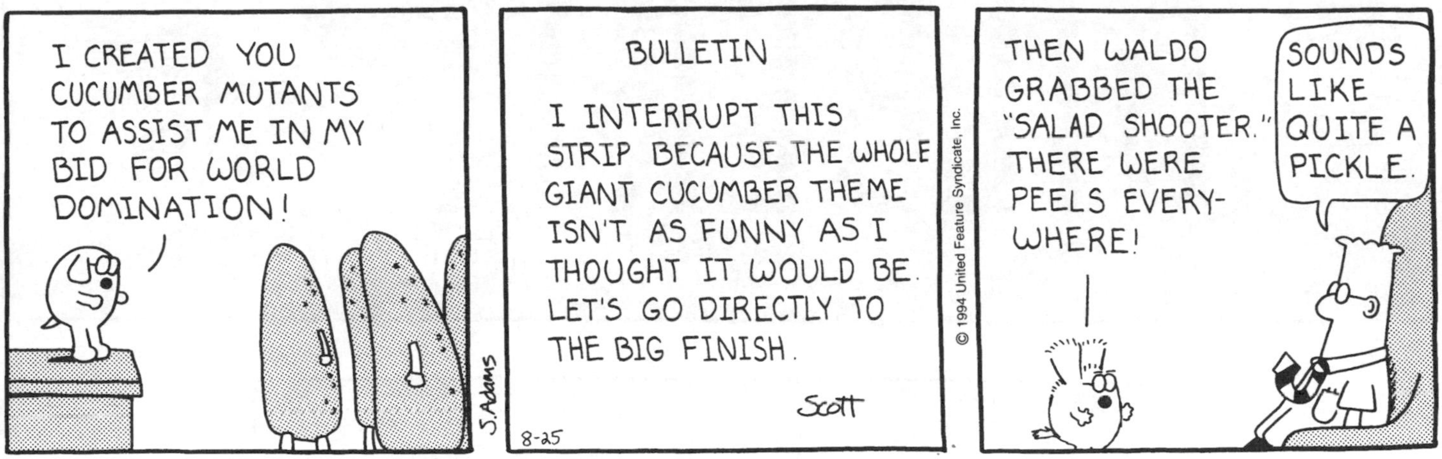
I CREATED YOU CUCUMBER MUTANTS TO ASSIST ME IN MY BID FOR WORLD DOMINATION!
S. Adams
BULLETIN
I INTERRUPT THIS STRIP BECAUSE THE WHOLE GIANT CUCUMBER THEME ISN'T AS FUNNY AS I THOUGHT IT WOULD BE. LET'S GO DIRECTLY TO THE BIG FINISH.
Scott
8-25
© 1994 United Feature Syndicate, Inc.
THEN WALDO GRABBED THE "SALAD SHOOTER." THERE WERE PEELS EVERYWHERE!
SOUNDS LIKE QUITE A PICKLE.

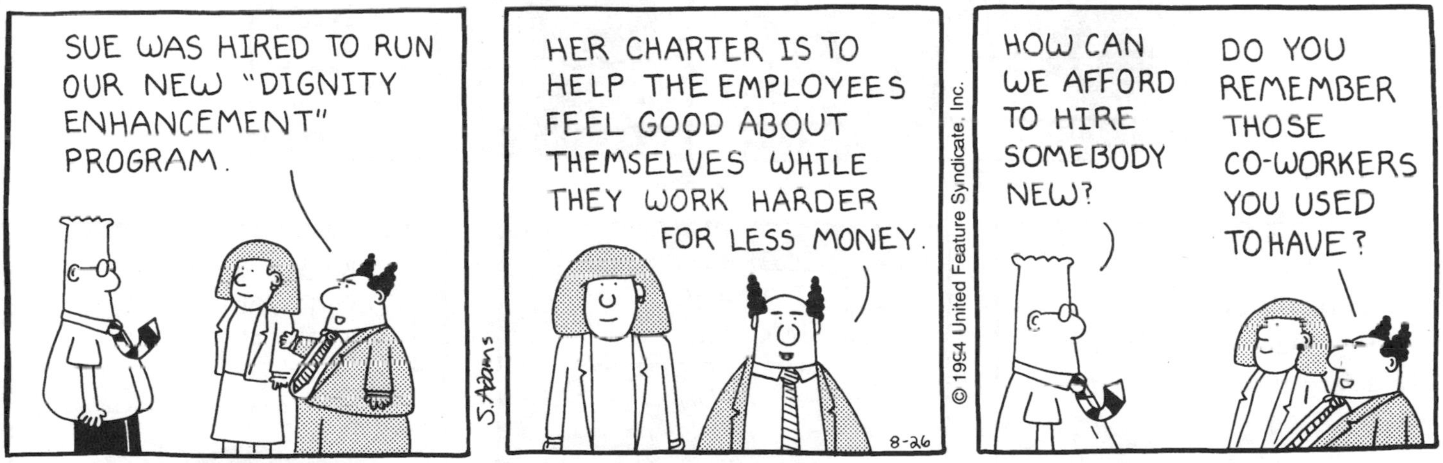
SUE WAS HIRED TO RUN OUR NEW "DIGNITY ENHANCEMENT" PROGRAM.
S. Adams
HER CHARTER IS TO HELP THE EMPLOYEES FEEL GOOD ABOUT THEMSELVES WHILE THEY WORK HARDER FOR LESS MONEY.
8-26
© 1954 United Feature Syndicate, Inc.
HOW CAN WE AFFORD TO HIRE SOMEBODY NEW?
DO YOU REMEMBER THOSE CO-WORKERS YOU USED TO HAVE?

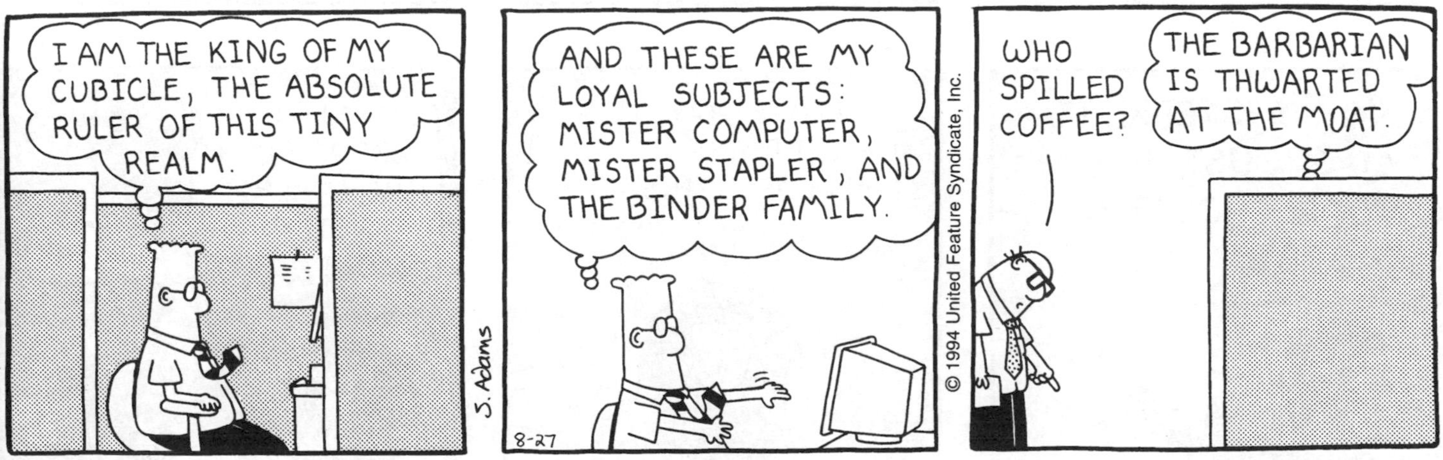
I AM THE KING OF MY CUBICLE, THE ABSOLUTE RULER OF THIS TINY REALM.
S. Adams
AND THESE ARE MY LOYAL SUBJECTS: MISTER COMPUTER, MISTER STAPLER, AND THE BINDER FAMILY.
8-27
© 1994 United Feature Syndicate, Inc.
WHO SPILLED COFFEE?
THE BARBARIAN IS THWARTED AT THE MOAT.

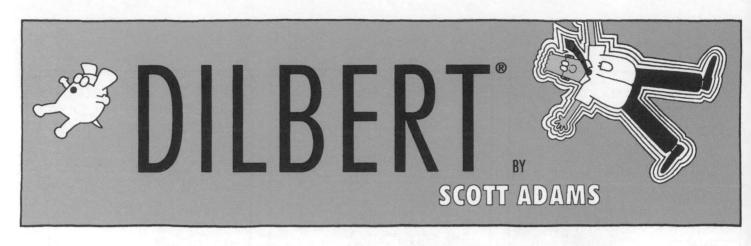

DILBERT BY SCOTT ADAMS

THE IMAGE IS FUZZY BECAUSE THE MONITOR HAS AN ACUTE DESIGN FLAW.

S Adams

ACUTE? THAT'S AN UNUSUAL CHOICE OF WORDS.

WOULD YOU HAVE SAID "ACUTE" TO A MALE CO-WORKER? I THINK NOT.

IT MEANS CRUCIAL, THAT'S ALL!!

I KNOW WHAT THE WORD MEANS! DO YOU THINK I DON'T SEE RIGHT THROUGH YOUR SEXIST PUNS?!

NO! I SWEAR, IT WAS JUST A POOR CHOICE OF WORDS!!

WELL... OKAY I ACCEPT YOUR APOLOGY. THIS TIME.

8-28

SO, WHAT'S WRONG WITH THE OTHER MONITOR?

WHICH?

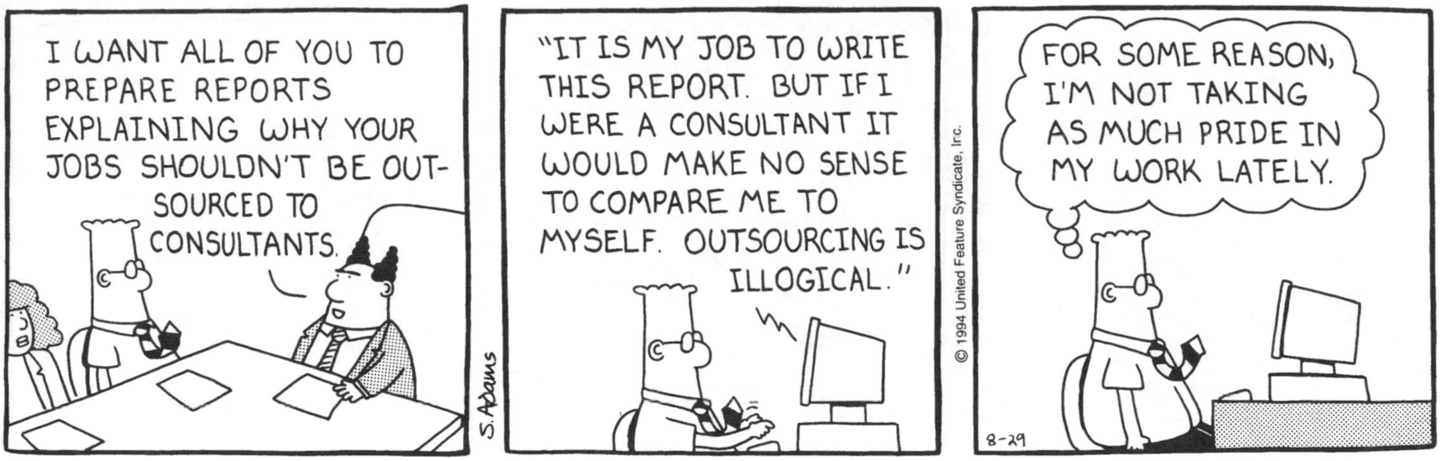
I WANT ALL OF YOU TO PREPARE REPORTS EXPLAINING WHY YOUR JOBS SHOULDN'T BE OUT-SOURCED TO CONSULTANTS.
"IT IS MY JOB TO WRITE THIS REPORT. BUT IF I WERE A CONSULTANT IT WOULD MAKE NO SENSE TO COMPARE ME TO MYSELF. OUTSOURCING IS ILLOGICAL."
FOR SOME REASON, I'M NOT TAKING AS MUCH PRIDE IN MY WORK LATELY.
S. Adams
© 1994 United Feature Syndicate, Inc.
8-29

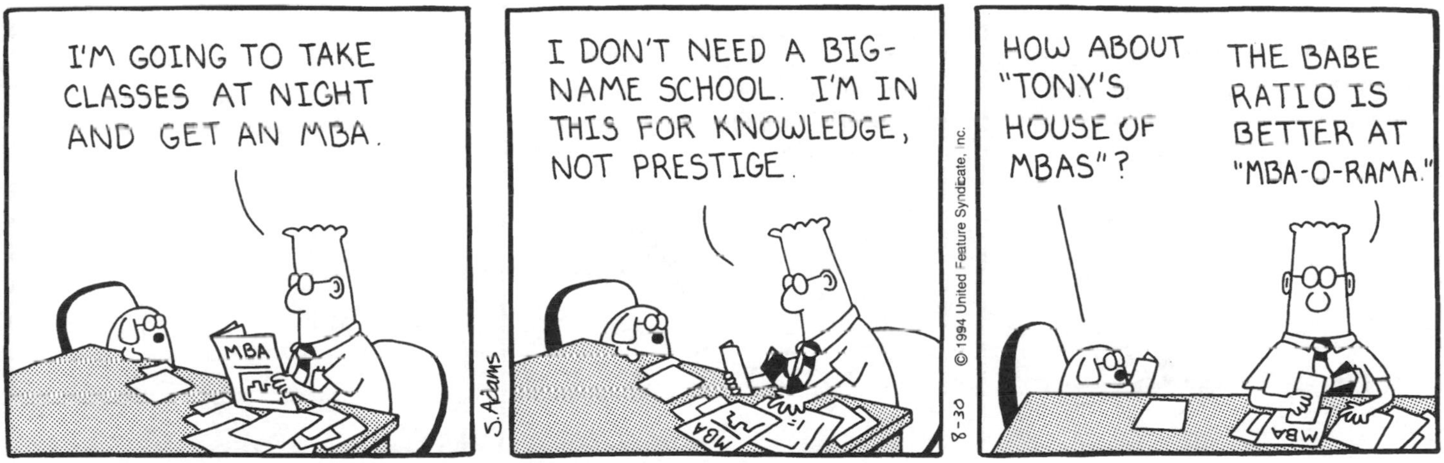
I'M GOING TO TAKE CLASSES AT NIGHT AND GET AN MBA.
MBA
I DON'T NEED A BIG-NAME SCHOOL. I'M IN THIS FOR KNOWLEDGE, NOT PRESTIGE.
HOW ABOUT "TONY'S HOUSE OF MBAS"?
THE BABE RATIO IS BETTER AT "MBA-O-RAMA."
S. Adams
© 1994 United Feature Syndicate, Inc.
8-30

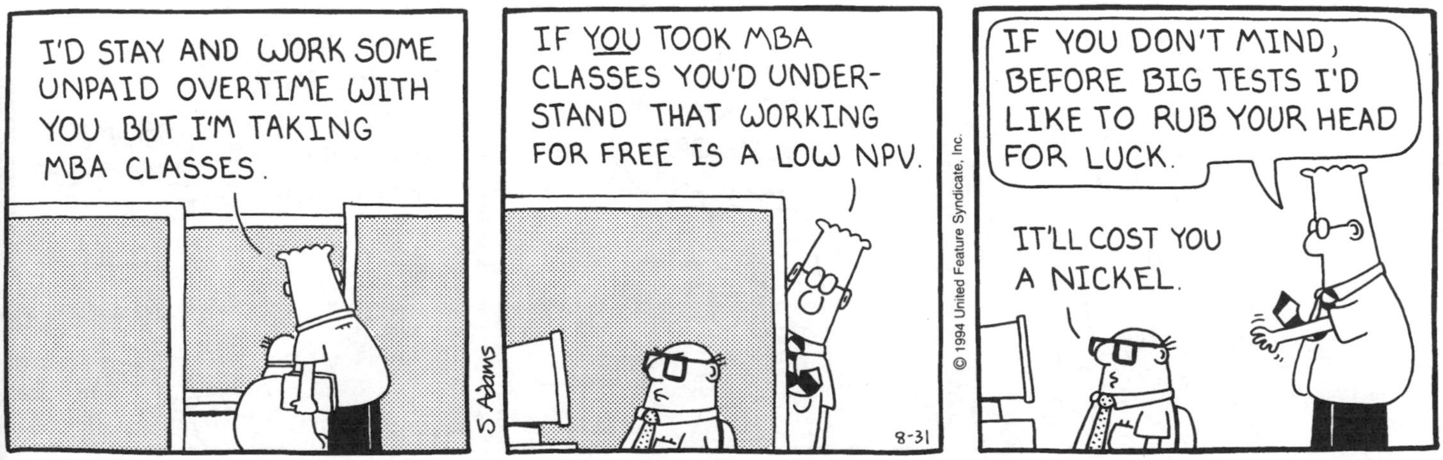
I'D STAY AND WORK SOME UNPAID OVERTIME WITH YOU BUT I'M TAKING MBA CLASSES.
IF YOU TOOK MBA CLASSES YOU'D UNDER-STAND THAT WORKING FOR FREE IS A LOW NPV.
IF YOU DON'T MIND, BEFORE BIG TESTS I'D LIKE TO RUB YOUR HEAD FOR LUCK.
IT'LL COST YOU A NICKEL.
S. Adams
© 1994 United Feature Syndicate, Inc.
8-31

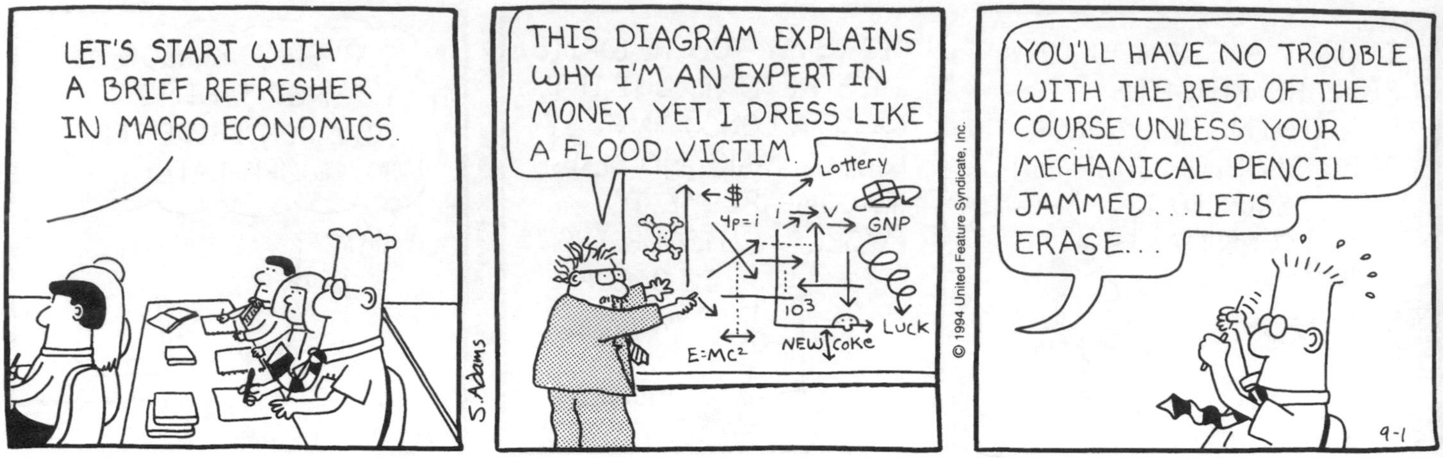
LET'S START WITH A BRIEF REFRESHER IN MACRO ECONOMICS.
S. Adams
THIS DIAGRAM EXPLAINS WHY I'M AN EXPERT IN MONEY YET I DRESS LIKE A FLOOD VICTIM.
Lottery
$
4p=i
i
V
GNP
10³
E=MC²
NEW COKE
LUCK
© 1994 United Feature Syndicate, Inc.
YOU'LL HAVE NO TROUBLE WITH THE REST OF THE COURSE UNLESS YOUR MECHANICAL PENCIL JAMMED...LET'S ERASE...
9-1

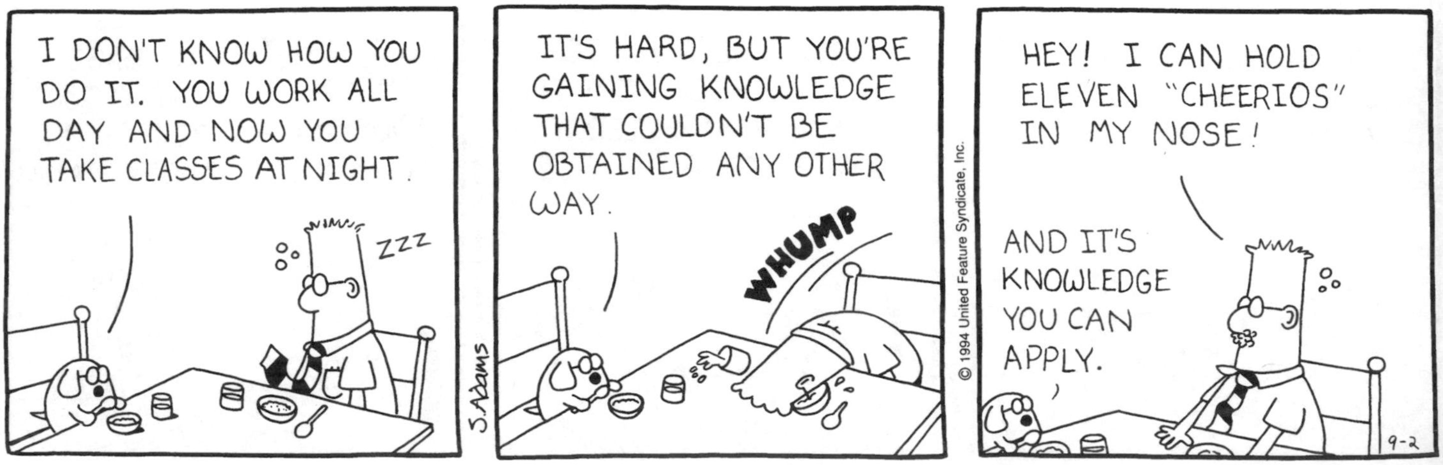
I DON'T KNOW HOW YOU DO IT. YOU WORK ALL DAY AND NOW YOU TAKE CLASSES AT NIGHT.
ZZZ
S. Adams
IT'S HARD, BUT YOU'RE GAINING KNOWLEDGE THAT COULDN'T BE OBTAINED ANY OTHER WAY.
WHUMP
© 1994 United Feature Syndicate, Inc.
HEY! I CAN HOLD ELEVEN "CHEERIOS" IN MY NOSE!
AND IT'S KNOWLEDGE YOU CAN APPLY.
9-2

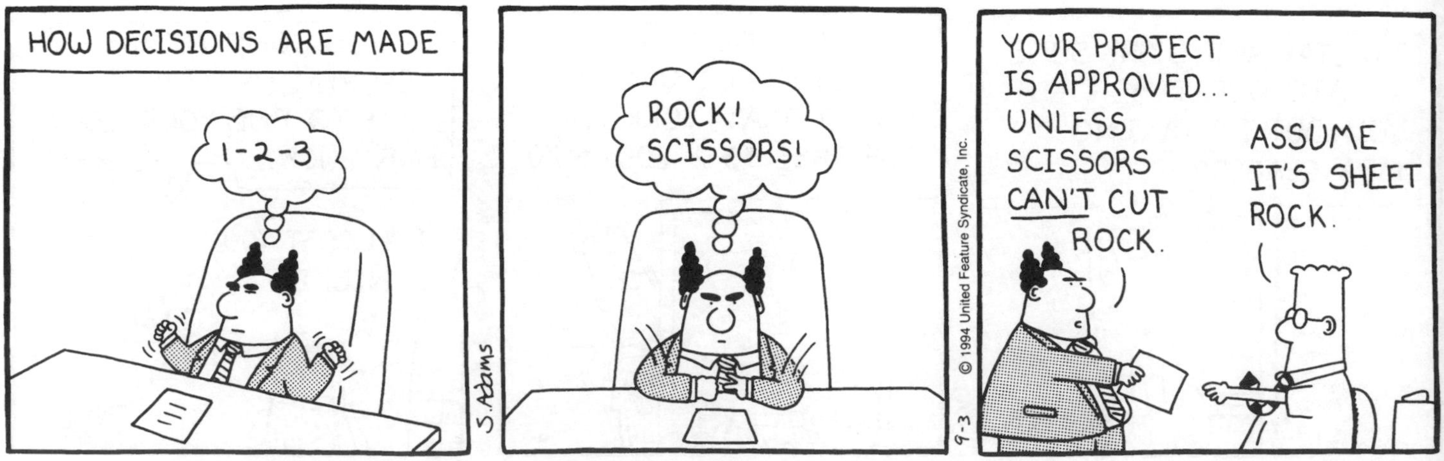
HOW DECISIONS ARE MADE
1-2-3
S. Adams
ROCK! SCISSORS!
9-3
© 1994 United Feature Syndicate, Inc.
YOUR PROJECT IS APPROVED... UNLESS SCISSORS CAN'T CUT ROCK.
ASSUME IT'S SHEET ROCK.

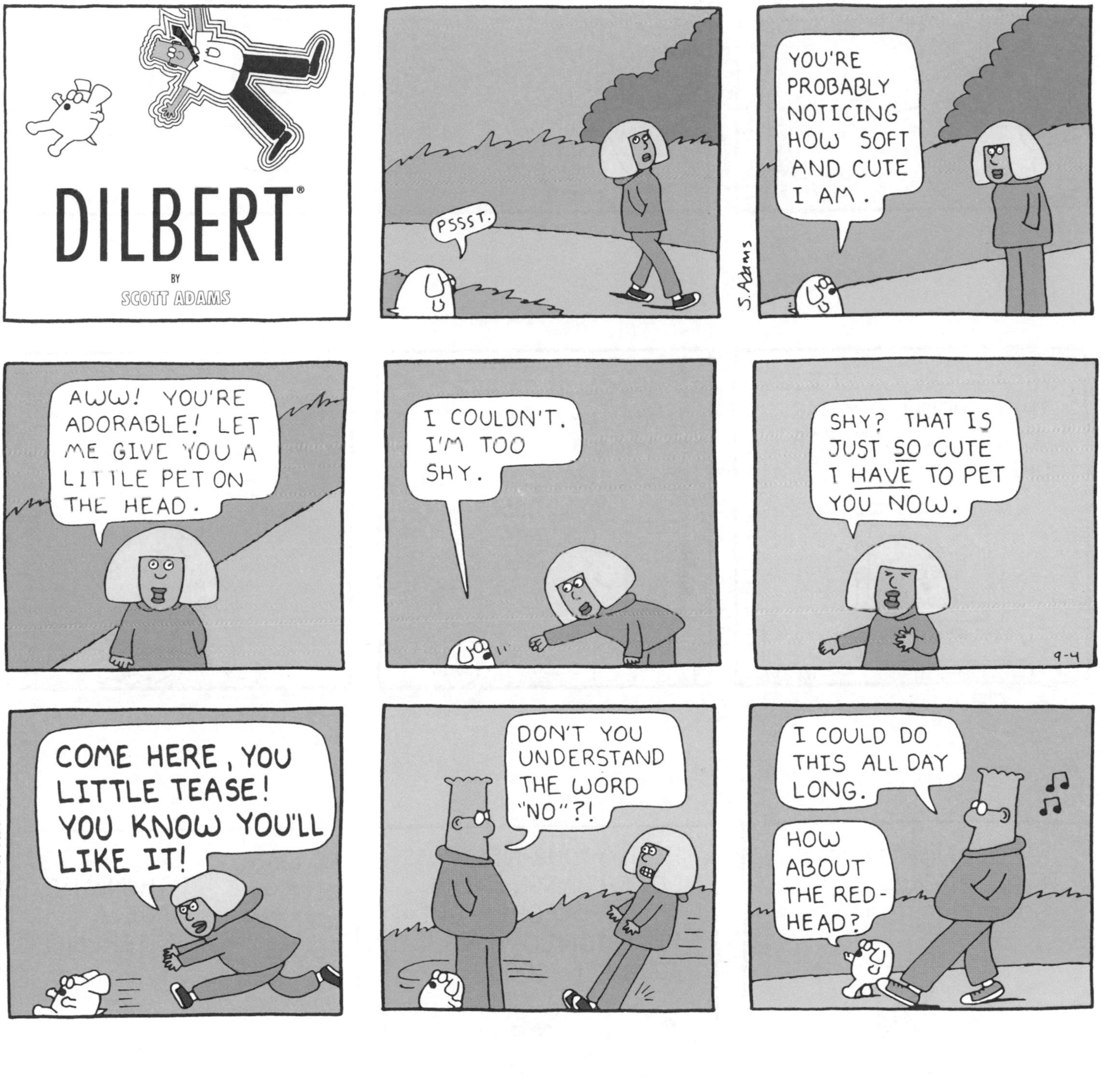
DILBERT®
BY
SCOTT ADAMS
PSSST.
S. Adams
YOU'RE PROBABLY NOTICING HOW SOFT AND CUTE I AM.
AWW! YOU'RE ADORABLE! LET ME GIVE YOU A LITTLE PET ON THE HEAD.
I COULDN'T. I'M TOO SHY.
SHY? THAT IS JUST SO CUTE I HAVE TO PET YOU NOW.
9-4
© 1994 United Feature Syndicate Inc
COME HERE, YOU LITTLE TEASE! YOU KNOW YOU'LL LIKE IT!
DON'T YOU UNDERSTAND THE WORD "NO"?!
I COULD DO THIS ALL DAY LONG.
HOW ABOUT THE RED-HEAD?

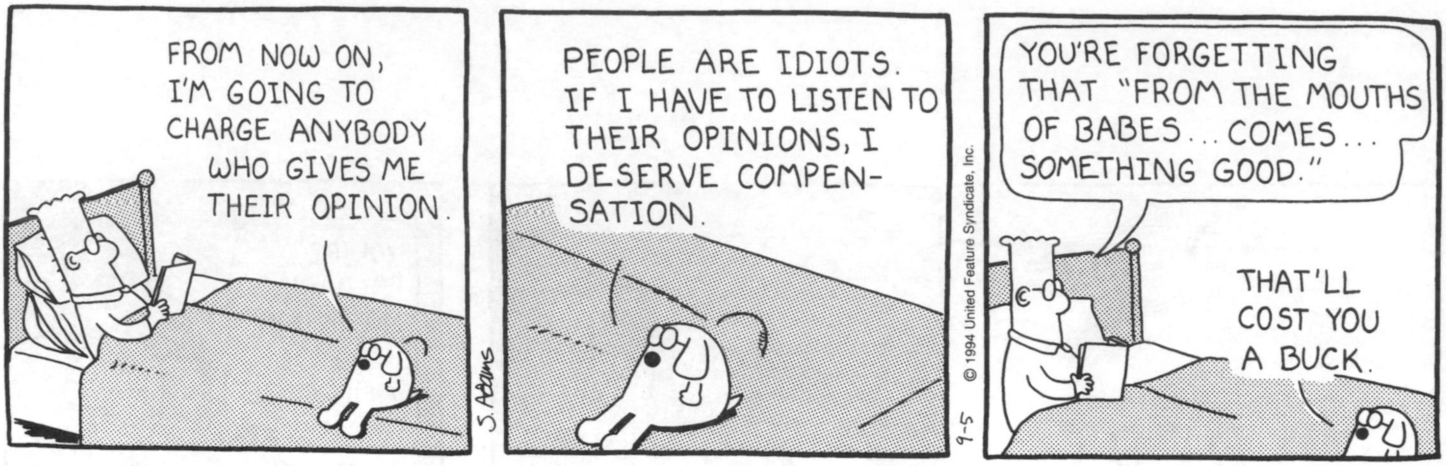
FROM NOW ON, I'M GOING TO CHARGE ANYBODY WHO GIVES ME THEIR OPINION.
PEOPLE ARE IDIOTS. IF I HAVE TO LISTEN TO THEIR OPINIONS, I DESERVE COMPEN-SATION.
YOU'RE FORGETTING THAT "FROM THE MOUTHS OF BABES... COMES... SOMETHING GOOD."
THAT'LL COST YOU A BUCK.
S. ADAMS
9-5
© 1994 United Feature Syndicate, Inc.

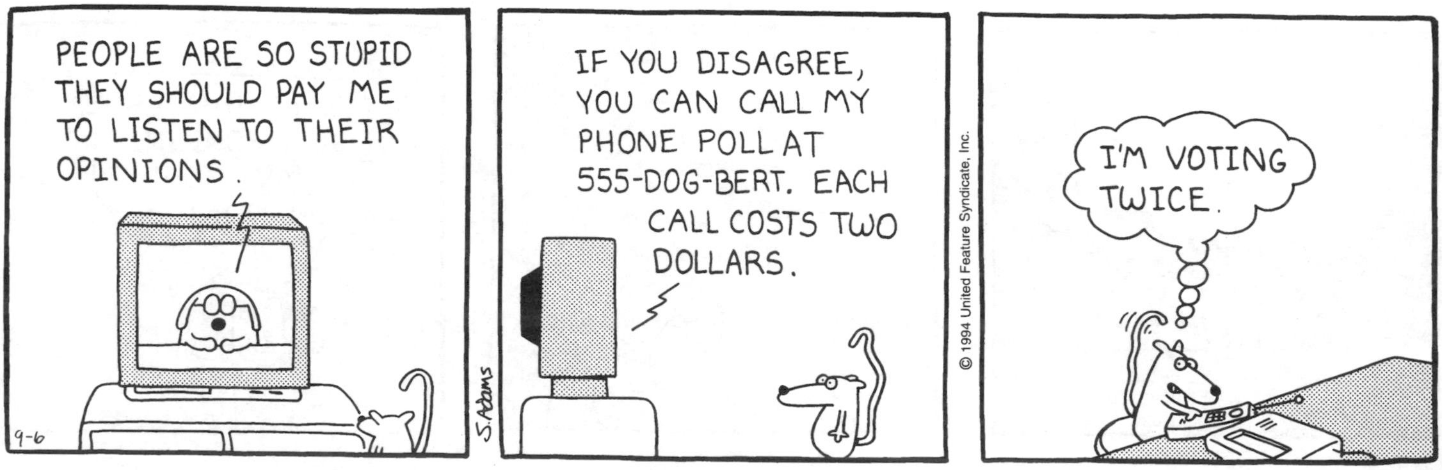
PEOPLE ARE SO STUPID THEY SHOULD PAY ME TO LISTEN TO THEIR OPINIONS.
9-6
S. ADAMS
IF YOU DISAGREE, YOU CAN CALL MY PHONE POLL AT 555-DOG-BERT. EACH CALL COSTS TWO DOLLARS.
© 1994 United Feature Syndicate, Inc.
I'M VOTING TWICE.

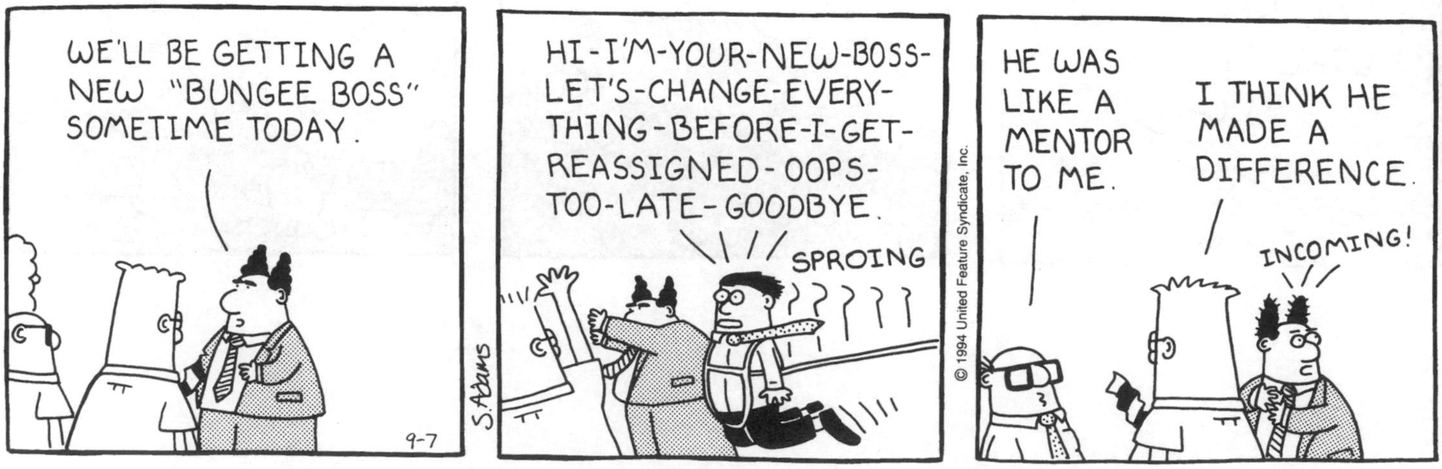
WE'LL BE GETTING A NEW "BUNGEE BOSS" SOMETIME TODAY.
9-7
S. ADAMS
HI-I'M-YOUR-NEW-BOSS-LET'S-CHANGE-EVERY-THING-BEFORE-I-GET-REASSIGNED-OOPS-TOO-LATE-GOODBYE.
SPROING
© 1994 United Feature Syndicate, Inc.
HE WAS LIKE A MENTOR TO ME.
I THINK HE MADE A DIFFERENCE.
INCOMING!

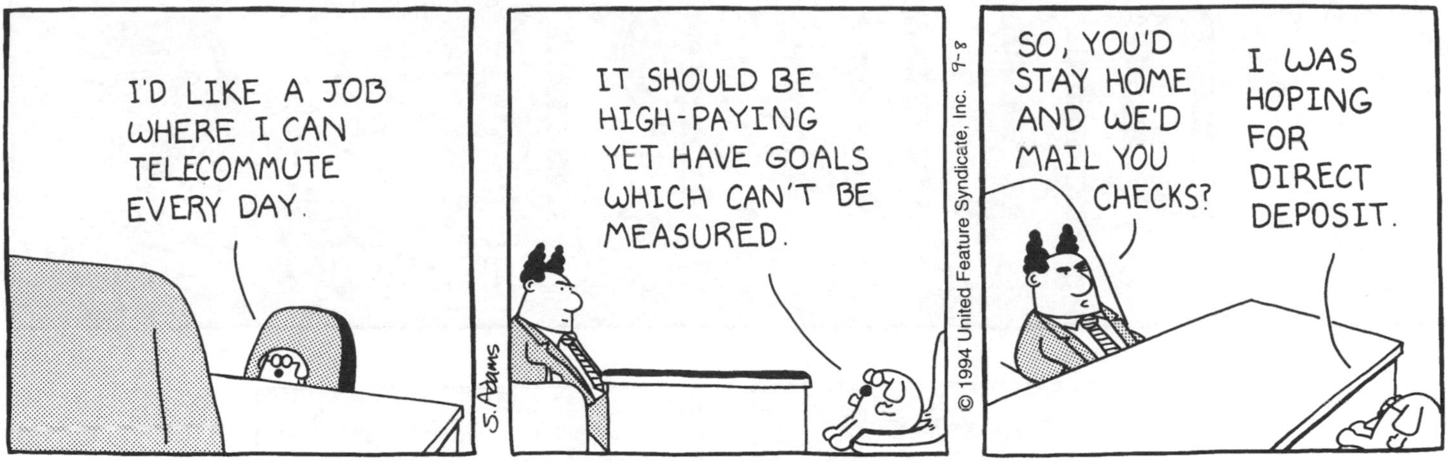

I'D LIKE A JOB WHERE I CAN TELECOMMUTE EVERY DAY.
IT SHOULD BE HIGH-PAYING YET HAVE GOALS WHICH CAN'T BE MEASURED.
SO, YOU'D STAY HOME AND WE'D MAIL YOU CHECKS?
I WAS HOPING FOR DIRECT DEPOSIT.
S. Adams
9-8
© 1994 United Feature Syndicate, Inc.

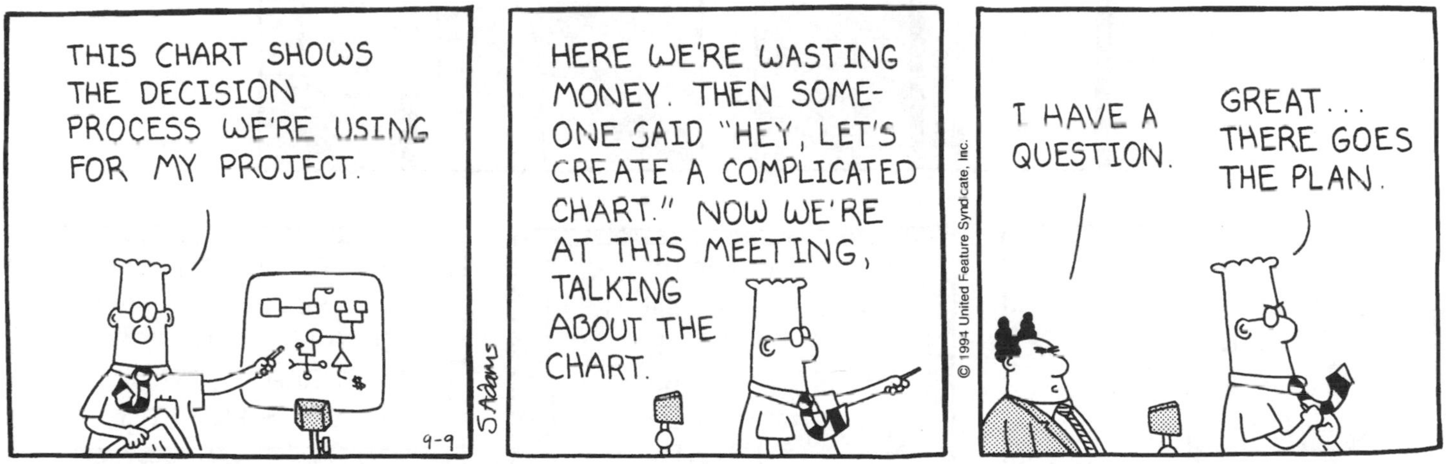

THIS CHART SHOWS THE DECISION PROCESS WE'RE USING FOR MY PROJECT.
9-9
S. Adams
HERE WE'RE WASTING MONEY. THEN SOMEONE SAID "HEY, LET'S CREATE A COMPLICATED CHART." NOW WE'RE AT THIS MEETING, TALKING ABOUT THE CHART.
I HAVE A QUESTION.
GREAT... THERE GOES THE PLAN.
© 1994 United Feature Syndicate, Inc.

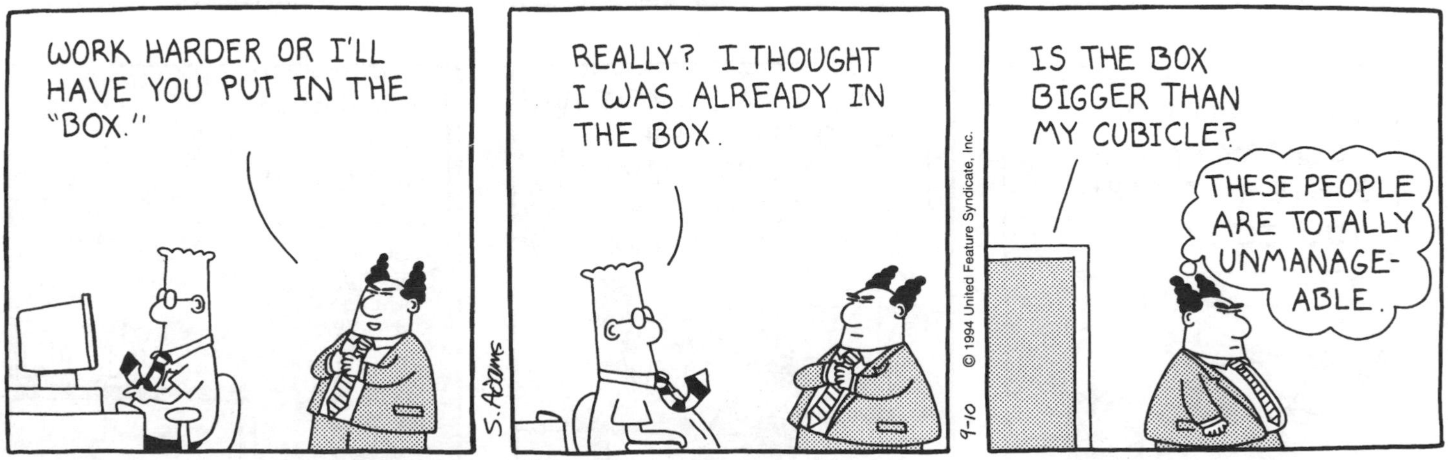

WORK HARDER OR I'LL HAVE YOU PUT IN THE "BOX."
S. Adams
REALLY? I THOUGHT I WAS ALREADY IN THE BOX.
IS THE BOX BIGGER THAN MY CUBICLE?
THESE PEOPLE ARE TOTALLY UNMANAGEABLE.
9-10
© 1994 United Feature Syndicate, Inc.

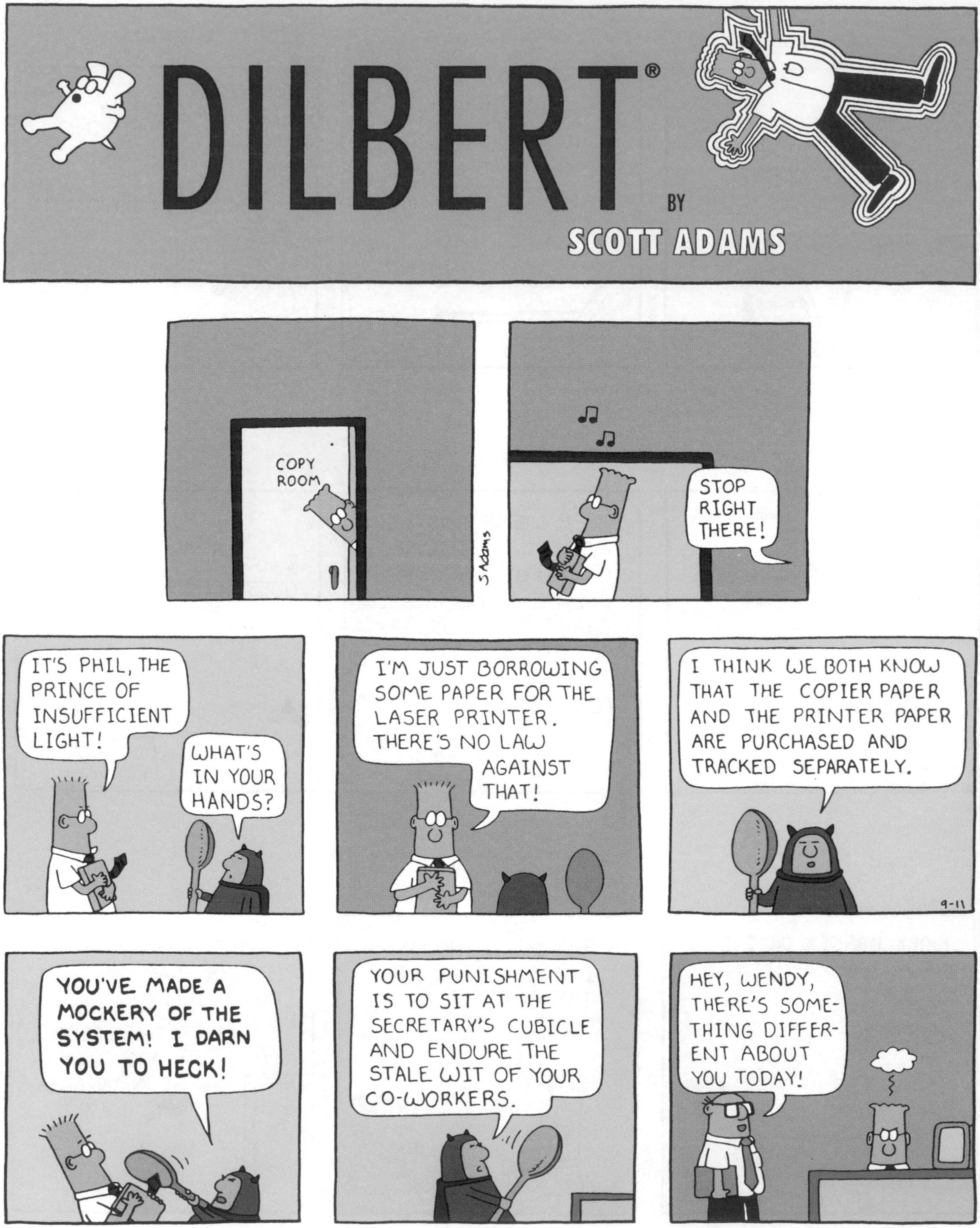
DILBERT®
BY
SCOTT ADAMS
COPY ROOM
S. Adams
STOP RIGHT THERE!
IT'S PHIL, THE PRINCE OF INSUFFICIENT LIGHT!
WHAT'S IN YOUR HANDS?
I'M JUST BORROWING SOME PAPER FOR THE LASER PRINTER. THERE'S NO LAW AGAINST THAT!
I THINK WE BOTH KNOW THAT THE COPIER PAPER AND THE PRINTER PAPER ARE PURCHASED AND TRACKED SEPARATELY.
© 1994 United Feature Syndicate, Inc.
9-11
YOU'VE MADE A MOCKERY OF THE SYSTEM! I DARN YOU TO HECK!
YOUR PUNISHMENT IS TO SIT AT THE SECRETARY'S CUBICLE AND ENDURE THE STALE WIT OF YOUR CO-WORKERS.
HEY, WENDY, THERE'S SOMETHING DIFFERENT ABOUT YOU TODAY!

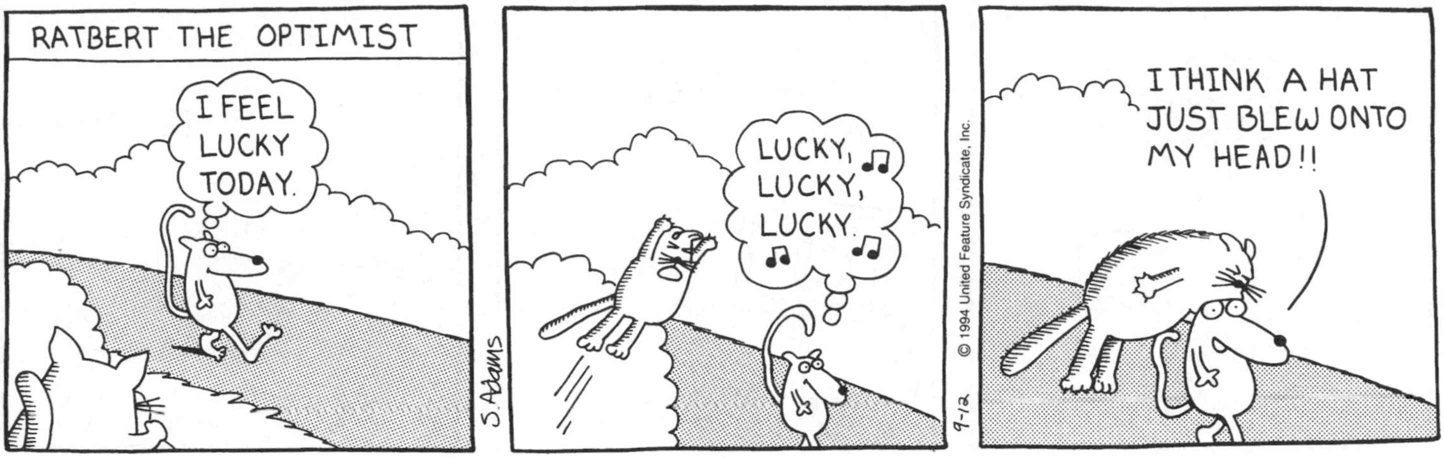
RATBERT THE OPTIMIST
I FEEL LUCKY TODAY.
LUCKY, LUCKY, LUCKY.
I THINK A HAT JUST BLEW ONTO MY HEAD!!
S. Adams
9-12
© 1994 United Feature Syndicate, Inc.

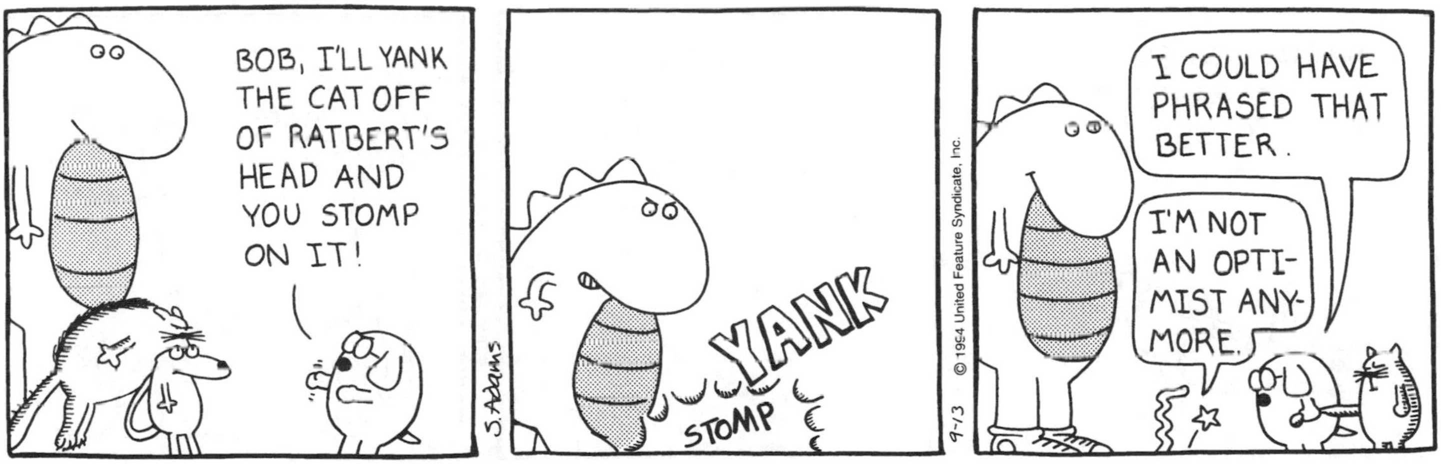
BOB, I'LL YANK THE CAT OFF OF RATBERT'S HEAD AND YOU STOMP ON IT!
YANK
STOMP
I COULD HAVE PHRASED THAT BETTER.
I'M NOT AN OPTI- MIST ANY- MORE.
S. Adams
9-13
© 1954 United Feature Syndicate, Inc.

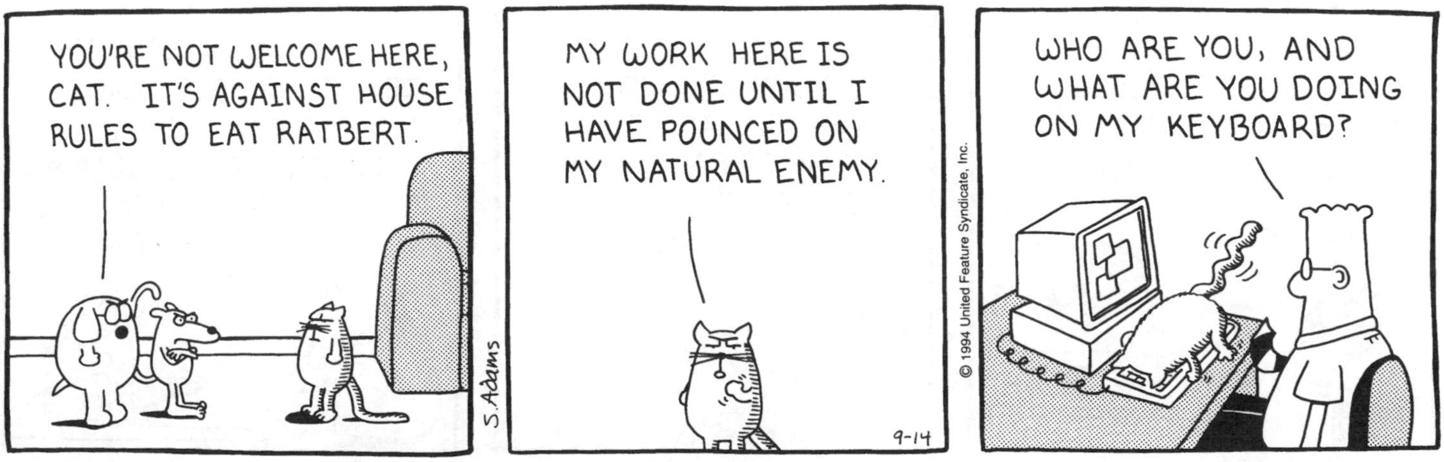
YOU'RE NOT WELCOME HERE, CAT. IT'S AGAINST HOUSE RULES TO EAT RATBERT.
MY WORK HERE IS NOT DONE UNTIL I HAVE POUNCED ON MY NATURAL ENEMY.
WHO ARE YOU, AND WHAT ARE YOU DOING ON MY KEYBOARD?
S. Adams
9-14
© 1994 United Feature Syndicate, Inc.

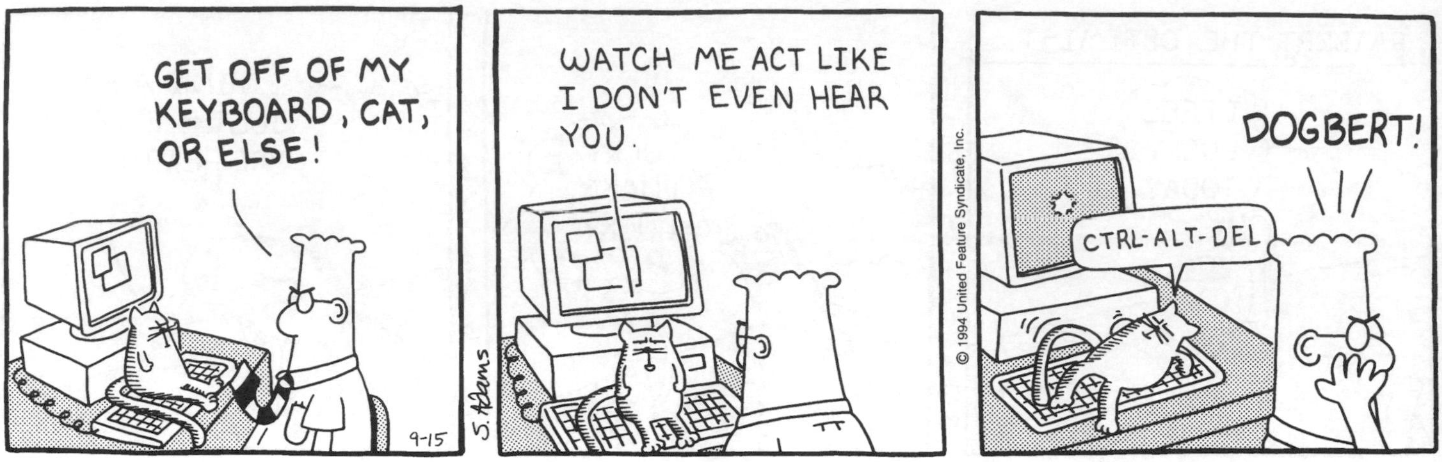
GET OFF OF MY KEYBOARD, CAT, OR ELSE!
9-15
WATCH ME ACT LIKE I DON'T EVEN HEAR YOU.
S. Adams
© 1994 United Feature Syndicate, Inc.
CTRL-ALT-DEL
DOGBERT!

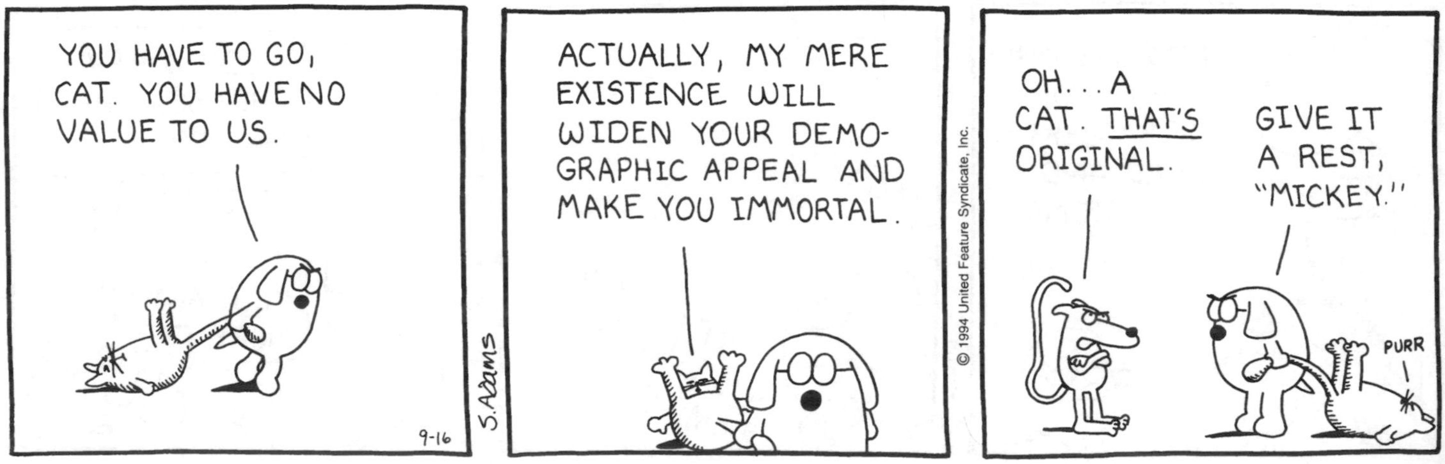
YOU HAVE TO GO, CAT. YOU HAVE NO VALUE TO US.
9-16
ACTUALLY, MY MERE EXISTENCE WILL WIDEN YOUR DEMO-GRAPHIC APPEAL AND MAKE YOU IMMORTAL.
S. Adams
© 1994 United Feature Syndicate, Inc.
OH... A CAT. THAT'S ORIGINAL.
GIVE IT A REST, "MICKEY."
PURR

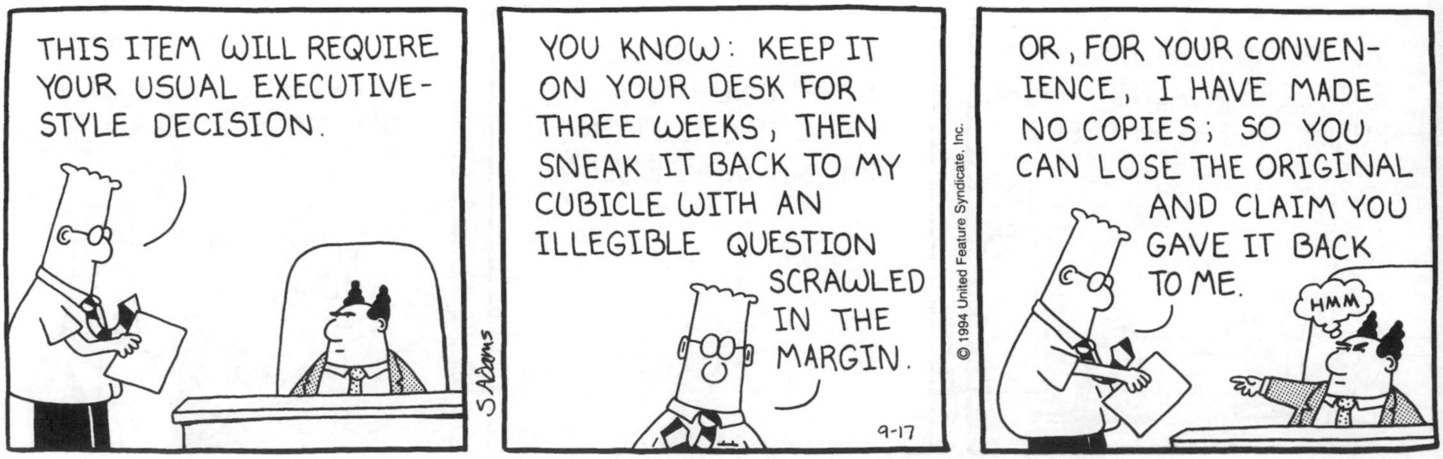
THIS ITEM WILL REQUIRE YOUR USUAL EXECUTIVE-STYLE DECISION.
S. Adams
YOU KNOW: KEEP IT ON YOUR DESK FOR THREE WEEKS, THEN SNEAK IT BACK TO MY CUBICLE WITH AN ILLEGIBLE QUESTION SCRAWLED IN THE MARGIN.
9-17
© 1994 United Feature Syndicate, Inc.
OR, FOR YOUR CONVEN-IENCE, I HAVE MADE NO COPIES; SO YOU CAN LOSE THE ORIGINAL AND CLAIM YOU GAVE IT BACK TO ME.
HMM

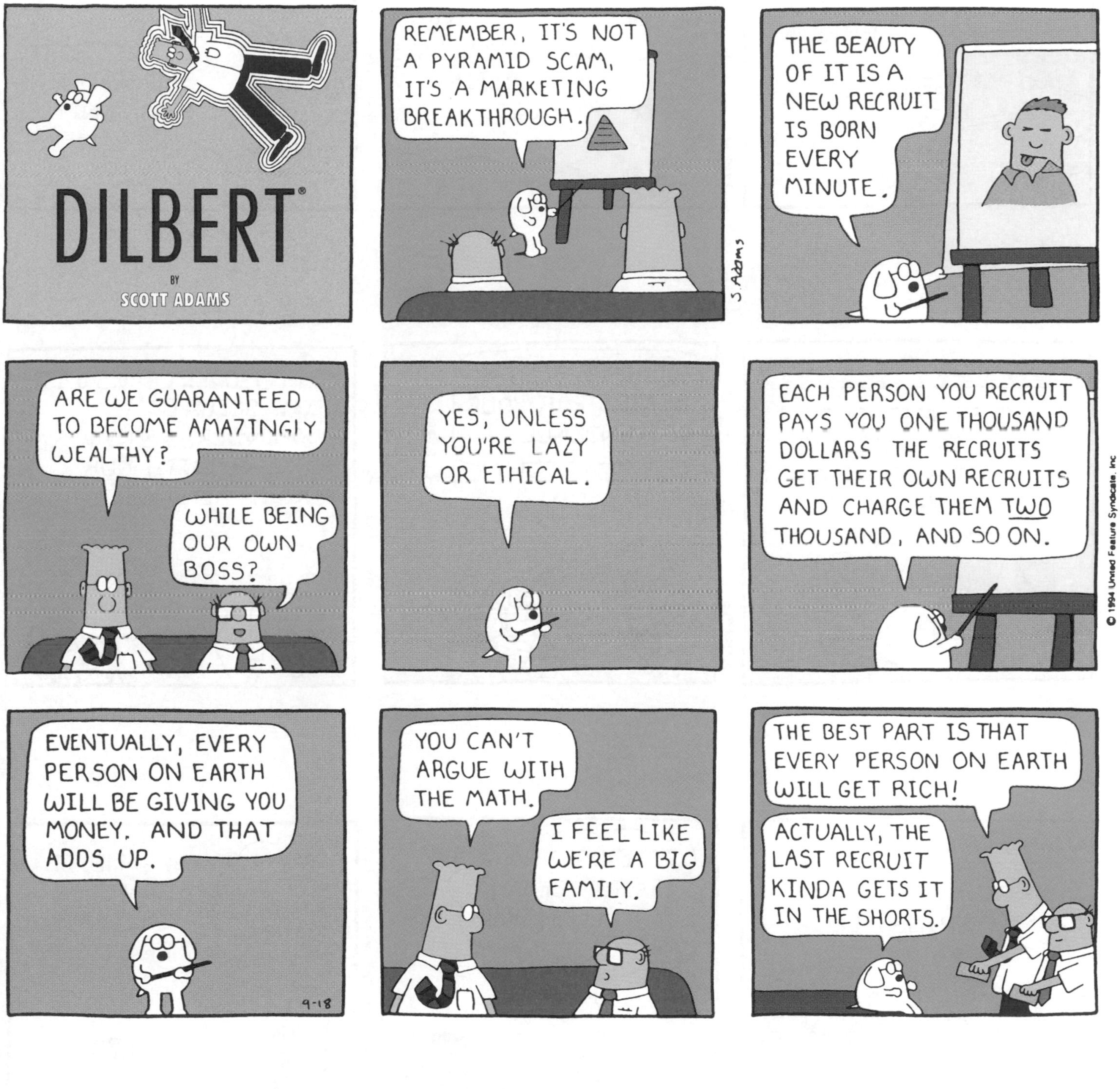
DILBERT®
BY
SCOTT ADAMS
REMEMBER, IT'S NOT A PYRAMID SCAM, IT'S A MARKETING BREAKTHROUGH.
S. Adams
THE BEAUTY OF IT IS A NEW RECRUIT IS BORN EVERY MINUTE.
ARE WE GUARANTEED TO BECOME AMAZINGLY WEALTHY?
WHILE BEING OUR OWN BOSS?
YES, UNLESS YOU'RE LAZY OR ETHICAL.
EACH PERSON YOU RECRUIT PAYS YOU ONE THOUSAND DOLLARS. THE RECRUITS GET THEIR OWN RECRUITS AND CHARGE THEM TWO THOUSAND, AND SO ON.
© 1994 United Feature Syndicate, Inc.
EVENTUALLY, EVERY PERSON ON EARTH WILL BE GIVING YOU MONEY. AND THAT ADDS UP.
9-18
YOU CAN'T ARGUE WITH THE MATH.
I FEEL LIKE WE'RE A BIG FAMILY.
THE BEST PART IS THAT EVERY PERSON ON EARTH WILL GET RICH!
ACTUALLY, THE LAST RECRUIT KINDA GETS IT IN THE SHORTS.

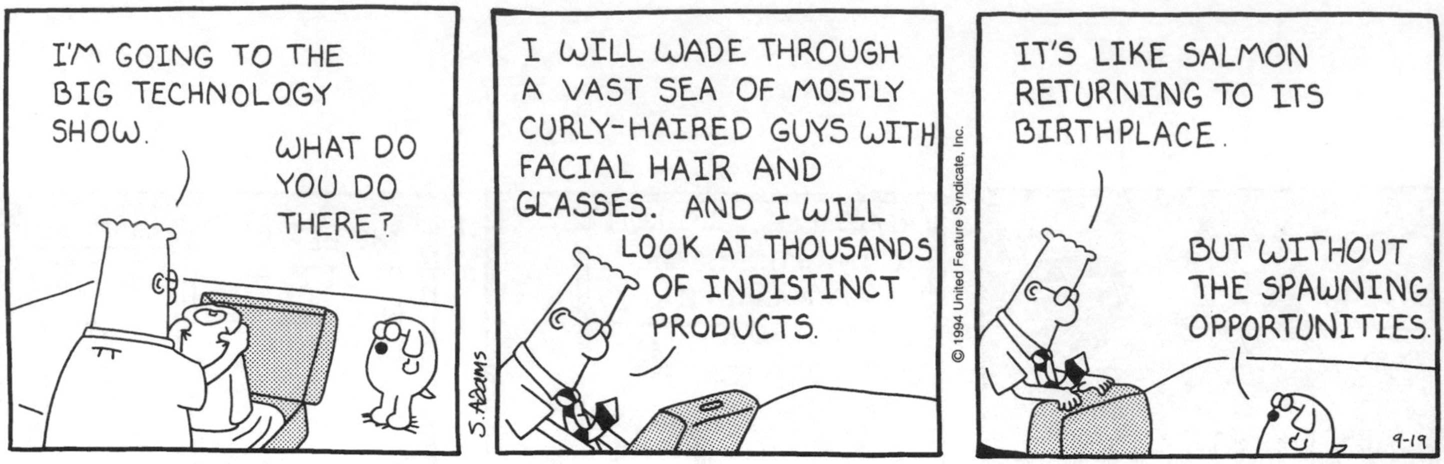
I'M GOING TO THE BIG TECHNOLOGY SHOW.
WHAT DO YOU DO THERE?
S. Adams
I WILL WADE THROUGH A VAST SEA OF MOSTLY CURLY-HAIRED GUYS WITH FACIAL HAIR AND GLASSES. AND I WILL LOOK AT THOUSANDS OF INDISTINCT PRODUCTS.
© 1994 United Feature Syndicate, Inc.
IT'S LIKE SALMON RETURNING TO ITS BIRTHPLACE.
BUT WITHOUT THE SPAWNING OPPORTUNITIES.
9-19

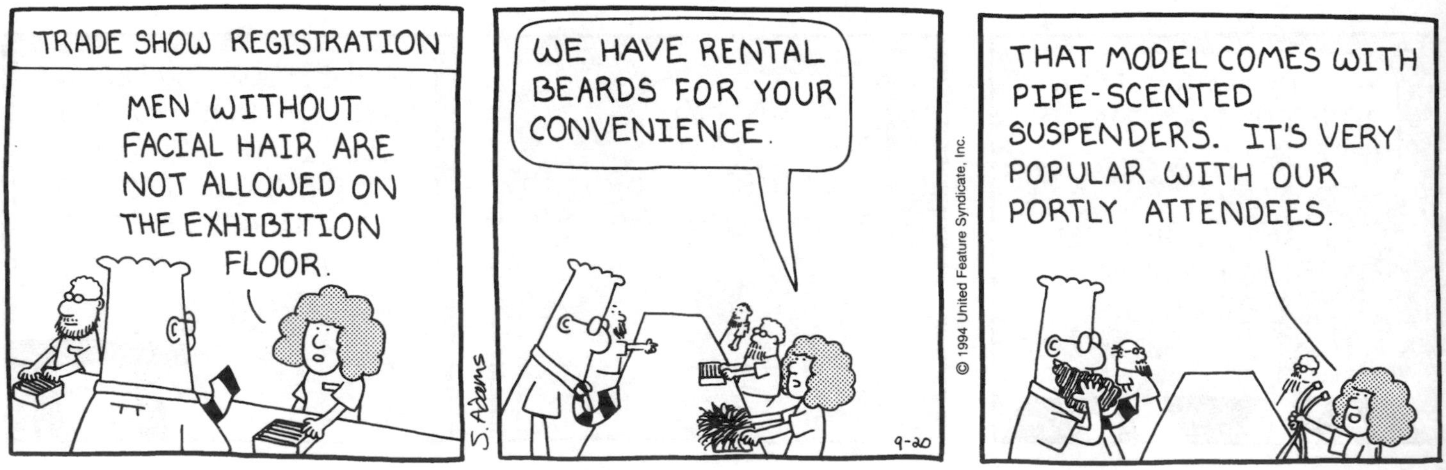
TRADE SHOW REGISTRATION
MEN WITHOUT FACIAL HAIR ARE NOT ALLOWED ON THE EXHIBITION FLOOR.
S. Adams
WE HAVE RENTAL BEARDS FOR YOUR CONVENIENCE.
9-20
© 1994 United Feature Syndicate, Inc.
THAT MODEL COMES WITH PIPE-SCENTED SUSPENDERS. IT'S VERY POPULAR WITH OUR PORTLY ATTENDEES.

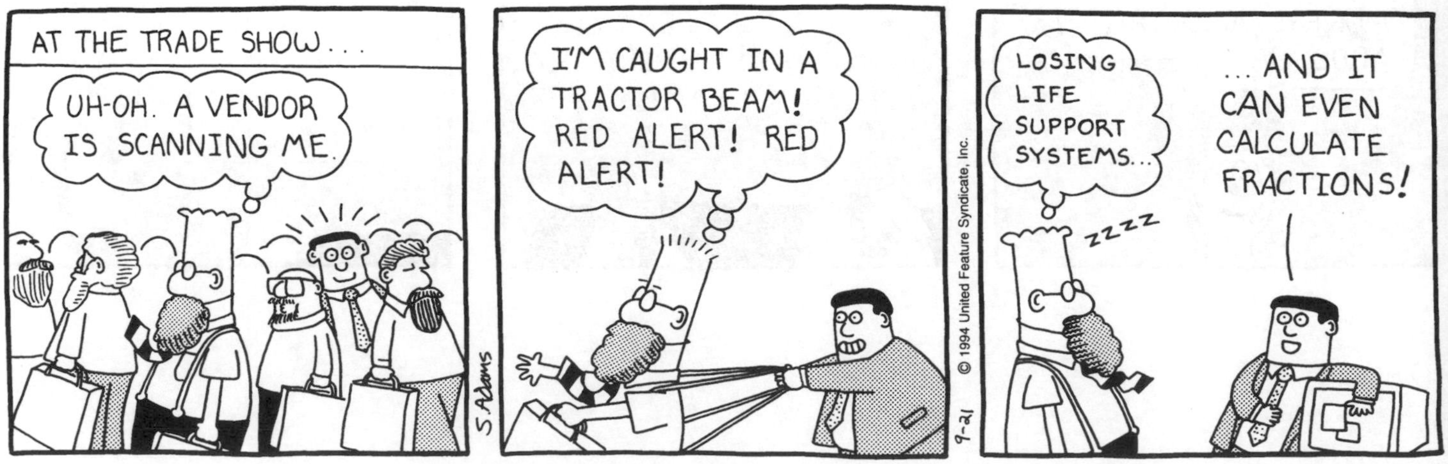
AT THE TRADE SHOW...
UH-OH. A VENDOR IS SCANNING ME.
S. Adams
I'M CAUGHT IN A TRACTOR BEAM! RED ALERT! RED ALERT!
9-21
© 1994 United Feature Syndicate, Inc.
LOSING LIFE SUPPORT SYSTEMS...
ZZZZ
... AND IT CAN EVEN CALCULATE FRACTIONS!

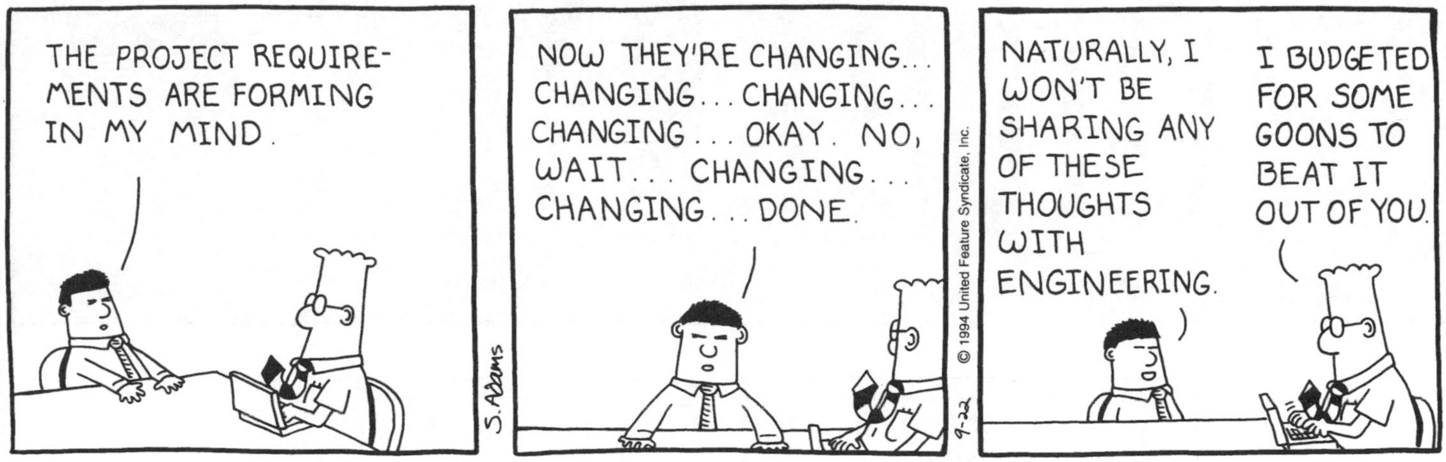
THE PROJECT REQUIREMENTS ARE FORMING IN MY MIND.
S. ADAMS
NOW THEY'RE CHANGING... CHANGING... CHANGING... CHANGING... OKAY. NO, WAIT... CHANGING... CHANGING... DONE.
9-22
© 1994 United Feature Syndicate, Inc.
NATURALLY, I WON'T BE SHARING ANY OF THESE THOUGHTS WITH ENGINEERING.
I BUDGETED FOR SOME GOONS TO BEAT IT OUT OF YOU.

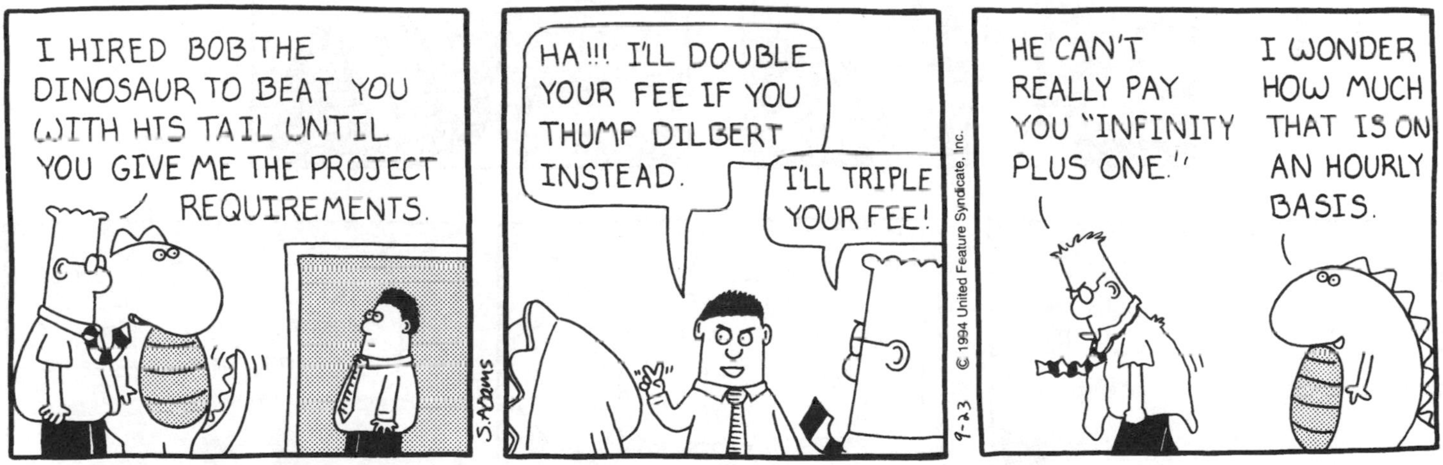
I HIRED BOB THE DINOSAUR TO BEAT YOU WITH HIS TAIL UNTIL YOU GIVE ME THE PROJECT REQUIREMENTS.
S. ADAMS
HA!!! I'LL DOUBLE YOUR FEE IF YOU THUMP DILBERT INSTEAD.
I'LL TRIPLE YOUR FEE!
9-23
© 1994 United Feature Syndicate, Inc.
HE CAN'T REALLY PAY YOU "INFINITY PLUS ONE."
I WONDER HOW MUCH THAT IS ON AN HOURLY BASIS.

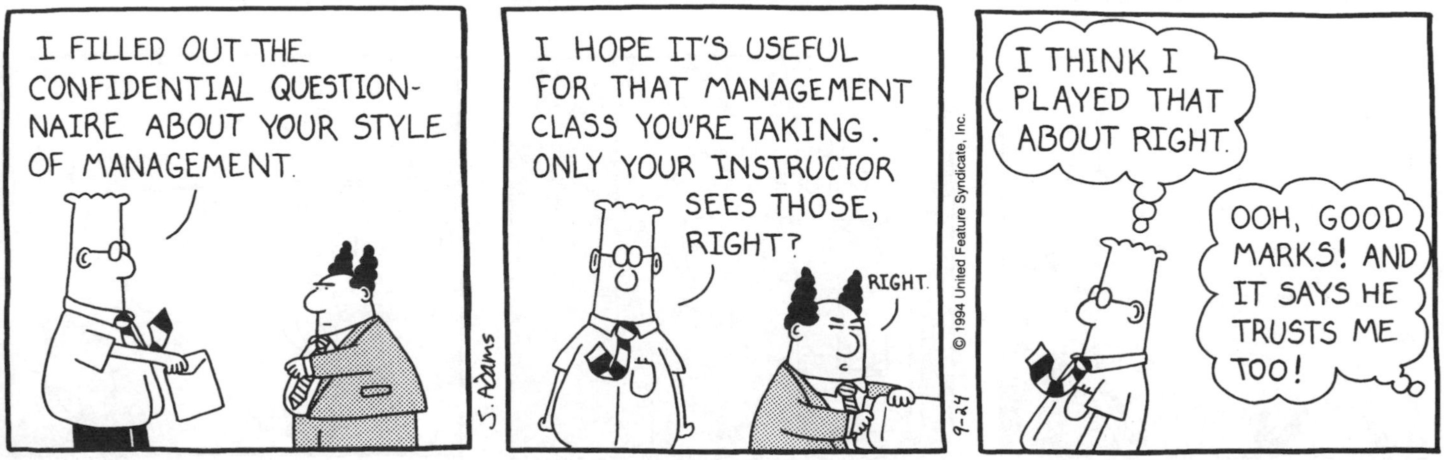
I FILLED OUT THE CONFIDENTIAL QUESTIONNAIRE ABOUT YOUR STYLE OF MANAGEMENT.
S. ADAMS
I HOPE IT'S USEFUL FOR THAT MANAGEMENT CLASS YOU'RE TAKING. ONLY YOUR INSTRUCTOR SEES THOSE, RIGHT?
RIGHT.
9-24
© 1994 United Feature Syndicate, Inc.
I THINK I PLAYED THAT ABOUT RIGHT.
OOH, GOOD MARKS! AND IT SAYS HE TRUSTS ME TOO!

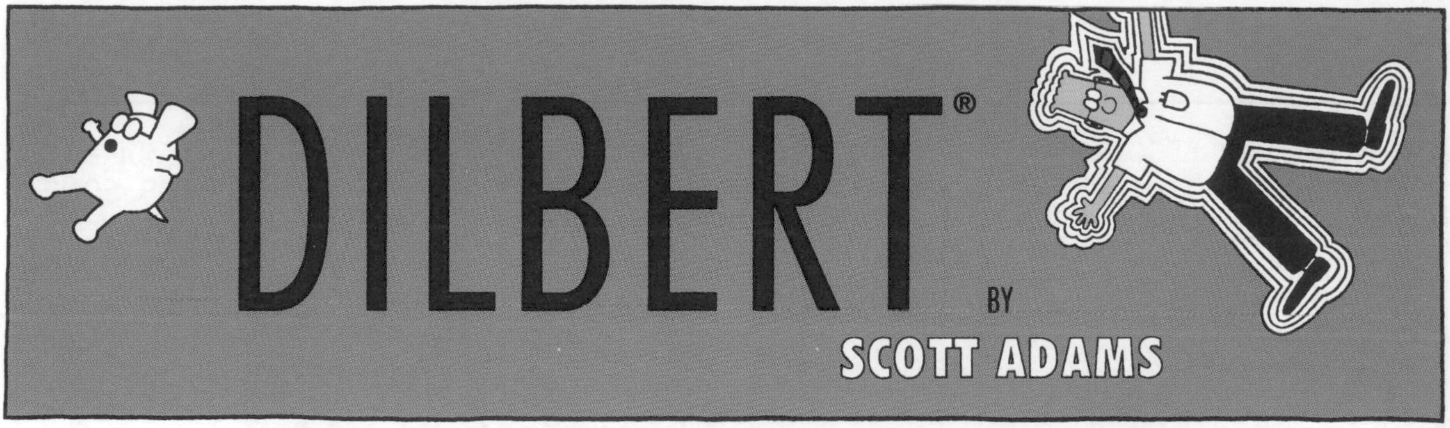
DILBERT®
BY
SCOTT ADAMS

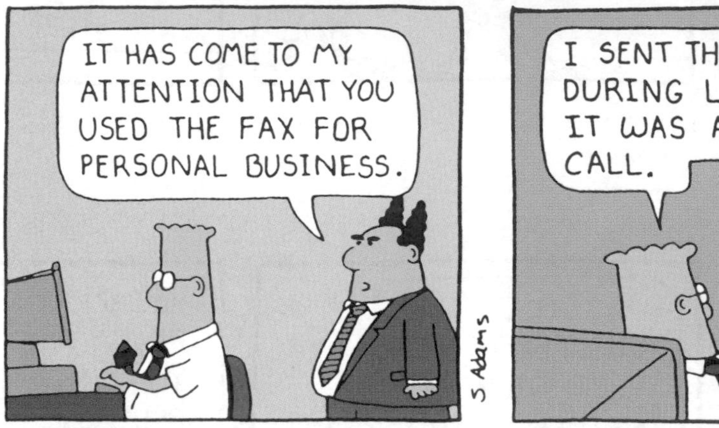
IT HAS COME TO MY ATTENTION THAT YOU USED THE FAX FOR PERSONAL BUSINESS.
S Adams
I SENT THE FAX DURING LUNCH. IT WAS A LOCAL CALL.

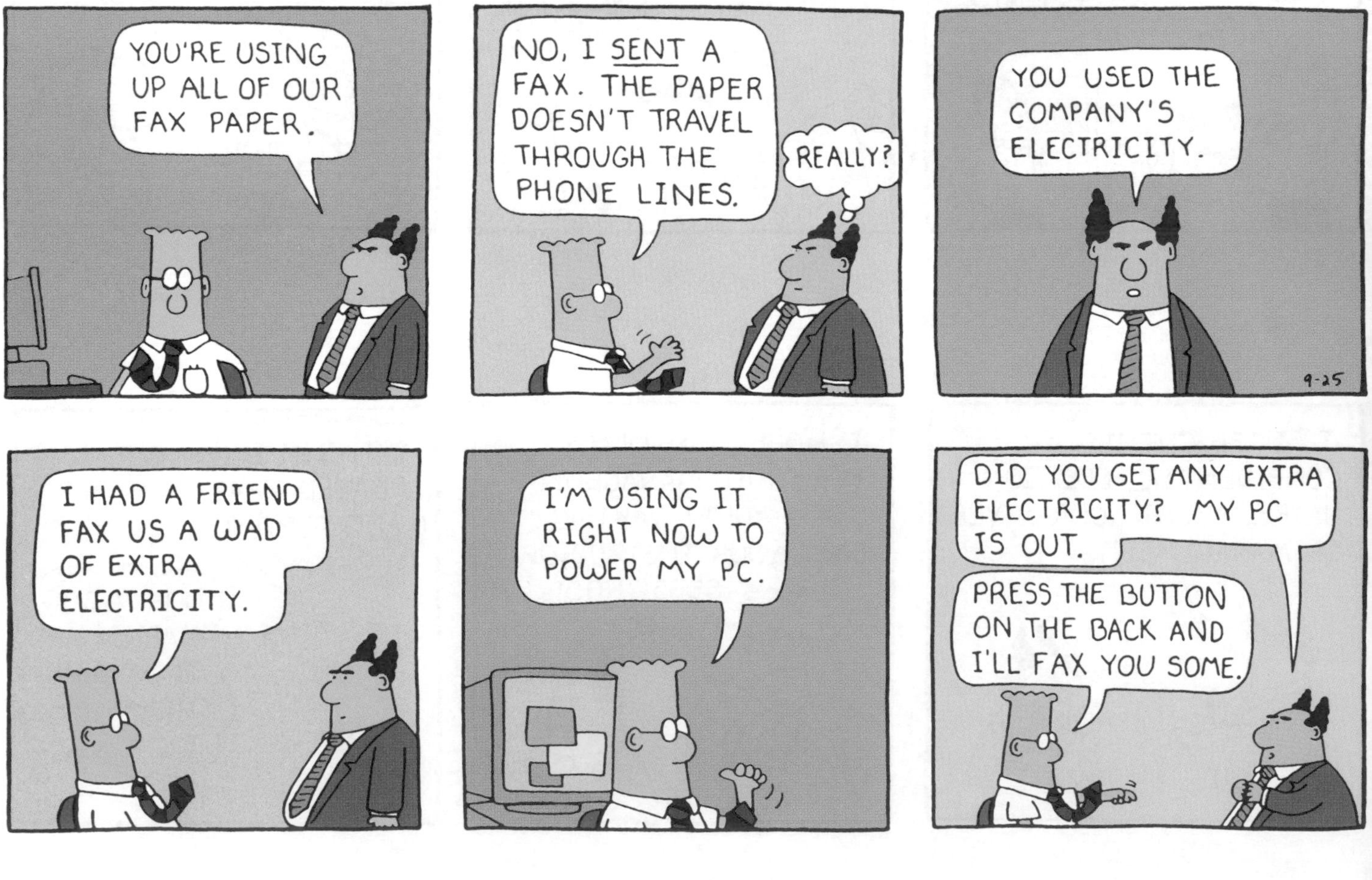
YOU'RE USING UP ALL OF OUR FAX PAPER.
NO, I SENT A FAX. THE PAPER DOESN'T TRAVEL THROUGH THE PHONE LINES.
REALLY?
YOU USED THE COMPANY'S ELECTRICITY.
9-25
I HAD A FRIEND FAX US A WAD OF EXTRA ELECTRICITY.
I'M USING IT RIGHT NOW TO POWER MY PC.
DID YOU GET ANY EXTRA ELECTRICITY? MY PC IS OUT.
PRESS THE BUTTON ON THE BACK AND I'LL FAX YOU SOME.

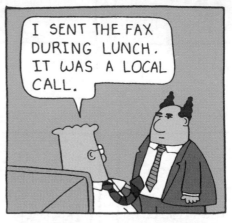

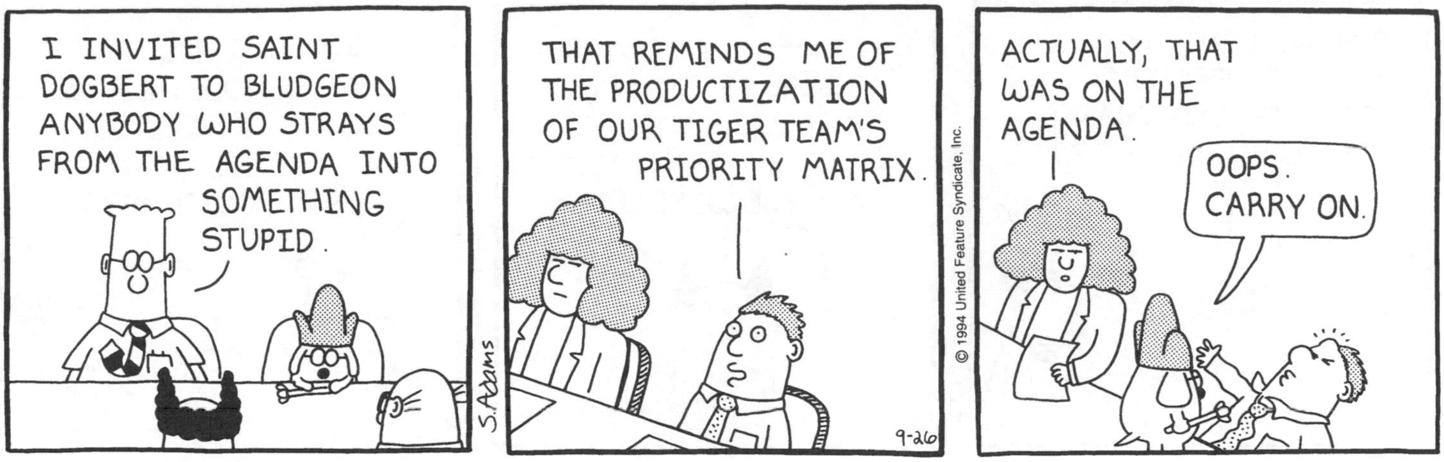
I INVITED SAINT DOGBERT TO BLUDGEON ANYBODY WHO STRAYS FROM THE AGENDA INTO SOMETHING STUPID.
S. Adams
THAT REMINDS ME OF THE PRODUCTIZATION OF OUR TIGER TEAM'S PRIORITY MATRIX.
9-26
© 1994 United Feature Syndicate, Inc.
ACTUALLY, THAT WAS ON THE AGENDA.
OOPS. CARRY ON.

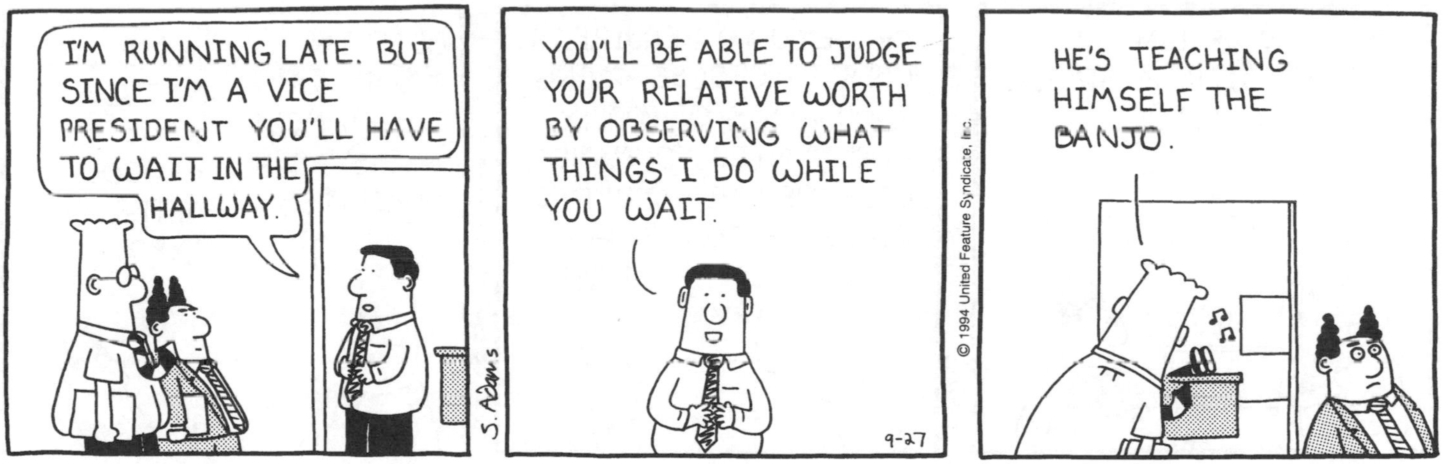
I'M RUNNING LATE. BUT SINCE I'M A VICE PRESIDENT YOU'LL HAVE TO WAIT IN THE HALLWAY.
S. Adams
YOU'LL BE ABLE TO JUDGE YOUR RELATIVE WORTH BY OBSERVING WHAT THINGS I DO WHILE YOU WAIT.
9-27
© 1994 United Feature Syndicate, Inc.
HE'S TEACHING HIMSELF THE BANJO.

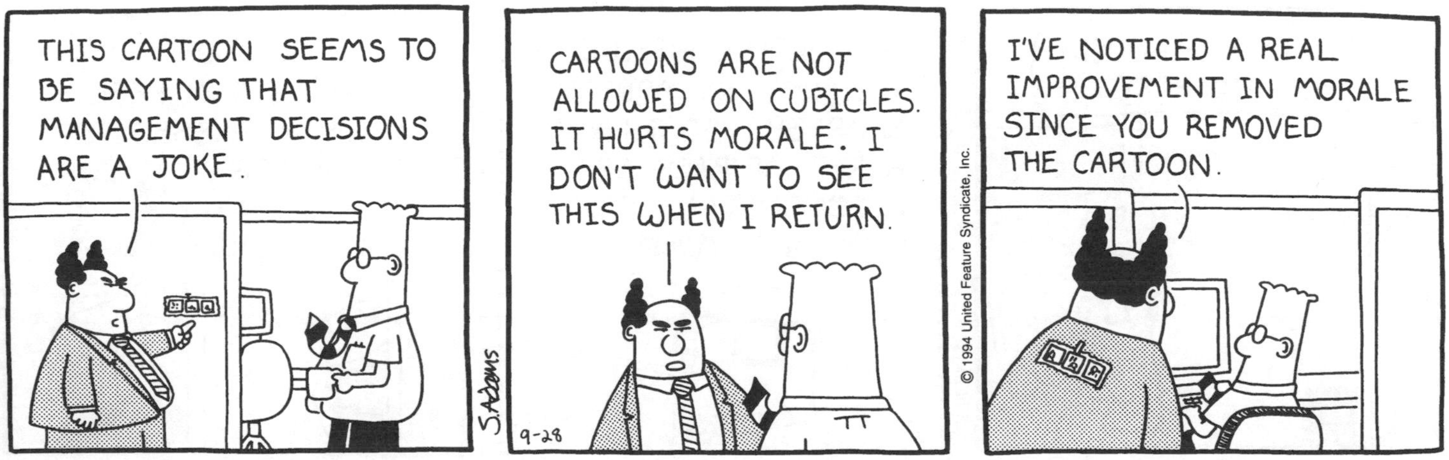
THIS CARTOON SEEMS TO BE SAYING THAT MANAGEMENT DECISIONS ARE A JOKE.
S. Adams
9-28
CARTOONS ARE NOT ALLOWED ON CUBICLES. IT HURTS MORALE. I DON'T WANT TO SEE THIS WHEN I RETURN.
© 1994 United Feature Syndicate, Inc.
I'VE NOTICED A REAL IMPROVEMENT IN MORALE SINCE YOU REMOVED THE CARTOON.

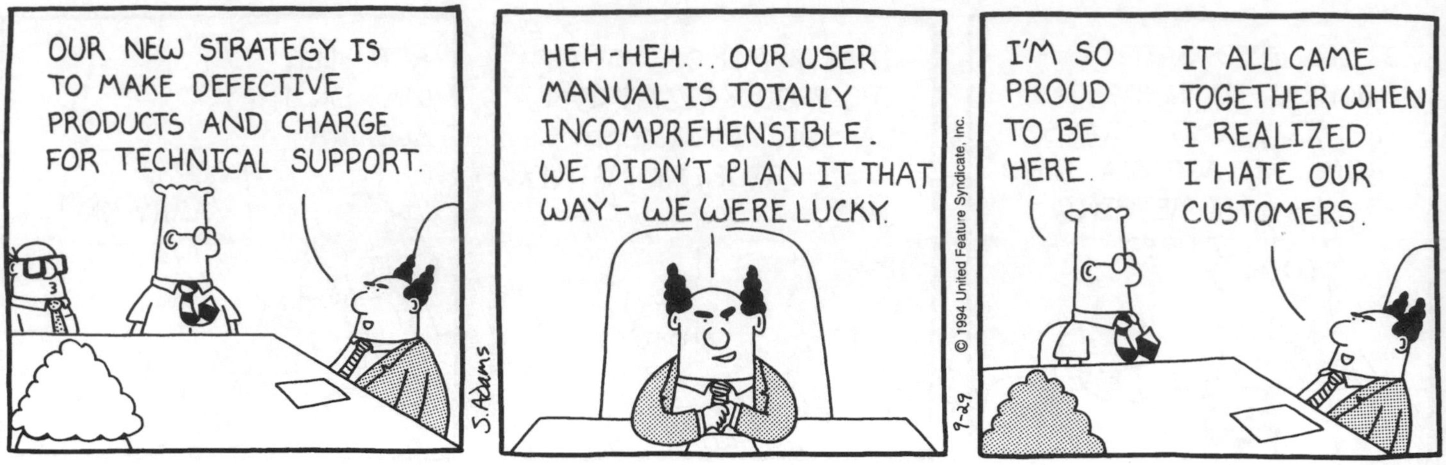
OUR NEW STRATEGY IS TO MAKE DEFECTIVE PRODUCTS AND CHARGE FOR TECHNICAL SUPPORT.
S. Adams
HEH-HEH... OUR USER MANUAL IS TOTALLY INCOMPREHENSIBLE. WE DIDN'T PLAN IT THAT WAY – WE WERE LUCKY.
9-29
© 1994 United Feature Syndicate, Inc.
I'M SO PROUD TO BE HERE.
IT ALL CAME TOGETHER WHEN I REALIZED I HATE OUR CUSTOMERS.

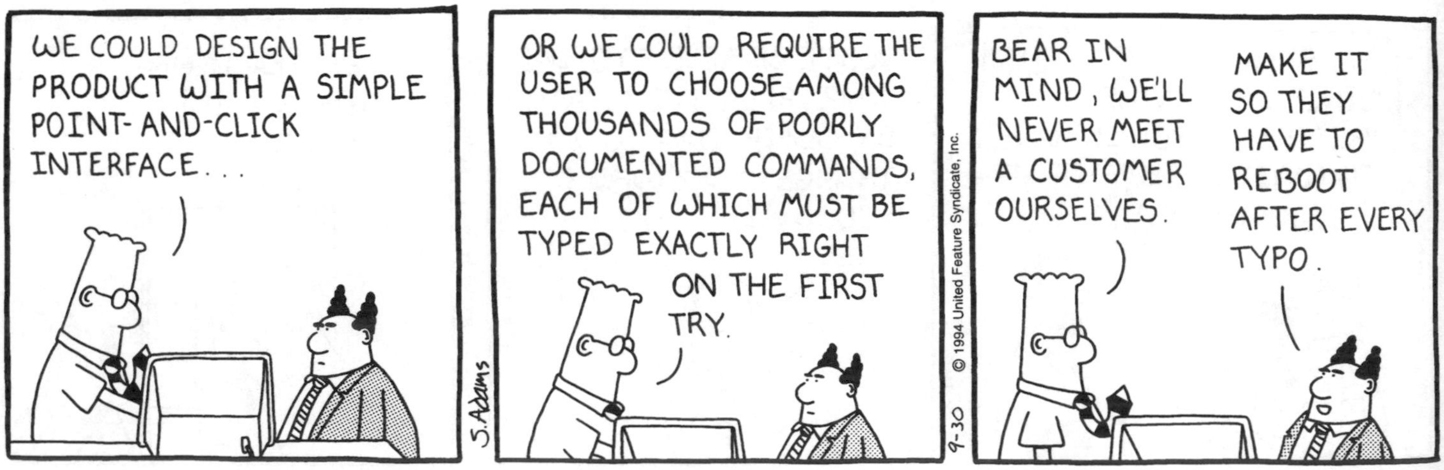
WE COULD DESIGN THE PRODUCT WITH A SIMPLE POINT-AND-CLICK INTERFACE...
S. Adams
OR WE COULD REQUIRE THE USER TO CHOOSE AMONG THOUSANDS OF POORLY DOCUMENTED COMMANDS, EACH OF WHICH MUST BE TYPED EXACTLY RIGHT
ON THE FIRST TRY.
9-30
© 1994 United Feature Syndicate, Inc.
BEAR IN MIND, WE'LL NEVER MEET A CUSTOMER OURSELVES.
MAKE IT SO THEY HAVE TO REBOOT AFTER EVERY TYPO.

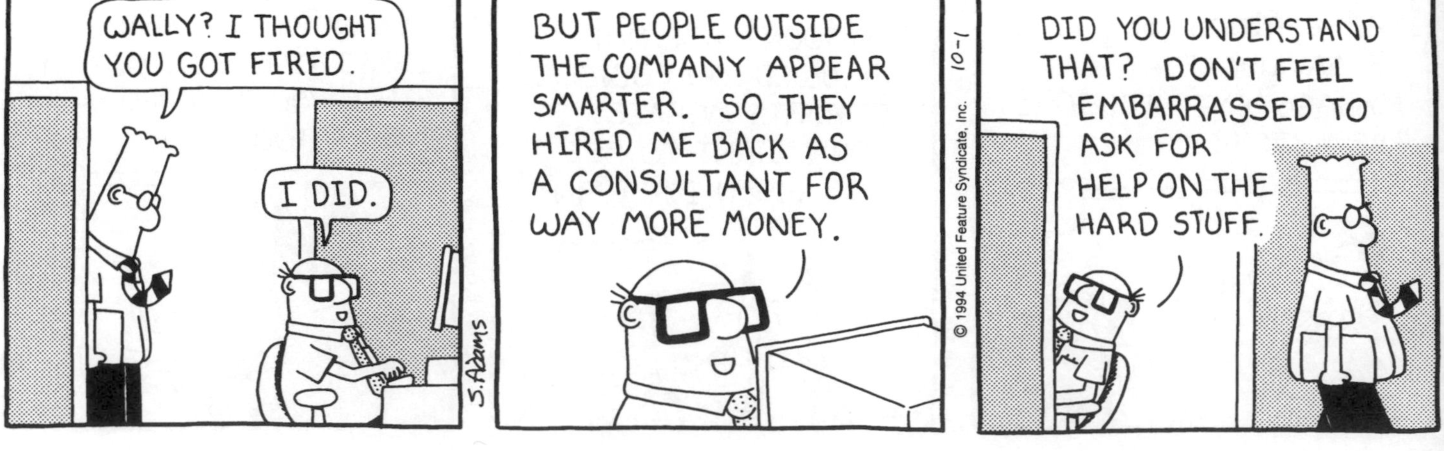
WALLY? I THOUGHT YOU GOT FIRED.
I DID.
S. Adams
BUT PEOPLE OUTSIDE THE COMPANY APPEAR SMARTER. SO THEY HIRED ME BACK AS A CONSULTANT FOR WAY MORE MONEY.
10-1
© 1994 United Feature Syndicate, Inc.
DID YOU UNDERSTAND THAT? DON'T FEEL EMBARRASSED TO ASK FOR HELP ON THE HARD STUFF.

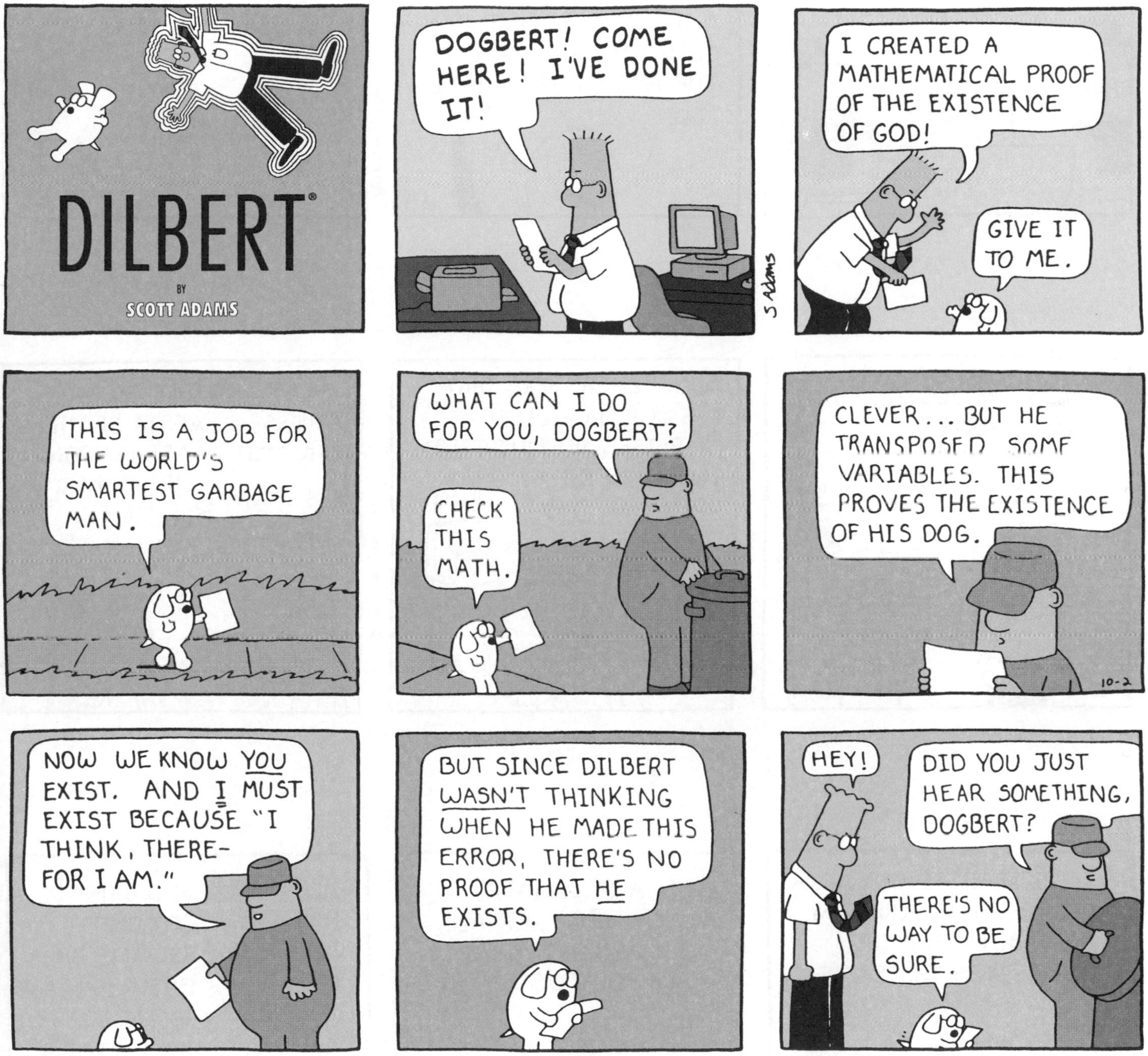
DILBERT®
BY
SCOTT ADAMS
DOGBERT! COME HERE! I'VE DONE IT!
S Adams
I CREATED A MATHEMATICAL PROOF OF THE EXISTENCE OF GOD!
GIVE IT TO ME.
THIS IS A JOB FOR THE WORLD'S SMARTEST GARBAGE MAN.
WHAT CAN I DO FOR YOU, DOGBERT?
CHECK THIS MATH.
CLEVER... BUT HE TRANSPOSED SOME VARIABLES. THIS PROVES THE EXISTENCE OF HIS DOG.
10-2
© 1994 United Feature Syndicate, Inc
NOW WE KNOW YOU EXIST. AND I MUST EXIST BECAUSE "I THINK, THERE-FOR I AM."
BUT SINCE DILBERT WASN'T THINKING WHEN HE MADE THIS ERROR, THERE'S NO PROOF THAT HE EXISTS.
HEY!
DID YOU JUST HEAR SOMETHING, DOGBERT?
THERE'S NO WAY TO BE SURE.

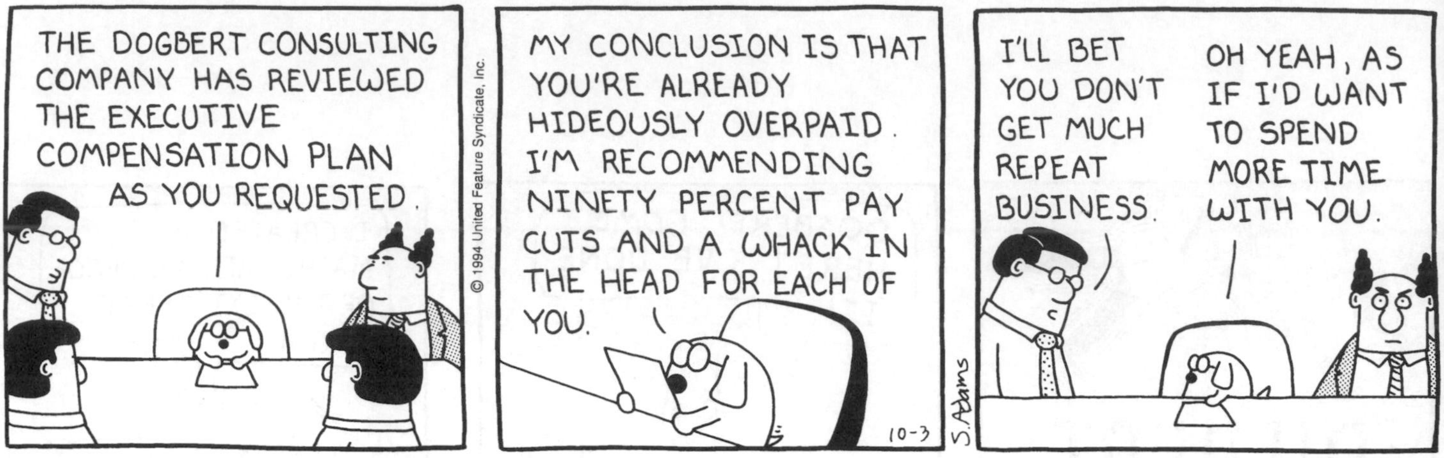
THE DOGBERT CONSULTING COMPANY HAS REVIEWED THE EXECUTIVE COMPENSATION PLAN AS YOU REQUESTED.
© 1994 United Feature Syndicate, Inc.
MY CONCLUSION IS THAT YOU'RE ALREADY HIDEOUSLY OVERPAID. I'M RECOMMENDING NINETY PERCENT PAY CUTS AND A WHACK IN THE HEAD FOR EACH OF YOU.
10-3
S. Adams
I'LL BET YOU DON'T GET MUCH REPEAT BUSINESS.
OH YEAH, AS IF I'D WANT TO SPEND MORE TIME WITH YOU.

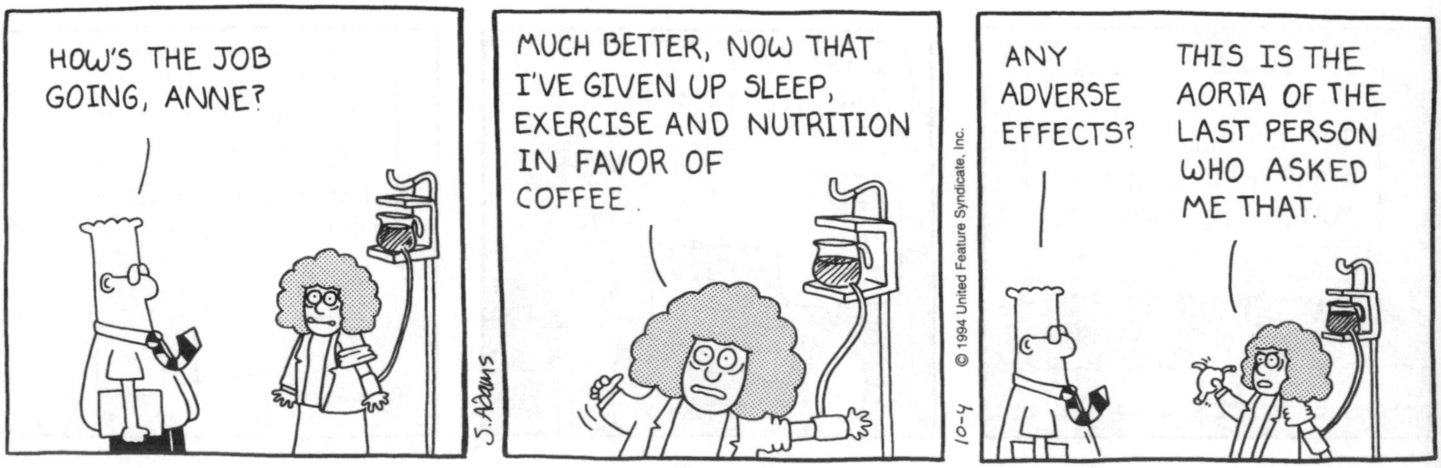
HOW'S THE JOB GOING, ANNE?
S. Adams
MUCH BETTER, NOW THAT I'VE GIVEN UP SLEEP, EXERCISE AND NUTRITION IN FAVOR OF COFFEE.
10-4
© 1994 United Feature Syndicate, Inc.
ANY ADVERSE EFFECTS?
THIS IS THE AORTA OF THE LAST PERSON WHO ASKED ME THAT.

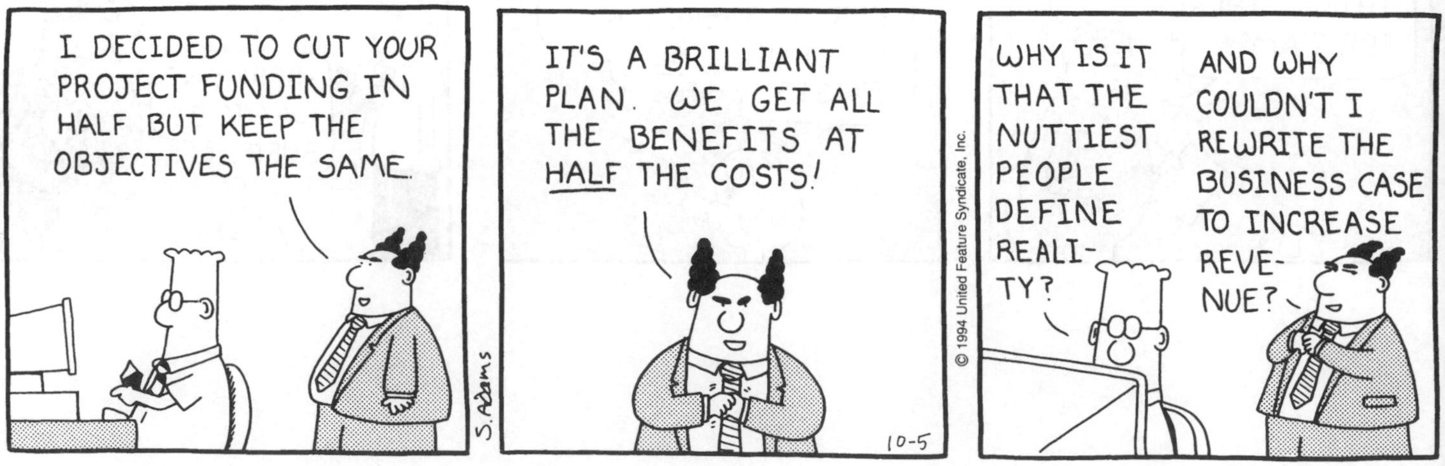
I DECIDED TO CUT YOUR PROJECT FUNDING IN HALF BUT KEEP THE OBJECTIVES THE SAME.
S. Adams
IT'S A BRILLIANT PLAN. WE GET ALL THE BENEFITS AT HALF THE COSTS!
10-5
© 1994 United Feature Syndicate, Inc.
WHY IS IT THAT THE NUTTIEST PEOPLE DEFINE REALI-TY?
AND WHY COULDN'T I REWRITE THE BUSINESS CASE TO INCREASE REVE-NUE?

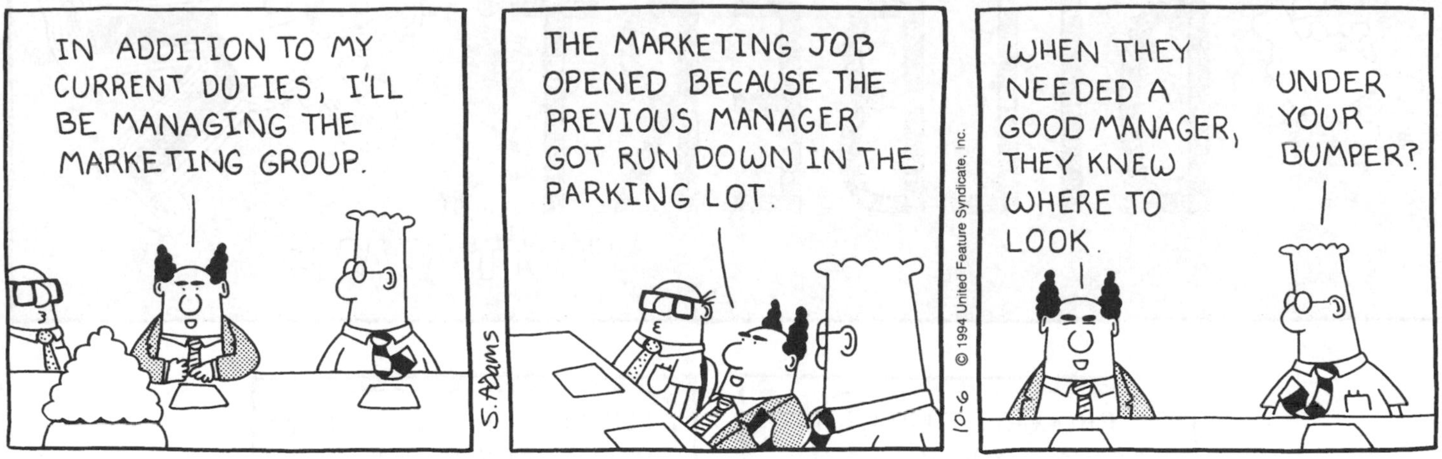
IN ADDITION TO MY CURRENT DUTIES, I'LL BE MANAGING THE MARKETING GROUP.
S. ADAMS
THE MARKETING JOB OPENED BECAUSE THE PREVIOUS MANAGER GOT RUN DOWN IN THE PARKING LOT.
10-6 © 1994 United Feature Syndicate, Inc.
WHEN THEY NEEDED A GOOD MANAGER, THEY KNEW WHERE TO LOOK.
UNDER YOUR BUMPER?

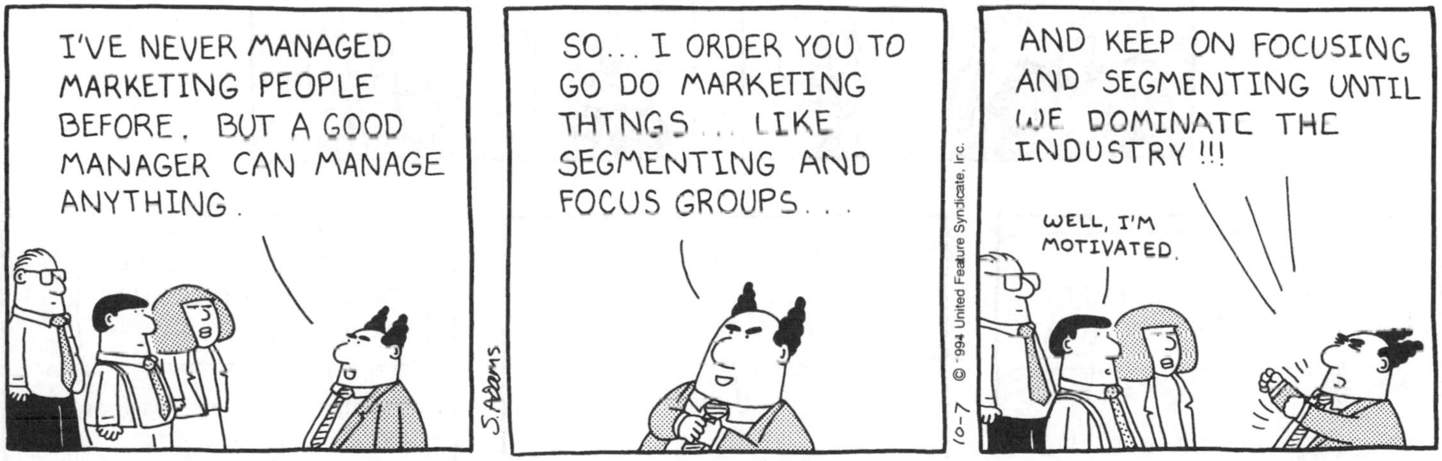
I'VE NEVER MANAGED MARKETING PEOPLE BEFORE. BUT A GOOD MANAGER CAN MANAGE ANYTHING.
S. ADAMS
SO... I ORDER YOU TO GO DO MARKETING THINGS... LIKE SEGMENTING AND FOCUS GROUPS...
10-7 © 1994 United Feature Syndicate, Inc.
AND KEEP ON FOCUSING AND SEGMENTING UNTIL WE DOMINATE THE INDUSTRY!!!
WELL, I'M MOTIVATED.

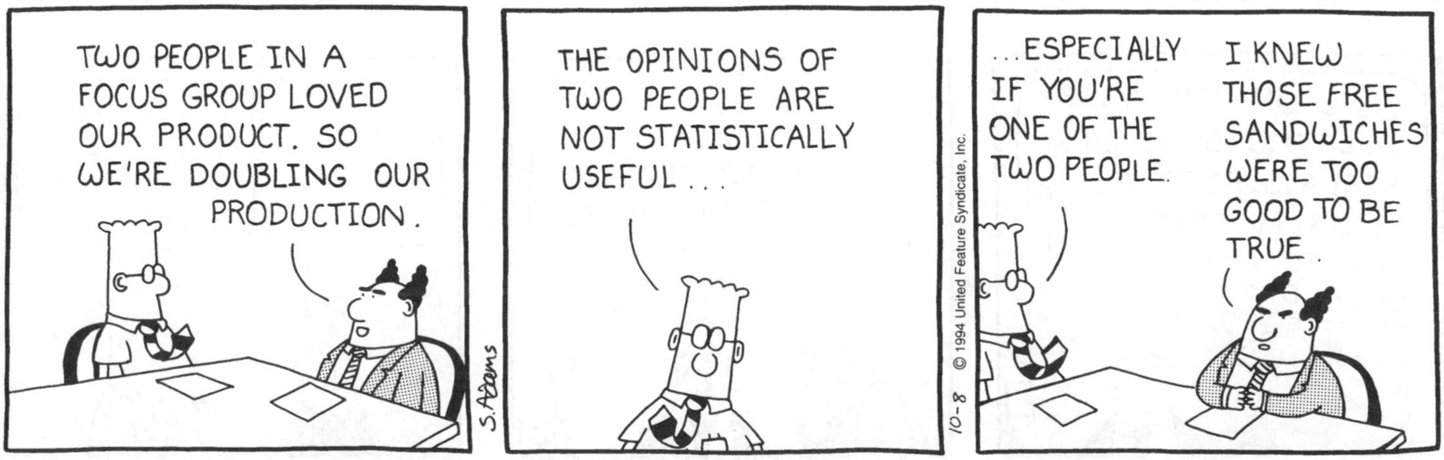
TWO PEOPLE IN A FOCUS GROUP LOVED OUR PRODUCT. SO WE'RE DOUBLING OUR PRODUCTION.
S. ADAMS
THE OPINIONS OF TWO PEOPLE ARE NOT STATISTICALLY USEFUL...
10-8 © 1994 United Feature Syndicate, Inc.
...ESPECIALLY IF YOU'RE ONE OF THE TWO PEOPLE.
I KNEW THOSE FREE SANDWICHES WERE TOO GOOD TO BE TRUE.

DILBERT®
BY
SCOTT ADAMS
I BROUGHT DILBERT, IN CASE YOU HAVE ANY TECHNICAL QUESTIONS ABOUT OUR PRODUCT.
S Adams
HEH-HEH... ENGINEERS DON'T KNOW HOW TO LIE. THE TRUTH WILL BE MINE.
UH-OH.
TED SAID YOUR PRODUCT IS BUG-FREE. IS THAT TRUE, DILBERT?
WELL... YES, THAT'S TRUE
I MEAN... BASICALLY TRUE...TECHNICALLY TRUE... SORT OF...
PHEW.
NO-O-O!! IT'S A LIE! ALL THE BUGS WERE RECLASSIFIED AS SECURITY FEATURES JUST TO MAKE THE SHIP DATE!!
10-9
AND WE BOTH THINK YOU COULD BE ATTRACTIVE IF YOU'D JUST DO SOMETHING WITH YOUR HAIR.
WHY DID I BRING YOU ALONG?
THE EVIDENCE SUGGESTS THAT YOU'RE STUPID.

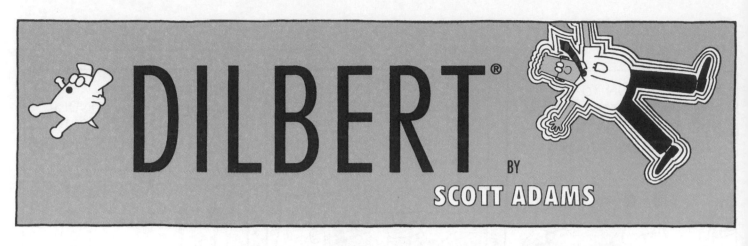

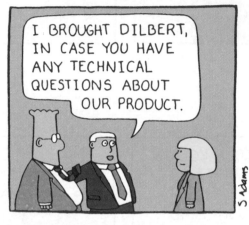

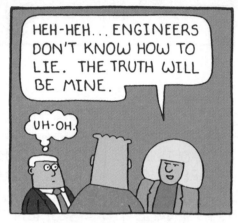

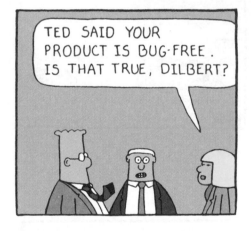

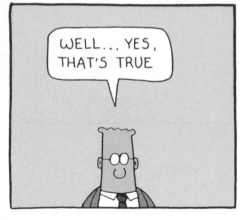

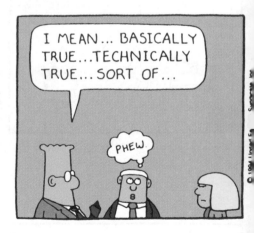

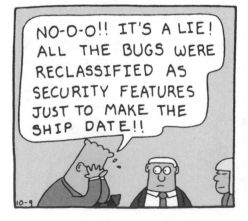

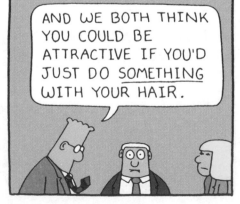

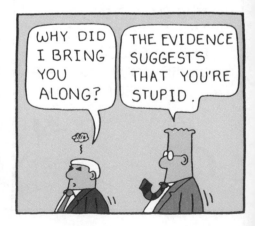

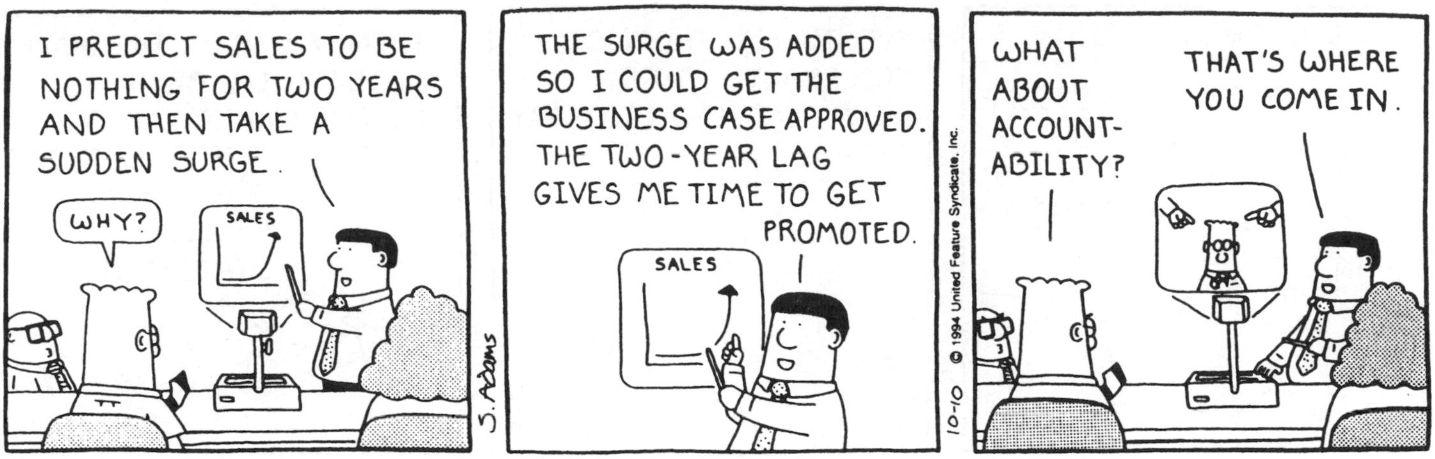
I PREDICT SALES TO BE NOTHING FOR TWO YEARS AND THEN TAKE A SUDDEN SURGE.
WHY?
SALES
S. Adams
THE SURGE WAS ADDED SO I COULD GET THE BUSINESS CASE APPROVED. THE TWO-YEAR LAG GIVES ME TIME TO GET PROMOTED.
SALES
10-10 © 1994 United Feature Syndicate, Inc.
WHAT ABOUT ACCOUNT-ABILITY?
THAT'S WHERE YOU COME IN.

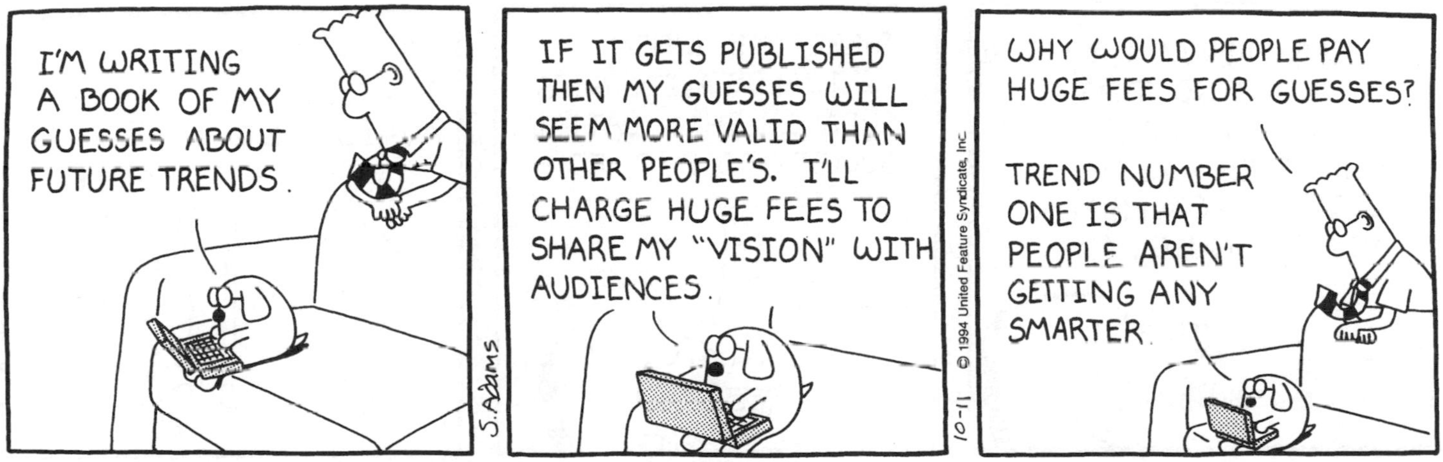
I'M WRITING A BOOK OF MY GUESSES ABOUT FUTURE TRENDS.
S. Adams
IF IT GETS PUBLISHED THEN MY GUESSES WILL SEEM MORE VALID THAN OTHER PEOPLE'S. I'LL CHARGE HUGE FEES TO SHARE MY "VISION" WITH AUDIENCES.
10-11 © 1994 United Feature Syndicate, Inc.
WHY WOULD PEOPLE PAY HUGE FEES FOR GUESSES?
TREND NUMBER ONE IS THAT PEOPLE AREN'T GETTING ANY SMARTER.

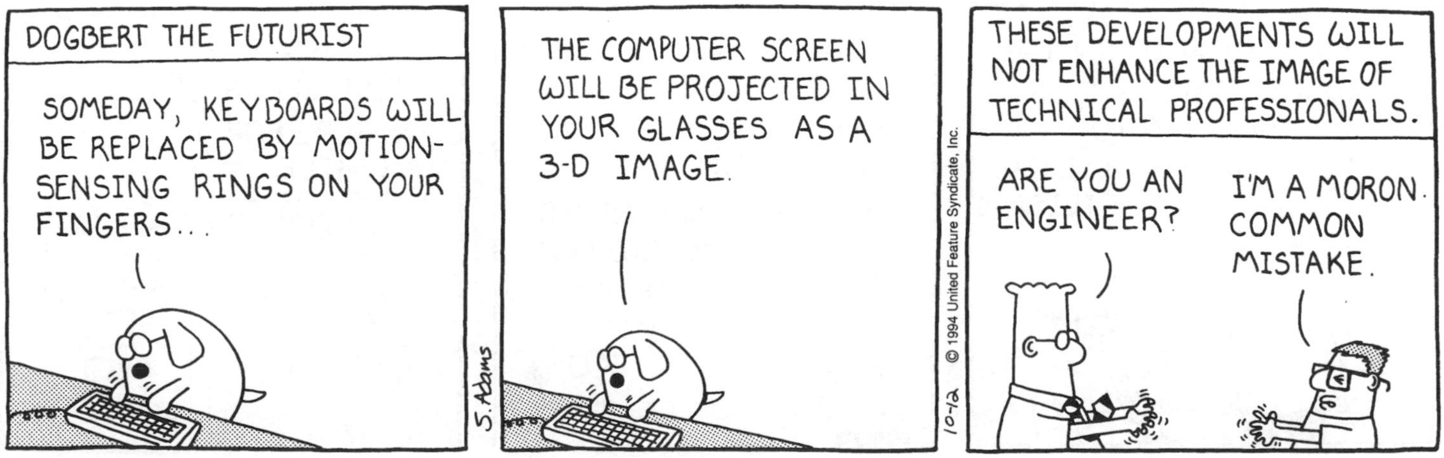
DOGBERT THE FUTURIST
SOMEDAY, KEYBOARDS WILL BE REPLACED BY MOTION-SENSING RINGS ON YOUR FINGERS...
S. Adams
THE COMPUTER SCREEN WILL BE PROJECTED IN YOUR GLASSES AS A 3-D IMAGE.
10-12 © 1994 United Feature Syndicate, Inc.
THESE DEVELOPMENTS WILL NOT ENHANCE THE IMAGE OF TECHNICAL PROFESSIONALS.
ARE YOU AN ENGINEER?
I'M A MORON. COMMON MISTAKE.

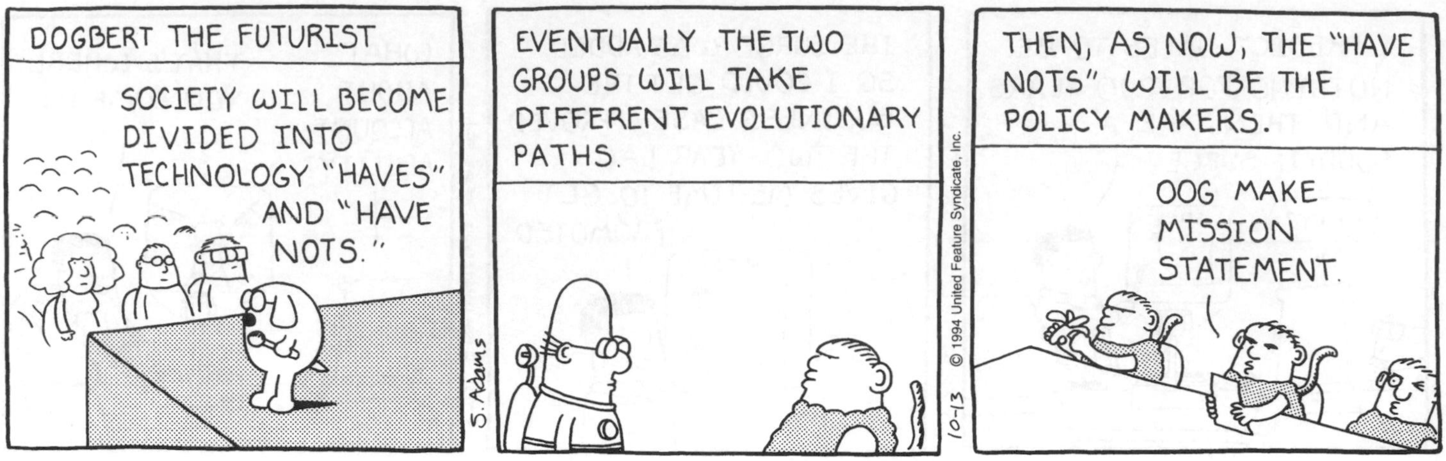
DOGBERT THE FUTURIST
SOCIETY WILL BECOME DIVIDED INTO TECHNOLOGY "HAVES" AND "HAVE NOTS."
S. Adams
EVENTUALLY THE TWO GROUPS WILL TAKE DIFFERENT EVOLUTIONARY PATHS.
© 1994 United Feature Syndicate, Inc.
10-13
THEN, AS NOW, THE "HAVE NOTS" WILL BE THE POLICY MAKERS.
OOG MAKE MISSION STATEMENT.

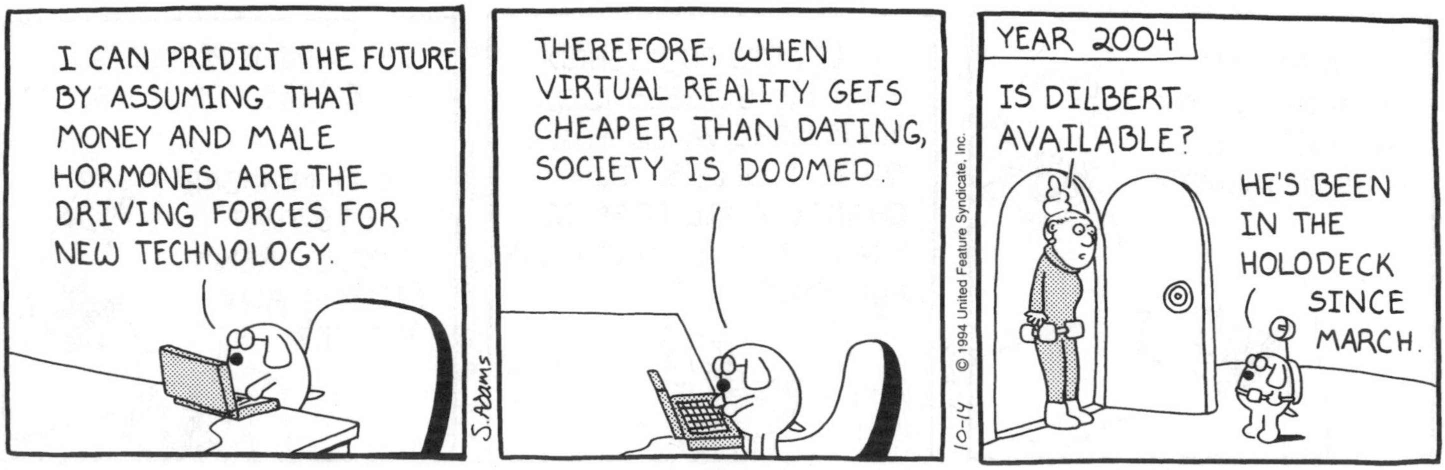
I CAN PREDICT THE FUTURE BY ASSUMING THAT MONEY AND MALE HORMONES ARE THE DRIVING FORCES FOR NEW TECHNOLOGY.
S. Adams
THEREFORE, WHEN VIRTUAL REALITY GETS CHEAPER THAN DATING, SOCIETY IS DOOMED.
© 1994 United Feature Syndicate, Inc.
10-14
YEAR 2004
IS DILBERT AVAILABLE?
HE'S BEEN IN THE HOLODECK SINCE MARCH.

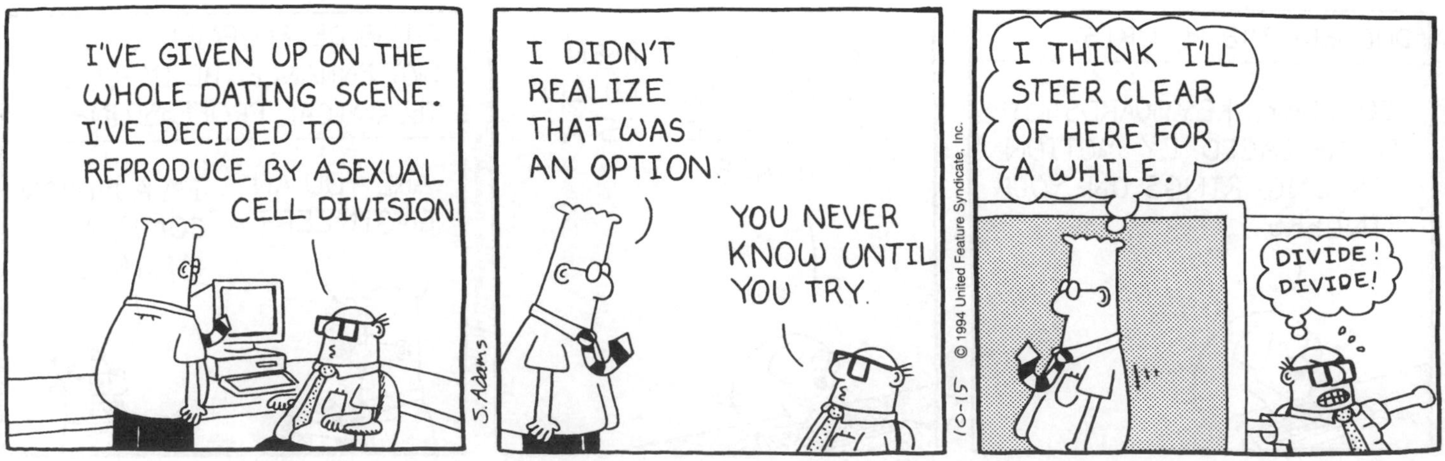
I'VE GIVEN UP ON THE WHOLE DATING SCENE. I'VE DECIDED TO REPRODUCE BY ASEXUAL CELL DIVISION.
S. Adams
I DIDN'T REALIZE THAT WAS AN OPTION.
YOU NEVER KNOW UNTIL YOU TRY.
© 1994 United Feature Syndicate, Inc.
10-15
I THINK I'LL STEER CLEAR OF HERE FOR A WHILE.
DIVIDE! DIVIDE!

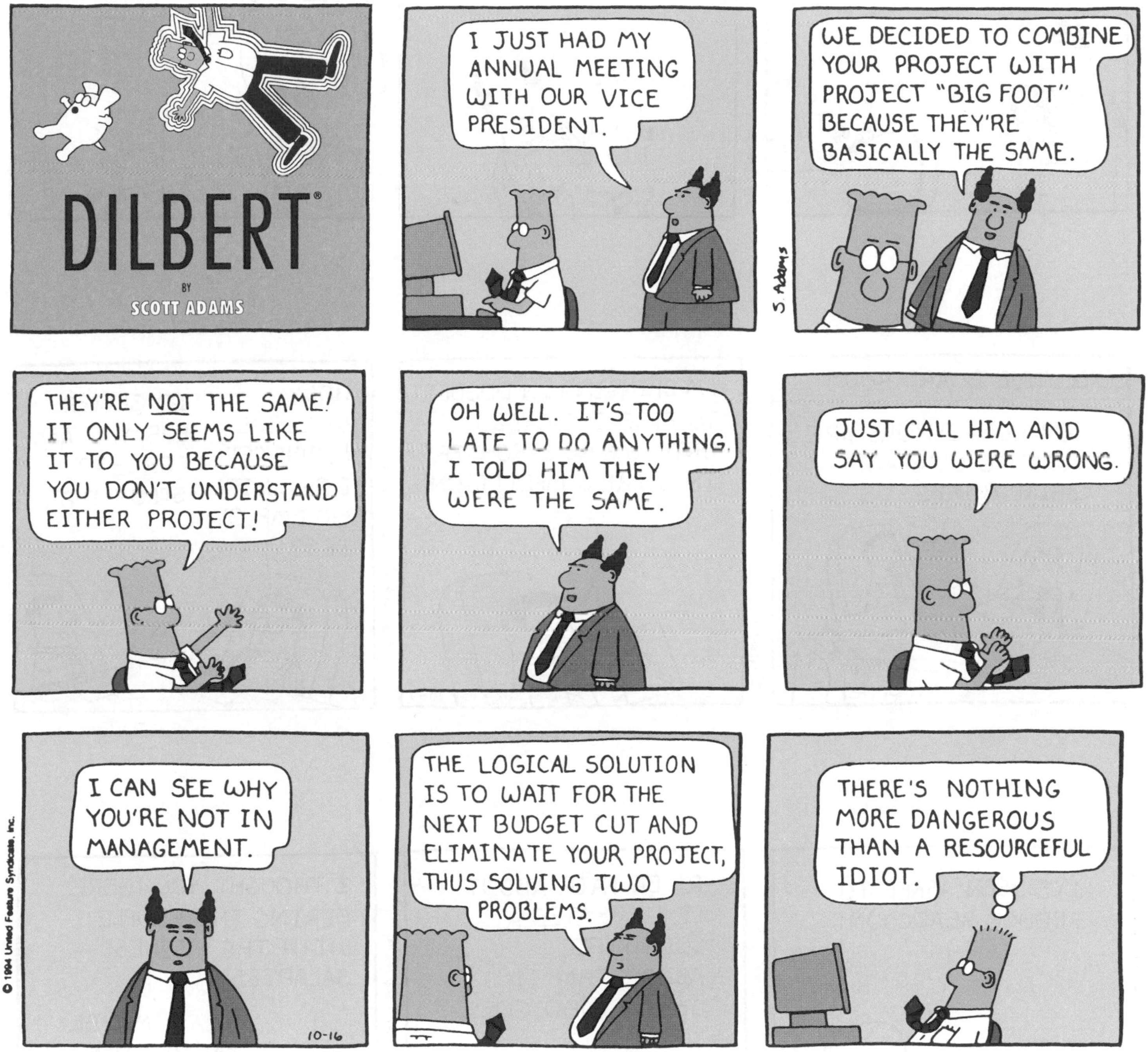
DILBERT®
BY
SCOTT ADAMS
I JUST HAD MY ANNUAL MEETING WITH OUR VICE PRESIDENT.
WE DECIDED TO COMBINE YOUR PROJECT WITH PROJECT "BIG FOOT" BECAUSE THEY'RE BASICALLY THE SAME.
S. Adams
THEY'RE NOT THE SAME! IT ONLY SEEMS LIKE IT TO YOU BECAUSE YOU DON'T UNDERSTAND EITHER PROJECT!
OH WELL. IT'S TOO LATE TO DO ANYTHING. I TOLD HIM THEY WERE THE SAME.
JUST CALL HIM AND SAY YOU WERE WRONG.
I CAN SEE WHY YOU'RE NOT IN MANAGEMENT.
© 1994 United Feature Syndicate, Inc.
10-16
THE LOGICAL SOLUTION IS TO WAIT FOR THE NEXT BUDGET CUT AND ELIMINATE YOUR PROJECT, THUS SOLVING TWO PROBLEMS.
THERE'S NOTHING MORE DANGEROUS THAN A RESOURCEFUL IDIOT.

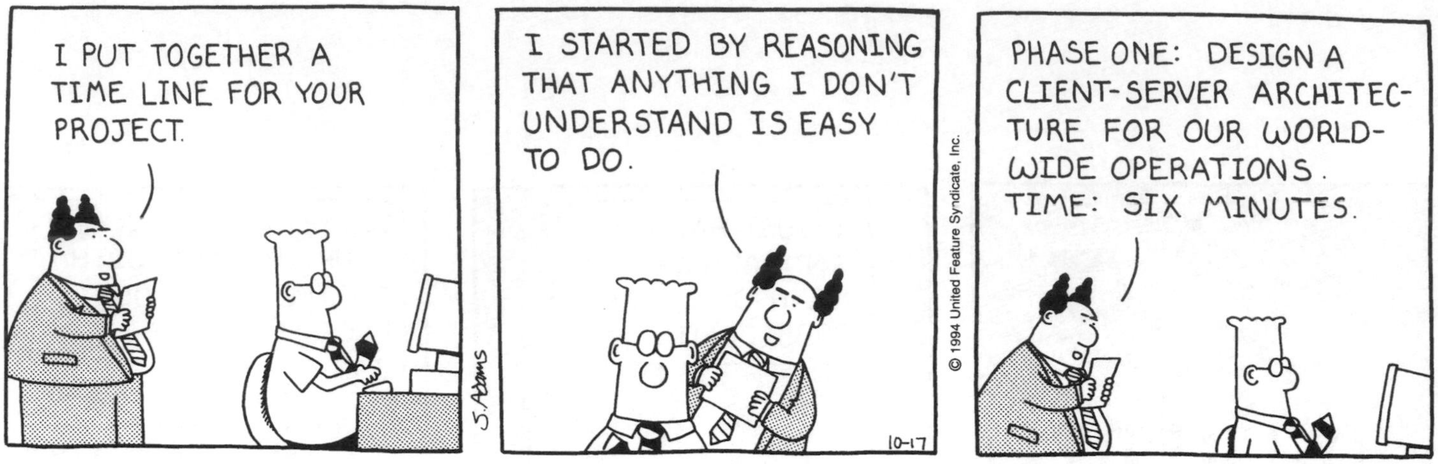
I PUT TOGETHER A TIME LINE FOR YOUR PROJECT.
S. Adams
I STARTED BY REASONING THAT ANYTHING I DON'T UNDERSTAND IS EASY TO DO.
10-17
© 1994 United Feature Syndicate, Inc.
PHASE ONE: DESIGN A CLIENT-SERVER ARCHITECTURE FOR OUR WORLD-WIDE OPERATIONS. TIME: SIX MINUTES.

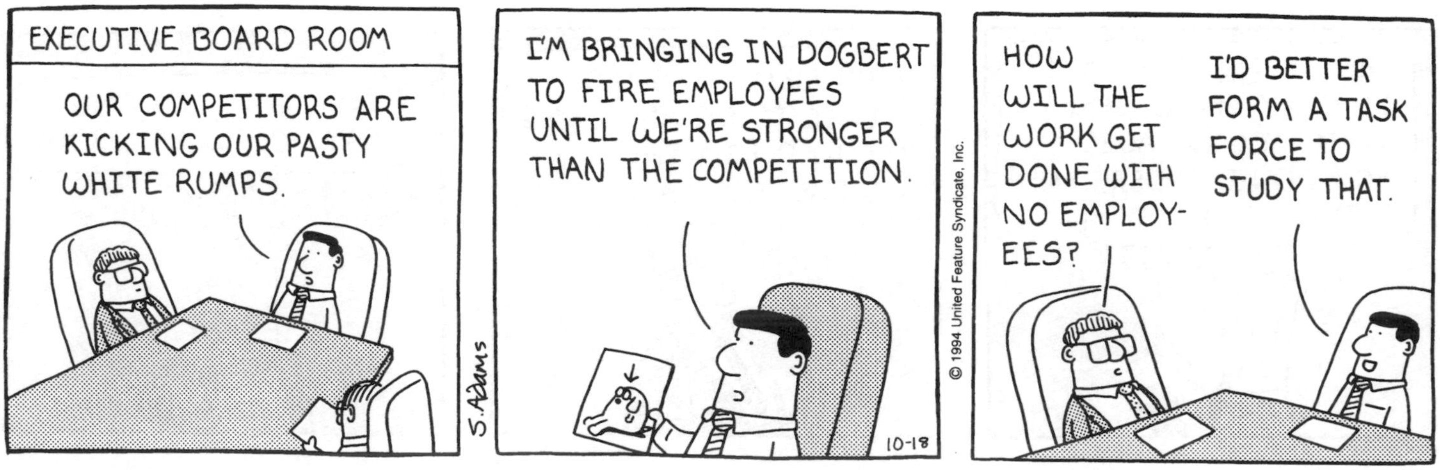
EXECUTIVE BOARD ROOM
OUR COMPETITORS ARE KICKING OUR PASTY WHITE RUMPS.
S. Adams
I'M BRINGING IN DOGBERT TO FIRE EMPLOYEES UNTIL WE'RE STRONGER THAN THE COMPETITION.
10-18
© 1994 United Feature Syndicate, Inc.
HOW WILL THE WORK GET DONE WITH NO EMPLOYEES?
I'D BETTER FORM A TASK FORCE TO STUDY THAT.

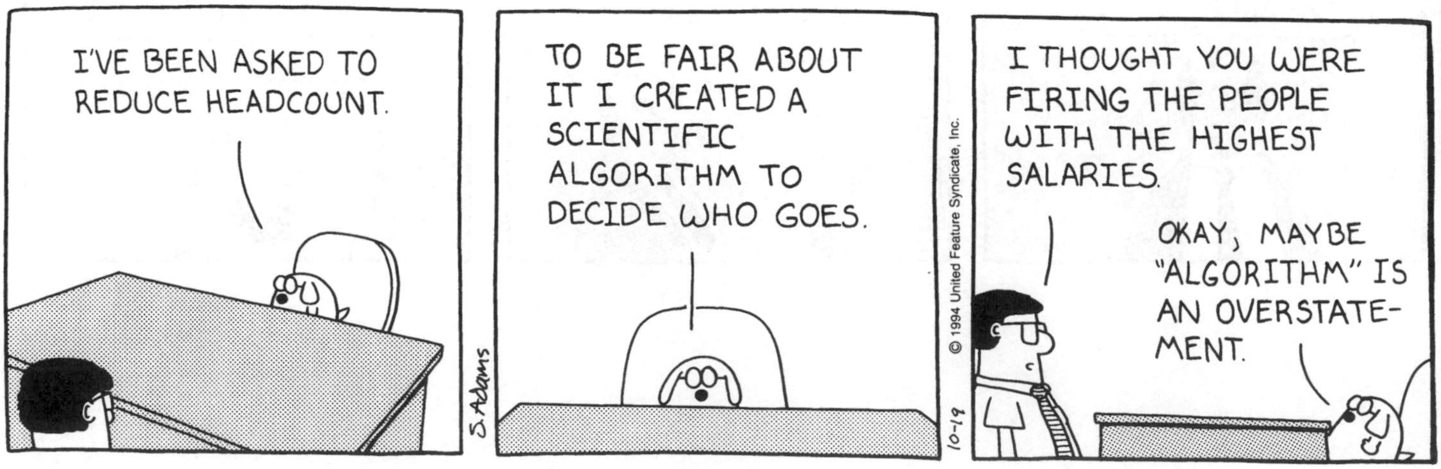
I'VE BEEN ASKED TO REDUCE HEADCOUNT.
S. Adams
TO BE FAIR ABOUT IT I CREATED A SCIENTIFIC ALGORITHM TO DECIDE WHO GOES.
10-19
© 1994 United Feature Syndicate, Inc.
I THOUGHT YOU WERE FIRING THE PEOPLE WITH THE HIGHEST SALARIES.
OKAY, MAYBE "ALGORITHM" IS AN OVERSTATEMENT.

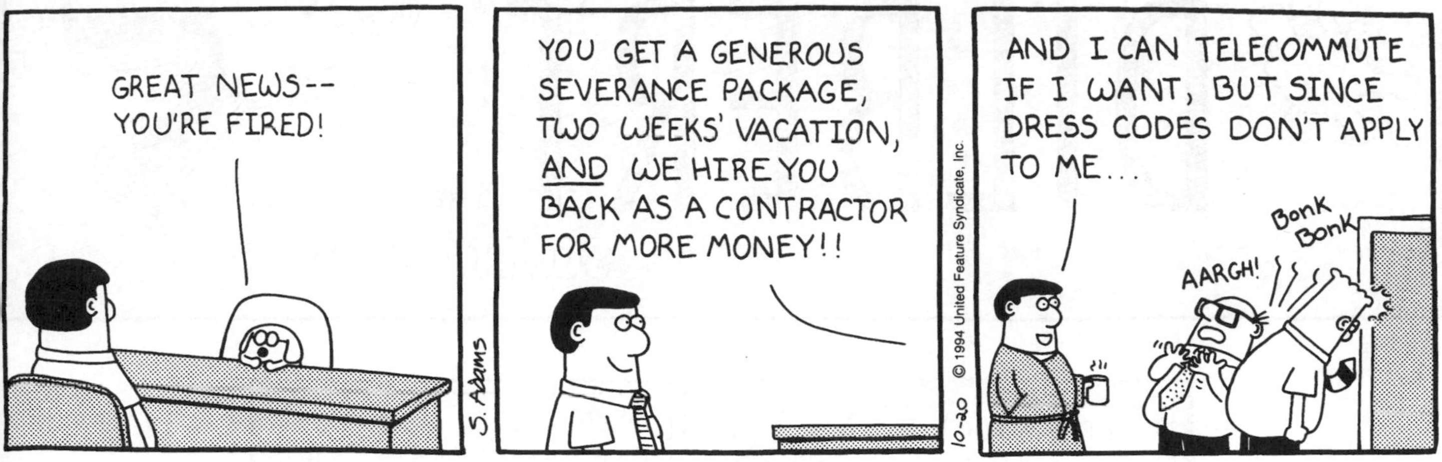
GREAT NEWS-- YOU'RE FIRED!
S. Adams
YOU GET A GENEROUS SEVERANCE PACKAGE, TWO WEEKS' VACATION, AND WE HIRE YOU BACK AS A CONTRACTOR FOR MORE MONEY!!
10-20 © 1994 United Feature Syndicate, Inc.
AND I CAN TELECOMMUTE IF I WANT, BUT SINCE DRESS CODES DON'T APPLY TO ME...
Bonk Bonk
AARGH!

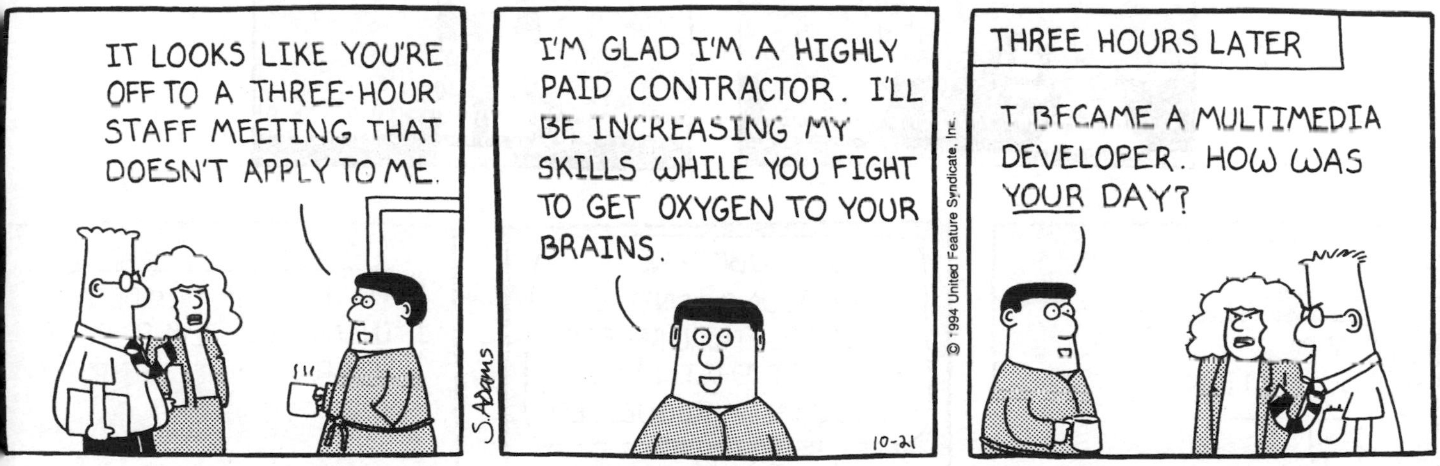
IT LOOKS LIKE YOU'RE OFF TO A THREE-HOUR STAFF MEETING THAT DOESN'T APPLY TO ME.
S. Adams
I'M GLAD I'M A HIGHLY PAID CONTRACTOR. I'LL BE INCREASING MY SKILLS WHILE YOU FIGHT TO GET OXYGEN TO YOUR BRAINS.
10-21
© 1994 United Feature Syndicate, Inc.
THREE HOURS LATER
I BECAME A MULTIMEDIA DEVELOPER. HOW WAS YOUR DAY?

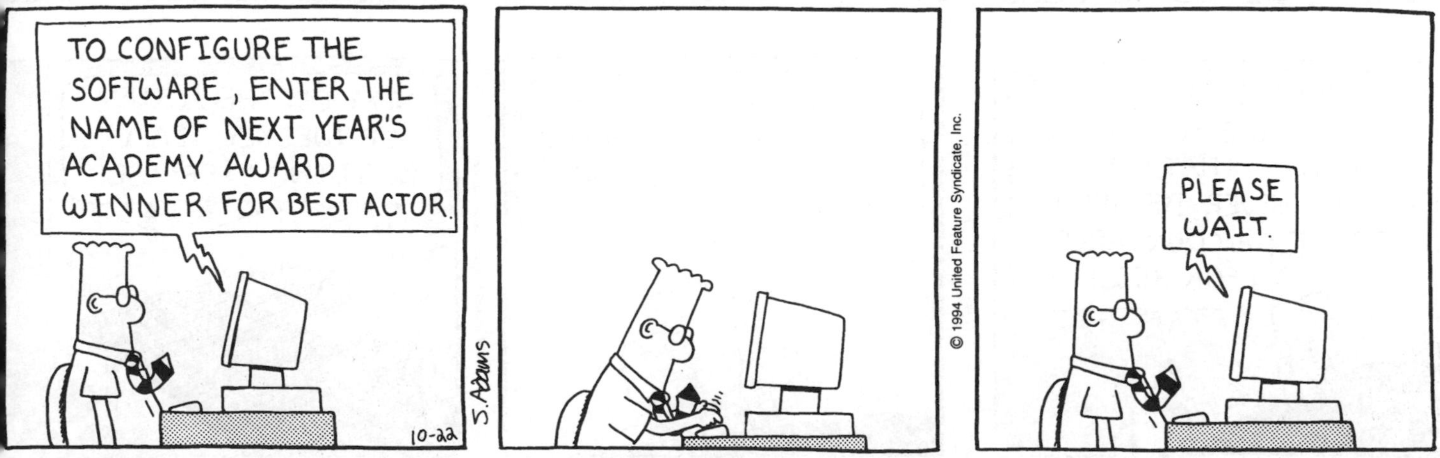
TO CONFIGURE THE SOFTWARE, ENTER THE NAME OF NEXT YEAR'S ACADEMY AWARD WINNER FOR BEST ACTOR.
10-22
S. Adams
© 1994 United Feature Syndicate, Inc.
PLEASE WAIT.

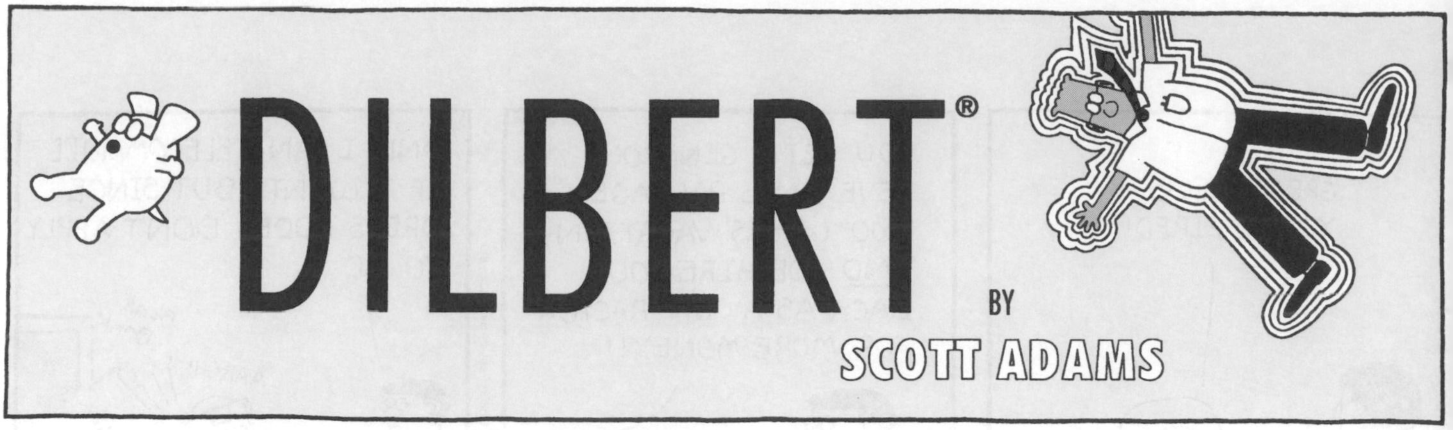
DILBERT®
BY
SCOTT ADAMS

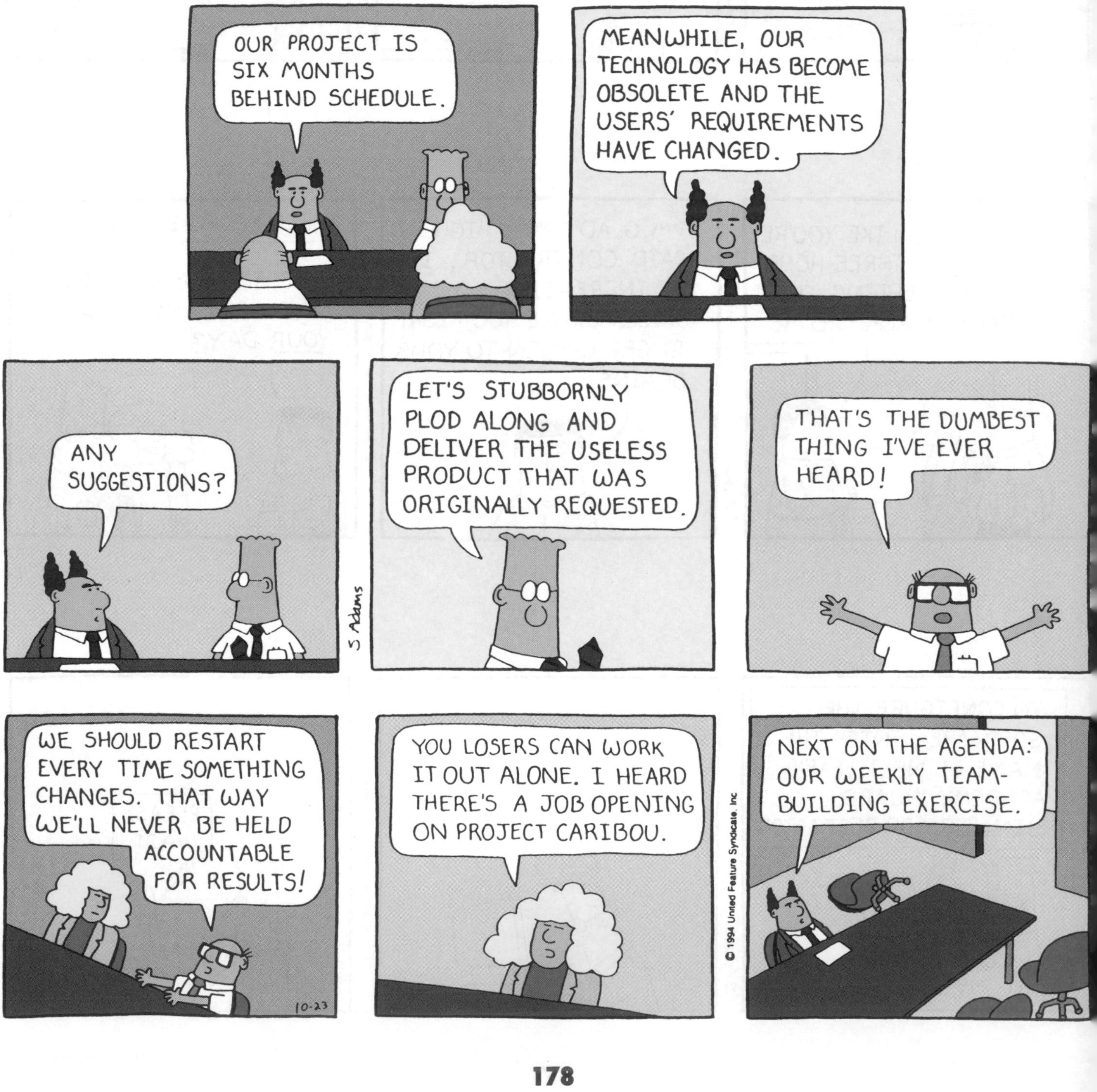
OUR PROJECT IS SIX MONTHS BEHIND SCHEDULE.
MEANWHILE, OUR TECHNOLOGY HAS BECOME OBSOLETE AND THE USERS' REQUIREMENTS HAVE CHANGED.
ANY SUGGESTIONS?
S Adams
LET'S STUBBORNLY PLOD ALONG AND DELIVER THE USELESS PRODUCT THAT WAS ORIGINALLY REQUESTED.
THAT'S THE DUMBEST THING I'VE EVER HEARD!
WE SHOULD RESTART EVERY TIME SOMETHING CHANGES. THAT WAY WE'LL NEVER BE HELD ACCOUNTABLE FOR RESULTS!
10-23
YOU LOSERS CAN WORK IT OUT ALONE. I HEARD THERE'S A JOB OPENING ON PROJECT CARIBOU.
© 1994 United Feature Syndicate, Inc
NEXT ON THE AGENDA: OUR WEEKLY TEAM-BUILDING EXERCISE.

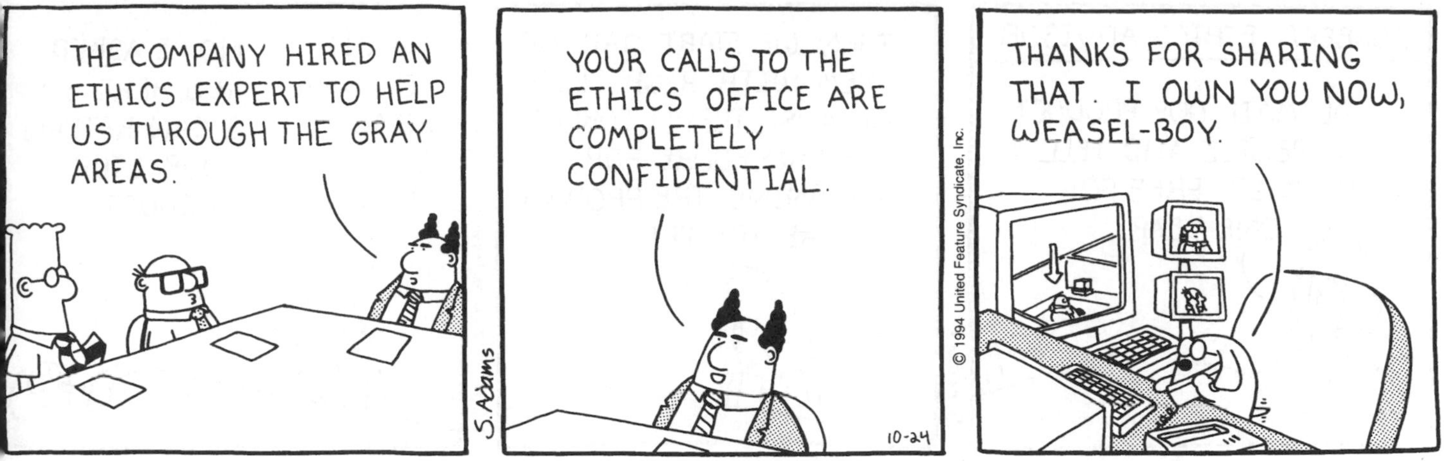
THE COMPANY HIRED AN ETHICS EXPERT TO HELP US THROUGH THE GRAY AREAS.
S. Adams
YOUR CALLS TO THE ETHICS OFFICE ARE COMPLETELY CONFIDENTIAL.
10-24
© 1994 United Feature Syndicate, Inc.
THANKS FOR SHARING THAT. I OWN YOU NOW, WEASEL-BOY.

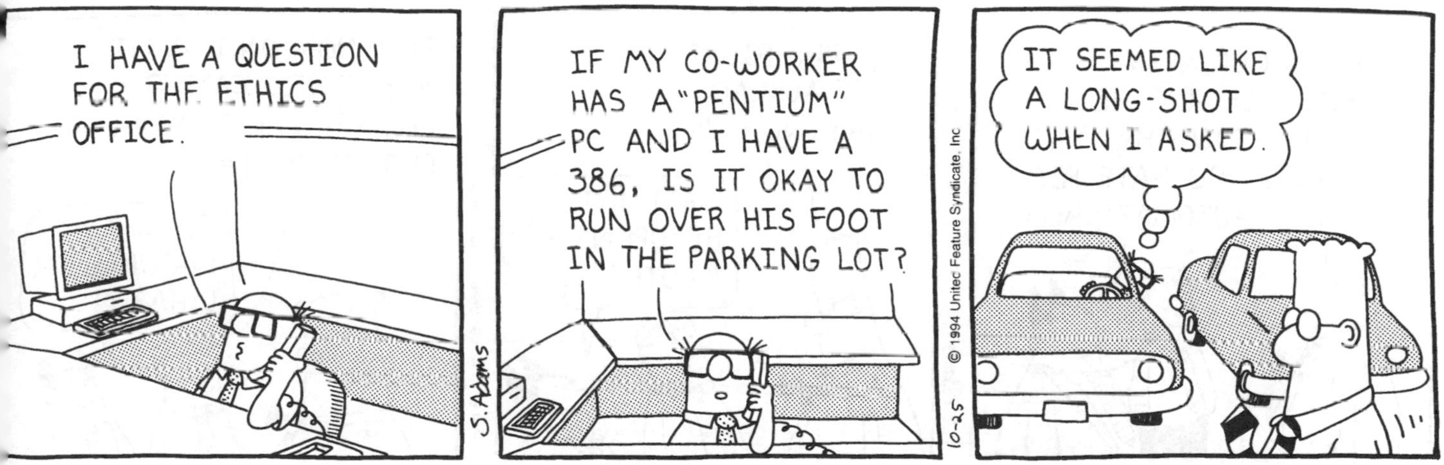
I HAVE A QUESTION FOR THE ETHICS OFFICE.
S. Adams
IF MY CO-WORKER HAS A "PENTIUM" PC AND I HAVE A 386, IS IT OKAY TO RUN OVER HIS FOOT IN THE PARKING LOT?
10-25
© 1994 United Feature Syndicate, Inc
IT SEEMED LIKE A LONG-SHOT WHEN I ASKED.

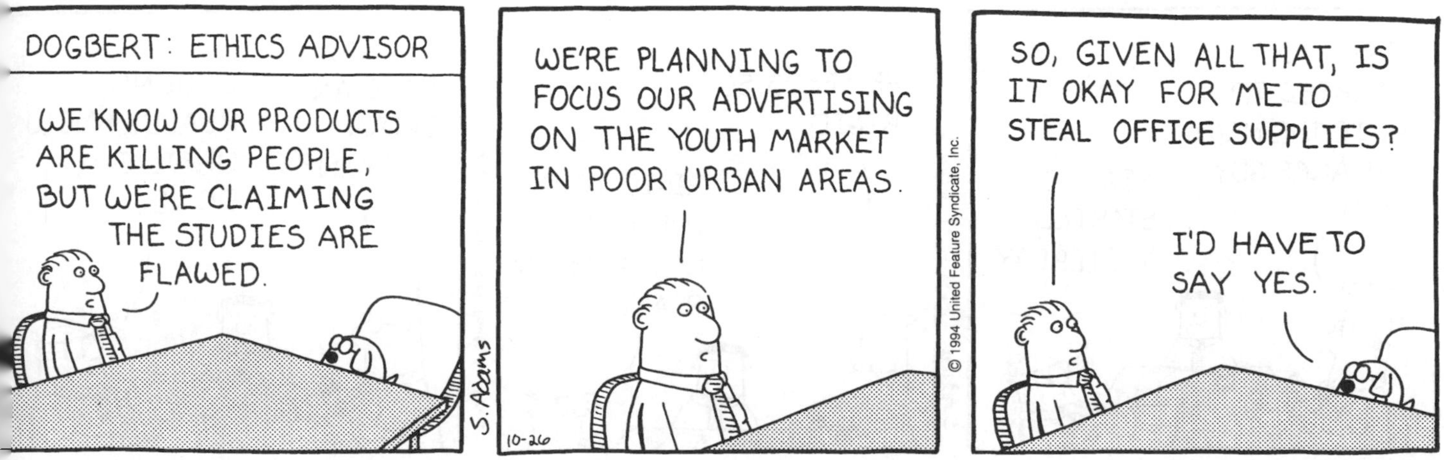
DOGBERT: ETHICS ADVISOR
WE KNOW OUR PRODUCTS ARE KILLING PEOPLE, BUT WE'RE CLAIMING THE STUDIES ARE FLAWED.
S. Adams
WE'RE PLANNING TO FOCUS OUR ADVERTISING ON THE YOUTH MARKET IN POOR URBAN AREAS.
10-26
© 1994 United Feature Syndicate, Inc.
SO, GIVEN ALL THAT, IS IT OKAY FOR ME TO STEAL OFFICE SUPPLIES?
I'D HAVE TO SAY YES.

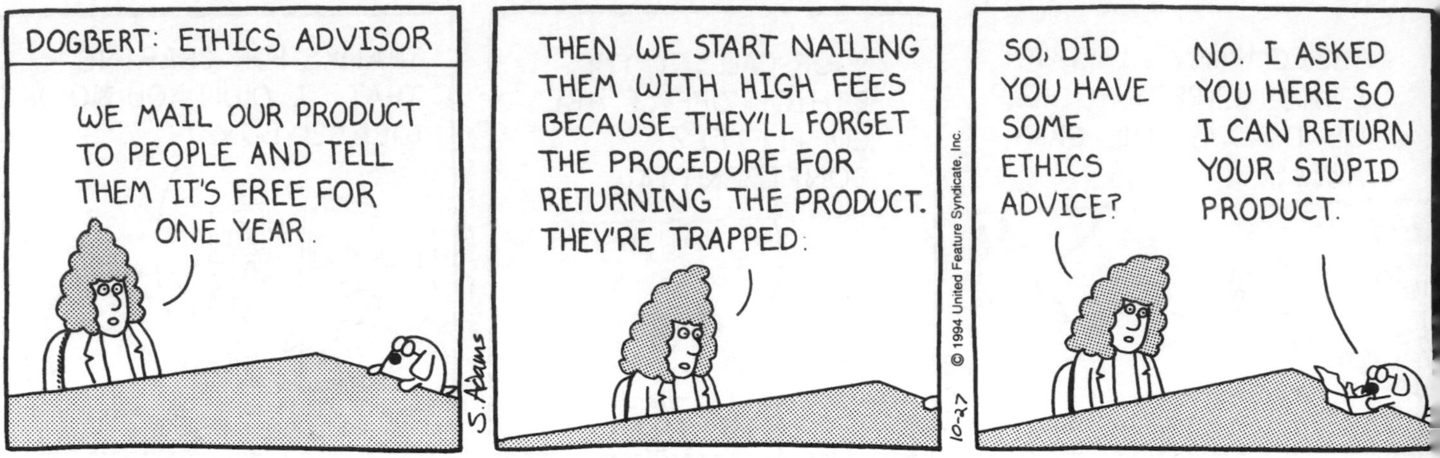
DOGBERT: ETHICS ADVISOR
WE MAIL OUR PRODUCT TO PEOPLE AND TELL THEM IT'S FREE FOR ONE YEAR.
S. Adams
THEN WE START NAILING THEM WITH HIGH FEES BECAUSE THEY'LL FORGET THE PROCEDURE FOR RETURNING THE PRODUCT. THEY'RE TRAPPED.
10-27
© 1994 United Feature Syndicate, Inc.
SO, DID YOU HAVE SOME ETHICS ADVICE?
NO. I ASKED YOU HERE SO I CAN RETURN YOUR STUPID PRODUCT.

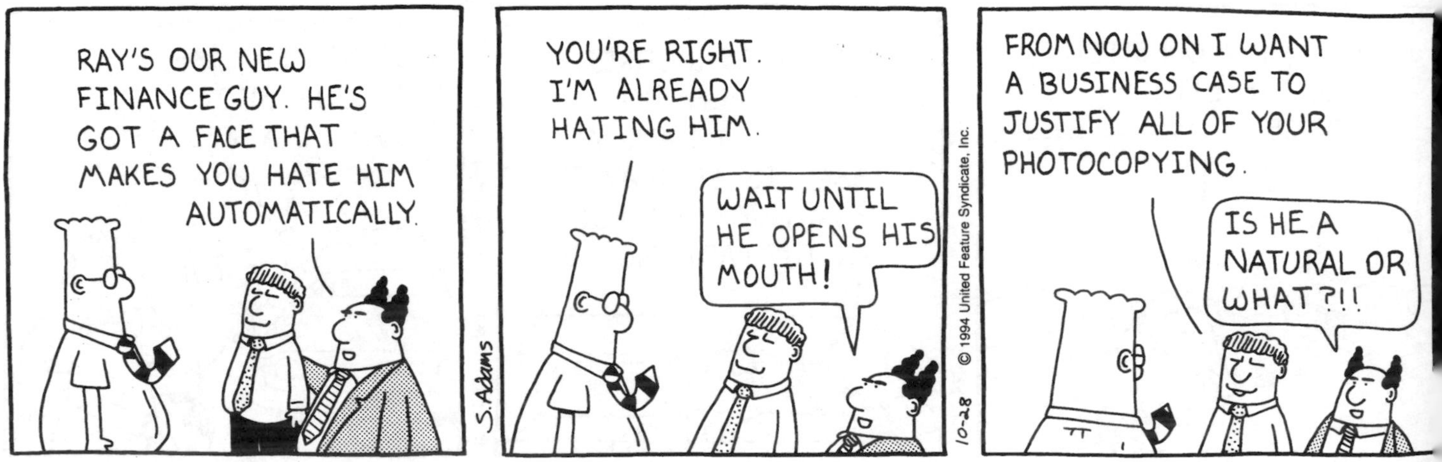
RAY'S OUR NEW FINANCE GUY. HE'S GOT A FACE THAT MAKES YOU HATE HIM AUTOMATICALLY.
S. Adams
YOU'RE RIGHT. I'M ALREADY HATING HIM.
WAIT UNTIL HE OPENS HIS MOUTH!
10-28
© 1994 United Feature Syndicate, Inc.
FROM NOW ON I WANT A BUSINESS CASE TO JUSTIFY ALL OF YOUR PHOTOCOPYING.
IS HE A NATURAL OR WHAT?!!

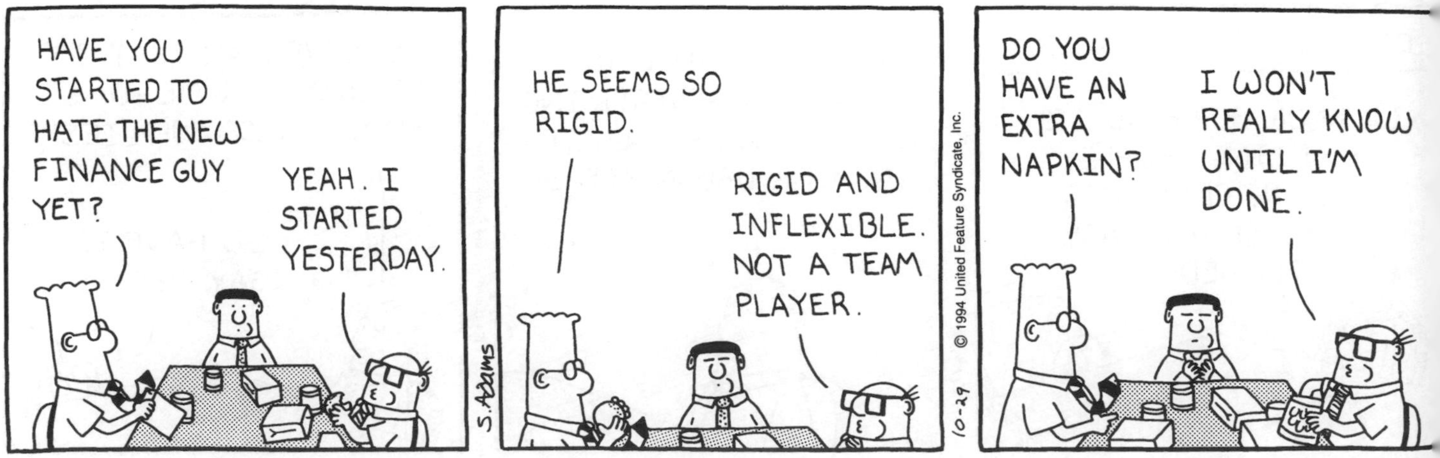
HAVE YOU STARTED TO HATE THE NEW FINANCE GUY YET?
YEAH. I STARTED YESTERDAY.
S. Adams
HE SEEMS SO RIGID.
RIGID AND INFLEXIBLE. NOT A TEAM PLAYER.
10-29
© 1994 United Feature Syndicate, Inc.
DO YOU HAVE AN EXTRA NAPKIN?
I WON'T REALLY KNOW UNTIL I'M DONE.

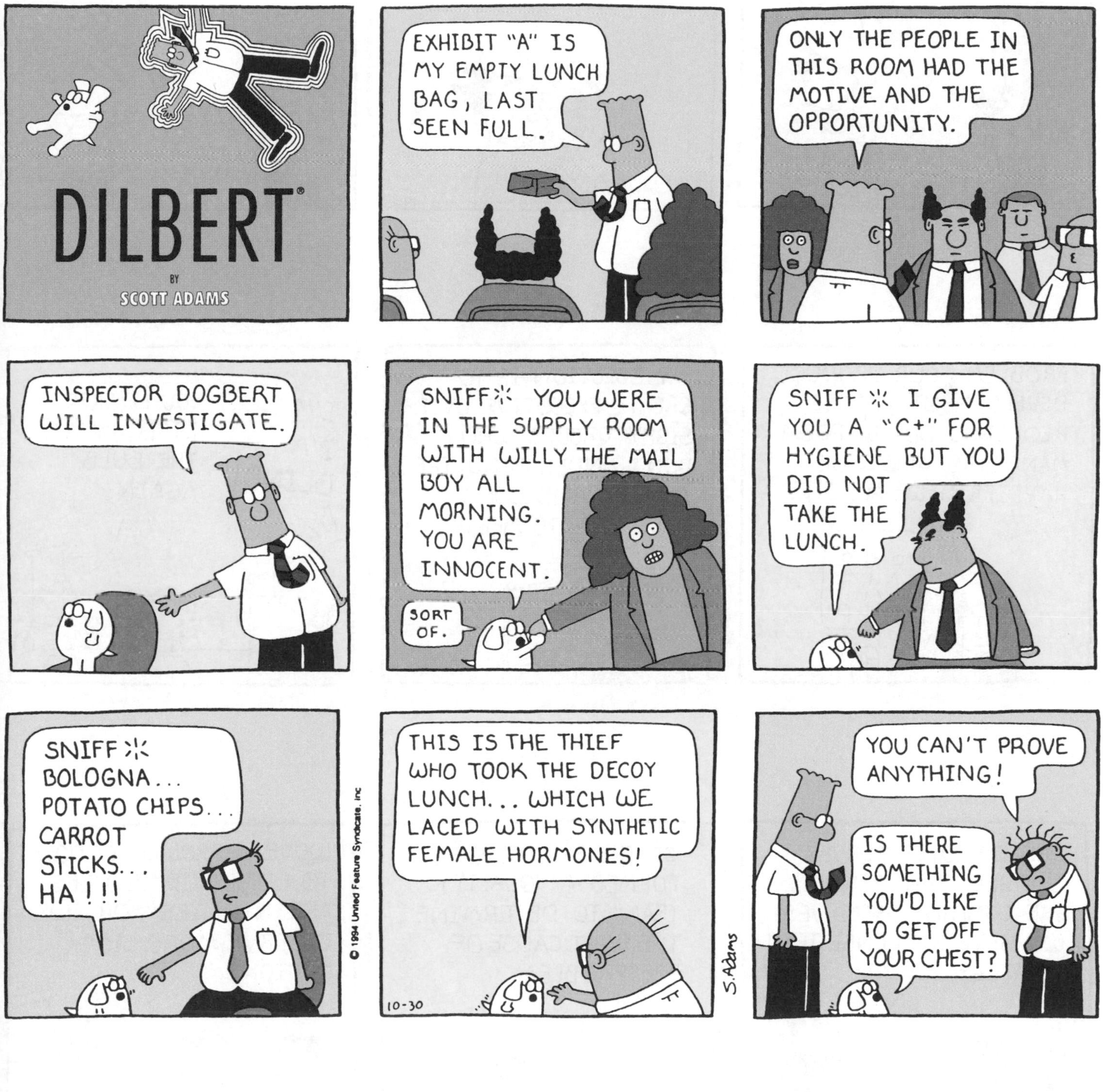
DILBERT®
BY SCOTT ADAMS
EXHIBIT "A" IS MY EMPTY LUNCH BAG, LAST SEEN FULL.
ONLY THE PEOPLE IN THIS ROOM HAD THE MOTIVE AND THE OPPORTUNITY.
INSPECTOR DOGBERT WILL INVESTIGATE.
SNIFF* YOU WERE IN THE SUPPLY ROOM WITH WILLY THE MAIL BOY ALL MORNING. YOU ARE INNOCENT.
SORT OF.
SNIFF * I GIVE YOU A "C+" FOR HYGIENE BUT YOU DID NOT TAKE THE LUNCH.
SNIFF* BOLOGNA... POTATO CHIPS... CARROT STICKS... HA!!!
© 1994 United Feature Syndicate, Inc
THIS IS THE THIEF WHO TOOK THE DECOY LUNCH... WHICH WE LACED WITH SYNTHETIC FEMALE HORMONES!
10-30
S. Adams
YOU CAN'T PROVE ANYTHING!
IS THERE SOMETHING YOU'D LIKE TO GET OFF YOUR CHEST?

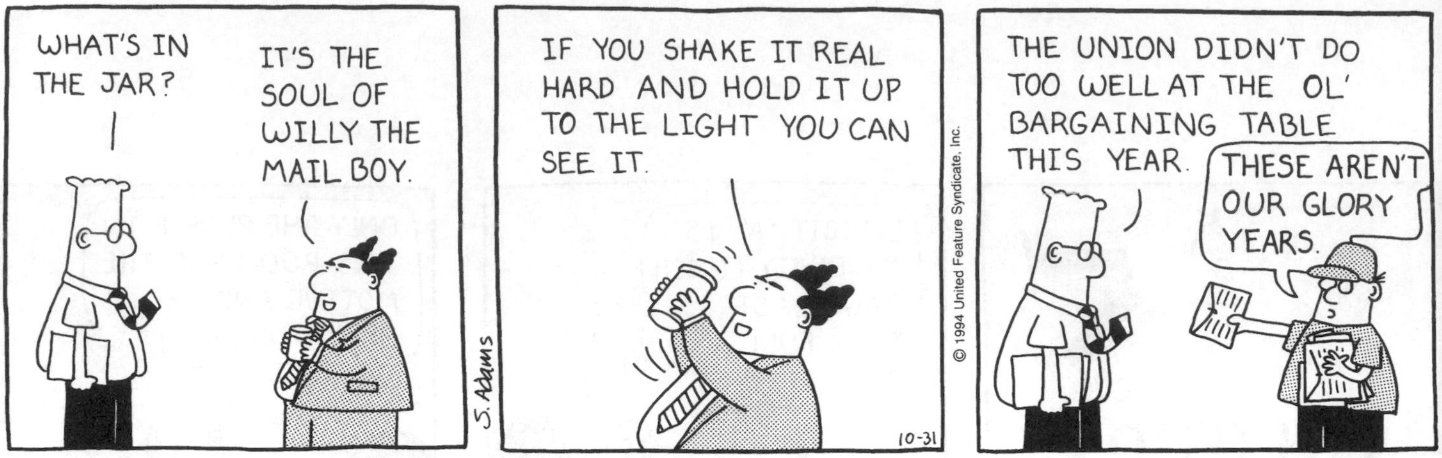
WHAT'S IN THE JAR?
IT'S THE SOUL OF WILLY THE MAIL BOY.
S. Adams
IF YOU SHAKE IT REAL HARD AND HOLD IT UP TO THE LIGHT YOU CAN SEE IT.
10-31
© 1994 United Feature Syndicate, Inc.
THE UNION DIDN'T DO TOO WELL AT THE OL' BARGAINING TABLE THIS YEAR.
THESE AREN'T OUR GLORY YEARS.

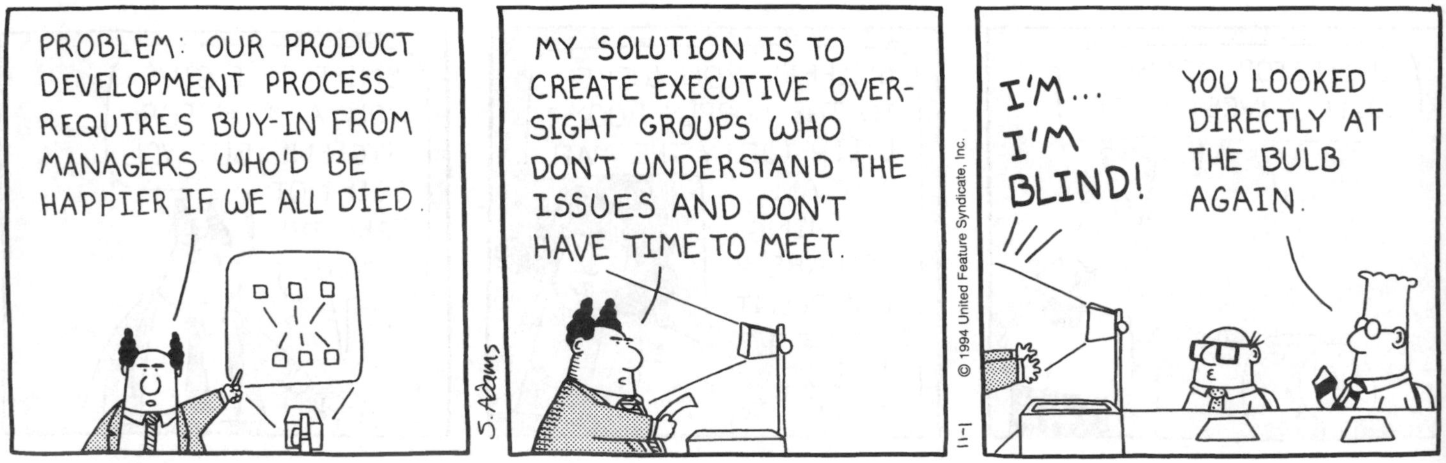
PROBLEM: OUR PRODUCT DEVELOPMENT PROCESS REQUIRES BUY-IN FROM MANAGERS WHO'D BE HAPPIER IF WE ALL DIED.
S. Adams
MY SOLUTION IS TO CREATE EXECUTIVE OVER-SIGHT GROUPS WHO DON'T UNDERSTAND THE ISSUES AND DON'T HAVE TIME TO MEET.
11-1
© 1994 United Feature Syndicate, Inc.
I'M... I'M BLIND!
YOU LOOKED DIRECTLY AT THE BULB AGAIN.

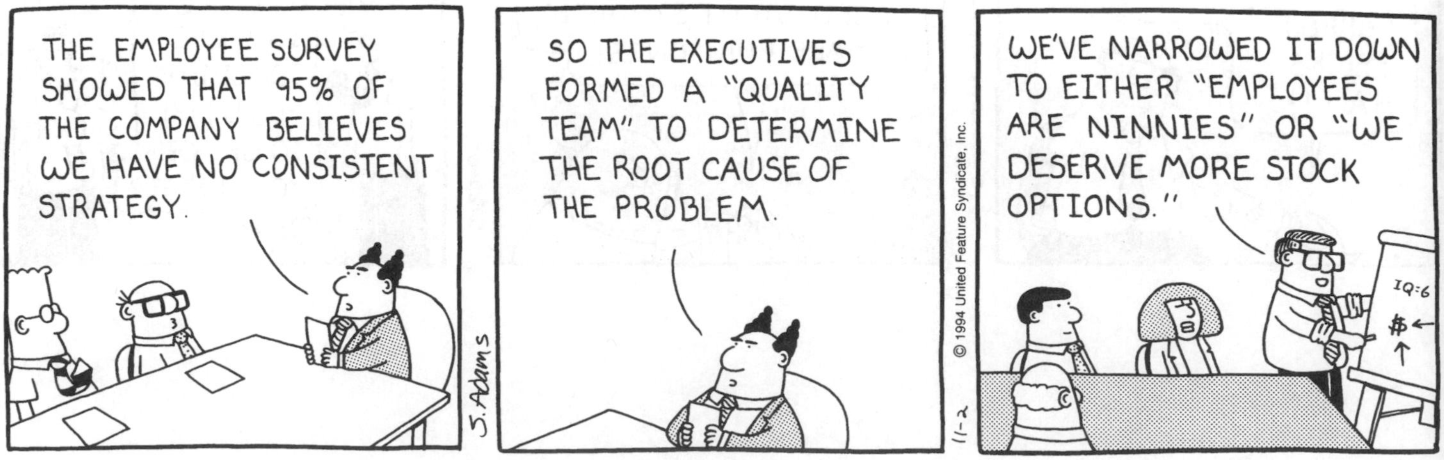
THE EMPLOYEE SURVEY SHOWED THAT 95% OF THE COMPANY BELIEVES WE HAVE NO CONSISTENT STRATEGY.
S. Adams
SO THE EXECUTIVES FORMED A "QUALITY TEAM" TO DETERMINE THE ROOT CAUSE OF THE PROBLEM.
11-2
© 1994 United Feature Syndicate, Inc.
WE'VE NARROWED IT DOWN TO EITHER "EMPLOYEES ARE NINNIES" OR "WE DESERVE MORE STOCK OPTIONS."
IQ:6
$

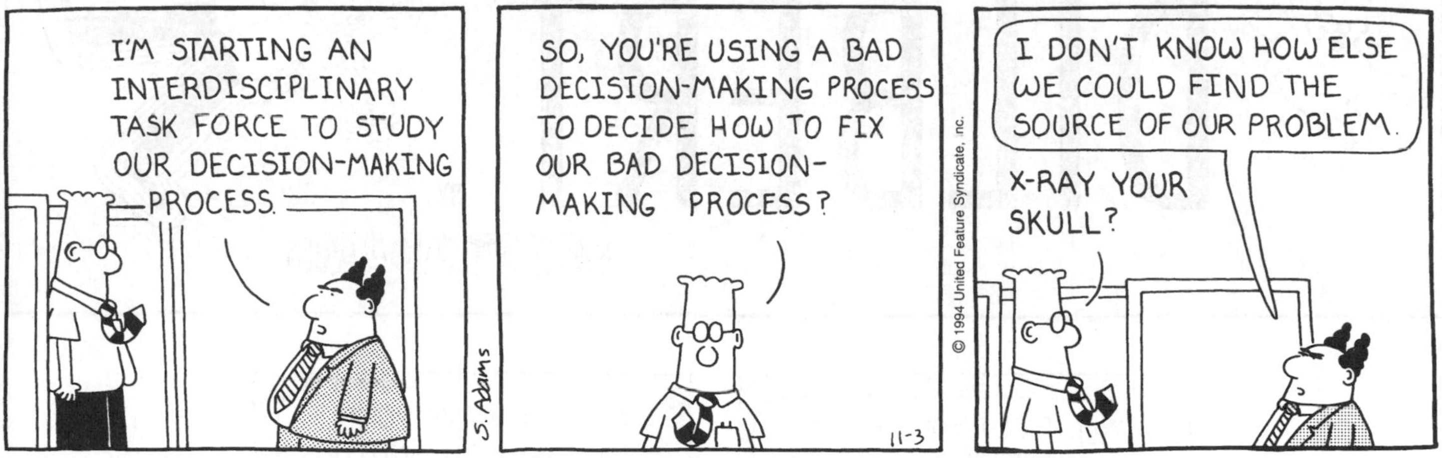
I'M STARTING AN INTERDISCIPLINARY TASK FORCE TO STUDY OUR DECISION-MAKING PROCESS.
SO, YOU'RE USING A BAD DECISION-MAKING PROCESS TO DECIDE HOW TO FIX OUR BAD DECISION-MAKING PROCESS?
I DON'T KNOW HOW ELSE WE COULD FIND THE SOURCE OF OUR PROBLEM.
X-RAY YOUR SKULL?
S. Adams
11-3
© 1994 United Feature Syndicate, Inc.

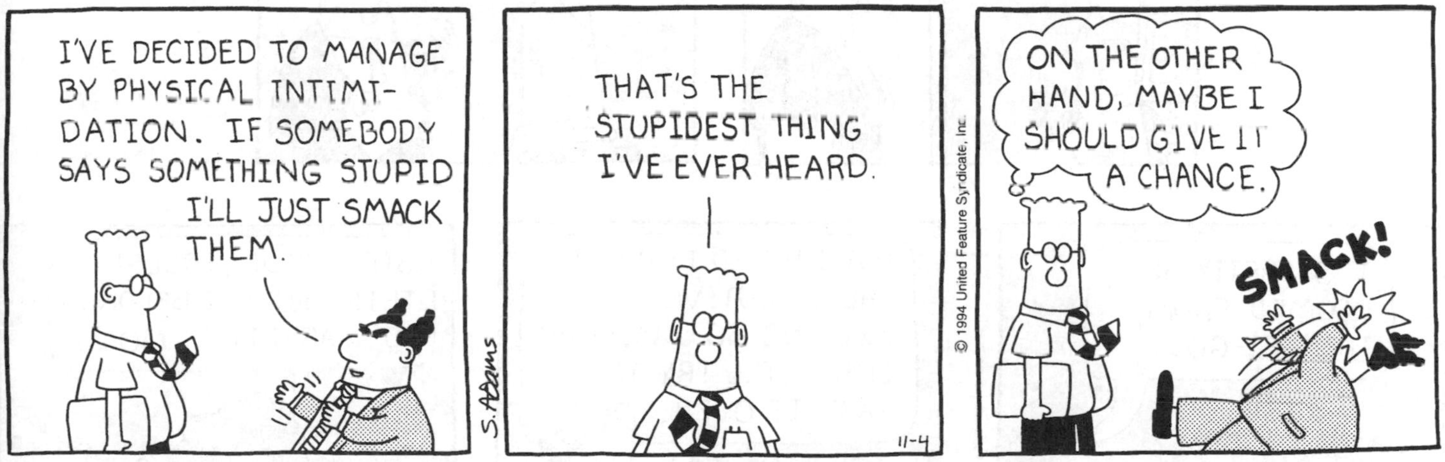
I'VE DECIDED TO MANAGE BY PHYSICAL INTIMIDATION. IF SOMEBODY SAYS SOMETHING STUPID I'LL JUST SMACK THEM.
THAT'S THE STUPIDEST THING I'VE EVER HEARD.
ON THE OTHER HAND, MAYBE I SHOULD GIVE IT A CHANCE.
SMACK!
S. Adams
11-4
© 1994 United Feature Syndicate, Inc.

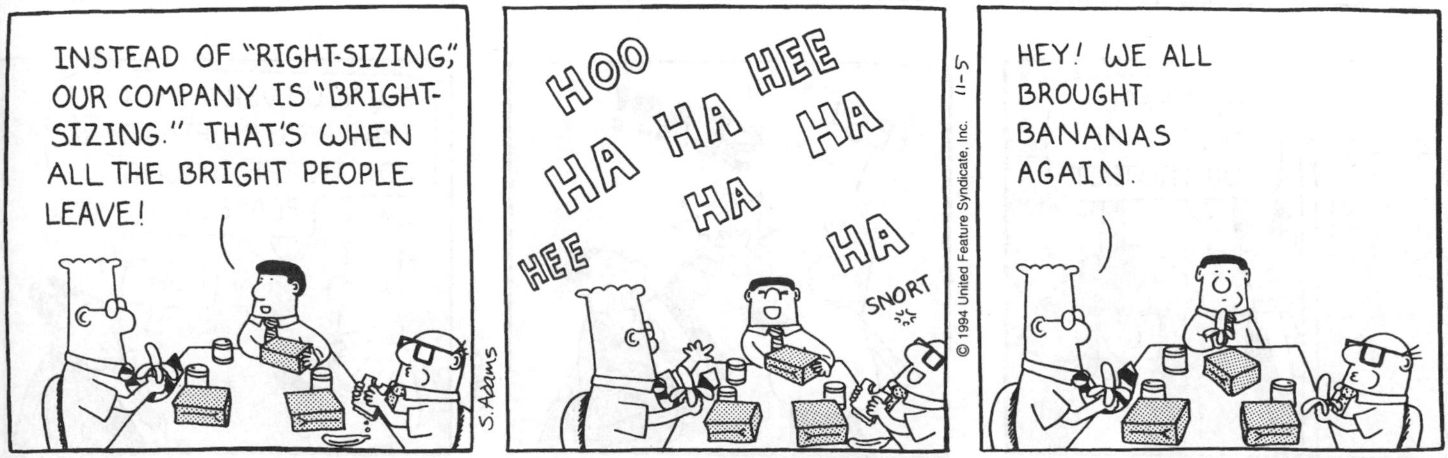
INSTEAD OF "RIGHT-SIZING," OUR COMPANY IS "BRIGHT-SIZING." THAT'S WHEN ALL THE BRIGHT PEOPLE LEAVE!
HOO
HEE
HA HA
HA
HA
HEE
HA
SNORT
HEY! WE ALL BROUGHT BANANAS AGAIN.
S. Adams
11-5
© 1994 United Feature Syndicate, Inc.

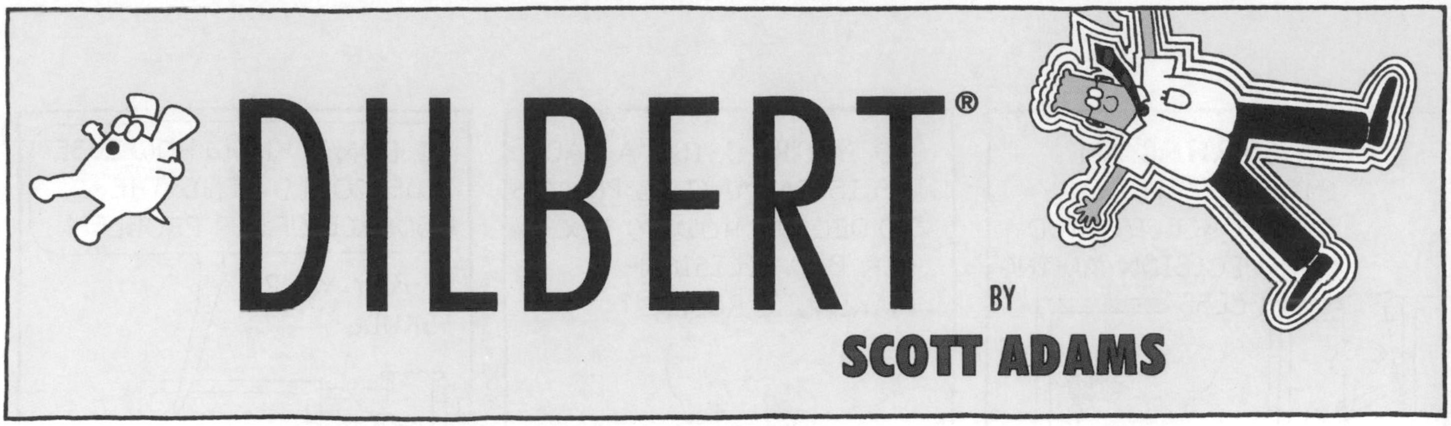
DILBERT®
BY
SCOTT ADAMS

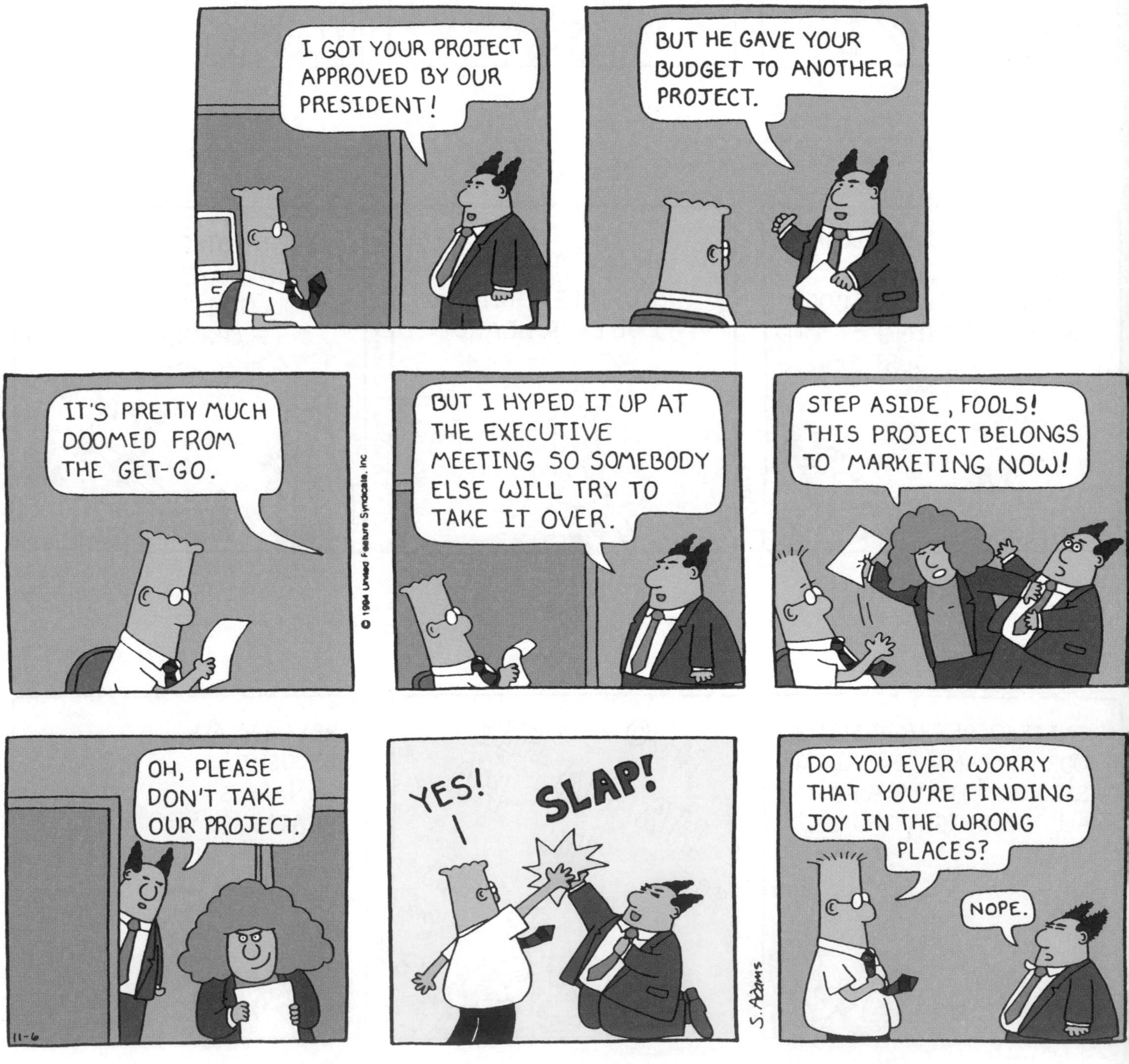
I GOT YOUR PROJECT APPROVED BY OUR PRESIDENT!
BUT HE GAVE YOUR BUDGET TO ANOTHER PROJECT.
IT'S PRETTY MUCH DOOMED FROM THE GET-GO.
© 1994 United Feature Syndicate, Inc
BUT I HYPED IT UP AT THE EXECUTIVE MEETING SO SOMEBODY ELSE WILL TRY TO TAKE IT OVER.
STEP ASIDE, FOOLS! THIS PROJECT BELONGS TO MARKETING NOW!
11-6
OH, PLEASE DON'T TAKE OUR PROJECT.
YES!
SLAP!
S. ADAMS
DO YOU EVER WORRY THAT YOU'RE FINDING JOY IN THE WRONG PLACES?
NOPE.

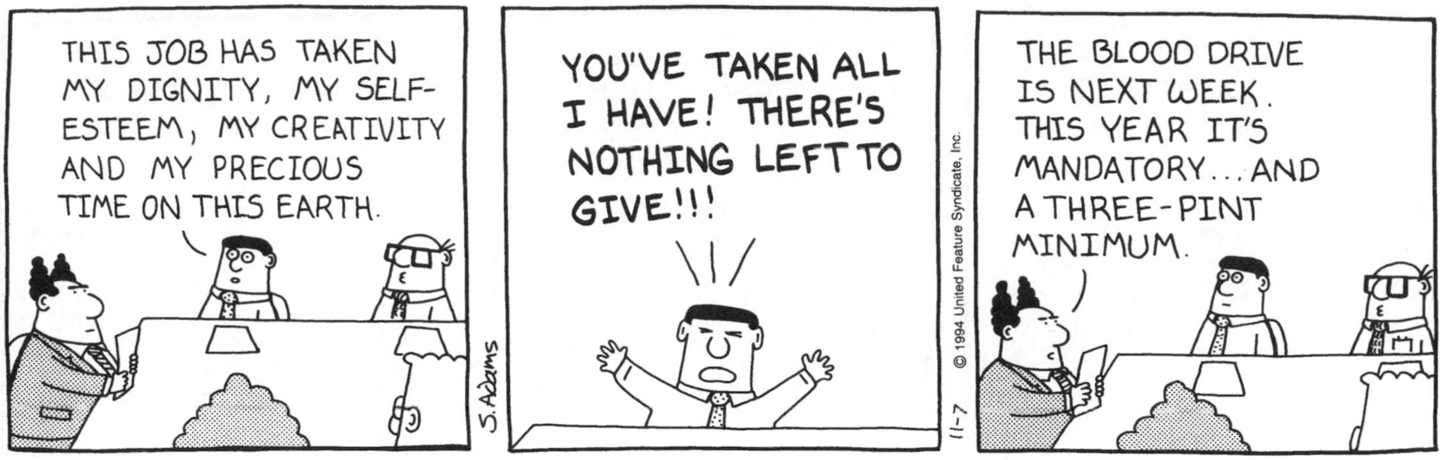
THIS JOB HAS TAKEN MY DIGNITY, MY SELF-ESTEEM, MY CREATIVITY AND MY PRECIOUS TIME ON THIS EARTH.
YOU'VE TAKEN ALL I HAVE! THERE'S NOTHING LEFT TO GIVE!!!
THE BLOOD DRIVE IS NEXT WEEK. THIS YEAR IT'S MANDATORY... AND A THREE-PINT MINIMUM.
S. Adams
11-7
© 1994 United Feature Syndicate, Inc.

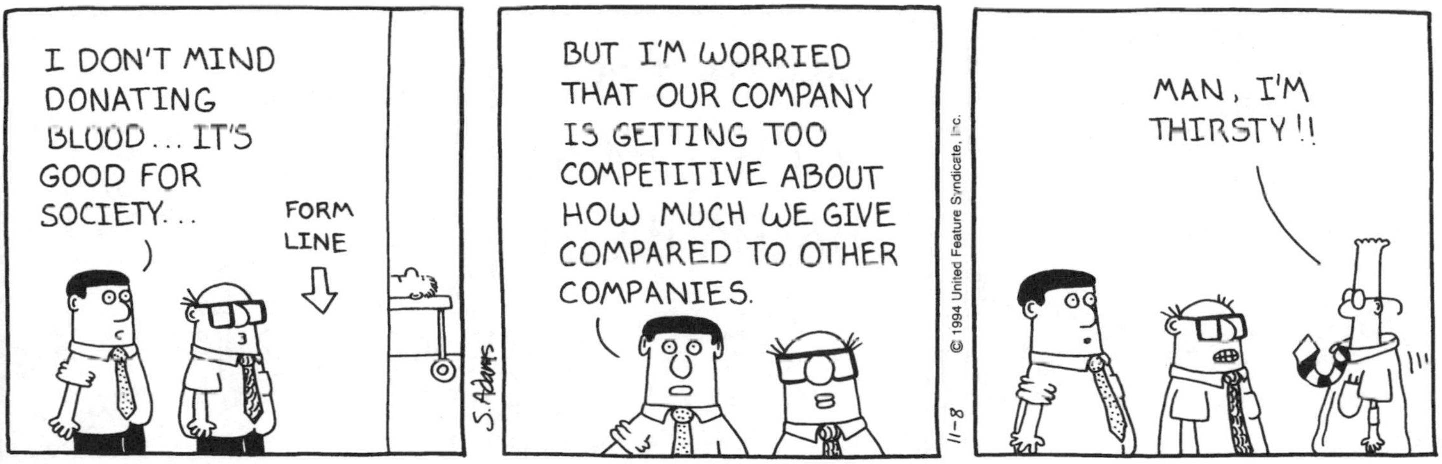
I DON'T MIND DONATING BLOOD... IT'S GOOD FOR SOCIETY...
FORM LINE
BUT I'M WORRIED THAT OUR COMPANY IS GETTING TOO COMPETITIVE ABOUT HOW MUCH WE GIVE COMPARED TO OTHER COMPANIES.
MAN, I'M THIRSTY!!
S. Adams
11-8
© 1994 United Feature Syndicate, Inc.

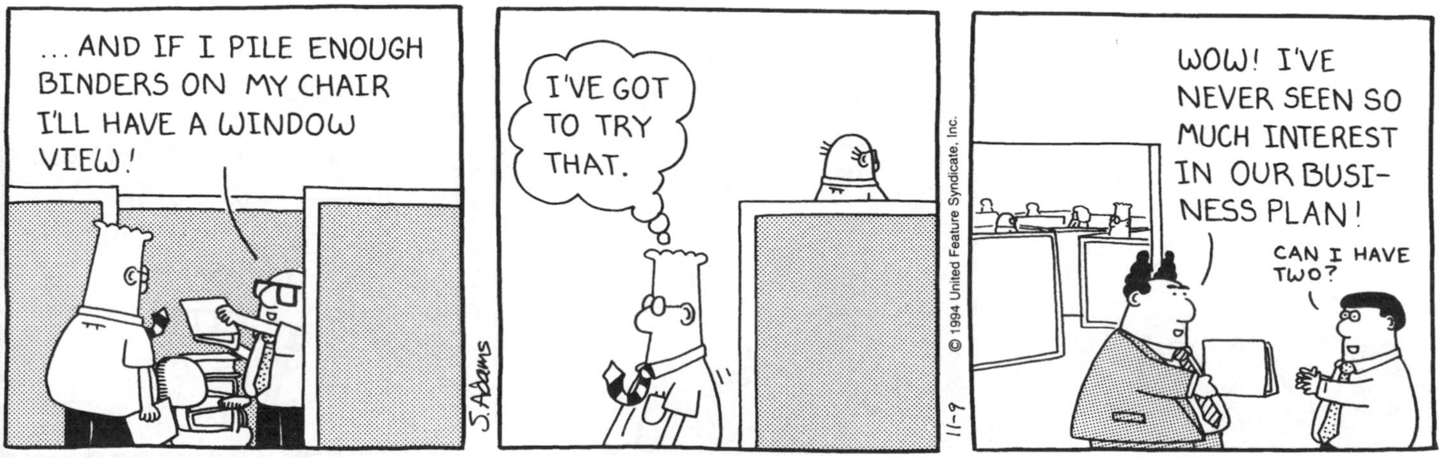
... AND IF I PILE ENOUGH BINDERS ON MY CHAIR I'LL HAVE A WINDOW VIEW!
I'VE GOT TO TRY THAT.
WOW! I'VE NEVER SEEN SO MUCH INTEREST IN OUR BUSINESS PLAN!
CAN I HAVE TWO?
S. Adams
11-9
© 1994 United Feature Syndicate, Inc.

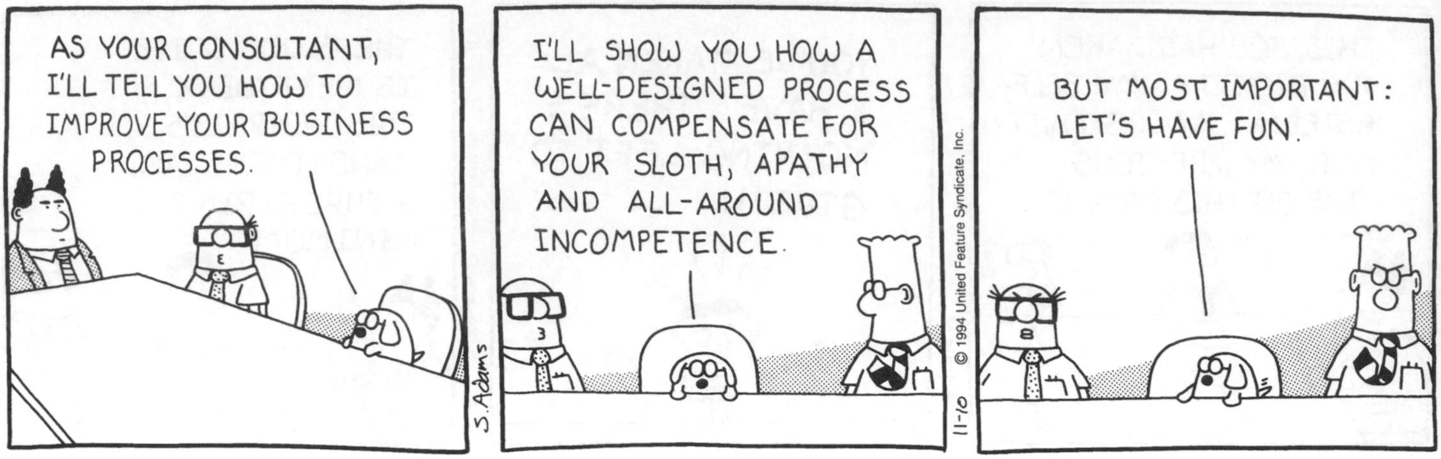
AS YOUR CONSULTANT, I'LL TELL YOU HOW TO IMPROVE YOUR BUSINESS PROCESSES.
I'LL SHOW YOU HOW A WELL-DESIGNED PROCESS CAN COMPENSATE FOR YOUR SLOTH, APATHY AND ALL-AROUND INCOMPETENCE.
BUT MOST IMPORTANT: LET'S HAVE FUN.
S. Adams
11-10
© 1994 United Feature Syndicate, Inc.

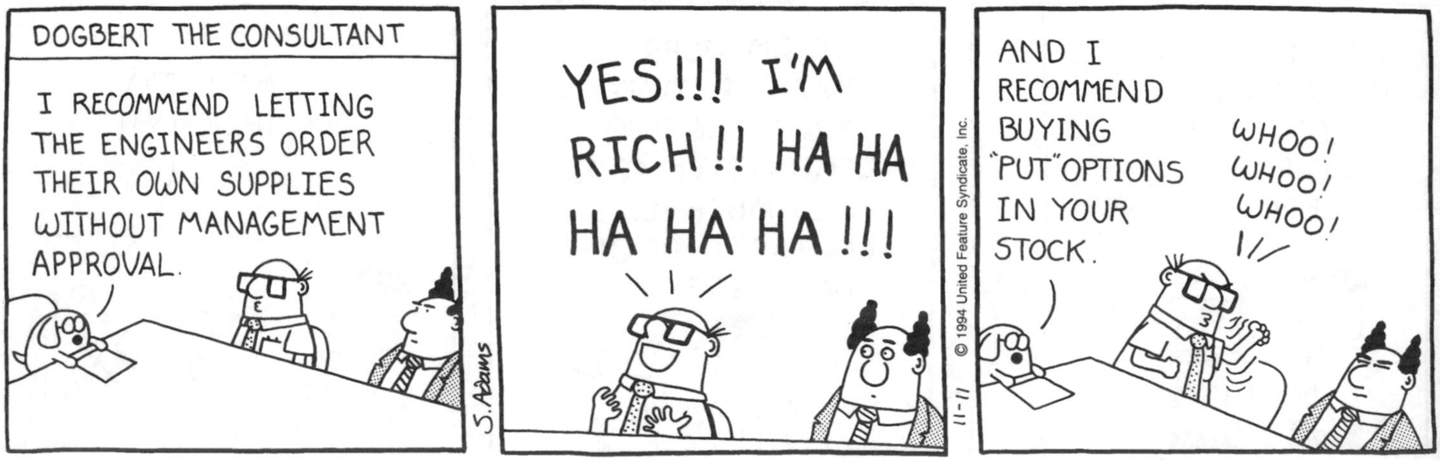
DOGBERT THE CONSULTANT
I RECOMMEND LETTING THE ENGINEERS ORDER THEIR OWN SUPPLIES WITHOUT MANAGEMENT APPROVAL.
YES!!! I'M RICH!! HA HA HA HA HA!!!
AND I RECOMMEND BUYING "PUT" OPTIONS IN YOUR STOCK.
WHOO! WHOO! WHOO!
S. Adams
11-11
© 1994 United Feature Syndicate, Inc.

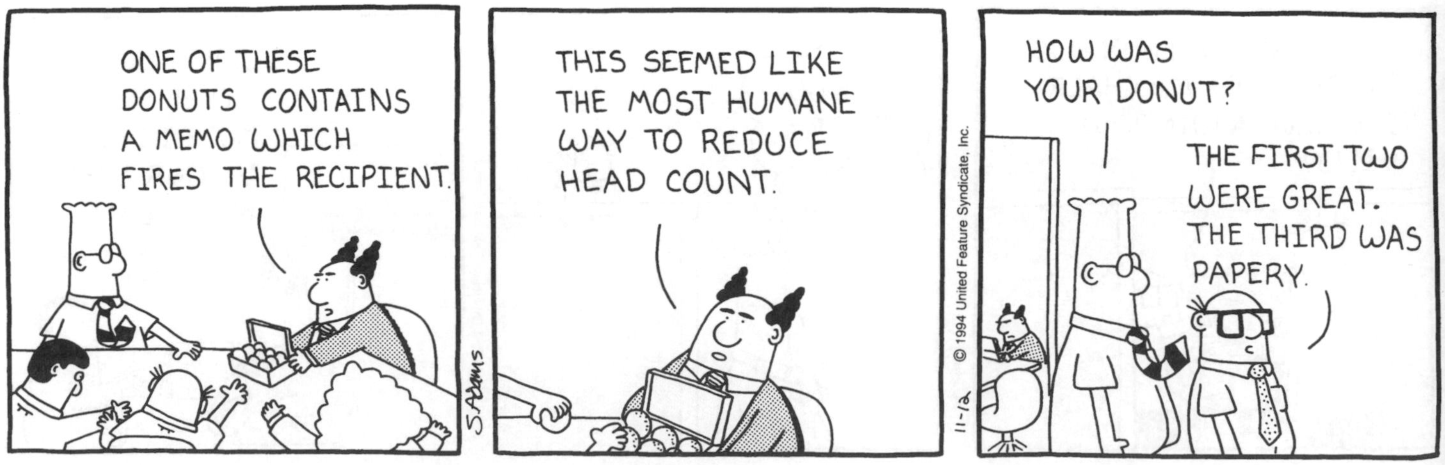
ONE OF THESE DONUTS CONTAINS A MEMO WHICH FIRES THE RECIPIENT.
THIS SEEMED LIKE THE MOST HUMANE WAY TO REDUCE HEAD COUNT.
HOW WAS YOUR DONUT?
THE FIRST TWO WERE GREAT. THE THIRD WAS PAPERY.
S. Adams
11-12
© 1994 United Feature Syndicate, Inc.

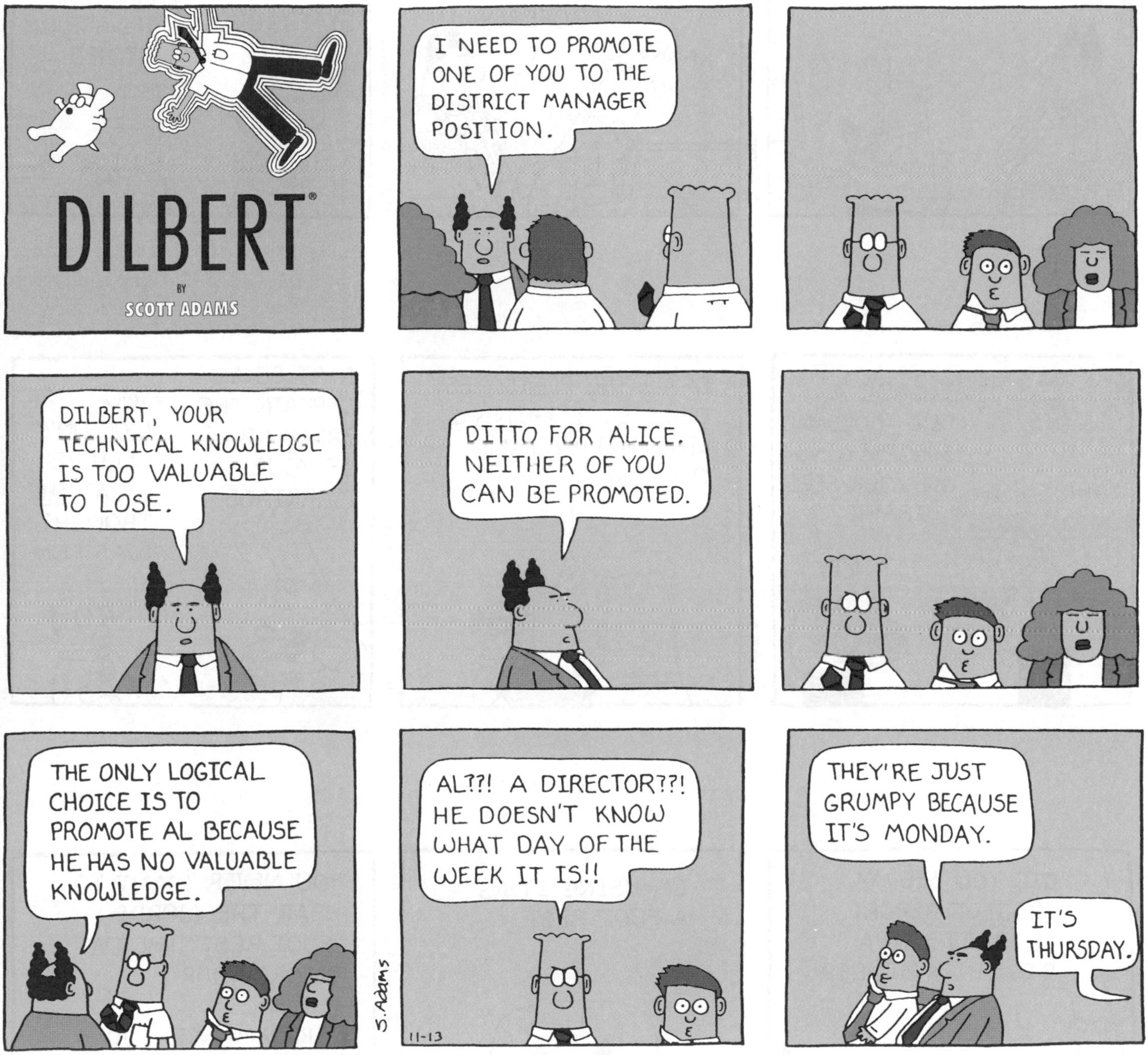
DILBERT®
BY
SCOTT ADAMS
I NEED TO PROMOTE ONE OF YOU TO THE DISTRICT MANAGER POSITION.
DILBERT, YOUR TECHNICAL KNOWLEDGE IS TOO VALUABLE TO LOSE.
DITTO FOR ALICE. NEITHER OF YOU CAN BE PROMOTED.
THE ONLY LOGICAL CHOICE IS TO PROMOTE AL BECAUSE HE HAS NO VALUABLE KNOWLEDGE.
S. Adams
AL??! A DIRECTOR??! HE DOESN'T KNOW WHAT DAY OF THE WEEK IT IS!!
11-13
THEY'RE JUST GRUMPY BECAUSE IT'S MONDAY.
IT'S THURSDAY.

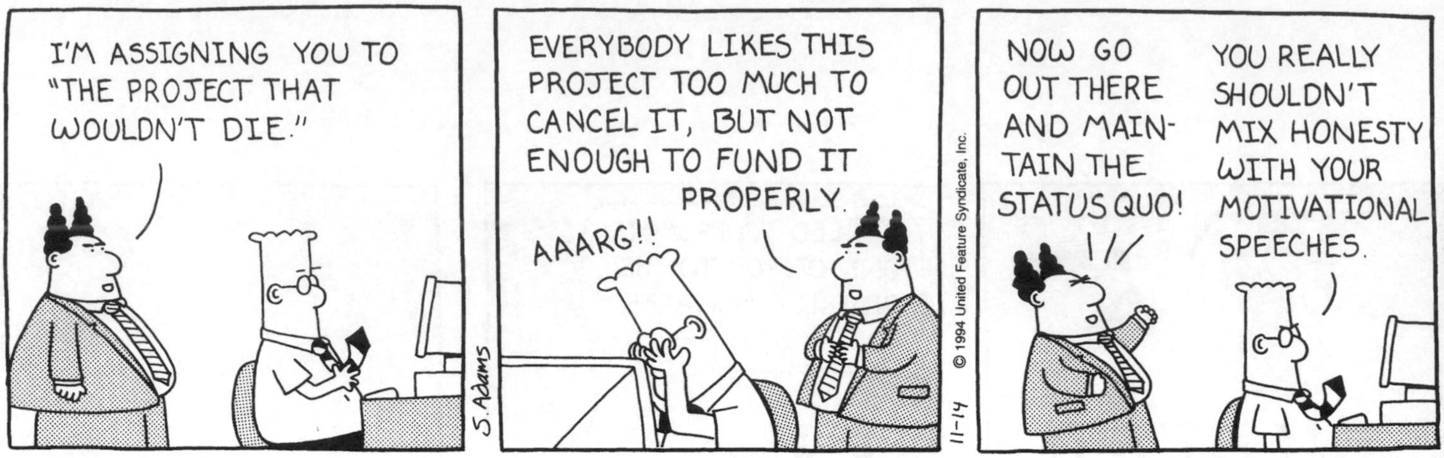
I'M ASSIGNING YOU TO "THE PROJECT THAT WOULDN'T DIE."
S. Adams
EVERYBODY LIKES THIS PROJECT TOO MUCH TO CANCEL IT, BUT NOT ENOUGH TO FUND IT PROPERLY.
AAARG!!
11-14 © 1994 United Feature Syndicate, Inc.
NOW GO OUT THERE AND MAIN-TAIN THE STATUS QUO!
YOU REALLY SHOULDN'T MIX HONESTY WITH YOUR MOTIVATIONAL SPEECHES.

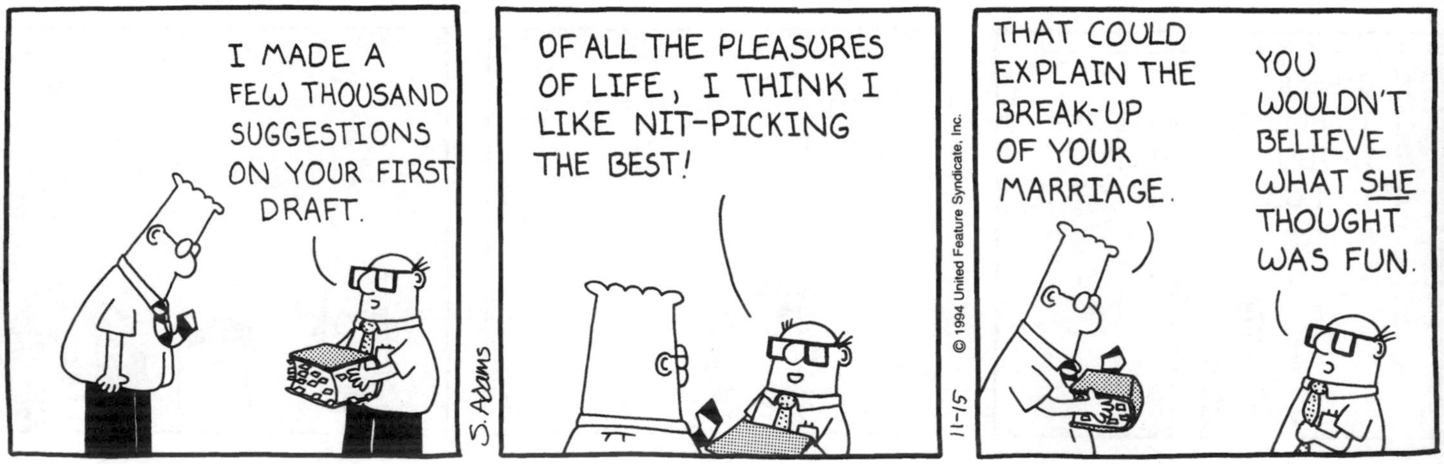
I MADE A FEW THOUSAND SUGGESTIONS ON YOUR FIRST DRAFT.
S. Adams
OF ALL THE PLEASURES OF LIFE, I THINK I LIKE NIT-PICKING THE BEST!
11-15 © 1994 United Feature Syndicate, Inc.
THAT COULD EXPLAIN THE BREAK-UP OF YOUR MARRIAGE.
YOU WOULDN'T BELIEVE WHAT SHE THOUGHT WAS FUN.

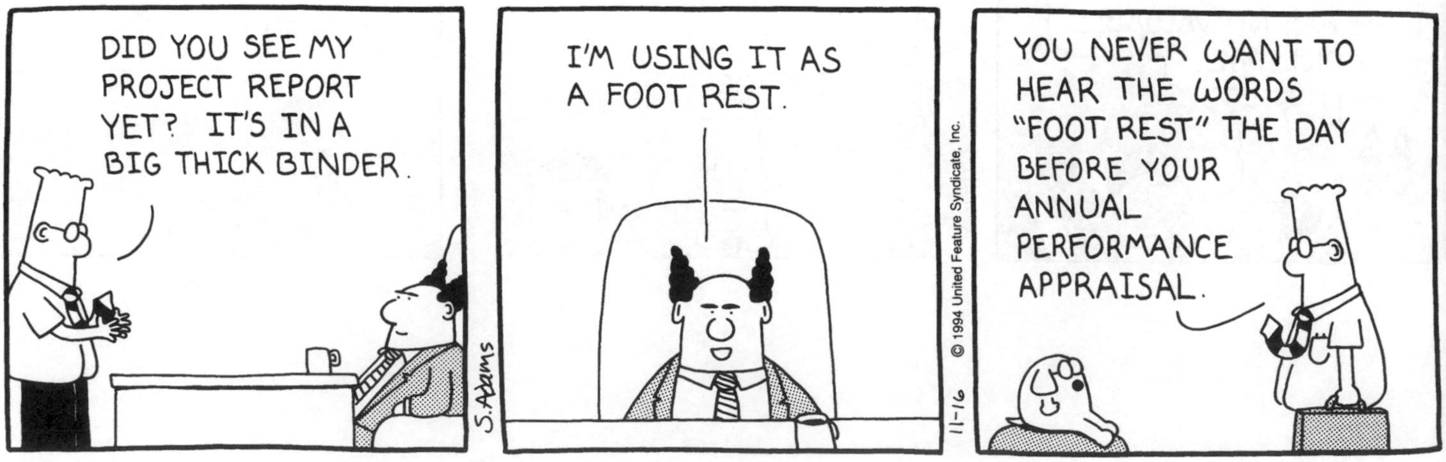
DID YOU SEE MY PROJECT REPORT YET? IT'S IN A BIG THICK BINDER.
S. Adams
I'M USING IT AS A FOOT REST.
11-16 © 1994 United Feature Syndicate, Inc.
YOU NEVER WANT TO HEAR THE WORDS "FOOT REST" THE DAY BEFORE YOUR ANNUAL PERFORMANCE APPRAISAL.

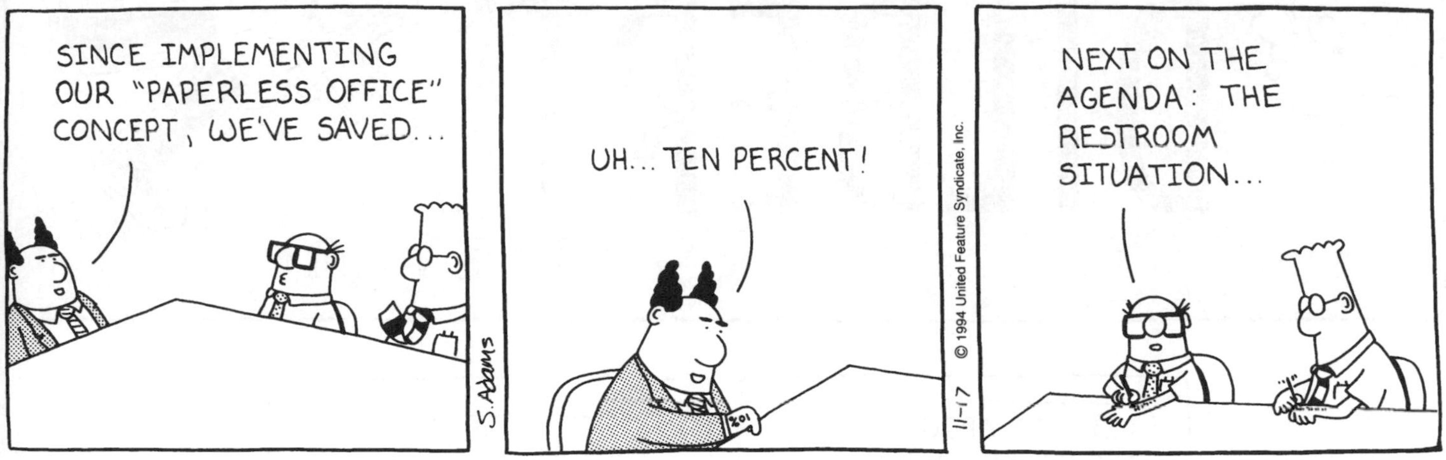
SINCE IMPLEMENTING OUR "PAPERLESS OFFICE" CONCEPT, WE'VE SAVED...
UH... TEN PERCENT!
NEXT ON THE AGENDA: THE RESTROOM SITUATION...
S. Adams
11-17
© 1994 United Feature Syndicate, Inc.

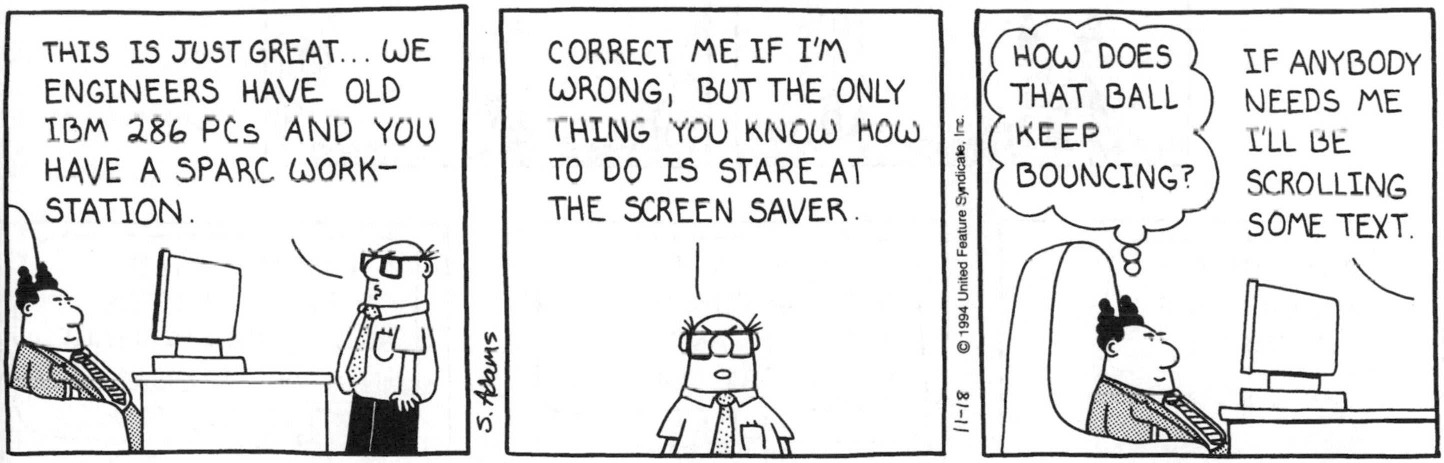
THIS IS JUST GREAT... WE ENGINEERS HAVE OLD IBM 286 PCs AND YOU HAVE A SPARC WORK-STATION.
CORRECT ME IF I'M WRONG, BUT THE ONLY THING YOU KNOW HOW TO DO IS STARE AT THE SCREEN SAVER.
HOW DOES THAT BALL KEEP BOUNCING?
IF ANYBODY NEEDS ME I'LL BE SCROLLING SOME TEXT.
S. Adams
11-18
© 1994 United Feature Syndicate, Inc.

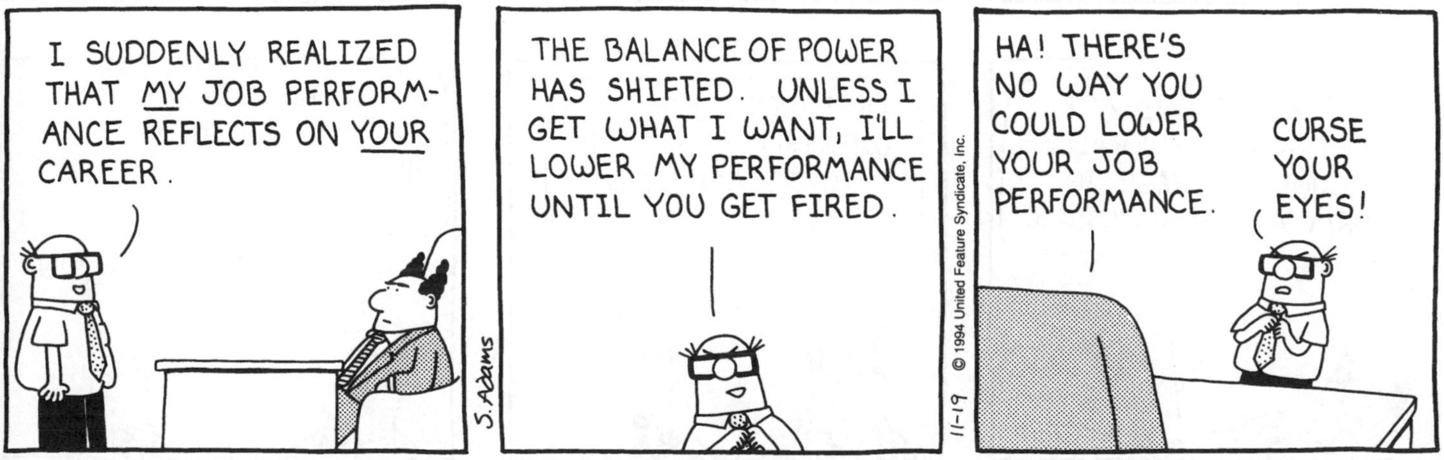
I SUDDENLY REALIZED THAT MY JOB PERFORM-ANCE REFLECTS ON YOUR CAREER.
THE BALANCE OF POWER HAS SHIFTED. UNLESS I GET WHAT I WANT, I'LL LOWER MY PERFORMANCE UNTIL YOU GET FIRED.
HA! THERE'S NO WAY YOU COULD LOWER YOUR JOB PERFORMANCE.
CURSE YOUR EYES!
S. Adams
11-19
© 1994 United Feature Syndicate, Inc.

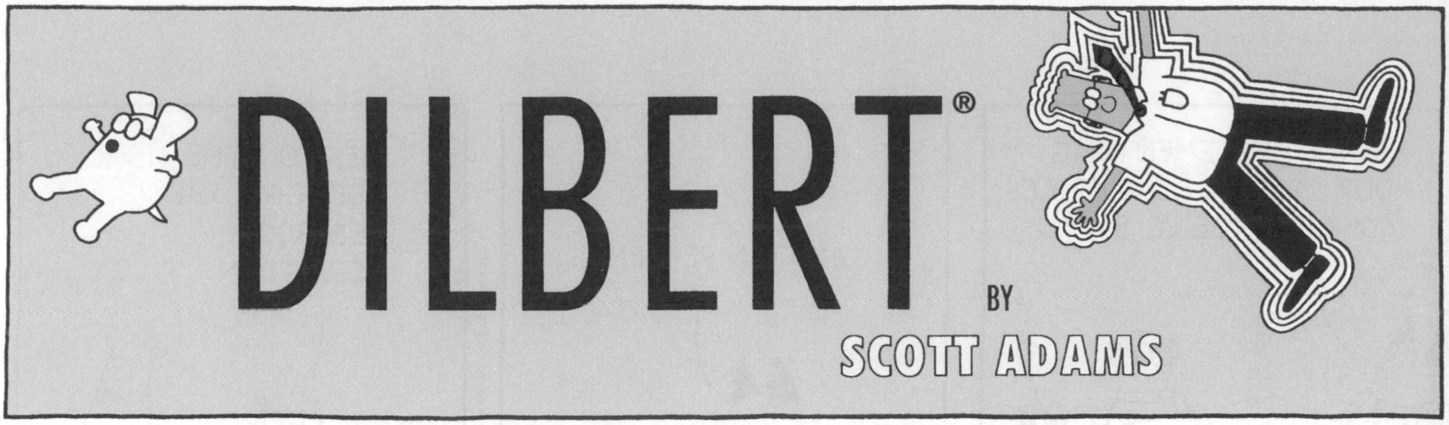
DILBERT®
BY
SCOTT ADAMS

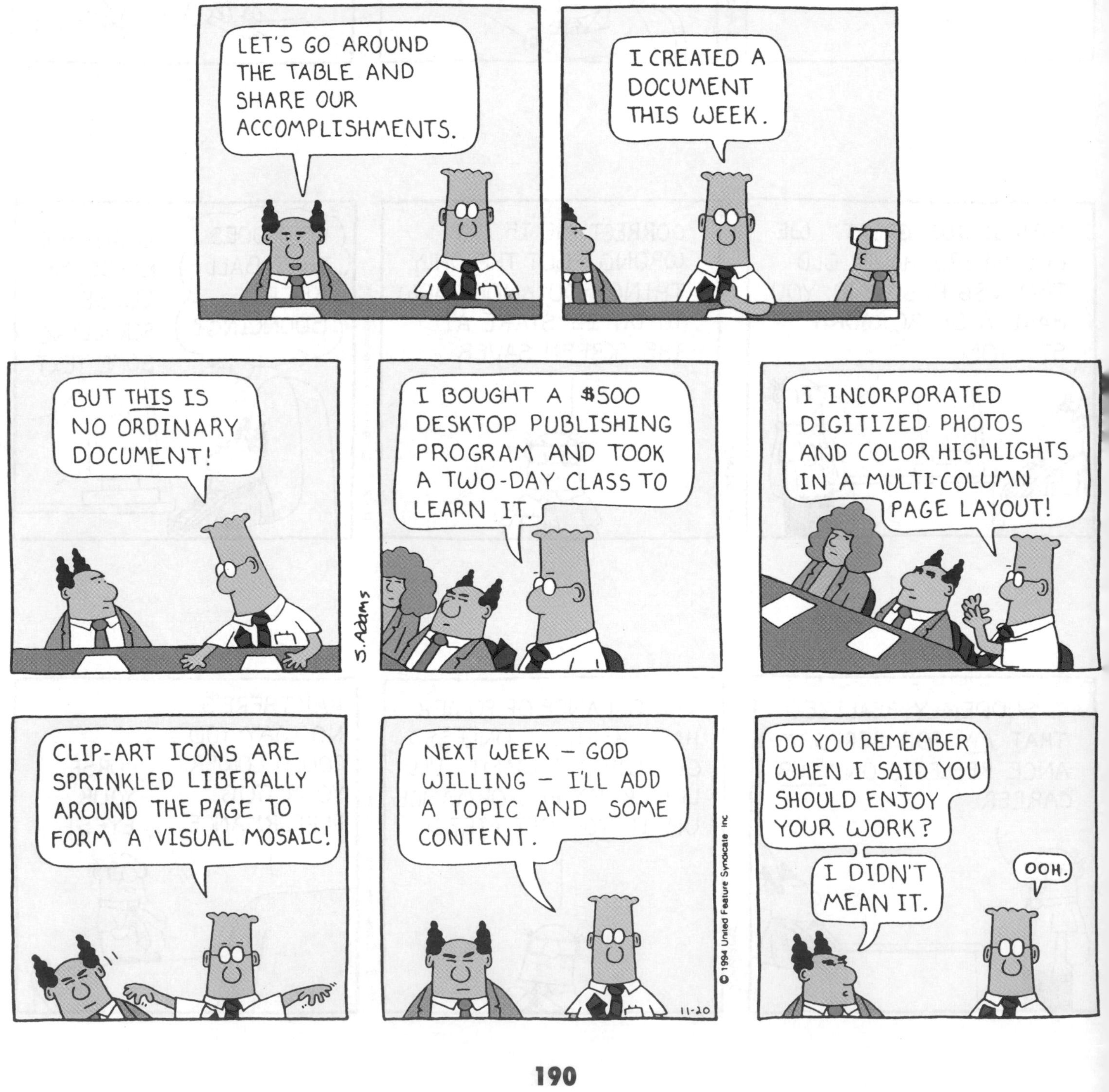
LET'S GO AROUND THE TABLE AND SHARE OUR ACCOMPLISHMENTS.
I CREATED A DOCUMENT THIS WEEK.
BUT THIS IS NO ORDINARY DOCUMENT!
S. Adams
I BOUGHT A $500 DESKTOP PUBLISHING PROGRAM AND TOOK A TWO-DAY CLASS TO LEARN IT.
I INCORPORATED DIGITIZED PHOTOS AND COLOR HIGHLIGHTS IN A MULTI-COLUMN PAGE LAYOUT!
CLIP-ART ICONS ARE SPRINKLED LIBERALLY AROUND THE PAGE TO FORM A VISUAL MOSAIC!
NEXT WEEK – GOD WILLING – I'LL ADD A TOPIC AND SOME CONTENT.
© 1994 United Feature Syndicate Inc
11-20
DO YOU REMEMBER WHEN I SAID YOU SHOULD ENJOY YOUR WORK?
I DIDN'T MEAN IT.
OOH.

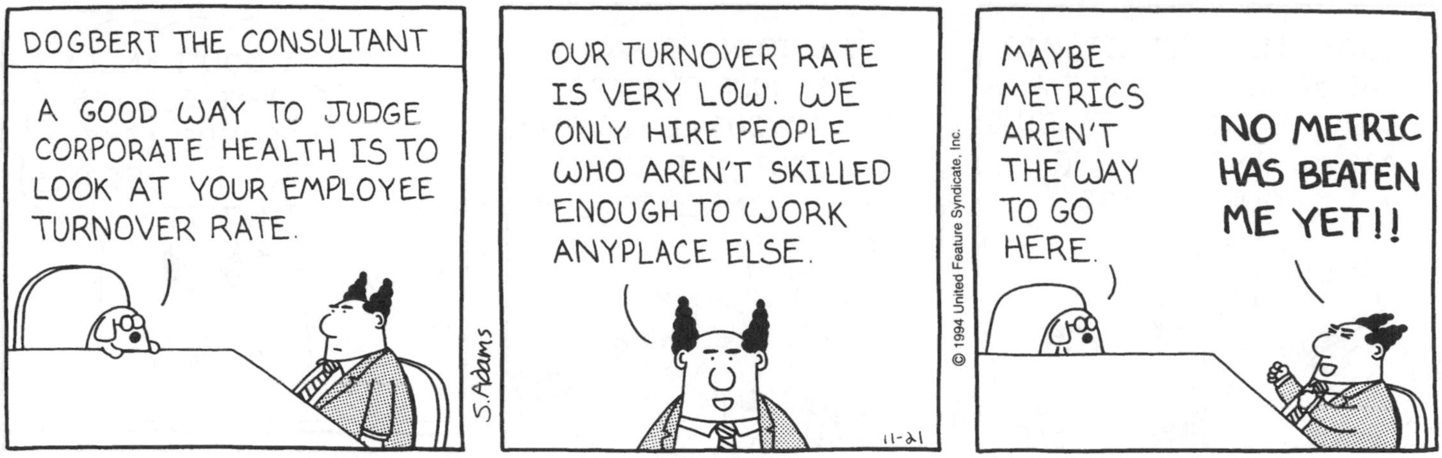
DOGBERT THE CONSULTANT
A GOOD WAY TO JUDGE CORPORATE HEALTH IS TO LOOK AT YOUR EMPLOYEE TURNOVER RATE.
S. Adams
OUR TURNOVER RATE IS VERY LOW. WE ONLY HIRE PEOPLE WHO AREN'T SKILLED ENOUGH TO WORK ANYPLACE ELSE.
11-21
© 1994 United Feature Syndicate, Inc.
MAYBE METRICS AREN'T THE WAY TO GO HERE.
NO METRIC HAS BEATEN ME YET!!

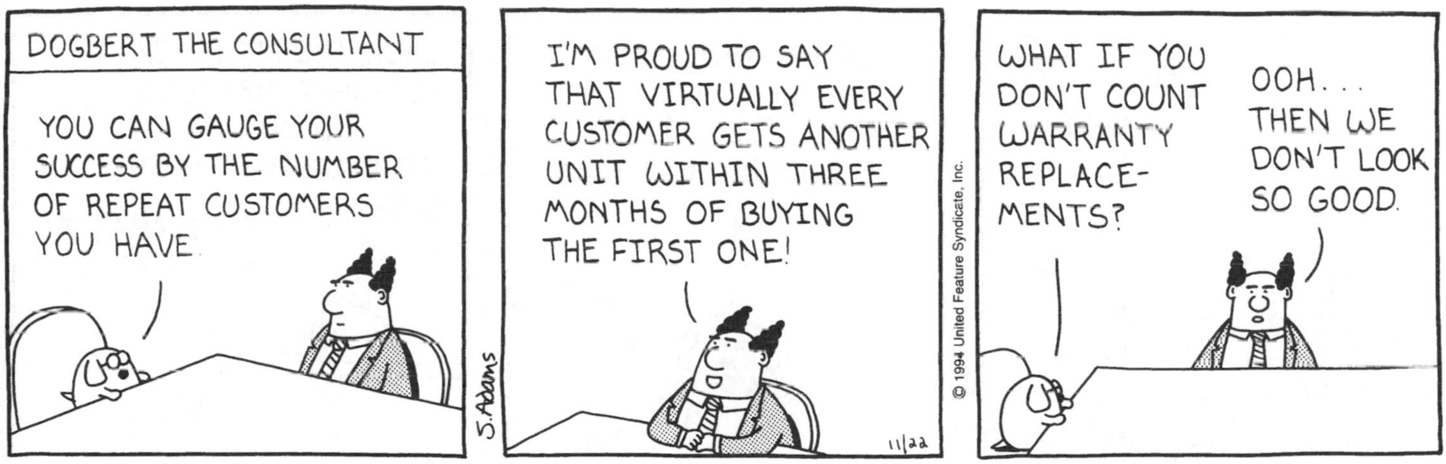
DOGBERT THE CONSULTANT
YOU CAN GAUGE YOUR SUCCESS BY THE NUMBER OF REPEAT CUSTOMERS YOU HAVE.
S. Adams
I'M PROUD TO SAY THAT VIRTUALLY EVERY CUSTOMER GETS ANOTHER UNIT WITHIN THREE MONTHS OF BUYING THE FIRST ONE!
11/22
© 1994 United Feature Syndicate, Inc.
WHAT IF YOU DON'T COUNT WARRANTY REPLACE-MENTS?
OOH... THEN WE DON'T LOOK SO GOOD.

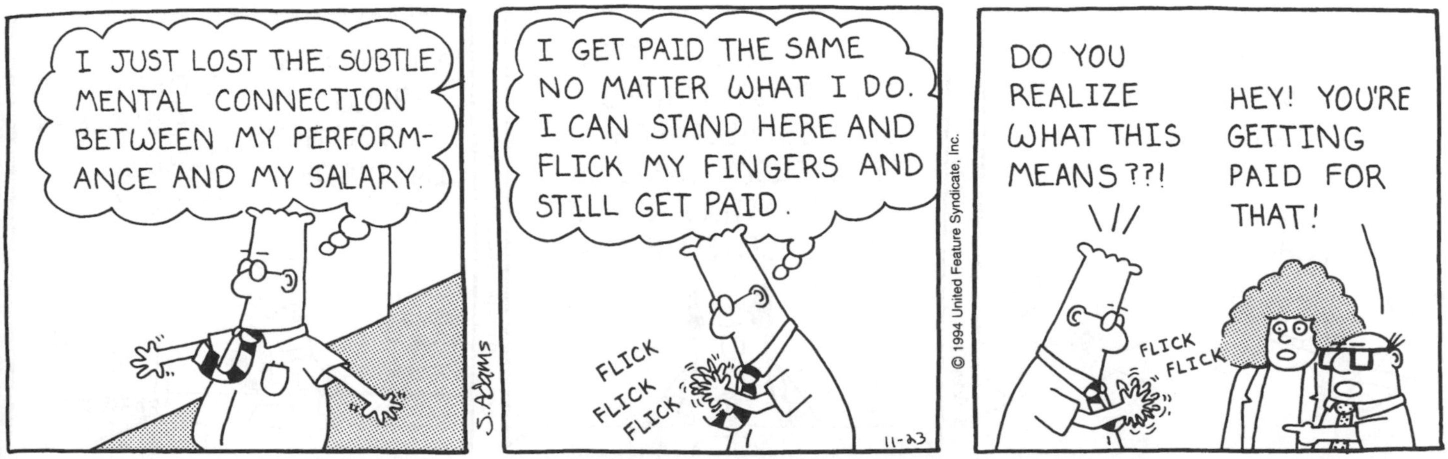
I JUST LOST THE SUBTLE MENTAL CONNECTION BETWEEN MY PERFORM-ANCE AND MY SALARY.
S. Adams
I GET PAID THE SAME NO MATTER WHAT I DO. I CAN STAND HERE AND FLICK MY FINGERS AND STILL GET PAID.
FLICK
FLICK
FLICK
11-23
© 1994 United Feature Syndicate, Inc.
DO YOU REALIZE WHAT THIS MEANS??!
FLICK
FLICK
HEY! YOU'RE GETTING PAID FOR THAT!

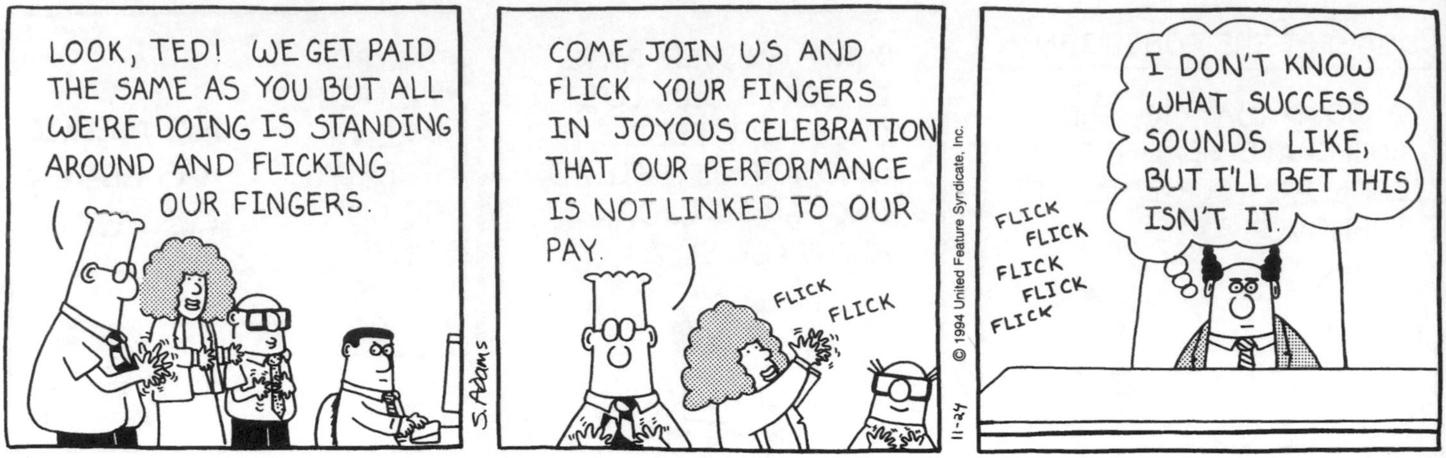
LOOK, TED! WE GET PAID THE SAME AS YOU BUT ALL WE'RE DOING IS STANDING AROUND AND FLICKING OUR FINGERS.
S. Adams
COME JOIN US AND FLICK YOUR FINGERS IN JOYOUS CELEBRATION THAT OUR PERFORMANCE IS NOT LINKED TO OUR PAY.
FLICK
FLICK
11-24
© 1994 United Feature Syndicate, Inc.
FLICK
FLICK
FLICK
FLICK
FLICK
I DON'T KNOW WHAT SUCCESS SOUNDS LIKE, BUT I'LL BET THIS ISN'T IT.

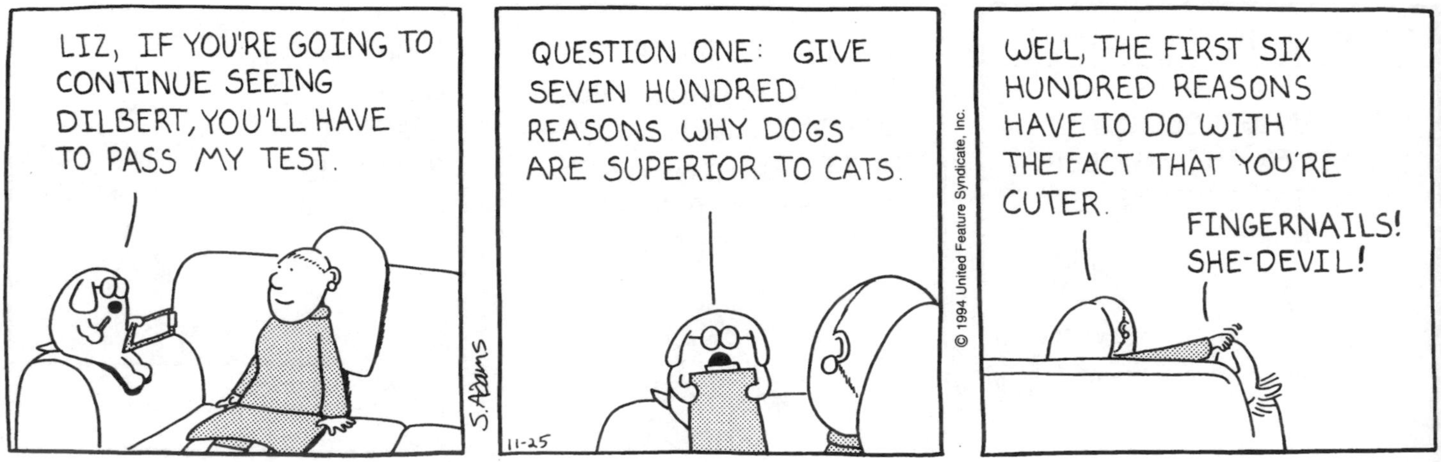
LIZ, IF YOU'RE GOING TO CONTINUE SEEING DILBERT, YOU'LL HAVE TO PASS MY TEST.
S. Adams
QUESTION ONE: GIVE SEVEN HUNDRED REASONS WHY DOGS ARE SUPERIOR TO CATS.
11-25
© 1994 United Feature Syndicate, Inc.
WELL, THE FIRST SIX HUNDRED REASONS HAVE TO DO WITH THE FACT THAT YOU'RE CUTER.
FINGERNAILS! SHE-DEVIL!

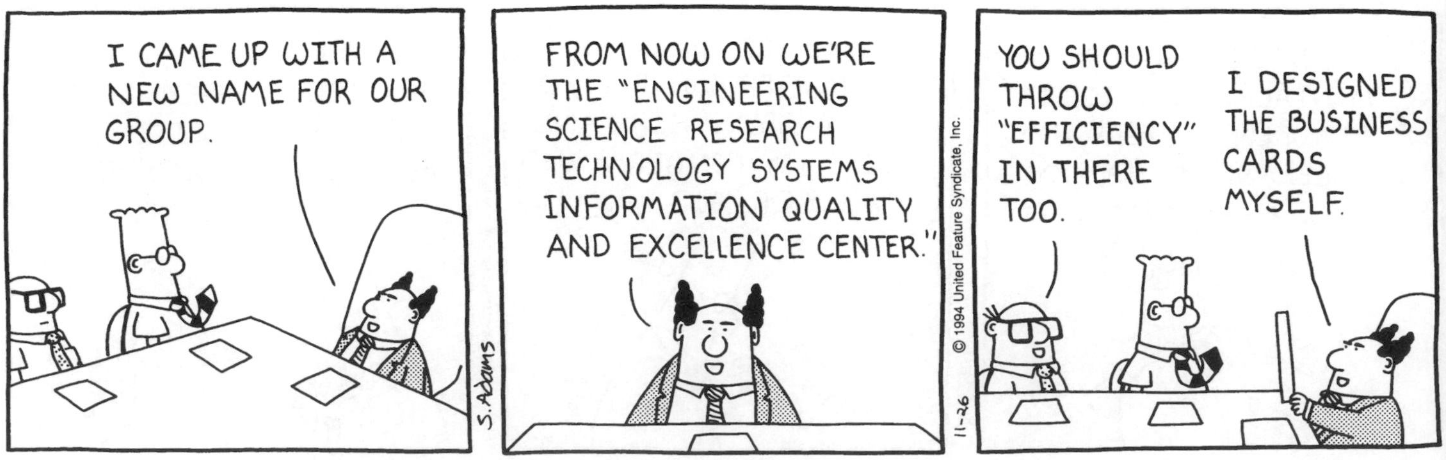
I CAME UP WITH A NEW NAME FOR OUR GROUP.
S. Adams
FROM NOW ON WE'RE THE "ENGINEERING SCIENCE RESEARCH TECHNOLOGY SYSTEMS INFORMATION QUALITY AND EXCELLENCE CENTER."
11-26
© 1994 United Feature Syndicate, Inc.
YOU SHOULD THROW "EFFICIENCY" IN THERE TOO.
I DESIGNED THE BUSINESS CARDS MYSELF.

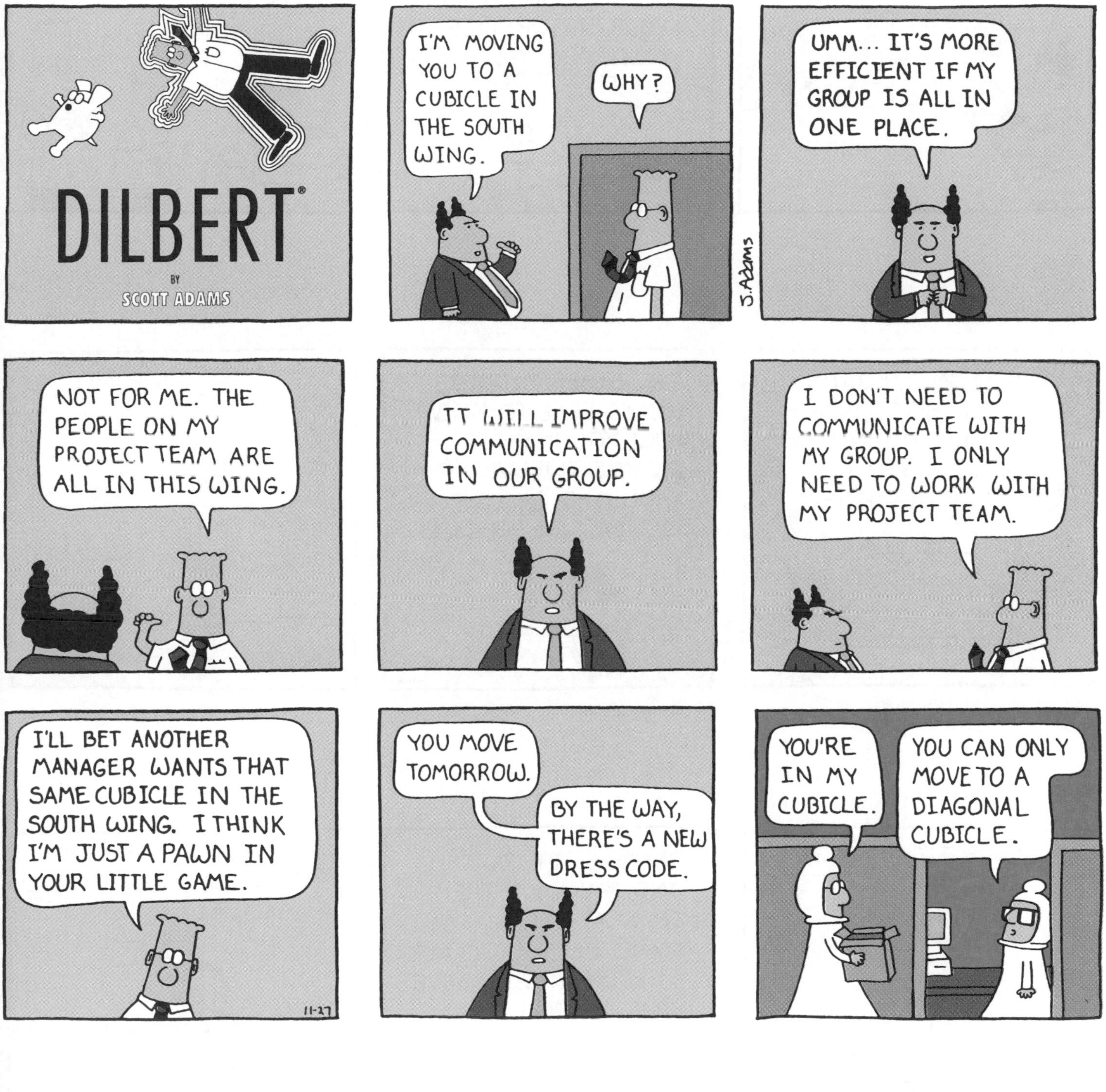
DILBERT®
BY
SCOTT ADAMS
I'M MOVING YOU TO A CUBICLE IN THE SOUTH WING.
WHY?
S. Adams
UMM... IT'S MORE EFFICIENT IF MY GROUP IS ALL IN ONE PLACE.
NOT FOR ME. THE PEOPLE ON MY PROJECT TEAM ARE ALL IN THIS WING.
IT WILL IMPROVE COMMUNICATION IN OUR GROUP.
I DON'T NEED TO COMMUNICATE WITH MY GROUP. I ONLY NEED TO WORK WITH MY PROJECT TEAM.
I'LL BET ANOTHER MANAGER WANTS THAT SAME CUBICLE IN THE SOUTH WING. I THINK I'M JUST A PAWN IN YOUR LITTLE GAME.
11-27
YOU MOVE TOMORROW.
BY THE WAY, THERE'S A NEW DRESS CODE.
YOU'RE IN MY CUBICLE.
YOU CAN ONLY MOVE TO A DIAGONAL CUBICLE.

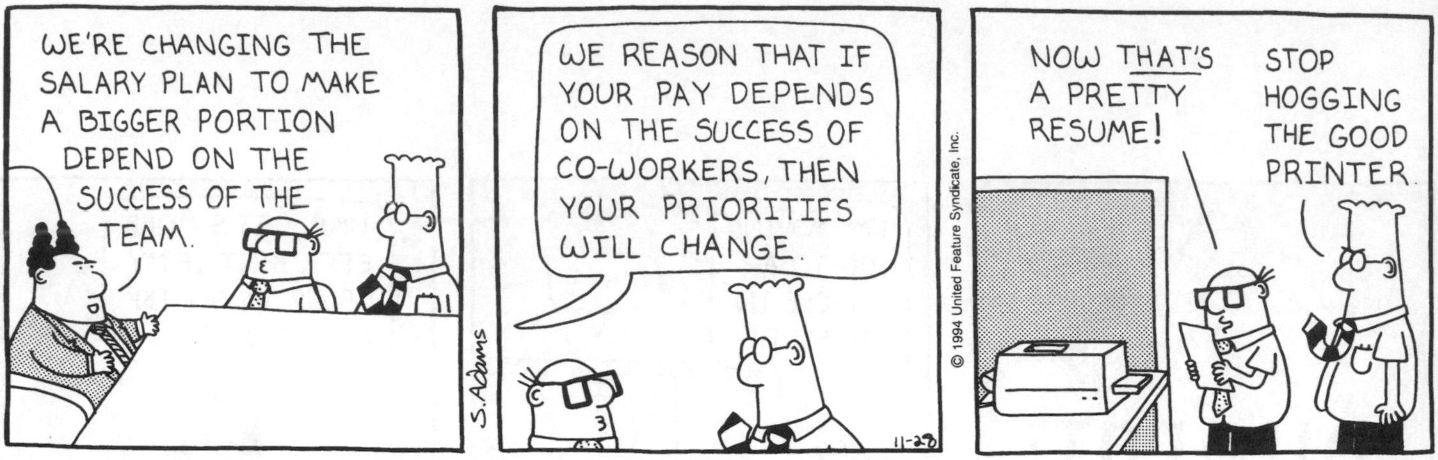
WE'RE CHANGING THE SALARY PLAN TO MAKE A BIGGER PORTION DEPEND ON THE SUCCESS OF THE TEAM.
S. Adams
WE REASON THAT IF YOUR PAY DEPENDS ON THE SUCCESS OF CO-WORKERS, THEN YOUR PRIORITIES WILL CHANGE.
11-28
© 1994 United Feature Syndicate, Inc.
NOW THAT'S A PRETTY RESUME!
STOP HOGGING THE GOOD PRINTER.

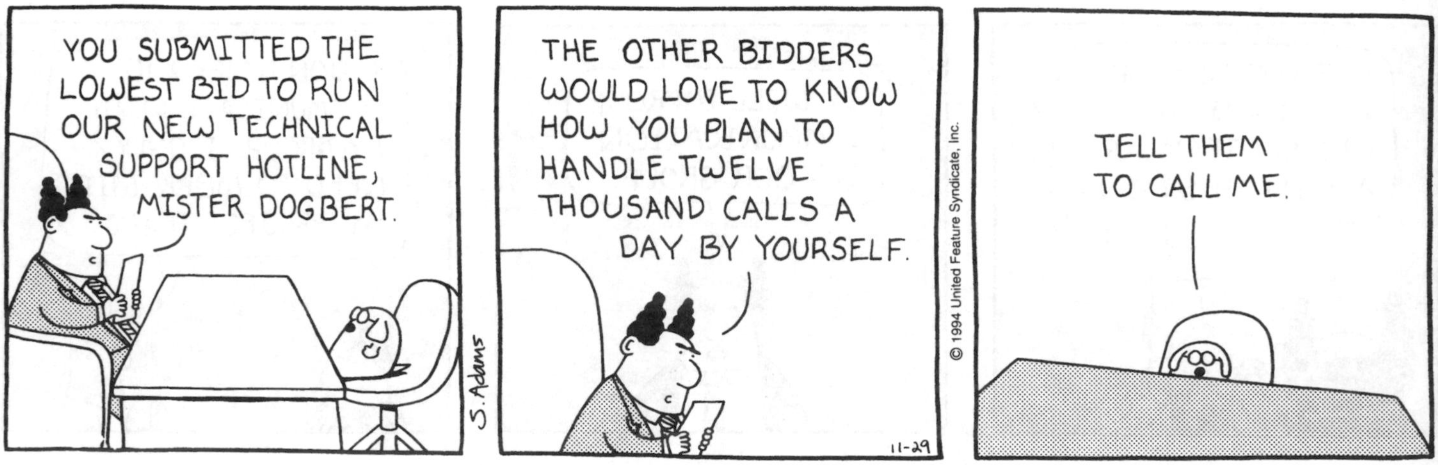
YOU SUBMITTED THE LOWEST BID TO RUN OUR NEW TECHNICAL SUPPORT HOTLINE, MISTER DOGBERT.
S. Adams
THE OTHER BIDDERS WOULD LOVE TO KNOW HOW YOU PLAN TO HANDLE TWELVE THOUSAND CALLS A DAY BY YOURSELF.
11-29
© 1994 United Feature Syndicate, Inc.
TELL THEM TO CALL ME.

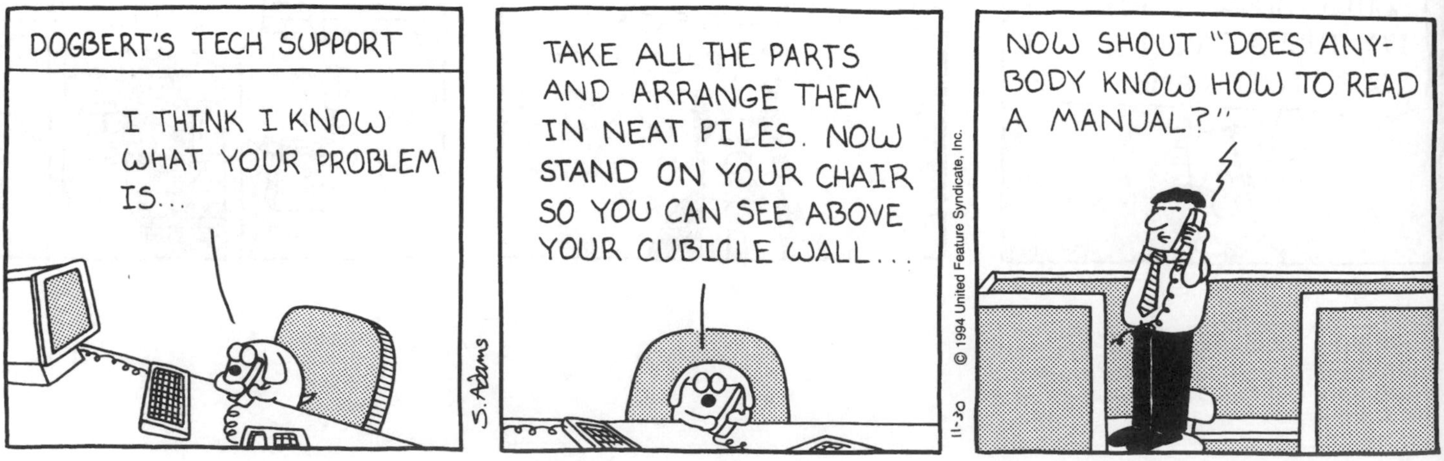
DOGBERT'S TECH SUPPORT
I THINK I KNOW WHAT YOUR PROBLEM IS...
S. Adams
TAKE ALL THE PARTS AND ARRANGE THEM IN NEAT PILES. NOW STAND ON YOUR CHAIR SO YOU CAN SEE ABOVE YOUR CUBICLE WALL...
11-30
© 1994 United Feature Syndicate, Inc.
NOW SHOUT "DOES ANYBODY KNOW HOW TO READ A MANUAL?"

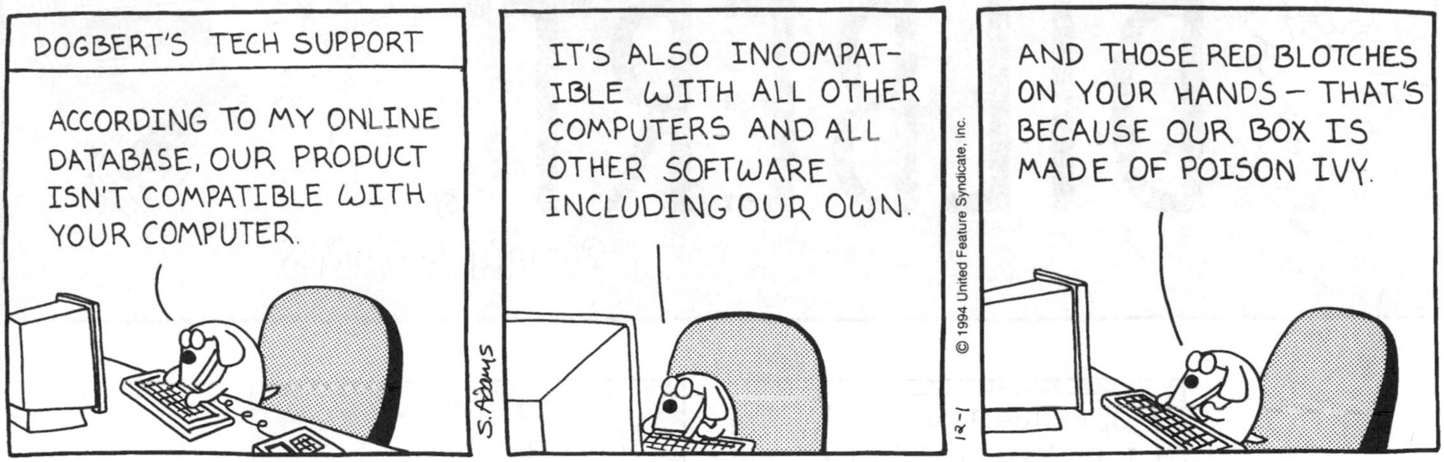
DOGBERT'S TECH SUPPORT
ACCORDING TO MY ONLINE DATABASE, OUR PRODUCT ISN'T COMPATIBLE WITH YOUR COMPUTER.
S. Adams
IT'S ALSO INCOMPATIBLE WITH ALL OTHER COMPUTERS AND ALL OTHER SOFTWARE INCLUDING OUR OWN.
12-1
© 1994 United Feature Syndicate, Inc.
AND THOSE RED BLOTCHES ON YOUR HANDS – THAT'S BECAUSE OUR BOX IS MADE OF POISON IVY.

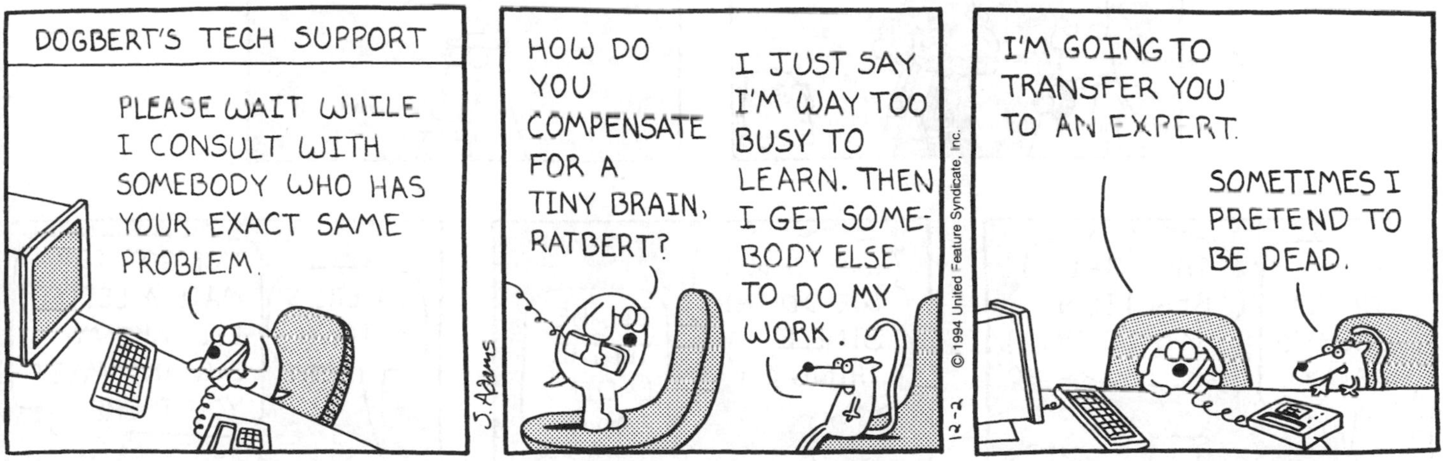
DOGBERT'S TECH SUPPORT
PLEASE WAIT WHILE I CONSULT WITH SOMEBODY WHO HAS YOUR EXACT SAME PROBLEM.
S. Adams
HOW DO YOU COMPENSATE FOR A TINY BRAIN, RATBERT?
I JUST SAY I'M WAY TOO BUSY TO LEARN. THEN I GET SOMEBODY ELSE TO DO MY WORK.
12-2
© 1994 United Feature Syndicate, Inc.
I'M GOING TO TRANSFER YOU TO AN EXPERT.
SOMETIMES I PRETEND TO BE DEAD.

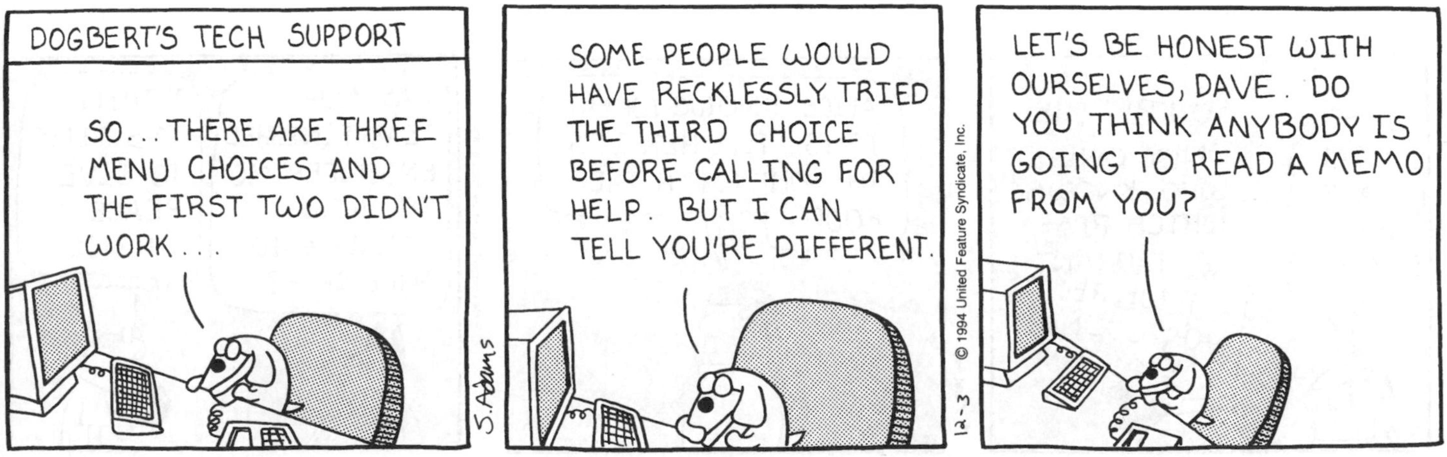
DOGBERT'S TECH SUPPORT
SO... THERE ARE THREE MENU CHOICES AND THE FIRST TWO DIDN'T WORK...
S. Adams
SOME PEOPLE WOULD HAVE RECKLESSLY TRIED THE THIRD CHOICE BEFORE CALLING FOR HELP. BUT I CAN TELL YOU'RE DIFFERENT.
12-3
© 1994 United Feature Syndicate, Inc.
LET'S BE HONEST WITH OURSELVES, DAVE. DO YOU THINK ANYBODY IS GOING TO READ A MEMO FROM YOU?

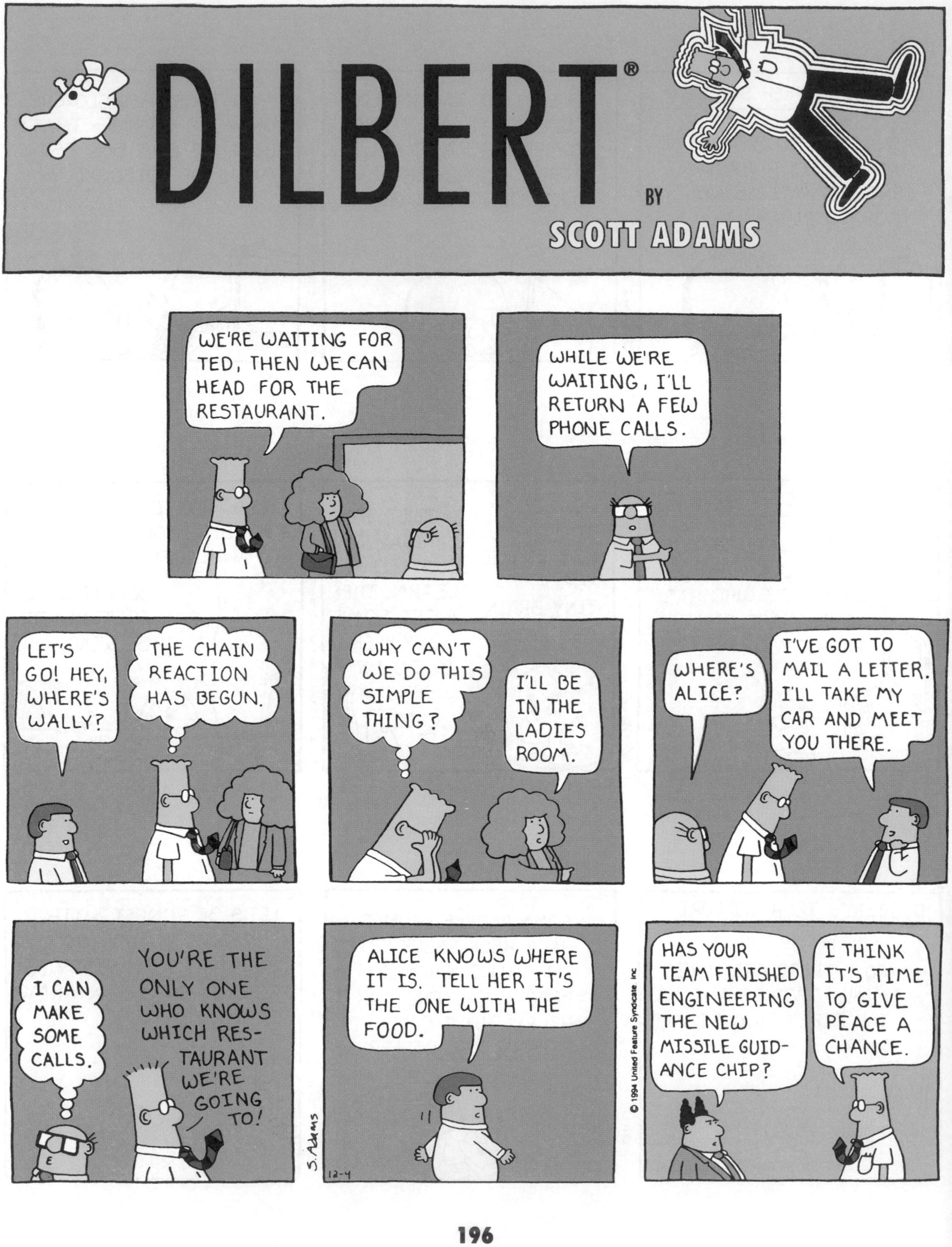
DILBERT®
BY
SCOTT ADAMS
WE'RE WAITING FOR TED, THEN WE CAN HEAD FOR THE RESTAURANT.
WHILE WE'RE WAITING, I'LL RETURN A FEW PHONE CALLS.
LET'S GO! HEY, WHERE'S WALLY?
THE CHAIN REACTION HAS BEGUN.
WHY CAN'T WE DO THIS SIMPLE THING?
I'LL BE IN THE LADIES ROOM.
WHERE'S ALICE?
I'VE GOT TO MAIL A LETTER. I'LL TAKE MY CAR AND MEET YOU THERE.
I CAN MAKE SOME CALLS.
YOU'RE THE ONLY ONE WHO KNOWS WHICH RES-TAURANT WE'RE GOING TO!
S. Adams
12-4
ALICE KNOWS WHERE IT IS. TELL HER IT'S THE ONE WITH THE FOOD.
© 1994 United Feature Syndicate, Inc
HAS YOUR TEAM FINISHED ENGINEERING THE NEW MISSILE GUID-ANCE CHIP?
I THINK IT'S TIME TO GIVE PEACE A CHANCE.

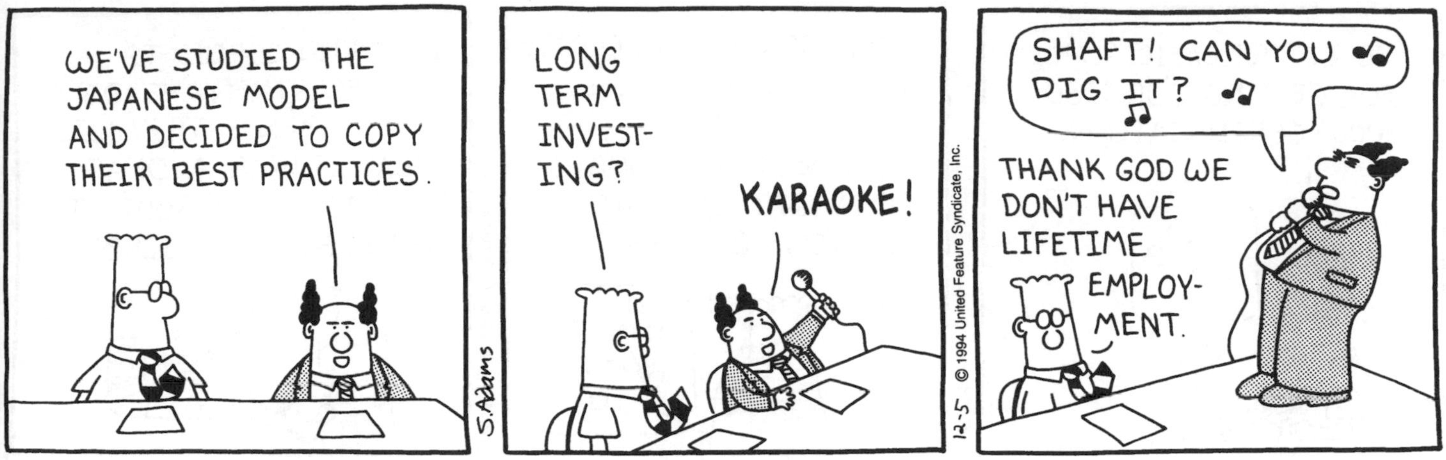
WE'VE STUDIED THE JAPANESE MODEL AND DECIDED TO COPY THEIR BEST PRACTICES.
S. Adams
LONG TERM INVEST-ING?
KARAOKE!
12-5 © 1994 United Feature Syndicate, Inc.
SHAFT! CAN YOU DIG IT?
THANK GOD WE DON'T HAVE LIFETIME EMPLOY-MENT.

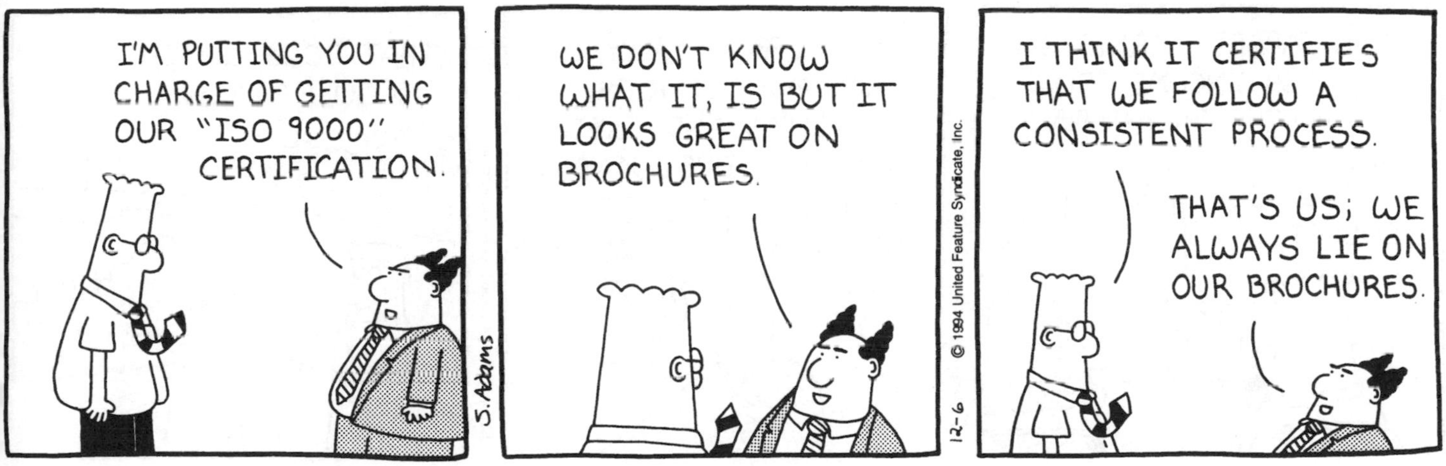
I'M PUTTING YOU IN CHARGE OF GETTING OUR "ISO 9000" CERTIFICATION.
S. Adams
WE DON'T KNOW WHAT IT, IS BUT IT LOOKS GREAT ON BROCHURES.
12-6 © 1994 United Feature Syndicate, Inc.
I THINK IT CERTIFIES THAT WE FOLLOW A CONSISTENT PROCESS.
THAT'S US; WE ALWAYS LIE ON OUR BROCHURES.

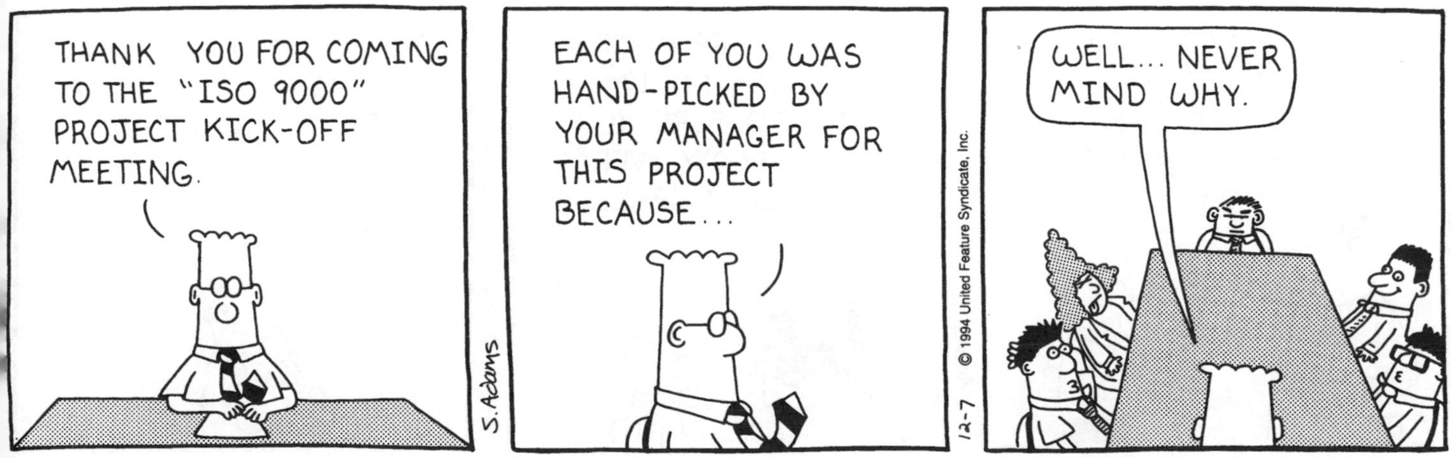
THANK YOU FOR COMING TO THE "ISO 9000" PROJECT KICK-OFF MEETING.
S. Adams
EACH OF YOU WAS HAND-PICKED BY YOUR MANAGER FOR THIS PROJECT BECAUSE...
12-7 © 1994 United Feature Syndicate, Inc.
WELL... NEVER MIND WHY.

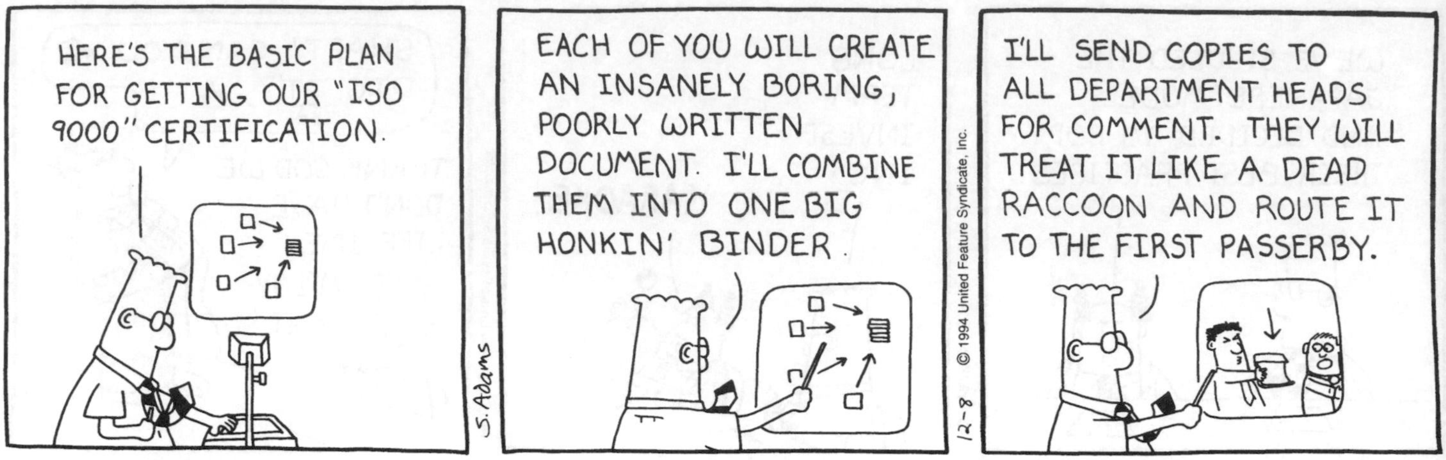
HERE'S THE BASIC PLAN FOR GETTING OUR "ISO 9000" CERTIFICATION.
S. Adams
EACH OF YOU WILL CREATE AN INSANELY BORING, POORLY WRITTEN DOCUMENT. I'LL COMBINE THEM INTO ONE BIG HONKIN' BINDER.
12-8
© 1994 United Feature Syndicate, Inc.
I'LL SEND COPIES TO ALL DEPARTMENT HEADS FOR COMMENT. THEY WILL TREAT IT LIKE A DEAD RACCOON AND ROUTE IT TO THE FIRST PASSERBY.

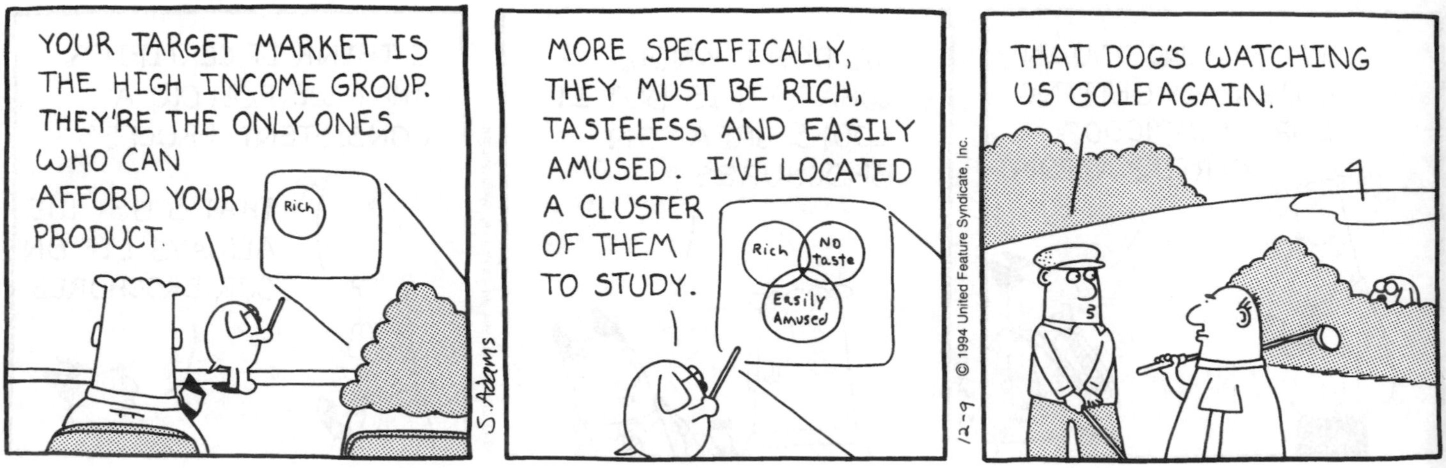
YOUR TARGET MARKET IS THE HIGH INCOME GROUP. THEY'RE THE ONLY ONES WHO CAN AFFORD YOUR PRODUCT.
Rich
S. Adams
MORE SPECIFICALLY, THEY MUST BE RICH, TASTELESS AND EASILY AMUSED. I'VE LOCATED A CLUSTER OF THEM TO STUDY.
Rich
No taste
Easily Amused
12-9
© 1994 United Feature Syndicate, Inc.
THAT DOG'S WATCHING US GOLF AGAIN.

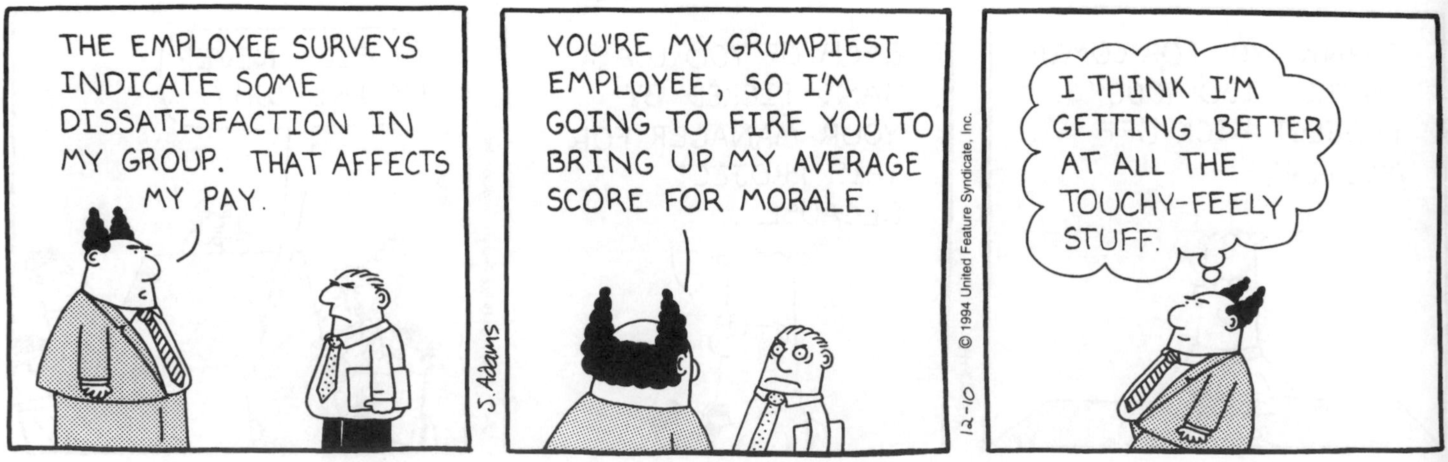
THE EMPLOYEE SURVEYS INDICATE SOME DISSATISFACTION IN MY GROUP. THAT AFFECTS MY PAY.
S. Adams
YOU'RE MY GRUMPIEST EMPLOYEE, SO I'M GOING TO FIRE YOU TO BRING UP MY AVERAGE SCORE FOR MORALE.
12-10
© 1994 United Feature Syndicate, Inc.
I THINK I'M GETTING BETTER AT ALL THE TOUCHY-FEELY STUFF.

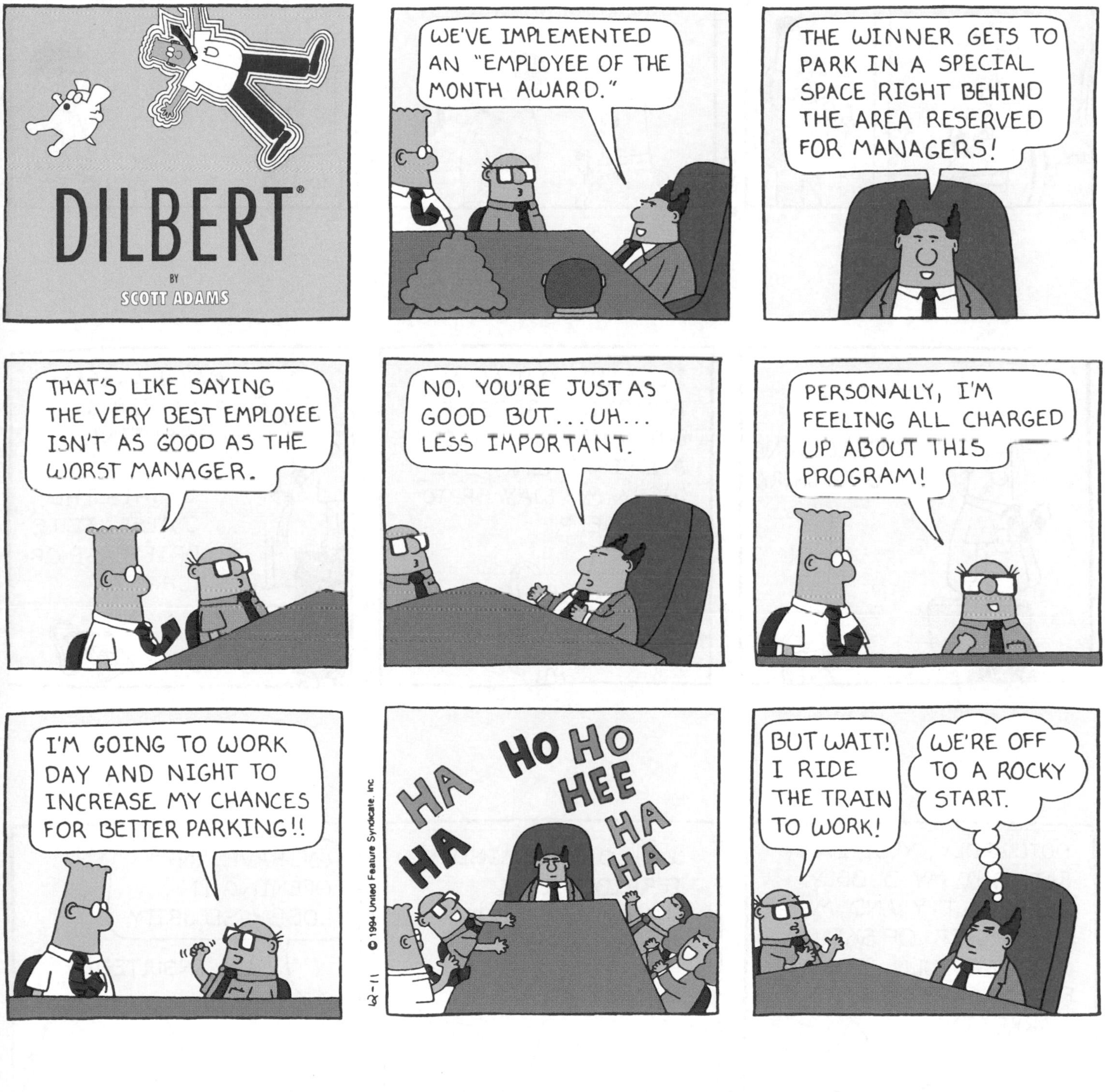
DILBERT®
BY
SCOTT ADAMS
WE'VE IMPLEMENTED AN "EMPLOYEE OF THE MONTH AWARD."
THE WINNER GETS TO PARK IN A SPECIAL SPACE RIGHT BEHIND THE AREA RESERVED FOR MANAGERS!
THAT'S LIKE SAYING THE VERY BEST EMPLOYEE ISN'T AS GOOD AS THE WORST MANAGER.
NO, YOU'RE JUST AS GOOD BUT... UH... LESS IMPORTANT.
PERSONALLY, I'M FEELING ALL CHARGED UP ABOUT THIS PROGRAM!
I'M GOING TO WORK DAY AND NIGHT TO INCREASE MY CHANCES FOR BETTER PARKING!!
© 1994 United Feature Syndicate, Inc
HO HO
HA HA
HEE
HA HA
HA
BUT WAIT! I RIDE THE TRAIN TO WORK!
WE'RE OFF TO A ROCKY START.

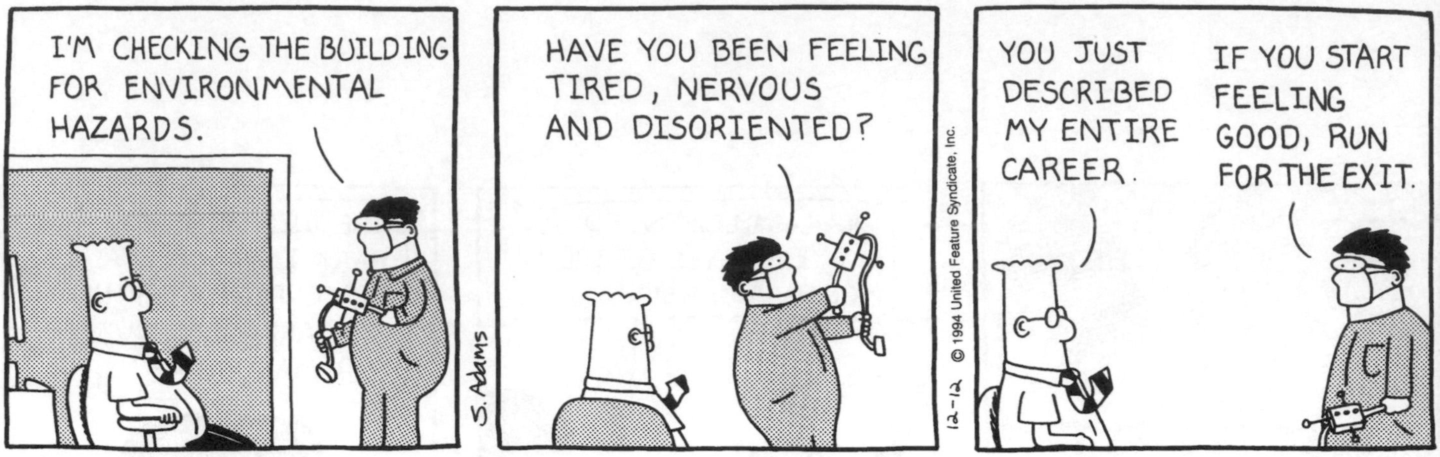
I'M CHECKING THE BUILDING FOR ENVIRONMENTAL HAZARDS.
S. Adams
HAVE YOU BEEN FEELING TIRED, NERVOUS AND DISORIENTED?
12-12 © 1994 United Feature Syndicate, Inc.
YOU JUST DESCRIBED MY ENTIRE CAREER.
IF YOU START FEELING GOOD, RUN FOR THE EXIT.

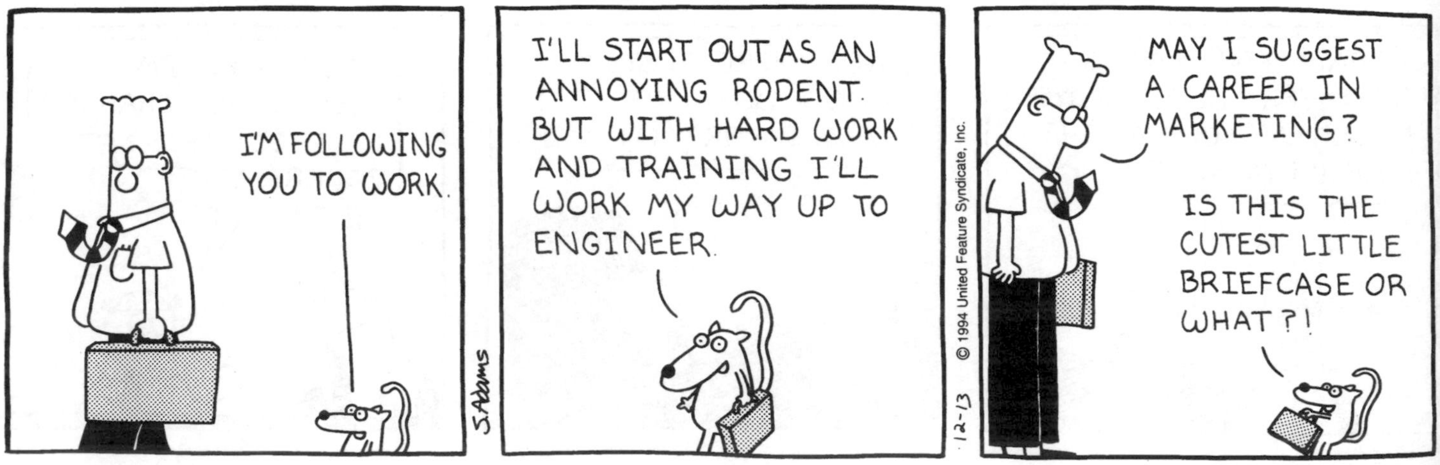
I'M FOLLOWING YOU TO WORK.
S. Adams
I'LL START OUT AS AN ANNOYING RODENT. BUT WITH HARD WORK AND TRAINING I'LL WORK MY WAY UP TO ENGINEER.
12-13 © 1994 United Feature Syndicate, Inc.
MAY I SUGGEST A CAREER IN MARKETING?
IS THIS THE CUTEST LITTLE BRIEFCASE OR WHAT?!

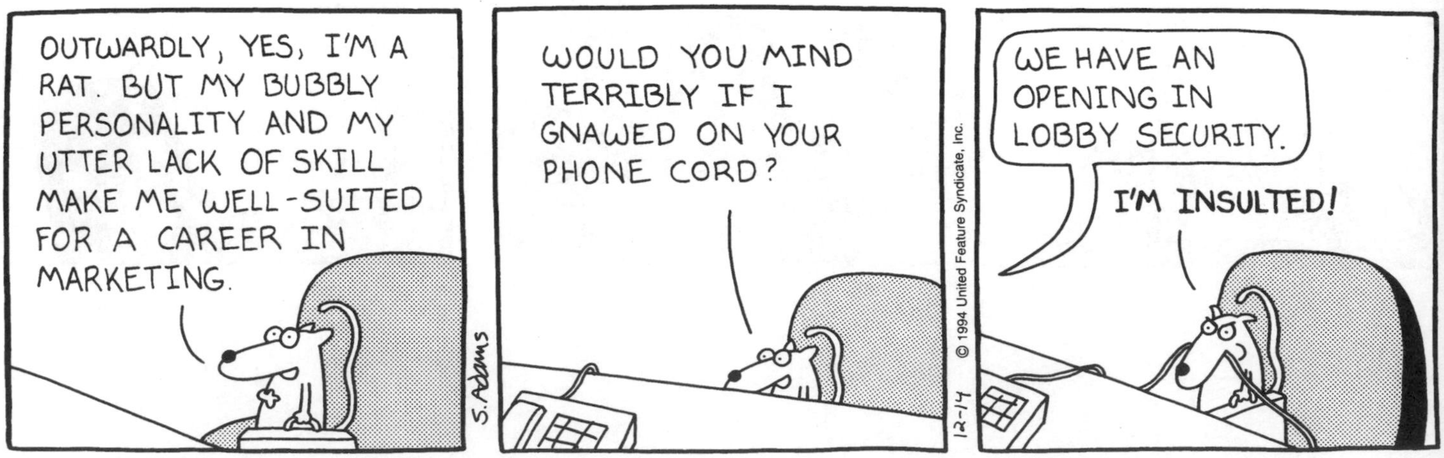
OUTWARDLY, YES, I'M A RAT. BUT MY BUBBLY PERSONALITY AND MY UTTER LACK OF SKILL MAKE ME WELL-SUITED FOR A CAREER IN MARKETING.
S. Adams
WOULD YOU MIND TERRIBLY IF I GNAWED ON YOUR PHONE CORD?
12-14 © 1994 United Feature Syndicate, Inc.
WE HAVE AN OPENING IN LOBBY SECURITY.
I'M INSULTED!

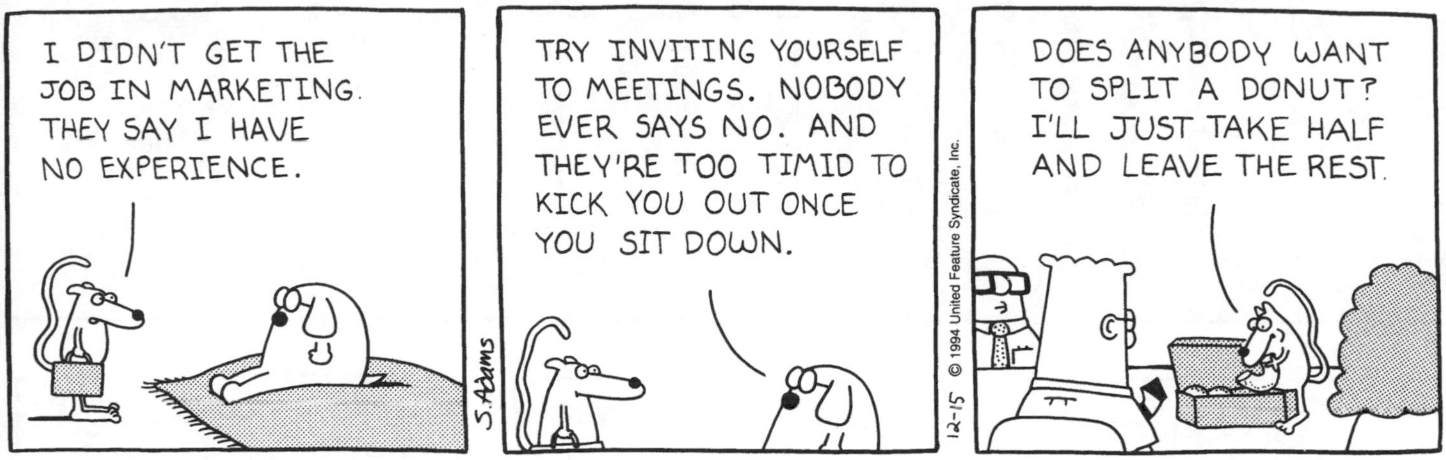
I DIDN'T GET THE JOB IN MARKETING. THEY SAY I HAVE NO EXPERIENCE.
S. Adams
TRY INVITING YOURSELF TO MEETINGS. NOBODY EVER SAYS NO. AND THEY'RE TOO TIMID TO KICK YOU OUT ONCE YOU SIT DOWN.
12-15
© 1994 United Feature Syndicate, Inc.
DOES ANYBODY WANT TO SPLIT A DONUT? I'LL JUST TAKE HALF AND LEAVE THE REST.

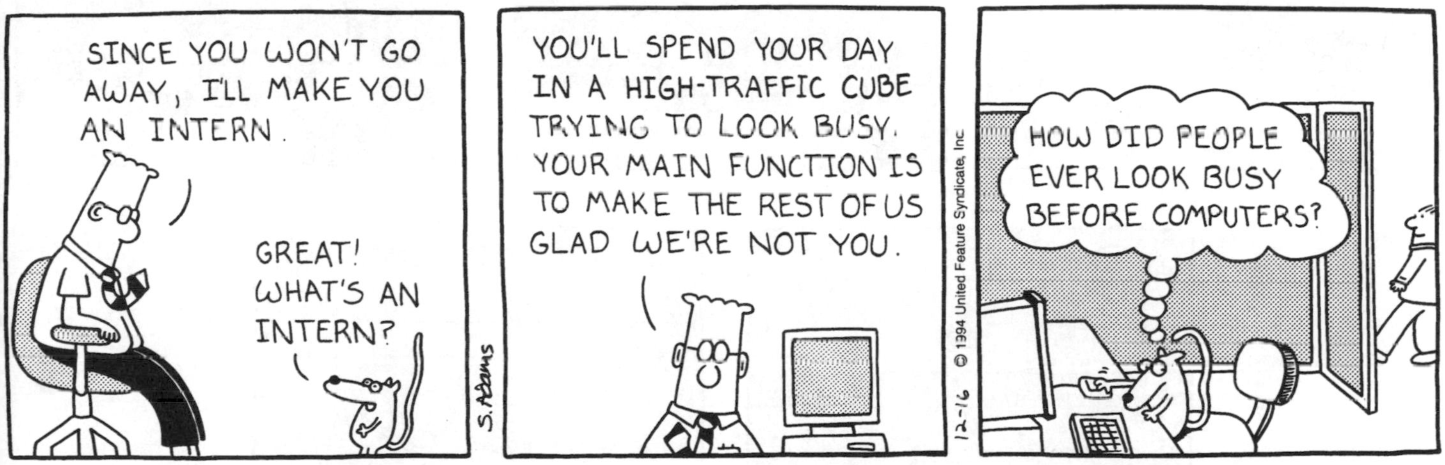
SINCE YOU WON'T GO AWAY, I'LL MAKE YOU AN INTERN.
GREAT! WHAT'S AN INTERN?
S. Adams
YOU'LL SPEND YOUR DAY IN A HIGH-TRAFFIC CUBE TRYING TO LOOK BUSY. YOUR MAIN FUNCTION IS TO MAKE THE REST OF US GLAD WE'RE NOT YOU.
12-16
© 1994 United Feature Syndicate, Inc.
HOW DID PEOPLE EVER LOOK BUSY BEFORE COMPUTERS?

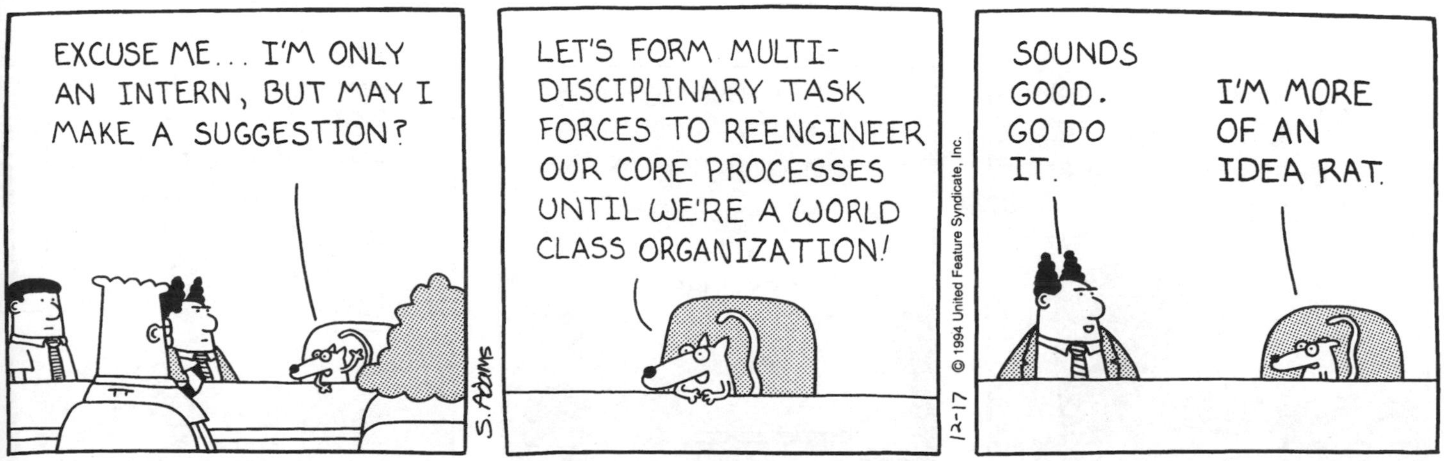
EXCUSE ME... I'M ONLY AN INTERN, BUT MAY I MAKE A SUGGESTION?
S. Adams
LET'S FORM MULTI-DISCIPLINARY TASK FORCES TO REENGINEER OUR CORE PROCESSES UNTIL WE'RE A WORLD CLASS ORGANIZATION!
12-17
© 1994 United Feature Syndicate, Inc.
SOUNDS GOOD. GO DO IT.
I'M MORE OF AN IDEA RAT.

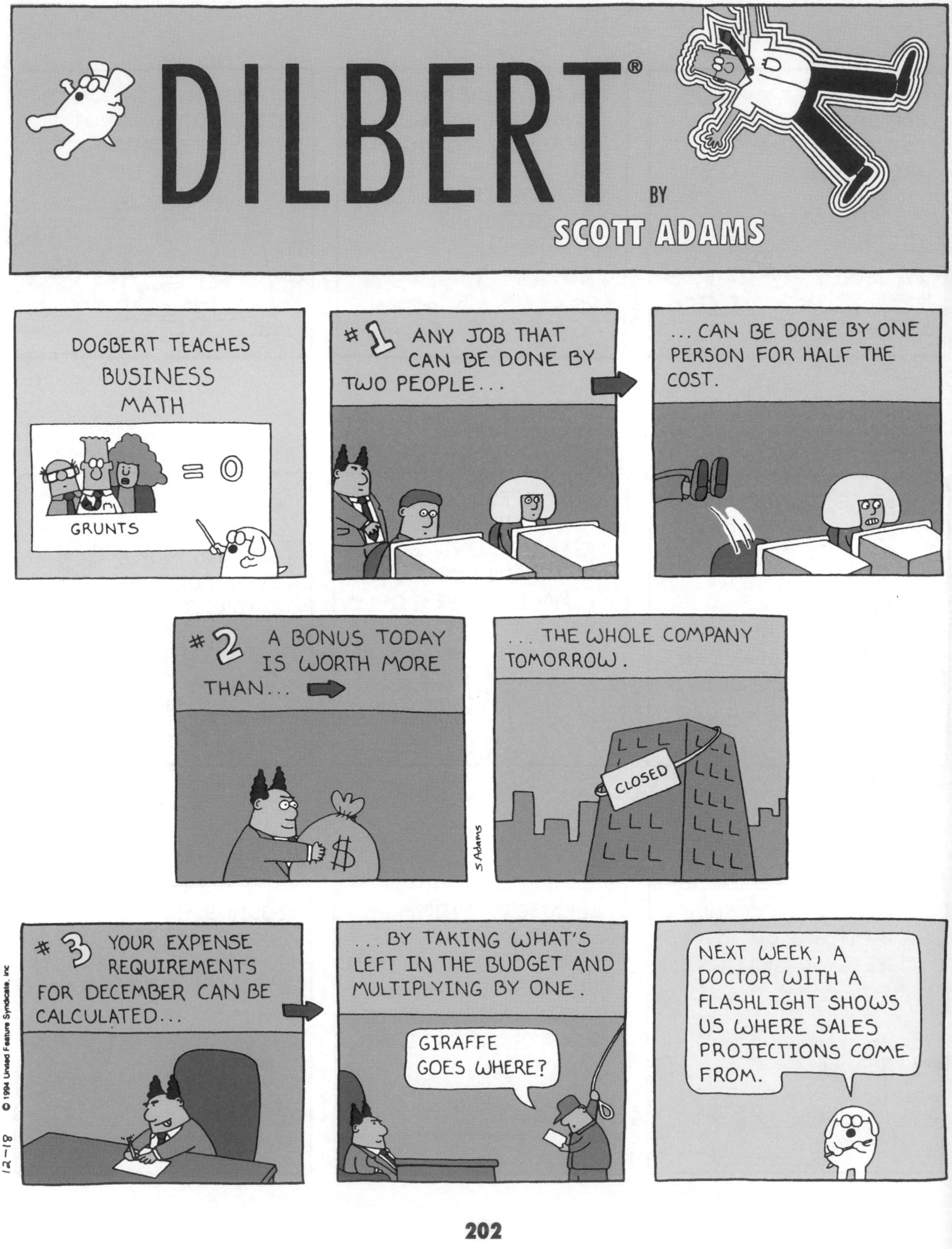
DILBERT®
BY
SCOTT ADAMS
DOGBERT TEACHES
BUSINESS
MATH
GRUNTS
= 0
#1 ANY JOB THAT CAN BE DONE BY TWO PEOPLE...
... CAN BE DONE BY ONE PERSON FOR HALF THE COST.
#2 A BONUS TODAY IS WORTH MORE THAN...
... THE WHOLE COMPANY TOMORROW.
CLOSED
S Adams
#3 YOUR EXPENSE REQUIREMENTS FOR DECEMBER CAN BE CALCULATED...
... BY TAKING WHAT'S LEFT IN THE BUDGET AND MULTIPLYING BY ONE.
GIRAFFE GOES WHERE?
NEXT WEEK, A DOCTOR WITH A FLASHLIGHT SHOWS US WHERE SALES PROJECTIONS COME FROM.
12-18
© 1994 United Feature Syndicate, Inc

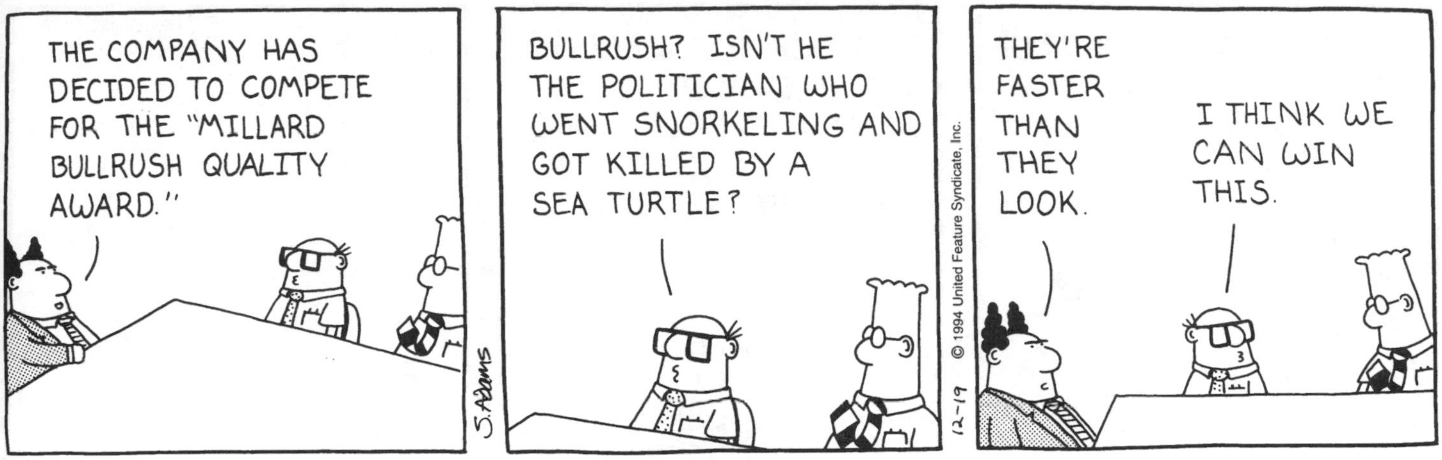
THE COMPANY HAS DECIDED TO COMPETE FOR THE "MILLARD BULLRUSH QUALITY AWARD."
S. Adams
BULLRUSH? ISN'T HE THE POLITICIAN WHO WENT SNORKELING AND GOT KILLED BY A SEA TURTLE?
12-19
© 1994 United Feature Syndicate, Inc.
THEY'RE FASTER THAN THEY LOOK.
I THINK WE CAN WIN THIS.

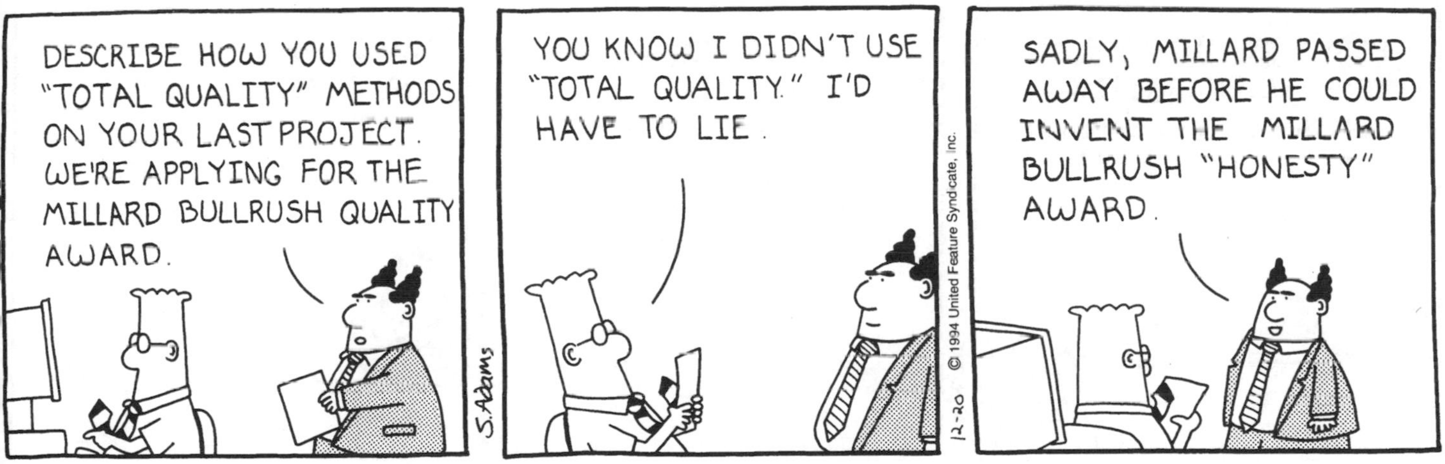
DESCRIBE HOW YOU USED "TOTAL QUALITY" METHODS ON YOUR LAST PROJECT. WE'RE APPLYING FOR THE MILLARD BULLRUSH QUALITY AWARD.
S. Adams
YOU KNOW I DIDN'T USE "TOTAL QUALITY." I'D HAVE TO LIE.
12-20
© 1994 United Feature Syndicate, Inc.
SADLY, MILLARD PASSED AWAY BEFORE HE COULD INVENT THE MILLARD BULLRUSH "HONESTY" AWARD.

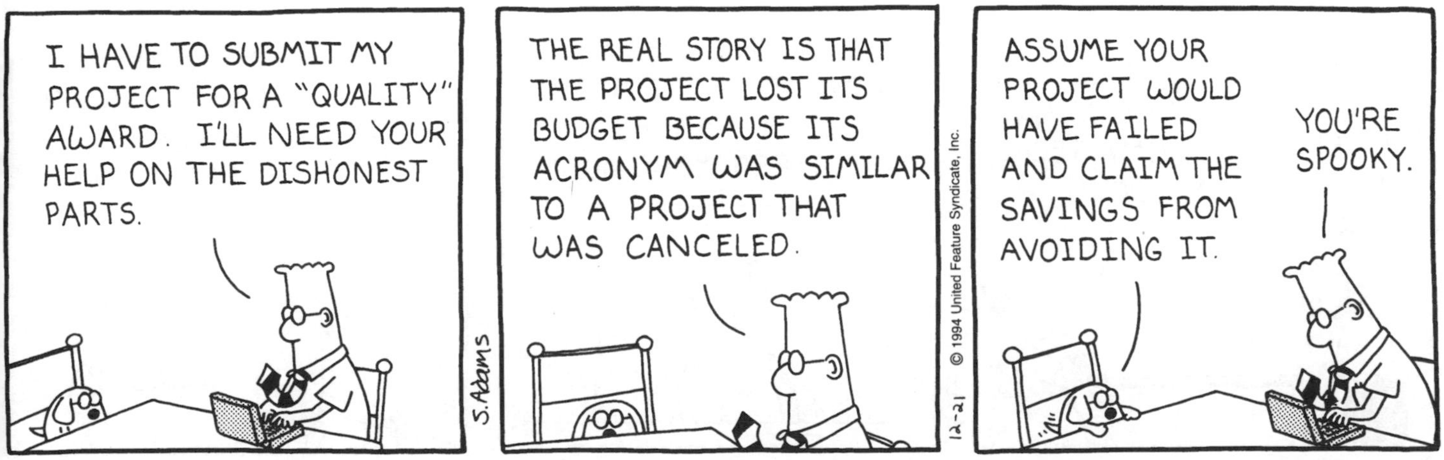
I HAVE TO SUBMIT MY PROJECT FOR A "QUALITY" AWARD. I'LL NEED YOUR HELP ON THE DISHONEST PARTS.
S. Adams
THE REAL STORY IS THAT THE PROJECT LOST ITS BUDGET BECAUSE ITS ACRONYM WAS SIMILAR TO A PROJECT THAT WAS CANCELED.
12-21
© 1994 United Feature Syndicate, Inc.
ASSUME YOUR PROJECT WOULD HAVE FAILED AND CLAIM THE SAVINGS FROM AVOIDING IT.
YOU'RE SPOOKY.

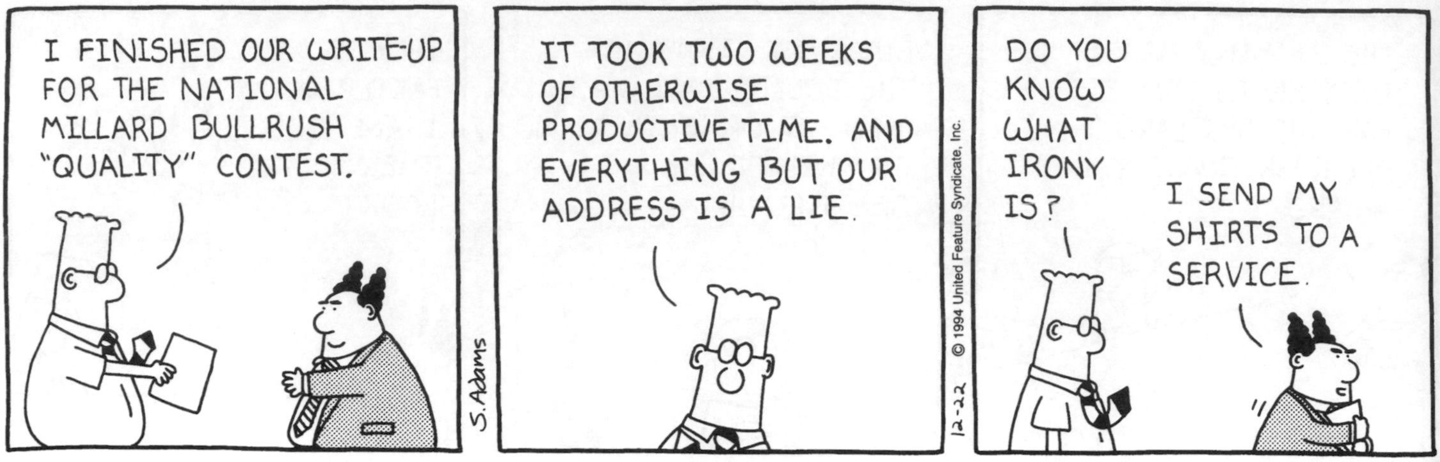
I FINISHED OUR WRITE-UP FOR THE NATIONAL MILLARD BULLRUSH "QUALITY" CONTEST.
S. Adams
IT TOOK TWO WEEKS OF OTHERWISE PRODUCTIVE TIME. AND EVERYTHING BUT OUR ADDRESS IS A LIE.
12-22
© 1994 United Feature Syndicate, Inc.
DO YOU KNOW WHAT IRONY IS?
I SEND MY SHIRTS TO A SERVICE.

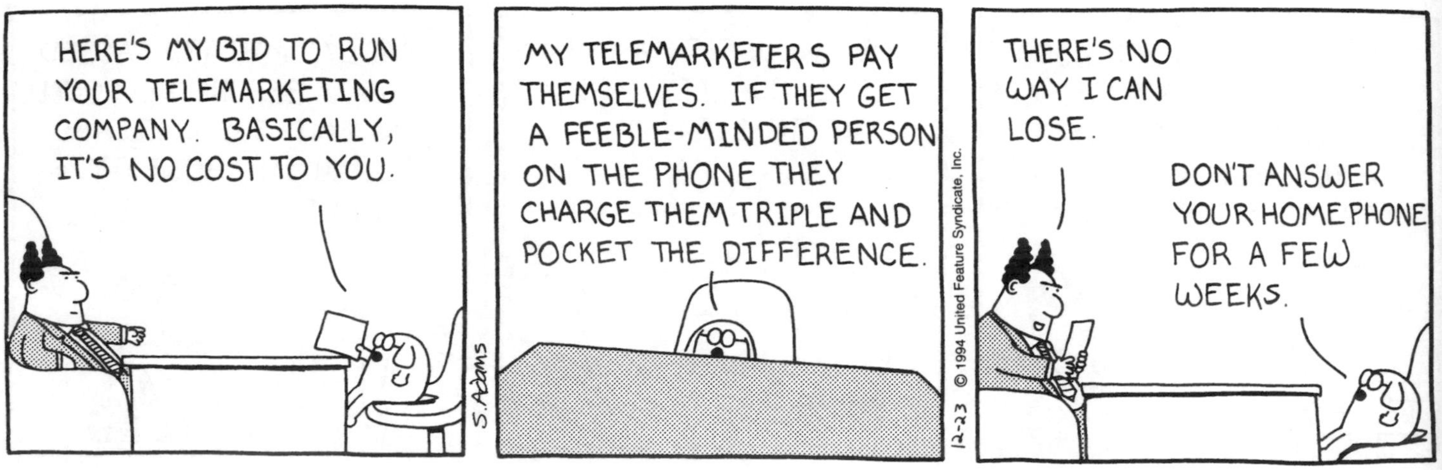
HERE'S MY BID TO RUN YOUR TELEMARKETING COMPANY. BASICALLY, IT'S NO COST TO YOU.
S. Adams
MY TELEMARKETERS PAY THEMSELVES. IF THEY GET A FEEBLE-MINDED PERSON ON THE PHONE THEY CHARGE THEM TRIPLE AND POCKET THE DIFFERENCE.
12-23
© 1994 United Feature Syndicate, Inc.
THERE'S NO WAY I CAN LOSE.
DON'T ANSWER YOUR HOME PHONE FOR A FEW WEEKS.

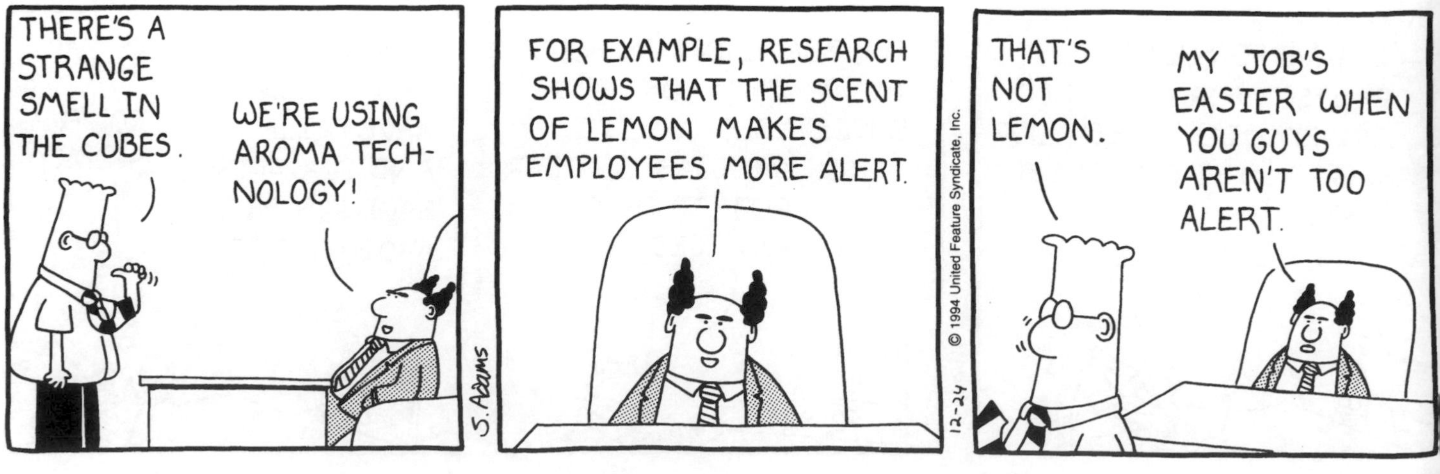
THERE'S A STRANGE SMELL IN THE CUBES.
WE'RE USING AROMA TECH-NOLOGY!
S. Adams
FOR EXAMPLE, RESEARCH SHOWS THAT THE SCENT OF LEMON MAKES EMPLOYEES MORE ALERT.
12-24
© 1994 United Feature Syndicate, Inc.
THAT'S NOT LEMON.
MY JOB'S EASIER WHEN YOU GUYS AREN'T TOO ALERT.

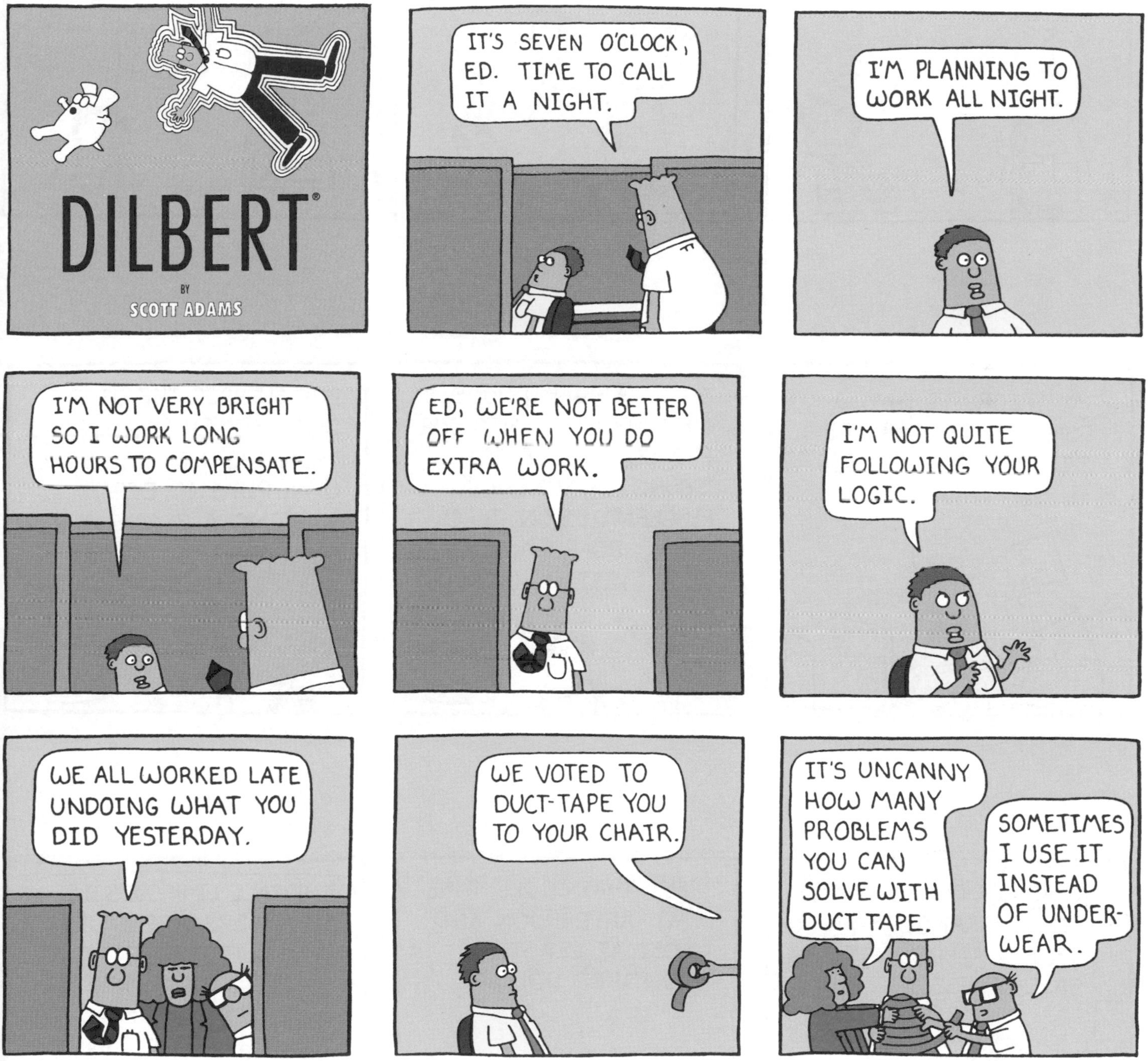
DILBERT®
BY
SCOTT ADAMS
IT'S SEVEN O'CLOCK, ED. TIME TO CALL IT A NIGHT.
I'M PLANNING TO WORK ALL NIGHT.
I'M NOT VERY BRIGHT SO I WORK LONG HOURS TO COMPENSATE.
ED, WE'RE NOT BETTER OFF WHEN YOU DO EXTRA WORK.
I'M NOT QUITE FOLLOWING YOUR LOGIC.
WE ALL WORKED LATE UNDOING WHAT YOU DID YESTERDAY.
WE VOTED TO DUCT-TAPE YOU TO YOUR CHAIR.
IT'S UNCANNY HOW MANY PROBLEMS YOU CAN SOLVE WITH DUCT TAPE.
SOMETIMES I USE IT INSTEAD OF UNDER-WEAR.

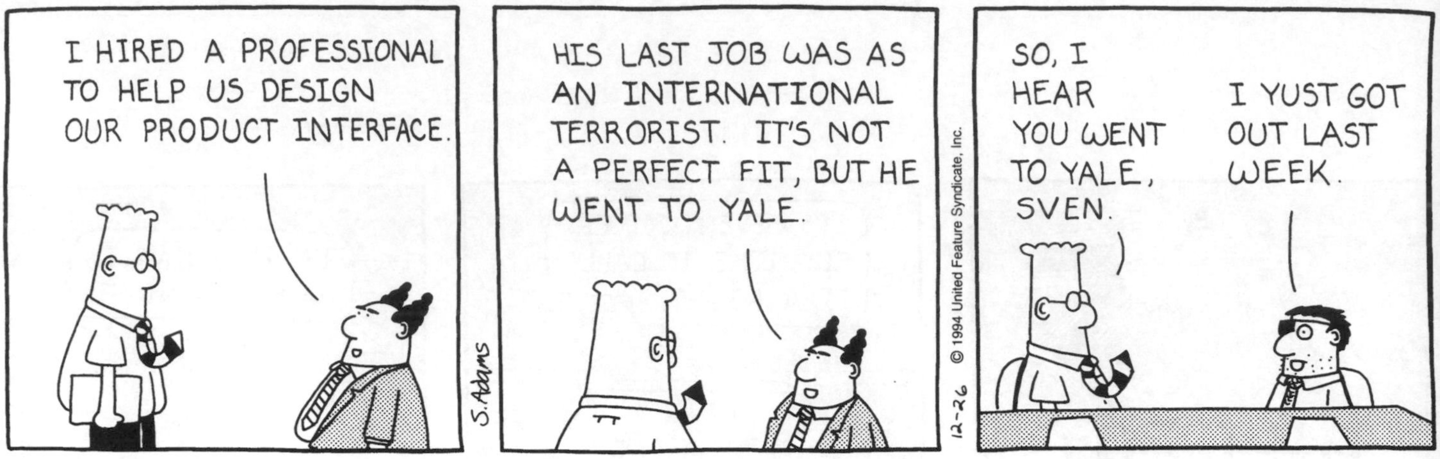
I HIRED A PROFESSIONAL TO HELP US DESIGN OUR PRODUCT INTERFACE.
S. Adams
HIS LAST JOB WAS AS AN INTERNATIONAL TERRORIST. IT'S NOT A PERFECT FIT, BUT HE WENT TO YALE.
12-26
© 1994 United Feature Syndicate, Inc.
SO, I HEAR YOU WENT TO YALE, SVEN.
I YUST GOT OUT LAST WEEK.

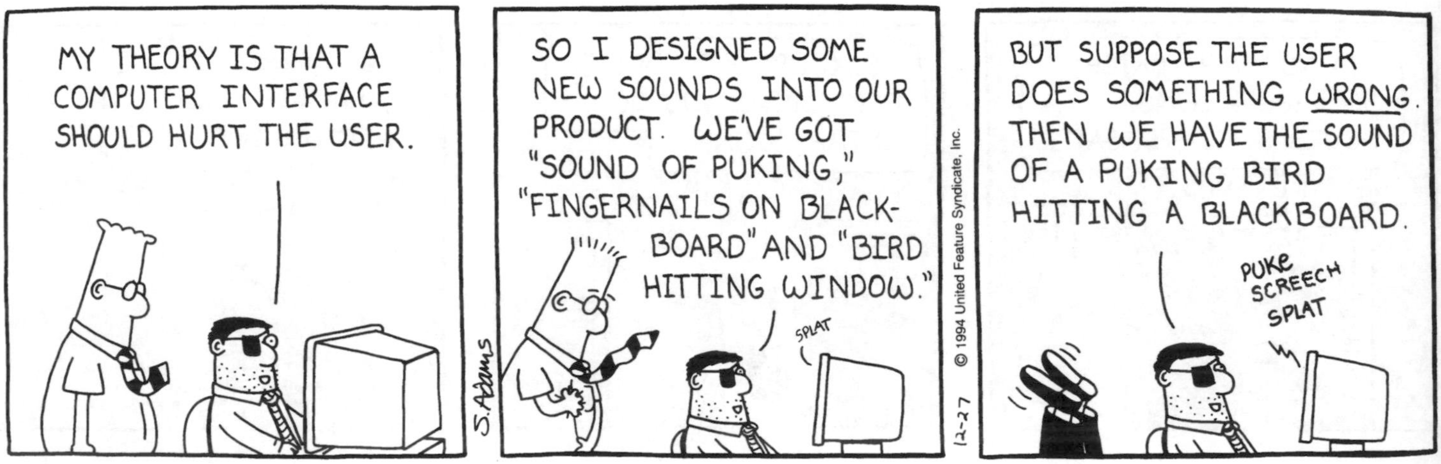
MY THEORY IS THAT A COMPUTER INTERFACE SHOULD HURT THE USER.
S. Adams
SO I DESIGNED SOME NEW SOUNDS INTO OUR PRODUCT. WE'VE GOT "SOUND OF PUKING," "FINGERNAILS ON BLACKBOARD" AND "BIRD HITTING WINDOW."
SPLAT
12-27
© 1994 United Feature Syndicate, Inc.
BUT SUPPOSE THE USER DOES SOMETHING WRONG. THEN WE HAVE THE SOUND OF A PUKING BIRD HITTING A BLACKBOARD.
PUKE
SCREECH
SPLAT

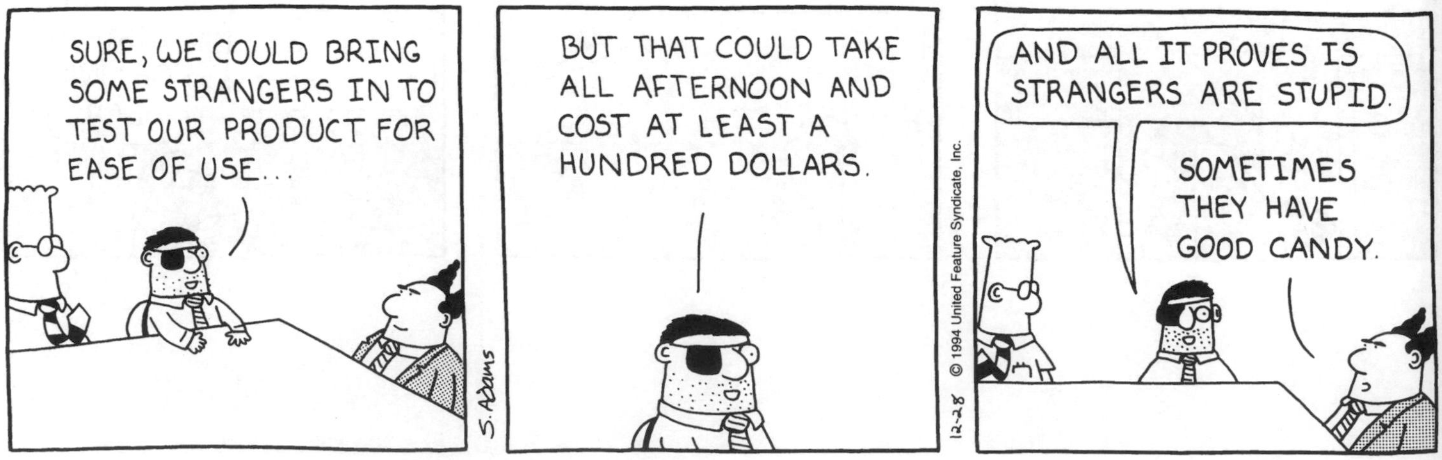
SURE, WE COULD BRING SOME STRANGERS IN TO TEST OUR PRODUCT FOR EASE OF USE...
S. Adams
BUT THAT COULD TAKE ALL AFTERNOON AND COST AT LEAST A HUNDRED DOLLARS.
12-28
© 1994 United Feature Syndicate, Inc.
AND ALL IT PROVES IS STRANGERS ARE STUPID.
SOMETIMES THEY HAVE GOOD CANDY.

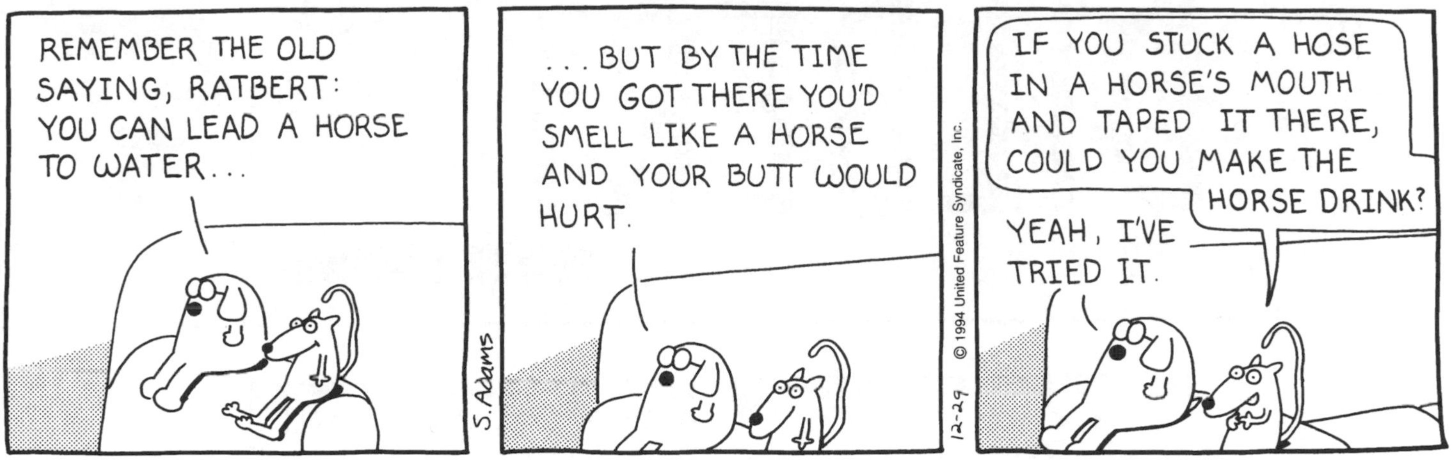
REMEMBER THE OLD SAYING, RATBERT: YOU CAN LEAD A HORSE TO WATER...
S. Adams
...BUT BY THE TIME YOU GOT THERE YOU'D SMELL LIKE A HORSE AND YOUR BUTT WOULD HURT.
12-29 © 1994 United Feature Syndicate, Inc.
IF YOU STUCK A HOSE IN A HORSE'S MOUTH AND TAPED IT THERE, COULD YOU MAKE THE HORSE DRINK?
YEAH, I'VE TRIED IT.

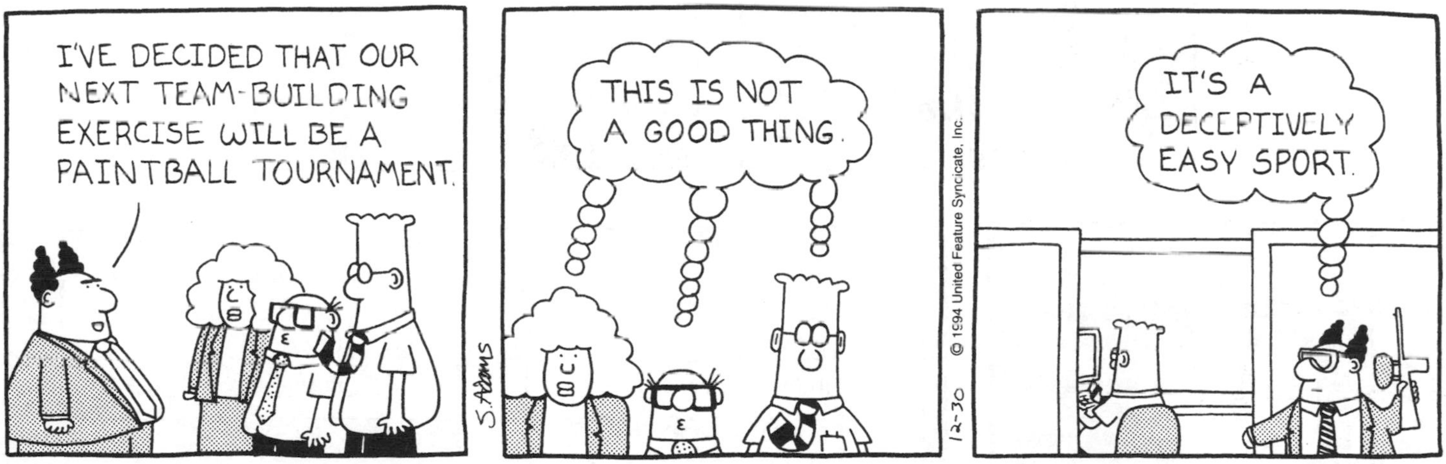
I'VE DECIDED THAT OUR NEXT TEAM-BUILDING EXERCISE WILL BE A PAINTBALL TOURNAMENT.
S. Adams
THIS IS NOT A GOOD THING.
12-30 © 1994 United Feature Syndicate, Inc.
IT'S A DECEPTIVELY EASY SPORT.

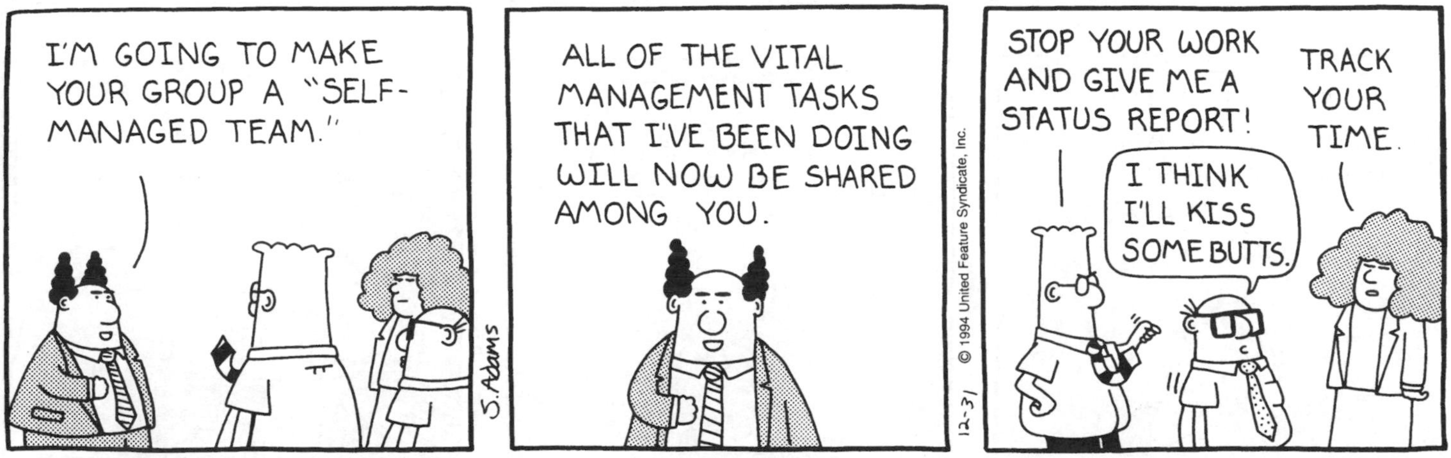
I'M GOING TO MAKE YOUR GROUP A "SELF-MANAGED TEAM."
S. Adams
ALL OF THE VITAL MANAGEMENT TASKS THAT I'VE BEEN DOING WILL NOW BE SHARED AMONG YOU.
12-31 © 1994 United Feature Syndicate, Inc.
STOP YOUR WORK AND GIVE ME A STATUS REPORT!
TRACK YOUR TIME.
I THINK I'LL KISS SOME BUTTS.

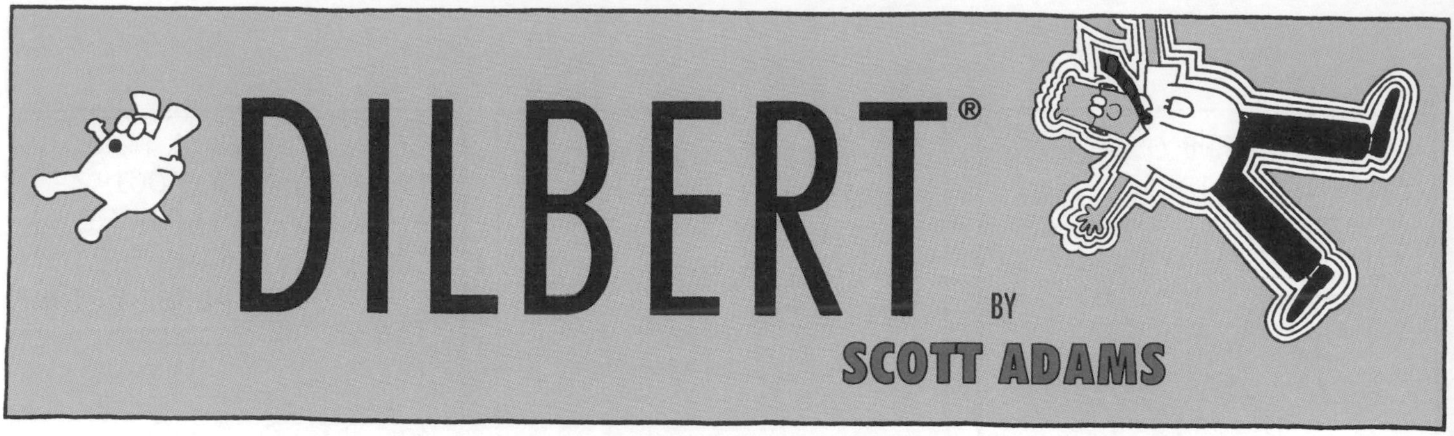
DILBERT®
BY
SCOTT ADAMS

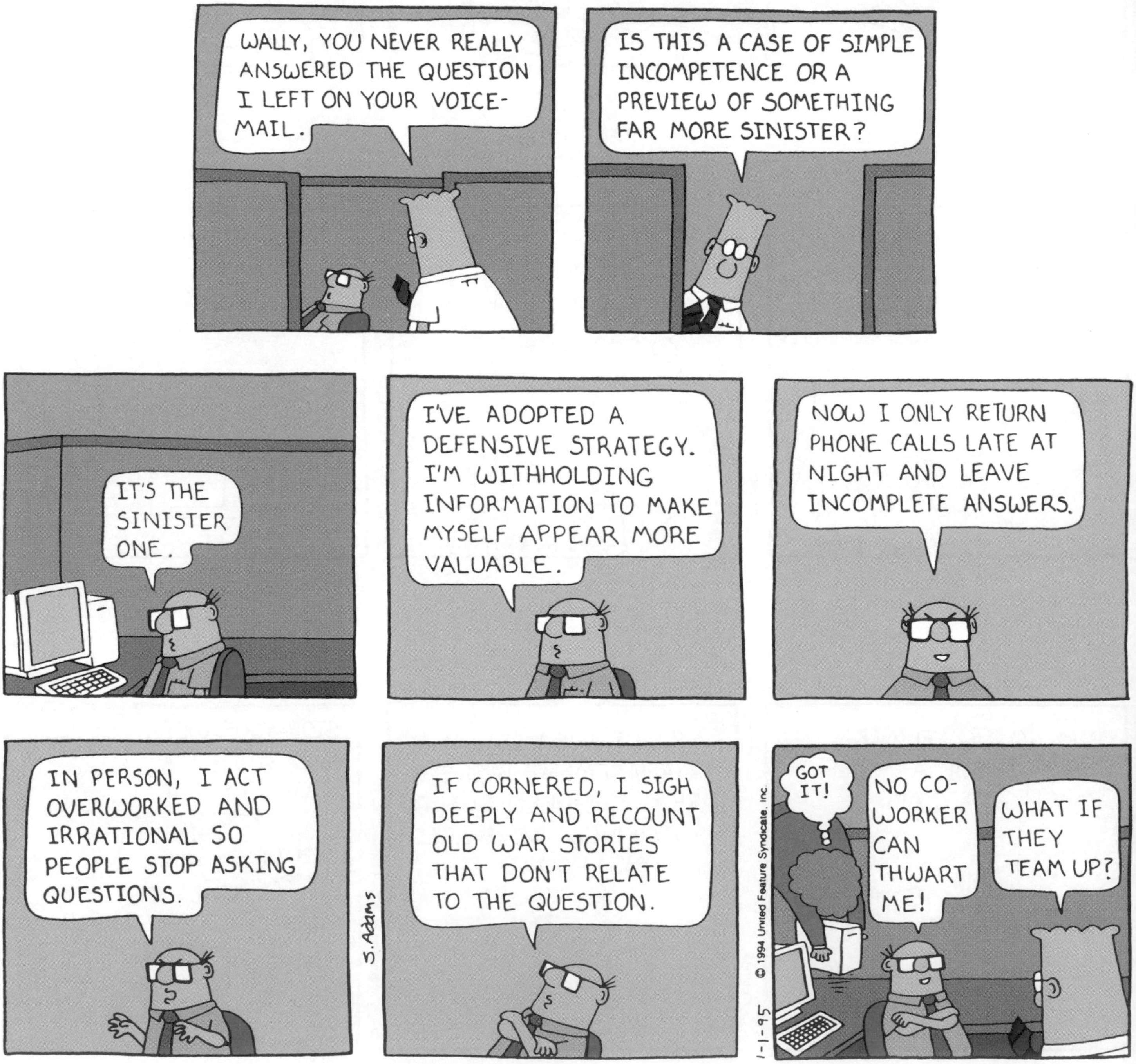
WALLY, YOU NEVER REALLY ANSWERED THE QUESTION I LEFT ON YOUR VOICE-MAIL.
IS THIS A CASE OF SIMPLE INCOMPETENCE OR A PREVIEW OF SOMETHING FAR MORE SINISTER?
IT'S THE SINISTER ONE.
I'VE ADOPTED A DEFENSIVE STRATEGY. I'M WITHHOLDING INFORMATION TO MAKE MYSELF APPEAR MORE VALUABLE.
NOW I ONLY RETURN PHONE CALLS LATE AT NIGHT AND LEAVE INCOMPLETE ANSWERS.
IN PERSON, I ACT OVERWORKED AND IRRATIONAL SO PEOPLE STOP ASKING QUESTIONS.
S. Adams
IF CORNERED, I SIGH DEEPLY AND RECOUNT OLD WAR STORIES THAT DON'T RELATE TO THE QUESTION.
© 1994 United Feature Syndicate, Inc.
1-1-95
GOT IT!
NO CO-WORKER CAN THWART ME!
WHAT IF THEY TEAM UP?

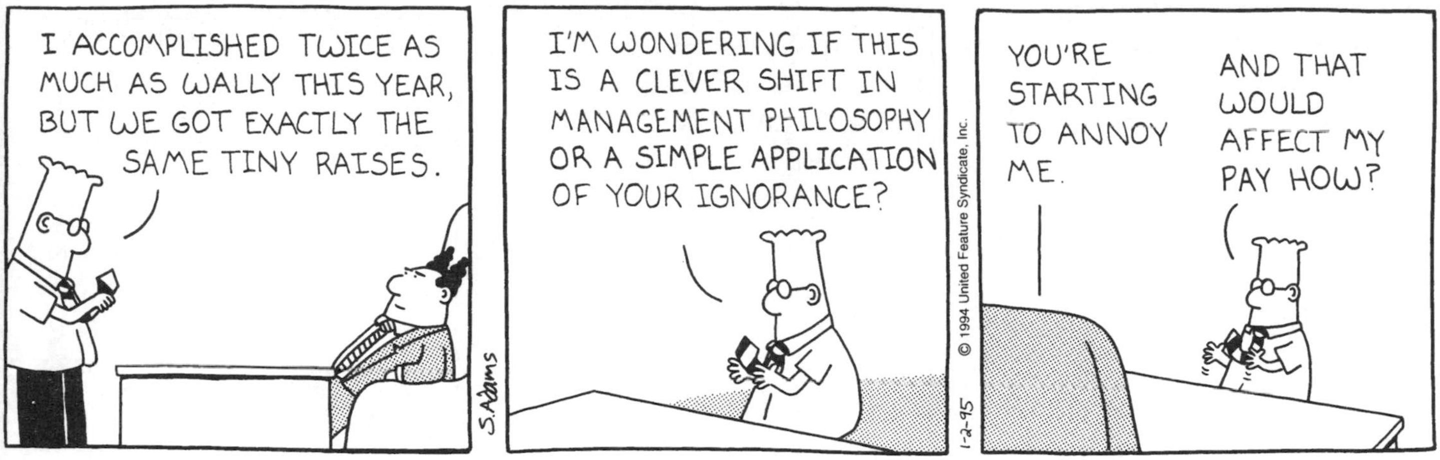
I ACCOMPLISHED TWICE AS MUCH AS WALLY THIS YEAR, BUT WE GOT EXACTLY THE SAME TINY RAISES.
S. Adams
I'M WONDERING IF THIS IS A CLEVER SHIFT IN MANAGEMENT PHILOSOPHY OR A SIMPLE APPLICATION OF YOUR IGNORANCE?
1-2-95
© 1994 United Feature Syndicate, Inc.
YOU'RE STARTING TO ANNOY ME.
AND THAT WOULD AFFECT MY PAY HOW?

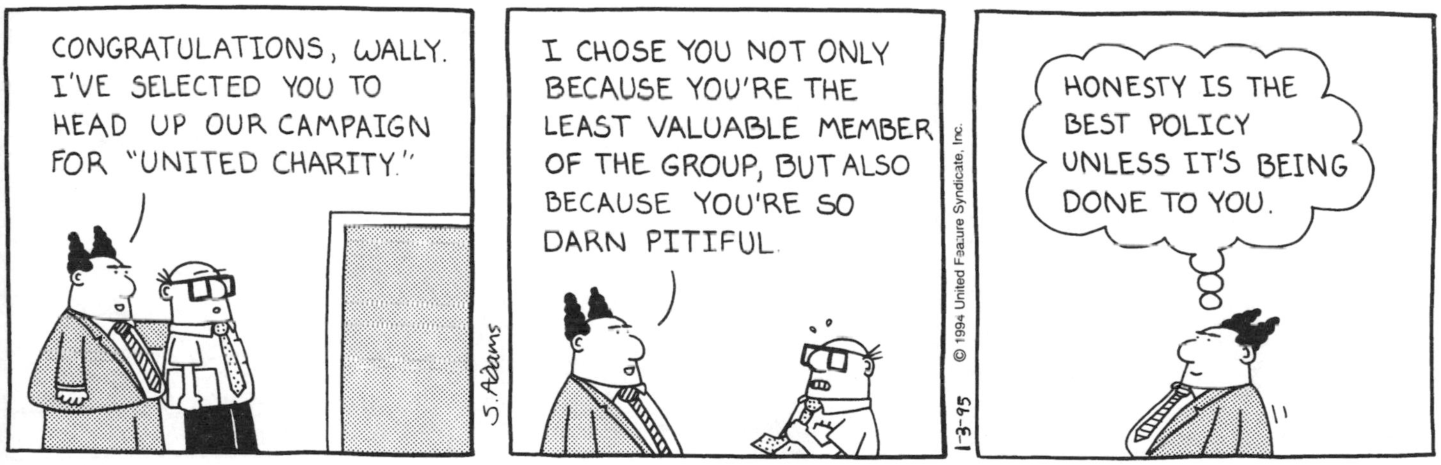
CONGRATULATIONS, WALLY. I'VE SELECTED YOU TO HEAD UP OUR CAMPAIGN FOR "UNITED CHARITY."
S. Adams
I CHOSE YOU NOT ONLY BECAUSE YOU'RE THE LEAST VALUABLE MEMBER OF THE GROUP, BUT ALSO BECAUSE YOU'RE SO DARN PITIFUL.
1-3-95
© 1994 United Feature Syndicate, Inc.
HONESTY IS THE BEST POLICY UNLESS IT'S BEING DONE TO YOU.

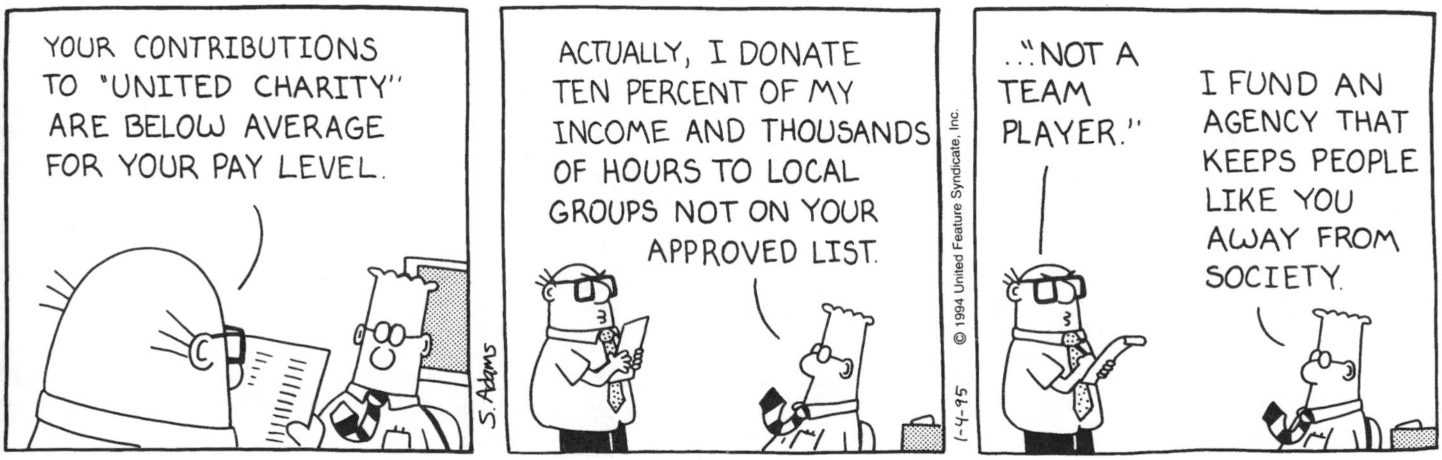
YOUR CONTRIBUTIONS TO "UNITED CHARITY" ARE BELOW AVERAGE FOR YOUR PAY LEVEL.
S. Adams
ACTUALLY, I DONATE TEN PERCENT OF MY INCOME AND THOUSANDS OF HOURS TO LOCAL GROUPS NOT ON YOUR APPROVED LIST.
1-4-95
© 1994 United Feature Syndicate, Inc.
..."NOT A TEAM PLAYER."
I FUND AN AGENCY THAT KEEPS PEOPLE LIKE YOU AWAY FROM SOCIETY.

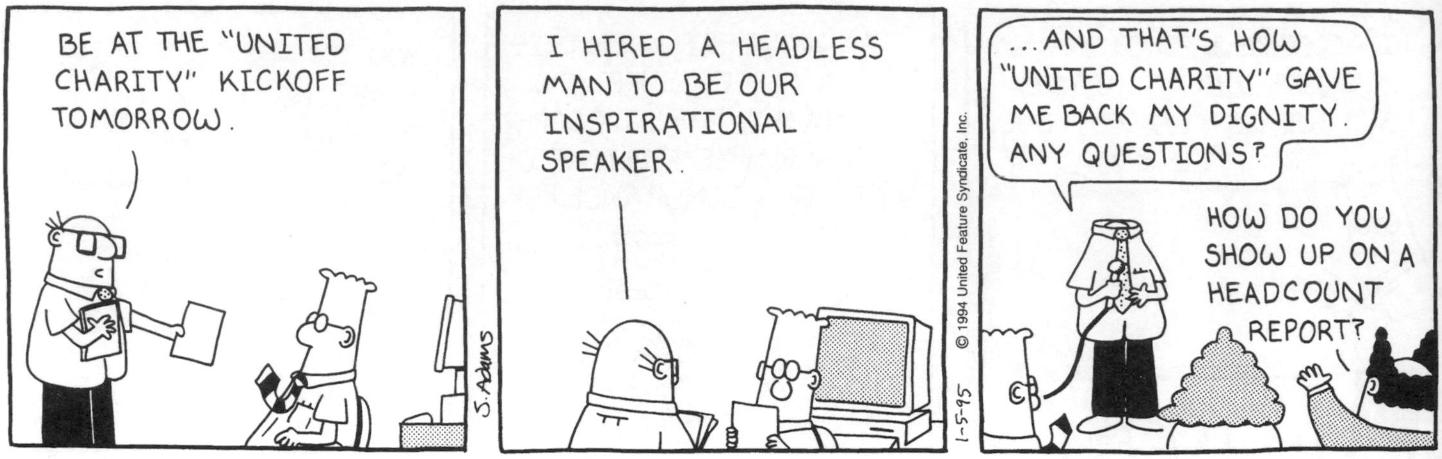
BE AT THE "UNITED CHARITY" KICKOFF TOMORROW.
I HIRED A HEADLESS MAN TO BE OUR INSPIRATIONAL SPEAKER.
...AND THAT'S HOW "UNITED CHARITY" GAVE ME BACK MY DIGNITY. ANY QUESTIONS?
HOW DO YOU SHOW UP ON A HEADCOUNT REPORT?
S. Adams
1-5-95
© 1994 United Feature Syndicate, Inc.

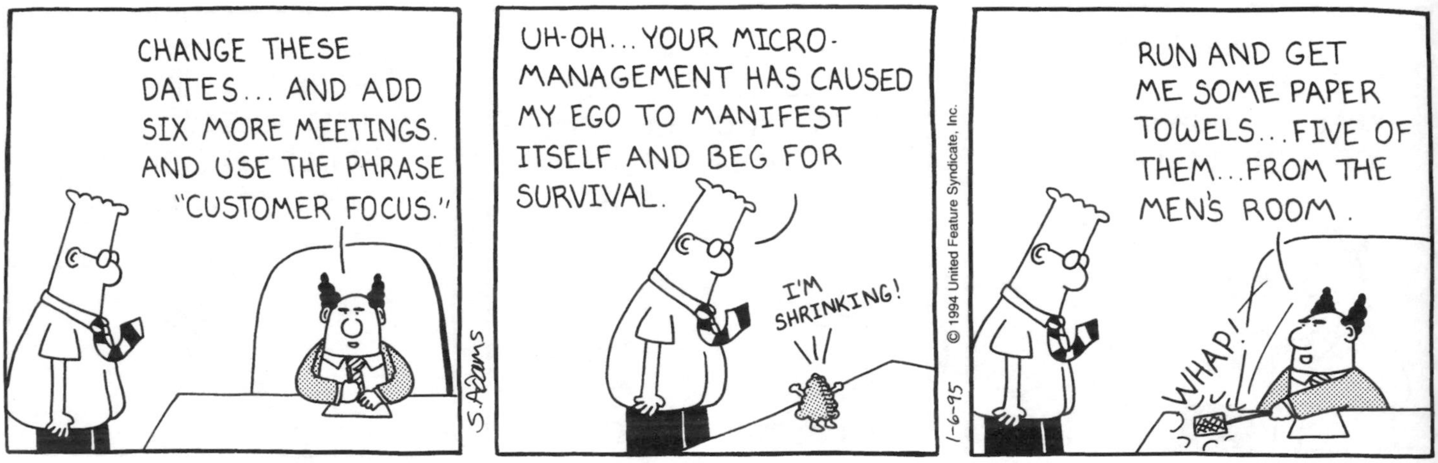
CHANGE THESE DATES... AND ADD SIX MORE MEETINGS. AND USE THE PHRASE "CUSTOMER FOCUS."
UH-OH...YOUR MICRO-MANAGEMENT HAS CAUSED MY EGO TO MANIFEST ITSELF AND BEG FOR SURVIVAL.
I'M SHRINKING!
RUN AND GET ME SOME PAPER TOWELS...FIVE OF THEM...FROM THE MEN'S ROOM.
WHAP!
S. Adams
1-6-95
© 1994 United Feature Syndicate, Inc.

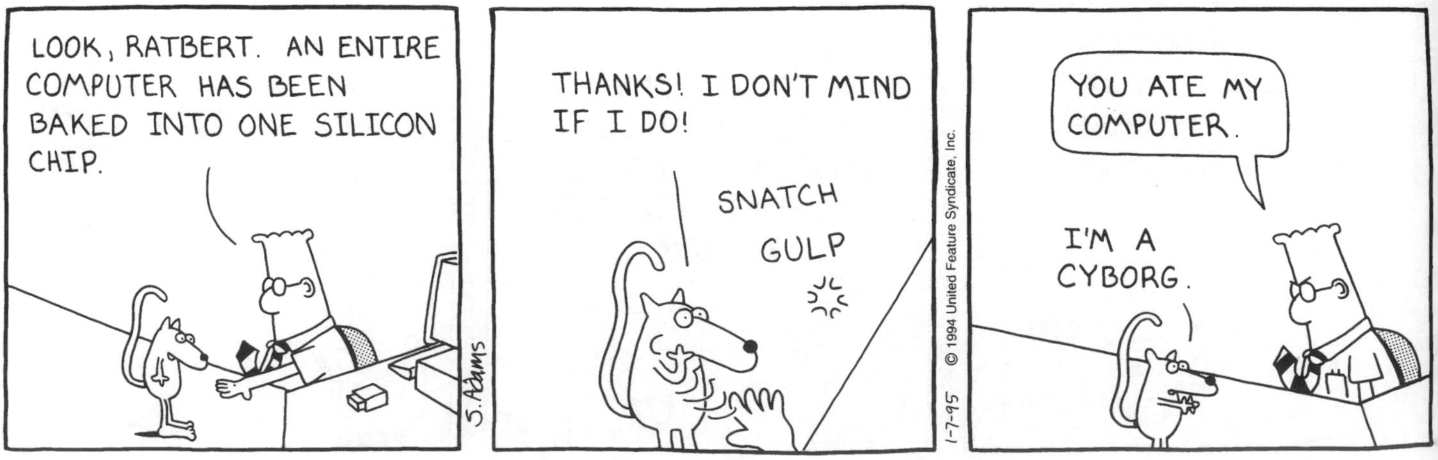
LOOK, RATBERT. AN ENTIRE COMPUTER HAS BEEN BAKED INTO ONE SILICON CHIP.
THANKS! I DON'T MIND IF I DO!
SNATCH
GULP
YOU ATE MY COMPUTER.
I'M A CYBORG.
S. Adams
1-7-95
© 1994 United Feature Syndicate, Inc.

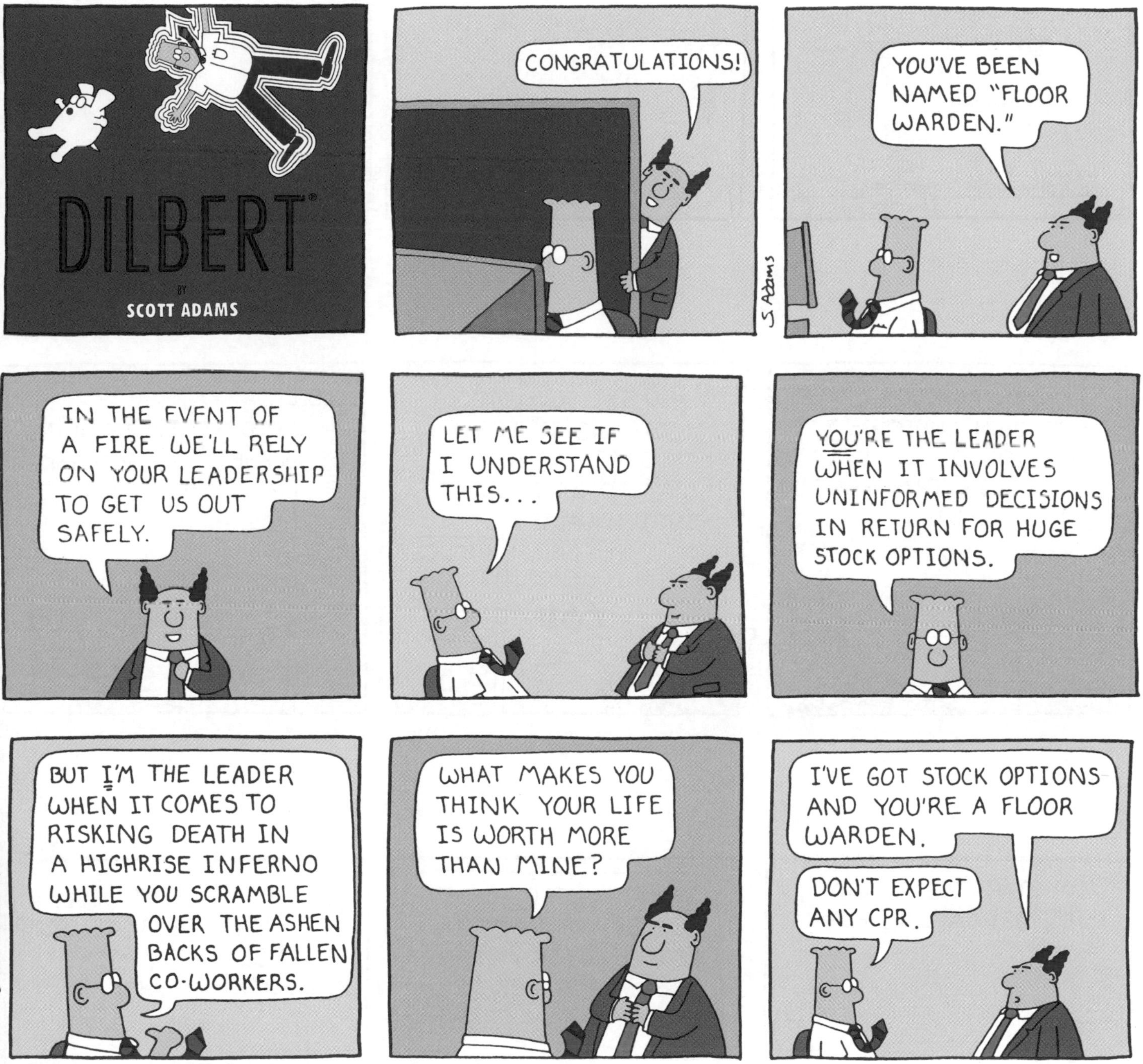
DILBERT®
BY
SCOTT ADAMS
CONGRATULATIONS!
YOU'VE BEEN NAMED "FLOOR WARDEN."
S. Adams
IN THE EVENT OF A FIRE WE'LL RELY ON YOUR LEADERSHIP TO GET US OUT SAFELY.
LET ME SEE IF I UNDERSTAND THIS...
YOU'RE THE LEADER WHEN IT INVOLVES UNINFORMED DECISIONS IN RETURN FOR HUGE STOCK OPTIONS.
BUT I'M THE LEADER WHEN IT COMES TO RISKING DEATH IN A HIGHRISE INFERNO WHILE YOU SCRAMBLE OVER THE ASHEN BACKS OF FALLEN CO-WORKERS.
WHAT MAKES YOU THINK YOUR LIFE IS WORTH MORE THAN MINE?
I'VE GOT STOCK OPTIONS AND YOU'RE A FLOOR WARDEN.
DON'T EXPECT ANY CPR.

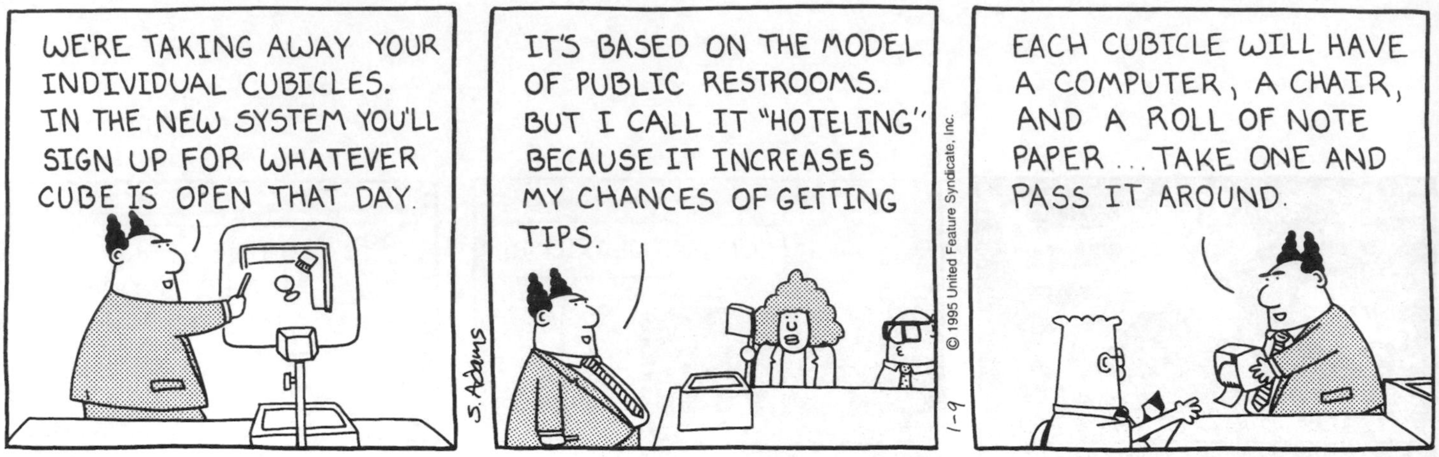
WE'RE TAKING AWAY YOUR INDIVIDUAL CUBICLES. IN THE NEW SYSTEM YOU'LL SIGN UP FOR WHATEVER CUBE IS OPEN THAT DAY.
IT'S BASED ON THE MODEL OF PUBLIC RESTROOMS. BUT I CALL IT "HOTELING" BECAUSE IT INCREASES MY CHANCES OF GETTING TIPS.
EACH CUBICLE WILL HAVE A COMPUTER, A CHAIR, AND A ROLL OF NOTE PAPER ... TAKE ONE AND PASS IT AROUND.
S. Adams
1-9
© 1995 United Feature Syndicate, Inc.

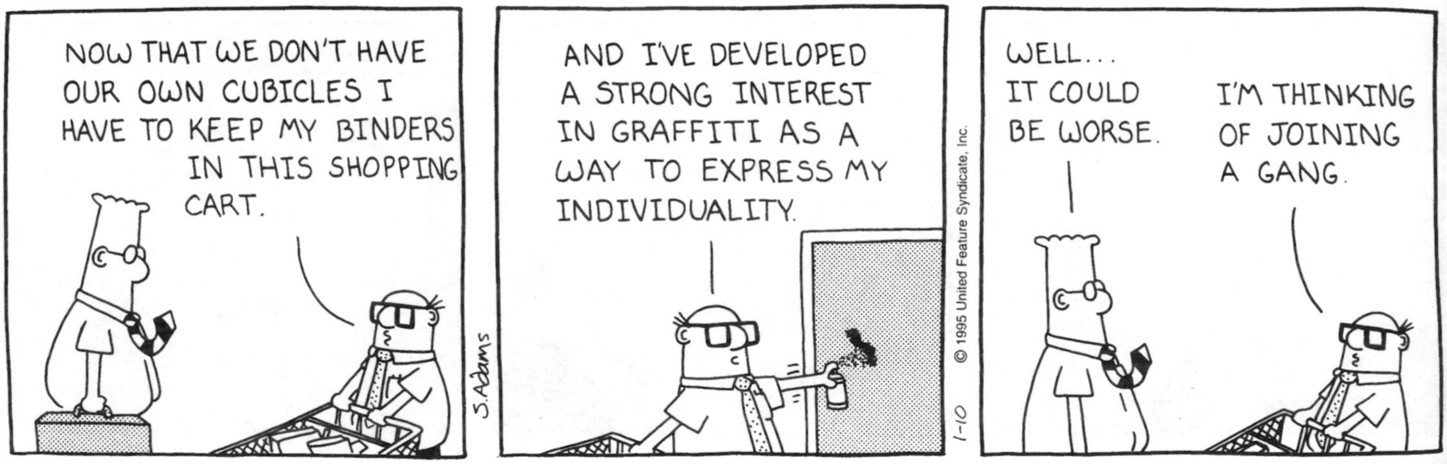
NOW THAT WE DON'T HAVE OUR OWN CUBICLES I HAVE TO KEEP MY BINDERS IN THIS SHOPPING CART.
AND I'VE DEVELOPED A STRONG INTEREST IN GRAFFITI AS A WAY TO EXPRESS MY INDIVIDUALITY.
WELL... IT COULD BE WORSE.
I'M THINKING OF JOINING A GANG.
S. Adams
1-10
© 1995 United Feature Syndicate, Inc.

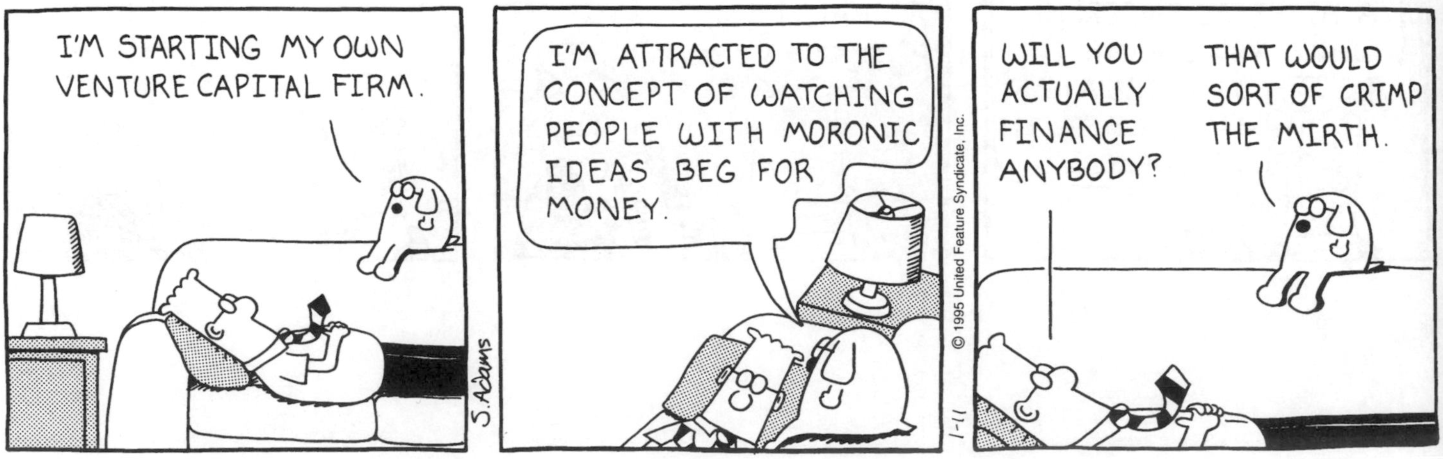
I'M STARTING MY OWN VENTURE CAPITAL FIRM.
I'M ATTRACTED TO THE CONCEPT OF WATCHING PEOPLE WITH MORONIC IDEAS BEG FOR MONEY.
WILL YOU ACTUALLY FINANCE ANYBODY?
THAT WOULD SORT OF CRIMP THE MIRTH.
S. Adams
1-11
© 1995 United Feature Syndicate, Inc.

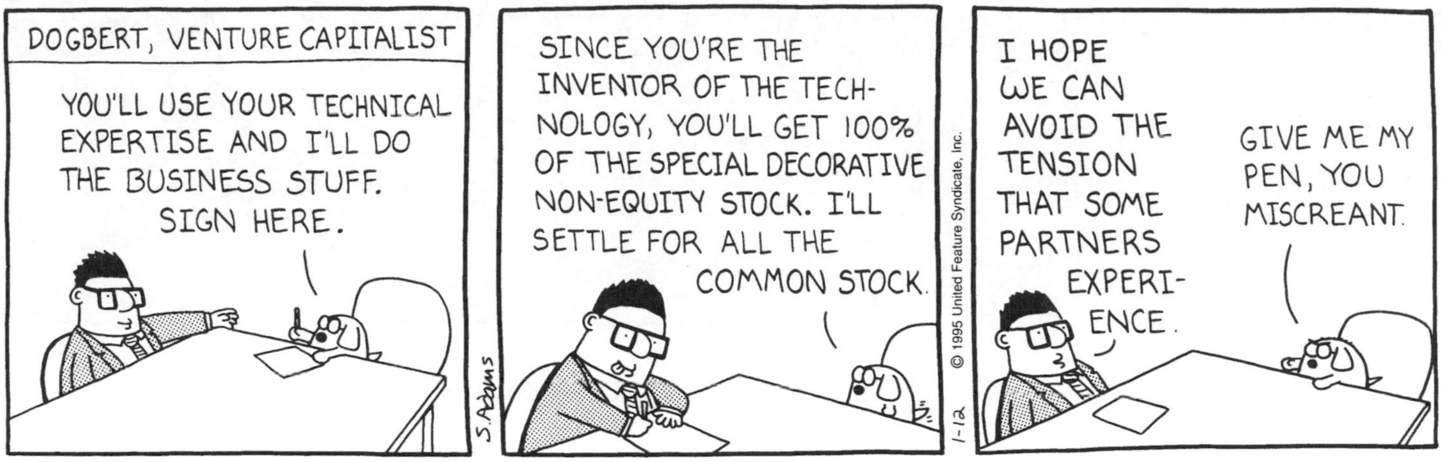
DOGBERT, VENTURE CAPITALIST
YOU'LL USE YOUR TECHNICAL EXPERTISE AND I'LL DO THE BUSINESS STUFF. SIGN HERE.
S. Adams
SINCE YOU'RE THE INVENTOR OF THE TECHNOLOGY, YOU'LL GET 100% OF THE SPECIAL DECORATIVE NON-EQUITY STOCK. I'LL SETTLE FOR ALL THE COMMON STOCK.
1-12 © 1995 United Feature Syndicate, Inc.
I HOPE WE CAN AVOID THE TENSION THAT SOME PARTNERS EXPERIENCE.
GIVE ME MY PEN, YOU MISCREANT.

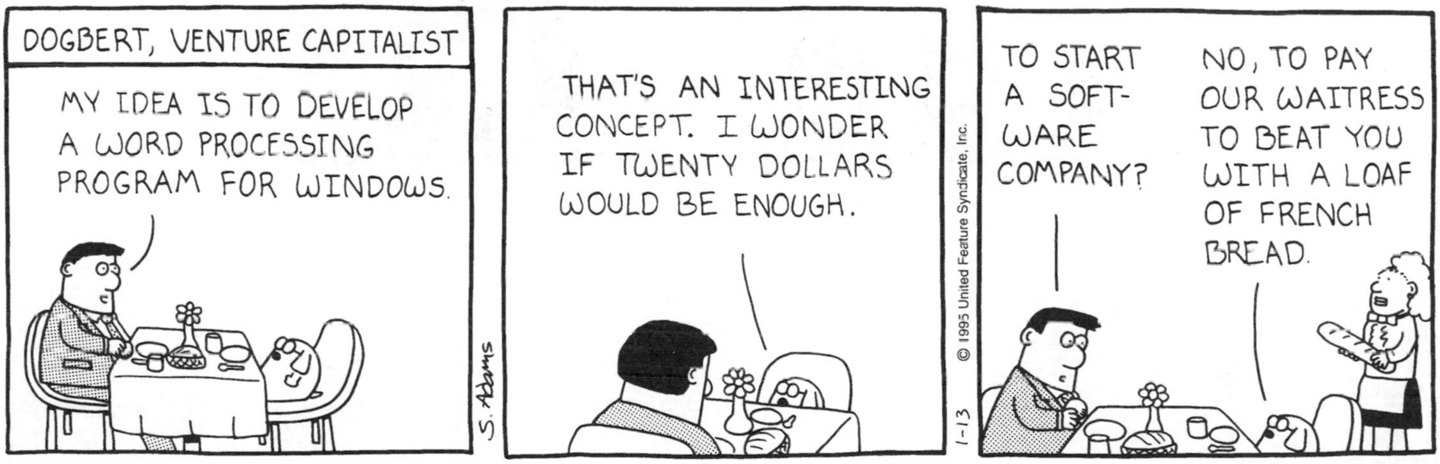
DOGBERT, VENTURE CAPITALIST
MY IDEA IS TO DEVELOP A WORD PROCESSING PROGRAM FOR WINDOWS.
S. Adams
THAT'S AN INTERESTING CONCEPT. I WONDER IF TWENTY DOLLARS WOULD BE ENOUGH.
1-13 © 1995 United Feature Syndicate, Inc.
TO START A SOFTWARE COMPANY?
NO, TO PAY OUR WAITRESS TO BEAT YOU WITH A LOAF OF FRENCH BREAD.

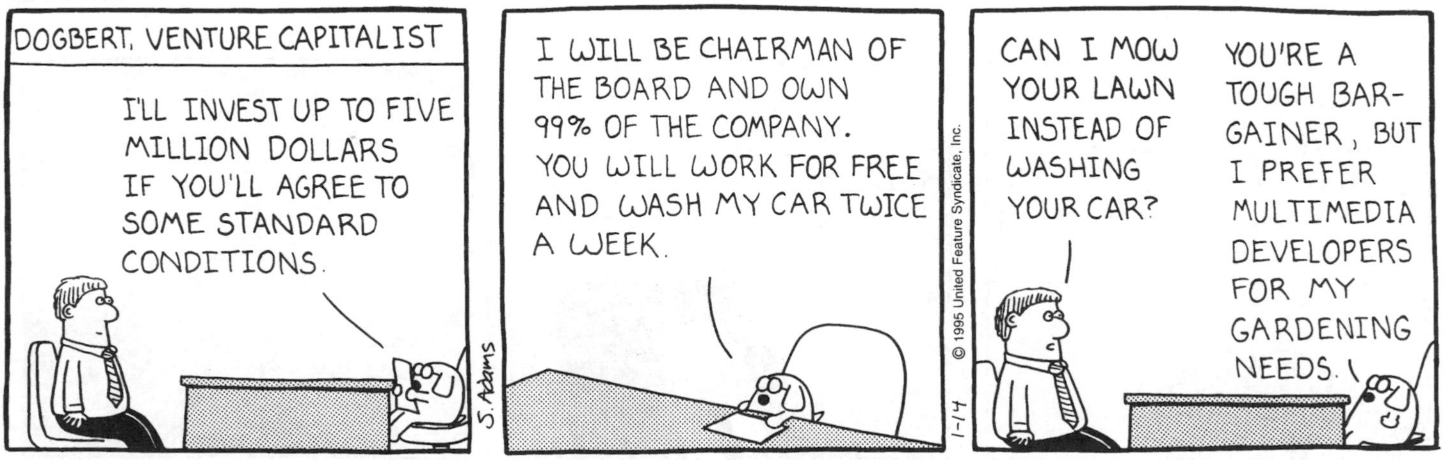
DOGBERT, VENTURE CAPITALIST
I'LL INVEST UP TO FIVE MILLION DOLLARS IF YOU'LL AGREE TO SOME STANDARD CONDITIONS.
S. Adams
I WILL BE CHAIRMAN OF THE BOARD AND OWN 99% OF THE COMPANY. YOU WILL WORK FOR FREE AND WASH MY CAR TWICE A WEEK.
1-14 © 1995 United Feature Syndicate, Inc.
CAN I MOW YOUR LAWN INSTEAD OF WASHING YOUR CAR?
YOU'RE A TOUGH BARGAINER, BUT I PREFER MULTIMEDIA DEVELOPERS FOR MY GARDENING NEEDS.

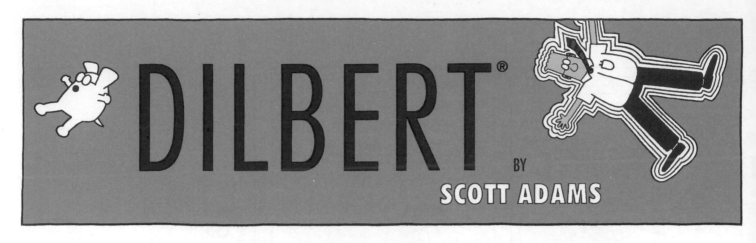

DILBERT
BY SCOTT ADAMS

OUR NEW PHILOSOPHY IS "WE DO IT RIGHT THE FIRST TIME."

THIS WILL INSPIRE YOU TO HIGHER QUALITY BECAUSE YOU'LL REALIZE MISTAKES ARE NOT TOLERATED.

QUESTION.

SINCE MISTAKES ARE INEVITABLE, WOULDN'T YOUR PHILOSOPHY INSPIRE US TO AVOID COMPLETING ANYTHING?

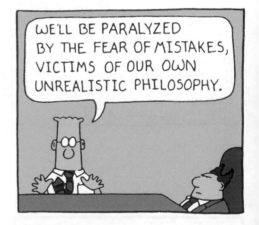

WE'LL BE PARALYZED BY THE FEAR OF MISTAKES, VICTIMS OF OUR OWN UNREALISTIC PHILOSOPHY.

YOU MIGHT AS WELL HAVE A PHILOSOPHY THAT SAYS "WE PUNISH ANYBODY WHO DOES ANYTHING."

I VALUE YOUR OPINION.

WALLY, I WANT YOU TO MAKE SOME POSTERS THAT SAY "WE DO IT RIGHT THE FIRST TIME."

WALLY'S PARALYZED.

NEXT ITEM: WHY IS EMPLOYEE MORALE SO LOW?

© 1995 United Feature Syndicate, Inc.

1-15

214

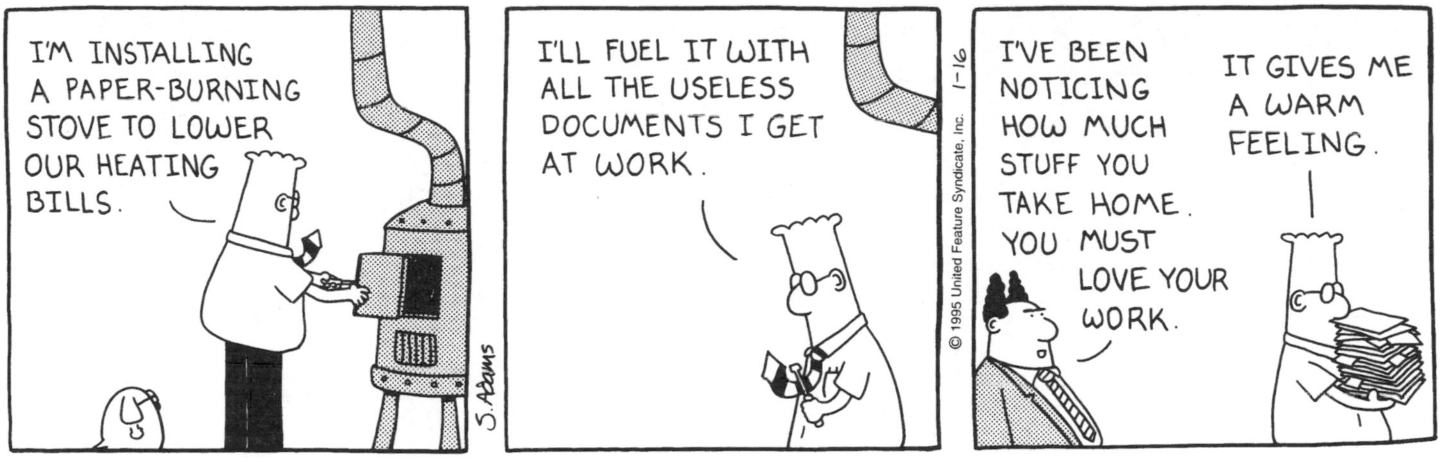
I'M INSTALLING A PAPER-BURNING STOVE TO LOWER OUR HEATING BILLS.
S. Adams
I'LL FUEL IT WITH ALL THE USELESS DOCUMENTS I GET AT WORK.
1-16
© 1995 United Feature Syndicate, Inc.
I'VE BEEN NOTICING HOW MUCH STUFF YOU TAKE HOME. YOU MUST LOVE YOUR WORK.
IT GIVES ME A WARM FEELING.

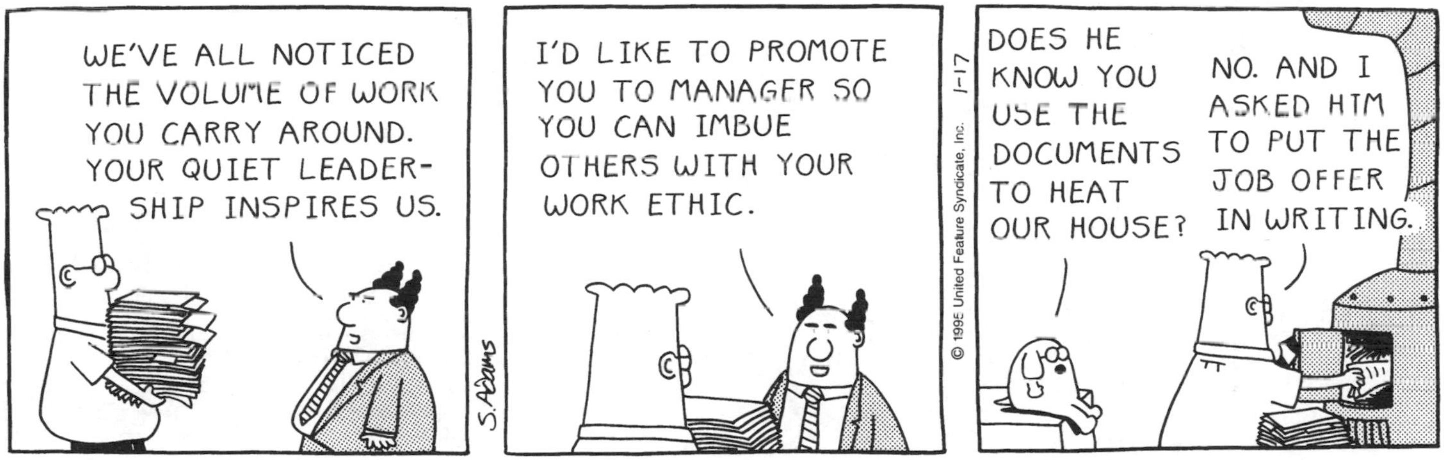
WE'VE ALL NOTICED THE VOLUME OF WORK YOU CARRY AROUND. YOUR QUIET LEADERSHIP INSPIRES US.
S. Adams
I'D LIKE TO PROMOTE YOU TO MANAGER SO YOU CAN IMBUE OTHERS WITH YOUR WORK ETHIC.
1-17
© 1995 United Feature Syndicate, Inc.
DOES HE KNOW YOU USE THE DOCUMENTS TO HEAT OUR HOUSE?
NO. AND I ASKED HIM TO PUT THE JOB OFFER IN WRITING.

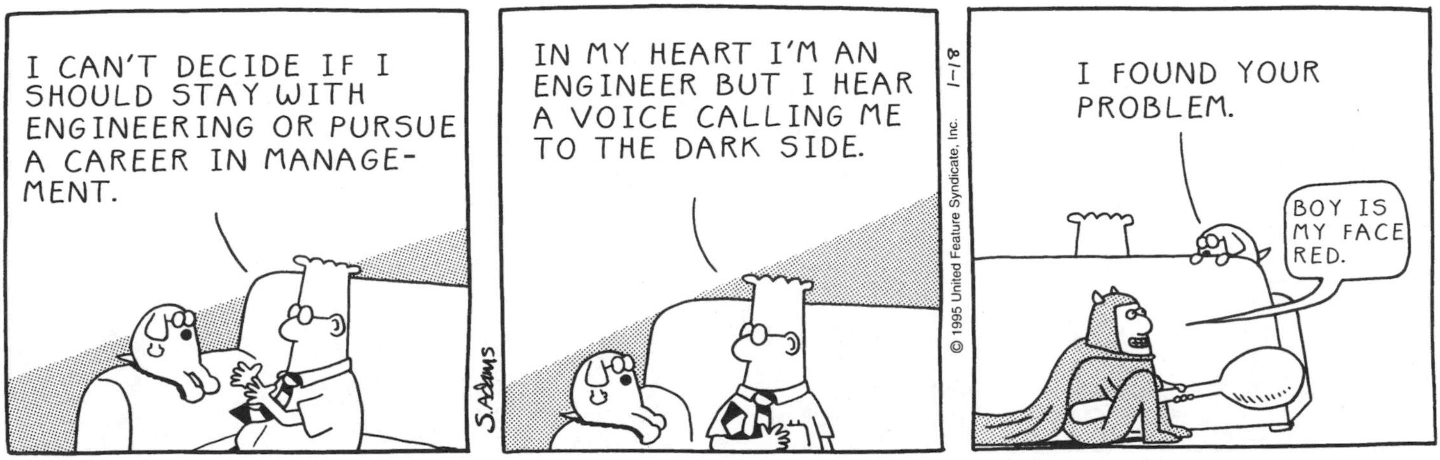
I CAN'T DECIDE IF I SHOULD STAY WITH ENGINEERING OR PURSUE A CAREER IN MANAGEMENT.
S. Adams
IN MY HEART I'M AN ENGINEER BUT I HEAR A VOICE CALLING ME TO THE DARK SIDE.
1-18
© 1995 United Feature Syndicate, Inc.
I FOUND YOUR PROBLEM.
BOY IS MY FACE RED.

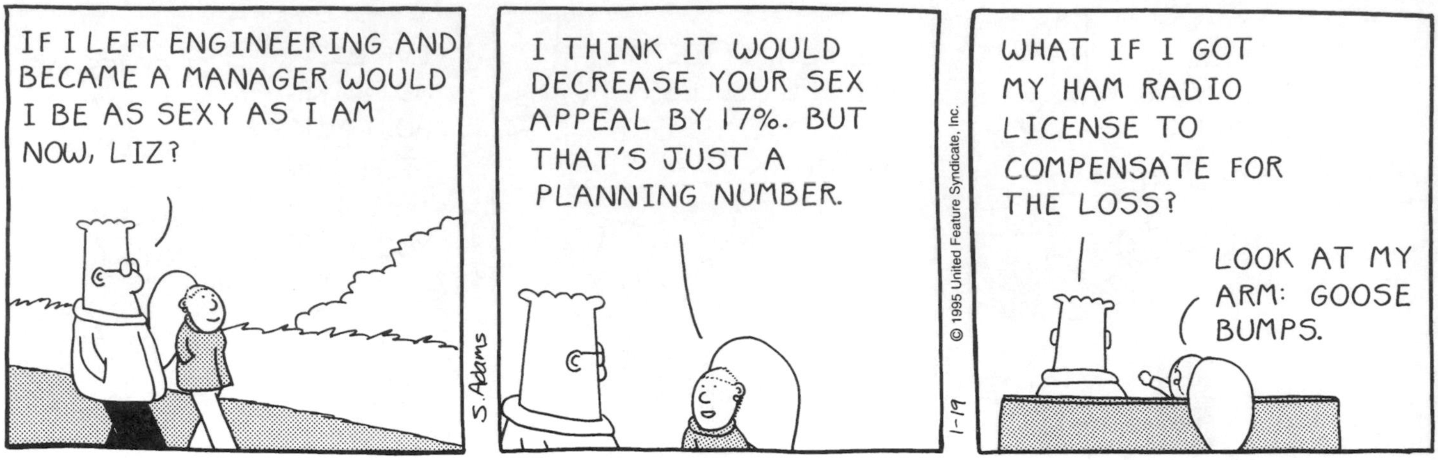
IF I LEFT ENGINEERING AND BECAME A MANAGER WOULD I BE AS SEXY AS I AM NOW, LIZ?
I THINK IT WOULD DECREASE YOUR SEX APPEAL BY 17%. BUT THAT'S JUST A PLANNING NUMBER.
WHAT IF I GOT MY HAM RADIO LICENSE TO COMPENSATE FOR THE LOSS?
LOOK AT MY ARM: GOOSE BUMPS.
S. Adams
1-19
© 1995 United Feature Syndicate, Inc.

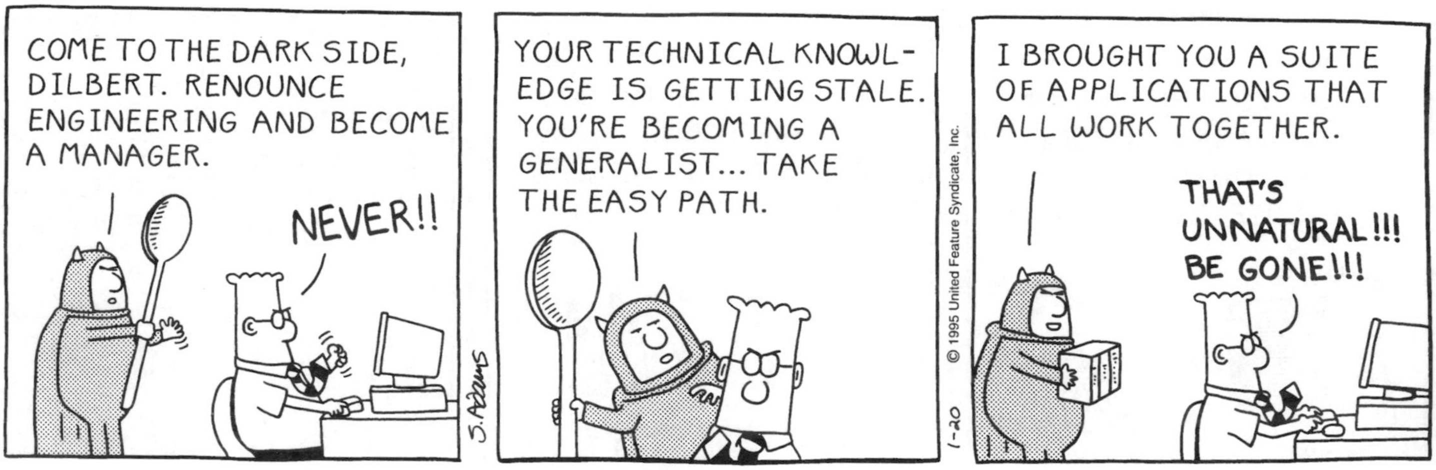
COME TO THE DARK SIDE, DILBERT. RENOUNCE ENGINEERING AND BECOME A MANAGER.
NEVER!!
YOUR TECHNICAL KNOWL-EDGE IS GETTING STALE. YOU'RE BECOMING A GENERALIST... TAKE THE EASY PATH.
I BROUGHT YOU A SUITE OF APPLICATIONS THAT ALL WORK TOGETHER.
THAT'S UNNATURAL!!! BE GONE!!!
S. Adams
1-20
© 1995 United Feature Syndicate, Inc.

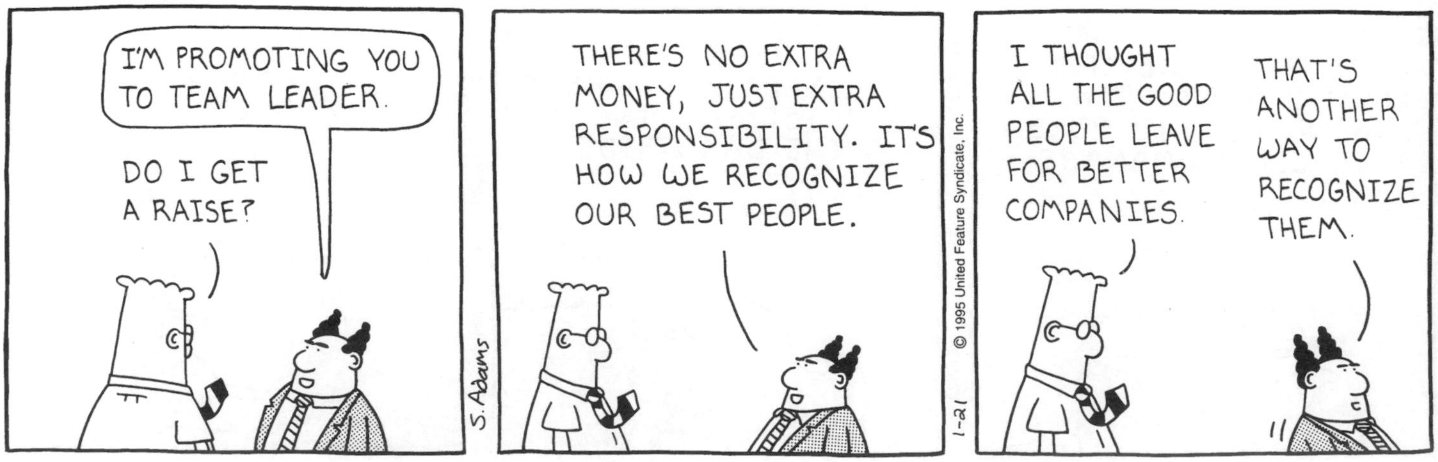
I'M PROMOTING YOU TO TEAM LEADER.
DO I GET A RAISE?
THERE'S NO EXTRA MONEY, JUST EXTRA RESPONSIBILITY. IT'S HOW WE RECOGNIZE OUR BEST PEOPLE.
I THOUGHT ALL THE GOOD PEOPLE LEAVE FOR BETTER COMPANIES.
THAT'S ANOTHER WAY TO RECOGNIZE THEM.
S. Adams
1-21
© 1995 United Feature Syndicate, Inc.

DILBERT®
BY
SCOTT ADAMS
HOW NATURE PROTECTS WEAK PRODUCTS
FIRST, THE ENGINEER PADS HIS SCHEDULE.
SIX MONTHS?
AT LEAST.
ONE MONTH TO BUILD THE PRODUCT AND FIVE MONTHS TO PLAY "DOOM" ON MY COMPUTER.
THEN THE MANAGER PADS THE SCHEDULE AS A CLEVER NEGOTIATING PLOY.
ONE YEAR... UNLESS YOU ADD PEOPLE TO MY TINY EMPIRE.
THEN THE VICE PRESIDENT PADS THE SCHEDULE TO AVOID LOOKING BAD TO THE PRESIDENT.
EIGHTEEN MONTHS.
S. Adams
MEANWHILE, THE SALES PEOPLE ARE MAKING UP NUMBERS BECAUSE NOBODY TELLS THEM ANYTHING.
TWO MONTHS... AND IT SOLVES EVERY PROBLEM YOU HAVE!
1-22-95
THIS CAUSES THE CUSTOMERS TO DEVELOP IRRATIONAL DESIRE FOR THE PRODUCT.
GIVE ME THE "BETA" TEST VERSION IN ONE MONTH.
© 1995 United Feature Syndicate, Inc.
THUS NATURE DISGUISES WEAK PRODUCTS AS "BETA".
CARDBOARD? THAT'S STUPID.
OH... THEN IT'S BETA.

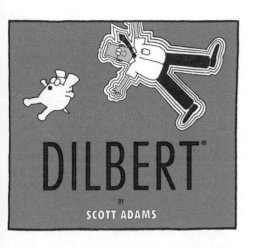

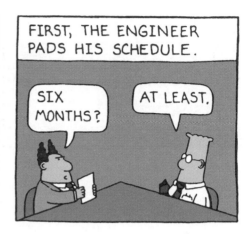

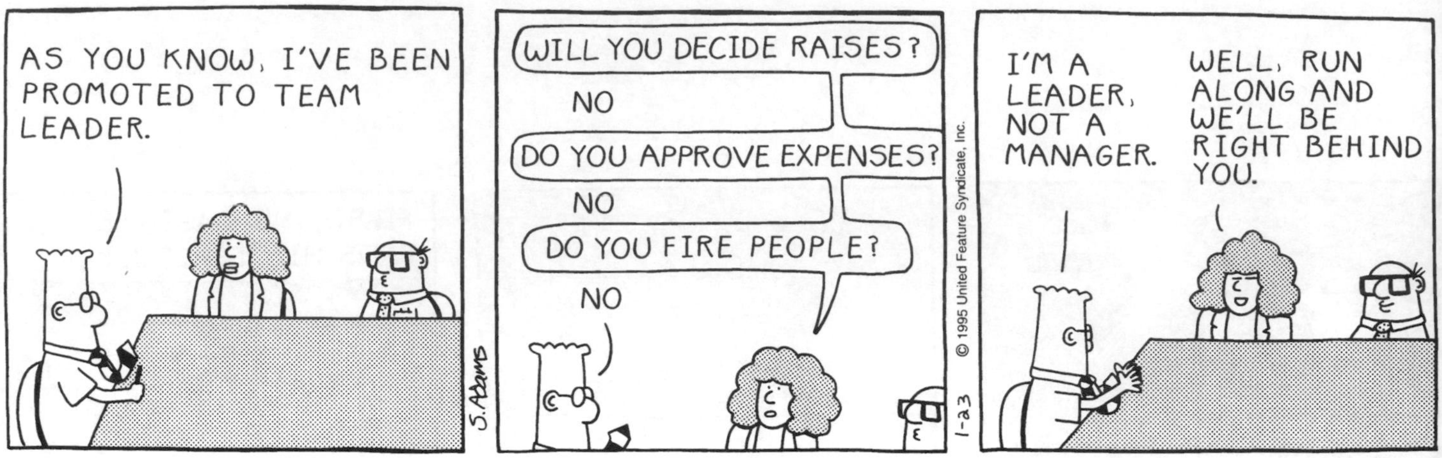
AS YOU KNOW, I'VE BEEN PROMOTED TO TEAM LEADER.
S. Adams
WILL YOU DECIDE RAISES?
NO
DO YOU APPROVE EXPENSES?
NO
DO YOU FIRE PEOPLE?
NO
1-23
© 1995 United Feature Syndicate, Inc.
I'M A LEADER, NOT A MANAGER.
WELL, RUN ALONG AND WE'LL BE RIGHT BEHIND YOU.

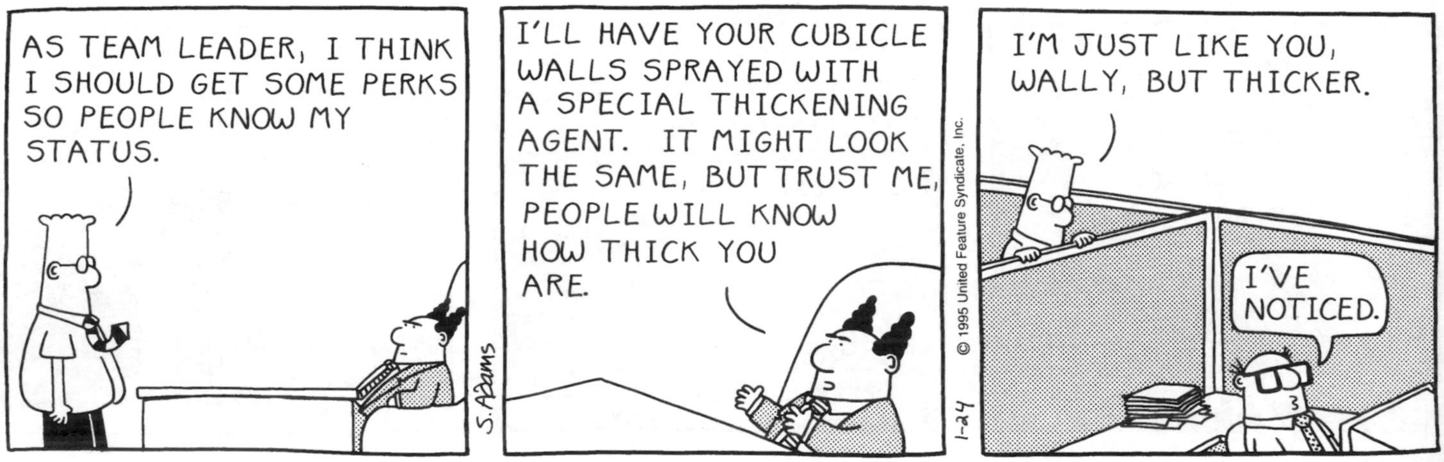
AS TEAM LEADER, I THINK I SHOULD GET SOME PERKS SO PEOPLE KNOW MY STATUS.
S. Adams
I'LL HAVE YOUR CUBICLE WALLS SPRAYED WITH A SPECIAL THICKENING AGENT. IT MIGHT LOOK THE SAME, BUT TRUST ME, PEOPLE WILL KNOW HOW THICK YOU ARE.
1-24
© 1995 United Feature Syndicate, Inc.
I'M JUST LIKE YOU, WALLY, BUT THICKER.
I'VE NOTICED.

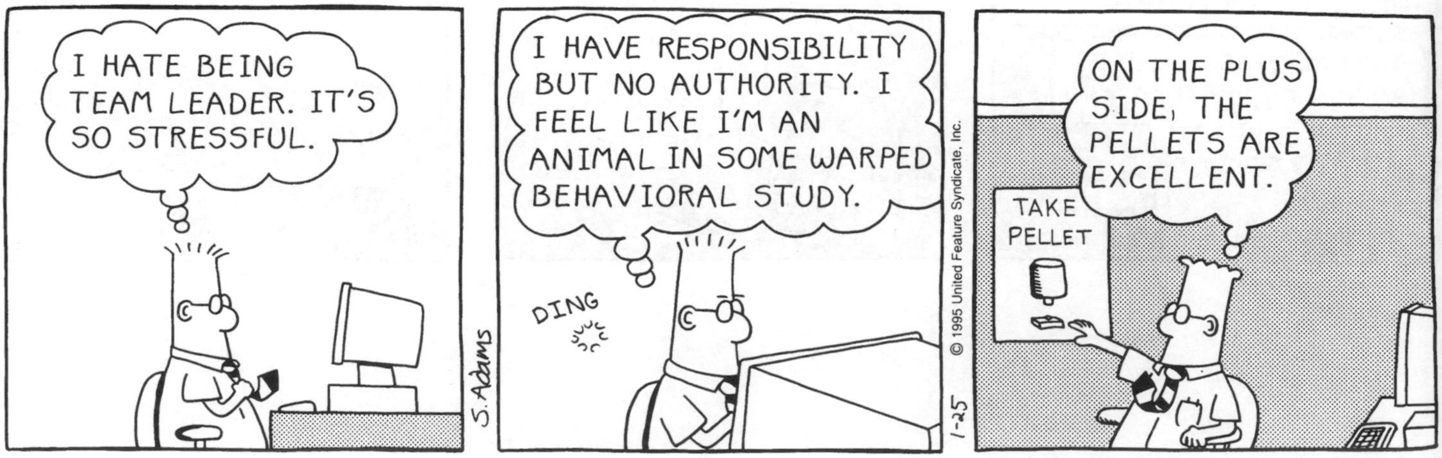
I HATE BEING TEAM LEADER. IT'S SO STRESSFUL.
S. Adams
I HAVE RESPONSIBILITY BUT NO AUTHORITY. I FEEL LIKE I'M AN ANIMAL IN SOME WARPED BEHAVIORAL STUDY.
DING
1-25
© 1995 United Feature Syndicate, Inc.
ON THE PLUS SIDE, THE PELLETS ARE EXCELLENT.
TAKE PELLET

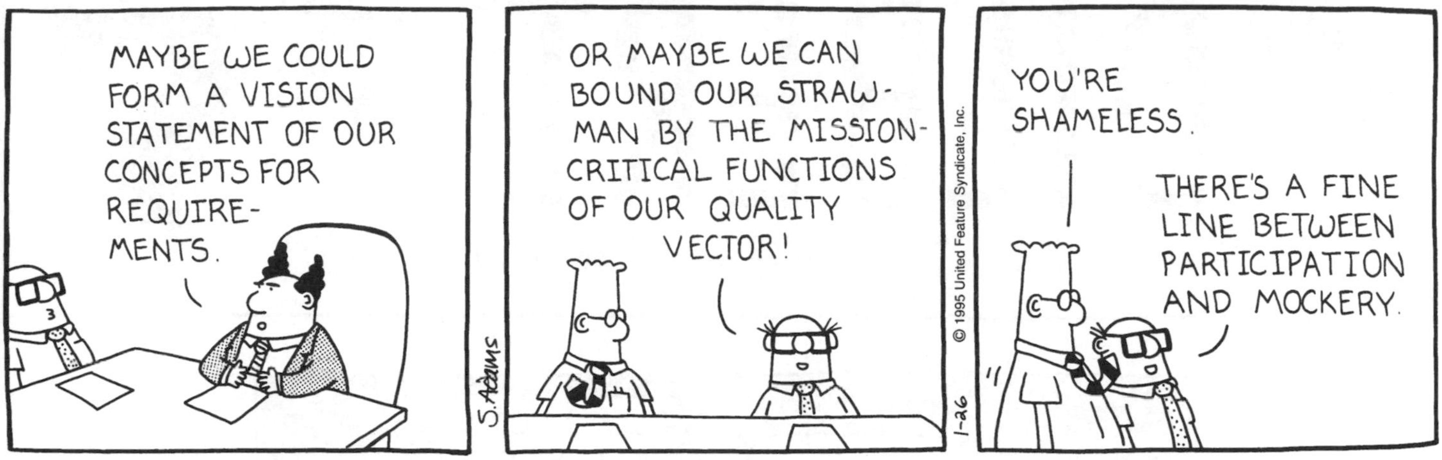
MAYBE WE COULD FORM A VISION STATEMENT OF OUR CONCEPTS FOR REQUIREMENTS.
OR MAYBE WE CAN BOUND OUR STRAWMAN BY THE MISSION-CRITICAL FUNCTIONS OF OUR QUALITY VECTOR!
YOU'RE SHAMELESS.
THERE'S A FINE LINE BETWEEN PARTICIPATION AND MOCKERY.
S. Adams
1-26
© 1995 United Feature Syndicate, Inc.

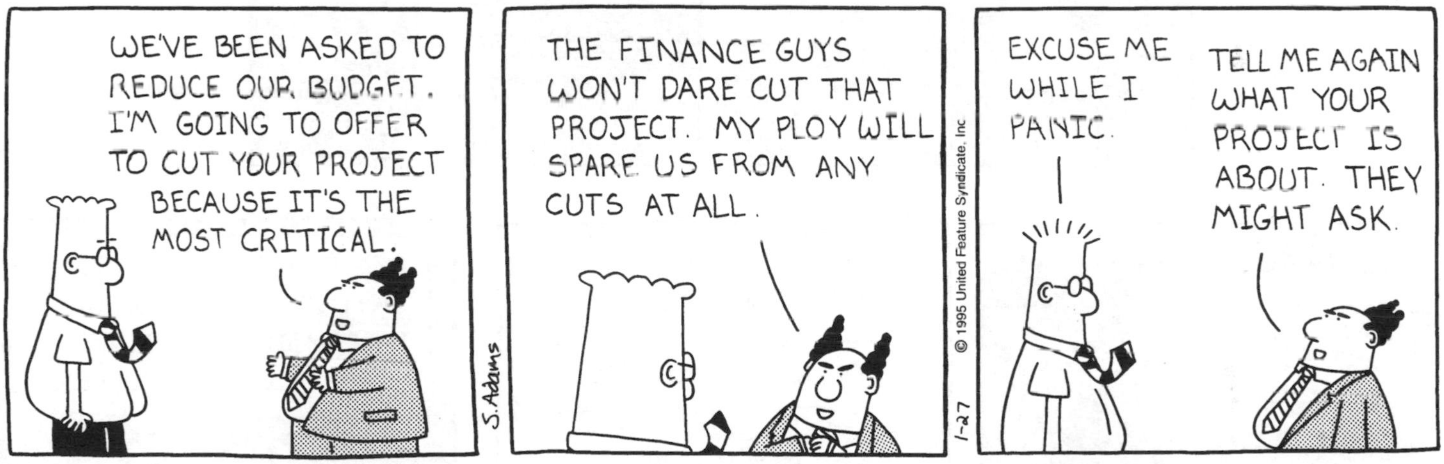
WE'VE BEEN ASKED TO REDUCE OUR BUDGET. I'M GOING TO OFFER TO CUT YOUR PROJECT BECAUSE IT'S THE MOST CRITICAL.
THE FINANCE GUYS WON'T DARE CUT THAT PROJECT. MY PLOY WILL SPARE US FROM ANY CUTS AT ALL.
EXCUSE ME WHILE I PANIC.
TELL ME AGAIN WHAT YOUR PROJECT IS ABOUT. THEY MIGHT ASK.
S. Adams
1-27
© 1995 United Feature Syndicate, Inc.

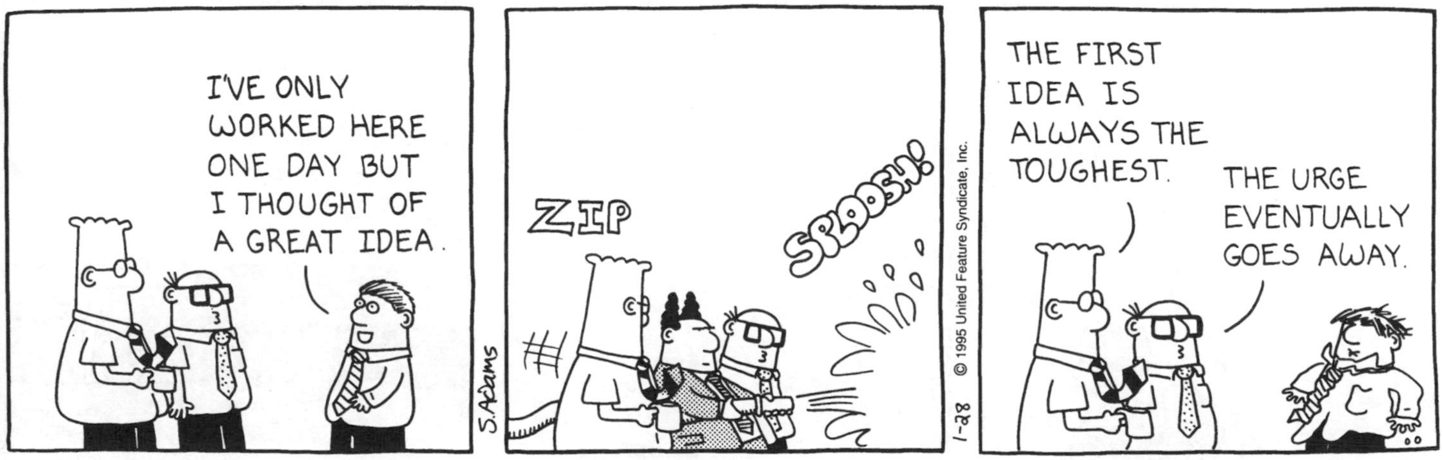
I'VE ONLY WORKED HERE ONE DAY BUT I THOUGHT OF A GREAT IDEA.
ZIP
SPLOOSH!
THE FIRST IDEA IS ALWAYS THE TOUGHEST.
THE URGE EVENTUALLY GOES AWAY.
S. Adams
1-28
© 1995 United Feature Syndicate, Inc.

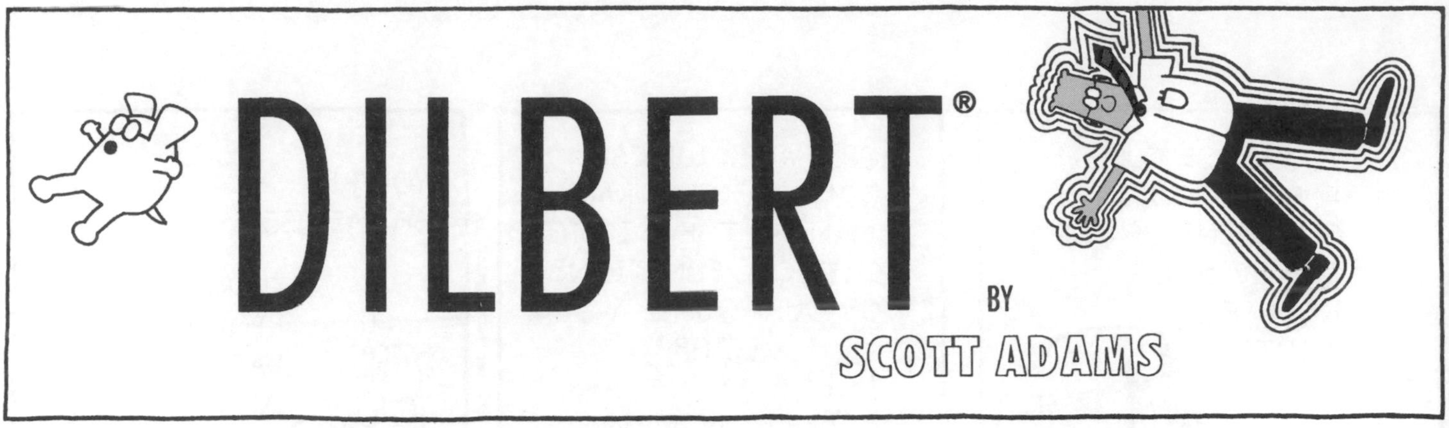
DILBERT®
BY
SCOTT ADAMS

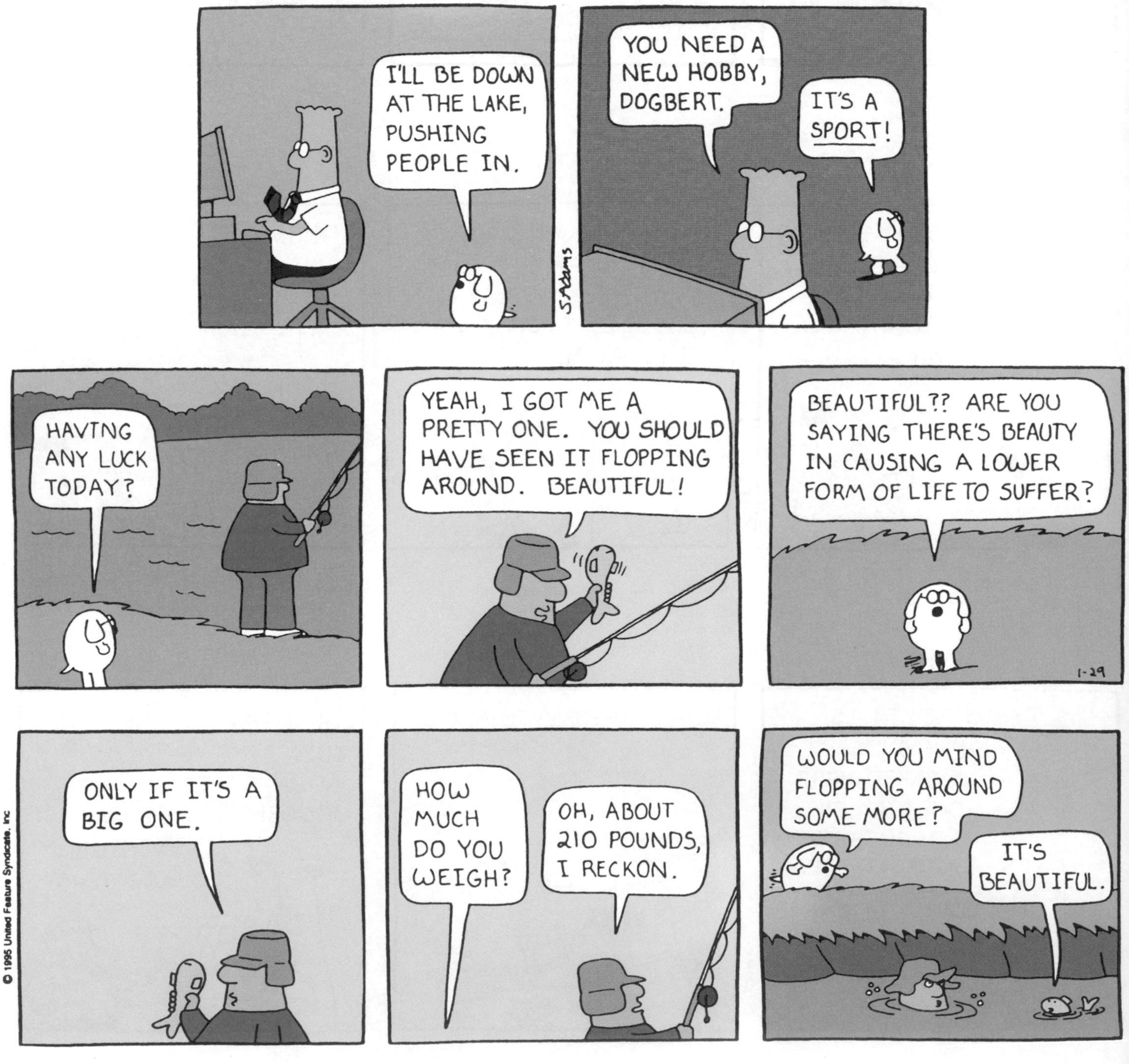
I'LL BE DOWN AT THE LAKE, PUSHING PEOPLE IN.
S. Adams
YOU NEED A NEW HOBBY, DOGBERT.
IT'S A SPORT!
HAVING ANY LUCK TODAY?
YEAH, I GOT ME A PRETTY ONE. YOU SHOULD HAVE SEEN IT FLOPPING AROUND. BEAUTIFUL!
BEAUTIFUL?? ARE YOU SAYING THERE'S BEAUTY IN CAUSING A LOWER FORM OF LIFE TO SUFFER?
1-29
ONLY IF IT'S A BIG ONE.
HOW MUCH DO YOU WEIGH?
OH, ABOUT 210 POUNDS, I RECKON.
WOULD YOU MIND FLOPPING AROUND SOME MORE?
IT'S BEAUTIFUL.

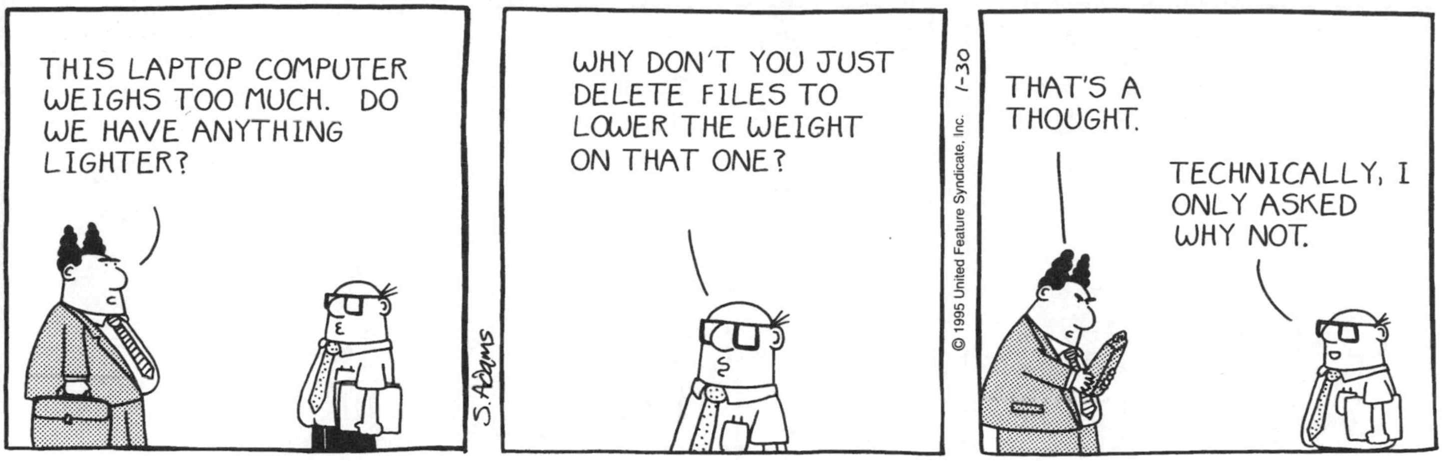
THIS LAPTOP COMPUTER WEIGHS TOO MUCH. DO WE HAVE ANYTHING LIGHTER?
S. Adams
WHY DON'T YOU JUST DELETE FILES TO LOWER THE WEIGHT ON THAT ONE?
1-30
© 1995 United Feature Syndicate, Inc.
THAT'S A THOUGHT.
TECHNICALLY, I ONLY ASKED WHY NOT.

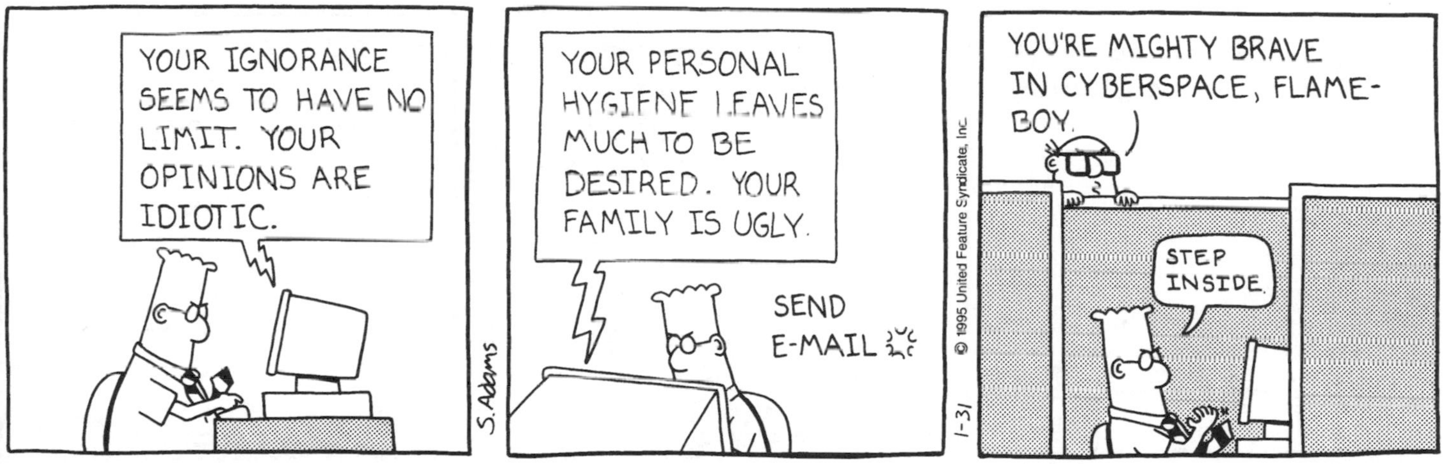
YOUR IGNORANCE SEEMS TO HAVE NO LIMIT. YOUR OPINIONS ARE IDIOTIC.
S. Adams
YOUR PERSONAL HYGIENE LEAVES MUCH TO BE DESIRED. YOUR FAMILY IS UGLY.
SEND E-MAIL
1-31
© 1995 United Feature Syndicate, Inc.
YOU'RE MIGHTY BRAVE IN CYBERSPACE, FLAME-BOY.
STEP INSIDE.

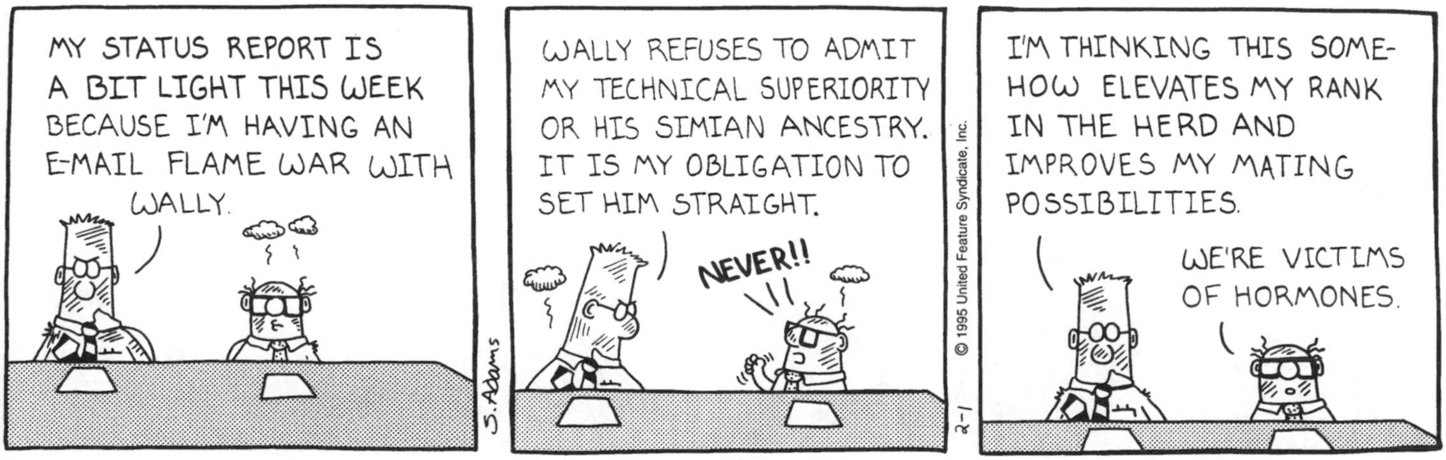
MY STATUS REPORT IS A BIT LIGHT THIS WEEK BECAUSE I'M HAVING AN E-MAIL FLAME WAR WITH WALLY.
S. Adams
WALLY REFUSES TO ADMIT MY TECHNICAL SUPERIORITY OR HIS SIMIAN ANCESTRY. IT IS MY OBLIGATION TO SET HIM STRAIGHT.
NEVER!!
2-1
© 1995 United Feature Syndicate, Inc.
I'M THINKING THIS SOMEHOW ELEVATES MY RANK IN THE HERD AND IMPROVES MY MATING POSSIBILITIES.
WE'RE VICTIMS OF HORMONES.

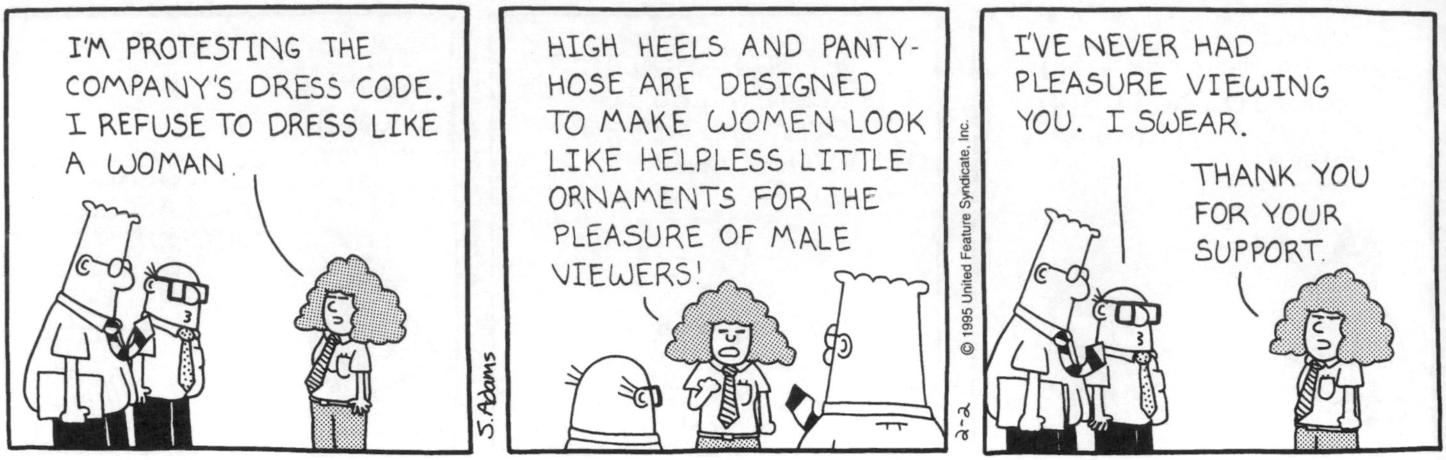
I'M PROTESTING THE COMPANY'S DRESS CODE. I REFUSE TO DRESS LIKE A WOMAN.
HIGH HEELS AND PANTY-HOSE ARE DESIGNED TO MAKE WOMEN LOOK LIKE HELPLESS LITTLE ORNAMENTS FOR THE PLEASURE OF MALE VIEWERS!
I'VE NEVER HAD PLEASURE VIEWING YOU. I SWEAR.
THANK YOU FOR YOUR SUPPORT.
S. Adams
2-2
© 1995 United Feature Syndicate, Inc.

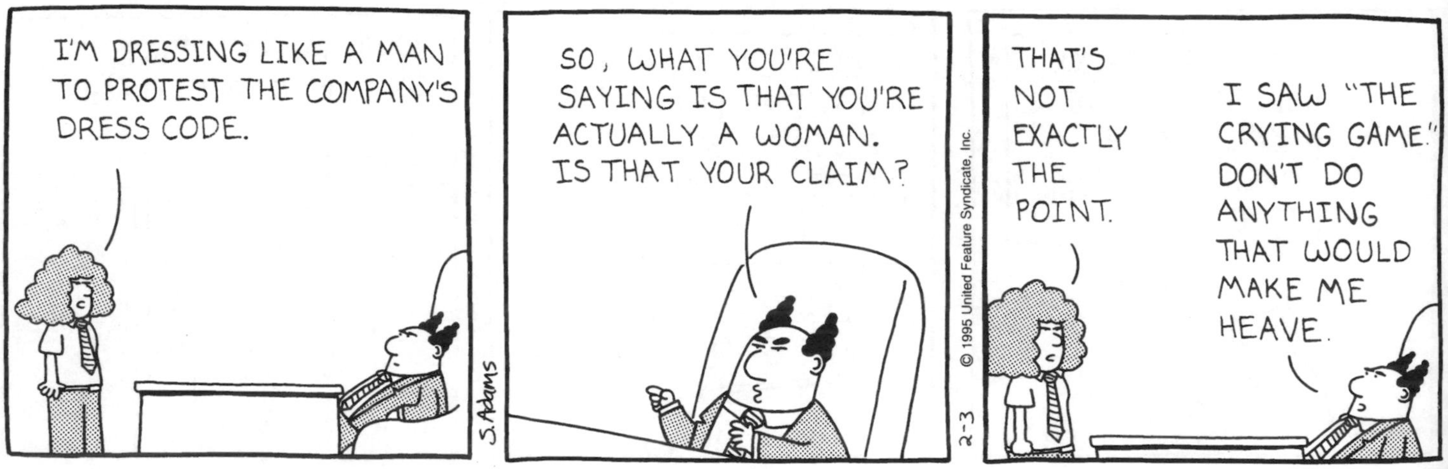
I'M DRESSING LIKE A MAN TO PROTEST THE COMPANY'S DRESS CODE.
SO, WHAT YOU'RE SAYING IS THAT YOU'RE ACTUALLY A WOMAN. IS THAT YOUR CLAIM?
THAT'S NOT EXACTLY THE POINT.
I SAW "THE CRYING GAME." DON'T DO ANYTHING THAT WOULD MAKE ME HEAVE.
S. Adams
2-3
© 1995 United Feature Syndicate, Inc.

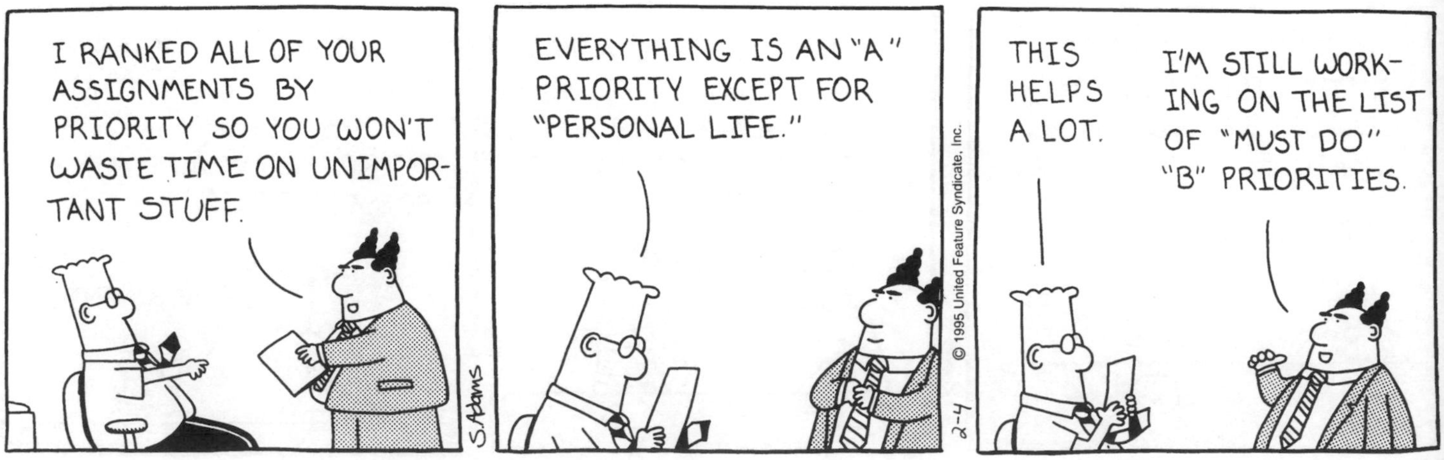
I RANKED ALL OF YOUR ASSIGNMENTS BY PRIORITY SO YOU WON'T WASTE TIME ON UNIMPORTANT STUFF.
EVERYTHING IS AN "A" PRIORITY EXCEPT FOR "PERSONAL LIFE."
THIS HELPS A LOT.
I'M STILL WORKING ON THE LIST OF "MUST DO" "B" PRIORITIES.
S. Adams
2-4
© 1995 United Feature Syndicate, Inc.

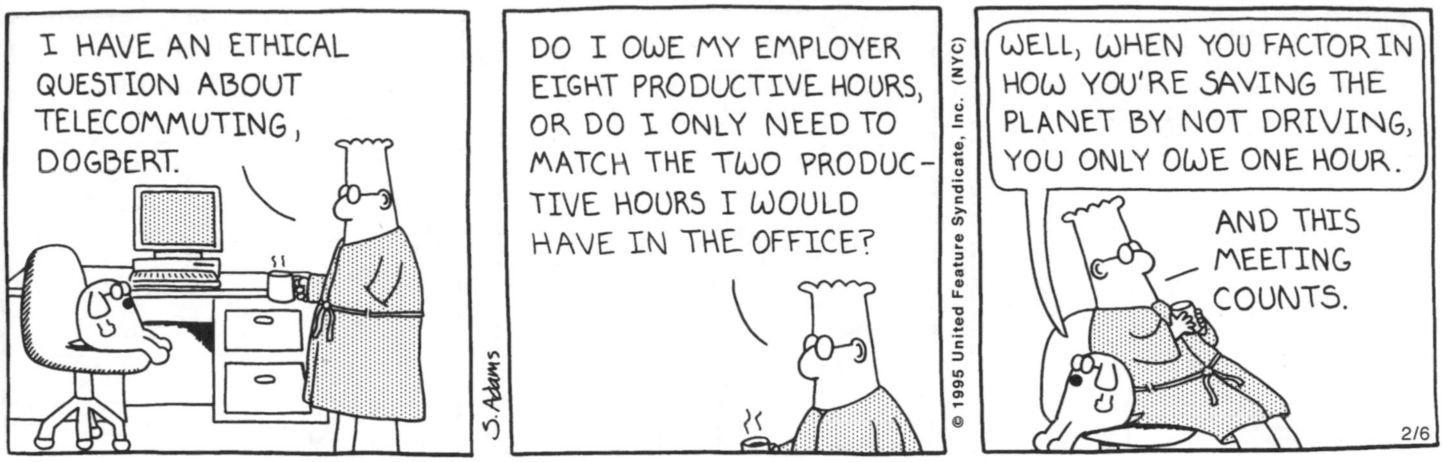
I HAVE AN ETHICAL QUESTION ABOUT TELECOMMUTING, DOGBERT.
S. Adams
DO I OWE MY EMPLOYER EIGHT PRODUCTIVE HOURS, OR DO I ONLY NEED TO MATCH THE TWO PRODUCTIVE HOURS I WOULD HAVE IN THE OFFICE?
© 1995 United Feature Syndicate, Inc. (NYC)
WELL, WHEN YOU FACTOR IN HOW YOU'RE SAVING THE PLANET BY NOT DRIVING, YOU ONLY OWE ONE HOUR.
AND THIS MEETING COUNTS.
2/6

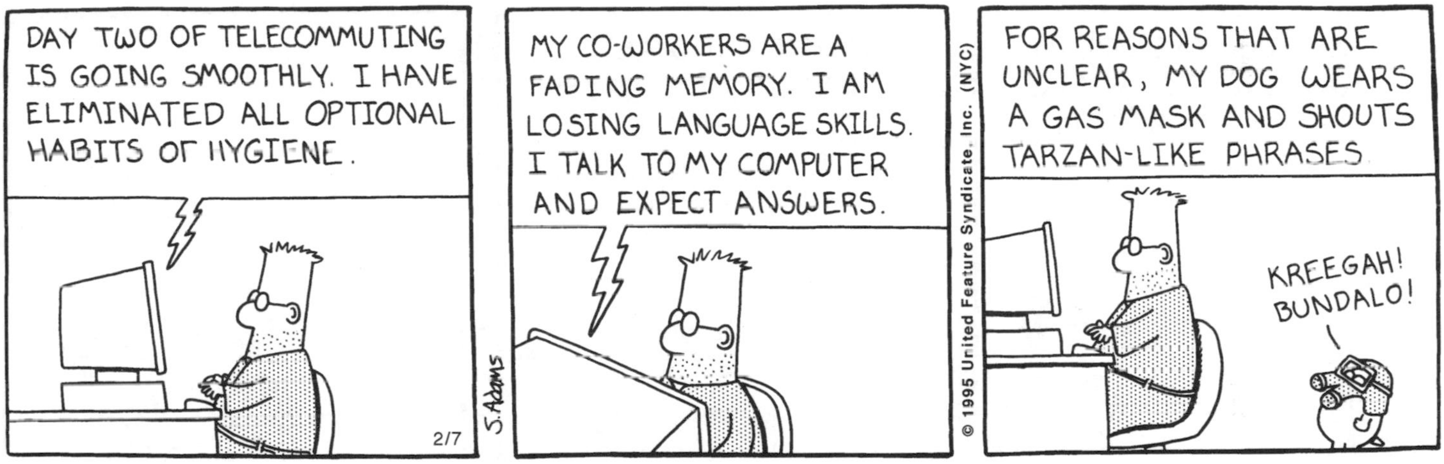
DAY TWO OF TELECOMMUTING IS GOING SMOOTHLY. I HAVE ELIMINATED ALL OPTIONAL HABITS OF HYGIENE.
2/7
S. Adams
MY CO-WORKERS ARE A FADING MEMORY. I AM LOSING LANGUAGE SKILLS. I TALK TO MY COMPUTER AND EXPECT ANSWERS.
© 1995 United Feature Syndicate, Inc. (NYC)
FOR REASONS THAT ARE UNCLEAR, MY DOG WEARS A GAS MASK AND SHOUTS TARZAN-LIKE PHRASES.
KREEGAH! BUNDALO!

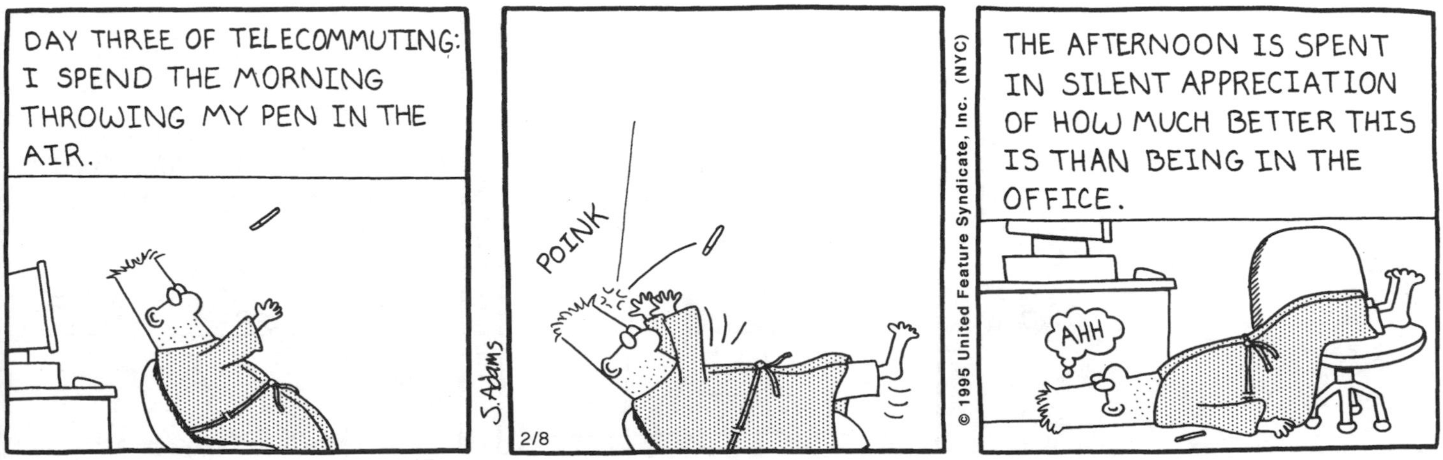
DAY THREE OF TELECOMMUTING: I SPEND THE MORNING THROWING MY PEN IN THE AIR.
S. Adams
POINK
2/8
© 1995 United Feature Syndicate, Inc. (NYC)
THE AFTERNOON IS SPENT IN SILENT APPRECIATION OF HOW MUCH BETTER THIS IS THAN BEING IN THE OFFICE.
AHH

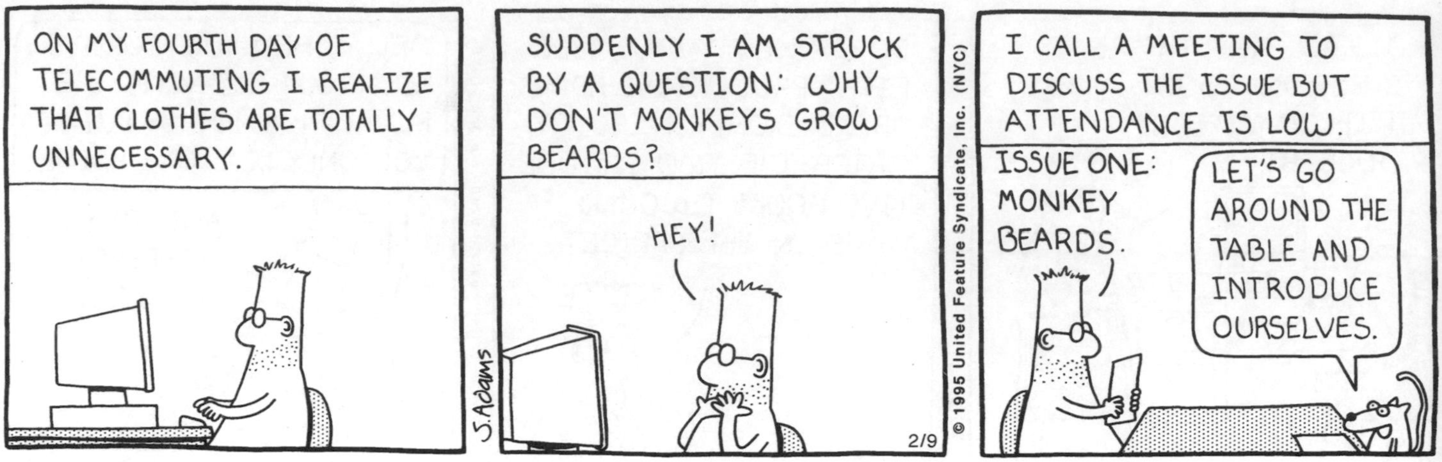
ON MY FOURTH DAY OF TELECOMMUTING I REALIZE THAT CLOTHES ARE TOTALLY UNNECESSARY.
SUDDENLY I AM STRUCK BY A QUESTION: WHY DON'T MONKEYS GROW BEARDS?
HEY!
I CALL A MEETING TO DISCUSS THE ISSUE BUT ATTENDANCE IS LOW.
ISSUE ONE: MONKEY BEARDS.
LET'S GO AROUND THE TABLE AND INTRODUCE OURSELVES.
S.Adams
2/9
© 1995 United Feature Syndicate, Inc. (NYC)

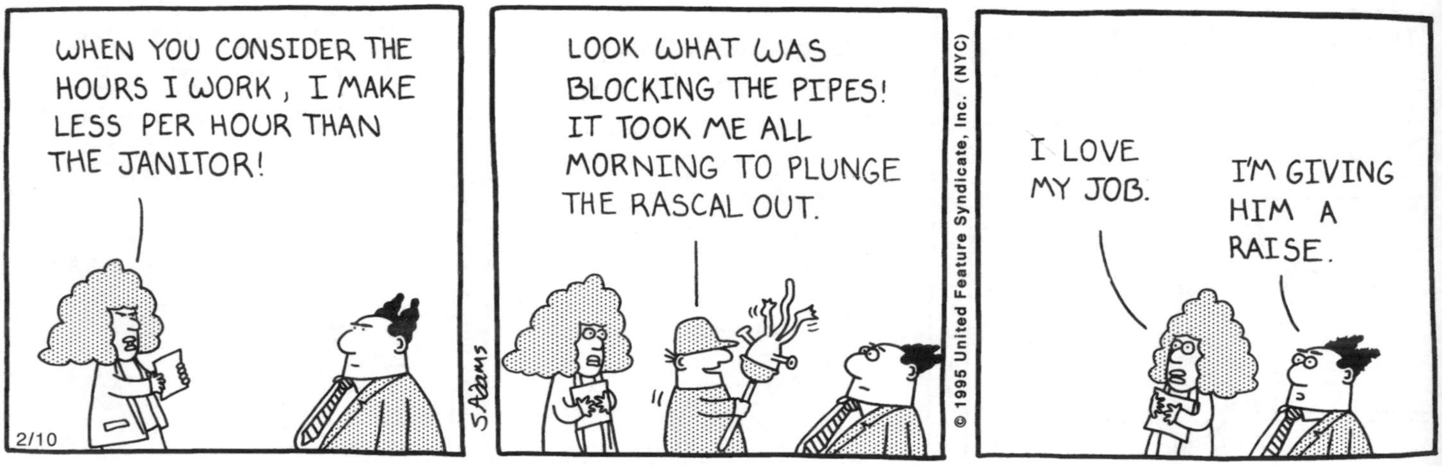
WHEN YOU CONSIDER THE HOURS I WORK, I MAKE LESS PER HOUR THAN THE JANITOR!
2/10
S.Adams
LOOK WHAT WAS BLOCKING THE PIPES! IT TOOK ME ALL MORNING TO PLUNGE THE RASCAL OUT.
© 1995 United Feature Syndicate, Inc. (NYC)
I LOVE MY JOB.
I'M GIVING HIM A RAISE.

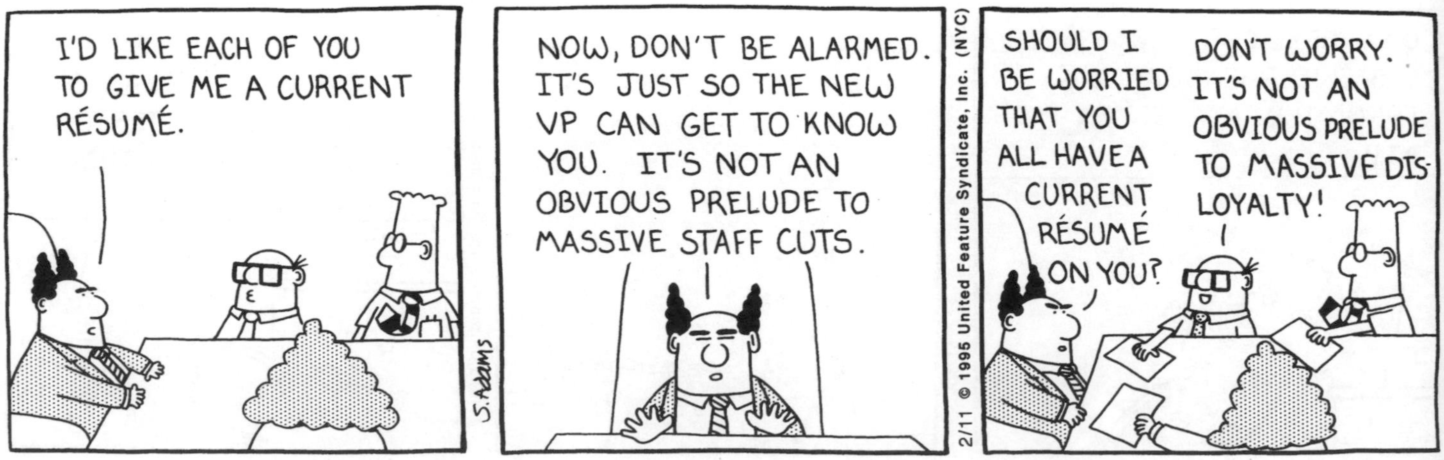
I'D LIKE EACH OF YOU TO GIVE ME A CURRENT RÉSUMÉ.
S.Adams
NOW, DON'T BE ALARMED. IT'S JUST SO THE NEW VP CAN GET TO KNOW YOU. IT'S NOT AN OBVIOUS PRELUDE TO MASSIVE STAFF CUTS.
2/11 © 1995 United Feature Syndicate, Inc. (NYC)
SHOULD I BE WORRIED THAT YOU ALL HAVE A CURRENT RÉSUMÉ ON YOU?
DON'T WORRY. IT'S NOT AN OBVIOUS PRELUDE TO MASSIVE DISLOYALTY!